Research Methods in Human-Computer Interaction

Research Methods in Human-Computer Interaction

Second Edition

Jonathan Lazar
Jinjuan Heidi Feng
Harry Hochheiser

MORGAN KAUFMANN PUBLISHERS

AN IMPRINT OF ELSEVIER

Morgan Kaufmann is an imprint of Elsevier
50 Hampshire Street, 5th Floor, Cambridge, MA 02139, United States

Notices
Knowledge and best practice in this field are constantly changing. As new research and experience broaden our understanding, changes in research methods, professional practices, or medical treatment may become necessary.

Practitioners and researchers must always rely on their own experience and knowledge in evaluating and using any information, methods, compounds, or experiments described herein. In using such information or methods they should be mindful of their own safety and the safety of others, including parties for whom they have a professional responsibility.

To the fullest extent of the law, neither the Publisher nor the authors, contributors, or editors, assume any liability for any injury and/or damage to persons or property as a matter of products liability, negligence or otherwise, or from any use or operation of any methods, products, instructions, or ideas contained in the material herein.

Library of Congress Cataloging-in-Publication Data
A catalog record for this book is available from the Library of Congress

British Library Cataloguing-in-Publication Data
A catalogue record for this book is available from the British Library

ISBN: 978-0-12-805390-4

For information on all Morgan Kaufmann publications visit our website at https://www.elsevier.com/books-and-journals

Working together
to grow libraries in
developing countries

www.elsevier.com • www.bookaid.org

Publisher: Todd Green
Acquisition Editor: Todd Green
Editorial Project Manager: Lindsay Lawrence
Production Project Manager: Punithavathy Govindaradjane
Cover Designer: Matthew Limbert

Critical Acclaim for *Research Methods in Human Computer Interaction,* Second Edition

"This book is an outstanding contribution to HCI's pedagogical and reference literature, reviewing and explaining the numerous research methods in common use. It motivates with numerous examples the methods in terms of posing questions and designing research to answer those questions. It covers well both quantitative and qualitative methods. The treatment is accessible and lively. The book should be considered for adoption by all HCI instructors."

—**Ron Baecker,** Member of the CHI Academy, Founder and Co-Director, Technologies for Aging Gracefully lab (TAGlab), and Professor Emeritus of Computer Science, University of Toronto

"This is *the* research methods book I recommend to my students and colleagues. And it's a time-saver: my students make fewer methodological mistakes and we can now engage in deeper and more insightful discussions about specific challenges of their research work. With this improved and updated edition, the bar is even higher! With increasing traces of our lives online and availability of Big Data in many research projects, the new chapter on online and ubiquitous HCI research was a welcome addition to the already comprehensive, multi-method research book. Every HCI student, researcher, and practitioner must read it!"

—**Simone Barbosa,** Professor, PUC-Rio, Brazil, and co-Editor-in-Chief of *ACM Interactions*

"Research Methods in HCI is an excellent resource for newcomers and seasoned HCI professionals alike. Covering all the basic methods for conducting research in HCI, concepts are explained clearly and brought alive through case studies and examples. In addition to offering how-to details, the text offers detailed rationale for why and when to use different methods. Some historical context and controversial viewpoints are also offered. Clear discussions around how to select participants and work with different populations are offered, as are ethical issues in conducting research. The attention to these kinds of details makes this a truly engaging, readable text. The extensive list of references offers plenty of scope for follow-up for those wishing to deepen their knowledge even further. The 2nd edition offers new and refreshed content, updated examples and case studies, and new references and resources."

—**Elizabeth Churchill,** Member of the CHI Academy, Secretary/ Treasurer of ACM, currently Director of User Experience at Google, formerly Director of Human Computer Interaction at eBay

"This book by Lazar, Feng, and Hochheiser is a must read for anyone in the field of Human-Computer Interaction. Their multi-discipline approach, housed in the reality of the technological world today, makes for a practical and informative guide for user interface designers, software and hardware engineers and anyone doing user research."

—**Mary Czerwinski,** Principal Research Manager, Microsoft Research, Recipient of the ACM SIGCHI Lifetime Service Award, Member of the CHI Academy, and ACM Fellow

"This is a superb book for all researchers, practitioners, and students interested in the investigation of anything related to HCI. This new edition has much needed information on research methods in HCI that have become prevalent, including crowdsourcing as well as new creative ways to collect and analyze qualitative data, two examples of essential skills for today's HCI students! Highly recommended!"

—**Vanessa Evers,** Full Professor and Chair of Human Media Interaction, Scientific Director of the DesignLab, University of Twente, the Netherlands

"I recommend this book to all my PhD students. It provides excellent coverage of a range of HCI research methods, and importantly, the context for researchers to know how the methods relate to each other and how to choose a method that is appropriate for their own research question. The book is a very nice read. It is an excellent reference for HCI researchers, not only for those just starting out, but also for experienced researchers who would like to firm up their knowledge of HCI methods."

—**Faustina Hwang,** Associate Professor of Digital Health, Biomedical Engineering, University of Reading, UK

"This is the book for you! Whether you are a seasoned practitioner, a student starting out, an established professor, or someone just curious about how HCI finds answers to research questions. Clear, coherent and comprehensive, it covers the classical - like surveys and ethnography - and the highly contemporary, including online and automated methods. Written in an accessible, engaging style and illustrated with examples and case studies from Google, Yahoo and the authors' own extensive experiences, this book should be on the desk of everyone doing HCI and UX design, development and research".

—**Matt Jones,** Author of *Mobile Interaction Design* (Wiley) & *There's Not an App for that: Mobile UX Design for Life* (Morgan Kaufmann). Professor of Computer Science, Future Interaction Technology Lab, Swansea University, UK

"This book is a must-read for those who seek a broad view and in-depth understanding of HCI research methodologies. I have had the privilege of using the earlier version of this book for my HCI research method classes for both academic and professional programs -- it was extraordinarily useful for students and researchers in the HCI field. Now, this 2nd edition becomes even more valuable as it not only includes more content regarding quantitative methods, such as statistical analysis, but also totally revamped qualitative data analysis. This updated version will be an indispensable reference for both students and practitioners who want to enhance their research skills in HCI."

—**Jinwoo Kim,** Professor of HCI at Yonsei
University, Korea, Founder and CEO at HAII

"As an educator and a researcher who frequently makes use of methods for gathering data from users, I was excited to see the variety and range of techniques for working with people presented in this book. It is also refreshing to see the book's emphasis on issues such as bias and ethics in research. The chapter that explicitly discusses best practices for working with participants with disabilities truly makes this book stand out. First, there is no equivalent resource that I know of on this topic. Second, I believe the lessons presented in this chapter can help to illustrate the importance of understanding and working with any population that is significantly different from the average undergraduate research participant featured in so many studies! Since HCI is expanding its domain more and more, this is a very timely lesson."

—**Jen Mankoff,** Professor, Human Computer
Interaction Institute, Carnegie Mellon University,
Chair of the SIGCHI Accessibility Community

"If you care about HCI research, then this book is a must-read. The book contains a broad coverage of methods and techniques for HCI research. This edition contains major additions to the previous version that are extremely timely, dealing with evolutions of interactive technologies and evolutions of knowledge in the area of HCI research. It is clear that the authors have applied the methods described in the book to understand their audience, building a book that is very pedagogic, blending a lot of knowledge in the field of HCI but still remaining easy to read, to understand and to apply for practitioners, students and lecturers in HCI."

—**Philippe Palanque,** Professor of Computer Science at Université
Toulouse III, France, Chair of the CHI Conference Steering
Committee, member of the CHI Academy, and co-editor of *The
Handbook of Formal Methods in Human-Computer Interaction*

"This is the book that every researcher will want to read. Comprehensive and at the same time 'hand-holding', this book guides researchers through designing and running their own studies using both qualitative and quantitative methods. Even seasoned researchers will want to dip in to check out details, while students will find this book particularly inspiring. There's something in the book for everyone."

—**Jenny Preece,** Professor, iSchool and Human-Computer Interaction Lab, University of Maryland, Member of the CHI Academy, co-author of *Interaction Design* (4th edition)

"Over the last 20 years research and practice in Human-Computer-Interaction have matured. An in-depth understanding of methods in this field is essential and is the key to success in research as well as in industry. The big question is how we teach and learn about these methods. Is a book in the digital age, in times when people are excited about MOOCs, and when video tutorials are everywhere, still an appropriate medium? Absolutely! This book is at the same time an accessible text book as well as a comprehensive reference. The topics are well selected and are highly relevant for students, researchers, and practitioners. Each chapter has a focus, communicates the basics, and teaches how to practically apply it. The new edition includes all the basics I would teach, and additionally provides a profound introduction to new topics, including Human-Computer Interaction in the context of online systems and ubiquitous computing."

—**Albrecht Schmidt,** Professor of Computer Science, Human Computer Interaction Group - VIS, University of Stuttgart, Germany

"Aspiring accessibility researchers will find the final chapter packed with invaluable tips for avoiding common pitfalls when working with populations with disabilities. The authors' passion and deep experience shine through."

—**Shari Trewin,** IBM Research, Chair of the ACM Special Interest Group on Accessible Computing (SIGACCESS)

"As a fan of the first edition who used it extensively in my research methods courses, I am thrilled to see the second edition expanded in exciting ways, especially around quantitative and qualitative data analysis. Also, the industrial case studies add real-world relevance to an already essential book. I highly recommend this new edition, whether you are conducting academic HCI research, or user research in a startup or large company. It is an invaluable resource."

—**Jacob O. Wobbrock,** Professor at the Information School, University of Washington, Recipient of the 2017 ACM SIGCHI Social Impact Award

Contents

About the Authors

Jonathan Lazar is a professor in the Department of Computer and Information Sciences at Towson University and has served as director of the Undergraduate Program in Information Systems since 2003. He also founded the Universal Usability Laboratory at Towson University and served as director from 2003 to 2014. In the area of human-computer interaction, Lazar is involved in teaching and research on web accessibility for people with disabilities, user-centered design methods, assistive technology, and law and public policy related to HCI. He has previously authored or edited 10 books, including *Ensuring Digital Accessibility Through Process and Policy* (coauthored with Dan Goldstein and Anne Taylor), *Disability, Human Rights, and Information Technology Accessibility* (coedited with Michael Stein), *Universal Usability: Designing Computer Interfaces for Diverse User Populations*, and *Web Usability: A User-Centered Design Approach*. He has published over 140 refereed articles in journals, conference proceedings, and edited books, and has been granted two US patents for his work on accessible web-based security features for blind users. He frequently serves as an adviser to government agencies and regularly provides testimony at federal and state levels, and multiple US federal regulations cite his research publications. His research has been funded by the National Science Foundation; National Institute on Disability, Independent Living, and Rehabilitation Research (NIDILRR); American Library Association; and TEDCO. He currently serves on the executive board of the Friends of the Maryland Library for the Blind and Physically Handicapped and the State of Maryland Work Group on Increasing the Teaching of IT Accessibility Concepts in State Universities. He has served in multiple roles in the Association for Computing Machinery Special Interest Group on Computer-Human Interaction (ACM SIGCHI), most recently, adjunct chair of public policy (2010–15) and Digital Accessibility Chair (CHI 2014). Lazar has been honored with the 2017 University System of Maryland Board of Regents Award for Excellence in Research, the 2016 SIGCHI Social Impact Award, given annually to an individual who has promoted the application of human-computer interaction research to pressing societal needs, the 2015 AccessComputing Capacity Building Award (sponsored by the University of Washington and the National Science Foundation) for advocacy on behalf of people with disabilities in computing fields, the 2011 University System of Maryland Board of Regents Award for Excellence in Public Service, and the 2010 Dr. Jacob Bolotin Award from the National Federation of the Blind, for working towards achieving the full integration of the blind into society on a basis of equality. In 2012, Lazar was selected to be the Shutzer Fellow at the Radcliffe Institute for Advanced Study at Harvard University, where he investigates the relationship between human-computer interaction for people with disabilities and US disability rights law.

Jinjuan Heidi Feng is a professor in the Department of Computer and Information Sciences at Towson University. She conducts research in the areas of human-computer interaction, universal accessibility, health informatics, and usable and accessible security. She works closely with national and local communities to improve the quality of life for people with disabilities through information technology. Her current research projects focus on assistive technologies for people with cognitive disabilities in educational and professional settings, mobile applications for health related activities, and accessible security techniques for individuals with visual or cognitive disabilities. Her research has been funded by various national and state agencies such as the National Science Foundation (NSF), the National Institute on Disability, Independent Living, and Rehabilitation Research (NIDILRR), and TEDCO. Her work has been published in various top-notch journals and presented at conferences such as Human-Computer Interaction, ACM Transactions on Computer-Human Interaction, and ACM Transactions on Accessible Computing. She has received the Maryland Daily Record's "Innovator of The Year Award" twice, in 2009 and 2016. Dr. Feng was appointed as the director for the School of Emerging Technologies in Fall 2015 and is leading the effort to promote interdisciplinary collaboration across the Towson University campus. She currently serves on the editorial board of ACM Transactions on Accessible Computing. She also served as the general conference chair for the 18th ACM SIGACCESS International Conference on Computers and Accessibility (ASSETS 2016).

Harry Hochheiser is currently a faculty member in the Department of Biomedical Informatics and the Intelligent Systems Program at the University of Pittsburgh, where he is actively involved in the Biomedical Informatics Training Program. Previously, Hochheiser served as an assistant professor at Towson University, and worked at Massachusetts General Hospital, Tufts University School of Medicine, AT & T Bell Labs, IBM T.J. Watson Labs, and the National Institutes on Aging. Working at the intersection of human-computer interaction and healthcare informatics, his research has covered a range of topics, including human-computer interaction, information visualization, bioinformatics, clinical informatics, universal usability, security, privacy, and public policy implications of computing systems. His research has been funded by the National Cancer Institute, National Library of Medicine, the Centers for Disease Control and Prevention, and the Baobab Health Trust, among others. Hochheiser has taught and developed several courses at both undergraduate and graduate levels, including introductory computer science, introduction to algorithms, information visualization, advanced web development, and human-computer interaction. He is a member of the US Public Policy Committee of the Association of Computing Machinery, and of the American Medical Informatics Association (AMIA) public policy committee. Hochheiser is co-recipient of the 2009 Maryland Daily Record's "Innovator of the Year Award" with Lazar and Feng, for the development of improved web-based security features for blind users.

Foreword

Many disciplines are hyphenated combinations, such as bio-informatics or physical-chemistry, but human-computer interaction (HCI) spans a broader range of topics than most. As a result, HCI researchers often draw on multiple diverse research methods, even in a single paper. It is just possible that HCI's remarkable successes in academic publishing and in widely used technologies stem from its diverse research methods.

While the traditional scientific method was a solid foundation for HCI, controlled laboratory studies with tests for statistically significant differences were never quite enough to deal with the ambitions of HCI researchers. We also embraced interviews, surveys, and focus groups, sometimes in fresh ways, to capture impressions of distinctive users and elicit suggestions, reactions, frustrations, and fears. Ethnographic observation and anthropological methods were also applied to study computer users "in the wild," which meant going to the place where people worked, lived, or played to see what actual use was like. As researchers shifted from studying the immediate out-of-the-box experience to understanding the evolution of user experiences over weeks and months, long-term case studies and time diaries became more common.

A larger step for HCI researchers was to incorporate iterative engineering processes and design thinking. They had to overcome resistance from traditional researchers who believed that controlled experiments were the best way forward. Over the years still newer methods tuned to the needs of businesses were developed, such as usability testing and expert reviews, to accelerate the development process, rather than refine theories. A major step forward was the development of A/B testing which contrasted two slightly different user interfaces in actual use over a period of days or weeks with thousands of actual users. Web designers were able to make rapid progress in determining which features led to greater commercial success.

Another novel approach has been to crowdsource research, by putting up online experiments available to many users or to use services like Amazon Turk to hire hundreds of participants for experimental studies. In recent years still newer methods based on big data analyses of millions of tweets or social media posts changed the game dramatically. The online availability of so much data about human performance led theoreticians and practitioners to study whole communities at scale in realistic settings.

I am pleased that the authors have used the distinction between micro-HCI and macro-HCI to organize thinking about when to apply one research method or another. Short-term perceptual, motor, or cognitive tasks can be studied by micro-HCI methods such as controlled experiments, but long-term trust, community development, or satisfaction are better studied by macro-HCI methods. I am also pleased that the authors encourage readers to reach out to other research communities to learn of their methods, to partner with them in policy initiatives, and to convey the opportunities that HCI presents for bold new directions and powerful impact.

The continuing discussions about which methods to use make this book a vital resource for new students, active researchers, and serious practitioners. It provides a comprehensive introduction with ample references for those who want more information and for those who are ready to invent still newer research methods, tailored to the issues they are studying.

This book also testifies to the vitality and ambition of HCI researchers, who have moved from narrow studies about pointing times for different target sizes to broader goals such as promoting information and communication technology for development (ICT4D), ensuring universal usability, countering cyberbullying, and reducing fake news. In a world where technology plays an increasing role, HCI is maturing into a larger field that is becoming a necessary component of new ideas in business, education, healthcare, community safety, energy sustainability, and environmental protection. There is an astonishing history of success in enabling 8 billion people to use novel technologies. This book celebrates that history and points to future directions that will yield new theories and still further benefits. There is also a great deal of work to be done by the next generation of creative researchers.

Ben Shneiderman
University of Maryland

Preface

Many textbooks arise from a perceived need—in our case, the lack of a research methods book specifically focusing on Human-Computer Interaction (HCI). When we first began writing the first edition of this book in 2007, we remembered our own experiences as doctoral students, primarily using research methods books in other fields, trying to determine how to properly apply the methods in HCI. As doctoral students, we took courses on research methods—from education, sociology, or psychology departments—or asked mentors. As professors, we found ourselves repeatedly returning to sources from outside our field to learn about unfamiliar research techniques. This gap in the literature led us to believe that the time was ripe for a research methods book specifically on HCI.

In the 10 years since we initially began writing the first edition of the book, academic offerings in HCI have grown immensely. Many universities now offer degrees with the name "Human-Computer Interaction" or "Human-Centered Computing." We are thrilled with this increased focus, and are honored to have played a role, however small, in that growth. We have also witnessed an evolution in the scope of HCI research. Although basic challenges—which research questions to ask, how to go about designing studies that would lead to answers, and how to interpret the results of those studies—remain the same, the range of available methods and techniques has grown. Crowdsourcing, social media, ubiquitous computing, and big data approaches have led to new uses of computing and new opportunities for research. Social networking sites offer billions of pieces of text and multimedia, suitable for analyzing patterns and describing conversations and information flows between users. Ubiquitous devices enable tracking of literally "every step we take," allowing detailed understanding of physical activity. Increased use of information tools in vital areas such as healthcare provides new challenges in understanding computing use in context, as doctors and patients routinely include electronic health records as key elements in medical care. Eye-tracking tools have dropped in price, allowing more researchers to afford them and integrate these tools into their research. More research now takes place outside of the laboratory to better understand usage of portable technology such as tablet computers and smart phones.

We have tried to present the various research methods in this text from the perspective of their use in HCI. Thus our description of experimental design (Chapter 4) discusses experiments with as few as 16 participants—a sample size much smaller than those often found in psychology experiments. Similarly, Chapter 5 (on surveys) discusses how nonrandom sample surveys are acceptable in HCI research—a sharp contrast with the strict sampling methodologies often found in social sciences.

We hope that you use this textbook on a daily basis, as you are faced with the challenges involved in doing data collection. We hope that this book helps inspire you, the reader, to do groundbreaking research, to change the way we all think about HCI, to do something different, something noteworthy, and something important.

Jonathan Lazar
Jinjuan Heidi Feng
Harry Hochheiser

Acknowledgments

Writing a book can be a long and often difficult process, even when you are working in a productive team with valued co-authors. We have been pleased to have the support of a great publisher and many people in a supportive professional community.

The first edition of Research Methods in Human-Computer Interaction was published in 2009 by John Wiley and Sons. We thank those who worked with us at Wiley on the first edition: Jonathan Shipley, Claire Jardine, Georgia King, Sam Crowe, Nicole Burnett, and Celine Durand-Watts. We are excited to be working with Morgan Kaufmann/Elsevier Publishers for the second edition. We appreciate the efforts of Todd Green, Meg Dunkerley, Punitha Radjane, and especially Lindsay Lawrence, at Morgan Kaufmann/Elsevier Publishers.

The chapters of the book have been reviewed numerous times, by careful and critical reviewers who have provided feedback to strengthen the content of the book. Angela Bah, Louise Barkhaus, Julia Galliers, Hilary Johnson, and Joseph Kaye provided reviews of the first edition. We especially thank Maxine Cohen and all of her students, who implemented the second edition in their Fall 2016 doctoral Human-Computer Interaction class at Nova Southeastern University and provided many fantastic suggestions. In addition to the formal reviews collected through publishers, colleagues have provided informal feedback on specific chapters. We thank John Bertot, Weiqin Chen, Beth Hanst, Kasper Hornbaek, Juan-Pablo Hourcade, Paul Jaeger, Sri Kurniawan, Jenny Preece, Ben Shneiderman, and Brian Wentz, for their feedback on specific chapters, both in the first and second editions. We greatly appreciate the contribution of case studies in chapter 10, from Gary Moulton at Yahoo!, and Laura Granka from Google. Jonathan and Heidi would like to acknowledge the support of the Department of Computer and Information Sciences at Towson University, and Harry would like to acknowledge the support of the Department of Biomedical Informatics at the University of Pittsburgh in the development and preparation of this manuscript. Jonathan would also like to thank the Radcliffe Institute for Advanced Study at Harvard University, which awarded him a 2016 summer fellowship, to work on the second edition of this book. Finally, we would like to thank the many supportive colleagues, researchers, teachers, practitioners, and students, who have expressed their enthusiasm for the book, and encouraged us to work on writing a second edition.

Introduction to HCI research

1.1 INTRODUCTION

Research in the area of human-computer interaction (HCI) is fascinating and complex. It is fascinating because there are so many interesting questions and so many changes over time (due to technical advancements). It is complex because we borrow research methods from a number of different fields, modify them, and create our own "standards" for what is considered acceptable research. It is also complex because our research involves human beings who are, to put it mildly, complex. It is important to understand the roots of the field, to understand the development of research methods in HCI, understand how HCI research has changed over time, and understand the multiple dimensions that must be considered when doing HCI research.

1.1.1 HISTORY OF HCI

There is a general consensus that the field of HCI was formally founded in 1982. This is the date of the first conference on Human Factors in Computing Systems in Gaithersburg (Maryland, United States), that later turned into the annual ACM SIGCHI conference. So, at the publication time of this book (2017), the field of human-computer interaction (HCI) is around 35 years old. However, this is a deceptively simple description of the history of HCI. The field draws on expertise existing in many other areas of study. People were doing work before 1982 that could be considered HCI work. There is a fascinating article (Pew, 2007) that describes work on a project for the Social Security Administration in the United States starting in 1977. The work on this project could easily be described as HCI work, including task analyses, scenario generation, screen prototyping, and building a usability laboratory. Pew also describes presenting some of his work at the annual meeting of the Human Factors Society in 1979. Ben Shneiderman published *Software Psychology*, considered one of the first books on the topic of HCI, in 1980. The terms "office automation" and "office information systems" were popular in the late 1970s. At that time, you could find articles that could be considered HCI-related, in fields such as management, psychology, software engineering, and human factors. In an interesting article on the history of office automation systems, Jonathan Grudin describes 1980 as the "banner year" for the study of office automation systems, after which, the number of people studying the topic dwindled, and many of them refocused under the title of HCI (Grudin, 2006b). The computer mouse was first publicly demoed by

Research Methods in Human-Computer Interaction. http://dx.doi.org/10.1016/B978-0-12-805390-4.00001-7

Doug Engelbart in 1968 (Engelbart, 2016). Still others point to seminal papers as far back as Vannevar Bush's "As We May Think," which looks surprisingly relevant, even today (Bush, 1945).

In the late 1970s and early 1980s, computers were moving out of the research laboratory and "secure, cooled room" into the home and the office. The use of mainframes was transitioning into the use of mini- and then microcomputers, and the more popular personal computers were making their debut: Apple II series, IBM PC/XT, and the Commodore/Vic. It was this move, away from large computers in secure rooms used only by highly trained technical people, to personal computers on desktops and in home dens used by nontechnical people in much greater numbers that created the need for the field of HCI. Suddenly, people were using computers just as a tool to help them in their jobs, with limited training, and personal computers became a product marketed to home users, like stoves or vacuum cleaners. The interaction between the human and the computer was suddenly important. Nonengineers would be using computers and, if there wasn't a consideration of ease of use, even at a basic level, then these computers were doomed to failure and nonuse. In the current context, where everyone is using computers, that may sound a bit odd, but back in the 1970s, almost no one outside of computing, engineering, and mathematics specialists were using computers. Personal computers weren't in school classrooms, they weren't in homes, there were no bank cash machines, or airline self check-in machines, before this shift towards nonengineering use happened. This shift created a sudden need for the field of HCI, drawing on many different fields of study.

1.2 TYPES OF HCI RESEARCH CONTRIBUTIONS

The field of HCI draws on many different disciplines, including computer science, sociology, psychology, communication, human factors engineering, industrial engineering, rehabilitation engineering, and many others. The research methods may have originated in these other disciplines. However, they are modified for use in HCI. For instance, techniques such as experimental design and observation from psychology, have been modified for use in HCI research. Because HCI draws on the work in so many different disciplines, people often ask "what is considered HCI research? What types of effort are considered research contributions?" In a recent article that we believe will become a classic read, Wobbrock and Kientz (2016) discuss seven types of research contributions:

Empirical contributions—data (qualitative or quantitative) collected through any of the methods described in this book: experimental design, surveys, focus groups, time diaries, sensors and other automated means, ethnography, and other methods.

Artifact contributions—the design and development of new artifacts, including interfaces, toolkits, and architectures, mock-ups, and "envisionments." These artifacts, are often accompanied by empirical data about feedback or usage. This type of contribution is often known as HCI systems research, HCI interaction techniques, or HCI design prototypes.

Methodological contributions—new approaches that influence processes in research or practice, such as a new method, new application of a method, modification of a method, or a new metric or instrument for measurement. Theoretical contributions—concepts and models which are vehicles for thought, which may be predictive or descriptive, such as a framework, a design space, or a conceptual model. Dataset contributions—a contribution which provides a corpus for the benefit of the research community, including a repository, benchmark tasks, and actual data. Survey contributions—a review and synthesis of work done in a specific area, to help identify trends and specific topics that need more work. This type of contribution can only occur after research in a certain area has existed for a few years so that there is sufficient work to analyze. Opinion contributions—writings which seek to persuade the readers to change their minds, often utilizing portions of the other contributions listed above, not simply to inform, but to persuade.

The majority of HCI research falls into either empirical research or artifact contributions, and this book specifically addresses empirical research using all of the potential data collection methods utilized in empirical research. In their analysis of research papers submitted to the CHI 2016 conference, Wobbrock and Kientz found that paper authors indicated in the submission form that over 70% of the papers submitted were either empirical studies of system use or empirical studies of people, and 28.4% were artifact/system papers (it is important to note that authors could select more than one category, so percentages can add up to more than 100%). There were a fair number of papers submitted on methodological contributions, but submissions in all of the other categories of contributions were rare (Wobbrock and Kientz, 2016). This provides some empirical data for what we (as book authors) have observed, that most HCI research is either empirical or systems research (or sometimes, a combination of both, such as when you develop a prototype and have users evaluate it).

1.3 CHANGES IN TOPICS OF HCI RESEARCH OVER TIME

The original HCI research in the 1980s was often about how people interacted with simple (or not so simple) office automation programs, such as word processing, database, and statistical software. The basics of interfaces, such as dialog boxes, and error messages, were the focus of much research. Some of the classic HCI articles of the 1980s, such as Norman's analysis of human error (Norman, 1983), Carroll's "training wheels" approach to interface design (Carroll and Carrithers, 1984), and Shneiderman's work on direct manipulation (Shneiderman, 1983) are still very relevant today. Towards the late 1980s, graphical user interfaces started to take hold. In the late 1980s and early 1990s, there was growth in the area of usability engineering methods (and the Usability Professionals' Association, now known as UXPA, was founded in 1991). But there was a major shift in the field of HCI research during the early to mid 1990s, as the Internet and the web gained wide acceptance. New types of interfaces and communication, such as web pages, e-mail, instant messaging, and groupware, received attention from the research community. This caused an increased number of research fields to be included under the umbrella of HCI, especially communication. A recent article by Liu et al. (2014) on trends of HCI research topics, determined a big difference between research in 1994–2003, which focused on fixed technology, and research from 2004–13, which focused on mobile and portable computing (such as tablets and smart phones).

Around 2004–05, the focus of research shifted more towards user-generated content that was shared, such as photos, videos, blogs, and wikis, and later grew into research on social networking. On Dec. 26, 2006, Time Magazine famously named "You" as the "person of the year" for generating much of the content on the web. The topic of user diversity gained more attention, with more research studying how younger users, older users, and users with disabilities, interact with technologies. In the late 2000s, research increased on touch screens, especially multitouch screens, with studies on motor movement focused on pointing using fingers, rather than computer mice. It is important to note that while multitouch screens only entered common public use in the late 2000s, multitouch screens had been developed and researched as far back as the early 1980s (Buxton, 2016).

The research focus in the late 2010s (the publication date of the book) is no longer on something as simple as task performance in statistical software, but is now more focused on collaboration, connections, emotion, and communication (although, again, research on collaboration has existed since the early 1980s, even if it's now just gaining attention). The focus is not just on workplace efficiency any more, but is on whether people like an interface and want to use it, and in what environment they will be using the technology. Today's research focuses on topics such as mobile devices, multitouch screens, gestures and natural computing, sensors, embedded and wearable computing, sustainability, big data, social and collaborative computing, accessibility, and other topics (Liu et al., 2014). But, of course, that will change over time! The topics of HCI research continue to change based on factors such as technological developments, societal needs, government funding priorities, and even user frustrations.

1.4 CHANGES IN HCI RESEARCH METHODS OVER TIME

There are many reasons why, over time, research methods naturally evolve and change. For instance, tools for research that were originally very expensive, such as eye-tracking, sensors, drones, facial electromyography (EMG), and electroencephalography (EEG) are now relatively inexpensive or at least are more reasonable, allowing more researchers to afford them and integrate these tools into their research. New tools develop over time, for instance, Amazon's Mechanical Turk. New opportunities present themselves, such as with social networking, where suddenly, there are billions of pieces of text and multimedia that can be evaluated, looking for patterns. Or with personal health tracking, or electronic health records, which allow for analysis of millions of data points, which have already been collected. Some types of research are now fully automated. For instance, years ago, researchers would do a citation analysis to understand trends in research, but most of that analysis is now easily available using tools such as Google Scholar. On the other hand, automated tools for testing interface accessibility, are still imperfect and have not yet replaced the need for human evaluations (either with representative users or interface experts).

One important difference between HCI research and research in some of the other social sciences (such as sociology and economics), is that, large entities or government agencies collect, on an annual basis, national data sets, which are then open for researchers to analyze. For instance, in the United States, the General Social Survey, or government organizations such as the National Center on Health Statistics, the US Census Bureau, or the Bureau of Labor Statistics, collect data using strict and well-established methodological controls. Outside of the US, agencies such as Statistics Canada, and EuroStat, collect excellent quality data, allowing researchers to, in many cases, to focus less on data collection and more on data analysis. However, this practice of national and/or annual data sets, does not exist in the area of HCI. Most HCI researchers must collect their own data. So that alone makes HCI research complex.

Typically, HCI research has utilized smaller size datasets, due to the need for researchers to recruit their own participants and collect their own datasets. However, as the use of big data approaches (sensors, text analysis, combining datasets collected for other purposes) has recently increased, many researchers now utilize larger pools of participant data in their research. Whereas, studies involving participants might have had 50 or 100 users, it is common now to see data from 10,000–100,000 users. That is not to say that researchers have actually been interacting with all of those users (which would be logistically impossible), but data has been collected from these large data sets. Doing research involving 100,000 users versus 50 users provides an interesting contrast. Those 100,000 users may never interact with the researchers or even be aware that their data is being included in research (since the terms of service of a social networking service, fitness tracking, or other device, may allow for data collection). Also, those participants will never get to clarify the meaning of the data, and the researchers, having no opportunity to interact with participants, may find it hard to get a deeper understanding of the meaning of the data, from the participants themselves. Put another way, big data can help us determine correlations (where there are relationships), but might not help us determine causality (why there are relationships) (Lehikoinen and Koistinen, 2014). On the other hand, by interacting with participants in a smaller study of 50 participants, researchers may get a deeper understanding of the meaning of the data. Combining big data approaches with researcher interaction with a small sampling of users (through interviews or focus groups) can provide some of the benefits of both approaches to data collection, understanding not only the correlations, but also the causality (Lehikoinen and Koistinen, 2014).

Another important difference between HCI research and research in some of the other fields of study is that longitudinal studies in HCI are rare. Fields such as medicine may track health outcomes over a period of decades. National census data collection can occur over centuries. However, longitudinal data generally does not exist in the area of HCI. There could possibly be a number of reasons for this. Technology in general, and specific tools, change so rapidly that, a comparison of computer usage in 1990, or even

2000, versus 2017 might simply not be relevant. What would you compare? However, a trend analysis over time might be useful, because there are some audiences for HCI research, for whom trend analyses, over time, are considered a primary approach for data collection (such as the CSCW researchers described in Section 1.6 and the policy-makers described in Section 1.7). Furthermore, there are areas of HCI research where longitudinal data would be both appropriate and very relevant. For instance, Kraut has examined, over a 15-year period, how internet usage impacts psychological well-being, and how the types of communication, and the trends, have changed over time (Kraut and Burke, 2015). There are other similar longitudinal studies that are also very useful, for instance, documenting that 65% of American adults use social networking tools in 2015, up from 7% in 2005 (Perrin, 2015), or documenting internet usage trends over a 15 year period (Perrin and Duggan, 2015). One could easily imagine other longitudinal studies that would be useful, such as how much "screentime" someone spends each day, over a 20 year period. The lack of longitudinal research studies in HCI, is a real shortcoming, and in some cases, limits the value that communities outside of computer science, place on our research.

Another reason why HCI research is complex is that, for much of the research, not just any human being is appropriate for taking part as a participant. For instance, a practice in many areas of research, is simply to recruit college students to partici-pate in the research. This would certainly be appropriate if the focus of the research is on college students. Or this potentially *could* be appropriate if the focus of the research is on something like motor performance (in which the main factors are age and physiological factors). However, for much of HCI research, there is a focus on the users, tasks, and environments, which means that not only must the users be representative in terms of age, educational experience, and technical experience, but also in terms of the task domain (it is often said that you must "know thy user"). For instance, that means that to study interfaces designed for lawyers, you must actually have practicing lawyers taking part in the research. It will take time to recruit them, and they will need to be paid appropriately for their participation in a research study. Perhaps it is possible, although not ideal, to substitute law students in limited phases of the research, but you would still need to have actual practicing lawyers, with the right task domain knowledge, taking part in the research at the most critical phases. Recruitment of participants is much more complex than just "find some people," and it can be actually quite complex and take a fair amount of time. For someone coming from a background of, say, sociology, the number of participants involved in HCI studies can seem small, and the focus may be different (strict random sampling in sociology, versus representativeness in HCI). But our goals are also different: in HCI, we are primarily trying to study interfaces, and how people interact with interfaces, we are not primarily studying people, so we don't always necessarily have to claim representativeness.

Despite historic roots in the early 1980s, only in the last 10–15 years or so have individuals been able to graduate from universities with a degree that is titled "Human-Computer Interaction" (and the number of people with such a degree is still incredibly small). Many people in the field of HCI may have degrees in computer science, information systems, psychology, sociology, or engineering. This means that these individuals come to the field with different approaches to research, with a certain view of the field. Even students studying HCI frequently take classes in psychology research methods or educational research methods. But taking just an educational or psychological approach to research methods doesn't cover the full breadth of potential research methods in HCI. Ben Shneiderman said that "The old computing is about what computers can do, the new computing is about what people can do" (Shneiderman, 2002). Since HCI focuses on what people can do, it involves multiple fields that involve the study of people, how they think and learn, how they communicate, and how physical objects are designed to meet their needs. Basically, HCI researchers need all of the research methods used in almost all of the social sciences, along with some engineering and medical research methods.

1.5 UNDERSTANDING HCI RESEARCH METHODS AND MEASUREMENT

HCI research requires both rigorous methods and relevance. It is often tempting to lean more heavily towards one or the other. Some other fields of research do focus more on theoretical results than on relevance. However, HCI research must be practical and relevant to people, organizations, or design. The research needs to be able to influence interface design, development processes, user training, public policy, or something else. Partially due to the philosophies of the founders of the field, HCI has had a historic focus on practical results that improve the quality of life (Hochheiser and Lazar, 2007). Is there a tension sometimes between researchers and practitioners? Absolutely. But all HCI research should at least consider the needs of both audiences. At the same time, the research methods used (regardless of the source discipline) must be rigorous and appropriate. It is not sufficient to develop a new computer interface without researching the need for the interface and without following up with user evaluations of that interface. HCI researchers are often placed in a position of evangelism where they must go out and convince others of the need for a focus on human users in computing. The only way to back up statements on the importance of users and human-centered design is with solid, rigorous research.

Due to this interdisciplinary focus and the historical development of the field, there are many different approaches to measurement and research currently used in the field of HCI. A group of researchers, all working on HCI-related topics, often disagree on what "real HCI research" means. There are major differences in how various leaders in the field perceive the existence of HCI. Be aware that, as an HCI researcher, you may run into people who don't like your research methods, are not comfortable with them, or simply come from a different research background and are unfamiliar with them. And that's OK. Think of it as another opportunity to be an HCI evangelist. (Note: As far as we know, the term "interface evangelist" was first used to describe Bruce Tognazzini. But we really think that the term applies to all of us who do HCI-related work.) Since the goal of this book is to provide a guide that introduces the reader to the set of generally accepted empirical research practices within the field of HCI, a central question is, therefore, how do we carry out measurement in the field of HCI research? What do we measure?

In the early days of HCI research, measurement was based on standards for human performance from human factors and psychology. How fast could someone complete a task? How many tasks were completed successfully, and how many errors were made? These are still the basic foundations for measuring interface usability and are still relevant today. These metrics are very much based on a task-centered model, where specific tasks can be separated out, quantified, and measured. These metrics include task correctness, time performance, error rate, time to learn, retention over time, and user satisfaction (see Chapters 5 and 10 for more information on measuring user satisfaction with surveys). These types of metrics are adopted by industry and standards-related organizations, such as the National Institute of Standards and Technology (in the United States) and the International Organization for Standardization (ISO). While these metrics are still often used and well-accepted, they are appropriate only in situations where the usage of computers can be broken down into specific tasks which themselves can be measured in a quantitative and discrete way.

Shneiderman has described the difference between micro-HCI and macro-HCI. The text in the previous paragraph, improving a user's experience using well-established metrics and techniques to improve task and time performance, could be considered micro-HCI (Shneiderman, 2011). However, many of the phenomena that interest researchers at a broader level, such as motivation, collaboration, social participation, trust, and empathy, perhaps having societal-level impacts, are not easy to measure using existing metrics or methods. Many of these phenomena cannot be measured in a laboratory setting using the human factors psychology model (Obrenovic, 2014; Shneiderman, 2008). And the classic metrics for performance may not be as appropriate when the usage of a new technology is discretionary and about enjoyment, rather than task performance in a controlled work setting (Grudin, 2006a). After all, how do you measure enjoyment or emotional gain? How do you measure why individuals use computers when they don't have to? Job satisfaction? Feeling of community? Mission in life? Multimethod approaches, possibly involving case studies, observations, interviews, data logging, and other longitudinal techniques, may be most appropriate for understanding what makes these new socio-technical systems successful. As an example, the research area of Computer-Supported Cooperative Work (CSCW) highlights the sociological perspectives of computer usage more than the psychological perspectives, with a focus more on observation in the field, rather than controlled lab studies (Bannon, 2011).

The old methods of research and measurement are comfortable: hypothesis testing, statistical tests, control groups, and so on. They come from a proud history of scientific research, and they are easily understood across many different academic, scientific, and research communities. However, they alone are not sufficient approaches to measure all of today's phenomena. The same applies to the "old standard" measures of task correctness and time performance. Those metrics may measure "how often?" or "how long?" but not "why?" However, they are still well-understood and well-accepted metrics, and they allow HCI researchers to communicate their results to other research communities where the cutting-edge tools and research methods may not be well-understood or well-accepted.

You may not be able to use experimental laboratory research to learn why people don't use technology. If you want to examine how people use portable or mobile technology such as smart phones and wearable computing, there are limitations to studying that in a controlled laboratory setting. If you want to study how people communicate with trusted partners, choose to perform business transactions with someone they don't know on another continent (as often happens with Ebay), or choose to collaborate, you need to find new ways of research and new forms of measurement. These are not research questions that can be answered with quantitative measurements in a short-term laboratory setting.

Consider Wikipedia, a collaborative, open-source encyclopedia. Currently, more than five million articles exist in English on Wikipedia, with an estimate of 70,000 active contributors (https://www.wikipedia.org), who spend their own time creating and editing Wikipedia entries. What causes them to do so? What do they get out of the experience? Clearly, task and time performance would not be appropriate metrics to use. But what metrics should be used? Joy? Emotion? A feeling of community? Lower blood pressure? This may not be a phenomenon that can be studied in a controlled laboratory setting (Menking and Erickson, 2015). The field of HCI has begun to apply more research methods from the social sciences, and we encourage the reader to start using some new research approaches that are not even in this textbook! Please be aware that people from other disciplines, as well as your "home discipline," will probably challenge the appropriateness of those research methods!

1.6 THE NATURE OF INTERDISCIPLINARY RESEARCH IN HCI

Interdisciplinary research using multiple research methods, is not always easy to do. There are many challenges that can arise, in many cases due to the individual cultures of each of the disciplines involved. The HCI community might be considered by some to be an interdisciplinary community, a multidisciplinary community, or its own discipline (Blackwell, 2015). Regardless of the status of HCI as interdisciplinary, multidisciplinary, or its own discipline, many conferences, professional organizations, and academic departments keep the focus on their primary discipline. When interdisciplinary research gets filtered through single-discipline evaluations, there are many challenges that can occur. Some of the challenges are well-known, such as how some disciplines (e.g., computer science) focus more on conference publications and others (e.g., management information systems) focus on journal publications (Grudin, 2006a). Some disciplines focus on single-author publications, while others focus primarily on group-author publications. Some disciplines are very open about sharing their results, while others keep their results more confidential. Some disciplines are very self-reflective and do research studies about their discipline (trends of research, rankings, funding, collaborations), while others do not. Some disciplines are primarily focused on getting grant money, while other disciplines are less interested, or can even be leery of the influences of outside sponsors. Even the appropriate dress at conferences for each discipline can vary widely. It is important, for a number of reasons, to become familiar with the research methods and preferences in different disciplines. You need to be able to communicate your research methods, and the reasons why you chose some and not others, in a very convincing way. When you submit journal articles, conference papers, grant proposals, or book chapters, you never know who will be reviewing your work. The chances are good that your work will be reviewed by people who come from very different research backgrounds, and interdisciplinary researchers can sometimes have problems convincing others at their workplace of the quality and seriousness of their work. But all of these are primarily concerns with an individual's professional career or with administrative issues (Sears et al., 2008).

There are more serious, but less well-known, challenges related to interdisciplinary research. As discussed earlier in this chapter, no research method, approach, or discipline is perfect. A research project is a series of steps and decisions related to data collection. For instance, there is a theoretical foundation for the data collection effort, there is a research method involved, often human participants are recruited and involved, there is data analysis, and then there is the discussion of implications involved. The development of a proof-of-concept or prototype is also frequently involved. Depending on the majority disciplinary background of those involved in the research, there may be different perspectives, value systems, and expectations (Hudson and Mankoff, 2014). For instance, there could be a distinction between technical HCI research (focused on interface building) versus behavioral HCI research (focused on cognitive foundations) which would likely have different expectations in terms of number and background of participants, development of a tool or interface, and outcomes (Hudson and Mankoff, 2014)

Different disciplines can sometimes be most interested in, and more focused on, different steps in the research process. While no one would ever say, "I'm not interested in the research methods," in many cases, there are steps that are considered to be of less interest to people from a certain discipline. And there may be historical roots for that. For instance, as described earlier and in other chapters, there are large data collection efforts that use strict controls, in fields such as sociology, and those data sets are available for researchers internationally to analyze. However, as previously discussed, no such central data sets exist for HCI and it is not considered a standard practice to publish your data sets or make them available to others. It is a very different model in other fields. That may lead to a focus on certain stages of research more than others.

(Please note: we expect the following paragraphs to be a bit controversial; however, we do believe strongly, based on our experience, that they are true.) One discipline might have an expectation that a specific step (such as research design) is done "perfectly," but that it is acceptable to give more flexibility in other steps (such as the types of participants). The management information systems community of

HCI researchers has a well-known focus on the theoretical underpinnings of any research. Computer science-based HCI researchers often have less interest in theory and much more of an interest in the practical outcomes of the research on interfaces (although Carroll, 2003 is a noteworthy effort on theory in HCI). This distinction is seen, for instance, in the Technology Acceptance Model, which is core theory and has central importance for HCI researchers focused on management information systems (Davis, 1989; Venkatesh and Davis, 2000), but is not well-known to the HCI researchers focused on computer science. While general computer science researchers have a great deal of theory in, say, algorithms, HCI research in computer science does not have a major focus on theory.

When having interdisciplinary discussions and working on interdisciplinary teams, it's important to be aware of these distinctions. Sociology-based HCI research tends to focus on the demographics of the research participants and determining if they are a true random sample, while this is not considered critical in computer science, where computer science students are often used as participants (even when it is not appropriate). Psychology-based HCI research tends to focus on an ideal and clean research design. HCI research based on computer science and on design is focused more on the implications for interfaces, although computer science may focus more on the technical underpinnings while design focuses more on the look and feel of the interface. These are just generalizations, obviously; all disciplines want excellence at all stages of research, but it is true that disciplines tend to focus more intensely on particular stages of research. The good news is that we want all of these different groups focusing on improving each stage of the research process. We WANT different groups looking at research through their different lenses. We want to get that triangulation (described more in Section 1.8), where people look at the same research questions, using different methods, different approaches, and different lenses, over time, with the goal of discovering some scientific truths.

1.7 WHO IS THE AUDIENCE FOR YOUR RESEARCH?

Most researchers in HCI often, unknowingly, target their HCI research towards other researchers. The metrics that are used most often to ascertain impact of a research publication, relate to the number of times that a paper is cited in other publications, and impact factor of the journal or conference proceeding. Metrics used in many areas of science, such as the h-index, can be used to ascertain productivity of an individual researcher, rather than a specific article, but again, it is based primarily on how the specific researcher has impacted other researchers. Alternative metrics, such as tracking number of downloads, using microblogging (e.g., Twitter), online reference managers (e.g., Zotero and Mendeley) and blogging to track impact, are also gaining in popularity (Bornmann, 2015). However, these metrics are reflections of how a research publication impacts other researchers, not how a research publication has impact outside of the research world. The idea of societal impact outside of other publications, is not something that most researchers receive training on, or even consider, and unless an individual is working in an industrial research lab or as a practitioner (where the goal is often to influence design and development) it is just perceived that the goal is to be cited by other researchers. However, there are other audiences for HCI research, aside from other researchers. Doing research targeted at other audiences requires different approaches to research, and different ways of communicating the findings of that research.

Outside of HCI researchers, the other audience that most HCI researchers would be familiar with, is the audience of individuals who do systems development and interface design, as practitioners. Often, industrial HCI labs focus on HCI systems research, with the goals of doing good, publishable research while testing out designs and/or influencing the next generation of product interfaces at the company or organization. Researchers at universities, may also partner with industry, to influence the interaction design in corporations or nonprofit organizations. Unlike HCI research aimed at researchers taking place in a university setting without industrial partners, there may be issues about disclosure, about sharing results publicly, about corporate secrecy. There also may be much more concern about the control of intellectual property resulting from the research.

Furthermore, the types of controls or inclusion criteria used in HCI research targeted at industrial impact, may differ from the types of controls utilized in HCI research targeted at other researchers. For instance, it can be expected that a company would be most interested in evaluating aspects related to their own products. So, when doing research to impact design and development, the company might only be interested in their own products and the specific configurations that the product is designed to work with. As an example, a company, researching how their new software application might be utilized for blind people, might only test it on certain operating systems (e.g., iOS only, rather than Windows, or only Windows 8 and later), or with certain screen readers (e.g., JAWS 14 or later, or Window-Eyes, but not VoiceOver). The product being evaluated by users, may have a specific configuration that it is designed to work with, and so the research may need to be limited to that configuration, even if that is an unrealistic configuration. For instance, a configuration may be unrealistic, either because no one is currently using that configuration, or because the configuration would bias the research since it would only allow for very advanced users who are on the cutting edge. Companies often face this challenge—there is a large installed base of users who utilize old versions of software or operating systems, yet this is not represented in the user research which involves only advanced users utilizing only the newest technologies, a situation that is not very representative.

Another potential target audience for HCI research is policymakers. Public policymakers need to have data to inform their decisions related to HCI issues, in the areas of statutory laws, regulations, executive orders, and everything from legal cases to human rights documents such as treaties. While many areas of science and technology have well-developed policy outreach, such community infrastructure does not yet exist for public policy issues related to HCI. There are a number of areas, where in the past, individual HCI researchers have been successful in informing and guiding public policy, and these include accessibility and ergonomics (Lazar et al., 2016). Furthermore, individuals from the HCI community have taken leadership roles as government policymakers in countries such as the United States and Sweden. Many more areas exist where public policies have been created that influence HCI research work, often (and unfortunately) without the benefit of feedback from the HCI community. These areas where HCI research has been impacted include laws and regulations for human subjects research, standards for measurement, areas of research funding, language requirements for interface design, data privacy laws, and specific domains such as e-government, education, libraries, voting, and healthcare (Lazar et al., 2016). Because there is not an existing lobbying infrastructure, or entrenched interests on most HCI-related topics, this is a great opportunity for HCI researchers to have a true impact on public policies. Furthermore, some governments have legal limitations on how much data can be collected from citizens, so research studies (even a usability test involving 25 users) can be logistically hard for government to implement or even get approval for. However, the requirements of a university Institutional Review Board are often easier, and therefore, HCI researchers can often do data collection to inform policymakers, that a government agency may simply not be allowed to do.

When trying to perform HCI research with the target audience of public policymakers, there are some logistical considerations to be aware of. Policymakers in general, are very concerned with the number of people who are impacted (e.g., how many children or people with disabilities are within their representation area), and which specific laws or policies relate to your HCI work. So, computer scientists tend to make generalizations about items outside of computer science (e.g., "there is a law" or "lots of people") but research targeted towards policymakers needs to be much more specific in terms of coverage. In general, policymakers like longitudinal research, because they like to know the trends in how people are being affected (e.g., is the situation getting better or worse?). Furthermore, it is important to understand the timelines of policymakers (e.g., when public comments are due on a regulatory process, when legislation is being considered, when legal proceedings occur), because, unlike in academia where there is always another conference to submit to, or another journal to submit your research to, when dealing with the timelines of policymakers, often there is no flexibility and if you miss a deadline, you will have zero impact (Lazar, 2014). Policymakers are not likely to communicate in the same way as researchers, so if you think that you can have an impact by just emailing or skyping with a policymaker, or sending them your research paper, you are mistaken. Policymakers tend to work only via face-to-face contact, so if you want to build relationships with policymakers, you need to schedule an appointment to meet with them. You also would be wise to provide summaries of research, designed for people who do not have a background in your area of HCI research (Lazar, 2014).

1.8 UNDERSTANDING ONE RESEARCH PROJECT IN THE CONTEXT OF RELATED RESEARCH

There is no such thing as a perfect data collection method or a perfect data collection effort. All methods, all approaches, all projects have a flaw or two. One data collection effort does not lead to a definitive answer on a question of research. In scientific communities, the goal is generally for multiple teams to examine the same research question from multiple angles over time. Research results should be reported, with enough detail so that other teams can attempt to replicate the findings and expand upon them. Replication is considered an important part of validating research findings, even though it is rare in HCI and often gets very little attention (Hornbaek et al., 2014) (and many other fields of research have similar complaints). All of these efforts, if they come up with the same general findings over time, give evidence for the scientific truth of the findings. This is often known as "triangulation." One data collection effort, yielding one paper, is interesting in itself but does not prove anything. If you have 15 teams of researchers, looking at similar research questions, over a period of 10 years, using multiple research methods, and they all come to the same general conclusion about a phenomenon, then there is some scientific proof for the phenomenon. The proof is even stronger when multiple research methods have been used in data collection. If all of the research teams replicate the exact same research methods over 10 years, then there is the remote possibility that the methods themselves are flawed. However, the weight of evidence is strengthened when multiple research methods are used.

Researchers often speak of a "research life cycle," describing the specific steps in a research project. Depending on who you ask, the steps can differ: for instance, (1) designing research, (2) running data collection, and (3) reporting research (Hornbaek, 2011).

But there is another type of life cycle to consider: when you are entering a new area or subspecialty of research, which methods are likely to be utilized first? On the other hand, which methods require first having additional research in place? For instance, two of the three coauthors of this book have been involved with performing research to understand how people with Down syndrome (both children and adults) utilize technology and what their interface needs are. When we decided to do this research, there was no existing HCI research on people with Down syndrome. There was no base of literature to draw from. So we first started with an exploratory survey to understand how children and young adults utilize technology. Then we did a series of observations of adults with Down syndrome who were expert users about what their skills were, and how they gained those skills. Then we utilized a usability testing methodology to understand how adults with Down syndrome utilize social networking and touch screens. Once we had a base of understanding about the research topic with those three studies, only then did we do an experimental design (to understand the effectiveness of different authentication methods for people with Down syndrome). It would have been too premature to start with an experimental design method first, when so little was known about the population of users and how they interact with technology. The controls necessary for an experimental design, would have not yet been understood, so there would have been lots of phenomenon that were unknown and not controlled for. Often, when a research topic is new, it is important to start with a research method that can utilized in a more exploratory way—such as surveys, interviews, focus groups, and ethnography. Then, with a basis of understanding from a few exploratory studies, research studies utilizing more structured research methods—such as experimental design, automated data collection, and time diaries, could be performed. That's not to say that such an order must occur—but such an order often does occur, because more background research, more structure, is required for certain types of research methods. Shneiderman describes this as a three-step process: observation, intervention, and controlled experimentation. The understanding through the exploratory research, can be utilized to build prototypes or hypotheses for experimental design (Shneiderman, 2016).

Another aspect of the research life cycle is determining when controlled, in-laboratory studies should occur, versus studies "in the wild" (also known as field studies or in-situ studies). There is a great discussion in the research community about when each approach is situationally appropriate. For instance, some authors argue that field studies are most appropriate for mobile device research, since mobile devices are utilized in the field, with weather, noise, motion, and competing cognitive demands playing an important role in usage (Kjeldskov and Skov, 2014). Controlled environments and precise measurement may simply not be realistic for the usage of certain types of technologies, such as mobile devices. Another argument for the increased use of field studies, is that, as researchers come to understand more about what specific aspects of design lead to increased usability, then the next step is to understand how those technologies fit into the complex work, leisure, and family lives of individuals (Kjeldskov and Skov, 2014). Field studies may present interesting challenges related to informed consent, since the period of data collection, and who participates, in a controlled environment, may be easy to ascertain. But for example, data collection in a public space (in the wild), such as marathon or a rock concert, may pose questions about the inclusion of data from people who are not aware of the data collection and did not consent to participate (Anstead et al., 2014). One can imagine multiple approaches for which research methods to utilize and in what order (as described in previous paragraphs). So perhaps researchers might first do exploratory research in the wild, before moving to more controlled laboratory settings. Or perhaps researchers might first do controlled laboratory experiments, and then move their research into the wild and do field studies. There is not one answer that is right or wrong.

From personal experience, the authors can verify that both approaches are useful, and the combination of controlled studies and field studies, often gives you interesting findings that make you rethink your approaches. For instance, from the authors of this textbook, there were three research studies of a web-based security prototype, in a combination of controlled settings (university lab, workplace, home, and always on a consistent laptop), from three different groups of users, where the average task performance rate on a specific prototype was always over 90%. When that same web-based security prototype was placed on the web, with a much more diverse set of users utilizing the prototype, generally with a lower level of technical experience, and with technical environment being another factor (older browsers, slow download speeds, etc.), the average task performance rate was under 50%, a significant drop. No research method is ever perfect, and trying out different research methods to investigate similar phenomenon, helps you to more fully understand your area of study. It is important to note that an individual's viewpoint on controlled laboratory experiments versus field studies, may also be influenced by their individual disciplinary background, so, for instance, those with engineering backgrounds may lean more naturally towards laboratory experiments compared to those with an anthropology background.

In HCI, there are some situations where the evidence over time supports a specific finding. One clear example is the preference for broad, shallow tree structures in menu design (see the "Depth vs Breadth in Menus" sidebar). Multiple research studies have documented that broad, shallow tree structures are superior (in terms of user performance) to narrow, deep tree structures.

DEPTH VS BREADTH IN MENUS

Multiple research studies by different research teams, throughout the history of the HCI field, have examined the issue of the trade-off between depth and breadth in menus. Generally, tree structures in menu design can be implemented as narrow and deep (where there are fewer choices per level but more levels) or as broad and shallow (where there are more choices per level but fewer levels). Figure **1.1** shows three menu structures.

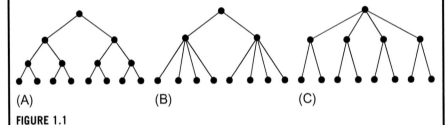

(A)   (B)   (C)

FIGURE 1.1

Types of tree structure in menu design: (A) narrow-deep: three levels with two choices at each level, (B) broad-shallow: two choices followed by four choices, (C) broad-shallow: four choices followed by two choices.

The research has consistently pointed to broad, shallow tree structures as being superior to narrow, deep structures. There are many possible reasons: users get more frustrated and more lost, the more levels they must navigate; users are capable of dealing with more than the 7 ± 2 options often cited in the research literature (since menus deal with recognition, not recall), and strategies for scanning can lead to superior performance. Different research methods and different research teams, examining different users, have all come to the same conclusion. So over time, the superiority of broad, shallow tree structures has become well-accepted as a foundation of interface design. Some of the better-known articles on this topic include:

Hochheiser, H., Lazar, J., 2010. Revisiting breadth vs. depth in menu structures for blind users of screen readers. Interacting with Computers 22 (5), 389–398.
Kiger, J.I., 1984. The depth/breadth trade-off in the design of menu-driven user interfaces. International Journal of Man-Machine Studies 20 (2), 201–213.
Landauer, T.K., Nachbar, D.W., 1985. Selection from alphabetic and numeric menu trees using a touch screen: breadth, depth, and width.

Proceedings of the SIGCHI Conference on Human Factors in Computing Systems, pp. 73–78.

Larson, K., Czerwinski, M., 1998. Web page design: implications of memory, structure and scent for information retrieval. Proceedings of the SIGCHI Conference on Human Factors in Computing Systems, pp. 25–32.

Miller, D., 1981. The depth/breadth tradeoff in hierarchical computer menus. Proceedings of the Human Factors Society 25th Annual Meeting, pp. 296–300.

Snowberry, K., Parkinson, S., Sisson, N., 1983. Computer display menus. Ergonomics 6 (7), 699–712.

Wallace, D.F., Anderson, N.S., Shneiderman, B., 1987. Time stress effects on two menu selection systems. Proceedings of the Human Factors and Ergonomics Society 31st Annual Meeting, pp. 727–731.

Zaphiris, P., Mtei, L., 2000. Depth vs breadth in the arrangement of web links. Proceedings of the Human Factors and Ergonomics Society, 44th Annual Meeting, pp. 139–144.

In contrast to the example in the sidebar, other research topics in HCI still have no clear answer, with multiple studies that yield conflicting findings. For instance, what is the minimum number of people required for usability testing? See Chapter 10, where the debate still rages on, as there is no agreed answer. The commonly repeated number is that 5 users is sufficient (although the research really doesn't say this), and more recent studies have suggested 10 ± 2 users (Hwang and Salvendy, 2010) or even more than 10 users (Schmettow, 2012). We suggest that readers turn to Chapter 10 to continue this debate. There may also be some research questions to which the answers change over time. For instance, in the late 1990s, web users tended to find download speed to be one of the biggest frustrations (Lightner et al., 1996; Pitkow and Kehoe, 1996). User habits and preferences are fluid and there may be changes over, say, a 20-year period (factors such as increased availability of broadband Internet access may also play a role). The biggest frustration for web users right now would most likely be viruses or spam. When the web first became popular in the mid-1990s, web-wide subject lists and in-site navigation were popular methods for finding items; now, search boxes are far more popular methods for finding what you want (and it is possible that the introduction of Google played a role). When it comes to user preferences, there can be many different influences, and these preferences may change over time. This is yet another reason why one research project, at one point in time, does not make a scientific fact.

You should never get disappointed or upset when you find out that another research team is working on a similar research question. You should get excited, because it means that both research teams are moving closer to the end goal of some definitive scientific answers. The chances are very high that your research method won't be exactly the same, your research questions won't be exactly the same, and your human participants won't be exactly the same. The fact that other research teams are interested in this topic shows the importance of the research area and strengthens your findings. Perhaps you should be more worried if no one else is interested in your research.

1.9 INHERENT TRADE-OFFS IN HCI

It would at first seem that, with enough research, you could simply decide which design is best by optimizing some specific measurement, such as task performance or time performance. First of all, as discussed earlier in this chapter, socio-technical systems can rarely be reduced to two or three measurements, and there are many factors to be controlled for. We can do comparison studies of small differences in menu structure or some detailed aspect of interface design, but it is much harder to compare fundamental recastings of tasks. In addition, there are inherent conflicts in HCI research and design. We make trade-offs and accept "better solutions" rather than optimal solutions. We have multiple stakeholders and not all of them can be satisfied. Design is not simple and it's not an optimization problem. Good HCI research allows us to understand the various factors at play, which design features may work well for which users, and where there are potential conflicts or trade-offs.

For example, we can learn how to make interfaces that are far better than our current interfaces. However, users may not prefer those interfaces because they are so different from the current interfaces. So maybe we should modify our interfaces gradually, making only minor changes each time? Keyboards are a perfect example of this. We know how to make keyboards that are more ergonomic, with key layouts that allow for much faster typing. However, the keyboard layout predominantly used with the Roman alphabet is still the QWERTY key layout. Why? We have far superior designs. However, people have been comfortable with the QWERTY layout for years and the other key layouts have not caught on (despite their clear superiority from a design and usability point of view). So we still use the QWERTY layout. It's a trade-off. You want to make interfaces that are much better but users want consistency. In the short-term, a totally new interface lowers user performance, increases user error, and lowers user satisfaction. In the long-term, a modified interface may improve performance and result in higher satisfaction. This focus on very minor tweaks can be seen in the attention currently being paid, in industry and government, to the idea of A/B testing, where you test very minor interface changes, barely noticeable by the user, and then roll out those that are deemed to be successful, increasing traffic, increasing sales, and reducing costs (Wolfers, 2015). Of course, there are sometimes new interfaces, new devices, that just leap ahead with a totally different design and users love it, such as the Apple iPad tablet device. You shouldn't create a totally new design, apparently, unless it's something so cool that users want to spend the time to learn how to use it. Well, how do you measure that? How do you decide that? How do you plan for that? It's not easy.

Other examples of trade-offs in HCI also exist. For instance, the intersection of usability and security (Bardram, 2005; DeWitt and Kuljis, 2006). In HCI, we want interfaces that are 100% easy to use. People focused on computer security want computers that are 100% secure. By definition, many security features are designed to present a roadblock, to make users stop and think, to be hard. They are designed so that users may not be successful all of the time. The best way to make a 100% usable interface would be to remove all security features. Clearly, we can't do that. From the HCI point of view, our goal is to reduce unnecessary difficulty. Right now, the typical user has so many passwords that they simply can't remember them or they choose easy-to-remember (and easy to crack) passwords (Chiasson et al., 2008). Users may write their passwords on a sheet of paper kept in their wallet, purse, or desk drawer (none of which are secure), or they click on the feature that most web sites have saying, "Can't remember your password? Click here!" and their password is e-mailed to them (also not secure!). We suggest to readers to check out the annual ACM Symposium on Usable Privacy and Security (SOUPS) for research on the intersection of usability and security. Other inherent trade-offs occur in the area of sustainability. While people working in the field of information technology may often be focused on new and better devices and design, faster machines, and faster processing, this can lead to high energy usage and a lot of waste. Sustainability means trying to encourage users to limit their energy usage (Chetty et al., 2009), to keep using current devices, and to reduce the amount of technology waste by allowing current devices to be repaired or retrofitted, rather than just throwing the device out (Mankoff et al., 2007a). Millions of current personal computers end up in landfills, poisoning the earth and water.

Being user centered, as HCI tends to be, also means being concerned about the impacts of technology on human life. In the past, this meant that HCI researchers were interested in reducing repetitive strain injuries from computer usage, whether spending lots of time on the Internet made you depressed, and whether computer frustration could impact on your health. How does all of our technology creation, usage, and disposal impact on the quality of our life and the lives of future generations? Can persuasive devices and social networking be used to encourage us to lower our ecological footprint? (Gustafsson and Gyllenswärd, 2005; Mankoff et al., 2007b). Let's go back to our keyboard example: if all keyboards in the English-speaking world were changed over to a different key layout (say, the DVORAK layout), there might be some initial resistance by users but, eventually, user performance might improve. However, how would those millions of keyboards in landfill impact on the quality of human life? This is a new point to evaluate when considering how we do research in HCI. What is the ecological impact of our research? What is the ecological impact of new interfaces or devices that we build? While it is likely that we won't know in advance what type of ecological impact our research work will lead to, it's an important consideration as we do our research, yet another inherent challenge in HCI.

1.10 SUMMARY OF CHAPTERS

Given that the topic of research methods in HCI is so broad, we have tried to give approximately one chapter to each research method. However, the book starts out with three chapters revolving around the topic of experimental design. Whole books and semesters have focused on experimental design and, when you include all of the statistical tests, this simply cannot be contained in one chapter. Chapter 4 can be useful for methods other than experimental design (for instance, statistical analysis is often used in survey research). And for researchers using statistical software and advanced statistical analysis, additional reading resources are likely to be necessary.

Chapters 5 and 6 cover surveys and diaries, two key research approaches from the field of sociology. While surveys are used far more often than diaries in HCI research, there are some emerging research projects using the time diary method. Again, a number of textbooks have been written solely on the topic of survey design. Chapters 7–9 are based on research approaches popular in the social sciences. Case studies, interviews/focus groups, and ethnography have also been popular approaches in business school research for years. The five research approaches in Chapters 5–9—surveys, time diaries, case studies, interviews, and ethnography—are often useful for understanding "why?" questions, whereas experimental research is often better at understanding "how often?" or "how long?" questions.

Chapter 10 provides useful information on how to manage structured usability tests, in cases where usability testing is a part of the package of research approaches. Chapter 11 focuses on analyzing qualitative data, which might have been collected from case studies, ethnography, time diaries, and other methods. Chapters 12 and 13 focus on methods of collecting research data through automated means. One method is automated data collection indirectly from humans, through their actions on a computer, including key logging and web site logs. The other method involves data collection directly from humans through sensors focused on the body, such as facial EMG and eye-tracking. While all of the chapters have been updated for the second edition of the book, Chapter 14 is our chapter that is strictly new, focusing on online data collection, crowdsourcing, and big data. Chapters 15 and 16 focus on issues that arise in working with human subjects. Chapter 15 covers general issues, such as informed consent, while Chapter 16 deals with issues specific to participants with disabilities.

As with any overview of such a broad and rich field, this book is not and cannot be exhaustive. We have provided content that provides a background understanding on HCI research, and the processes involved with research, along with details on implementing many of the methods. Where possible, we have tried to provide detailed descriptions of how various methods can be used. For methods needing greater detail for implementation (e.g., eye-tracking), we have tried to provide pointers to more in-depth discussions, including examples of how those methods were used. We hope that we have provided enough detail to be useful and informative, without being overwhelming. We would love to hear from readers about areas where we might have hit the mark, and (more likely) those where we've fallen short. At the end of the day, we hope that you enjoy reading this book as much as we enjoyed writing it! We hope that the book helps you in your journey, of doing HCI research that has an impact on making the lives of computer users everywhere, easier, safer, and happier!

DISCUSSION QUESTIONS

1. What were some of the major shifts in the topics of HCI research from the original focus on word processing and other office automation software? Discuss at least two shifts in the focus of research.

2. What are the standard quantitative metrics that have been used in HCI research since the early 1980s?

3. What are some newer metrics used in HCI research?

4. What is triangulation? Why is it important?

5. Why doesn't one published research paper equate to scientific truth?

6. Name four disciplines that have helped contribute to the field of human-computer interaction.

7. What are the seven types of research contributions described by Wobbrock and Kientz? Which two types are the most commonly performed types of HCI research?

8. Are there any national or international data sets collected on a yearly basis for HCI researchers?

9. What types of research questions in HCI does big data help us understand? What types of research questions does big data not help us understand? What types of research questions could longitudinal data help us understand?

10. When researchers are doing research in an industrial setting to influence new technologies being built for that company, what considerations do they have, that HCI researchers working in a university, may not have considered?

11. What are three suggestions for how to inform public policy makers about your HCI research, relevant to their legislative, executive, or judicial work?

12. Give one benefit and one drawback of controlled laboratory studies versus field studies.

13. Describe three professional challenges of interdisciplinary research.

14. Describe three research design challenges in interdisciplinary research.

15. Describe three inherent conflicts in human-computer interaction.

16. What do you think the field of HCI research will look like in 20 years?

RESEARCH DESIGN EXERCISE

Imagine that you are going to be researching the topic of why people choose to take part in an online community for parents of children with autism. What are some of the reference disciplines that you should be looking into? What types of people might you want to talk with? What types of metrics might be appropriate for understanding this community? Come up with three approaches that you could take in researching this online community.

REFERENCES

Anstead, E., Flintham, M., Benford, S., 2014. Studying MarathonLive: consent for in-the-wild research. In: Proceedings of the 2014 ACM International Joint Conference on Pervasive and Ubiquitous Computing: Adjunct Publication. pp. 665–670.

Bannon, L., 2011. Reimagining HCI: toward a more human-centered perspective. Interactions 18 (4), 50–57.

Bardram, E., 2005. The trouble with login: on usability and computer security in ubiquitous computing. Personal and Ubiquitous Computing 9 (6), 357–367.

Blackwell, A., 2015. HCI as an inter-discipline. In: Proceedings of the 33rd Annual ACM Conference Extended Abstracts on Human Factors in Computing Systems, pp. 503–516.

Bornmann, L., 2015. Alternative metrics in scientometrics: a meta-analysis of research into three altmetrics. Scientometrics 103 (3), 1123–1144.

Bush, V., 1945. As we may think. The Atlantic Monthly 176, 101–108.

Buxton, B., 2016. Multi-touch systems that I have known and loved. Available at: http://www.billbuxton.com/multitouchOverview.html.

Carroll, J. (Ed.), 2003. HCI models, theories, and frameworks: toward a multidisciplinary science. Morgan Kaufmann Publishers, San Francisco, CA.

Carroll, J., Carrithers, C., 1984. Training wheels in a user interface. Communications of the ACM 27 (8), 800–806.

Chetty, M., Brush, A.J.B., Meyers, B., Johns, P., 2009. It's not easy being green: understanding home computer power management, In: Proceedings of the 27th ACM Conference on Human Factors in Computing Systems, pp. 1033–1042.

Chiasson, S., Forget, A., Biddle, R., Van Oorschot, P., 2008. Influencing users towards better passwords: persuasive cued click-points. In: Proceedings of the 22nd British HCI Group Annual Conference on HCI 2008: People and Computers, pp. 121–130.

Davis, F., 1989. Perceived usefulness, perceived ease of use, and user acceptance of information technology. MIS Quarterly 13 (3), 319–340.

DeWitt, A., Kuljis, J., 2006. Aligning usability and security: a usability study of Polaris. In: Proceedings of the Second Symposium on Usable Privacy and Security, pp. 1–7.

Engelbart, D., 2016. Highlights of the 1968 "Mother of All Demos". Available at: http://dougengelbart.org/events/1968-demo-highlights.html.

Grudin, J., 2006a. Is HCI homeless? In search of inter-disciplinary status. Interactions 13 (1), 54–59.

Grudin, J., 2006b. A missing generation: office automation/information systems and human–computer interaction. Interactions 13 (3), 58–61.

Gustafsson, A., Gyllenswärd, M., 2005. The power-aware cord: energy awareness through ambient information display. In: Proceedings of the ACM Conference on Human Factors in Computing Systems, pp. 1423–1426.

Hochheiser, H., Lazar, J., 2007. HCI and societal issues: a framework for engagement. International Journal of Human–Computer Interaction 23 (3), 339–374.

Hornbæk, K., 2011. Some whys and hows of experiments in human–computer interaction. Foundations and Trends in Human-Computer Interaction 5 (4), 299–373.

Hornbæk, K., Sander, S.S., Bargas-Avila, J.A., Grue Simonsen, J., 2014. Is once enough?: on the extent and content of replications in human-computer interaction. In: Proceedings of the SIGCHI Conference on Human Factors in Computing Systems, pp. 3523–3532.

Hudson, S., Mankoff, J., 2014. Concepts, values, and methods for technical human-computer interaction research. In: Olson, J., Kellogg, W. (Eds.), Ways of Knowing in HCI. Springer, New York, pp. 69–93.

Hwang, W., Salvendy, G., 2010. Number of people required for usability evaluation: the 10 ± 2 rule. Communications of the ACM 53 (5), 130–133.

Kjeldskov, J., Skov, M.B., 2014. Was it worth the hassle? Ten years of mobile HCI research discussions on lab and field evaluations. In: Proceedings of the 16th International Conference on Human-Computer Interaction With Mobile Devices & Services (MobileHCI), pp. 43–52.

Kraut, R., Burke, M., 2015. Internet use and psychological well-bring: effects of activity and audience. Communications of the ACM 58 (12), 94–99.

Lazar, J., 2014. Engaging in information science research that informs public policy. The Library Quarterly 84 (4), 451–459.

Lazar, J., Abascal, A., Barbosa, S., Barksdale, J., Friedman, B., Grossklags, J., et al., 2016. Human-computer interaction and international public policymaking: a framework for understanding and taking future actions. Foundations and Trends in Human-Computer Interaction 9 (2), 69–149.

Lehikoinen, J., Koistinen, V., 2014. In big data we trust? Interactions 21 (5), 38–41.

Lightner, N., Bose, I., Salvendy, G., 1996. What is wrong with the world wide web? A diagnosis of some problems and prescription of some remedies. Ergonomics 39 (8), 995–1004.

Liu, Y., Goncalves, J., Ferreira, D., Xiao, B., Hosio, S., Kostakos, V., 2014. CHI 1994-2013: mapping two decades of intellectual progress through co-word analysis. In: Proceedings of the 32nd Annual ACM Conference on Human Factors in Computing Systems, pp. 3553–3562.

Mankoff, J., Blevis, E., Borning, A., Friedman, B., Fussell, S., Hasbrouck, J., et al., 2007a. Environmental sustainability and interaction. In: Proceedings of the ACM Conference on Human Factors in Computing Systems, pp. 2121–2124.

Mankoff, J., Matthews, D., Fussell, S., Johnson, M., 2007b. Leveraging social networks to motivate individuals to reduce their ecological footprints. In: Proceedings of the 2007 Hawaii International Conference on System Sciences, pp. 87.

Menking, A., Erickson, I., 2015. The heart work of Wikipedia: Gendered, emotional labor in the world's largest online encyclopedia. In: Proceedings of the 33rd Annual ACM Conference on Human Factors in Computing Systems. pp. 207–210.

Norman, D., 1983. Design rules based on analyses of human error. Communications of the ACM 26 (4), 254–258.

Obrenovic, Z., 2014. The hawthorne studies and their relevance to HCI research. Interactions 21 (6), 46–51.

Perrin, A., 2015. Social Media Usage: 2005–2015. Pew Research Center. Available at: http://www.pewinternet.org/2015/10/08/social-networking-usage-2005-2015/.

Perrin, A., Duggan, M., 2015. Americans' Internet Access: 2000–2015. Pew Research Center. Available at: http://www.pewinternet.org/2015/06/26/americans-internet-access-2000-2015/.

Pew, R., 2007. An unlikely HCI frontier: the Social Security Administration in 1978. Interactions 14 (3), 18–21.

Pitkow, J., Kehoe, C., 1996. Emerging trends in the WWW population. Communications of the ACM 39 (6), 106–110.

Schmettow, M., 2012. Sample size in usability studies. Communications of the ACM 55 (4), 64–70.

Sears, A., Lazar, J., Ozok, A., Meiselwitz, G., 2008. Human-centered computing: defining a research agenda. International Journal of Human–Computer Interaction 24 (1), 2–16.

Shneiderman, B., 1983. Direct manipulation: a step beyond programming languages. IEEE Computer 9 (4), 57–69.

Shneiderman, B., 2002. Leonardo's laptop: human needs and the new computing technologies. MIT Press, Cambridge, MA.

Shneiderman, B., 2008. Science 2.0. Science 319, 1349–1350.

Shneiderman, B., 2011. Claiming success, charting the future: micro-HCI and macro-HCI. Interactions 18 (5), 10–11.

Shneiderman, B., 2016. The new ABCs of research: achieving breakthrough collaborations. Oxford University Press, Oxford.

Venkatesh, V., Davis, F., 2000. A theoretical extension of the technology acceptance model: four longitudinal field studies. Management Science 46 (2), 186–204.

Wobbrock, J., Kientz, J., 2016. Research contributions in human-computer interaction. Interactions 23 (3), 38–44.

Wolfers, J., 2015. A better government, one tweak at a time. The New York Times. Sept 25, 2015. Available at: http://www.nytimes.com/2015/09/27/upshot/a-better-government-one-tweak-at-a-time.html?_r=0.

Experimental research

2

A variety of laboratory and nonlaboratory research methods are available for human-computer interaction (HCI) researchers or practitioners when studying interfaces or applications. The most frequently used include observations, field studies, surveys, usability studies, interviews, focus groups, and controlled experiments (Shneiderman et al., 2017). In order to study how users enter information into their mobile phones, researchers may choose to observe mobile phone users in a natural setting, such as individuals who are using a cell phone in a company lobby, an airport, or a park. They may develop a survey that addresses questions that they would like to have answered and ask mobile phone users to respond to the survey. They may interview a number of mobile phone users to find out how they enter information into their phones. They may also choose to recruit a number of participants and run a usability test in a lab-based environment. Another option is to specify several conditions and run a strictly controlled lab-based experiment.

We can continue to add more options to the researchers' list: focus groups, field studies, and so on. Each of these options has its own strengths and weaknesses. Unobtrusively observing users in natural settings may allow the researcher to identify the patterns that are most representative of the use of the mobile phone in natural settings, but observation studies can be extremely time consuming. The researchers may wait for hours only to find that none of the individuals being observed has used the functions in which they are most interested. The survey approach may allow the researchers to reach a large number of users, say over a hundred, in a short period of time, but the participants may misunderstand the questions, the data collected may not represent depth in understanding, and the participant sample can be highly biased. Interviews allow the researchers to clarify questions and dig deeper with follow-up questions when a participant provides interesting feedback. However, interviews cost significantly more time and money than surveys. Usability tests provide a quick and comparatively low-cost method of identifying key usability problems in an interface or application, but they cannot guarantee that all critical design problems can be identified.

Choosing which method to use is a highly context-dependent issue related to a variety of factors including the primary purpose of the study, time constraints, funding, the participant pool, and the researchers' experience. We discuss in more detail in Chapter 3 on how to select the best research method. This chapter examines experimental research in general and focuses on the very basics of conducting experimental studies. We discuss how to develop research hypotheses and how to test the validity of a hypothesis. Important concepts related to hypothesis testing, such as Type I and Type II errors and their practical implications, are examined in detail.

2.1 TYPES OF BEHAVIORAL RESEARCH

Viewed broadly, all of the methods mentioned above are kinds of empirical investigation that can be categorized into three groups: descriptive investigations, relational investigations, and experimental investigations (Rosenthal and Rosnow, 2008). Descriptive investigations, such as observations, surveys, and focus groups, focus on constructing an accurate description of what is happening. For example, a researcher may observe that 8 out of 10 teenagers in a class who frequently play a specific computer game can touch type while only 2 out of 12 teenagers in the same class who do not play the game can touch type. This raises an interesting observation. But it does not allow the establishment of a relationship between the two factors: playing the game and typing. Neither does it enable the researcher to explain why this happens.

Relational investigations enable the researcher to identify relations between multiple factors. That is, the value of factor X changes as the value of factor Y changes. For example, the researcher may collect data on the number of hours that the teenagers play the computer game per week and measure their typing speed. The researcher can run a correlation analysis[1] between the number of hours and typing speed. If the result is significant, it suggests that there is a relationship between typing speed and the time spent playing the game. The results of relational studies usually carry more weight than what can be learned through descriptive studies. However, relational studies can rarely determine the causal relationship between multiple factors (Cooper and Schindler, 2000; Rosenthal and Rosnow, 2008).

Using the same example, the significant correlation result does not allow the researcher to determine the cause of the observed relationship. It is possible that playing the computer game improves typing speed. It is also possible that teenagers who type well tend to like the game more and spend more time on it. To complicate matters even more, the correlation can be due to hidden factors that the researcher has not considered or studied. For example, it is possible that teenagers who read well tend to type faster and that teenagers who read well tend to like the game more and spend more time on it. In this case, playing the computer game has no impact on the typing speed of the teenagers.

How, then, can the researchers determine the causal effect between two factors? The answer lies in experimental research (Kirk, 1982; Oehlert, 2000). The researchers may recruit teenagers in the same age group and randomly assign the teenagers to two groups. One group will spend a certain amount of time playing the computer game every week and the other group will not. After a period of time (e.g., 3 months or longer), the researchers can measure each teenager's typing speed. If the teenagers who play the computer game type significantly faster than the teenagers who do not

---

[1] Correlation analysis is a statistical test designed to identify relationships between two or more factors. Details of correlation analysis are discussed in Chapter 4.

play the game, the researchers can confidently draw the conclusion that playing this computer game improves the typing skills of teenagers.

As shown in the above example and summarized in Table 2.1, the most notable difference between experimental research and the other two types of investigation is that experimental research enables the identification of causal relationships. Simply put, it can tell how something happens and, in some cases, why it happens. The ability of experimental research to identify the true cause of a phenomenon allows researchers to manipulate the way we do research and achieve the desired results. To give a few examples, experimental studies are widely adopted in the field of medicine to identify better drugs or treatment methods for diseases. Scientists also use experimental research to investigate various questions originating from both the macro-world, such as the impact of acid rain on plants, and the micro-world, such as how nerves and cells function.

Table 2.1 Relationship Between Descriptive Research, Relational Research, and Experimental Research

Type of Research	Focus	General Claims	Typical Methods
Descriptive	Describe a situation or a set of events	X is happening	Observations, field studies, focus groups, interviews
Relational	Identify relations between multiple variables	X is related to Y	Observations, field studies, surveys
Experimental	Identify causes of a situation or a set of events	X is responsible for Y	Controlled experiments

The three kinds of research methods are not totally independent but highly inter-twined. Typical research projects include a combination of two or even three kinds of investigation. Descriptive investigations are often the first step of a research program, enabling researchers to identify interesting phenomena or events that establish the cornerstone of the research and identify future research directions. Relational investi-gations enable researchers or practitioners to discover connections between multiple events or variables. Ultimately, experimental research provides the opportunity to explore the fundamental causal relations. Each of the three kinds of investigation is of great importance in the process of scientific discovery.

2.2 RESEARCH HYPOTHESES

An experiment normally starts with a research hypothesis. A hypothesis is a pre-cise problem statement that can be directly tested through an empirical investigation. Compared with a theory, a hypothesis is a smaller, more focused statement that can be examined by a single experiment (Rosenthal and Rosnow, 2008). In contrast, a theory normally covers a larger scope and the establishment of a theory normally requires a sequence of empirical studies. A concrete research hypothesis lays the foundation of an experiment as well as the basis of statistical significance testing.

THEORY VS HYPOTHESIS

The differences between theories and hypotheses can be clearly demonstrated by the extensive HCI research into Fitts' law (Fitts, 1954), one of the most widely accepted theories in the HCI field. It states a general relationship between movement time, navigation distance, and target size for pointing tasks in an interface:

> *In movement tasks, the movement time increases as the movement distance increases and the size of the target decreases. The movement time has a log linear relationship with the movement distance and the width of the target.*

Fitts' law is a general theory that may apply to various kinds of pointing devices. It is impossible to validate Fitts' law in a few experiments. Since Fitts' law was proposed, hundreds of user studies have been conducted on various pointing devices and tasks to validate and modify Fitts' law. The research hypothesis of each of those studies is a much more focused statement covering a small, testable application domain.

For example, Miniotas (2000) examined hypotheses about the performance of two pointing devices: a mouse and an eye tracker. Movement time was shorter for the mouse than for the eye tracker. Fitts' law predicted the navigation time fairly well for both the mouse and the eye tracker, indicating the potential to apply Fitts' law to technologies that do not rely on hand-based control. Accot and Zhai (2003) investigated Fitts' law in the context of two-dimensional targets. More recently, Bi et al. (2013) developed a FFitts law model that expanded Fitts' law to finger touch input.

2.2.1 NULL HYPOTHESIS AND ALTERNATIVE HYPOTHESIS

An experiment normally has at least one null hypothesis and one alternative hypothesis. A null hypothesis typically states that there is no difference between experimental treatments. The alternative hypothesis is always a statement that is mutually exclusive with the null hypothesis. The goal of an experiment is to find statistical evidence to refute or nullify the null hypothesis in order to support the alternative hypothesis (Rosenthal and Rosnow, 2008). Some experiments may have several pairs of null hypotheses and alternative hypotheses. The characteristics of null and alternative hypotheses can be better explained through the following hypothetical research case.

Suppose the developers of a website are trying to figure out whether to use a pull-down menu or a pop-up menu in the home page of the website. The developers decide to conduct an experiment to find out which menu design will allow the users to navigate the site more effectively. For this research case, the null and alternative hypotheses[2] can be stated in classical statistical terms as follows:

- H_0: There is no difference between the pull-down menu and the pop-up menu in the time spent locating pages.
- H_1: There is a difference between the pull-down menu and the pop-up menu in the time spent locating pages.

From this example, we can see that the null hypothesis usually assumes that there is no difference between two or more conditions. The alternative hypothesis and the null hypothesis should be mutually exclusive. That is, if the null hypothesis is true, the alternative hypothesis must be false, and vice versa. The goal of the experiment is to test the null hypothesis against the alternative hypothesis and decide which one should be accepted and which one should be rejected. The results of any significance test tell us whether it is reasonable to reject the null hypothesis and the likelihood of being wrong if rejecting the null hypothesis. We explain this topic in more detail in Section 2.5.

Many experiments examine multiple pairs of null and alternative hypotheses. For example, in the research case above, the researchers may study the following additional hypotheses:

- H_0: There is no difference in user satisfaction rating between the pull-down menu and the pop-up menu.
- H_1: There is a difference in user satisfaction rating between the pull-down menu and the pop-up menu.

There is no limit on the number of hypotheses that can be investigated in one experiment. However, it is generally recommended that researchers should not attempt to study too many hypotheses in a single experiment. Normally, the more hypotheses to be tested, the more factors that need to be controlled and the more variables that need to be measured. This results in very complicated experiments, subject to a higher risk of design flaws.

In order to conduct a successful experiment, it is crucial to start with one or more good hypotheses (Durbin, 2004). A good hypothesis normally satisfies the following criteria:

- is presented in precise, lucid language;
- is focused on a problem that is testable in one experiment;
- clearly states the control groups or conditions of the experiment.

In the early stages of a research project, researchers usually find themselves confronted with a broad and vague task. There are no well-defined research questions. There are no focused, testable research hypotheses. The common way to initiate a research project is to conduct exploratory descriptive investigations such as observations, interviews, or focus groups. Well-conducted descriptive investigations help researchers identify key research issues and come up with appropriate control groups to be manipulated as well as dependent variables to be measured.

---

[2] Traditionally, H_0 is used to represent the null hypothesis and H_1 to represent the alternative hypothesis.

2.2.2 DEPENDENT AND INDEPENDENT VARIABLES

A well-defined hypothesis clearly states the dependent and independent variables of the study. Independent variables refer to the factors that the researchers are interested in studying or the possible "cause" of the change in the dependent variable. The term "independent" is used to suggest that the variable is independent of a participant's behavior. Dependent variables refer to the outcome or effect that the researchers are interested in. The term "dependent" is used to suggest that the variable is dependent on a participant's behavior or the changes in the independent variables. In experiments, the primary interest of researchers is to study the relationship between dependent variables and independent variables. More specifically, the researcher wants to find out whether and how changes in independent variables induce changes in dependent variables.

A useful rule of thumb to differentiate dependent variables from independent variables is that independent variables are usually the treatments or conditions that the researchers can control while dependent variables are usually the outcomes that the researchers need to measure (Oehlert, 2000). For example, consider the null hypothesis proposed in the research case in Section 2.2.1:

> *There is no difference between the pull-down menu and the pop-up menu in the time spent locating pages.*

The independent variable is the type of menu (pull-down or pop-up). The dependent variable is the time spent in locating web pages. During the experiment, the researchers have full control over the types of menu with which each participant interacts by randomly assigning each participant to an experimental condition. In contrast, "time" is highly dependent on individual behavioral factors that the researchers cannot fully control. Some participants will be faster than others due to a number of factors, such as the type of menu, previous computer experience, physical capabilities, reading speed, and so on. The researchers need to accurately measure the time that each participant spends in locating pages and to relate the results to the independent variable in order to make a direct comparison between the two types of menu design.

2.2.3 TYPICAL INDEPENDENT VARIABLES IN HCI RESEARCH

Independent variables are closely related to the specific research field. It is obvious that the factors frequently investigated in medical science are drastically different from those examined in physics or astronomy. In the HCI field, independent variables are usually related to technologies, users, and the context in which the technology is used. Typical independent variables that relate to technology include:

- different types of technology or devices, such as typing versus speech-based dictation, mouse versus joystick, touch pad, and other pointing devices;
- different types of design, such as pull-down menu versus pop-up menu, font sizes, contrast, background colors, and website architecture.

Typical independent variables related to users include age, gender, computer experience, professional domain, education, culture, motivation, mood, and disabilities. Using age as an example, we know that human capabilities change during their life span. Children have a physically smaller build and shorter attention span. Their reading skills, typing skills, and cognitive capabilities are all limited compared to typical computer users between ages 20 and 55. At the other end of the scale, senior citizens experience deterioration in cognitive, physical, and sensory capabilities. As a result, users in different age groups interact differently with computers and computer-related devices. Most computer applications are designed by people between 20 and 50 years of age who have little or no knowledge or experience in the interaction style or challenges faced by the younger and older user groups (Chisnell, 2007). In order to understand the gap created by age differences, a number of studies have been conducted to compare the interaction styles of users in different age groups (Zajicek, 2006; Zajicek and Jonsson, 2006).

Typical independent variables related to the context of use of technologies include both physical factors, such as environmental noise, lighting, temperature, vibration, users' status (e.g., seated, walking or jogging) (Price et al., 2006), and social factors, such as the number of people surrounding the user and their relation to the user.

2.2.4 TYPICAL DEPENDENT VARIABLES IN HCI RESEARCH

Dependent variables frequently measured can be categorized into five groups: efficiency, accuracy, subjective satisfaction, ease of learning and retention rate, and physical or cognitive demand.

Efficiency describes how fast a task can be completed. Typical measures include time to complete a task and speed (e.g., words per minute, number of targets selected per minute)

Accuracy describes the states in which the system or the user makes errors. The most frequently used accuracy measure is error rate. Numerous metrics to measure error rate have been proposed for various interaction tasks, such as the "minimum string distance" proposed for text entry tasks (Soukoreff and Mackenzie, 2003). In HCI studies, efficiency and accuracy are not isolated but are highly related factors. There is usually a trade-off between efficiency and accuracy, meaning that, when the other factors are the same, achieving a higher speed will result in more errors and ensuring fewer errors will lower the speed. Consequently, any investigation that only measures one of the two factors misses a critical side of the picture.

Subjective satisfaction describes the user's perceived satisfaction with the interaction experience. The data is normally collected using Likert scale ratings (e.g., numeric scales from 1 to 5) through questionnaires.

Ease of learning and retention rate describe how quickly and how easily an individual can learn to use a new application or complete a new task and how long they retain the learned skills (Feng et al., 2005). This category is less studied than the previous three categories but is highly important for the adoption of information technology.

Variables in the fifth category describe the cognitive and physical demand that an application or a task exerts on an individual or how long an individual can interact with an application without significant fatigue. This category of measures is less studied but they play an important role in technology adoption.

2.3 BASICS OF EXPERIMENTAL RESEARCH

In order to understand why experimental research can allow causal inference while descriptive and relational investigations do not, we need to discuss the characteristics of experimental research. In a true experimental design, the investigator can fully control or manipulate the experimental conditions so that a direct comparison can be made between two or more conditions while other factors are, ideally, kept the same. One aspect of the full control of factors is complete randomization, which means that the investigator can randomly assign participants to different conditions. The capability to effectively control for variables not of interest, therefore limiting the effects to the variables being studied, is the feature that most differentiates experimental research from quasi-experimental research, descriptive investigations, and relational investigations.

2.3.1 COMPONENTS OF AN EXPERIMENT

After a research hypothesis is identified, the design of an experiment consists of three components: treatments, units, and assignment method (Oehlert, 2000). Treatments, or conditions, refer to the different techniques, devices, or procedures that we want to compare. Units are the objects to which we apply the experiment treatments. In the field of HCI research, the units are normally human subjects with specific characteristics, such as gender, age, or computing experience. Assignment method refers to the way in which the experimental units are assigned different treatments.

We can further explain these three terms through an example. Suppose a researcher is running an experiment to compare typing speed using a traditional QWERTY keyboard and a DVORAK keyboard.[3] The treatment of this experiment is the type of keyboard: QWERTY or DVORAK. The experiment units are the participants recruited to join the study. To achieve the goal of fair comparison, the researchers would have to require that the participants have no previous experience using either keyboard. If most participants can touch type using the QWERTY keyboard but have never used a DVORAK keyboard before, it is obvious that the results will be highly biased towards the QWERTY keyboard. The researcher can employ different methods to randomly assign the participants into each of the two conditions. One well-known traditional method is to toss a coin. If a head is tossed, the participant is assigned to the QWERTY condition. If a tail is tossed, the participant is assigned to the DVORAK condition. Obviously, researchers are not busy tossing coins in their lab; more convenient randomization methods are used today. We discuss those methods in Section 2.3.2.

---

[3] Dvorak keyboard is an ergonomic alternative to the commonly used "QWERTY keyboard." The design of the Dvorak keyboard emphasizes typist comfort, high productivity, and ease of learning.

The keyboard comparison case illustrates a simple between-subject[4] design with two conditions. There are much more complicated designs involving multiple treatments and both between-subject and within-subject[5] comparisons. No matter how complicated the design is, all experiments consist of these three major components: treatments, units, and assignment methods.

2.3.2 RANDOMIZATION

The power of experimental research lies in its ability to uncover causal relations. The major reason why experimental research can achieve this goal is because of complete randomization. Randomization refers to the random assignment of treatments to the experimental units or participants (Oehlert, 2000).

In a totally randomized experiment, no one, including the investigators themselves, is able to predict the condition to which a participant is going to be assigned. For example, in the QWERTY vs. DVORAK experiment, when a participant comes in, the researchers do not know whether the participant will be using the QWERTY keyboard or the DVORAK keyboard until they toss a coin and find out whether it settles as heads or tails. Since the outcome of tossing the coin is totally random and out of the control of the researchers, the researchers have no influence, whether intentionally or subconsciously, on the assignment of the treatment to the participant. This effectively controls the influence of hidden factors and allows a clean comparison between the experiment conditions.

Traditional randomization methods include tossing a coin, throwing dice, spinning a roulette wheel, or drawing capsules out of an urn. However, these types of randomization are rarely used in behavioral research and HCI studies nowadays. One method to randomize the selection of experimental conditions or other factors is the use of a random digit table. Table 2.2 is an abbreviated random digit table taken from the large random digit table generated by RAND (1955). The original table consisted of a million random digits.

Table 2.2 An Abbreviated Random Digit Table

Line	Random Digits				
000	10097	32533	76520	13586	34673
001	37542	04805	64894	74296	24805
002	08422	68953	19645	09303	23209
003	99019	02529	09376	70715	38311
004	12807	99970	80157	36147	64032
005	66065	74717	34072	76850	36697

There are several ways to use this table. Suppose we are running a study that compares three types of navigation schemes for a website: topical, audience split,

---

[4] A between-subject design means each participant only experiences one task condition. The details of between-subject design are discussed in Chapter 3.

[5] A within-subject design means each participant experiences multiple task conditions. The details of within-subject design is discussed in Chapter 3.

and organizational. We recruit 45 participants and need to assign each of them to one of the three conditions. We can start anywhere in the random digit table and count in either direction. For example, if we start from the third number on the first row and count to the right for three numbers, we get 76520, 13586, and 34673. We can assign the first three participants to the conditions according to the order of the three random numbers. In this case, 76520 is the largest, corresponding to condition 3; 13586 is the smallest, corresponding to condition 1; and 34673 corresponds to condition 2. This means that the first participant is assigned to the design with the organizational navigation scheme, the second participant to the topical scheme, and the third participant to the audience split scheme. We can continue counting the numbers and repeating the process until all 45 participants are assigned to specific conditions.

Nowadays, software-driven randomization is also commonly used among researchers and practitioners. A large number of randomization software resources are available online, some of them free of charge, such as the services offered at http://www.randomization.com. Randomization functions are also available in most of the commercial statistical software packages, such as SAS, SPSS, and SYSTAT.

In a well-designed experiment, you will frequently find that you not only need to randomize the assignment of experiment conditions, but other factors as well. In a longitudinal study[6] reported by Sears et al. (2001, 2003), the researchers investigated the use of recognition software to generate text documents. Each of the 15 participants completed a total of nine tasks on different days. During each task, the participant composed a text document of approximately 500 words in response to one of nine predefined scenarios. The researchers found it necessary to randomize the order of the scenarios being used in the nine tasks. If the order of the scenarios were not randomized, it is likely that the characteristics of the scenarios would become a factor that influences the results. Randomizing the order of the scenarios cancels out the potential errors introduced by differences in scenarios.[7]

Counter balancing is commonly used in experiments to address the problem of systematic differences between successive conditions. In this case, researchers usually rotate the sequences of treatments or conditions through a "Latin Square Design" illustrated in Table 2.3 (Rosenthal and Rosnow, 2008). In this table, letters A, B, C,

Table 2.3 Latin Square Design

	Order of Administration			
	1	2	3	4
Sequence 1	A	B	C	D
Sequence 2	B	C	D	A
Sequence 3	C	D	A	B
Sequence 4	D	A	B	C

---

[6] A study in which data is gathered for the same participants repeatedly over a period of time.
[7] Special attention was paid during the development of the scenarios so that they are similar to each other in the degree of difficulty in responding, which was confirmed by the reported results. However, it is good practice to randomize the order of the scenarios in case there are unanticipated differences between them.

D each represents a condition. Each row represents a sequence of four conditions to which one participant can be randomly assigned. Note that each condition only appears once in each row and column, suggesting that the order of the conditions is completely counter balanced for these four participants.

2.4 SIGNIFICANCE TESTS
2.4.1 WHY DO WE NEED THEM?

Almost all experimental investigations are analyzed and reported through significance tests. If you randomly pick up an HCI-related journal article or a conference paper, it is very likely that you will encounter statements similar to the following:

> On average, participants performed significantly better ($F(1,25) = 20.83$, $p < 0.01$) ... in the dynamic peephole condition ... rather than the static peephole condition. (Mehra et al., 2006)
> A t test showed that there was a significant difference in the number of lines of text entered ($t(11) = 6.28$, $p < 0.001$) with more entered in the tactile condition. (Brewster et al., 2007)

Why do you need to run significance tests on your data? What is wrong with the approach of comparing two mean values of error rate and then claiming that the application with the lower mean value is more accurate than the other application? Here we encounter a fundamental issue in statistics that has to be clarified in order to understand the numerous concepts, terms, and methods that will be discussed in the rest of this chapter and in Chapters 4 and 5. Let us consider the following two statements:

1. Mike's height is 6'2". Mary's height is 5'8". So Mike is taller than Mary.
2. The average height of three males (Mike, John, and Ted) is 5'5". The average height of three females (Mary, Rose, and Jessica) is 5'10". So females are taller than males.

It should not be difficult for you to tell that the first statement is correct while the second one is not. In the first statement, the targets being compared are the heights of two individuals, both known numbers. Based on the two numbers, we know that Mike is taller than Mary. This is simple to understand, even for a child. When the values of the members of the comparison groups are all known, you can directly compare them and draw a conclusion. No significance test is needed since there is no uncertainty involved.

What is wrong with the second statement? People may give various responses to this question, such as:

- Well, by common sense, I know males are generally taller than females.
- I can easily find three other males and three other females, in which the average height of the three males is higher than that of the three females.
- There are only three individuals in each group. The sizes of the comparison groups are too small.
- The individuals in both the male group and the female group are not representative of the general population.

All of the above responses are well grounded, though the last two responses have deeper statistical roots. The claim that females are taller than males is wrong due to inappropriate sampling. The distribution of the heights of the human population (and many other things in our life) follows a pattern called "normal distribution." Data sets that follow normal distribution can be illustrated by a bell-shaped curve (see Figure 2.1), with the majority of the data points falling in the central area surrounding the mean of the population (μ). The further a value is from the population mean, the fewer data points would fall in the area around that value.

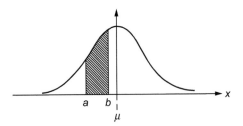

FIGURE 2.1

Normal distribution curve.

When you compare two large populations, such as males and females, there is no way to collect the data from every individual in the population. Therefore, you select a smaller group from the large population and use that smaller group to represent the entire population. This process is called sampling. In the situation described in statement 2 above, the three males selected as the sample population happened to be shorter than average males, while the three females selected as samples happened to be taller than average females, thus resulting in a misleading conclusion. Randomization methods and large sample sizes can greatly reduce the possibility of making this kind of error in research.

Since we are not able to measure the heights of all males and females, we can only sample a subgroup of people from the entire population. Significance tests allow us to determine how confident we are that the results observed from the sampling population can be generalized to the entire population. For example, a t test that is significant at $P < 0.05$ suggests that we are confident that 95% of the time the test result correctly applies to the entire population. We further explore the concept of significance tests in the next section.

2.4.2 TYPE I AND TYPE II ERRORS

In technical terms, significance testing is a process in which a null hypothesis (H_0) is contrasted with an alternative hypothesis (H_1) to determine the likelihood that the null hypothesis is true. All significance tests are subject to the risk of Type I and Type II errors.

A Type I error (also called an α error or a "false positive") refers to the mistake of rejecting the null hypothesis when it is true and should not be rejected. A Type II error (also called a β error or a "false negative") refers to the mistake of not rejecting the null hypothesis when it is false and should be rejected (Rosenthal and Rosnow, 2008). A widely used example to demonstrate Type I and Type II errors is the judicial case. In the US justice system, a defendant is presumed innocent. This presumption leads to the following null and alternative hypotheses:

- H_0: The defendant is innocent.
- H_1: The defendant is guilty.

A Type I error occurs when the jury decides that the defendant is guilty when he is actually innocent, meaning that the null hypothesis is rejected when it is true. A Type II error occurs when the jury decides that the defendant is innocent when he is actually guilty, meaning that the null hypothesis is accepted when it is false. Table 2.4 illustrates these errors. In the ideal case, the jury should always reach the decision that the defendant is guilty when he is actually guilty and vice versa. But in reality, the jury makes mistakes occasionally. Each type of error has costs. When a Type I error occurs, an innocent person would be sent to prison or may even lose his life; when a Type II error occurs, a criminal is set free and may commit another crime.

Table 2.4 Type I and Type II Errors in the Judicial Case

		Jury Decision	
		Not Guilty	Guilty
Reality	Not guilty	√	Type I error
	Guilty	Type II error	√

Let us further examine Type I and Type II errors through a study in the HCI domain. Suppose a bank hires several HCI researchers to evaluate whether ATMs with a touch-screen interface are easier to use than the ATMs with buttons that the bank branches are currently using. In this case, the null hypothesis and the alternative hypothesis are:

- H_0: There is no difference between the ease of use of ATMs with touch screens and ATMs with buttons.
- H_1: ATMs with touch screens are easier to use than ATMs with buttons.

The possible Type I and Type II errors in this study are illustrated in Table 2.5. A Type I error occurs when the research team decides that touch-screen ATMs are easier to use than ATMs with buttons, when they are actually not. A Type II error occurs when the research team decides that touch-screen ATMs are no better than ATMs with buttons, when they are. Again, each type of error can induce negative consequences. When a Type I error occurs, the bank may spend money to switch to touch-screen ATMs that do not provide better service to the customers. When a Type II error occurs, the bank chooses to stay with ATMs with buttons and loses the opportunity to improve the service that it provides to its customers.

Table 2.5 Type I and Type II Errors in a Hypothetical HCI Experiment

		Study Conclusion	
		No Difference	**Touchscreen ATM is Easier to Use**
Reality	No difference	√	Type I error
	Touchscreen ATM is easier to use	Type II error	√

It is generally believed that Type I errors are worse than Type II errors. Statisticians call Type I errors a mistake that involves "gullibility." A Type I error may result in a condition worse than the current state. For example, if a new medication is mistakenly found to be more effective than the medication that patients are currently taking, the patients may switch to new medication that is less effective than their current treatment. Type II errors are mistakes that involve "blindness" and can cost the opportunity to improve the current state. In the medication example, a Type II error means the test does not reveal that the new medication is more effective than the existing treatment; the patients stick with the existing treatment and miss the opportunity of a better treatment.

2.4.3 CONTROLLING THE RISKS OF TYPE I AND TYPE II ERRORS

When designing experiments and analyzing data, you have to evaluate the risk of making Type I and Type II errors. In statistics, the probability of making a Type I error is called alpha (or significance level, P value). The probability of making a Type II error is called beta. The statistical power of a test, defined as $1 - \beta$, refers to the probability of successfully rejecting a null hypothesis when it is false and should be rejected (Cohen, 1988).[8]

It should be noted that alpha and beta are interrelated. Under the same conditions, decreasing alpha reduces the chance of making Type I errors but increases the chance of making Type II errors. Simply put, if you want to reduce the chance of making Type I errors with all other factors being the same, you can do so by being less gullible. However, in doing so, you increase the odds that you miss something that is in fact true, meaning that your research is more vulnerable to Type II errors.

In experimental research, it is generally believed that Type I errors are worse than Type II errors. So a very low P value (0.05) is widely adopted to control the occurrence of Type I errors. If a significance test returns a value that is significant at $P < 0.05$, it means that the probability of making a Type I error is below 0.05. In other words, the probability of mistakenly rejecting a null hypothesis is below 0.05. In order to reduce Type II errors, it is generally suggested that you use a relatively

---

[8] How alpha and beta are calculated is beyond the scope of this book. For detailed discussion of the calculation, please refer to Rosenthal and Rosnow (2008).

large sample size so that the difference can be observed even when the effect size is relatively small. If interested, you can find more detailed discussions on statistical power in Rosenthal and Rosnow (2008).

2.5 LIMITATIONS OF EXPERIMENTAL RESEARCH

Experimental research methods originated from behavioral research and are largely rooted in the field of psychology. Experimental research has been a highly effective research approach and has led to many groundbreaking findings in behavioral science in the 20th century. Experimental research certainly plays an important role in the field of HCI. A large number of studies that explored fundamental interaction theories and models, such as Fitts' law, employed the approach of experimental research. To date, experimental research remains one of the most effective approaches to making findings that can be generalized to larger populations.

On the other hand, experimental research also has notable limitations. It requires well-defined, testable hypotheses that consist of a limited number of dependent and independent variables. However, many problems that HCI researchers or practitioners face are not clearly defined or involve a large number of potentially influential factors. As a result, it is often very hard to construct a well-defined and testable hypothesis. This is especially true when studying an innovative interaction technique or a new user population and in the early development stage of a product.

Experimental research also requires strict control of factors that may influence the dependent variables. That is, except the independent variables, any factor that may have an impact on the dependent variables, often called potential confounding variables, needs to be kept the same under different experiment conditions. This requirement can hardly be satisfied in many HCI studies. For example, when studying how older users and young users interact with computer-related devices, there are many factors besides age that are different between the two age groups, such as educational and knowledge background, computer experience, frequency of use, living conditions, and so on. If an experiment is conducted to study the two age groups, those factors will become confounding factors and may have a significant impact on the observed results. This problem can be partially addressed in the data collection and data analysis stages. In the data collection stage, extra caution should be taken when there are known confounding factors. Increasing the sample size may reduce the impact of the confounding factors. When recruiting participants, prescreening should be conducted to make the participants in different groups as homogeneous as possible. When confounding factors are inevitable, specific data analysis methods can be applied so that the impact of the confounding factors can be filtered out. A common method for this purpose is the analysis of covariables.

Lab-based experiments may not be a good representation of users' typical interaction behavior. It has been reported that participants may behave differently in lab-based experiments due to the stress of being observed, the different environment, or the rewards offered for participation. This phenomenon, called the "Hawthorne effect," was documented around 60 years ago (Landsberger, 1958). In many cases, being observed can cause users to make short-term improvements that typically do not last once the observation is over.

However, it should be noted that the context of the Hawthorne studies and HCI-related experiments is significantly different (Macefield, 2007). First, the Hawthorne studies were all longitudinal while most HCI experiments are not. Secondly, all the participants in the Hawthorne studies were experts in the tasks being observed while most HCI experiments observe novice users. Thirdly, the Hawthorne studies primarily focused on efficiency while HCI experiments value other important measures, such as error rates. Finally, the participants in the Hawthorne study had a vested interest in a successful outcome for the study since it was a point of contact between them and their senior management. In contrast, most HCI studies do not carry this motivation. Based on those reasons, we believe that the difference between the observed results of HCI experiments and the actual performance is not as big as that observed in the Hawthorne studies. But still, we should keep this potential risk in mind and take precautions to avoid or alleviate the impact of the possible Hawthorne effect.

EMPIRICAL EVALUATION IN HCI

The validity of empirical experiments and quantitative evaluation in HCI research has been doubted by some researchers. They argue that the nature of research in HCI is very different from traditional scientific fields, such as physics or chemistry, and, therefore, the results of experimental studies that suggest one interface is better than another may not be truly valid.

The major concern with the use of empirical experiments in HCI is the control of all possible related factors (Lieberman, 2007). In experiments in physics or chemistry, it is possible to strictly control all major related factors so that multiple experimental conditions are only different in the states of the independent variables. However, in HCI experiments, it is very difficult to control all potential factors and create experimental conditions that are exactly the same with the only exception of the independent variable. For instance, it is almost impossible to recruit two or more groups of participants with exactly the same age, educational background, and computer experience. All three factors may impact the interaction experience as well as the performance. It is argued that the use of significance tests in the data analysis stage only provides a veneer of validity when the potentially influential factors are not fully controlled (Lieberman, 2007).

We agree that experimental research has its limitations and deficiencies, just as any other research method does. But we believe that the overall validity of experimental research in the field of HCI is well-grounded. Simply observing a few users trying two interfaces does not provide convincing results on the performance and preference of the target population. Controlled experiments have allowed us to make critical and generalizable findings that other methods would not be able to provide. The truth is, experimental research and significance testing is the only approach that enables us to make judgments with systematically measured confidence and reliability. The control of confounding factors is challenging but the impact of those factors can be reduced to acceptable levels through well-designed and implemented experiments, which we discuss in detail in Chapter 3.

2.6 SUMMARY

Research in HCI examines human behavior in relation to computers or computer-related devices. There are three major types of research methods for studying human behavior: descriptive, relational, and experimental. The major strength of experimental research, compared to the other two types, is that it allows the identification of causal relationships between entities or events.

After a hypothesis is constructed, the design of an experiment consists of three components: treatments, units, and the assignment method. In an experiment, the process of sample selection needs to be randomized or counter-balanced, as does the assignment of treatments, or experiment conditions. Many methods can be used to randomly select samples or assign experiment conditions, including, but not limited to, the random digit table and software-generated randomization schemes.

Successful experimental research depends on well-defined research hypotheses that specify the dependent variables to be observed and the independent variables to be controlled. Usually a pair of null and alternative hypotheses is proposed and the goal of the experiment is to test whether the null hypothesis can be rejected or the alternative hypothesis can be accepted. Good research hypotheses should have a reasonable scope that can be tested within an experiment; clearly defined independent variables that can be strictly controlled; and clearly defined dependent variables that can be accurately measured.

Significance testing allows us to judge whether the observed group means are truly different. All significance tests are subject to two types of error. Type I errors refer to the situation in which the null hypothesis is mistakenly rejected when it is actually true. Type II errors refer to the situation of not rejecting the null hypothesis when it is actually false. It is generally believed that Type I errors are worse than Type II errors, therefore the alpha threshold that determines the probability of making Type I errors should be kept low. The widely accepted alpha threshold is 0.05. With its notable strengths, experimental research also has notable limitations when applied in the field of HCI: difficulty in identifying a testable hypothesis, difficulty in controlling potential confounding factors, and changes in observed behavior as compared to behavior in a more realistic setting. Therefore, experimental research methods should only be adopted when appropriate.

DISCUSSION QUESTIONS

1. What is descriptive research?

2. What is relational research?

3. What is experimental research?

4. What is randomization in experimental research? Discuss several examples of randomization methods.

5. What is a research hypothesis? What are the characteristics of a good research hypothesis?

6. What is a dependent variable?

7. What is an independent variable?

8. What is a significance test? Why do we need to run significance tests?

9. What is a Type I error? What is a Type II error?

10. Discuss the practical implications of Type I errors and Type II errors.

RESEARCH DESIGN EXERCISES

1. A research team is investigating three possible navigation architectures for an e-commerce website. Thirty participants are recruited to test the website, with 10 participants testing each architecture. How should the participants be assigned to the three conditions?

2. Read the following hypotheses and identify the dependent variables and independent variables in each hypothesis.

    1. There is no difference in users' reading speed and retention rate when they view news on a desktop computer or a PDA.

    2. There is no difference in the target selection speed and error rate between joystick, touch screen, and gesture recognition.

    3. There is no difference in the technology adoption rate between two speech-based applications with different dialog designs.

    4. There is no difference in the reading skills of children who used educational software for 6 months compared to those who have never used the software.

3. A spam filter assigns ratings to all incoming emails. If the rating of an email is higher than a specific threshold, the email is deleted before it reaches the inbox. Answer the following questions based on this scenario:
  a. What is a Type I error in this scenario?
  b. What is a Type II error in this scenario?
  c. If the rating is assigned using a scale of 1–10, with 1 representing "definitely not spam" and 10 representing "definitely spam," what happens if the threshold is set to 1, 2, 3, …, 10?
  d. What do you think the appropriate threshold should be? Why?

REFERENCES

Accot, J., Zhai, S., 2003. Refining Fitts' law models for bivariate pointing. In: Proceedings of the SIGCHI Conference on Human Factors in Computing Systems, pp. 193–200.

Bi, X., Li, Y., Zhai, S., 2013. FFitts law: modeling finger touch with Fitts' Law. In: Proceeding of the SIGCHI Conference on Human Factors in Computing Systems, pp. 1363–1372.

Brewster, S., Chohan, F., Brown, L., 2007. Mobile interaction: tactile feedback for mobile interactions. In: Proceedings of the SIGCHI Conference on Human Factors in Computing Systems, pp. 159–162.

Chisnell, D., 2007. Where technology meets green bananas. Interactions 14 (2), 10–11.

Cohen, J., 1988. Statistical Power Analysis for the Behavioral Sciences, second ed. Academic Press, New York.

Cooper, D., Schindler, P., 2000. Business Research Methods, seventh ed. McGraw Hill, Boston, MA.

Durbin, C., 2004. How to come up with a good research question: framing the hypothesis. Respiratory Care 49 (10), 1195–1198.

Feng, J., Karat, C.-M., Sears, A., 2005. How productivity improves in hands-free continuous dictation tasks: lessons learned from a longitudinal study. Interacting with Computers 17 (3), 265–289.

Fitts, P.M., 1954. The information capacity of the human motor system in controlling the amplitude of movement. Journal of Experimental Psychology 47 (6), 381–391.

Kirk, R., 1982. Experimental Design: Procedures for the Behavioral Sciences, second ed Brooks/Cole Publishing Company, Pacific Grove, CA.

Landsberger, H., 1958. Hawthorne Revisited. Cornell University, Ithaca, NY.

Lieberman, H., 2007. The tyranny of evaluation. http://web.media.mit.edu/~lieber/Misc/Tyranny-Evaluation.html (retrieved 16.11.07.).

Macefield, R., 2007. Usability studies and the Hawthorne Effect. Journal of Usability Studies 2 (3), 145–154.

Mehra, S., Werkhoven, P., Worring, M., 2006. Navigating on handheld displays: dynamic versus static peephole navigation. ACM Transactions on Computer-Human Interaction 13 (4), 448–457.

Miniotas, D., 2000. Application of Fitts' Law to eye gaze interaction. In: Proceedings of the SIGCHI Conference on Human Factors in Computing Systems, pp. 339–340.

Oehlert, G., 2000. A First Course in Design and Analysis of Experiments. Freeman and Company, New York.

Price, K.J., Lin, M., Feng, J., Goldman, R., Sears, A., Jacko, J.A., 2006. Motion does matter: an examination of speech-based-text entry on the move. Universal Access in the Information Society 4 (3), 246–257.

RAND Corporation, 1955. A Million Random Digits with 100,000 Normal Deviates. Free Press, New York.

Rosenthal, R., Rosnow, R., 2008. Essentials of Behavioral Research: Methods and Data Analysis, third ed McGraw Hill, Boston, MA.

Sears, A., Karat, C.-M., Oseitutu, K., Karimullah, A., Feng, J., 2001. Productivity, satisfaction, and interaction strategies of individuals with spinal cord injuries and traditional users interacting with speech recognition software. Universal Access in the Information Society 1 (1), 4–15.

Sears, A., Feng, J., Oseitutu, K., Karat, C.-M., 2003. Speech-based navigation during dictation: difficulties, consequences, and solutions. Human–Computer Interaction 18 (3), 229–257.

Shneiderman, B., Plaisant, C., Cohen, M., Jacobs, S., 2017. Designing the User Interface: Strategies for Effective Human–Computer Interaction, sixth ed. Addison-Wesley, Boston, MA.

Soukoreff, W., MacKenzie, S., 2003. Metrics for text entry research: an evaluation of MSD and KSPC, and a new unified error metric. In: Proceedings of the ACM Conference on Human Factors in Computing Systems, pp. 113–120.

Zajicek, M., 2006. Aspects of HCI research for older people. Universal Access in the Information Society 5 (3), 279–386.

Zajicek, M., Jonsson, I., 2006. In-car speech systems for older adults: can they help and does the voice matter? International Journal of Technology, Knowledge, and Society 2 (6), 55–64.

Experimental design

3

Experiments help us answer questions and identify causal relationships. Well-designed experiments can reveal important scientific findings. By contrast, ill-designed experiments may generate results that are false or misleading. Experiments have been widely used in the human-computer interaction (HCI) field to develop and modify user models or task models, evaluate different design solutions, and answer various other critical questions, such as technology adoption.

Before we discuss specific experimental design methods, we need to differentiate three groups of studies: experiments, quasi-experiments, and nonexperiments (Cooper and Schindler, 2000; Rosenthal and Rosnow, 2008). Figure 3.1 demonstrates the relationship among the three types of studies. If a study involves multiple groups or conditions and the participants are randomly assigned to each condition, it is a true experiment. If a study involves multiple groups or conditions but the participants are not randomly assigned to different conditions, it is a quasi-experiment. Finally, if there is only one observation group or only one condition involved, it is a nonexperiment. True experiments possess the following characteristics:

- A true experiment is based on at least one testable research hypothesis and aims to validate it.
- There are usually at least two conditions (a treatment condition and a control condition) or groups (a treatment group and a control group).
- The dependent variables are normally measured through quantitative measurements.
- The results are analyzed through various statistical significance tests.
- A true experiment should be designed and conducted with the goal of removing potential biases.
- A true experiment should be replicable with different participant samples, at different times, in different locations, and by different experimenters.

In this chapter, we focus on the design of true experiments, which means that all the studies we discuss have multiple conditions or measures and the participants are randomly assigned to different conditions. We start with the issues that need to be considered when designing experiments, followed by discussions of simple experiments that involve only one independent variable. We then examine more complicated experiments that involve two or more independent variables. Three major types of experiment design are discussed: between-group design, within-group design, and split-plot design. Section 3.5 focuses on potential sources of systematic errors

Research Methods in Human-Computer Interaction. http://dx.doi.org/10.1016/B978-0-12-805390-4.00003-0

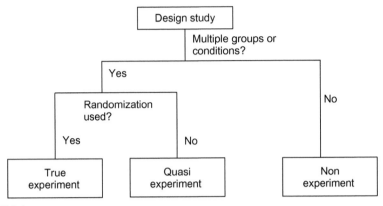

FIGURE 3.1

Defining true experiments, quasi-experiments, and nonexperiments.

(biases) and guidelines for effectively avoiding or controlling those biases. The chapter ends with a discussion of typical procedures for running HCI experiments.

3.1 WHAT NEEDS TO BE CONSIDERED WHEN DESIGNING EXPERIMENTS?

We need to consider several issues when designing an experiment that investigates HCI-related questions. Some of these issues are universal for all scientific experiments, such as research hypotheses, the measurement of the dependent variables, and the control of multiple conditions. Other issues are unique to experiments that involve human subjects, such as the learning effect, participants' knowledge background, and the size of the potential participant pool. Detailed discussions of measurement and generation of research hypotheses are provided in Chapter 2. A complete review on conducting research involving human subjects is provided in Chapter 15.

Most successful experiments start with a clearly defined research hypothesis with a reasonable scope (Oehlert, 2000). The research hypothesis is generated based on results of earlier exploratory studies and provides critical information needed to design an experiment. It specifies the independent and dependent variables of the experiment. The number and values of independent variables directly determine how many conditions the experiment has. For example, consider designing an experiment to investigate the following hypothesis:

> *There is no difference between the target selection speed when using a mouse, a joystick, or a trackball to select icons of different sizes (small, medium, and large).*

There are two independent variables in this hypothesis: the type of pointing device and the size of icon. Three different pointing devices will be examined: a mouse, a joystick, and a trackball, suggesting three conditions under this independent variable. Three different target sizes will be examined: small, medium, and large, suggesting three conditions under this independent variable as well. Since we need to test each combination of values of the two independent variables, combining the two independent variables results in a total of nine ($3 \times 3 = 9$) conditions in the experiment.

The identification of dependent variables will allow us to further consider the appropriate metric for measuring the dependent variables. In many cases, multiple approaches can be used to measure the dependent variables. For example, typing speed can be measured by the number of words typed per minute, which is equal to the total number of words typed divided by the number of minutes used to generate those words. It may also be measured by number of correct words typed per minute, which is equal to the total number of correct words typed divided by the number of minutes used to generate those words. We need to consider the objective of the experiment to determine which measure is more appropriate.

Another issue to consider when designing experiments is how to control the independent variables to create multiple experimental conditions (Kirk, 1982). In some experiments, control of the independent variable is quite easy and straightforward. For instance, when testing the previously stated hypothesis, we can control the type of pointing device by presenting participants with a mouse, a joystick, or a trackball. In many other cases, the control of the independent variable can be challenging. For instance, if we are developing a speech-based application and need to investigate how recognition errors impact users' interaction behavior, we may want to compare two conditions. Under the control condition, the speech recognizer would be error free and recognize every word that the user says correctly. Under the comparison condition, the speech recognizer would make errors and recognize a percentage of the words incorrectly. This sounds straightforward, theoretically. But in practice, all speech recognizers make errors. There is no way to find a recognizer that would satisfy the requirements of the controlled condition. A possible solution to meet the needs of this experiment is the Wizard-of-Oz approach (Feng and Sears, 2009). That is, we can have a human acting as a speech recognizer, listening to what the user says and entering the user's dictation into the system. The truth would normally not be revealed to the participants until the end of the experiment. Therefore, all participants would believe that they are interacting with the speech recognizer when completing the task. The Wizard-of-Oz approach allows us to test ideal applications that do not exist in the real world. This approach is not without its limitations. Humans also make errors. It is very likely that the human "wizard" would make errors when listening to the dictation or when typing the words. Therefore, it is very difficult to control the independent variable to achieve the desired condition (Feng and Sears, 2009; Li et al., 2006). One approach that addresses this problem is the development of technical tools to assist the human wizard (Li et al., 2006).

3.2 DETERMINING THE BASIC DESIGN STRUCTURE

At the first stage of experimental design, we need to construct the experiment based on the research hypotheses that have been developed. This enables us to draw a big picture of the general scope of the experiment and, accordingly, come up with a reasonable estimation of the timeline of the experiment and the budget. The basic structure of an experiment can be determined by answering two questions:

- How many independent variables do we want to investigate in the experiment?
- How many different values does each independent variable have?

The answer to the first question determines whether we need a basic design or a factorial design. If there is one independent variable, we need only a basic one-level design. If there are two or more independent variables, factorial design is the way to go. The answer to the second question determines the number of conditions needed in the experiment (see Figure 3.2). In a basic design, the number of conditions in the experiment is an important factor when we consider whether to adopt a between-group or within-group design. In a factorial design, we have a third option: the split-plot design. Again, the number of conditions is a crucial factor when weighing up the three options.

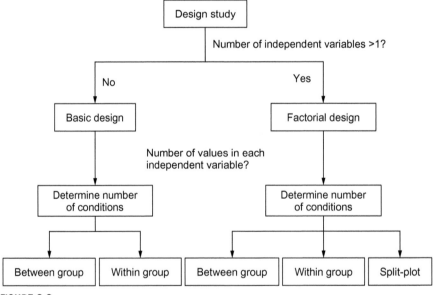

FIGURE 3.2

Determining the experiment structure.

In the following sections, we first consider the basic design scenarios involving one independent variable and focus on the characteristics of between-group design and within-group design. After that, we consider more complicated designs involving multiple independent variables, to which understanding split-plot design is the key.

3.3 INVESTIGATING A SINGLE INDEPENDENT VARIABLE

When we study a single independent variable, the design of the experiment is simpler than cases in which multiple variables are involved. The following hypotheses all lead to experiments that investigate a single independent variable:

- H1: There is no difference in typing speed when using a QWERTY keyboard, a DVORAK keyboard,[1] or an alphabetically ordered keyboard.
- H2: There is no difference in the time required to locate an item in an online store between novice users and experienced users.
- H3: There is no difference in the perceived trust toward an online agent among customers who are from the United States, Russia, China, and Nigeria.

The number of conditions in each experiment is determined by the possible values of the independent variable. The experiment conducted to investigate hypothesis H1 would involve three conditions: the QWERTY keyboard, the DVORAK keyboard, and the alphabetically ordered keyboard. The experiment conducted to investigate hypothesis H2 would involve two conditions: novice users and experienced users. And the experiment conducted to investigate hypothesis H3 would involve four conditions: customers from the United States, Russia, China, and Nigeria.

Once the conditions are set, we need to determine the number of conditions to which we would allow each participant to be exposed by selecting either a between-group design or a within-group design. This is a critical step in experimental design and the decision made has a direct impact on the quality of the data collected as well as the statistical methods that should be used to analyze the data.

3.3.1 BETWEEN-GROUP DESIGN AND WITHIN-GROUP DESIGN

Between-group design is also called "between-subject design." In a between-group design, each participant is only exposed to one experimental condition. The number of participant groups directly corresponds to the number of experimental conditions. Let us use the experiment on types of keyboard as an example. As shown in Figure 3.3, three

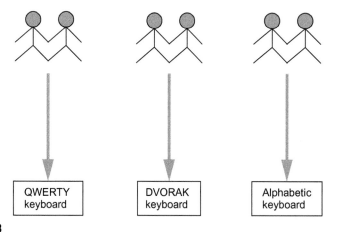

FIGURE 3.3

Between-group design.

---

[1] Dvorak keyboard is an ergonomic alternative to the commonly used "QWERTY keyboard." The design of the Dvorak keyboard emphasizes typist comfort, high productivity, and ease of learning.

groups of participants take part in the experiment and each group only uses one specific type of keyboard. If the task is to type a document of 500 words, then each participant types one document using one of the keyboards.

In contrast, a within-group design (also called "within-subject design") requires each participant to be exposed to multiple experimental conditions. Only one group of participants is needed for the entire experiment. If we use the keyboard experiment as an example, as shown in Figure 3.4, one group of participants uses all three types of keyboard during the experiment. If the task is to type a document of 500 words, then each participant types three documents, using each of the three keyboards for one document.

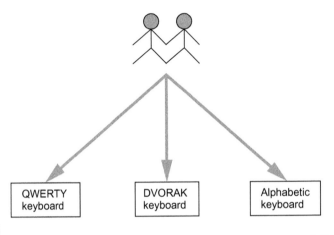

FIGURE 3.4

Within-group design.

Please note that different statistical approaches are needed to analyze data collected from the two different design methods. The details of statistical analysis are discussed in Chapter 4.

3.3.1.1 Advantages and disadvantages of between-group design

From the statistical perspective, between-group design is a cleaner design. Since the participant is only exposed to one condition, the users do not learn from different task conditions. Therefore, it allows us to avoid the learning effect. In addition, since the participants only need to complete tasks under one condition, the time it takes each participant to complete the experiment is much shorter than in a within-group design. As a result, confounding factors such as fatigue and frustration can be effectively controlled.

On the other hand, between-group design also has notable disadvantages. In a between-group experiment, we are comparing the performance of one group of participants against the performance of another group of participants. The results are subject to substantial impacts from individual differences: the difference between the multiple values that we expect to observe can be buried in a high level of "noise" caused by individual differences. Therefore, it is harder to detect significant differences and Type II errors are more likely to occur.

In order to effectively exclude the impact of noise and make significant findings, a comparatively larger number of participants are needed under each condition. This leads to the second major disadvantage of the between-group design: large sample size. Since the number of participants (m) in each condition should be comparatively larger than that in a within group design and approximately the same number of participants are needed for each condition (let n be the number of conditions), the total number of participants needed for the experiment ($m \times n$) is usually quite large. For example, if an experiment has 4 conditions and 16 participants are needed under each condition, the total number of participants needed is 64. Recruiting the number of participants needed for a between-group experiment can be a very challenging task.

3.3.1.2 Advantages and disadvantages of within-group design
Within-group design, in contrast, requires a much smaller sample size. When analyzing the data coming from within-group experiments, we are comparing the performances of the same participants under different conditions. Therefore, the impact of individual differences is effectively isolated and the expected difference can be observed with a relatively smaller sample size. If we change the design of the experiment with 4 conditions and 16 participants from a between-group design into a within-group design, the total number of participants needed would be 16, rather than 64. The benefit of a reduced sample size is an important factor for many studies in the HCI field when qualified participants may be quite difficult to recruit. It may also help reduce the cost of the experiments when financial compensation is provided.

Within-group designs are not free of limitations. The biggest problem with a within-group design is the possible impact of learning effects. Since the participants complete the same types of task under multiple conditions, they are very likely to learn from the experience and may get better in completing the tasks. For instance, suppose we are conducting a within-group experiment that evaluates two types of ATM: one with a button interface and one with a touch-screen interface. The task is to withdraw money from an existing account. If the participant first completes the task using the ATM with the button interface, the participant gains some experience with the ATM interface and its functions. Therefore, the participant may perform better when subsequently completing the same tasks using the ATM with the touch-screen interface. If we do not isolate the learning effect, we might draw a conclusion that the touch-screen interface is better than the button interface when the observed difference is actually due to the learning effect. Normally, the potential bias of the learning effect is the biggest concern of experimenters when considering adopting a within-group design. A Latin Square Design is commonly adopted to control the impact of the learning effect.

Another potential problem with within-group designs is fatigue. Since there are multiple conditions in the experiment, and the participants need to complete one or more tasks under each condition, the time it takes to complete the experiment may be quite long and participants may get tired or bored during the process. Contrary to the learning effect, which favors conditions completed toward the end of the experiment, fatigue negatively impacts on the performance of conditions completed toward the end of the experiment. For instance, in the ATM experiment, if the touch-screen interface is always tested after the button interface, we might draw a conclusion that the touch-screen interface is not as effective as the button interface when the observed difference is actually due to the participants' fatigue. We might fail to identify that the touch-screen interface is better than the button interface because the impact of fatigue offsets the gain of the touch-screen interface. Similarly, the potential problem of fatigue can also be controlled through the adoption of the Latin Square Design.

3.3.1.3 Comparison of between-group and within-group designs

The pros and cons of the between- and within-group designs are summarized in Table 3.1. You can see from the table that the advantages and limitations of the two design methods are exactly opposite to each other.

Table 3.1 Advantages and Disadvantages of Between-Group Design and Within-Group Design

	Type of Experiment Design	
	Between-Group Design	**Within-Group Design**
Advantages	Cleaner Avoids learning effect Better control of confounding factors, such as fatigue	Smaller sample size Effective isolation of individual differences More powerful tests
Limitations	Larger sample size Large impact of individual differences Harder to get statistically significant results	Hard to control learning effect Large impact of fatigue

3.3.2 CHOOSING THE APPROPRIATE DESIGN APPROACH

It is quite common for experimenters to argue back and forth when deciding which of the two design approaches to adopt. Many times the decision is quite hard to make since the advantages and disadvantages of the between-group design and within-group design are exactly opposite to each other. It should be emphasized that each experiment is unique and the decision should be made on a case-by-case basis with full consideration of the specific context of the experiment. In some cases, a hybrid design may be adopted that involves both between-group factors and within-group factors. The hybrid approach is discussed in detail in Section 3.4.2. This section discusses the general guidelines that help us choose the appropriate approach for a specific user study.

3.3.2.1 Between-group design

Generally speaking, between-group design should be adopted when the experiment investigates: simple tasks with limited individual differences; tasks that would be greatly influenced by the learning effect; or problems that cannot be investigated through a within-group design.

The size of the individual differences is very hard to estimate. However, it is empirically confirmed that individual differences are smaller when the tasks are simple and involve limited cognitive process (Dillon, 1996; Egan, 1988). In contrast, individual differences are larger when the task is complicated or involves significant cognitive functions. For example, when the task mainly involves basic motor skills, such as selecting a target on the screen, the individual differences among participants might be comparatively small.[2] But when the task involves more complicated cognitive or perceptual functions, such as reading, comprehension, information retrieval, and problem solving, the individual differences have a much larger impact. So when the task is simple, the impact of individual differences is limited and a between-group design would be appropriate.

Depending on the types of task, some experiments are more vulnerable to the learning effect than others. For example, in an experiment that compares the navigation effectiveness of two types of menu within a website, a participant who completes the navigation tasks under one condition would have gained a significant amount of knowledge of the website architecture. The knowledge would make a great impact on the participant's performance when completing the tasks under the other condition. Therefore, within-group design is highly inappropriate for this type of task and between-group design would have to be adopted.

There are many circumstances when it is totally impossible to adopt a within-group design. Taking hypotheses H2 and H3, previously stated, as examples:

- H2: There is no difference in the time required to locate an item in an online store between novice users and experienced users.
- H3: There is no difference in the perceived trust toward an online agent among customers who are from the United States, Russia, China, and Nigeria.

You can see that there is no way to compare the performances of novice users and experienced users through a within-group design because an individual cannot be both a novice user and an experienced user of the online store at the same time. For the same reason, a within-group design is not appropriate for H3 since any participant can only represent one of the four cultures. Under those circumstances, a between-group design is obviously the only option we have.

After choosing a between-group design for an experiment, we need to take special caution to control potential confounding factors. Participants should be randomly assigned to different conditions whenever possible.[3] When assigning participants, we need to try our best to counterbalance potential confounding factors, such as gender, age, computing experience, and internet experience,

---

[2] Note that the individual differences in these types of tasks can be quite substantial when the participants come from different age groups or when individuals with motor disabilities are involved.

[3] We cannot randomly assign participants to different conditions in the cases of H2 and H3, obviously.

across conditions. In other words, we need to make sure that the groups are as similar as possible, except for the personal characteristics that are experimental variables under investigation.

3.3.2.2 Within-group design

Within-group design is more appropriate when the experiment investigates tasks with large individual differences, tasks that are less susceptible to the learning effect, or when the target participant pool is very small. As discussed previously, complicated tasks that involve substantial human cognitive and perceptual capabilities generally encounter much larger individual differences than simple tasks. Therefore, when an experiment investigates complicated tasks such as reading, comprehension, information retrieval, and problem solving, a within-group design might be more appropriate since it effectively isolates individual differences from the main effects.

Most of the tasks that examine complicated or learned skills or knowledge—such as typing, reading, composition, and problem solving—are less susceptible to learning effects. For example, if an experiment investigates the impact of two fonts (i.e., Times New Roman and Arial) on participants' reading speed, the learning effect between the two conditions would be very limited. Reading one text document of several hundred words is unlikely to improve an individual's reading speed. Therefore, a within-group design would be appropriate as long as the text materials presented to the participant under the two conditions are different in content but similar in levels of difficulty.

Difficulty in finding and recruiting qualified participants is a problem frequently faced by many HCI researchers. One typical example is the field of universal usability, which focuses on developing applications usable by diverse user populations. Numerous studies in this field examine how individuals with disabilities interact with computers or computer-related devices. Although the total number of people falling into a specific disability or disease category is quite large, the number of such individuals living in a particular area is very limited. Therefore, the sample sizes are normally smaller than that in studies examining users without disabilities (e.g., Taylor et al., 2016).

Recruiting participants with specific disabilities is always a challenging task. For more detailed discussion on working with participants with disabilities, please refer to Chapter 16. The same problem also occurs when the target population is well trained, highly experienced, professionals, such as business executives or experienced project managers, simply because they are too busy to be bothered. Under those circumstances, it is almost impossible to recruit the number of participants needed for a between-group design, forcing the experimenters to adopt a within-group design.

Having decided to adopt a within-group design, you need to consider how to control the negative impact of learning effects, fatigue, and other potential problems associated with a within-group design. As discussed previously, a general approach to control these negative impacts is counterbalancing the condition or treatment orders through a Latin Square Design.

When the objective of the study is not initial interaction with the application, an effective approach to reduce the impact of the learning effect is to provide sufficient time for training. Research suggests that, for many types of tasks, the learning curve tends to be steeper during the initial interaction stages and flatter after that stage (see Figure 3.5). People achieve quicker progress in learning during initial stages, followed by gradual lesser improvement with further practice. Therefore, providing sufficient training time for users to get acquainted with the system or the task greatly reduces the learning effect during the actual task sessions. Of course, training cannot completely eliminate the learning effect. It only reduces its impact. This approach, combined with the counterbalancing of task conditions, is widely adopted in HCI studies to control the impact of learning.

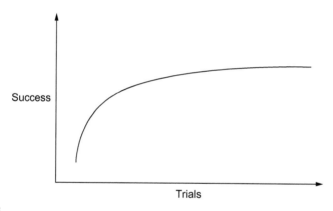

FIGURE 3.5

Typical learning curve.

To address the problem of fatigue caused by multiple experimental tasks, we need to design experiment tasks frugally, reducing the required number of tasks and shortening the experiment time whenever possible. It is generally suggested that the appropriate length of a single experiment session should be 60 to 90 minutes or shorter (Nielsen, 2005). When a session lasts longer than 90 minutes, the participant may get tired or frustrated. It is strongly suggested that a single session should definitely not last longer than 2 hours. During the experiment, the participant should be provided with opportunities to take breaks as needed. Interestingly, even when the experimenter encourages the participants to take breaks, the participants may not realize that they are getting tired and tend to ignore the suggestion to take a break. Therefore, some researchers find it helpful to force the participants to take a break during an experiment. For more discussion regarding the benefit of breaks in HCI studies, please refer to Chapter 15.

3.4 INVESTIGATING MORE THAN ONE INDEPENDENT VARIABLE

3.4.1 FACTORIAL DESIGN

Factorial designs are widely adopted when an experiment investigates more than one independent variable or factor. Using this method, we divide the experiment groups or conditions into multiple subsets according to the independent variables. It allows us to simultaneously investigate the impact of all independent variables as well as the interaction effects between multiple variables.

The number of conditions in a factorial design is determined by the total number of independent variables and the level of each independent variable. The equation for calculating the number of conditions is:

$$C = \prod_{a=1}^{n} Va$$

where C is the number of conditions, V is the number of levels in each variable, and $\prod$ is the product of V_1 through V_n.

The best way to explain a factorial design and this equation is through an example. Consider running an experiment to compare the typing speed when using three types of keyboard (QWERTY, DVORAK, and Alphabetic). We are also interested in examining the effect of different tasks (composition vs transcription) on the typing speed. This suggests that two independent variables are investigated in the experiment: type of keyboards and type of tasks. The variable "type of keyboards" has three levels: QWERTY, DVORAK, and Alphabetic. The variable "type of tasks" has two levels: transcription and composition. Therefore, the total number of conditions in this experiment is calculated according to the following equation:

$$\text{Number of conditions} = 3 \times 2 = 6$$

Table 3.2 illustrates the six conditions in this experiment. In the first three conditions, the participants would all complete composition tasks using different kinds of keyboard. In the other three conditions, the participants would all complete transcription tasks using different keyboards. When analyzing the data, we can compare conditions in the same row to examine the impact of keyboards. The effect of the tasks can be examined through comparing conditions in the same column. As a result, the effect of both independent variables can be examined simultaneously through a single experiment.

Table 3.2 A Factorial Design

	QWERTY	DVORAK	Alphabetic
Composition	1	2	3
Transcription	4	5	6

Either a between-group design or a within-group design may be adopted in this experiment. In a between-group design, each participant completes tasks under only one of the six conditions. As a result, six groups of participants would be required, one group for each condition. In a within-group design, each participant completes tasks under all six conditions. The advantages and disadvantages of between-group design and within-group design that we discussed in Section 3.3.2 also apply to factorial designs. No matter which design is adopted, it is important to counterbalance the orders and conditions in the experiment. In a between-group design, the participants need to be randomly assigned to the conditions. In a within-group design, the order in which the participant completes the six tasks needs to be counterbalanced.

3.4.2 SPLIT-PLOT DESIGN

In experiments that study one independent variable, we can choose to implement the study as a between-group design or a within-group design. In a factorial study, we can also choose a split-plot design. A split-plot design has both between-group components and within-group components. That is, one or more independent variables are investigated through a between-group approach and the other variables are investigated through a within-group approach.

Table 3.3 illustrates an experiment that employs a split-plot design. The experiment investigates two independent variables: age and the use of GPS. The variable "age" has three levels: people who are 20–40 years old, people who are 41–60 years old, and people who are older than 60. The second variable has two levels: driving without GPS and driving with GPS assistance. Therefore, the total number of conditions in this experiment is six.

Table 3.3 A Split-Plot Design

	20–40 Years Old	41–60 Years Old	Above 60
Driving without GPS assistance	1	2	3
Driving with GPS assistance	4	5	6

The impact of age is investigated through a between-group design since three groups of participants from different age ranges are studied. The impact of the use of GPS can be examined through a within-group approach. We can require each participant to complete the same driving task both with and without the assistance of the GPS. This gives us a typical split-plot design that involves both a between-group component (age analysis is based on the columns) and a within-group component (GPS use is analyzed by comparing condition 1 with condition 4, condition 2 with condition 5, and condition 3 with condition 6).

> **FACTORIAL DESIGN IN HCI RESEARCH**
>
> Factorial design has been commonly adopted in user studies in the HCI field. For example, Warr et al. (2016) used a 3×3 factorial design to investigate the differences between three window switching methods in a desktop environment.
>
> The between-group factor of the study was the window switching method: the *Cards* interface, the *Exposé* interface, and the *Mosaic* interface. Three groups of participants took part in the study, each completing tasks under one of the assigned window switching conditions. The within-group factor of the study was the number of open windows on the screen (3, 6, and 9). Under a specific window switching condition, each participant completed the same number of trials with 3 open windows, 6 open windows, and 9 open windows, respectively.
>
> Learning and fatigue might occur during the experiment. In order to address these two factors, participants were given time to practice selecting windows until they were comfortable with the procedure. The order of the 3, 6, and 9 window conditions was counterbalanced through a Latin Square Design.

3.4.3 INTERACTION EFFECTS

One advantage of a factorial design is that it allows us to study the interaction effects between two or more independent variables. According to Cozby (1997), an interaction effect can be described as "the differing effect of one independent variable on the dependent variable, depending on the particular level of another independent variable." When a significant interaction exists between independent variables X and Y, the means of the dependent variable Z would be determined jointly by X and Y.

Let us explain interaction effect through an example. Suppose we are conducting an experiment that investigates how types of device (mouse and touchscreen) and experience impact the effectiveness of target selection tasks. Two types of user are studied: novice users and experienced users. Based on the data collected, we draw a diagram as shown in Figure 3.6. As you can see, novice users can select targets faster with a touchscreen than with a mouse. Experienced users can select targets faster with a mouse than with a touchscreen. The target selection speeds for both the mouse and the touchscreen increase as the user gains more experience with the device. However, the increase in speed is much larger for the mouse than for the touchscreen.

It is critical to study interaction effects in HCI studies since performance may be affected by multiple factors jointly. There are numerous studies that did not identify any significant effect in individual independent variables but found significant results in interaction effects.

Interaction effects may have important implications for design. For example, the interaction effect in Figure 3.6 would suggest that the touchscreen performs better than the mouse during the initial interaction. But users can make greater progress in learning the mouse than the touchscreen and eventually achieve higher efficiency with the mouse. This result may imply that a touchscreen is a more appropriate input

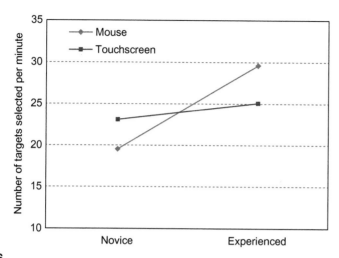

FIGURE 3.6

Interaction effects.

device when the interaction is normally brief and the opportunities for training are limited, such as an ATM interface. In contrast, a mouse might be more appropriate for long-term, frequent tasks, such as interacting with a computer desktop.

3.5 RELIABILITY OF EXPERIMENTAL RESULTS

All experimental research strives for high reliability. Reliable experiments can be replicated by other research teams in other locations and yield results that are consistent, dependable, and stable. One big challenge in HCI studies is that in contrast to the "hard sciences," such as physics, chemistry, and biology, measurements of human behavior and social interaction are normally subject to higher fluctuations and, therefore, are less replicable. The fluctuations in experimental results are referred to as errors.

3.5.1 RANDOM ERRORS

We may observe a participant typing several text documents during five sessions and obtain an actual typing speed of 50 words per minute. It is very unlikely that we would get the same typing speed for all five sessions. Instead, we may end up with data like this:

Session 1: 46 words per minute
Session 2: 52 words per minute
Session 3: 47 words per minute
Session 4: 51 words per minute
Session 5: 53 words per minute

The general relationship between the actual value we are looking for and the observed values can be expressed as follows:

$$\text{Observed values} = \text{Actual value} + \text{Random error}$$

Random errors are also called "chance errors" or "noise." They occur by chance and are not correlated with the actual value. Random errors push the observed values to move up or down around the exact value. There is no way to eliminate or control random errors but we can reduce the impact of random errors by enlarging the observed sample size. When a sample size is small, the random errors may have significant impact on the observed mean and the observed mean may be far from the actual value. When a sample size is large enough, the random errors should offset each other and the observed mean should be very close to the actual value. For example, in the typing task earlier, if we observe only Session 1, the mean would be 46, which is 4 words from the true value of 50 words per minute. If we increase the number of observed sessions to 5, the mean of the observed values is 49.8, very close to the actual value. In reality, we can never claim that we are 100% confident that the observed value is the actual value. But we can be 100% confident that the larger our sample size is, the closer the observed value is to the actual value.

3.5.2 SYSTEMATIC ERRORS

Systematic errors, also called "biases," are completely different in nature from random errors. While random errors cause variations in observed values in both directions around the actual value, systematic errors always push the observed values in the same direction. As a result, systematic errors never offset each other in the way that random errors do and they cause the observed mean to be either too high or too low.

Using the typing task example, the participant might consistently underperform during all five observation sessions, because of tiredness or nervousness, and we may collect the following data:

Session 1: 47 words per minute
Session 2: 44 words per minute
Session 3: 45 words per minute
Session 4: 42 words per minute
Session 5: 46 words per minute

In this case, the mean of the observed values is 44.8, 5 words lower than the actual value. Figure 3.7 shows the performance of the participant in each case. Under the unbiased conditions, the observed values fluctuate due to random errors, but the fluctuations occur in both directions around the actual value and offset each other. However, under the biased condition, the systematic error consistently pushes all values down, causing the mean of the observed values to be significantly below the actual value.

Systematic errors can greatly reduce the reliability of experimental results; therefore, they are the true enemy of experimental research. We can counter systematic errors in two stages: we should try to eliminate or control biases during the experiment

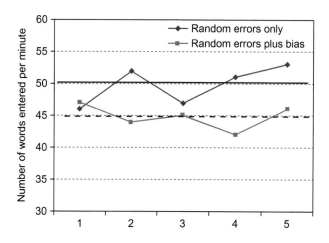

FIGURE 3.7

Comparison of random and systematic errors.

when biases are inevitable, and we need to isolate the impact of them from the main effect when analyzing the data. There are five major sources of systematic error:

- measurement instruments;
- experimental procedures;
- participants;
- experimenter behavior; and
- experimental environment.

3.5.2.1 Bias caused by measurement instruments

When the measurement instruments used are not appropriate, not accurate, or not configured correctly, they may introduce systematic errors. For instance, when observing participants searching for an item on an e-commerce website, we may use a stop watch to measure the time it takes to locate the specific item. If the stop watch is slow and misses 5 minutes in every hour, then we consistently record less time than the actual time used. As a consequence, the observed performance will be better than the actual value. In order to control biases introduced by the measurement instruments, we need to carefully examine the instruments used before experiment sessions. Another approach is to use extensively tested, reliable, and software-driven instruments. A bonus of software-driven instruments is that they can avoid human errors as well.

3.5.2.2 Bias caused by experimental procedures

Inappropriate or unclear experimental procedures may introduce biases. As discussed previously, if the order of task conditions is not randomized in an experiment with a within-group design, the observed results will be subject to the impact of the learning effect and fatigue: conditions tested later may be consistently better than conditions tested earlier due to learning effect; on the other hand, conditions tested earlier may be consistently better than later conditions due to fatigue. The biases caused by the learning effect and fatigue push the observed value in opposite directions and the combined effect is determined by the specific context of the experiment. If the tasks are simple and less susceptible to the learning effect, but tedious and long, the impact of fatigue and frustration may outweigh the impact of the learning effect, causing participants to consistently underperform in later sessions. If the tasks are complicated and highly susceptible to the learning effect, but short and interesting, the impact of the learning effect may outweigh the impact of fatigue, causing participants to consistently perform better in later sessions.

The instructions that participants receive play a crucial role in an experiment and the wording of the experiment instructions should be carefully scrutinized before a study. Slightly different wording in instructions may lead to different participant responses. In a reported HCI study (Wallace et al., 1993), participants were instructed to complete the task "as quickly as possible" under one condition. Under the other condition, participants were instructed to "take your time, there is no rush." Interestingly, participants working under the no-time-stress condition completed the tasks faster than those under the time-stress condition. This suggests the importance of critical wording in instructions. It also implies that the instructions that participants receive need to be highly consistent. When a study is conducted under the supervision of multiple investigators, it is more likely that the investigators give inconsistent instructions to the participants. Instructions and procedures on a written document or prerecorded instructions are highly recommended to ensure consistency across experimental sessions.

Many times, trivial and unforeseen details introduce biases into the results. For instance, in an experiment that studies data entry on a PDA, the way the PDA is physically positioned may have an impact on the results. If no specification is given, some participants may hold the PDA in one hand and enter data using the other hand, other participants may put the PDA on a table and enter data using both hands. There are notable differences between the two conditions regarding the distance between the PDA screen and the participant's eyes, the angle of the PDA screen, and the number of hands involved for data entry. Any of those factors may introduce biases into the observed results. In order to reduce the biases attributed to experimental procedures, we need to

- randomize the order of conditions, tasks, and task scenarios in experiments that adopt a within-group design or a split-plot design;
- prepare a written document with detailed instructions for participants;
- prepare a written document with detailed procedures for experimenters; and
- run multiple pilot studies before actual data collection to identify potential biases.

A pilot study is not a luxury that we conduct only when we have plenty of time or money to spend. On the contrary, years of experience tells us that pilot studies are critical for all HCI experiments to identify potential biases. No matter how well you think you have planned the study, there are always things that you overlook. A pilot study is the only chance you have to fix your mistakes before you run the main study. Pilot studies should be treated very seriously and conducted in exactly the same way as planned for the actual experiment. Participants of the pilot study should be from the target population. Having one or two members from the research team completing the designed tasks is not a pilot study in its true sense (Preece et al., 1994).

3.5.2.3 Bias caused by participants

Many characteristics of the participants may introduce systematic errors into the results. Potential contributors may be in a specific age range or have particular computer or internet experience, domain knowledge, education, professional experience and training, or personal interests. For instance, if we are running an experiment to test the user interface of a new mobile phone model, we might recruit participants by posting announcements on a popular blog on https://www.cnet.com. Since this website features highly technical news and reviews related to information technology, its visitors normally have a strong technical background and rich experience in using IT devices. As a consequence, the observed data would tend to outperform what we would observe from the general public. The following guidelines can help us reduce systematic errors from the participants:

- Recruit participants carefully, making sure the participant pool is representative of the target user population (Broome, 1984; Smart, 1966).
- Create an environment or task procedure that causes the least stress to the users.
- Reassure the participants that you are testing the interface, not them, so they are calm and relaxed during the experiment.
- Reschedule a session or give participants some time to recover if they arrive tired, exhausted, or very nervous.

3.5.2.4 Bias due to experimenter behavior

Experimenter behavior is one of the major sources of bias. Experimenters may intentionally or unintentionally influence the experiment results. Any intentional action to influence participants' performance or preference is unethical in research and should be strictly avoided. However, experimenters may unknowingly influence the observed data. Spoken language, body language, and facial expressions frequently serve as triggers for bias. Let us examine the following scenarios:

1. An experimenter is introducing an interface to a participant. The experimenter says, "Now you get to the pull-down menus. I think you will really like them.... I designed them myself!"
2. An experimenter is loading an application for a participant. The response time is a bit long. The experimenter is frustrated and says, "Damn! It's slower than a snail."
3. An experimenter is loading an application for a participant. The response time is a bit long. The experimenter waits uneasily, tapping fingers on the desk and frequently changing body position while staring at the screen impatiently.
4. A participant arrives on time for a study scheduled at 9 a.m. The experimenter does not arrive until 9:10 a.m. After guiding the participant into the lab, the experimenter takes 10 minutes to set up all the equipment. Once the experiment starts, the experimenter finds that the task list is missing and runs out of the lab to print a copy.

In Scenario 1, the experimenter is very demanding and the comment may make the participant reluctant to provide negative feedback about the interface in case it hurts the experimenter's feelings. Therefore, the data collected from the participant, especially the subjective data, are likely to be better than the actual value. In Scenarios 2 and 3, the experimenter's spoken language or body language reveals negative attitude toward the application. Participants would register those cues and would form a negative perspective even before their first encounter with the application and the collected subjective ratings and feedback would be biased against the application. In Scenario 4, the unprofessional and slack style of the experimenter would give a negative impression to the participant, which may impact the participant's performance as well as the subjective ratings and feedback.

When multiple experimenters are involved in the experiment, bias is likely to occur due to inconsistency in instructions and training, as well as individual styles and attitudes. If one of the experimenters is very patient, offers long training sessions, and demonstrates all related commands to the participants before the actual task, while the other experimenter is pushy, offers shorter training sessions, and only demonstrates a subset of the commands, the participants who complete the experiment under the guidance of the first experimenter may systematically outperform the participants who complete the experiment with the second experimenter. In order to control possible biases triggered by experimenters, we need to

- Offer training opportunities to experimenters and teach them to be neutral, calm, and patient when supervising experiments.
- Make sure that the experimenter arrives at least 10 minutes before the scheduled sessions and gets everything ready before the session starts.
- Whenever possible, have two experimenters supervise a session together, one as the lead experimenter and the other as the assistant experimenter. The lead experimenter is responsible for interacting with the participants. The assistant experimenter observes the session closely, fixes errors if noted, and takes notes when necessary.
- Prepare written documents with detailed procedures for experimenters and require all experimenters to follow the same procedure strictly.
- When appropriate, record important instructions before the experiment and play the recording to the participants during the experiment. In this way, we can guarantee that all participants go through the same training process and receive the same instructions.

3.5.2.5 Bias due to environmental factors

Environmental factors play an increasingly important role in HCI research due to the rapid development in mobile computing, universal accessibility, and recognition-based technologies. Environmental factors can be categorized into two groups: physical environmental factors and social environmental factors. Examples of physical environmental factors include noise, temperature, lighting, vibration, and humidity. Examples of social environmental factors include the number of people in the surrounding environment and the relationship between those people and the participant.

Both physical and social environmental factors may introduce systematic errors into the observed data. For instance, a study that examines the performance of a speech-recognition application may yield lower recognition error rates than the actual value if there is a significant level of ambient noise during the experiment session. Even when the study investigates applications other than speech, loud environmental noise may distract the participants or induce fatigue. Regarding social factors, a participant with a person watching over his shoulder may perform differently from a participant who is seated alone. Environmental factors may cause more problems when the experiment is not conducted in a lab, but in locations such as the participant's home or workplace. The following guidelines can help us avoid or control environment-induced biases:

- In a lab setting, make sure the room is quiet, the lighting is appropriate, and the chairs and tables are comfortable. The room should be clean and tidy, without notable distractions.
- Whenever possible, the participant should be seated alone and the experimenter can observe the session from another room via a one-way mirror or monitors.
- In a field study, the experimenters should visit the location before the scheduled time to confirm that the setting meets the requirements of the study.

Finally, it is important to realize that, no matter how hard you try to avoid biases, they can never be completely eliminated. A well-designed experiment with lots of consideration for controlling bias can improve the data, making the observed results closer to the actual values, but still subject to the impact of biases. Therefore, we should be careful when reporting the findings, even when the study results are statistically significant.

3.6 EXPERIMENTAL PROCEDURES

Experiments are conducted in dramatically different fields to answer a myriad of questions. Experiments in the HCI field, similar to many studies in sociology or psychology, typically involve human subjects. Studying human subjects is quite different from studying metal or plant reactions, or other animals, and introduces many interesting issues or challenges. The concerns and practices of working with human subjects are discussed in detail in Chapter 15. In this section, we briefly introduce the procedures for experiments that study human subjects.

In the lifecycle of an HCI experiment, we typically go through the following process:

1. Identify a research hypothesis.
2. Specify the design of the study.
3. Run a pilot study to test the design, the system, and the study instruments.
4. Recruit participants.
5. Run the actual data collection sessions.
6. Analyze the data.
7. Report the results.

Within a specific experiment session, we typically go through the following steps:

1. Ensure that the systems or devices being evaluated are functioning properly, the related instruments are ready for the experiment.
2. Greet the participants.
3. Introduce the purpose of the study and the procedures.
4. Get the consent of the participants.
5. Assign the participants to a specific experimental condition according to the predefined randomization method.
6. Participants complete training tasks.
7. Participants complete actual tasks.
8. Participants answer questionnaires (if any).
9. Debriefing session.
10. Payment (if any).

Some experiments may require more complicated steps or procedures. For example, longitudinal studies involve multiple trials. We need to make sure that the tasks used in each trial are randomized in order to control the impact of the learning effect.

A number of open source platforms have been developed to help researchers design experiments, collect data, and analyze the results. One example is the Touchstone experimental design platform. The Touchtone system includes a "design" platform for examining alternative, controlled experimental designs, a "run" platform for running subjects, and an "analysis" platform that provides advices on statistical analysis (Mackay et al., 2007).

3.7 SUMMARY

Experiment design starts with a clearly defined, testable research hypothesis. During the design process, we need to answer the following questions:

- How many dependent variables are investigated in the experiment and how are they measured?
- How many independent variables are investigated in the experiment and how are they controlled?
- How many conditions are involved in the experiment?
- Which of the three designs will be adopted: between-group, within-group, or split-plot?
- What potential bias may occur and how can we avoid or control those biases?

When an experiment studies only one independent variable, we need to choose between the between-group design and the within-group design. When there is more than one independent variable, we need to select among the between-group design, the within-group design, and the split-plot design.

The between-group design is cleaner, avoids the learning effect, and is less likely to be affected by fatigue and frustration. But this design is weaker due to the high noise level of individual differences. In addition, larger numbers of participants are usually required for a between-group design. The within-group design, on the other hand, effectively isolates individual differences and, therefore, is a much stronger test than the between-group design. Another bonus is that fewer participants are required. But within-group designs are more vulnerable to learning effects and fatigue. The appropriate design method needs to be selected based on the nature of the application, the participant, and the tasks examined in the experiment.

All experiments strive for clean, accurate, and unbiased results. In reality, experiment results are highly susceptible to bias. Biases can be attributed to five major sources: the measurement instruments, the experiment procedure, the participants, the experimenters, and the physical and social environment. We should try to avoid or control biases through accurate and appropriate measurement devices and scales; clearly defined and detailed experimental procedures; carefully recruited participants; well-trained, professional, and unbiased experimenters; and well-controlled environments.

DISCUSSION QUESTIONS

1. Explain the differences among the three types of study: experiment, quasi-experiment, and nonexperiment.

2. What are the major issues that need to be considered when designing experiments?

3. What is a between-group design? Explain the advantages and disadvantages of a between-group design.

4. What is a within-group design? Explain the advantages and disadvantages of a within-group design.

5. When should a between-group design be considered for an experiment?

6. When should a within-group design be considered for an experiment?

7. What is the benefit of a factorial design compared to experiments that investigate one factor at a time?

8. What is a split-plot design?

9. Explain the differences between random errors and systematic errors.

10. What are the major sources of systematic errors, or biases?

11. What can we do to reduce systematic errors in experiments?

12. Describe the typical procedure of an experiment that involves human subjects.

RESEARCH DESIGN EXERCISES

1. Read the following scenarios. Identify actions or conditions that may induce systematic errors in each scenario and explain the direction of the impact (i.e., whether the observed data will be pulled up or down from the actual value).
Scenario 1: In an experiment that investigates how novice users learn to use the T9 method to enter data into a PDA, a participant has actually used T9 for over a year.
Scenario 2: An experimenter is introducing a website to a participant. The experimenter says, "My team has spent six months on this site. The site is like our baby."
Scenario 3: In an experiment that examines how individuals with severe motor disabilities interact with computers using a brain-computer interface, all participants recruited are healthy individuals without any disability.
Scenario 4: In an experiment that examines speech-based dictation techniques, the experimenter forgets to switch the speech profiles between experiment sessions, so a participant used another person's speech profile to complete the dictation tasks.
Scenario 5: In an experiment that examines the design of an e-commerce website, participants complete multiple tasks to retrieve specific information on the site. However, the network speed is very slow and the participants have to wait significant amounts of time for each page to be loaded.

2. Read the following scenarios. Discuss the type of experiment design (between-group, within-group, or split-plot) that is appropriate for each scenario.
Scenario 1: A study investigates whether people who have attended a security training program generate and use more secure passwords than people who have not received any security training.
Scenario 2: A research team examines the effectiveness of joysticks and trackballs for selecting static targets and moving targets.
Scenario 3: A research team examines whether the gender of an online agent affects the perception of trust for young users, middle-aged users, and older users.
Scenario 4: A research team examines whether virtual teams who use video conferencing are more productive than teams who use phone-based teleconferencing.
Scenario 5: A study examines the effectiveness of three menu structures. The first structure has two levels, with 8 items in the first level and 64 items in the second level. The second structure has three levels, with 4 items in the first level, 16 items in the second level, and 64 items in the third level. The third menu has six levels, with 2 items in the first level and 2^n items in the nth level.

REFERENCES

Broome, J., 1984. Selecting people randomly. Ethics 95 (1), 38–55.
Cooper, D., Schindler, P., 2000. Business Research Methods, seventh ed. McGraw Hill, Boston, MA.

Cozby, P.C., 1997. Methods in Behavioral Research, sixth ed. Mayfield Publishing, Mountain View, CA.

Dillon, A., 1996. User analysis in HCI: the historical lesson from individual differences research. International Journal of Human-Computer Studies 45 (6), 619–637.

Egan, D., 1988. Individual differences in human–computer interaction. In: Helander, M. (Ed.), Handbook of Human–Computer Interaction. Elsevier, North-Holland, pp. 543–568.

Feng, J., Sears, A., 2009. Beyond errors: measuring reliability for error-prone interaction devices. Behaviour & Information Technology, 1–15.

Kirk, R., 1982. Experimental Design: Procedures for the Behavioral Sciences, second ed Brooks/Cole Publishing Company, Pacific Grove, CA.

Li, Y., Welbourne, E., Landay, J., 2006. Novel methods: emotions, gestures, events: design and experimental analysis of continuous location tracking techniques for wizard of Oz testing. In: Proceedings of the SIGCHI Conference on Human Factors in Computing Systems, pp. 1019–1022.

Mackay, W.E., Appert, C., Beaudouin-Lafon, M., Chapuis, O., Du, Y., Fekete, J.-D., et al., 2007. Usability evaluation: Touchstone: exploratory design of experiments. In: Proceedings of the SIGCHI Conference on Human Factors in Computing Systems, pp. 1425–1434.

Nielsen, J., 2005. Time budgets for usability sessions. Alert Box. September 12. Retrieved from http://www.useit.com/alertbox/usability_sessions.html.

Oehlert, G., 2000. A First Course in Design and Analysis of Experiments. Freeman and Company, New York.

Preece, J., Rogers, Y., Sharp, H., Benyon, D., Holland, S., Carey, T., 1994. Human–Computer Interaction. Addison-Wesley Longman Ltd., Essex, UK.

Rosenthal, R., Rosnow, R., 2008. Essentials of Behavioral Research: Methods and Data Analysis, third ed. McGraw Hill, Boston, MA.

Smart, R.G., 1966. Subject selection bias in psychological research. Canadian Psychology 7a, 115–121.

Taylor, B., Dey, A., Siewiorek, D., Smailagic, A., 2016. Customizable 3D printed tactile maps as interactive overlays. In: Proceedings of the 18th International ACM SIGACCESS Conference on Computers and Accessibility, pp. 71–79.

Wallace, D., Anderson, N., Shneiderman, B., 1993. Time stress effects on two menu selection systems. In: Shneiderman, B. (Ed.), Sparks of Innovation in Human–Computer Interaction. Ablex Publishing Corporation, Norwood, NJ.

Warr, A., Chi, E., Harris, H., Kuscher, A., Chen, J., Flack, R., et al., 2016. Window shopping: a study of desktop window switching. In: Proceedings of the SIGCHI Conference on Human Factors in Computing Systems, pp. 3335–3338.

Statistical analysis

4

In Chapter 2, we discussed why we need to run statistical analysis on data collected through various methods. Appropriate selection of statistical analysis methods and accurate interpretation of the test results are essential for user studies. After weeks, months, or even years of arduous preparation and data collection, you finally have a heavy set of data on hand and may feel the need to lie back and enjoy a hard-earned break. Well, it is a little too early to relax and celebrate at this point. With many studies, the data analysis stage is equally or even more labor intensive than the data collection stage. Many critical decisions need to be made when analyzing the data, such as the type of statistical method to be used, the confidence threshold, as well as the interpretation of the significance test results. Incorrect selection of statistical methods or inappropriate interpretation of the results can lead to erroneous conclusions that let high-quality data go to waste.

This chapter discusses general data analysis procedures and commonly used statistical methods, including independent-samples t test, paired-samples t test, one-way analysis of variance (ANOVA), factorial ANOVA, repeated measures ANOVA, correlation, regression, chi-squared test, and four other nonparametric tests.[1] The focus of this chapter is not on the mathematical computation behind each method or how to use statistical software to conduct each analysis. Instead, we focus on the contexts of use and the assumptions of each method. We also discuss how to appropriately interpret the results of each significance test. Through this chapter, we hope that you will be able to choose appropriate statistical methods for data analysis, run the corresponding tests using statistical software, and accurately interpret the analysis results for your own studies. You will also learn how to assess the validity of the findings reported in academic articles based on the experimental design and the statistical analysis procedure.

4.1 PREPARING DATA FOR STATISTICAL ANALYSIS

In most cases, the original data collected from lab-based experiments, usability tests, field studies, surveys, and various other channels need to be carefully processed before any statistical analysis can be conducted. There are several reasons for the need for preprocessing. First, the original data collected, especially if they are entered

---

[1] Tests to be used when the assumptions of the parametric tests are not met. More details will be discussed in Sections 4.6 and 4.8.

Research Methods in Human-Computer Interaction. http://dx.doi.org/10.1016/B978-0-12-805390-4.00004-2

manually by participants, may contain errors or may be presented in inconsistent formats. If those errors or inconsistencies are not filtered out or fixed, they may contaminate the entire data set. Second, the original data collected may be too primitive and higher level coding may be necessary to help identify the underlying themes. Third, the specific statistical analysis method or software may require the data to be organized in a predefined layout or format so that they can be processed (Delwiche and Slaughter, 2008).

4.1.1 CLEANING UP DATA

The first thing that you need to do after data collection is to screen the data for possible errors. This step is necessary for any type of data collected, but is particularly important for data entered manually by participants. To err is human. All people make mistakes (Norman, 1988). Although it is not possible to identify all the errors, you want to trace as many errors as possible to minimize the negative impact of human errors. There are various ways to identify errors depending on the nature of the data collected.

Sometimes you can identify errors by conducting a reasonableness check. For instance, if the age of a participant is entered as "223," you can easily conclude that there is something wrong. Your participant might have accidentally pushed the number "2" button twice, in which case the correct age should be 23, or he might have accidentally hit the number "3" button after the correct age, 22, has been entered. Sometimes you need to check multiple data fields in order to identify possible errors. For example, you may compare the participant's "age" and "years of computing experience" to check whether there is an unreasonable entry.

For automatically collected data, error checking usually boils down to time consistency issues or whether the performance is within a reasonable range. Something is obviously wrong if the logged start time of an event is later than the logged end time of the same event. You should also be on alert if any unreasonably high or low performance levels are documented.

In many studies, data about the same participant are collected from multiple channels. For example, in a study investigating multiple data-entry techniques, the performance data (such as time and number of keystrokes) might be automatically logged by data-logging software. The participants' subjective preference and satisfaction data might be manually collected via paper-based questionnaires. In this case, you need to make sure that all the data about the same participant are correctly grouped together. The result will be invalid if the performance data of one participant is grouped with the subjective data of another participant.

After errors are identified, how shall we deal with them? It is obvious that you always want to fix errors and replace them with accurate data. This is possible in some cases. If the age of a participant is incorrect, you can contact that participant and find out the accurate information. In many cases, fixing errors in the preprocessing stage is impossible. In many online studies or studies in which the participant remains anonymous, you may have no means of reaching participants after the data is collected. Under those circumstances, you need to remove the problematic data items and treat them as missing values in the statistical data analysis.

Sometimes, the data collected need to be cleaned up due to inappropriate formatting. Using age as an example, participants may enter age in various formats. In an online survey, most respondents used numeric values such as "9" to report their age (Feng et al., 2008). Some used text such as "nine" or "nine and a half." A number of participants even entered detailed text descriptions such as "He will turn nine in January." The entries in text formats were all transformed to numeric values before the data was analyzed by statistical software.

4.1.2 CODING DATA

In many studies, the original data collected need to be coded before any statistical analysis can be conducted. A typical example is the data about the demographic information of your participants. Table 4.1 shows the original demographic data of three participants. The information on age is numerical and does not need to be coded. The information on gender, highest degree earned, and previous software experience needs to be coded so that statistical software can interpret the input. In Table 4.2, gender information is coded using 1 to represent "male" and 0 to represent "female." Highest degree earned has more categories, with 1 representing a high school degree, 2 representing a college degree, and 3 representing a graduate degree. Previous software experience is also coded, with 1 representing "Yes" and 0 representing "No." Usually we use codes "0" and "1" for dichotomous variables (categorical variables with exactly two possible values). When coding variables with three or more possible values, the codes used may vary depending on the specific context. For

Table 4.1 Sample Demographic Data in Its Original Form

	Age	Gender	Highest Degree	Previous Experience In Software A
Participant 1	34	Male	College	Yes
Participant 2	28	Female	Graduate	No
Participant 3	21	Female	High school	No

Table 4.2 Sample Demographic Data in Coded Form

	Age	Gender	Highest Degree	Previous Experience In Software A
Participant 1	34	1	2	1
Participant 2	28	0	3	0
Participant 3	21	0	1	0

example, in Table 4.2, I used "1" to represent "high school degree" rather than "0." However, when the data is processed by a statistics software, a coding scheme of "0, 1, 2" is exactly the same as a scheme of "1, 2, 3."

In various studies such as surveys, interviews, and focus groups, content analysis needs to be conducted in which text reflecting different themes or critical events is coded and counted (Stemler, 2001). Detailed discussion on content analysis is provided in Chapter 11. Event coding is also quite common in usability tests or lab-based studies. For example, Hu and Feng (2015) used extensive coding schemes to analyze the causes for failed browsing or search tasks in an online environment. The coding scheme allowed the authors to further understand the difficulties that users experience when finding information online.

When coding your data, it is critical to ensure the coding is consistent. This is particularly challenging when the coding is completed by more than one person. If the coding is inconsistent, the validity of the analysis results will be greatly affected. Various statistical methods, such as Cronbach's alpha, can be used to assess the reliability of coding completed by multiple coders (Weber, 1990). Please see Chapter 11 for more details on this topic.

4.1.3 ORGANIZING DATA

Statistical and other data-processing software normally has predefined requirements for how data should be laid out for specific statistical analysis. In SPSS, for example, when running an independent-samples t test to compare two groups of data, the data of the two groups need to be listed in the same column. In contrast, when running a paired-samples t test to compare two means, the two groups of data need to be laid out parallel to each other in two separate columns. Similarly, other statistical methods such as ANOVA, repeated measures, and correlation all have different data organization requirements that need to be followed closely.

4.2 DESCRIPTIVE STATISTICS

After the collected data is cleaned up, you may want to run a number of basic descriptive statistical tests to understand the nature of your data set. For instance, you may want to know the range into which most of your data points fall; you may also want to know how your data points are distributed. The most commonly used descriptive measures include means, medians, modes, variances, standard deviations, and ranges.

4.2.1 MEASURES OF CENTRAL TENDENCY

When we study a data set, we often want to find out where the bulk of the data is located. In statistical terms, this characteristic is called the "central tendency." Various measures can be used to describe the central tendency of a data set, including the mean, the median, and the mode (Rosenthal and Rosnow, 2008).

The mean is also called the "arithmetic average" of a data set. When multiple groups are involved in a study, comparing their means can provide preliminary insights on how the groups relate to each other. If you find that the mean of one group is notably higher than the other group, you may conduct significance tests, such as a *t* test, to examine whether that difference is statistically significant. The median is the middle score in a data set. Consider the following data set of typing speeds collected from seven users:

$$\{15,\ 19,\ 22,\ 29,\ 33,\ 45,\ 50\}$$

The mean of this data set is 30.4 while the median of the data set is 29.

The mode is the value that occurs with the greatest frequency in a data set. Suppose we collected the following data from seven participants about the number of hours they spend on the Internet every week:

$$\{12,\ 15,\ 22,\ 22,\ 22,\ 34,\ 34\}$$

The mode of the data set is 22.

4.2.2 MEASURES OF SPREAD

Another important group of descriptive measures that we usually want to know is how much the data points deviate from the center of the data set. In other words, we want to know how spread out our data set is. Measures in this group include range, variances, and standard deviations.

The range measures the distance between the highest and lowest scores in the data set. In the typing-speed data set of Section 4.2.1, the range is $50-15=35$. The larger the range, the more distributed the data set is.

The variance of a data set is the mean of the squared distances of all the scores from the mean of the data set. The square root of the variance is called the standard deviation. As with range, higher variances or standard deviations indicate that the data set is more distributed.

A commonly used method for describing the distribution of a data set is the normal distribution, a special bell-shaped distribution that can be defined by the mean and the standard deviation (see Figure 4.1). The pattern of normal distribution is very

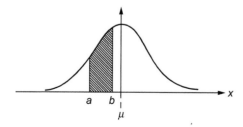

FIGURE 4.1

Normal distribution curve.

important and useful for data analysis since many attributes from various fields of study are distributed normally, such as the heights of a population, student grades, and various performance measures.

Testing a data set to determine whether it is normally distributed is a necessary step when selecting the type of significance tests to conduct. Parametric tests assume that the data set is normally distributed or approximately normally distributed. If you find that the data collected is not normally distributed, you may need to consider transforming the data so that they are normally distributed or you may adopt nonparametric tests for the analysis.

For detailed calculation of each of the measures, please refer to statistical textbooks, such as Hinkle et al. (2002), Newton and Rudestam (1999), Rosenthal and Rosnow (2008), and Albert and Tullis (2013). Microsoft Excel offers built-in functions that allow you to conveniently calculate or count various descriptive measures.

4.3 COMPARING MEANS

In user studies involving multiple conditions or groups, the ultimate objective of the researcher is to find out whether there is any difference between the conditions or groups. Suppose you are evaluating the effectiveness of two search engines; you may adopt a between-group design, in which case you will recruit two groups of participants and have each group use one of the two search engines to complete a number of search tasks. If you choose a within-group design, you will recruit one group of participants and have each participant complete a series of tasks using both search engines. In either case, you want to compare the performance measures of the two groups or conditions to find out whether there is any difference between the two search engines.

Many studies involve three or more conditions that need to be compared. Due to variances in the data, you should not directly compare the means of the multiple conditions and claim that a difference exists as long as the means are different. Instead, you have to use statistical significance tests to evaluate the variances that can be explained by the independent variables and the variances that cannot be explained by them. The significance test will suggest the probability of the observed difference occurring by chance. If the probability that the difference occurs by chance is fairly low (e.g., less than 5%), we can claim with high confidence that the observed difference is due to the difference in the controlled independent variables.

Various significance tests are available to compare the means of multiple groups. Commonly used tests include t tests and the ANOVA. A t test is a simplified ANOVA involving only two groups or conditions. Two commonly used t tests are the independent-samples t test and the paired-samples t test. When a study involves more than two conditions, an ANOVA test has to be used. Various ANOVA methods are available to fit the needs of different experimental designs. Commonly used ANOVA tests include one-way ANOVA, factorial ANOVA, repeated measures ANOVA, and ANOVA for split-plot design.

Table 4.3 summarizes the major types of empirical study regarding design methodology and the appropriate significance test for each design. For studies with between-group design that only investigate one independent variable with two conditions, an independent-samples *t* test can be used. When the independent variable has three or more conditions, a one-way ANOVA can be used. When a between-group study investigates two or more independent variables, a factorial ANOVA test should be considered. For studies that adopt a within-group design, if the study investigates only one independent variable with two conditions, a paired-samples *t* test can be used. If the study's independent variables have three or more conditions, a repeated measures ANOVA test can be used. Finally, a study may adopt a split-plot design that involves both a between-group component and a within-group component. In this case, a split-plot ANOVA test can be used.

Table 4.3 Commonly Used Significance Tests for Comparing Means and Their Application Context

Experiment Design	Independent Variables (IV)	Conditions for each IV	Types of Test
Between-group	1	2	Independent-samples *t* test
	1	3 or more	One-way ANOVA
	2 or more	2 or more	Factorial ANOVA
Within-group	1	2	Paired-samples *t* test
	1	3 or more	Repeated measures ANOVA
	2 or more	2 or more	Repeated measures ANOVA
Between- and within-group	2 or more	2 or more	Split-plot ANOVA

4.4 *T* TESTS

The most widely adopted statistical procedure for comparing two means is the *t* test (Rosenthal and Rosnow, 2008). Different types of *t* test should be adopted according to the specific design of the study. When the two groups being compared are presumably unrelated, an independent-samples *t* test can be used. When the two means are contributed by the same group, a paired-samples *t* test can be considered.

Suppose you want to investigate whether the use of specific word-prediction software has an impact on typing speed. The hypothesis of the test is:

There is no significant difference in the task completion time between individuals who use the word-prediction software and those who do not use the software.

The following two sections will demonstrate how we investigate this hypothesis through two different designs that lead to the use of the independent-samples *t* test and the paired-samples *t* test.

4.4.1 INDEPENDENT-SAMPLES *T* TEST

You can test the hypothesis by recruiting two groups of participants and have one group type some text using standard word-processing software only and another group using the word-processing software with word-prediction functions. If a random-sampling method is used, the two groups are presumably independent from each other. In this case, the independent-samples *t* test is appropriate for data analysis.

If you use SPSS to run an independent-samples *t* test, the data points of the two groups should be listed in the same column. You need to create an additional column to mark the group to which each data point belongs. In Table 4.4, each condition has eight participants. The Coding column marks the group information, with 0 representing the participants who completed the tasks without word prediction and 1 representing the participants who completed the tasks with word prediction. When using SPSS, only the third and the fourth columns need to be entered.

Table 4.4 Sample Data for Independent-Samples *t* Test

Group	Participants	Task Completion Time	Coding
No prediction	Participant 1	245	0
No prediction	Participant 2	236	0
No prediction	Participant 3	321	0
No prediction	Participant 4	212	0
No prediction	Participant 5	267	0
No prediction	Participant 6	334	0
No prediction	Participant 7	287	0
No prediction	Participant 8	259	0
With prediction	Participant 9	246	1
With prediction	Participant 10	213	1
With prediction	Participant 11	265	1
With prediction	Participant 12	189	1
With prediction	Participant 13	201	1
With prediction	Participant 14	197	1
With prediction	Participant 15	289	1
With prediction	Participant 16	224	1

4.4.2 PAIRED-SAMPLES *T* TEST

An alternative strategy for the word-prediction software study is to recruit one group of participants and have each participant complete comparable typing tasks under both conditions. Since the data points contributed by the same participant are related, a paired-samples *t* test should be used.

If you use SPSS to run a paired-samples *t* test, the two data points contributed by the same participant should be listed parallel to each other in the same row. In Table 4.5, the two numeric values in each row were contributed by the same participant. When using SPSS to run the test, only the second and third columns need to be entered.

Table 4.5 Sample Data for Paired-Samples *t* Test

Participants	No Prediction	With Prediction
Participant 1	245	246
Participant 2	236	213
Participant 3	321	265
Participant 4	212	189
Participant 5	267	201
Participant 6	334	197
Participant 7	287	289
Participant 8	259	224

4.4.3 INTERPRETATION OF *T* TEST RESULTS

The *t* tests return a value, *t*, with larger *t* values suggesting higher probability of the null hypothesis being false. In other words, the higher the *t* value, the more likely the two means are different. As stated in Chapter 2, we normally use a 95% confidence interval in significance tests. So any *t* value that is higher than the corresponding *t* value at the 95% confidence interval suggests that there is a significant difference between participants (e.g., between users who use word-prediction software and those who do not).

SPSS generates a summary table for the results, containing both the *t* test results and additional test results that examine the data distribution. If we run an independent-samples *t* test using the data set provided in Table 4.4, the returned *t* value is 2.169, which is higher than the *t* value for the specific degree of freedom ($df = 15$) at the 95% confidence interval ($t = 2.131$).[2] In statistical terms, the result can be reported as:

> An independent-samples t test suggests that there is significant difference in the task completion time between the group who used the standard word-processing software and the group who used word-processing software with word prediction functions ($t(15) = 2.169$, $p < 0.05$).

Note that the *t* value needs to be reported together with the degree of freedom and the level of significance. Presenting the degree of freedom helps readers evaluate whether the data analysis is done correctly and interpret the results appropriately.

---

[2] The *t* value can be found in a summary table of *t*, which is available in many statistics books.

4.4.4 TWO-TAILED *T* TESTS AND ONE-TAILED *T* TESTS

In some empirical studies, the hypothesis indicates the direction of the difference. For example, you may expect the use of word-prediction software to improve typing speed. In this case, the hypothesis of the study will be:

> *Individuals who use word-prediction software can type faster than those who do not use word-prediction software.*

How does this hypothesis differ from the original hypothesis? In the original hypothesis, the direction of the difference is not specified, implying that the use of word-prediction software may improve typing speed, reduce typing speed, or have no impact on typing speed. In the hypothesis specified in this section, we expect the use of the word-prediction software to either improve typing speed, or have no impact at all. In this case, a "one-tailed *t* test" is appropriate. A *t* value that is larger than the 90% confidence interval suggests that the null hypothesis is false and that the difference between the two means is significant.

4.5 ANALYSIS OF VARIANCE

ANOVA is a widely used statistical method to compare the means of two or more groups. When there are only two means to be compared, the calculation of ANOVA is simplified to *t* tests. ANOVA tests normally return a value called the omnibus *F*. Therefore, ANOVA tests are also called "*F* tests."

4.5.1 ONE-WAY ANOVA

One-way ANOVA is appropriate for empirical studies that adopt a between-group design and investigate only one independent variable with three or more conditions. Let us revisit the word-prediction software study from Section 4.4.

Suppose you are also interested in a speech-based data-entry method and would like to compare three conditions: text entry using standard word-processing software, text entry using word-prediction software, and text entry using speech-based dictation software. The independent variable of the study has three conditions. With a between-group design, you need to recruit three groups of participants and have each group complete the text entry task using one of the three methods.

The data layout for running one-way ANOVA using SPSS is similar to that for the independent-samples *t* test. Table 4.6 presents a data set for the one-way ANOVA test. The Coding column marks the group that each data point belongs to. Normally we use 0 to mark the control group (those who used the basic word-processing software); 1 and 2 are used to mark the group who used the word-prediction software and the group who used the speech-based dictation software. When using SPSS, only the third and the fourth columns need to be entered.

Table 4.6 Sample Data for One-Way ANOVA Test

Group	Participants	Task Completion Time	Coding
Standard	Participant 1	245	0
Standard	Participant 2	236	0
Standard	Participant 3	321	0
Standard	Participant 4	212	0
Standard	Participant 5	267	0
Standard	Participant 6	334	0
Standard	Participant 7	287	0
Standard	Participant 8	259	0
Prediction	Participant 9	246	1
Prediction	Participant 10	213	1
Prediction	Participant 11	265	1
Prediction	Participant 12	189	1
Prediction	Participant 13	201	1
Prediction	Participant 14	197	1
Prediction	Participant 15	289	1
Prediction	Participant 16	224	1
Speech-based dictation	Participant 17	178	2
Speech-based dictation	Participant 18	289	2
Speech-based dictation	Participant 19	222	2
Speech-based dictation	Participant 20	189	2
Speech-based dictation	Participant 21	245	2
Speech-based dictation	Participant 22	311	2
Speech-based dictation	Participant 23	267	2
Speech-based dictation	Participant 24	197	2

Table 4.7 presents a simplified summary report provided by SPSS for the one-way ANOVA test. The between-group's sum of squares represents the amount of variances in the data that can be explained by the use of text entry methods. The within-group's sum of squares represents the amount of variances in the data that cannot be explained by the text entry methods. The mean square is calculated by dividing the sum of squares by the degree of freedom. The returned F value of

Table 4.7 Result of the One-Way ANOVA Test

Source	Sum of Squares	df	Mean Square	F	Significance
Between-group	7842.250	2	3921.125	2.174	0.139
Within-group	37,880.375	21	1803.827		

2.174 is lower than the value at the 95% confidence interval, suggesting that there is no significant difference among the three conditions. The results can be reported as follows:

> *A one-way ANOVA test using task completion time as the dependent variable and group as the independent variable suggests that there is no significant difference among the three conditions (F(2, 21) = 2.174, n.s.).*

4.5.2 FACTORIAL ANOVA

Factorial ANOVA is appropriate for empirical studies that adopt a between-group design and investigate two or more independent variables.

Let us continue with the data-entry evaluation study. You may also want to know whether different types of task, such as composition or transcription, have any impact on performance. In this case, you can introduce two independent variables to your study: data-entry method and task type. There are three conditions for the data-entry method variable: standard word-processing software, word-prediction software, and speech-based dictation software. There are two conditions for the task type variable: transcription and composition. Accordingly, the empirical study has a total of $3 \times 2 = 6$ conditions. With a between-group design (see Table 4.8), you need to recruit six groups of participants and have each group complete the text entry task under one of the six conditions.

Table 4.8 A Between-Group Factorial Design With Two Independent Variables

	Standard	Prediction	Speech
Transcription	Group 1	Group 2	Group 3
Composition	Group 4	Group 5	Group 6

If you use SPSS to run the analysis, the data layout for running the factorial ANOVA test is more complicated than that of a one-way ANOVA test. Table 4.9 shows part of the data table for the factorial ANOVA test of the text entry study. The task completion time for all participants is listed in a single column. A separate coding column is created for each independent variable involved in the study. In Table 4.9, the fifth column shows whether a participant completed the transcription task or the composition task. The sixth column shows whether the participants completed the task using standard word-processing software, word-prediction software, or speech-based dictation software. When using SPSS to run the test, only columns 4, 5, and 6 need to be entered.

The SPSS procedure for a factorial ANOVA test is the univariate analysis. Table 4.10 presents the summary of the analysis results, with the first and second rows listing the information for the two independent variables, respectively. The third row lists the information for the interaction effect between the two independent variables. The analysis result suggests that there is no significant difference between participants who completed the transcription tasks and those who completed the composition tasks ($F(1, 42) = 1.41$, n.s.). There is significant difference among participants who used different text entry methods ($F(2, 42) = 4.51$, $p < 0.05$).

Table 4.9 Sample Data for the Factorial ANOVA Test

Task type	Entry method	Participant Number	Task time	Task Type coding	Entry Method coding
Transcription	Standard	Participant 1	245	0	0
Transcription	Standard	Participant 2	236	0	0
...	...	...	...	...	...
Transcription	Prediction	Participant 9	246	0	1
Transcription	Prediction	Participant 10	213	0	1
...	...	...	...	...	...
Transcription	Speech-based dictation	Participant 17	178	0	2
Transcription	Speech-based dictation	Participant 18	289	0	2
...	...	...	...	...	...
Composition	Standard	Participant 25	256	1	0
Composition	Standard	Participant 26	269	1	0
...	...	...	...	...	...
Composition	Prediction	Participant 33	265	1	1
Composition	Prediction	Participant 34	232	1	1
...	...	...	...	...	...
Composition	Speech-based dictation	Participant 41	189	1	2
Composition	Speech-based dictation	Participant 42	321	1	2
...	...	...	...	...	...
Composition	Speech-based dictation	Participant 48	202	1	2

Table 4.10 Result of the Factorial ANOVA Test

Source	Sum of Square	df	Mean Square	F	Significance
Task type	2745.188	1	2745.188	1.410	0.242
Entry method	17,564.625	2	8782.313	4.512	0.017
Task*entry	114.875	2	57.437	0.030	0.971
Error	81,751.625	42	1946.467		

4.5.3 REPEATED MEASURES ANOVA

Repeated measures ANOVA tests are appropriate for empirical studies that adopt a within-group design. As stated in Section 4.5.2, the investigation of the text entry method and task type variables requires six conditions. If you adopt a between-group design, you need to recruit six groups of participants. If 12 participants are needed for each group, you must recruit a total of 72 participants. It is quite difficult to recruit such a large sample size in many HCI studies, especially those that involve participants with disabilities or specific expertise. To address that problem, you may decide to use a within-group design, in which case you recruit just one group of participants and have each participant complete the tasks under all conditions.

Repeated measures ANOVA tests can involve just one level or multiple levels. A one-way, repeated measures ANOVA test can be used for within-group studies that investigate just one independent variable. For example, if you are interested only in the impact of the text entry method, a one-way, repeated measures ANOVA test would be appropriate for the data analysis. If you use SPSS to run the test, the three data points contributed by each participant should be listed in the same row. Table 4.11 demonstrates the sample data layout for the analysis.

Table 4.11 Sample Data for One-Way, Repeated Measures ANOVA

	Standard	Prediction	Speech
Participant 1	245	246	178
Participant 2	236	213	289
Participant 3	321	265	222
Participant 4	212	189	189
Participant 5	267	201	245
Participant 6	334	197	311
Participant 7	287	289	267
Participant 8	259	224	197

Table 4.12 is the simplified summary table for the one-way, repeated measures ANOVA test generated by SPSS. The returned F value with degree of freedom (2, 14) is 2.925. It is below the 95% confidence interval, suggesting that there is no significant difference between the three text entry methods.

Table 4.12 Result of the One-Way, Repeated Measures ANOVA Test

Source	Sum of Square	df	Mean Square	F	Significance
Entry method	7842.25	2	3921.125	2.925	0.087
Error	18,767.083	14	1340.506		

Multiple-level, repeated measures ANOVA tests are needed for within-group studies that investigate two or more independent variables. If you are interested in the impact of both the text entry method and the types of task, the study involves six conditions as illustrated in Table 4.13. A two-way, repeated measures ANOVA test can be used to analyze the data collected under this design.

Table 4.13 Experiment Design of a Two-Way, Repeated Measures ANOVA Test

	Standard	Prediction	Speech
Transcription	Group 1	Group 1	Group 1
Composition	Group 1	Group 1	Group 1

When using SPSS to run the analysis, the data need to be carefully arranged to avoid potential errors. The data points contributed by the same participant need to be listed in the same row. It is recommended that you repeat the same pattern when arranging the columns (see Table 4.14).

Table 4.14 Sample Data for Two-Way, Repeated Measures ANOVA Test

	Transcription			Composition		
	Standard	Prediction	Speech	Standard	Prediction	Speech
Participant 1	245	246	178	256	265	189
Participant 2	236	213	289	269	232	321
Participant 3	321	265	222	333	254	202
Participant 4	212	189	189	246	199	198
Participant 5	267	201	245	259	194	278
Participant 6	334	197	311	357	221	341
Participant 7	287	289	267	301	302	279
Participant 8	259	224	197	278	243	229

Table 4.15 presents the simplified summary table for the two-way, repeated measures ANOVA test. The task type has a significant impact on the time spent to complete the task $(F(1, 7)=14.217, p<0.01)$. There is no significant difference among the three text entry methods $(F(2, 14)=2.923, \text{n.s.})$. The interaction effect between the two independent variables is not significant either $(F(2, 14)=0.759, \text{n.s.})$.

Table 4.15 Result of the Two-Way, Repeated Measures ANOVA Test

Source	Sum of Square	df	Mean Square	F	Significance
Task type	2745.187	1	2745.187	14.217	0.007
Error (task type)	1351.646	7	193.092		
Entry method	17,564.625	2	8782.313	2.923	0.087
Error (entry method)	42,067.708	14	3004.836		
Task type*entry method	114.875	2	57.438	0.759	0.486
Error (task type*entry method)	1058.792	14	75.628		

4.5.4 ANOVA FOR SPLIT-PLOT DESIGN

Sometimes you may choose a study design that involves both between-group factors and within-group factors. In the text entry study, you may recruit two groups of participants. One group completes transcription tasks using all three data-entry methods. The other group completes composition tasks using all three data-entry methods (see Table 4.16). In this case, the type of task is a between-group factor and the text entry method is a within-group factor. There are two benefits of this design as compared to a pure within-group design. First, it greatly reduces the time of the study and the participants are less likely to feel tired or bored. Second, it controls the learning effect to some extent. Compared to a pure between-group study, the mixed design allows you to compare the same number of conditions with a fairly small sample size.

Table 4.16 Split-Plot Experiment Design

	Keyboard	Prediction	Speech
Transcription	Group 1	Group 1	Group 1
Composition	Group 2	Group 2	Group 2

Table 4.17 demonstrates the sample data table for the mixed design when running the test using SPSS. Note that one column needs to be added to specify the value of the between-group variable (types of task). Data points collected from the same participant need to be listed parallel to each other in the same row.

Table 4.17 Sample Data for the Split-Plot ANOVA Test

Task Type	Participant Number	Task Type Coding	Standard	Prediction	Speech
Transcription	Participant 1	0	245	246	178
Transcription	Participant 2	0	236	213	289
Transcription	Participant 3	0	321	265	222
Transcription	Participant 4	0	212	189	189
Transcription	Participant 5	0	267	201	245
Transcription	Participant 6	0	334	197	311
Transcription	Participant 7	0	287	289	267
Transcription	Participant 8	0	259	224	197
Composition	Participant 9	1	256	265	189
Composition	Participant 10	1	269	232	321
Composition	Participant 11	1	333	254	202
Composition	Participant 12	1	246	199	198
Composition	Participant 13	1	259	194	278
Composition	Participant 14	1	357	221	341
Composition	Participant 15	1	301	302	279
Composition	Participant 16	1	278	243	229

The results of a mixed design are presented in two tables in the outputs of SPSS. Table 4.18 provides the result for the between-group factor (task type). Table 4.19 provides the result for the within-group factor (text entry method). Table 4.18 suggests that there is no significant difference between participants who complete composition or transcription tasks ($F(1, 14)=0.995$, n.s.). Table 4.19 suggests that there is a significant difference among the three text entry methods ($F(2, 28)=5.702$, $p<0.01$). The interaction effect between task types and text entry methods is not significant ($F(2, 28)=0.037$, n.s.).

Table 4.18 Results of the Split-Plot Test for the Between-Group Variable

Source	Sum of Square	df	Mean Square	F	Significance
Task type	2745.187	1	2745.187	0.995	0.335
Error	38,625.125	14	2758.937		

Table 4.19 Results of the Split-Plot Test for the Within-Group Variable

Source	Sum of Square	df	Mean Square	F	Significance
Entry method	17,564.625	2	8782.313	5.702	0.008
Entry method*task type	114.875	2	57.437	0.037	0.963
Error (entry method)	43,126.5	28	1540.232		

4.6 ASSUMPTIONS OF *T* TESTS AND *F* TESTS

Before running a *t* test or an *F* test, it is important to examine whether your data meet the assumptions of the two tests. If the assumptions are not met, you may make incorrect inferences from those tests. Both *t* tests and *F* tests typically require three assumptions for the data:

First, the errors of all data points should be independent of each other. If they are not independent of each other, the result of the test can be misleading (Snedecor and Cochran, 1989). For example, in the text-entry method study, if two investigators conducted the study and one investigator consistently gave the participants more detailed instructions than the other investigator, the participants who completed the study with more detailed instructions might perform consistently better than those who received less detailed instructions. In this case, the errors of the participants who were instructed by the same investigator are no longer independent and the test results would be spurious.

Second, the errors in the data need to be identically distributed. This assumption is also called "homogeneity of variance." When multiple group means are compared, the *t* test or the *F* test is more accurate if the variances of the sample population are nearly equal. This assumption does not mean that we can only run *t* tests or *F* tests when the variances in the populations are exactly the same. Actually, we only become concerned when the population variances are very different or when the two sample sizes are very different (Rosenthal and Rosnow, 2008). In cases when this assumption is violated, you can use transformation techniques, such as square roots, logs, and the reciprocals of the original data (Hamilton, 1990), to make the variances in the sample population nearly equal.

Third, the errors in the data should be normally distributed. Similar to the assumption of "homogeneity of variance," this assumption is only considered to be violated when the sample data is highly skewed. When the errors are not normally distributed, nonparametric tests (discussed in Section 4.8) should be used to analyze the data.

4.7 IDENTIFYING RELATIONSHIPS

One of the most common objectives for HCI-related studies is to identify relationships between various factors. For example, you may want to know whether there is a relationship between age, computing experience, and target selection speed. In statistical terms, two factors are correlated if there is a significant relationship between them.

4.7.1 CORRELATION

The most widely used statistical method for testing correlation is the Pearson's product moment correlation coefficient test (Rosenthal and Rosnow, 2008). This test returns a correlation coefficient called Pearson's r. The value of Pearson's r ranges from -1.00 to 1.00. When the Pearson's r value between two variables is -1.00, it suggests a perfect negative linear relationship between the two variables. In other words, any specific increase in the scores of one variable will perfectly predict a specific amount of decrease in the scores of the other variable. When the Pearson's r value between two variables is 1.00, it suggests a perfect positive linear relationship between the two variables. That is, any specific increase in the scores of one variable will perfectly predict a specific amount of increase in the scores of the other variable. When the Pearson's r value is 0, it means that there is no linear relationship between the two variables. In other words, the increase or decrease in one variable does not predict any changes in the other variable.

In the data-entry method example, suppose the eight participants each complete two tasks, one using standard word-processing software, the other using word-prediction software. Table 4.20 lists the number of years that each participant had used computers and the time they spent on each task. We can run three Pearson's correlation tests based on this data set to examine the correlation between:

Table 4.20 Sample Data for Correlation Tests

	Computer Experience	Standard	Prediction
Participant 1	12	245	246
Participant 2	6	236	213
Participant 3	3	321	265
Participant 4	19	212	189
Participant 5	16	267	201
Participant 6	5	334	197
Participant 7	8	287	289
Participant 8	11	259	224

- computer experience and task time under the standard word-processing software condition;
- computer experience and task time under the prediction software condition; and
- task times under the standard word-processing software condition and those under the prediction software condition.

Table 4.21 illustrates the correlation matrix between the three variables generated by SPSS. The three variables are listed in the top row and the left column in the same order. The correlation between the same variable is always 1, as indicated by the three r values on the diagonal line of the table. The correlation between computer experience and the time using the standard software is significant, with r value equal to -0.723. The negative r value suggests that as computer experience increases, the time spent on completing the task using the standard software decreases. The correlation between computer experience and time spent using prediction software is not significant $(r=-0.468)$. The correlation between the completion times using the standard software and using the prediction software is not significant either $(r=0.325)$.

Table 4.21 Results of the Correlation Tests

		Experience	Time Keyboard	Time Prediction
Experience	Pearson correlation	1	-0.723^a	-0.468
	Significance		0.043	0.243
	N	8	8	8
Time keyboard	Pearson correlation	-0.723^a	1	0.325
	Significance	0.043		0.432
	N	8	8	8
Time prediction	Pearson correlation	-0.468	0.325	1
	Significance	0.243	0.432	
	N	8	8	8

^{a} Correlation is significant at the 0.05 level (two-tailed).

In practice, the Pearson's r^2 is reported more often than the Pearson's r. The r^2 represents the proportion of the variance shared by the two variables. In other words, suppose we have two variables X and Y, the r^2 represents the percentage of variance in variable X that can be explained by variable Y. It also represents the percentage of variance in variable Y that can be explained by variable X. For many researchers, the r^2 is a more direct measure of the degree of correlation than the Pearson's r.

The most important thing to keep in mind about correlation is that it does not imply a causal relationship. That is, the fact that two variables are significantly correlated does not necessarily mean that the changes in one variable cause the changes in the other variable. In some cases, there is causal relationship between the two variables. In other cases, there is a hidden variable (also called the "intervening" variable, which is one type of confounding variable) that serves as the underlying cause of the change.

For example, in an experiment that studies how users interact with an e-commerce website, you may find a significant correlation between income and performance. More specifically, participants with higher income spend longer time finding a specific item and make more errors during the navigation process. Can you claim that earning a higher income causes people to spend longer time retrieving online items and make more errors? The answer is obviously no. The truth might be that people who earn a higher income tend to be older than those who earn a lower income. People in the older age group do not use computers as intensively as in the younger age group, especially when it comes to activities such as online shopping. Consequently, they may spend longer time to find items and make more errors. In this case, age is the intervening variable that is hidden behind the two variables examined in the correlation. Although income and performance are significantly correlated, there is no causal relationship between them. A correct interpretation of the relationship between the variables is listed in Figure 4.2.

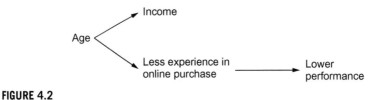

FIGURE 4.2

Relationship between correlated variables and an intervening variable.

This example demonstrates the danger of claiming causal relationship based on significant correlation. In data analysis, it is not uncommon for researchers to conduct pairwise correlation tests on all variables involved and then claim that "variable A has a significant impact on variable B" or "the changes in variable A cause variable B to change," which can be spurious in many cases. To avoid this mistake, you should keep in mind that empirical studies should be driven by hypothesis, not data. That is, your analysis should be based on a predefined hypothesis, not the other way around. In the earlier example, you are unlikely to develop a hypothesis that "income has a significant impact on online purchasing performance" since it does not make much sense. If your study is hypothesis driven, you will not be fooled by correlation analysis results. On the other hand, if you do not have a clearly defined hypothesis before the study, you will derive hypotheses driven by the data analysis, making it more likely that you will draw false conclusions.

4.7.2 **REGRESSION**

Unlike correlation analysis, which allows the study of only two variables, regression analysis allows you to investigate the relationship among one dependent variable and a number of independent variables. In HCI-related studies, regression analysis is used for two main purposes: model construction and prediction. In cases of model construction, we are interested in identifying the quantitative relationship between one dependent variable and a number of independent variables. That is, we want to find a mathematical equation based on the independent variables that best explains the variances in the dependent variable. In cases of prediction, we are interested in using a number of known factors, also called "predictor variables," to predict the value of the dependent variable, also called the "criterion variable" (Share, 1984). The two objectives are closely related. You need to build a robust model in order to predict the values of the criterion factor in which you are interested.

Depending on the specific research objective, you need to choose different regression procedures to construct the model. If the objective of the study is to find the relationship between the dependent variable and the independent variables as a group, you can enter all the independent variables simultaneously. This is the most commonly adopted regression procedure (Darlington, 1968). Using this approach, you will find out the percentage of variances in the dependent variable that can be explained by the independent variables as a group. This percentage is presented in the form of R^2. If the procedure returns a significant R^2, it suggests that the independent variables as a group have significant impact on the dependent variable. This procedure is useful but is insufficient if you are interested in the impact of each individual independent variable.

If you want to create a model that explains the relationship between the dependent variable and each individual independent variable, the hierarchical regression procedure is appropriate. Using this procedure, you will enter the independent variables one at a time into the regression equation. The order of the entry of the independent variables is determined by the predefined theoretical model. The independent variables that are entered into the equation first usually fall into two categories. One category includes variables that are considered to be important according to previous literature or observation; in this case, you want to evaluate the overall impact of this variable on the dependent variable. The second category includes the variables that are of no interest to you but have significant impact on the dependent variable (also called covariates); in this case, you want to exclude the variable's impact on the dependent variable before you study the variables that you are interested in. In other words, entering the covariates first allows you to remove the variances in the dependent variable that can be explained by the covariates, making it easier to identify significant relationships for the variables in which you are interested.

Suppose you conduct a user study that investigates target selection tasks using a standard mouse. One important dependent variable of interest is the task completion time and you want to know what factors have an impact on task completion time. There are a number of potential factors such as target size, distance, computer experience, age, etc. In order to find the relationships among the factors, you can conduct a regression analysis using task completion time as the dependent variable and the other factors as independent variables. Table 4.22 demonstrates a portion of the data from this study.

Table 4.22 Sample Data for the Regression Analysis

Age	Computer Experience	Target Size	Target Distance	Task Time
18	6	10	10	7
...	...	...	...	...
12	4	10	20	10
...	...	...	...	...
32	16	30	10	5
...	...	...	...	...
45	15	40	20	5
...	...	...	...	...

In this regression analysis, the dependent variable is the task completion time. The independent variables are age, computer experience (as represented by the number of years using computers), target size, and the distance between the current cursor location and the target. If you want to find out the relationship between task completion time and the independent variables as a group, simultaneous regression can be adopted. If you use SPSS to run the procedure, you enter task completion time into the dependent variable block and age, computer experience, target size, and distance into the same block for independent variables.

Table 4.23 shows the summary result of the simultaneous regression analysis. There is a significant relationship between task completion time and the independent variables as a group ($F(4, 59) = 41.147$, $p < 0.001$). The R^2 indicates the percentage of variance in the dependent variable that can be explained by the independent variables. Age, computer experience, target size, and navigation distance explain a total of 73.6% of the variance in task completion time. Please note that this percentage is unusually high since the data were made up by the authors.

Table 4.23 Result for Simultaneous Regression Procedure

Model	R	R^2	F	df1	df2	Significance
1	0.858	0.736	41.147	4	59	0.000

If you are interested in the impact that each independent variable has on task completion time, the hierarchical regression procedure can be adopted. Suppose target size and navigation distance are the most important factors that you want to examine; you can enter target size in the first block for independent variables and navigation distance, age, and computer experience into the subsequent blocks. Table 4.24 shows the summary result of this procedure. Since the four independent variables were entered separately, four regression models were constructed. Model 1 describes the relationship between task completion time and target size. It shows that target size explains a significant percentage of the variance (31.9%) in task completion time ($F(1, 62) = 29.054$, $p < 0.001$). The R^2 change column represents the additional variance in the dependent variable that can be explained by the newly entered independent variable. For example, Model 2 suggests that adding navigation distance to the regression model explains an additional 8.4% of the variance in task completion time. Navigation distance also has a significant impact on task completion time ($F(1, 61) = 8.615$, $p < 0.01$).

Table 4.24 Result for Hierarchical Regression Procedure

Model	R	R^2	R^2 change	F	df1	df2	Significance
1	0.565	0.319	0.319	29.054	1	62	0.000
2	0.635	0.403	0.084	8.615	1	61	0.005
3	0.767	0.588	0.184	26.817	1	60	0.000
4	0.858	0.736	0.148	33.196	1	59	0.000

4.8 NONPARAMETRIC STATISTICAL TESTS

All the analysis methods discussed in the previous sections are parametric tests that require several general assumptions. First, the data needs to be collected from a population that is normally distributed. Usually we consider this assumption as being met if the population has an approximately normal distribution. Second, the variables should be at least scaled by intervals. That is, the distance between any two adjacent data units should be equal. For example, when examining the age variable, the distances between 1 and 2, 2 and 3, and 80 and 81 are all equal to each other. And third, for tests that compare means of different groups, the variance in the data collected from different groups should be approximately equal.

In reality, you may encounter situations where one or more of the three assumptions are not met. Some studies may yield data that poorly approximates to normal distribution. Some hypotheses may have to be measured through categorical variables (e.g., race or gender) or ordinal variables (e.g., ranking scales) where different items are compared directly with each other. In these cases, the intervals between the values are not equally spaced. For example, when collecting subjective satisfaction about an application, you may use a Likert scale question, as shown in Figure 4.3. In this case, the distance between the two adjacent data points can be unequal. The same problem exists for questions that require "yes" or "no" answers or ask participants to rank a number of options.

I am satisfied with the time it took to complete the task

1	2	3	4	5
highly disagree	disagree	neutral	agree	highly agree

FIGURE 4.3

Likert scale question.

When the assumptions of parametric tests are not met, you need to consider the use of nonparametric analysis methods. Compared to parametric tests, nonparametric methods make fewer assumptions about the data. Although nonparametric tests are also called "assumption-free" tests, it should be noted that they are not actually free of assumptions. For example, the Chi-squared test, one of the most commonly used nonparametric tests, has specific requirements on the sample size and independence of data points.

Another important message to note about nonparametric analysis is that information in the data can be lost when the data tested are actually interval or ratio. The reason is that the nonparametric analysis collapses the data into ranks so all that matters is the order of the data while the distance information between the data points is lost. Therefore, nonparametric analysis sacrifices the power to use all available information to reject a false null hypothesis in exchange for less strict assumptions about the data (Mackenzie, 2013).

4.8.1 CHI-SQUARED TEST

In user studies, we frequently encounter situations where categorical data (e.g., yes or no) are collected and we need to determine whether there is any relationship in the variables. Those data are normally presented in tables of counts (also called contingency tables) that can be as simple as a 2-by-2 table or as complicated as tables with more than 10 columns or rows. The Chi-squared test is probably the most popular significance test used to analyze frequency counts (Rosenthal and Rosnow, 2008).

Let us explore the Chi-squared test through an example. Suppose you are examining the impact of age on users' preferences toward two target selection devices: a mouse and a touchscreen. You recruit two groups of users. One group consists of 20 adult users who are younger than 65 and the other consists of 20 users who are 65 or older. After completing a series of target selection tasks using both the mouse and the touchscreen, participants specify the type of device that they prefer to use. You can generate a contingency table (see Table 4.25) that summarizes the frequency counts of the preferred device specified by the two groups of participants.

Table 4.25 A 2-by-2 Frequency Count Table

Age	Preferred Device	
	Mouse	**Touchscreen**
<65	14	6
≥65	4	16

As demonstrated in Table 4.25, more participants under the age of 65 prefer the mouse while more senior participants prefer the touchscreen. In order to examine whether this result is merely by chance or there is indeed a relationship between age and the preference for pointing devices, you can run a Chi-squared test. The test returns a Chi-squared value and a P value that helps you determine whether the result is significant. The result for the data in Table 4.25 is ($\chi^2(1) = 10.1$, $p < 0.005$). It suggests that the probability of the difference between the rows and columns occurring by chance is less than 0.005. Using the 95% confidence interval, you reject the null hypothesis and conclude that there is a relationship between age and preferred pointing device.

The degree of freedom of a Chi-squared test is calculated by the following equation:

$$\text{Degree of freedom} = (\text{Number of rows} - 1) \times (\text{Number of columns} - 1)$$

In the earlier example, the degree of freedom is $(2-1) \times (2-1) = 1$. If you have a contingency data with 3 rows and 3 columns, the degree of freedom of the Chi-squared test will be $(3-1) \times (3-1) = 4$.

If you expand the study to three pointing devices and include children in it, you have three task conditions and three participant groups. Suppose the data collected are as demonstrated in Table 4.26. In this case, the Chi-squared test result is ($\chi^2(4) = 16.8$, $p < 0.005$), suggesting that there is significant difference among the three age groups regarding preference for the pointing devices.

Table 4.26 A 3-by-3 Frequency Count Table

Age	Preferred Device		
	Mouse	**Touchscreen**	**Stylus**
<18	4	9	7
18–65	12	6	2
≥65	4	15	1

As we mentioned before, nonparametric tests are not assumption free. The Chi-squared test requires two assumptions that the data must satisfy in order to make a valid judgment. First, the data points in the contingency table must be independent from each other. In other words, one participant can only contribute one data point in the contingency table. To give a more specific example, you cannot have a participant that prefers both the mouse and the touchscreen. All the numbers presented in Tables 4.25 and 4.26 have to be contributed by independent samples. Second, the Chi-squared test does not work well when the sample is too small. It is generally suggested that, to acquire a robust Chi-square, the total sample size needs to be 20 or larger (Camilli and Hopkins, 1978).

4.8.2 OTHER NONPARAMETRIC TESTS

Many parametric tests have corresponding nonparametric alternatives. If you are comparing data collected from two independent samples (e.g., data collected using a between-group design), the independent-samples t test can be used when the parametric analysis assumptions are met. When the assumptions are not met, the Mann-Whitney U test or the Wald-Wolfowitz runs test may be considered. If you are comparing two sets of data collected from the same user group (e.g., data collected using a within-group design), the paired-samples t test is typically adopted when the assumptions are met. If not, the Wilcoxon signed-rank test can be used instead.

The following example illustrates the use of the Mann-Whitney U test. Suppose you are evaluating two authentication techniques: the traditional alphanumeric password and an image-based password that contain several images preselected by the user. You recruit two groups of participants. Each group uses one authentication technique to complete a number of login tasks. In addition to performance measures such as task completion time, failed login tasks, and keystroke level data, you also ask the participants to answer a questionnaire at the end of the study. Each participant rates the general level of frustration when using the authentication technique through a 7-point Likert scale question (1=least frustrated, 7=most frustrated). Sample data for the test is demonstrated in Table 4.27. The mean score for the alphanumeric password is 3.88. The mean score for the image-based password is 5.50. In order to determine whether the difference is statistically significant, you need to use nonparametric tests to compare the two groups of data. Since the data is collected from two independent groups of participants, you can use the Mann-Whitney U test for this analysis.

The result of the Mann-Whitney test includes a U value and a z score with the corresponding P value. The z score is a normalized score calculated based on the

Table 4.27 Sample Data for Mann-Whitney U test

Group	Participants	Rating	Coding
Alphanumeric	Participant 1	4	0
Alphanumeric	Participant 2	3	0
Alphanumeric	Participant 3	6	0

Table 4.27 Sample Data for Mann-Whitney *U* test *Continued*

Group	Participants	Rating	Coding
Alphanumeric	Participant 4	4	0
Alphanumeric	Participant 5	3	0
Alphanumeric	Participant 6	2	0
Alphanumeric	Participant 7	4	0
Alphanumeric	Participant 8	5	0
Image-based	Participant 9	4	1
Image-based	Participant 10	6	1
Image-based	Participant 11	6	1
Image-based	Participant 12	7	1
Image-based	Participant 13	5	1
Image-based	Participant 14	6	1
Image-based	Participant 15	4	1
Image-based	Participant 16	6	1

U value. For this example, $U = 10.5$ and $p < 0.05$. Therefore, the null hypothesis is rejected. The data suggests that there is significant difference in the level of perceived frustration between the two authentication techniques. Participants experienced significantly lower level of frustration when using the image-based password than the alphanumeric password.

Let us examine another scenario in which you are interested in the use of the two authentication techniques by people with Down syndrome. Since recruiting participant with Down syndrome from the local area is quite challenging, you only successfully recruit 10 participants for the study. The small participant size suggests that a within-group design will be more appropriate. So each participant completes the study using both authentication techniques and answers a questionnaire after the interaction with each technique. Sample data for the test is demonstrated in Table 4.28. The mean score for the alphanumeric password is 3.9. The mean score for the image-based password is 4.7. Since the data is collected from one group of participants, you can use the Wilcoxon signed-rank test to examine whether there is significant difference in the perceived level of frustration between the two techniques.

The result of the Wilcoxon signed-rank test is a normalized *z* score. For this example, $z = -1.31$ and $p = 0.19$. There is no significant difference in the perceived level of frustration between the two techniques.

Table 4.28 Sample Data for Wilcoxon Signed-Rank Test

Participants	Alphanumeric	Image-Based
Participant 1	5	6
Participant 2	3	4
Participant 3	4	3

Continued

Table 4.28 Sample Data for Wilcoxon Signed-Rank Test *Continued*

Participants	Alphanumeric	Image-Based
Participant 4	5	5
Participant 5	2	7
Participant 6	3	4
Participant 7	4	6
Participant 8	6	5
Participant 9	4	3
Participant 10	3	4

In cases when three or more sets of data are compared and the parametric analysis assumptions are not met, the Kruskal-Wallis one-way ANOVA by ranks (an extension of the Mann-Whitney U test) may be considered when the samples are independent. When the data sets are dependent on each other, you can consider using Friedman's two-way ANOVA test.

In the authentication study discussed previously, suppose you would like to evaluate a drawing-based password technique in additional to the alphanumeric technique and the image-based technique, the study will include three conditions. If you recruit three groups of participants and let each group use one authentication technique during the study, the data will be collected from independent samples and the frustration rating can be analyzed through the Kruskal-Wallis one-way ANOVA by ranks. Sample data for the test is demonstrated in Table 4.29. The mean score for the alphanumeric password is 3.25. The mean score for the image-based password is 4.63. The mean score for the drawing-based password is 5.63.

The result of the Kruskal-Wallis test is an H value. In this example, $H(2) = 11.897$, $p < 0.05$. Therefore, the null hypothesis is rejected. The result suggests that there is significant difference in the perceived level of frustration between the three authentication techniques.

Table 4.29 Sample Data for Kruskal-Wallis One-Way Analysis of Variance by Ranks

Group	Participants	Rating	Coding
Alphanumeric	Participant 1	5	0
Alphanumeric	Participant 2	3	0
Alphanumeric	Participant 3	4	0
Alphanumeric	Participant 4	4	0
Alphanumeric	Participant 5	2	0
Alphanumeric	Participant 6	3	0
Alphanumeric	Participant 7	3	0
Alphanumeric	Participant 8	2	0
Image-based	Participant 9	3	1
Image-based	Participant 10	5	1
Image-based	Participant 11	6	1

Table 4.29 Sample Data for Kruskal-Wallis One-Way Analysis of Variance by Ranks *Continued*

Group	Participants	Rating	Coding
Image-based	Participant 12	4	1
Image-based	Participant 13	5	1
Image-based	Participant 14	4	1
Image-based	Participant 15	5	1
Image-based	Participant 16	5	1
Drawing-based	Participant 17	6	2
Drawing-based	Participant 18	4	2
Drawing-based	Participant 19	5	2
Drawing-based	Participant 20	5	2
Drawing-based	Participant 21	6	2
Drawing-based	Participant 22	7	2
Drawing-based	Participant 23	5	2
Drawing-based	Participant 24	7	2

Similarly, if you would like to evaluate the three authentication techniques when being used by people with Down syndrome, you may choose to adopt a within-group design that requires each participant to complete the tasks using all three authentication methods. In this case, the data can be analyzed through the Friedman's two-way ANOVA test. Sample data for the test is demonstrated in Table 4.30. The mean score for the alphanumeric password is 3.6. The mean score for the image-based password is 4. The mean score for the drawing-based password is 4.6.

The result of the Friedman's ANOVA test is an H value. In this example, $H(2)=2.722$, $p=0.256$. There is no significant difference in the perceived level of frustration between the three techniques.

All four nonparametric methods discussed earlier can only be used to analyze data that involves only one independent variable (factor). If you need to analyze

Table 4.30 Sample Data for Friedman's Two-Way Analysis of Variance Test

Participants	Alphanumeric	Image-Based	Drawing-Based
Participant 1	2	4	6
Participant 2	4	5	6
Participant 3	3	3	5
Participant 4	5	5	3
Participant 5	5	7	7
Participant 6	3	4	5
Participant 7	4	2	3
Participant 8	1	5	4
Participant 9	4	3	4
Participant 10	5	2	3

nonparametric data that involves two or more independent variables, you can consider using more recent approaches that extend nonparametric analysis to multifactor analysis (e.g., Kaptein et al., 2010; Wobbrock et al., 2011). For more information on this topic, please refer to sources that discuss the nonparametric analysis methods in depth, such as Conover (1999), Newton and Rudestam (1999), and Wasserman (2007).

4.9 SUMMARY

Statistical analysis is a powerful tool that helps us find interesting patterns and differences in the data as well as identify relationships between variables. Before running significance tests, the data needs to be cleaned up, coded, and appropriately organized to meet the needs of the specific statistical software package. The nature of the data collected and the design of the study determine the appropriate significance test that should be used. If the data are normally distributed and intervally scaled, parametric tests are appropriate. When the normal distribution and interval scale requirements are not met, nonparametric tests should be considered.

A number of statistical methods are available for comparing the means of multiple groups. A simple t test allows us to compare the means of two groups, with the independent-samples t test for the between-group design and the paired-samples t test for the within-group design. A one-way ANOVA test allows us to compare the means of three or more groups when a between-group design is adopted and there is only one independent variable involved. When two or more independent variables are involved in a between-group design, the factorial ANOVA test would be appropriate. If a study adopts a within-group design and involves one independent variable with more than two conditions, the one level repeated measures ANOVA test would be appropriate. When two or more independent variables are involved in a within-group design, the multiple-level repeated measures ANOVA test should be adopted. For studies that involve both a between-group factor and a within-group factor, the split-plot ANOVA test should be considered.

Correlation analysis allows us to identify significant relationships between two variables. When three or more variables are involved and a quantitative model is needed to describe the relationships between the dependent variables and the independent variables, regression analysis can be considered. Different regression procedures should be used based on the specific goals of the study.

Nonparametric statistical tests should be used when the data does not meet the required assumptions of parametric tests. The Chi-squared test is widely used to analyze frequency counts of categorical data. Other commonly used nonparametric tests include the Mann-Whitney U test, the Wilcoxon signed-rank test, the Kruskal-Wallis one-way ANOVA by ranks, and the Friedman's two-way ANOVA test. Although nonparametric tests have less strict requirements for the data, they are not assumption free and the data still need to be carefully examined before running any nonparametric tests.

DISCUSSION QUESTIONS

1. What are the major steps to prepare data for statistical analysis?

2. What are the measures of central tendency?

3. What are the measures of spread?

4. What is normal distribution? Why is it important to test whether a data sample is normally distributed?

5. What statistical methods are available for comparing group means?

6. What statistical method can be used to compare two group means contributed by two independent groups?

7. What statistical method can be used to compare two group means contributed by the same group?

8. When should a one-way ANOVA test be used? Describe a research study design that fits the one-way ANOVA test.

9. When should a factorial ANOVA test be used? Describe a research study design that fits the factorial ANOVA test.

10. When should a repeated measures ANOVA test be used? Describe a research study design that fits the repeated measures ANOVA test.

11. When should a split-plot ANOVA test be used? Describe a research study design that fits the split-plot ANOVA test.

12. When should correlation analysis be used? What does Pearson's r^2 represent?

13. When should regression analysis be used? Describe a research study that requires regression analysis.

14. Name two regression procedures and discuss when a specific procedure should be used.

15. What are the assumptions for parametric statistical tests?

16. When should nonparametric tests be considered?

17. Is the Chi-squared test "assumption free"? If not, what are the assumptions of a Chi-squared test?

18. What are the alternative nonparametric tests for the independent-samples t test, the paired-samples t test, the one-way ANOVA test, and the one-way repeated measures ANOVA test?

RESEARCH DESIGN EXERCISES

Read the following research questions and identify the appropriate statistical methods for each scenario.

1. Is there a difference in the time spent online per week for people who are single, people who are married without kids, and people who are married with kids?

2. Is there a difference between the weights of Americans and Canadians within the age ranges 20–40, 40–60, and above 60?

3. Is there a difference in the target selection speed between the mouse and the joystick for children who are 5–9 years old? (Each child uses both the mouse and the joystick during the study.)

4. Use the distance between the current cursor location and the target location to predict the amount of time needed to select a target.

5. Is there a difference between users in the United States and users in the United Kingdom when using three search engines? (Each user should use all three engines during the study.)

6. Do students in the English department have a higher GPA than students in the Education department?

7. Is there a relationship between the sales of Cheerios and the sales of milk in a grocery store?

8. Is there a difference between the blood pressures of people over 60 in the morning, at noon, and in the evening? (Each participant contributes three data points, each from a different time of the day.)

TEAM EXERCISES

Form a team of 4–5 members. Find a research topic that could be studied with existing resources available to your team. For example, comparing the time it takes to find a specific product on an e-Commerce website by two different user groups. Develop a research hypothesis and an appropriate experimental design to evaluate that hypothesis.

Recruit 10–20 participants and collect a set of data. The participants can be your classmates, friends, or relatives. Complete the following steps to analyze the data:

1. Clean up the data and code it if necessary.

2. Describe the data using descriptive statistics.

3. Select the appropriate statistical method for analyzing the data.

4. Run a significance test using statistical software.

5. Write a report to discuss the findings of the significant test. Include graphical presentations to help illustrate your findings.

Depending on how the data will be collected and used, IRB approval may or may not be needed for the study. Specific instructions should be provided by the instructors regarding the IRB requirement.

REFERENCES

Albert, W., Tullis, T., 2013. Measuring the User Experience: Collecting, Analyzing, and Presenting Usability Metrics, second ed. Morgan Kaufmann, Waltham, MA.

Camilli, G., Hopkins, K., 1978. Applicability of chi-square to 2×2 contingency tables with small expected cell frequencies. Psychological Bulletin 85 (1), 163–167.

Conover, W., 1999. Practical Nonparametric Statistics, third ed. John Wiley & Sons, Hoboken, NJ.

Darlington, R., 1968. Multiple regression in psychological research and practice. Psychological Bulletin 69 (3), 161–182.

Delwiche, L., Slaughter, S., 2008. The Little SAS Book: A Primer, fourth ed. SAS Institute Inc., Cary, NC.

Feng, J., Lazar, J., Kumin, L., Ozok, A., 2008. Computer usage by children with down syndrome: an exploratory study. In: Proceedings of the 10th ACM Conference on Computers and Accessibility (ASSETS). pp. 35–42.

Hamilton, L., 1990. Modern Data Analysis: A First Course in Applied Statistics. Wadsworth Publishing Company, Belmont, CA.

Hinkle, D., Wiersma, W., Jurs, S., 2002. Applied Statistics for the Behavioral Sciences, fifth ed. Houghton Mifflin Company, Boston, MA.

Hu, R., Feng, J., 2015. Investigating Information Search by People with Cognitive Disabilities. ACM Transactions on Accessible Computing 7 (1), 1–30.

Kaptein, M., Nass, C., Markopoulos, P., 2010. Powerful and consistent analysis of Likert type rating scales. In: Proceedings of the ACM SIGCHI Conference on Human Factors in Computing Systems. pp. 2391–2394.

MacKenzie, S., 2013. Human-Computer Interaction: An Empirical Research Perspective. Elsevier, Waltham, MA.

Newton, R., Rudestam, K., 1999. Your Statistical Consultant: Answers to Your Data Analysis Questions. Sage Publications, Thousand Oaks, CA.

Norman, D., 1988. The Design of Everyday Things. Basic Books, New York.

Rosenthal, R., Rosnow, R., 2008. Essentials of Behavioral Research: Methods and Data Analysis, third ed. McGraw Hill, Boston, MA.

Share, D., 1984. Interpreting the output of multivariate analyses: a discussion of current approaches. British Journal of Psychology 75 (3), 349–362.

Snedecor, G., Cochran, W., 1989. Statistical Methods, eighth ed. Iowa State University, Ames.

Stemler, S., 2001. An overview of content analysis. Practical Assessment, Research & Evaluation 7 (17) 137–146.

Wasserman, L., 2007. All of Nonparametric Statistics. Springer Science + Business Media, New York.

Weber, R.P., 1990. Basic Content Analysis: Quantitative Analysis in the Social Sciences, second ed. Sage Publications, Newbury Park, CA.

Wobbrock, J., Findlater, L., Gergle, D., Higgins, J., 2011. The aligned rank transform for nonparametric factorial analyses using only ANOVA procedures. In: Proceedings of the ACM SIGCHI Conference on Human Factors in Computing Systems. pp. 143–146.

Surveys

5

5.1 INTRODUCTION

Surveys are one of the most commonly used research methods, across all fields of research, not just human-computer interaction (HCI). Surveys are frequently used to describe populations, to explain behaviors, and to explore uncharted waters (Babbie, 1990). Surveys are also one of the most maligned methods. Surveys can be structured, well-tested, robust, and result in data with a high level of validity. However, surveys can be poorly done, resulting in data of questionable validity.

What is a survey? In short, it is a well-defined and well-written set of questions to which an individual is asked to respond. Surveys are typically self-administered by an individual, with no researcher present; because of this, the data collected is not as deep and in-depth as with other research methods (such as ethnography or focus groups). The strength of the survey is the ability to get a large number of responses quickly from a population of users that is geographically dispersed. Surveys allow you to capture the "big picture" relatively quickly, of how individuals are interacting with a certain technology, what problems they are facing, and what actions they are taking. Surveys also allow you to make statistically accurate estimates for a population, when structured using random sampling.

One of the reasons why surveys may be maligned is that they are often used not because they are the most appropriate method but because they are the easiest method. There are a lot of bad research projects, in which professors or students quickly write a survey, do not do sufficient pilot testing of the survey questions, distribute it to first-year students, and then claim that the survey results can generalize to other populations. Unless the actual focus of the research is university students, then this research example is misguided. As an example, an appropriate use of students was made in a survey study (Hanks et al., 2008), in which the goal of the research was to learn more about student perceptions of sustainable interaction design. It collected 435 surveys, from a cross-section of majors, not just computer science majors.

There are many HCI research projects in which a survey is the ideal method; in which the survey is well-designed, strict controls are used, and the resulting data has a high level of validity. Survey research may be the most appropriate methodology for measuring attitudes, awareness, intent, feedback about user experiences, characteristics of users, and over-time comparisons (Müller et al., 2014). Surveys may be less appropriate for precise measurements, or for solely identifying usability problems in an interface; however, surveys are often used appropriately in as one component of a full evaluation involving user-based testing (described more in Chapter 10) (Müller et al., 2014). Since surveys primarily rely on users to self-administer, remember data that occurred in a previous point in time, and return the survey, without a researcher being physically present, there are a lot of background details that must receive attention for the data collected to be valid and useful.

Is a survey the same thing as a questionnaire? Well, many people do use the two terms interchangeably. Others differentiate between the "questionnaire," which is the list of questions, and the "survey," which is the complete methodological approach, including sampling, reminders, and incentives. For instance, Dillman states clearly that "the questionnaire is only one element of a well-done survey" (Dillman, 2000, p. 149). While we acknowledge the difference, since the two terms are often used interchangeably, we use them interchangeably in this chapter.

5.2 BENEFITS AND DRAWBACKS OF SURVEYS

Surveys have many benefits and a few drawbacks. Using a survey, it is easy to collect data from a large number of people, at a relatively low cost. Surveys can be used for many different research goals. Because they allow access to a large number of people, surveys can be very useful for getting an overview, or a "snapshot," of a user population. Surveys do not require advanced tools for development; they can be distributed easily using e-mail or existing survey websites, or done on paper. From a practical point of view, surveys are among the research methods most likely to get approval from an institutional review board or human subjects board because they are relatively unobtrusive (see Chapter 15 for more information on institutional review boards).

There are a few drawbacks to using surveys as a research method. A survey is very good at getting limited "shallow" data from a large number of people but is not very good at getting "deep," detailed data. Since surveys are typically self-administered (either on paper, e-mail, or websites), if interesting phenomena start appearing, it is usually not possible to ask follow-up questions, or go back and change the original survey instrument to ask more detailed questions.

Another major drawback is that surveys can sometimes lead to biased data when the questions are related to patterns of usage, rather than clear factual phenomena. For instance, a question such as the user's age or gender is not subject to interpretation or memory. Clearly, on a given day, an individual has an age (say, 33 years old) and a gender (male). However, questions related to mood (e.g., "How were you feeling when you were using this software application?") are subject to recall bias if the event took place a significant amount of time earlier. Another example might be to ask people to recall how much money they have spent on e-commerce within a 6-month period or how many times they completed a certain task using a specific software application. Their response might be biased and either overestimate or underestimate the amount (Andrews et al., 2003). If data is of a factual nature and can instead be collected in an automated fashion using a computer, it may be a preferred method compared to asking users to recall how many times they completed a task. In that type of situation, a combination of computer-collected data and a user survey might make the most sense (see the sidebar on photo tagging and sharing). It is also possible that the individuals who you are most interested in studying may come from a culture that is more oriented toward oral (spoken) approaches to communication than written approaches. If that is the case, then interviews or ethnography might be a more appropriate research method than a survey.

RESEARCHING PHOTO TAGGING AND SHARING BEHAVIORS

Two separate studies researching photo tagging and photo sharing behaviors illustrate how a combination of a survey and computer-collected data could be performed in a research study.

Nov et al. (2008) were interested in learning more about tagging behavior on Flickr (a website on which people can post pictures and notes ["tags"] about those pictures). The researchers were aware that it would not make sense to ask users how many tags they had created in a certain time period, as their responses were likely to be only a guess or an estimate, not an accurate count. However, there were a number of research questions that could best be investigated using a survey, so a combination of a survey and data logging, was used.

The researchers contacted a random sample of Flickr users who had posted at least five unique tags on pictures, in English (although this might have limited the sample to certain nationalities, the researchers wanted to make sure that the respondents understood the survey questions). A random sample of 1373 users was selected and e-mailed with an invitation to participate in a survey. At the end of the survey, respondents were asked to authorize the researchers to access data about tagging from their Flickr account (if the user gives permission, Flickr allows access to data from a user's account). Once the respondents filled out the survey and authorized access to their account data, the researchers were able to collect data on the number of tags. There were 237 valid survey responses and the average respondent had used 370 tags.

In a separate study related to Flickr usage published 8 years later, Kairam et al. (2016) were interested in studying how users chose to share photos. The researchers recruited participants who were already active Flickr users, to respond to a survey, requesting permission to access their photos as a part of the study (and the participants were paid a few dollars through Amazon's Mechanical Turk). There were 96 respondents to the survey. As a part of the research, 20 photos were selected from each participant's account, stratified across the five possible privacy settings for each picture. Of those 20 photos, 10 photos were randomly selected to be presented to the participants during the survey, with questions related to the privacy and content of the picture.

(Continued)

RESEARCHING PHOTO TAGGING AND SHARING BEHAVIORS—CONT'D

In data collection related to the research questions, but not related to the participants who responded to the previously described survey, more data was collected, from a sample of 638,930 active Flickr users (meaning at least one photo was uploaded in Jan. 2015), collecting aggregate data about their activity (e.g., number of photos, social connections, and group participation).

5.3 GOALS AND TARGETED USERS FOR SURVEY RESEARCH

Surveys are appropriate research methods for a number of different research goals. Since surveys are good for getting responses from large numbers of people, they are often used for collecting thousands, or even millions, of responses. The population of interest is also known as the "target population" (Couper, 2000) or, in the case of HCI research, the targeted users. If it is a well-defined population of interest, the actual number of individuals in the population can be identified. It might be a group of 20 individuals or 300 million individuals. However, if it is a well-defined population, there will be a definitive number of people within the population and it will be clear who is and who is not part of the population (Couper, 2000).

Who are the targeted respondents for the survey? Why are these people of interest? It is rare that you can truly say "anyone can respond to the survey." Survey responses usually need to come from a specific population that is being studied—for instance, people of a certain age, users of a certain software application, people who work in a certain industry or company, or people who have a certain disability. You must first identify who they are and the limitations on this group. Do you limit responses to, say, people 30 years and older? People who are software engineers? People who have used the EndNote software application? People who are registered nurses? What demographic factors will decide whether a response from an individual is valid? It is important to note that the term "targeted respondents" from the world of survey design, can be used interchangeably with similar terms used throughout the book such as "user population" and "inclusion criteria." The inclusion criteria will specify, in great detail, who qualifies to be included in your survey study (or in any other type of research study).

Once you have decided what criteria to use for your survey study, the next question is how can you find contact information for these individuals? Is there a well-defined list or directory of who these individuals are? General sociological research tends to use phone books or e-mail lists for the general public. When a listing or set of listings is used to define the potential survey respondents, this is known as "defining the population frame" (Couper, 2000). It is important to note that phone surveys, while they used to be more frequent, are now used much less often in survey research. There are several reasons for this: due to telemarketing calls, people do not answer their phones as often; there are now several phones per individual; many people no longer have a landline phone; and government efforts in some countries have made it so that many individuals are placed on a "do not call" list because they do not want to receive many types of phone calls (Couper, 2005). When phone surveys are used now, there are often biases in the response.

For research into HCI, the population of interest is generally a bit more focused than just the general public, or a very broad set of criteria (e.g., registered voters). Often, there is a much more focused set of inclusion criteria. For example, if the inclusion criteria relate to being in a specific profession, websites, membership lists, and social networking for that profession, are great places to start. For instance, if the survey research targets researchers or practitioners in HCI, commonly used lists for HCI research are membership directories and social networking groups for professional organizations (such as SIGCHI, UXPA, and/or HFES). If inclusion criteria for a survey study relates to having a specific disability, membership directories of organizations for people with a specific impairment (such as organizations for people with spinal cord injuries) might be appropriate. If the survey relates to usage of a certain software application, lists of registered software users from a company might be appropriate. All of these types of lists may provide information on postal mailing addresses, phone numbers, or e-mail addresses. There may also be monthly or annual gatherings at which surveys, or information about surveys, can be distributed (Lazar, 2006). It is also possible that a website, online community, or social networking group might provide contact information for a group of potential respondents. Social networking applications can help recruit participants with a shared interest, for participation in a survey study (e.g., recruitment information can be posted on an interest group on Facebook or shared via someone on Twitter who has a lot of followers with a common interest). However, these methods alone may not work well for a lot of HCI research.

If the population for a survey is not easily well-defined, then the goal may be either to get a response that is diverse and represents multiple subgroups within the respondents or to get a survey response that matches what is known about the population (see Section 5.5).

5.4 PROBABILISTIC SAMPLING

The classic use of a survey in sociology is to make estimates for populations. The most accurate way to do this is by running a census, in which you attempt to get a survey response from every member of a population. Because a census is often very expensive and complex, they are not carried out very frequently. When a census is done, it tends to be sponsored by a large organization or governmental entity (see the US Census sidebar). If a population of interest is known and very small (say, up to a few thousand individuals), you might try to organize a modified census, in which everyone is invited to participate in the survey. However, it is not expected that everyone will take you up on the invitation and participate (Sue and Ritter, 2007).

US CENSUS—COUNTING EVERYONE

In the United States, a national census is taken every 10 years. Every person or family in the United States is supposed to fill out a paper survey. Responses to the Census Bureau are required by law, as the census count is used to distribute budgets and seats in congress and to make many governmental decisions. When a response is not received, individuals working for the Census Bureau visit residences to try and collect data from those who did not respond to the paper survey.

The Census Bureau tested a web-based form during the 2000 census. People who received the short form (five out of every six Americans) had the option of filling out the census form on the web. Each paper short form had an ID number. To ensure appropriate counting, the respondent had to enter the ID number on the web before filling out the actual survey.

Due to security and privacy concerns, the Census Bureau decided not to have a web-based form in 2010. However, the Census Bureau used a web survey for "reinterviewing" those who had already submitted their primary census form. See https://www.census.gov/ for more information.

Instead of running a census, a structured method called "random sampling" (or "probability sampling") is often used. In a probability sample, it is known exactly how likely it is for a participant to be selected for the sample, which is an equal, greater than zero chance, and everyone selected in the sample receives the same invitation to participate (Sue and Ritter, 2007; Müller et al., 2014).For instance, imagine that there are 10,000 members of a population of interest (the sampling frame). Perhaps 500 of these individuals are selected, at random, for requested inclusion in a survey study. All of these selected individuals must meet inclusion criteria (characteristics that they must have, such as being a nonsmoker or male) and not meet exclusion criteria (such as not being a native English speaker) (Sue and Ritter, 2007). See the sidebar on Random Sampling for an example of random sampling of a population of users.

A STUDY WITH RANDOM SAMPLING

When users are required to log into networked resources (such as an e-mail system, intranet, or social networking site), random sampling methods can be used, since a detailed list of who is considered to be within the population of interest does exist. For instance, a research study focused on Beehive, an enterprise social networking system from IBM. At the time of the study, it was estimated that there were at least 38,000 registered users of the site. A total of 500 users were randomly selected and invited to participate in the research study, based on having logged into Beehive during the last week and having enough data in their account so that friend recommendations could be made (the inclusion criteria). Each selected user received a personalized survey, asking them to respond to recommendations made by the social networking software. During the period of the research study, 415 out of the 500 users logged in, 258 responded to the survey, and when the data was cleaned (due to incomplete or missing responses), 230 users had submitted valid surveys (Chen et al., 2009).

It is important to note that the sample frame need not be individuals; it can also be organizations. A long-term survey has documented the level of Internet access in public libraries across the United States. See the "Use of Sampling Frames in Studying Internet Access" sidebar for an example of a random sampling of organizations.

5.4.1 STRATIFICATION

Sometimes a sample can be stratified. A stratified sample is when you divide your entire population in separate subpopulations (known as strata) and a separate sample is selected from within each subpopulation (Frankel, 1983). So, when collected, data analysis can be made for each subpopulation and can be combined for the entire population. Stratification can help ensure that you have an appropriate number of responses from each subset of your user population (Babbie, 1990). Stratification can also help when the subpopulations have unequal representation, so that the relative distribution of the subpopulations in the sample can be increased or decreased (Frankel, 1983). A simple example is a random sample of university students. A random sample of university students is likely to have freshmen, sophomores, juniors, and seniors represented; however, due to enrollment trends often some class years have much larger classes of students as compared to other years, and therefore, there very likely would be an unequal number from each class who were randomly selected. However, a **stratified** random sample would have an equal number of respondents invited to participate, from each of those class years. A stratified random sample was used in a study of how people use technology to keep in touch after they move (see the Stratification sidebar for more information), so that long-distance moves would be represented more than local moves (which in fact are the majority of moves).

USE OF SAMPLING FRAMES IN STUDYING INTERNET ACCESS

The American Library Association sponsors a survey on the implementation and use of the Internet in public libraries in the United States. The earliest survey was in 1994 and the survey has been repeated on an annual or biennial basis since then. The most recent survey was in 2012, after which this survey was folded into the Digital Inclusion Survey (see http://digitalinclusion.umd.edu/). The survey started out as a paper-based survey but, over the years, it moved to a web-based survey.

(Continued)

USE OF SAMPLING FRAMES IN STUDYING INTERNET ACCESS—CONT'D

Since the survey is used to make national population estimates, the research approach used must be highly structured and controlled. Data was more recently collected using a web-based survey, with a paper letter mailed to public libraries to inform them about the existence of the survey. The letter included an identification code so that the survey data collected was identified to a specific library system or branch. The 2008 survey included 16,457 library outlets, a 6984 sample frame, and 5488 library responses (78.6%). The 2011–12 survey (with data published in 2012) included 16,776 library outlets, an 8790 sample frame (stratified by state and proportional by state and metropolitan status), and 7260 responses (82.5% response rate). See http://www.plinternetsurvey.org/ for more information on methodological issues related to this survey.

STRATIFICATION

Shklovski et al. (2008) were interested in studying how technology influences the maintaining of friendships after a residential move. A sample of 6000 individuals was chosen from the US Postal Service's Change of Address Database. These were all individuals who had moved in the previous few months. The sample was stratified so that 1/3 of those selected had local moves, of 50 miles or less, while the other 2/3 selected had longer distance moves, of 50 miles or more. This stratification was done because the researchers were interested in studying long-distance moves. However, it is implied in their write-up that a majority of moves are local moves. Of the 6000 people selected from the database, 1779 (32%) responded to the survey. Two follow-up surveys were sent to the 1779 individuals who responded to the first survey. The second survey received 1156 responses, and a third survey received 910 responses. This research provides an example of stratification.

5.4.2 RESPONSE SIZE

If it is feasible for random sampling to be used in the research, this is preferable. However, the next question that comes up most often is, "how many responses do I need?" The statistics on this are not as clear as in, say, statistics in experimental design, where there is a clear threshold of significance or nonsignificance. In probabilistic sampling, the number of responses required depends on what level of confidence and margin of error are considered acceptable. For instance, for a simple random sample, a sample size of 384 may lead to a 95% confidence level with a $\pm 5\%$ margin of error (Sue and Ritter, 2007). That means that "if the survey were conducted 100 times, the true percentage would be within 5 percentage points of the sample percentage in about 95 of the 100 surveys" (Sue and Ritter, 2007, p. 30). To change the margin of error to $\pm 4\%$, 600 responses are needed; for $\pm 3\%$ margin of error, 1067 responses are needed. The margin of error is only valid using a true random sample. In this example, the actual size of the population sampled is irrelevant, since there is an automatic assumption that all populations being sampled are very large (Babbie, 2009). If the sample is relatively large compared to the population size (more than 5% or 10%), then the margin of error may be smaller, and can be calculated using the "finite population correction," which is beyond the scope of this book. Another way to look at this is that, in a small population size, a smaller sample may be needed. See Sue and Ritter (2007), Babbie (2009), or Dillman (2000) for more information on appropriate sample sizes, confidence levels, and margins of error. The reader is especially encouraged to read (Müller et al., 2014, pp. 238–239), which is specifically focused on sample sizes in HCI research.

5.4.3 ERRORS

Random sampling seems like an ideal method but it is subject to a number of potential errors and biases. Careful attention to these potential problems can increase the accuracy and validity of the research findings. For instance, sampling error occurs when there are not enough responses from those surveyed to make accurate population estimates (e.g., if 10,000 individuals are surveyed but only 100 responses are received).

Coverage error occurs when not all members of the population of interest have an equal chance of being selected for the survey (e.g., if you use e-mail lists or phone lists to create the sample and not all potential respondents are on those e-mail or phone lists) (Couper, 2000). Measurement error occurs when survey questions are poorly worded or biased, leading to data of questionable quality.

Nonresponse error occurs when there are major differences (in demographics, such as age or gender) between the people who responded to a survey and the people who were sampled (e.g., if the sampling frame is split evenly by gender, but 90% of responses are from males) (Dillman, 2000).

5.5 NONPROBABILISTIC SAMPLING

The assumption in Section 5.4 on probabilistic sampling is that the goal is to achieve a population estimate. In HCI research, population estimates are generally not the goal. And so, users are more often recruited in a nonprobabilistic manner. Often, there is not a clear, well-defined population of potential respondents. There is not a list or a central repository of people who meet a certain qualification and could be respondents. For instance, due to requirements for patient confidentiality, it would be very hard to create a sample frame and a strict random sample involving people who have, for example, HIV (Müller et al., 2014). That may just be the nature of the population that no centralized list of potential respondents exists. So strict random sampling cannot be done. However, valid data can still be collected through nonprobability-based samples. Nonprobabilistic samples include approaches such as volunteer opt-in panels, self-selected surveys (where people often click on links on a website or social networking), or snowball recruiting (where respondents recruit other potential respondents) (Müller et al., 2014).

It is important to note that different academic communities have different standards in how they apply sampling techniques. For instance, there are many people in the fields of social science and statistics who believe that without strict random sampling, no survey data is valid (Couper, 2000; Sue and Ritter, 2007). On the other hand, the HCI community has a long history of using surveys, in many different ways, without random sampling, and this is considered valid and acceptable. Part of this difference may stem from the nature of research in different communities. In some research communities, large national and international data sets are collected using rigorous, structured sampling methodologies. The general social survey in the United States (gss.norc.org) and the National Centre for Social Research in the United Kingdom (http://www.natcen.ac.uk/) are examples in the fields of sociology and public policy. Researchers can take these high-quality, probability-sampled data sets and perform analyses on the many variables in them. This is *not* the model of research used in HCI. In HCI, researchers must, typically, collect the data themselves. No large, well-structured data sets exist. The HCI researcher must go out, find users to take part in their research, and collect the data, as well as analyze the data. Because of this difference, both probability samples and nonprobability samples are considered valid in HCI research. There are a number of techniques for ensuring validity in nonprobability-based samples. The next sections detail the standard approaches for ensuring validity in nonprobability-based samples.

It is also important to note that, very often, surveys are used by HCI researchers, in conjunction with other research methods, when there is no claim of the representativeness of the survey responses, in fact, it is openly acknowledged that the responses represent a convenience sample. This is quite common, so, for instance, if you look at recent papers from the CHI conference, not only will you find surveys with over 1000 responses (such as Moser et al., 2016; Chilana et al., 2016), you will also find papers that combine small surveys with other research methods such as diary studies (Epstein et al., 2016), interviews (Dell and Kumar, 2016), usability testing (Kosmalla et al., 2016), and log analysis (Guy et al., 2016). These examples only scratch the surface; clearly, small, nonprobabilistic samples are used throughout HCI research on a regular basis, without concern.

5.5.1 DEMOGRAPHIC DATA

One way of determining the validity of survey responses is to ask respondents for a fair amount of demographic data. The goal should be to use the demographic data to ensure that either the responses represent a diverse, cross-section of respondents or the responses are somewhat representative of already-established, baseline data (if any exists). For instance, even basic demographic data on age, gender, education, job responsibility, or computer usage can help establish the validity and representativeness of survey responses when respondents are self-selected (Lazar and Preece, 2001). While this is not equivalent to the validity of a population estimate or random sampling, it is better than no check on the validity or representativeness of survey responses. Note that, in some cases, researchers may have a goal to get representative data from multiple countries to do a multinational comparison. A great example of this is Harbach et al.'s (2016) recent study examining smartphone locking in eight different countries, with over 8000 survey responses. In such cases, it may be necessary to collect detailed demographic and cultural data related to the country, and researchers are also encouraged to consult a guide on doing cross-cultural HCI research (e.g., Aykin, 2005).

5.5.2 OVERSAMPLING

When there is not a well-defined list of users and strict random sampling is not possible, then the number of responses becomes increasingly important. For instance, in a nonprobabilistic sample, 20 survey responses may not be sufficient. Even with demographic data present, there may just be too many biases present, relating to which users have responded. However, when the survey response reaches a certain number that is considered large in proportion to the estimated or perceived population size, this can help establish some informal validity. This is known as *oversampling*. While not all researchers agree that oversampling increases validity (Couper, 2000), simply having a large response can reduce the likelihood of excluding any segment of the population (Andrews et al., 2003). However, the key is that the response must be large in the context of the population of interest. For instance, 500 survey responses would be a large number if the estimated total population of interest is around 5000 individuals. However, 500 survey responses would not considered large if the population of interest is a country, such as Australia or France. One researcher suggests that 30 responses should be considered a baseline minimum number of responses for any type of survey research (Sue and Ritter, 2007). Fogg et al. used both demographic data and oversampling to learn more about web credibility in 2001 (see Demographic Data and Oversampling sidebar).

DEMOGRAPHIC DATA AND OVERSAMPLING

Fogg et al. (2001) wanted to learn more about how different elements of design on a website impact on the user's perception of credibility. To do this, they recruited survey responses through charitable groups in the United States and a news media organization in Finland. They received 1441 survey responses in 1 week. After discarding a number of responses due to inadequate information provided or responses that placed the respondent outside of the population frame, 1410 survey responses were considered valid.

The survey collected information on age, gender, country, education level, income, years on the Internet, average number of hours spent online per week, and average number of purchases online. The demographic information helped to confirm that the responses to the survey were, indeed, representative of the diversity of web users. The high number of responses helped to improve the validity of the study.

5.5.3 RANDOM SAMPLING OF USAGE, NOT USERS

Another approach to sampling is the random sampling of usage, not users (Lazar and Preece, 2001). For instance, it may be that every 10th time a web page is loaded, the user is asked to fill out a survey. Often, this survey appears in a pop-up window. This sampling technique is also known as intercept sampling (Sue and Ritter, 2007). While this gets an accurate picture of usage, a subset of users (those who use the web page often) is over-represented and those who do not view the web page often are under-represented.

5.5.4 SELF-SELECTED SURVEYS

In a "self-selected" survey, there is a link on a web page every time that it is loaded and everyone visiting the website is invited to fill out the survey. So, it is less about a certain group of people being recruited to participate and more about inviting everyone to participate. (Yes, it can be a bit fuzzy sometimes in nonprobabilistic surveys as to whether responses are invited or self-selected.)

If a self-selected survey is used, then both the number of survey responses and the demographic data on respondents become increasingly important in establishing the validity of the survey data. One of the earliest web-based survey studies came from the Georgia Institute of Technology. The entire population of web users was invited to participate. Banner ads about the survey, inviting people to participate, were placed on search engines, news sites, general advertising networks, mailing lists and newsgroups, and also in the popular press. Everyone was invited to participate in the surveys, which took place semiannually from 1994 to 1998. In the final survey, 5022 people responded. See Pitkow and Kehoe (1996) for a good summary of the studies and http://www.cc.gatech.edu/gvu/user_surveys/ for detailed data.

There may be reasons why a population could theoretically be well-defined and probabilistic sampling be used, but it is not logistically realistic. See the sidebar ("Probabilistic Sampling Probably Not Feasible") for an example of a situation where self-selected surveys are the only feasible approach for a population that theoretically (but not realistically) could be sampled using probabilistic methods.

PROBABILISTIC SAMPLING PROBABLY NOT FEASIBLE

A well-known, ongoing survey in the accessibility community is the "Screen Reader Survey" run by WebAIM at Utah State University, which has the goal of learning more about the preferences of screen reader users. Screen readers are software applications, such as JAWS, VoiceOver, Window-Eyes, and NVDA, that allow people who are Blind or low vision to listen to the content on the screen, from web pages, applications, and operating systems (and they are not only installed on desktop and laptop computers, but also on tablet computers and smartphones). The first Screen Reader Survey was run in Dec. 2008 and Jan. 2009, with 1121 responses to the survey. The most recent (the 6th) Screen Reader Survey was run in Jul. 2015, with 2515 responses.

Theoretically, it might be possible to do a random sampling of current screen reader users (people who are blind or low vision and are already using a screen reader). However, to do so would require the major screen reader companies (companies such as Freedom Scientific, AI Squared, and Apple) to collaborate, share sales data, and any data that they have on users, to come up with a list of current screen reader users which probabilistic sampling methods could be applied to. Because the screen reader market is highly competitive, there have been lawsuits over intellectual property infringement, and there are a number of partnerships in place (e.g., AI Squared partnered with Microsoft to allow users of Microsoft Office to download free versions of the Window-Eyes screen reader), the likelihood of these companies collaborating on research and sharing data is not very high. Because companies want the Screen Reader Survey to report favorably on their market share, there can be pressure to "get out the vote." While the Screen Reader Survey has a fair number of methodological flaws, it is the best set of data out there, over a 6-year period, about screen reader usage. For more information about the most recent Screen Reader Survey, see http://webaim.org/projects/screenreadersurvey6/. Chris Hofstader provides an in-depth criticism of the methodology of the screen reader survey at http://chrishofstader.com/screen-reader-market-figures-my-analysis-of-webaim-survey-6/. The inherent conflict between the need for the data and the wish for highly valid data when none is available can be seen in Chris's comment that "I love numbers and, while the WebAIM survey has some major flaws, it is by far the best data we have available to us regarding the questions it covers" right before he provides pages and pages of criticism. ☺

Finally, it is important to note that self-selected, nonprobability-based surveys may be the most natural data collection method for investigating new user populations or new phenomena of usage. For instance, if no data exists about a certain user population or usage pattern, then a self-selected survey of users, asking about usage, might make the most sense, just as a starting point. The population of interest can be informed about the survey by posting a message about the survey to a social networking group, listserver, or chat room where members of the population are known to congregate (Schmidt, 1997).

5.5.5 UNINVESTIGATED POPULATIONS

Surprisingly, there are user groups that have still not been investigated in much detail. For instance, people with certain types of cognitive impairments have yet to receive much attention, if any, in the HCI research literature (see Chapter 16). For these populations where no baseline data exists, not enough is already known to develop hypotheses, experimental design, or well-structured time diaries. Population estimates may exist on how many people are living with a certain impairment within a certain country; however, no data exists on how many individuals with a certain impairment are using computer technology. No baseline data exists, no estimate on the population size exists, no previous research exists, so all of the issues related to random sampling are really not appropriate. The goal of such a survey would be to establish the baseline data. In a case like this, the goal should be to simply get as large a response as possible. See the Computer Usage Patterns of People with Down Syndrome sidebar to see an example of where surveys were used to explore how young adults with Down Syndrome use computer technology.

COMPUTER USAGE PATTERNS OF PEOPLE WITH DOWN SYNDROME

When our team decided to pursue research about computer usage by people with Down syndrome in the mid-2000s, a search of multiple digital libraries and databases resulted in the determination that no research studies existed at that time, which examined how individuals with Down syndrome use computers and the Internet.

Only one design case study, where a website was being built to assist children with Down syndrome in learning about computers, was known to exist and be moving toward publication (Kirijian et al., 2007). Therefore, a survey methodology was the most appropriate approach, as a starting point for investigating the topic. We developed a large-scale survey, simply to gather baseline data about this user population. A 56-question survey was developed, covering demographic information, usage patterns, interaction techniques, and use of other electronic devices. Because it could be challenging to get accurate survey data from young adults with Down syndrome, it was decided that parents of children with Down syndrome would be recruited to respond to the survey.

The survey was placed on the web using survey monkey (a web-based tool), and responses were solicited through two organizations in the United States: the National Down Syndrome Congress and the National Down Syndrome Society. A total of 561 surveys were collected, which provides a rich foundation of data on which other studies and research projects can be built (Feng et al., 2008).

In communities where limited research has been done in the past, it may be challenging to find and recruit individuals to take part in the survey. There may be a lack of knowledge on the part of researchers, individuals may be reluctant to participate, or there might even be existing distrust.

Sometimes, snowball sampling can assist with getting survey responses. Snowball sampling is when individuals may not only respond to a survey, but also recruit someone else (usually a friend or colleague) to take part in the survey (Sue and Ritter, 2007). In a way, the role of contacting and recruiting participants shifts from the researchers to the survey respondents themselves. This method may work well when the population of interest is very small and hard to "break into," and individuals in the population of interest may know each other well. An outside researcher, coming into a community of individuals, may not have a high level of credibility, but another community member suggesting participation in a survey may come with a high level of credibility.

5.6 DEVELOPING SURVEY QUESTIONS

Once the goal and strategy for using a survey has been decided upon, the next step is to develop a survey tool. As mentioned earlier, some describe the survey tool itself as a "questionnaire." The main challenge is to develop well-written, nonbiased questions. The questions in a survey can often lead to answers that do not represent what the researchers were actually asking. Since a majority of surveys are self-administered, they must be easy enough to understand that users can fill them out by themselves. In a limited number of situations, an interviewer may ask survey questions. For more information on interviews, read Chapter 8.

It is important to understand that there are two different structures in a survey: the structure of single questions and the structure of the entire survey. More information on overall survey structure is presented in Section 5.7. Most survey questions can be structured in one of three ways: as open-ended questions, closed-ended questions with ordered response categories, or closed-ended questions with unordered response categories (Dillman, 2000).

5.6.1 OPEN-ENDED QUESTIONS

Open-ended questions are useful in getting a better understanding of phenomena, because they give respondents complete flexibility in their answers. However, aside from the obvious drawback of more complex data analysis, open-ended questions must be carefully worded. Otherwise, they may lead to responses that either do not really help researchers address the root question, or responses that simply do not provide enough information. Consider the following open-ended question:

Why did you stop using the Banjee Software product?

This open-ended question provides no information about the possible causes; instead it requires the respondent to think deeply about what the causes might be (Dillman, 2000). The respondent may be too busy to come up with a complete response or may simply say something like "I didn't like the software." It is a very broad question. More specific questions might be:

How did you feel about the usability (ease of use) of the Banjee software?
Did the Banjee software allow you to complete the tasks that you wanted to complete?

These questions address more specific topics: ease of use and task completion. The respondents cannot simply answer "I didn't like it," although they could just answer "yes" or "no" to the second question. Perhaps another way to reword that second question might be as:

What barriers did you face, in attempting to use the Banjee software to complete your tasks?

In that revision, the respondents could simply say, "none" but the question also invites the respondents to think carefully about the problems that they might have faced.

5.6.2 CLOSED-ENDED QUESTIONS

There are two types of closed-ended questions. One type has ordered response categories, and the other type does not. An ordered response is when a number of choices can be given, which have some logical order (Dillman, 2000). For instance, using a scale such as "excellent to poor" or "strongly agree to strongly disagree" would be an ordered response. Likert scale questions, which often take the form of a scale of 1 to 5, 7, or 9, ask users to note where they fall on a scale of, for example, "strongly agree" to "strongly disagree." Typically, closed-ended questions with an ordered response request respondents to choose only one item (see Figure 5.1).

Closed-ended questions with an unordered response allow for choices that do not have a logical order. For instance, asking about types of software applications, hardware items, user tasks, or even simple demographic information such as gender or type of Internet connection are unordered, but closed-ended questions. Figure 5.2 is an example of a closed-ended, unordered question.

What is your impression of using the website for www.veggieworld.com?

Please circle one number

Frustrating   Satisfying

1   2   3   4   5   6   7   8   9

FIGURE 5.1

A closed-ended question with an ordered response.

Source: QUIS, see http://www.lap.umd.edu/quis/.

Which application do you use most often for text editing? (please select only one)

___MS-Word

___WordPerfect

___Google Docs

___OpenOffice Writer

___WordPad

___QuickOffice

___Other (please specify)

FIGURE 5.2

A closed-ended question with an unordered response (single selection).

When using my primary computer, I use the following input devices or methods
on a daily basis (select as many as apply)

____Keyboard

____ Mouse

____Touchpad

____Trackball

____Voice recognition

___Multitouch screen

___Eye-tracking

FIGURE 5.3

A closed-ended question with an unordered response (multiple selection).

With unordered, closed-ended questions, you can often ask respondents to select more than one choice. On paper, this is not a challenge. However, it is important to note that if you are creating a web-based survey, different interface widgets
must be used. Option buttons only allow one choice, whereas checkboxes allow
for many choices. Figure 5.3 is an example of a question that allows multiple
responses.

5.6.3 COMMON PROBLEMS WITH SURVEY QUESTIONS

It is important to note that there are a number of common problems with survey questions. Researchers should carefully examine their questions to determine if any of
these problems are present in their survey questions (Babbie, 1990):

- A "double-barreled question" asks two separate, and possibly related questions
  (e.g., "How long have you used the Word processing software and which
  advanced features have you used?"). These questions need to be separated.
- The use of negative words in questions (e.g., "Do you agree that the e-mail
  software is not easy to use?") can cause confusion for the respondents.
- Biased wording in questions (such as starting a sentence with "Don't you agree
  that …") can lead to biased responses. If a question begins by identifying the
  position of a well-respected person or organization (e.g., "Oprah Winfrey [or
  David Beckham] takes the view that …"), this may also lead to a biased response.
- "Hot-button" words, such as "liberal," "conservative," "abortion," and
  "terrorism," can lead to biased responses.

5.7 OVERALL SURVEY STRUCTURE

Well-written questions are important, but so is the overall structure of the survey instrument. The questions do not exist in a vacuum, rather, they are part of an overall survey structure. For instance, a survey, in any format, must begin with instructions. These instructions must make clear how the respondent is to interact with the survey (Babbie, 1990). For instance, are respondents required to fill out all of the questions? Will respondents be required to enter their name or contact information? It is sometimes useful to put in a description, as a reminder, of who should be filling out the survey (e.g., you must be aged 65 years or older). If a survey is separated into multiple sections, then those divisions, and who should fill those different portions, must be made clear. Each section should be given an appropriate heading. Just as it is important to provide navigation on a website, a survey should provide navigation to the reader, whether the survey is paper, e-mail, or web-based. The user (respondent) needs to know where on the survey they should go, in what order. Sometimes, it is also helpful to provide contact information if the respondent has any questions (such as a telephone number or e-mail address).

Different formats of surveys (paper, e-mail, web-based) may require that information or instructions be presented to the respondent. For instance, in a paper survey, are there ovals or checkboxes? Should a checkmark be placed in them, should an X be placed in the box, or should the box be filled in? Should items be circled? Are respondents required to fill out all of the questions? These directions must be made clear. For an e-mail survey, should answers be typed in directly following the question on the same line, or on a line or two below it?

Layout of the survey instrument can also be important. For paper surveys, it is important to make sure that there is enough white space so that the respondent does not feel overwhelmed by the amount of information on a page (Babbie, 1990). Obviously, a balance needs to be struck. While respondents may worry if they see a 30-page survey, on the other hand, stuffing all of the survey questions onto two pages may prove to be problematic. Only white paper should be used, and a large enough font, in standard text, should be used (Dillman, 2000). Booklet printing (with two staples in the middle of the booklet) is preferred to one staple in the upper left-hand corner, but that is still preferred to any type of unusual folding or paper shapes that users may have trouble understanding (Dillman, 2000). In addition, do not use abbreviations to cut down on the amount of space needed, as they may cause confusion among respondents (Babbie, 1990). For a web-based survey, links are often provided directly in the survey, so that the respondent can click on the link and get a pop-up window with more detailed information. While pop-up windows are generally not good interface design, they work very well for giving short bits of information to users while they are in the process of responding to a survey.

Survey questions generally may be asked in any order which makes sense in the context of the research. However, it is important to keep in mind that questions relating to a similar topic or idea should be grouped together (Dillman, 2000). This tends to lower the cognitive load on respondents and allows them to think more deeply about the topic, rather than "switching gear" after every question. Because some questions may require knowledge or details presented in other survey questions, it is generally hard to randomize the order of questions (Babbie, 1990). Rather, provide interesting questions at the beginning of the survey, to help motivate people to read the survey and complete it. Generally, it is a good idea to leave demographic questions until the end of the survey, as these are the least interesting (Babbie, 1990). Also, if there are any sensitive or potentially objectionable questions (relating to income, health, or similar topics), then they should be placed near the end, once the respondent has already become interested in the survey (Dillman, 2000). Note that survey length is an important consideration. While you want to include as many questions as possible on the survey, at some point, a survey becomes too long for many people to complete, and very long surveys can lead to very low response rates. Try to ask all of the questions that you need, but be reasonable when it comes to the amount of time that individuals need to set aside to respond to the survey.

The easiest type of survey is when all respondents should answer all questions. But frequently some questions do not apply to all respondents. For instance, imagine that you are running a survey to learn more about the e-mail usage habits of users over the age of 65. You may ask if they use a specific e-mail application (and you will need to be clear about the version of the application, and whether it is desktop, web-based, or smartphone-based). If the answer is "yes," you may want them to answer a set of additional questions; if the answer is "no," you want them to skip to the next set of questions. This is sometimes called a "contingent question" (Babbie, 1990) because the respondent's need to respond to the second question is contingent on their response to the first question. This can be cause for confusion: if the directions and layout are not clear enough, a respondent who does not use Microsoft Office 365 may start reading questions relating to Microsoft Office 365 usage and be unsure of how to respond. On a paper survey, there are a number of ways to manage this. Babbie suggests using an indented box, with an arrow coming from the original question (see Figure 5.4). For a web-based survey, it may be possible either to provide a hyperlink to the next section (e.g., "If you answered no, please click here to move on to the next section") or to automatically make a section of the survey "disappear," so that the next question

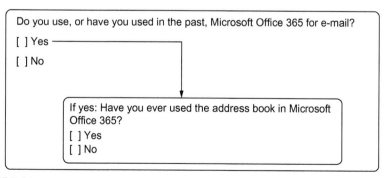

FIGURE 5.4

A contingent question on a paper survey.

presented is the one relevant to the respondent. This is similar to the "expand and collapse" menus that exist on many web pages. On a further note, the first question of the entire survey should always be a question that applies to everybody (Dillman, 2000).

5.8 EXISTING SURVEYS

It is important to note that there are many existing surveys that have already been tested and validated in the research literature in HCI. If a survey tool has already been developed, there is no need to create one from scratch.

For most research purposes, there will be a need to create a new survey tool. However, for tasks such as usability testing and evaluation, there are already a number of existing survey tools. Usually, these survey tools can be modified in minimal ways. For instance, one section of the survey tool can often be used independently of others. See Table 5.1 for a list of established survey tools.

Table 5.1 Survey Tools in HCI

Tool	Citations
Computer System Usability Questionnaire (CSUQ)	Lewis (1995)
Interface Consistency Testing Questionnaire (ICTQ)	Ozok and Salvendy (2001)
Perdue Usability Testing Questionnaire (PUTQ)	Lin et al. (1997)
Questionnaire for User Interaction Satisfaction (QUIS)	Chin et al. (1988) Slaughter et al. (1994) http://www.lap.umd.edu/quis/
Software Usability Measurement Inventory (SUMI)	http://sumi.uxp.ie/
Website Analysis and MeasureMent Inventory (WAMMI)	http://wammi.uxp.ie/

For more information about existing surveys for usability evaluation, the reader is encouraged to visit http://garyperlman.com/quest/.

5.9 PAPER OR ONLINE SURVEYS?

An important question is to determine if you want to distribute surveys using paper, the web, e-mail, or a combination of the three. The traditional method is to use paper-based surveys. A benefit of this is that a majority of individuals can use a paper survey; however, people who are blind, visually impaired, or have a print-related disability will not be able to use a paper survey (see Chapter 16 for more information on doing research with computer users with disabilities). If you only use an electronic survey (web or e-mail), you are automatically cutting out any potential respondents who do not have access to a computer and a network, which may include users who are economically disadvantaged, or ethnic or racial groups that have lower base rates of computer access (Andrews et al., 2003). In addition, if you are creating an electronic survey, you must make sure that the interface is usable by a wide range of individuals who may respond to your survey (such as users with disabilities and older users).

In reality, the relative strengths and weaknesses of online and paper surveys generally do not influence which one is used. One major influence on which method (or combination) is used is how the researchers have best access to the user population of interest. In some cases, the best access is to visit individuals at a weekly meeting where paper surveys can be passed out. In other situations, if a list of postal mailing addresses exists for potential respondents, paper surveys can be mailed. If a list of e-mail addresses exists, e-mailed surveys may be best. Another major influence on which method (paper, e-mail, or web) is used, is the ease of developing online surveys, using existing web-based tools which allow a survey to be posted and distributed in minutes (although, honestly, such a rushed job is likely to lead to design problems and errors). These web-based tools include SurveyMonkey, SurveyPlanet, FreeOnlineForms.com, and Google Forms, and they certainly influence many researchers to use a web-based survey, even if there are good methodological reasons to choose another format. Web-based surveys are now the most frequently used format of survey research.

Sometimes, a combination of paper and web-based surveys can be used to make sure that all portions of a target population are reached (Lazar et al., 1999). It is also sometimes helpful to offer respondents a choice between a paper and an electronic version of the survey, as some research suggests that some people may simply prefer filling out surveys on paper (Schonlau et al., 2003). These mixed-model designs, in which paper, e-mail, and web-based versions of a survey instrument are used together, can help improve the response rate, but caution must be taken to make sure that no biases are introduced into the data collection process (from three survey instruments that, in fact, do have minor differences) (Couper, 2005). Obviously, paper surveys must be used to study questions such as "why don't people go online?" and other research questions related to nonuse of technology (Lazar and Preece, 2001). Another potential complication is that you may need to offer your survey in multiple languages. In countries where there are multiple official languages, this may be a legal requirement (Normand et al., 2014). In other cases, you may be interested in studying a group of computer users who do not share the same primary language. If so, you need to ensure that the surveys in two or three different languages are in fact asking the same questions and that there are no mistranslations. Professional human translation is necessary in such a scenario (automated tools for translation are not sufficient for the task).

There are benefits to electronic (both e-mail and web-based) surveys. Copying costs, mailing, and related postage costs can be eliminated with electronic surveys (perhaps having only the cost of sending out paper letters notifying potential participants, when needed). While the set-up costs may be high for a custom developed web-based survey, using existing web-based survey tools when possible, make web-based surveys the most cost effective in terms of time and expenses (Sue and Ritter, 2007). In most cases, web-based surveys and even e-mailed surveys can automatically have responses saved in a spreadsheet or database, eliminating the need for time-consuming data entry and eliminating many data entry errors (Lazar and Preece, 2001). While response rates in online surveys may sometime be lower, the speed of response is certainly higher (Sue and Ritter, 2007), as is the speed of analysis by researchers (Müller et al., 2014).

The question is often asked if the responses from electronic (web-based or e-mail) surveys are as trustworthy or valid as paper surveys. There is no evidence to suggest that people are more dishonest in online surveys than in paper surveys, as people can lie easily in both. However, there is evidence that people, when delivering bad news, are more honest in online communication than face to face (Sussman and Sproull, 1999). There is also evidence that people, when they care about a topic, are likely to be very honest. If the surveys can be submitted anonymously, this may also lead to an increased level of self-disclosure (McKenna and Bargh, 2000; Spears and Lea, 1994). Therefore, web-based surveys can sometimes be superior to e-mailed surveys (which clearly identify the respondent) for dealing with sensitive information (Sue and Ritter, 2007). In addition, respondents to self-administered surveys tend to provide more honest answers to sensitive questions than in interviews (Couper, 2005). Overall, the likelihood that someone will lie in an electronic survey is the same as the likelihood that someone will lie in a paper-based survey.

In traditional paper-based surveys, individuals may have to sign an "informed consent form" (also known as an institutional review board [IRB] or human subjects form), acknowledging that they are aware that they are taking part in a research project and giving their consent. There is debate as to how individuals can best give informed consent when they respond to a survey online. For more information on informed consent online, please see Chapter 15.

5.10 PILOT TESTING THE SURVEY TOOL

After a survey tool is developed, it is very important to do a pilot study (also known as pretesting the survey) to help ensure that the questions are clear and unambiguous. There are really two different areas of interest within a pilot study: the questions themselves and the interface of the survey. While the interface features primarily refer to web-based or e-mailed surveys, there are also interface features on paper-based surveys. For instance, on a paper survey, there should be an examination of issues such as the font face and type size, spacing, use of grids, and cover designs (Dillman, 2000). While these are theoretically different pilot testing sessions for the questions and for the layout, in reality, they take place at the same time. See Chapter 10 for more information on usability testing of a computer interface.

Dillman (2000) suggests a three-stage process of pretesting a survey, while noting that it is rarely done thoroughly. The three stages are as follows:

1. Review of the survey tool by knowledgeable colleagues and analysts.
2. Interviews with potential respondents to evaluate cognitive and motivational qualities in the survey tool.
3. Pilot study of both the survey tool and implementation procedures.

The idea of this three-stage process is that you start first with people who are knowledgeable, but are not potential respondents. (Note that you start first with expert nonrespondents, just as in usability testing in Chapter 10.) You begin with expert evaluations before involving any representative users. You then ask a few potential respondents about the clarity and motivation of the questions in the survey. Finally, you do a pilot study where potential respondents complete an entire survey and the researchers can note any flaws. While this three-stage process is ideal, in reality, most research in HCI involves either a few colleagues examining the survey tool or a few potential respondents reading over the survey tool and giving some feedback, but even at this minimal level, the pilot study is still necessary and important.

A pilot study can help the researcher identify questions that are confusing or misleading. These pilot study efforts are aimed at determining the validity of the survey, that is, does the survey measure what it is claiming to measure? (Babbie, 1990; Ozok, 2007). There are usually a few common problems discovered in a pilot study, to keep an eye out for. For instance, questions that were not answered, questions where multiple answers were given (when only one was expected); and questions where respondents filled out "other" (Babbie, 1990). All of these are signs that a question might need to be reworded. A pilot study, ideally, will involve a small number of potential respondents (people who meet the inclusion criteria) answering the survey questions, with encouragement to provide specific feedback on the questions in the survey. For a small survey study (say, where the goal is 200–300 responses), perhaps 5–10 people taking part in the pilot study would be sufficient. However, for larger survey studies, where the goal is 100,000 survey responses, a corresponding larger number of individuals should take part in the pilot study. It is important to note that individuals who responded to the pilot study should generally not take part in the main study and their data should not be included. The process of participating in the pilot study could bias the future responses and therefore, they should not be included in the main data collection.

A different type of evaluation can take place at a later time. When a survey instrument has been used to collect data multiple times, then the reliability of that survey can be established. Reliability is the determination of whether a survey measures constructs consistently across time (Babbie, 1990; Ozok, 2007). Methods for measuring the internal reliability of questions, such as having the same question asked multiple times in a different way, can be used. The Cronbach's alpha coefficient is often used in that situation (Ozok, 2007).

Another approach to evaluating survey questions after data is collected from many people, especially if the survey has a large number of questions, is *exploratory factor analysis*. In factor analysis, statistical software creates an artificial dimension that would correlate highly with a set of chosen survey question data (Babbie, 1990). Researchers then determine how important the specific survey question is, based on the factor loading, which is the correlation level between the data item and the artificial dimension. Survey items with high factor loadings have high correlation, and are likely to be more predictive, and therefore, more relevant (Babbie, 1990). Exploratory factor analysis can help to cut down the number of questions in a survey (Ozok and Salvendy, 2001). For instance, in one of the two research projects described in the Flickr sidebar, the survey questions were validated using an exploratory factor analysis of 193 users. "Items showing factor loading higher than 0.6 and cross-loadings lower than 0.4 were retained, and others were dropped" (Nov et al., 2008, p. 1098).

5.11 **RESPONSE RATE**

A good sampling method and a well-written survey tool are important. However, those steps alone do not guarantee a sufficient number of responses to a survey. One of the main challenges of survey research is how to ensure a sufficient response rate. Other research methods tend to have fewer users taking part and higher incentives for taking part, than in survey research. For instance, if 70 people take part in an experimental research study, they may each be paid $100 for their participation. Obviously, this is not feasible when thousands of individuals are responding to a survey. Perhaps to increase the response rate, the names of respondents could be entered into a drawing to win a prize. Also, surveys are generally self-administered, regardless of whether they are paper, e-mail or web-based. Individuals often need to remember where the survey is located (the URL for a web-based survey, or where they have put the paper survey) and complete it in a timely manner, with the caveat being that they may not receive any major incentive for doing so. So it is important to motivate people to respond to surveys.

There are a number of tried and tested ways to increase the response rate to a survey. For all types of survey (paper, e-mail, and web-based), there should be some type of introductory letter, letting individuals know that they have been selected for inclusion in a survey study. The letter should tell people: who is sponsoring the research study, why it is important, what the expected timeframe is, and hopefully establish some authority or credibility. This is not the same thing as an informed consent form, this is all about establishing the importance and credibility of the survey study, to motivate people to respond. For instance, if an individual who is a trusted authority within the community of individuals helps to introduce the survey, this may help increase the response rate. Or if the survey comes from a well-respected government source, this should be clearly identified to help establish authority.

Aside from establishing the credibility of a survey, another method for increasing the response rate is to increase the ease in returning a survey. For instance, a paper survey should be accompanied by a self-addressed return envelope with postage included.

A multistep contact process tends to increase the response rate. Researchers should make multiple contacts with respondents. For instance, Dillman (2000) suggests the following process for paper surveys:

1. Send a precontact letter (usually with information from a trusted authority, as stated earlier), before the actual mailing.
2. Send a postal mailing, which includes the actual survey.
3. Send a thank you postcard (which thanks people for their time and serves as a reminder).

4. Send a replacement survey to nonrespondents 2–4 weeks after the original one was sent.
5. Make a final contact using a different mode. If the original survey was sent using postal mail, then maybe a phone call or e-mail should be used. If the survey was electronic, maybe a postal letter or phone call should be used. The idea is to have a different delivery method for the final contact that gets the attention of the respondent.

Depending on how the researchers have access to the potential respondents, different methods of postal mail, e-mail, phone calls, or even instant messaging, may be interchanged. So, for instance, in an electronic survey (web-based or e-mail), multiple reminders are important, and each time, the researchers should give the survey instrument (for a web-based survey).

A common question, mentioned earlier in the chapter, is the question "How many survey responses are enough?" This is not easy to answer, as it has to do with a number of different issues: What is the goal of the survey? What type of survey? What sampling method has been used? What level of confidence and margin of error is considered acceptable? See Section 5.4.2 earlier in this chapter, where these questions are discussed.

5.12 DATA ANALYSIS

There are several ways to analyze survey data. The analysis chosen will depend, in large part, on:

- whether it was a probabilistic or nonprobabilistic survey;
- how many responses were received; and
- whether a majority of questions were open-ended or closed-ended questions.

Generally, the quantitative and qualitative data is separated for analysis. The data is "cleaned," meaning that the researchers look through and make sure that each survey response is valid, and that none of the responses are either repeats (where the same person submitted more than one response), incomplete (where most questions were not answered), or invalid (due to a respondent not meeting the qualifications). The quantitative data is ready to analyze, whereas the qualitative data must first be coded (see Chapter 11 for more information on content analysis).

Often, the goal of quantitative data analysis is simply to have a set of "descriptive statistics" that simply describe the data collected in a manageable way (Babbie, 1990). No one but the researchers will read through every survey response so the descriptive statistics are simply a short, high-level summary of the data. Most often, descriptive statistics involve percentages, ratios, or matrices. Inferential statistics involve a higher level of understanding of the data, by understanding the relationships between variables and how they impact each other. For more information on statistical analysis, read Chapter 4.

5.13 SUMMARY

Surveys are a very powerful tool for collecting data from many individuals; however, there are only certain types of research questions in HCI for which surveys are the most appropriate research method. For an appropriate survey method, there must be a number of different steps that take place. To ensure validity and reliability, survey questions must be pilot tested, to ensure that they are clear, unambiguous, and unbiased. The overall survey design should make it easy for respondents to understand and use the instrument, whether web-based, e-mailed, or on paper. Appropriate sampling methods, even if they are nonprobabilistic, must be used to ensure a representative response that can answer the research questions. Good introductions, establishing the credibility and importance of the survey, as well as providing ongoing reminders to respond, can increase the likelihood that there will be a sufficient number of responses for the data to be considered valid. Other research methods can also be useful in conjunction with surveys, such as focus groups, interviews, or time diaries.

DISCUSSION QUESTIONS

1. Is a survey the same thing as a questionnaire? If not, how are they different?

2. What is the difference between the target population and the sampling frame?

3. Why are censuses done rarely? What is often used instead when population estimates need to be made?

4. What is the defining characteristic of a probability sample?

5. What is a stratified random sample? How is it different from a traditional random sample?

6. What is one of the major reasons that nonprobabilistic sampling is considered appropriate in human-computer interaction research but not in other research communities?

7. What is oversampling and why might it help improve validity of the research?

8. What is the difference between an open-ended and a closed-ended question?

9. Why might you want to use an existing survey instrument, when possible?

10. What is a double-barreled question and why is it not a good idea?

11. What is a contingent question and how might you deal with one in a survey layout?

12. What are two methods for testing a survey tool?

RESEARCH DESIGN EXERCISE

Consider that you want to learn more about how people use USB portable storage, as compared to network/cloud-based storage (in web accounts) or storage on their computer hard drives. More specifically, you want to learn how children and young adults (aged 10–18) and older users (aged 65–85) use these storage devices. You want to learn more about which devices individuals prefer and in what situations they use them. Would you use probabilistic or nonprobabilistic sampling? What questions might you ask? Come up with at least five questions. How would you structure the survey? Would you use contingent questions? How would you pretest the survey? How would you ensure that you receive a sufficient number of responses?

REFERENCES

Andrews, D., Nonnecke, B., Preece, J., 2003. Electronic survey methodology: a case study in reaching hard to involve Internet users. International Journal of Human–Computer Interaction 16 (2), 185–210.

Aykin, N. (Ed.), 2005. Usability and Internationalization of Information Technology. Lawrence Erlbaum Associates, Mahwah, NJ.

Babbie, E., 1990. Survey Research Methods, second ed. Wadsworth Publishing, Belmont, CA.

Babbie, E., 2009. The Practice of Social Research. Wadsworth Publishing, Belmont, CA.

Chen, C., Geyer, W., Dugan, C., Muller, M., Guy, I., 2009. Make new friends, but keep the old: recommending people on social networking sites. In: Proceedings of the ACM Conference on Human Factors in Computing Systems, pp. 201–210.

Chilana, P., Singh, R., Guo, P., 2016. Understanding conversational programmers: a perspective from the software industry. In: Proceedings of the 2016 CHI Conference on Human Factors in Computing Systems (CHI '16), pp. 1462–1472.

Chin, J.P., Diehl, V.A., Norman, K.L., 1988. Development of an instrument measuring user satisfaction of the human-computer interface. In: Proceedings of the ACM Conference on Human Factors in Computing Systems, pp. 213–218.

Couper, M., 2000. Web-based surveys: a review of issues and approaches. Public Opinion Quarterly 64, 464–494.

Couper, M., 2005. Technology trends in survey data collection. Social Science Computer Review 23 (4), 486–501.

Dell, N., Kumar, N., 2016. The ins and outs of HCI for development. In: Proceedings of the 2016 CHI Conference on Human Factors in Computing Systems (CHI '16), pp. 2220–2232.

Dillman, D., 2000. Mail and Internet Surveys: The Tailored Design Method. John Wiley & Sons, New York.

Epstein, D., Avrahami, D., Biehl, J., 2016. Taking 5: work-breaks, productivity, and opportunities for personal informatics for knowledge workers. In: Proceedings of the 2016 CHI Conference on Human Factors in Computing Systems (CHI '16), pp. 673–684.

Feng, J., Lazar, J., Kumin, L., Ozok, A., 2008. Computer usage and computer-related behavior of young individuals with Down Syndrome. In: Proceedings of the ACM Conference on Assistive Technology (ASSETS), pp. 35–42.

Fogg, B., Marshall, J., Laraki, O., Osipovich, A., Varma, C., Fang, N., Paul, J., Rangnekar, A., Shon, J., Swani, P., Treinen, M., 2001. What makes web sites credible? A report on a large quantitative study. In: Proceedings of the ACM Conference on Human Factors in Computing Systems, pp. 61–68.

Frankel, M., 1983. Sampling theory. In: Rossi, P.H., Wright, J.D., Anderson, A.B. (Eds.), Handbook of Survey Research. Academic Press, New York, pp. 21–67.

Guy, I., Ronen, I., Zwerdling, N., Zuyev-Grabovitch, I., Jacovi, M., 2016. What is your organization 'like'?: a study of liking activity in the enterprise. In: Proceedings of the 2016 CHI Conference on Human Factors in Computing Systems (CHI '16), pp. 3025–3037.

Hanks, K., Odom, W., Roedl, D., Blevis, E., 2008. Sustainable millennials: attitudes towards sustainability and the material effects of interactive technologies. In: Proceedings of the ACM Conference on Human Factors in Computing Systems, pp. 333–342.

Harbach, M., De Luca, A., Malkin, N., Egelman, S., 2016. Keep on lockin' in the free world: a multi-national comparison of smartphone locking. In: Proceedings of the 2016 CHI Conference on Human Factors in Computing Systems (CHI '16), pp. 4823–4827.

Kairam, S., Kaye, J., Guerra-Gomez, J., Shamma, D., 2016. Snap decisions?: how users, content, and aesthetics interact to shape photo sharing behaviors. In: Proceedings of the 2016 CHI Conference on Human Factors in Computing Systems (CHI '16), pp. 113–124.

Kirijian, A., Myers, M., Charland, S., 2007. Web fun central: online learning tools for individuals with Down syndrome. In: Lazar, J. (Ed.), Universal Usability: Designing Computer Interfaces for Diverse User Populations. John Wiley & Sons, Chichester, pp. 195–230.

Kosmalla, F., Wiehr, F., Daiber, F., Krüger, A., Löchtefeld, M., 2016. ClimbAware: investigating perception and acceptance of wearables in rock climbing. In: Proceedings of the 2016 CHI Conference on Human Factors in Computing Systems (CHI '16), pp. 1097–1108.

Lazar, J., 2006. Web Usability: A User-Centered Design Approach. Addison-Wesley, Boston, MA.

Lazar, J., Preece, J., 2001. Using electronic surveys to evaluate networked resources: from idea to implementation. In: McClure, C., Bertot, J. (Eds.), Evaluating Networked Information Services: Techniques, Policy, and Issues. Information Today, Medford, NJ, pp. 137–154.

Lazar, J., Tsao, R., Preece, J., 1999. One foot in cyberspace and the other on the ground: a case study of analysis and design issues in a hybrid virtual and physical community. WebNet Journal. Internet Technologies, Applications & Issues 1 (3), 49–57.

Lewis, J.R., 1995. IBM Computer usability satisfaction questionnaires: psychometric evaluation and instructions for use. International Journal of Human–Computer Interaction 7 (1), 57–78.

Lin, H.X., Choong, Y.-Y., Salvendy, G., 1997. A proposed index of usability: a method for comparing the relative usability of different software systems. Behaviour & Information Technology 16 (4/5), 267–278.

McKenna, K., Bargh, J., 2000. Plan 9 from cyberspace: the implications of the Internet for personality and social psychology. Personality and Social Psychology Review 4 (1), 57–75.

Müller, H., Sedley, A., Ferrall-Nunge, E., 2014. Survey research in HCI. In: Olson, J., Kellogg, W. (Eds.), Ways of Knowing in HCI. Springer, New York, pp. 229–266.

Moser, C., Schoenebeck, S., Reinecke, K., 2016. Technology at the table: attitudes about mobile phone use at mealtimes. In: Proceedings of the 2016 CHI Conference on Human Factors in Computing Systems (CHI '16), pp. 1881–1892.

Normand, L.M., Paternò, F., Winckler, M., 2014. Public policies and multilingualism in HCI. Interactions 21 (3), 70–73.

Nov, O., Naaman, M., Ye, C., 2008. What drives content tagging: the case of photos on Flickr. In: Proceedings of the ACM Conference on Human Factors in Computing Systems, pp. 1097–1100.

Ozok, A., 2007. Survey design and implementation in HCI. In: Sears, A., Jacko, J. (Eds.), The Human Computer Interaction Handbook. second ed. Lawrence Erlbaum Associates, New York, pp. 1151–1169.

Ozok, A., Salvendy, G., 2001. How consistent is your web design? Behaviour & Information Technology 20 (6), 433–447.

Pitkow, J., Kehoe, C., 1996. Emerging trends in the WWW population. Communications of the ACM 39 (6), 106–110.

Schmidt, W., 1997. World wide web survey research: benefits, potential problems, and solutions. Behavior Research Methods, Instruments, & Computers 29 (2), 274–279.

Schonlau, M., Asch, B., Du, C., 2003. Web surveys as part of a mixed-mode strategy for populations that cannot be contacted by e-mail. Social Science Computer Review 21 (2), 218–222.

Shklovski, I., Kraut, R., Cummings, J., 2008. Keeping in touch by technology: maintaining friendships after a residential move. In: Proceedings of the ACM Conference on Human Factors in Computing Systems, pp. 807–816.

Slaughter, L., Harper, B., Norman, K., 1994. Assessing the equivalence of paper and on-line versions of the QUIS 5.5. In: Proceedings of the 2nd Annual Mid-Atlantic Human Factors Conference, pp. 87–91.

Spears, R., Lea, M., 1994. Panacea or panopticon? The hidden power in computer-mediated communication. Communication Research 21 (4), 427–459.

Sue, V., Ritter, L., 2007. Conducting Online Surveys. Sage Publications, Los Angeles.

Sussman, S., Sproull, L., 1999. Straight talk: delivering bad news through electronic communication. Information Systems Research 10 (2), 150–166.

Diaries

6

6.1 INTRODUCTION

A diary is a document created by an individual who maintains regular recordings about events in their life, at the time that those events occur (Alaszewski, 2006). These recordings can be anything from a simple record of activities (such as a schedule) to an explanation of those activities to personal reflections on the meaning of those activities. When you are asking people to record information that is fluid and changes over time, such as their mood, or about multiple events that occur within the day, diaries are generally more accurate than other research methods (Alaszewski, 2006). Many people keep a diary and do not even realize it. Informal diaries are kept online and are known as blogs. Many people now send out tweets using "Twitter" or status updates using "Facebook" and both of these, where individuals record what they are doing, as they are doing it, are in fact a form of diary (although not primarily used for any research purposes).

The diary method used in human-computer interaction (HCI) has been adopted from other fields, primarily sociology and history (Hyldegard, 2006). For instance, diaries in history have been used to understand the feelings, experiences, and stories of both famous and unknown figures. Personal diaries of world leaders give insight to historians, while personal diaries of unknown individuals allow a documentation of the lives of those who are often left out of the official record of history (Alaszewski, 2006). In sociology, diaries are used to understand what individuals experience but otherwise seems ordinary and unremarkable to those individuals, and might be hard to understand by outsiders (Alaszewski, 2006). Other fields, such as medicine, also frequently use the diary method for research. While the focus of much experimental research in medicine is on measuring objective data that can be observed, other data which is not objective, such as the individual's feelings of pain or fatigue, can best be understood through the use of a diary (Alaszewski, 2006).

One form of diary is a time diary. A time diary focuses on how individuals utilize their time in different activities. The major difference between a general diary and a time diary is that general diary entries may be on an infrequent or nontemporal basis, whereas time diaries have a time focus. Individuals are asked to record entries on a regular basis, record entries when events occur and note time information, or a combination thereof. Because much of the research in HCI focuses on how long we spend in some software application, how much time we spend on a website, or how much time we lose due to frustrations or task switching, time diaries are often the prevailing type of diary used in HCI research. The sidebar on "time diaries to study user frustration" provides an example.

TIME DIARIES TO STUDY USER FRUSTRATION

Time diaries have been used in researching the presence of frustration among users interacting with computers. A series of research studies examined what frustrates users while using computers, how they respond to those frustrations, and how it impacts on the users' time. One study focused on 111 university students and their friends; one study focused on 50 workplace users; and a third on 100 blind users on the web (Ceaparu et al., 2004; Lazar et al., 2006, 2007).

The methodology was essentially the same for all three studies: users were asked to fill out a time diary of their computer usage over a given amount of time (such as a few hours). At the beginning and end of their usage session on the computer, the users were asked to record their mood by answering a series of questions. The users were requested to fill out a "frustration experience form" each time during the session that they felt frustrated, with no minimum or maximum number of forms. Throughout the process, the time of day was recorded by users, which helped both to validate the quality of the data and to ascertain how much time was lost due to these frustration experiences.

There are a number of different findings from these studies relating to causes of frustration and how users responded to the frustrations. One of the most interesting findings was how much time was lost due to frustrating situations. In the study of the student users, 38%–43% of the time spent on the computer was lost due to frustrating experiences. In the study of workplace users, 42.7% of time on the computer was lost due to frustrating experiences. In the study of blind users, 30.4% of time on the computer was lost due to frustrating experiences.

Below is the Frustration experience form (time diary) from Ceaparu et al. (2004).

Frustrating Experience

Please fill out this form for each frustrating experience that you encounter while using your computer during the reporting session. This should include both major problems such as computer or application crashes, and minor issues such as a program not responding the way that you need it to. Anything which frustrates you should be recorded.

1. What were you trying to do?
2. On a scale of 1 (not very important) to 9 (very important), how important was this task to you?

   Not very important   1   2   3   4   5   6   7   8   9   Very Important
3. What software or program did the problem occur in? If the problem was the computer system, please check the program that you were using when it occurred (check all that apply).

___ e-mail   ___ spreadsheet programs (e.g., Excel)

___ chat and instant   ___ graphic design
messaging

___ web browsing   ___ programming tools

___ other Internet use   ___ database programs

___ word processing   ___ presentation software
(e.g., PowerPoint)

___ file browsers   ___ other _____

4. Please write a brief description of the experience:

_____

5. How did you solve this problem?
   _____ I knew how to solve it because it has happened before
   _____ I figured out a way to fix it myself without help
   _____ I asked someone for help. Number of people asked ___
   _____ I consulted online help or the system/application tutorial
   _____ I consulted a manual or book
   _____ I rebooted
   _____ I ignored the problem or found an alternative solution
   _____ I was unable to solve it
   _____ I tried again
   _____ I restarted the program

6. Please provide a short step-by-step description of the process you used to resolve this incident.

_____

7. How often does this problem happen? ___ more than once a day ___ one time a day ___ several times a week ___ once a week ___ several times a month ___ once a month ___ several times a year ___ first time it happened

8. On a scale of 1 (not very frustrating) to 9 (very frustrating), how frustrating was this problem for you?

   Not very frustrating   1   2   3   4   5   6   7   8   9   Very frustrating

9. Of the following, did you feel: ___ Angry at the computer ___ angry at yourself ___ helpless/resigned ___ determined to fix it ___ other

10. How many minutes did it take you to solve this problem?

_____

11. Other than the amount of time it took you to solve the problem, how many minutes did you lose because of this problem? (If this has happened before, please account only for the current time lost)._____
Please explain:

6.2 WHY DO WE USE DIARIES IN HCI RESEARCH?

Diaries fill the gaps in HCI research methods between observation in naturalistic settings, observation in a fixed lab, and surveys (Hyldegard, 2006). Many say that controlled studies in controlled settings (such as usability labs) are ideal and others say that observing users in their natural settings (such as homes or workplaces) is ideal. However, in many cases, it is not feasible to either bring users into a fixed setting or visit the users in their natural setting. In addition, having observers present in either setting can sometimes change the actions of the users (Carter and Mankoff, 2005). Diaries are especially good at studying usage patterns that cross multiple technologies, multiple locations, and multiple environments (Hayashi and Hong, 2011). For instance, to study how people utilize passwords across multiple systems, devices, networks, and locations, at both home and work, a diary study was used, with 20 participants, who recorded 1500 password events over a 2-week period (Hayashi and Hong, 2011). Of the various research methods described in this book, very few of the methods could have accurately collected data from so many different technical and physical environments.

All research methods have strengths and weaknesses, and by using two or three different research methods, you can often get a much better understanding of phenomena than you would with only one research method. For instance, Kientz et al. developed a technical solution (called FETCH) to help blind people track everyday items, such as keys, iPod, remote controls, and sunglasses. A small Bluetooth tag was added to these items to help in tracking. While a laboratory study was conducted first, a controlled laboratory study clearly would not be sufficient to determine how this approach to finding items could be used in someone's daily life. After the laboratory study discovered some needed improvements in the interface, a diary study was used in which participants would track when they lost items that they needed and how long it took them to find the item. In the first 2-week phase of the diary study, the participants did not use FETCH. During the second 2-week phase, the participants used the FETCH system and recorded when they lost items and how long it took to find them (Kientz et al., 2006). The diary study was then followed up with interviews with the participants. The use of the diary in conjunction with other methods strengthened the findings of this research project. However, while ideal, it is sometimes not possible to use two or three different research methods, due to time, cost, or participant availability.

It might seem that surveys are an appropriate solution compared to diaries, as they allow users to record data in their own settings and time, and surveys reach a geographically distributed set of users. However, surveys can lead to biased data in behavioral research in some situations, and diaries offer some advantages over surveys in certain research situations. In many cases, diaries are used in conjunction with other methods; when this is possible, it is ideal, as adding one research method often ameliorates the shortcomings of another method. Diaries allow for collecting of more detailed research than surveys, which often use predefined questions and allow little flexibility for respondents. Alaszewski said it best, "While survey research is good at describing what people do, it is rather less effective at explaining or understanding why they do it" (Alaszewski, 2006, p. 36). Surveys ask users to recall information. This may be appropriate if you are asking users to recall information that does not change over time, such as their date of birth, their income, or other demographic data. Any data that is fluid, occurs only at a specific time, and changes, such as mood, feeling, perception, time, or response, needs a very short-time period between the occurrence of the event and the recording of the event. Surveys can skew this type of data because, when users are asked to recall their mood, their feeling, their response, or the time that an event took, their response to a survey can be biased or incorrect. In some cases, users might simply forget the details of what occurred. In other cases, an individual user's personality might bias the response. If you ask different people to recall a similar challenging event in their life, some will recall it with optimism and remember the event as being not so bad. Others, who are pessimistic, may look back and remember the event as being worse than it actually was. Differences in personality can skew the recollection. For instance, an 80-year-old friend of one of the authors recalled that when he owned a food store in the 1950s, he once had a robbery where a man held the employees up with a gun and forced them to go into a meat locker for hours. The next comment from the man was "You know, it was a hot day in July, so actually, a few hours in the cooler wasn't too bad!" His personality made him look back on what was most likely a traumatic event and remember a joke. A diary allows for a very small gap between the occurrence of the event and the recording of the event. Ideally, this gap is as close to zero as possible.

Diaries are a very good method for recording measurements that cannot be accurately collected by experimental or observational means, or may result in increased overall validity when used in conjunction with these other methods. For example, diaries were utilized in studying why older individuals (50+) decide to contribute to open source software projects for the first time (Davidson et al., 2014). Direct observation or experimentation would not be useful approaches to understand the motivations and benefits that the participants experienced from their first forays into open source contributions. Over a 2-month period, participants received daily reminder emails, to fill out diary entries, asking about their contributions to open source software, their motivations for doing so, the benefits that they received, and any barriers stopping them from continuing to contribute (Davidson et al., 2014).

While research methods such as experimental design focus on objectively measuring human performance and automated data collection methods focus on studying data that computers can collect unobtrusively, surveys and time diaries ask users about themselves. How did they perceive a certain experience with the computer or device? How did they feel? How did they respond? How much time did it take them? How did it impact on their mood? When did they use it? How did it impact on their feelings of self-efficacy? The diary elicits this information in a way that neither outside observation nor automated data collection can. For instance, how do you determine when a user intended to perform an action, but did not do so? (Carter and Mankoff, 2005) Neither observation nor automated data collection would be able to record that.

Despite all of the benefits of using diaries for HCI research, there are some potential disadvantages. If you are asking for participants to provide insights as a part of a diary entry, for some individuals, they may not be introspective or aware enough to do that. While time recording may be more accurate using a diary as compared to a survey, automated methods of data collection, when available, may still be more accurate. It can also be challenging sometimes, to get participants to record a sufficient number of diary entries. Furthermore, if a diary study requires a high number of diary entries, or very personal information, participants may not want to take part in the study, or again, may record diary entries relatively infrequently. A summary of the strengths and weaknesses of diaries appears in Table 6.1.

Table 6.1 Strengths and Weaknesses of Diaries

Advantages	Disadvantages
Good for understanding how individuals utilize technology in nonworkplace, noncontrolled, or on-the-go settings	Participants are sometimes not introspective and not aware of the specifics of what they are doing; they may therefore have trouble recording it in a diary entry
Good for understanding the "why" of user interaction with a technology or any technology phenomenon	Participants may not follow through and record a sufficient number of entries
More accurate time recording than in a survey	Time recording may be less accurate than in a controlled laboratory setting or automated data collection
Good for collecting data that is fluid, and changes over time (such as time, mood, perception, or response)	Generally harder to recruit participants for a diary study than for a less intrusive study, such as a survey
The limited gap between an event happening and it being recorded can help limit the impact of individual personality on interpretation of what occurred	Since data is both qualitative and quantitative, data analysis may take a long time
Good for collecting user-defined data (e.g., when a user intended to perform an action but did not do so)	Hard to strike a balance between a frequent-enough series of diary entries and infringement on daily activities (user participation may then trail off)

Diaries can investigate the use of technology that exists at multiple stages:

- Technology that does not exist yet but could (where researchers investigate communication or information usage patterns, separate from the technology).
- Technology that exists but needs to be improved (how people use existing technology).
- Prototypes of new technology that need to be evaluated.

Diaries are excellent for recording the existence and quantity of incidents that are user defined, and where there is little previous data documented on the topic. For instance, one study examined how often users feel that they have learned something while using a computer. The moment when the user realizes that they have learned something new about the computer interface, dubbed a "eureka moment," was recorded using a diary. Over a period of 5 days, 10 individuals recorded 69 eureka moments, but two of the individuals reported more than 50% of the moments (Rieman, 1993). In another study, "rendezvousing" (face-to-face meetings with friends and family) was studied using a diary method. It was determined that the 34 participants reported a total of 415 rendezvous incidents over a 2-week period (an average of six per day) (Colbert, 2001). Documenting in a diary the time involved, both for a specific incident and throughout the day, can help strengthen the validity of the data.

Diaries are very good at examining situations where users do not stay in one place during the time period of interest (i.e., users are on the go). Diaries are also good for studying the use of a technological device in a real-world setting, where a controlled setting would not be able to provide ecological validity. For instance, you could not examine the use of a global positioning system (GPS) device by studying how people use it within a laboratory setting. In the rendezvous study, diaries were used to examine how people "meet up," with the goal of understanding how technology could help support them in their meetings (Colbert, 2001). Clearly, this is a phenomenon that could not be studied in the laboratory and interviewing people or surveying them after-the-fact could lead to biased or incorrect data. Diaries are also good at examining situations that involve both computer usage and noncomputer usage. For instance, a time diary study was used to examine work-related reading, where the goal was to use an understanding of how people read at work, to inform the design of digital readers or electronic books. For the 15 participants in that diary study, an average of 82% of their work time was spent reading or writing documents (Adler et al., 1998).

Diaries are a research method used heavily in sociology. For instance, long-running studies of how people use their time have used a time diary, which requires users to account for all their time within specific guidelines (such as all time during the work day, all time while awake, or all time within a 24-hour period). While humans generally have problems remembering details of events that have occurred in the recent past, they are especially prone to inaccurately remembering details about time. For instance, in a number of national surveys, people have indicated that they did activities for more than the 168 hours within that week, which is impossible (Robinson and Godbey, 1997).

6.3 PARTICIPANTS FOR A DIARY STUDY

To develop a diary for appropriate use within a research study, there are a number of steps involved. Like any other type of research method, prior planning and testing are a requirement to ensure a valid outcome. When deciding to do a diary study, one of the first questions is who will take part in the diary study? While survey methods sometimes call for strict random sampling, this is not realistic for a diary study and it is generally not feasible to get 500 or 1000 users to record diaries. However, strict representation is not as important for diaries as it is for large-scale surveys or experimental design. Many research projects start out with a hypothesis that needs to be tested with statistics. However, diaries should be used when the goal is not to test a hypothesis, but rather, to learn more about situations or behaviors that are not well-understood (Alaszewski, 2006).

In survey research and experimental research, the goal generally is to recruit large numbers of individuals. However, with diary research, it is generally more important to connect with individuals who can provide useful insight (Alaszewski, 2006). Often, an initial set of users can provide access to other users that they know who are also willing to take part in the diary study, a technique called snowball sampling. An introduction from a trusted source (such as a well-known organization or individual) to potential diarists can help in recruiting potential diarists. It is important to make sure that potential diarists are representative of the user population of interest. Not only must the potential diarists meet certain demographic rules (e.g., women over 70 years old) but they must also have a appropriate level of computer experience and a willingness to take part. In the past, computer users, who were often primarily technically oriented people, might not have been as open about their lives. However, as technology has spread throughout the entire population, and as social networking sites (e.g., Facebook, Twitter, and Instagram) and blogging have become popular, many more individuals are likely to feel comfortable with the process of keeping a diary. The challenge may not be in recruiting people who are comfortable with and capable of keeping a diary, but rather making sure that you can recruit users that meet the demographic qualifications necessary. Potential diarists must not only meet demographic requirements but also possess three qualities (modified from Alaszewski (2006)):

- an understanding of the purposes of maintaining the diary;
- the motivation to keep a regular and accurate record; and
- competence in using the technology that is the subject of the diary and the method used to record the diary.

The diary study must be structured in a way that yields useful data without imposing an unreasonable burden on the lives of the diarists. For instance, keeping the diary should not in any way negatively impact on the diarists' employment, health, or relationships with others. A payment of some form (either money or a product) should be offered to the diarists for their participation. Sometimes, when diaries are used to understand new technology, the diarist is allowed to keep, free of charge, the technology about which they have been recording diary entries. Of course, as in any type of research, the participants need to be informed of their rights and their participation in the research should remain anonymous (see Chapter 15 for more information on human subjects protection).

6.4 WHAT TYPE OF DIARY?

There are a number of different methodological decisions to make when using diaries in HCI research: What type of diary? How will the diary be recorded (paper or electronic)? For what period will the users be asked to keep the diary? Diaries are typically kept for a period of 1 or 2 weeks (Rieman, 1993). Any longer than that and participation tends to drop off.

At a high level, diaries can be split into two types of purpose: feedback and elicitation (Carter and Mankoff, 2005). A feedback diary is one in which the data from the diary itself provides the feedback to the researchers. The feedback diary is the data collection method; the diary is not meant as a springboard to anything else. In an elicitation diary, the data recorded in the diary is used for prompting, when interviews take place at a later point, and the users are encouraged to expand upon each data point (see Chapter 8 for more information on interviews). Feedback diaries usually focus on the events that interest the researcher, whereas elicitation diaries usually focus on events that interest the user. Feedback diaries tend to have instructions for users that they should make a diary entry when a certain event or threshold occurs. Elicitation diaries tend to encourage users to make diary entries based more on events that have meaning to the user. Feedback diaries can be more accurate (since users record events on a regular basis as they occur) and more objective but elicitation diaries can provide a view that is more representative of what the user is feeling (Carter and Mankoff, 2005). In a similar fashion to a survey, with an elicitation diary users must recall in a later interview what has occurred and this can lead to bias. However, the data points recorded by the user in the elicitation diary can provide some level of validation, which does not exist in a survey.

6.4.1 FEEDBACK DIARY

Feedback diaries come in many different formats, but probably the most important research question in a feedback diary is how often a diary entry is made. For instance, what event, time, or threshold triggers the need for the user to make a diary entry? Users could be asked to make a diary recording when an event occurs, such as when they feel frustrated with an interface, or when they complete a certain task. Users could be asked to make a diary recording at a set time every day (say, 9 p.m.), or during a specified time period (say, from noon to 6 p.m.). Users could be interrupted throughout the day at random times, to get a random sample of the user's daily life (Carter and Mankoff, 2005). Historically, an individual in this type of time diary study wears a beeper and must record what they are doing whenever the beeper goes off (at random times) (Robinson and Godbey, 1997), although smartphones are often now used for this purpose.

Just as surveys can be very structured or very unstructured, diaries can have different levels of structure. For instance, diaries can be set up like a structured survey, with Likert scales (e.g., "on a scale of 1–7, with 1 being strongly disagree and 7 being strongly agree"), multiple-choice questions, and closed-ended questions. If the diary has a time focus, it can be set up where individuals must record all events within their day in 15-minute increments. Very structured diaries could include predefined categories, checkboxes, counts of how often things occurred such as events, and time stamps. On the other hand, a time diary could be set up in such a manner that it encourages general reflection ("how are you feeling right now about your computer?") (Hyldegard, 2006). Other common questions in an unstructured diary could include "how do you think an activity could be improved?" or "what is notable?" (Palen and Salzman, 2002). The most unstructured diaries would be similar to blogs, where users are not actually being solicited to take part in a study, but they are just recording their general thoughts on a topic. While blogs are not solicited or structured by researchers and may have issues with validity, there are many blogs on the web where users record their feelings about new technologies. It might be useful for you to examine any blogs that document user experience with the technology that is of interest to you as a researcher.

6.4.2 ELICITATION DIARY

The goal of an elicitation diary is to have users record only basic information about the important events occurring in their day. These data points are used as prompts to encourage users to expand the explanation during an interview at a later time. Typically, the data points recorded in elicitation diaries are very quick and simple. In many cases, for elicitation diaries, users simply record pictures, short audio clips, short snippets of text, or a combination (Brandt et al., 2007; Carter and Mankoff, 2005). By using digital cameras and smartphones, the number of diary entries might be higher. The trade-off is that a user taking many different photos and being asked to recall why they took all of those photos may not be able to remember why they made those diary entries (Carter and Mankoff, 2005). After the recordings are made, users are later asked to expand upon these recordings. For instance, in one study related to the development of a new handheld document scanner, 22 users were asked to record their diaries over 7 days by taking photos using a digital camera. Half of the users were asked to take a digital photo any time they felt that there was a paper document that they wanted to capture electronically and half of them were asked to take a digital photo any time there was any information that they wanted to capture electronically (e.g., audio or video). The pictures were then used during a series of semistructured interviews to prompt users to expand upon the photos that they took. Over the 7 days, the 22 users made 381 diary entries (Brown et al.,

2000). In another diary study, related to the information-seeking needs of mobile device users, the participants were asked to send in a short text message, identifying when they had an information need. These short text messages were not the main diary entry but they were used to remind the participants of what had occurred and, at the end of each day, the participants were requested to go to the project website and answer a series of questions (including "where were you?", "what were you doing?", and "what was your information need?") about that specific occurrence (Sohn et al., 2008). This is a great example of the elicitation approach to diaries.

6.4.3 HYBRID FEEDBACK AND ELICITATION DIARY

Like any other type of research method, the approaches used are modified to meet the needs of a specific research study. For instance, in one study, examining how students use transportation, aspects of both feedback and elicitation diaries were used (Carter and Mankoff, 2005). For a 2-week period, the users were asked to use their cell phones to call a specific phone number every time they made a transit decision. At that phone number, they were asked a series of questions about their choice. These aspects were similar to a feedback diary. At the same time, the location of the user at the time of each diary recording was noted, using the built-in GPS features of the phone. At a later time, during an interview, the users were presented with the recordings that they made via cell phone and the GPS information of their location and were prompted to expand their thoughts on that specific decision. These aspects were clearly similar to an elicitation diary.

6.5 DATA COLLECTION FOR THE DIARY STUDY

It is important for researchers to decide how the diaries will be recorded. Will the diaries be recorded on paper, in electronic format, text, voice, video, or pictures? Historically, diaries have been recorded on paper and, if that is the case, enough paper must be provided and appropriate columns and fields should be designated in a structured format. Within the field of HCI, it seems more natural to use technology as a tool to record diary entries (Ceaparu et al., 2004). Increasingly, portable electronic devices are being used for diary entries. This makes diary recording easy and natural, especially for younger users who may be very comfortable using tablets, smartphones, and other portable devices. In addition, when a smartphone or other portable device is used, it does not appear to others that a user is taking part in a study but, rather, that they are just doing a daily activity. This removes any potential stigma of taking part in a research study. This is similar to how many applications for people with cognitive impairments are implemented using standard mobile devices, because when a user with a cognitive impairment uses such a device, they look like any other individual, not "odd" or out of place in any way (Lazar, 2007). Also, digital devices can be utilized by participants for signifying when an event occurs for which a diary entry would be appropriate, even if the participant is unable to make an entry at that time, and the participants can then be reminded to make the diary entry as soon as possible (Chong et al., 2014).

The crucial factor in choosing the media should be the type of media that will be most natural for the diarists in their everyday life. For instance, if participants will be performing the tasks of interest while sitting at their computer, it might make sense to use word processing, spreadsheets, or web-based forms (see the Diary Study of Task Switching sidebar). However, if participants will be recording diary entries about the use of mobile devices, you would expect these entries to occur while the participants are on-the-go (see the Recording Entries on the Go sidebar).

DIARY STUDY OF TASK SWITCHING

Czerwinski et al. (2004) did a diary study of task switching between different projects (and related interruptions) during a week. They were trying to examine how interruptions impact on task switching, with the end goal of improving how user interfaces support users recovering from interruptions. They used a diary study, which they felt was most appropriate since there were no existing empirical studies of tools for dealing with task switching and recovery. In addition, diary studies, because they take place in the users' natural settings and tasks, have high ecological validity.

Eleven users took part; all were professionals who multitasked among at least three major projects or tasks. Before the diaries started, users filled out a baseline survey with demographic information and perceptions about computers. The diaries were recorded using an Excel spreadsheet, where the researchers had labeled columns for each parameter that they wanted to track. For instance, the researchers were interested in learning how users defined tasks, at what level of granularity. The diaries also tracked the difficulty of switching tasks and the amount of time spent on the tasks.

Due to the qualitative nature of the data, two researchers tested and validated the rich coding scheme. Using the coding scheme, first frequency counts and descriptive statistics were carried out on the diary data, followed by regression analysis. Among the significant findings were that users reported an average of 50 task shifts over the week, and that long-term projects, which involved multiple documents and involved more revisits, were very hard to return to, once interrupted.

A time diary form from Czerwinski et al. (2004) appears on the next page.

Please enter your daily activities in the columns below (you might need to scroll to the right to see all columns). For each activity, please enter:

(a) the time you started it

(b) a brief description of the task

(c) the application or the device you used to perform the task

(d) the priority of the task (hi, med, or low)

(e) what caused you to switch to the task

(f) level of difficulty getting started (hi, med, or low)

(g) what other documents or data you needed to find to start the task

(h) whether or not it was on your to do list

(i) whether you forgot anything related to the task, or any other comments you might have

Remember to use the worksheet at the bottom of the spreadsheet corresponding to the day of the week.

At the end of each day, please go to row 50 and fill out the 3 questions listed there. Thanks again!
Please email your diary as it stands at the end of each day [email address now outdated and removed]

Time (HH:MM)	Project/task description	Application or device	Priority (hi, med, low)?	What caused the switch?	Difficulty initiating task (hi, med, low)? Why?	What docs/ data needed to be found?	On ToDo List (if keep one)?	No. of Interruptions?	Time completed (if done)?	Forget anything? Comments?

RECORDING DIARY ENTRIES ON THE GO

Palen and Salzman (2002) carried out two studies, which used diaries to learn about the usage of new mobile phone users. They wanted to know how the mobile phones were used in various situations on a daily basis. If you want users to make diary entries in real time, it does not make sense to ask the diarists to record entries about mobile phone use on paper or desktop/laptop computers, since the diarists would then be likely to make entries at a later time (which would subject the diary entries to recall bias).

It was decided that voicemail entries would be used to record the diary entries. However, another challenge is that there could be complications stemming from the fact that the subject of the diary (the cell phone) might also be the method of making the diary entries. So participants were given the option to record voicemail messages using any type of phone that they wanted—a landline, their current mobile phone, or a different mobile phone. A phone number with voicemail was dedicated to the project, so that participants would not have to use any features on their mobile phone to record, just make a standard outgoing call. This aspect limited the complications of using the mobile phone to record data about the mobile phone.

The goal of the first study was to learn more about the usability of the features in the phone handset. In this portion of the research, 19 users participated and they were paid $1 per day for calling in. The goal was not to collect rigorous, qualitative data, but rather to get a better understanding of when they used their phones in a new environment, used new features, or contacted the phone service provider. Participants at first started phoning in their diary entries from landlines and then gradually switched to using their mobile phones. The second study had 18 participants, and the researchers used a much more structured approach, where they asked specific questions. In the second study, participants reported things such as confusion about services and signal coverage, and even the ergonomics of the phone (some asked if rubber grippers could be added so that the phone would not slip).

6.6 LETTING PARTICIPANTS KNOW WHEN TO RECORD A DIARY ENTRY

Regardless of whether the diary format is paper or electronic, participants should be given information about the goal of the study, the types of activities that are of interest, when to make diary recordings (at a given time every day or when a certain type of incident occurs), and definitions of terminology. Definitions of terminology are especially important, as many individuals may use different terms for the same events or similar terms for different events. For instance, if someone using a personal computer records a "crash," what does that mean? Does it mean that the application crashed but the operating system was OK? Did the operating system crash? Or was it a hard drive crash? It is necessary to provide participants with a list of terms and how they should be used, along with specific details of what should be recorded.

It is also very important to define for participants when they should make a diary recording. Just saying, "when you feel like it" is not sufficient as, many times, this will not provide enough motivation or clarity. Often, diarists do not immediately sense the importance of their entries and, especially with diaries that are relatively unstructured, one of the big challenges is convincing participants that what they are doing is important. They may feel that there is nothing to report, that what's going on is mundane. At the same time, the number of diary entries should not be linked directly to payment for participation. For instance, if participants are paid, $2 for each diary entry, there is a good chance that they will attempt to make many diary entries. In the Time Diaries to Study User Frustration sidebar, if the method had been modified so that users were paid $5 every time that they filled out a frustration experience report, the chances are good that users would get frustrated very often and fill out many reports, regardless of how they were feeling; this could bias the data so that it is unrepresentative. Any payment should be for regular participation but should not be linked directly to the number of entries. Participants should get paid for taking part in the study, regardless of the number of entries. Each diary entry should be triggered by an event, a time, or a sense of importance, not by financial compensation.

Throughout the period of the study (and 2 weeks is often an appropriate length of time), it might be necessary to encourage participants to keep making diary entries. If diary reports are turned in during the study period (not only at the end), you may be able to monitor the diary reports and give feedback to users who are not providing useful data. For instance, in a diary study of the information-seeking needs of mobile device users (Sohn et al., 2008), the participants were sent five text messages a day, reminding them to send in text messages which served as basic diary entries (and which were then followed up later in the day). It is always a good idea to give feedback to diary participants, not on their specific entries (which might bias the data) but on the existence of their diary entries, on a regular basis. Another interesting study reported on the use of smartwatches in the service of reminding participants when to record a diary entry. For a diary relating to tracking food items eaten, whenever the smartwatch detected hand gestures that typically represented hand-to-mouth eating, the smartwatch sent a message to a smartphone app, reminding the participant to record what they were eating (Ye et al., 2016).

6.7 ANALYSIS OF DIARIES

Once the diaries are collected, the next step is to analyze the diary entries or reports. Depending on the media used to collect the diary entries (such as paper), it may be necessary first to transfer the diary entries to an electronic format. Hopefully, if any handwriting was done in paper diaries, the handwriting is legible and not open to potential debate!

Some data collected in the diary will be relatively easy to analyze, if it is in quantitative format. Those types of data points can be entered in a spreadsheet and traditional statistical tests and measurements can be used (see Chapter 4 for more information on statistics). However, it is expected that much of the data in a diary will be of a qualitative nature. Since diaries are often used for more exploratory research, where little is known, it is expected that much of the diary data will be in qualitative format, in text described by the diarist. This descriptive text can then be subjected to some form of content analysis (see Chapter 11), in which researchers develop coding categories and code text according to the meaning of the descriptive text (Alaszewski, 2006). Content analysis can help in understanding the meaning of the text, allowing for a comparison between diary entries.

Assuming that the diary is somewhat structured in nature, coding and analysis should not be overwhelmingly challenging, although researchers analyzing unsolicited unstructured diaries (such as blogs) may find it very challenging to code diary entries. An example of a diary report that collects both qualitative and quantitative data is in the sidebar on task switching, earlier in this chapter. Follow-up interviews with participants who keep an elicitation diary may involve the participants themselves interpreting the data recorded. In many cases, even if the diary is not an elicitation diary, the researchers can contact the participants to ask for clarification of diary entries.

Finally, after data analysis is performed, it is always a good idea to note how, in the future, your approach to data collection through diaries might be modified and improved.

6.8 SUMMARY

Diaries have a long history as a research tool in sociology and history, but have only recently been adopted as a research tool in HCI. Diaries are very useful in a number of different research situations. For instance, diaries are appropriate where little is known about the usage patterns of a new technology, and there is not enough background research for an experimental study. Diaries are useful where technology is being used on the go and observation or experimental design would not be appropriate. Diaries are also useful where the research questions lead to data points that cannot easily be observed or measured (such as feelings of frustration). Finally, diaries are useful in triangulation: using multiple research methods to explore the same phenomenon from different points of view. Diaries can help with the understanding of why something happened, not only in documenting that it did happen.

DISCUSSION QUESTIONS

1. What is the major difference between diaries in general and time diaries?

2. What bias often present in survey responses do diaries sometimes eliminate?

3. Why are diaries good for collecting data on user-defined events?

4. What aspects of hand-held or mobile devices make them appropriate for diary studies?

5. Why is strict random sampling not necessary in diary studies?

6. What is the main difference between feedback diaries and elicitation diaries?

7. Why is it important to clearly define appropriate definitions of terminology for diary participants?

8. Why do you not want to pay participants for each diary entry?

9. What is generally considered to be the longest appropriate time period for a diary study?

RESEARCH DESIGN EXERCISE

Imagine designing a research study to learn more about the use of genealogy (the study of family history) websites, applications, and databases. Not much is previously known about the user habits for this type of work. What types of participants might be appropriate for a research study? What characteristics might they have? Why might a diary study be superior to a survey or observation study? Specifically, provide information on how a feedback diary and an elicitation diary might be implemented for this study. If the diary was relatively structured, what types of questions should be asked? Would time be an important consideration in this type of diary? Would random sampling of time be appropriate?

REFERENCES

Adler, A., Gujar, A., Harrison, B., O'Hara, K., Sellen, A., 1998. A diary study of work-related reading: design implications for digital reading devices. In: Proceedings of the ACM Conference on Human Factors in Computing Systems, pp. 241–248.

Alaszewski, A., 2006. Using Diaries for Social Research. Sage Publications, London.

Brandt, J., Weiss, N., Klemmer, S., 2007. txt 4 l8r: lowering the burden for diary studies under mobile conditions. In: Proceedings of the 2007 ACM Conference on Human Factors in Computing Systems, pp. 2303–2308.

Brown, B., Sellen, A., O'Hara, K., 2000. A diary study of information capture in working life. In: Proceedings of the 2000 ACM Conference on Human Factors in Computing Systems, pp. 438–445.

Carter, S., Mankoff, J., 2005. When participants do the capturing: the role of media in diary studies. In: Proceedings of the 2005 ACM Conference on Human Factors in Computing Systems, pp. 899–908.

Ceaparu, I., Lazar, J., Bessiere, K., Robinson, J., Shneiderman, B., 2004. Determining causes and severity of end-user frustration. International Journal of Human–Computer Interaction 17 (3), 333–356.

Chong, M.K., Whittle, J., Rashid, U., Ang, C.S., 2014. Squeeze the moment: denoting diary events by squeezing. In: Proceedings of the 2014 ACM International Joint Conference on Pervasive and Ubiquitous Computing: Adjunct Publication, pp. 219–222.

Colbert, M., 2001. A diary study of rendezvousing: implications for position-aware computing and communications for the general public. In: Proceedings of the 2001 ACM Conference on Groupware, pp. 15–23.

Czerwinski, M., Horvitz, E., Wilhite, S., 2004. A diary study of task switching and interruptions. In: Proceedings of the ACM Conference on Human Factors in Computing Systems, pp. 175–182.

Davidson, J.L., Mannan, U.A., Naik, R., Dua, I., Jensen, C., 2014. Older adults and free/open source software: a diary study of first-time contributors. In: Proceedings of the International Symposium on Open Collaboration, pp. 1–10.

Hayashi, E., Hong, J., 2011. A diary study of password usage in daily life. In: Proceedings of the SIGCHI Conference on Human Factors in Computing Systems, pp. 2627–2630.

Hyldegard, J., 2006. Using diaries in group based information behavior research: a methodological study. In: Proceedings of the Information Interaction in Context, pp. 153–161.

Kientz, J., Patel, S., Tyebkhan, A., Gane, B., Wiley, J., Abowd, G., 2006. Where's my stuff? design and evaluation of a mobile system for locating lost items for the visually impaired. In: Proceedings of the ACM Conference on Assistive Technology (ASSETS), pp. 103–110.

Lazar, J. (Ed.), 2007. Universal Usability: Designing Computer Interfaces for Diverse User Populations. John Wiley & Sons, Chichester.

Lazar, J., Jones, A., Shneiderman, B., 2006. Workplace user frustration with computers: an exploratory investigation of the causes and severity. Behaviour & Information Technology 25 (3), 239–251.

Lazar, J., Allen, A., Kleinman, J., Malarkey, C., 2007. What frustrates screen reader users on the web: a study of 100 blind users. International Journal of Human–Computer Interaction 22 (3), 247–269.

Palen, L., Salzman, M., 2002. Voice mail diary studies for naturalistic data capture under mobile conditions. In: Proceedings of the ACM Conference on Computer-supported Cooperative Work, pp. 87–95.

Rieman, J., 1993. The diary study: a workplace-oriented research tool to guide laboratory efforts. In: Proceedings of the ACM Conference on Human Factors in Computing Systems, pp. 321–326.

Robinson, J., Godbey, 1997. Time for Life: The Surprising Ways Americans Use Their Time, second ed. Pennsylvania State University Press, Pennsylvania.

Sohn, T., Li, K., Griswold, W., Hollan, J., 2008. A diary study of mobile information needs. In: Proceedings of the ACM Conference on Human Factors in Computing Systems, pp. 433–442.

Ye, X., Chen, G., Gao, Y., Wang, H., Cao, Y., 2016. Assisting food journaling with automatic eating detection. In: Proceedings of the 2016 CHI Conference Extended Abstracts on Human Factors in Computing Systems, pp. 3255–3262.

Case studies

7.1 INTRODUCTION

Research into human-computer interaction (HCI), like most other research, is often a numbers game: the more, the merrier. Whether you are collecting data to help you understand the requirements for a new system, evaluating the usability of a new system, or conducting an empirical study aimed at validating a new theory, more participants are better. It takes more time and effort to run 20 subjects than 10 and it may be harder to find 100 people than 30 for focus groups, but the advantages are significant. When you involve large numbers of people, you get a broader, more representative sample. With a small number of people, your chances of getting outliers—those who are significantly faster or slower, inexperienced or expert—are vastly increased. For empirical studies, results that may be statistically ambiguous with a small group may be much clearer with a larger sample.

Unfortunately, for some research projects, a large sample is extremely difficult, if not completely impossible. Fortunately, this is not a cause for despair. *Case studies*, in which researchers study a small number of participants (possibly as few as one) in depth, can be useful tools for gathering requirements and evaluating interfaces.

A case study is an in-depth study of a specific instance (or a small number of instances) within a specific real-life context. Close examination of individual cases can be used to build understanding, generate theories and hypotheses, present evidence for the existence of certain behavior, or to provide insight that would otherwise be difficult to gather. Case studies often use theoretical frameworks to guide both the collection of data from multiple sources and the analysis of the data (Yin, 2014). However, statistical analyses are not the goal. Instead, case studies use careful analysis of carefully selected subjects to generate interesting and novel insights, ideally with an eye on developing general principles that might facilitate understanding of other cases.

Case studies present a different set of challenges from studies involving larger numbers of participants. The first question you might face is determining whether or not a case study is appropriate. Given the small sample size, identifying appropriate participants may be even more important than it is for larger studies. The duration, content, and format of the study will depend upon your goals and resources. Finally, data analysis and interpretation are particularly important: you may want to be careful about making broad, sweeping claims based on your study of one case.

Research Methods in Human-Computer Interaction. http://dx.doi.org/10.1016/B978-0-12-805390-4.00007-8

In a truly reflective style, we look closely at an example of HCI case study research to understand what is involved. Close examination of this one case will illustrate when case studies are appropriate, how they might be designed, how cases are chosen, how data might be collected, and how the data can be interpreted. Examination of this specific case provides us with a clearer understanding of the application of case study research.

7.2 OBSERVING SARA: A CASE STUDY OF A CASE STUDY

Concerns over the limits of narrowly constructed usability studies led Shinohara and Tenenberg to conduct an in-depth examination of a blind person's use of assistive technologies (Shinohara and Tenenberg, 2007). By examining the use of a range of technologies in the user's home, they were able to address several questions that would have been difficult to consider in a lab-based usability study. Specifically, they looked at types of task that were common across multiple technologies, including both digital and physical objects, in order to identify general strategies and understand the trade-offs involved in hardware and software design.

Shinohara and Tenenberg used a series of semistructured interviews (see Chapter 8) to collect the observations that form the basis of the case study. In a series of 6, 2-hour sessions in her home, Sara (not her real name) demonstrated how she used technologies such as tactile wristwatches and screen readers; discussed early memories of using various objects and her reactions to them; and imagined improved designs for various objects or tasks. Notes, audio recordings, interviewer reactions, and photographs from these sessions provided the raw data for subsequent analysis. Insights and theories based on early observations were shared with the subject for validation and clarification.

Analysis and presentation of the case study data took multiple forms. Twelve tasks were recorded in terms of their intentions/goals, limitations, workarounds, and desires for future improvements (see excerpt in Table 7.1). This table can be used to compare and group seemingly unrelated tasks in search of common themes. Detailed descriptions—complete with representative quotations—of Sara's use of a tactile watch and screen-reader software complement this table with illustrative details. For example, discussion of the tactile watch led to a deeper understanding of the importance that Sara placed on aesthetics and her desire to be unobtrusive, as she preferred the comfortable, silent tactile watch to a talking watch, which was both noisier and larger. Examination of Sara's use of a screen reader led to the observation that she would examine all possible options, possibly even restarting from scratch, in order to achieve a goal (Shinohara and Tenenberg, 2007).

Building upon the insights from the individual tasks, Shinohara and Tenenberg identified several general insights that could guide the design of improved tools. Examples included the importance of designs that would not make users feel self-conscious when interacting with sighted friends or colleagues; the importance of control, efficiency, and portability; the need for tools that ease the process of

Table 7.1 Analysis of Sara's Tasks

Object/Task	Description	Intentions/Goals	Limitation (What Exactly is Going on?)	Explanation (Why Does the Limitation Happen?)	Workaround (How is the Limitation Overcome?)	Usability of Workaround (Efficiency, Memorability, Satisfaction)	Wish (Desires for the Future)
Navigating with JAWS	Incorrect key strokes may cause her to lose her bearings	Execute an action through specific hotkeys	JAWS is doing something other than the intended action	Other keys may have been hit by mistake	Keeps trying different key combinations to execute intended action	Satisfactory but not efficient	JAWS could help gather her bearings before executing commands
Searching for A CD to play	Linearly searches all CDs	To select a specific CD to listen to	She cannot quickly read CD covers	CD jewel cases not easily identifiable. Labels do not fit on case spines	Labeled CDs, mentally organized by preference, read one at a time	Slow but satisfactory	
Organizing CD collection	CD collection is placed on two shelves, in almost no particular order	To distinguish CDs in player, preferred ones from least favorites	Discs are not organized in conventional means	She does not have much time; she has a lot of CDs	Three discs currently in CD player have a special spot on CD shelf	Efficient, quick and straightforward	

JAWS refers to the assistive screen-reading software used to turn text on the screen into speech (http://www.freedomscientific.com/Products/Blindness/JAWS [accessed 19.03.16]).
Excerpted from Shinohara and Tenenberg (2007). Copyright ACM.

distinguishing between similar items (such as CDs); and the need for flexibility and interoperability.

Although Sara does not provide a comprehensive picture of the needs and concerns of blind people, the investigations of her needs and goals led to valuable insights that might apply to many other blind people.

The remainder of this chapter uses this specific case study to develop a broader understanding of case studies in general.

7.3 WHAT IS A CASE STUDY?

A case study is a detailed examination of one or more specific situations. The case study described above helped the researchers to understand how Sara used a variety of technologies to accomplish multiple tasks. They were specifically interested in understanding "what technologies were most valued and used, when they were used and for what purpose" (Shinohara and Tenenberg, 2007). Conducting the research in Sara's home helped the investigators gain insights into how she actually addressed real challenges, as opposed to the more contrived results that might have been seen in the lab.

Four key aspects of this design can be used to describe case studies:

- in-depth investigation of a small number of cases;
- examination in context;
- multiple data sources;
- emphasis on qualitative data and analysis.

7.3.1 IN-DEPTH INVESTIGATION OF A SMALL NUMBER OF CASES

The substantial effort needed to conduct a thorough investigation of each case leads directly to a practical limit on the number of cases that can be included in any given study. The entire Shinohara and Tenenberg (Shinohara and Tenenberg, 2007) study was focused on a single individual: data was collected in her house over the course of approximately 12 hours, with postmeeting debriefings, transcriptions of audio tapes, and photos compiled for analysis. The substantial effort required to collect and collate this body of data is difficult—if not impossible—to replicate for larger numbers of participants.

In this regard, case studies are quite different from experiments that ask large numbers of participants to perform specific, well-defined tasks, leading to results that can be interpreted as applying to a broad range of users. Case studies use in-depth, broad examinations of a small number of cases in order to discuss issues that might provide insights not available in larger user studies. However, this insight comes at a cost, as the focus on a small number of participants increases the risk that the chosen cases might be somehow unrepresentative, thus limiting the generalizability of the conclusions.

Although case studies are small, they need not be limited to only one case. Involving two or more cases is a highly recommended technique for increasing the credibility of both analyses and results (Yin, 2014). As we will see, the precise defini-tion of a case is not clear (Section 7.5.2). Was Sara's study an example of a case study with one case—the individual—or with twelve cases—the tasks? Answers to these questions are not necessarily obvious.

Case studies are closely related to ethnographic research (Chapter 9) in that both approaches involve close, qualitative examination of a small number—often only one—of situations. Although case studies often use ethnographic observation tech-niques, classic ethnographic studies are usually more in-depth, conducted over lon-ger periods of time, and more likely to involve a mix of participation and observation than case studies. As the line between case studies and ethnography is often some-what blurred, it is often best to focus on the techniques used for data collection and analysis, rather than on the label applied to the study.

7.3.2 EXAMINATION IN CONTEXT

Lab-based usability studies have a huge role to play in HCI research. The controlled environments of usability labs are wonderful for removing undesired external influ-ences, but they do not provide a very realistic picture of how people really work. Computer use generally takes place at homes or offices that have distractions, com-peting concerns demanding attention, and the stress of multitasking in the hopes of meeting competing deadlines. As these factors do not arise in controlled usability labs, observations made in the lab might not generalize to "real-world" behavior.

Unlike lab-based experiments, case studies focus on observation of phenomena in a meaningful context that is beyond the control of the investigator. By observing and closely watching activities as they occur in the real world, free from the prede-termined goals and narrowly defined questions that often accompany usability stud-ies and controlled experiments, researchers can use case studies to develop detailed understandings of interaction techniques and coping strategies—understandings that might be hard (if not impossible) to develop through usability studies. In this sense, case studies can be very similar to ethnographic research (Chapter 9), although case studies generally (although not always) lack the participatory aspect associated with some ethnographic studies. Further comparison between case studies and ethnogra-phies can be found in Chapter 9.

7.3.3 MULTIPLE DATA SOURCES

Case studies often rely upon multiple data collection techniques to act as sources of corroborating evidence. In Shinohara and Tenenberg (Shinohara and Tenenberg, 2007), three types of technology biographies (Blythe et al., 2002) were used: demonstrations of devices (*technology tours*), reflections on memories of early use of and reactions to devices (*personal histories*), and wishful thinking about possible technological innova-tions (*guided speculation*). More generally, these data sources are examples of three commonly used types of case study data: artifacts, observation, and interviews. The case study of Sara also involved the impressions and subjective responses of the researchers.

These three approaches to technology biography provide opportunities for gathering insights that might be difficult to acquire using only one method. By asking Sara to talk about both past experiences and future aspirations, the research design allowed for the possibility of understanding changes in her relationship to technology. Sara's demonstrations of the tools provided an example of current use of artifacts. The examination of tools (such as the tactile watch and screen-reading software) can be an important source of data for case studies, particularly when you are interested in understanding how users complete tasks.

Multiple data sources can also provide corroborating evidence to increase your confidence in observations. In a case study of workplace information management, you might start your data collection with interviews of employees. These discussions provide useful data but they are limited: participants may have different understandings of practices and habits, they may be unwilling to comment on the details of their work, or they may simply forget important details (Chapter 8). Investigation of the artifacts of their work—computer files, paper records, archives, and e-mail messages—can provide concrete understanding of actual practices, free from the limitations of interviews. This analysis may confirm statements made in interviews, thus increasing your confidence in their validity. The use of multiple sources to provide corroborating evidence is known as *data triangulation*—a reference to the practice of taking measurements relative to multiple known reference points in order to precisely measure location.

Multiple data sources can also help deal with any concerns about the quality of the data provided by any single source. Due to the relatively small number of cases involved, the use of any single data collection technique with a particular case may not give you the data that you really need. For example, if Sara had some residual vision that allowed her to make use of some visual display components on a computer screen she might not be an appropriate participant in the case study. We have more to say about selecting cases in Section 7.7, but for now, we mention that simply asking Sara about her use of technology might not have revealed her use of visual displays. A combination of interviews along with direct observation of her work might provide more appropriate measurements; logs of computer activity—taken when she wasn't being directly observed—might be even more realistic.

Of course, the use of multiple data sources does not guarantee nice, clean corroboration of results—if only it were that easy. Two scenarios may arise that make life more interesting. Your data sources might diverge, with each source of data covering different observations. This is not necessarily a problem, as all of the observations may have some validity. When this happens, your use of multiple data sources has not increased the validity of your analyses—you simply have many observations that fail to support each other. You may need to be cautious about your interpretation, refraining from strong claims until you can find some corroboration.

The possibility of contradiction is a more troubling concern. Suppose one source says that something is true, while another says that it is not? You may need to look carefully at the specific details of the claims and the specific sources, in order to determine which is plausible. Contradictions may also motivate you to dig deeper, asking additional questions of existing sources or consulting new data sources in order to develop explanations that resolve the inconsistencies.

Case studies often draw upon many data sources. Documents, data archives, direct observation, and participant observation (similar to ethnography—see Chapter 9) are just a few of the possibilities (Yin, 2014).

7.3.4 EMPHASIS ON QUALITATIVE DATA AND ANALYSIS

The researchers were not specifically interested in measuring how quickly Sara completed various tasks, how many errors she made, or how quickly she learned to use an interface. Case studies always contain a substantial qualitative component, focusing on questions that help describe or explain behavior (Yin, 2014). In Sara's case, questions might have included "How did she use technology to achieve various goals?" or "which tools did she use in a given circumstance?" The data needed to answer questions such as these tends to be more qualitative than quantitative.

Case studies can certainly include quantitative components measuring traditional metrics, such as task completion time, but these measures are not usually the sole focus of the investigation. In Sara's case, the investigators might have measured the time it took her to complete certain tasks or how frequently she used the tactile watch. As interesting as these measurements might have been, they would not have been sufficient to meet the goal of the study: a deeper understanding of her use of assistive technology. The qualitative interviews, which provided room for in-depth discussion, elaboration of concerns, and discussion of contextual issues, were crucial for achieving this goal.

Quantitative data might be used as a triangulation tool for corroborating results. In this case, Sara's frequency of use of the tactile watch might be used to provide supporting evidence for interview comments describing her perceptions of how she uses the watch. If you choose to use quantitative data in a case study, you should be acutely aware of its limitations: as your case or cases are unlikely to be representative of a larger class, statistical comparisons are generally not appropriate. Having collected data on the frequency of Sara's use of the tactile watch over a period of weeks, investigators might have sufficient data to investigate how Sara's use of the watch changed over time, but they would not have been able to make any comparison between Sara and other tactile watch wearers, or blind people in general.

7.4 GOALS OF HCI CASE STUDIES

Goals of traditional qualitative case studies generally fall into one of three categories (Yin, 2014):

- *exploration*: understanding novel problems or situations, often with the hopes of informing new designs;
- *explanation*: developing models that can be used to understand a context of technology use; and

- *description*: documenting a system, a context of technology use, or the process that led to a proposed design.

  HCI case studies address these and one additional goal:
- *demonstration*: showing how a new tool was successfully used.

7.4.1 EXPLORATION

New research projects—whether in a lab or in a product development environment—often begin with an incomplete or preliminary understanding of a problem and its context. Case studies can provide invaluable feedback when a project team is in the early stages of understanding both the problem and the merits of possible solutions. Such studies would have members of the project team examining the goals and constraints facing likely users. Using processes similar to those used in ethnographic work (see Chapter 9), researchers might observe how potential users currently accomplish tasks, use available tools, and respond to problematic situations. The insights that result from this inquiry can inform both system design and further investigation.

7.4.2 EXPLANATION

Technologies in general, and computer systems in particular, are often used in ways that were not considered in the initial design, often with impacts that are completely unexpected. Case studies of tools in use can provide understanding of these uses and outcomes. An examination of the use of a tool for browsing photo collections on mobile devices provides an example of an explanatory study: in-depth interviews with nine users provided substantial insight into how the tool was used and how specific designs might engage users (Naaman et al., 2008).

The Extreme Cases sidebar describes a case study of the use of GPS location devices for tracking parolees. In addition to explaining how these systems affect—often in surprising ways—the behavior of the individuals required to wear them, this case study provided the basis for reconsideration of broader issues regarding mobility and privacy.

EXTREME CASES

Cases are not always selected because they are representative or typical. *Edge cases*—extreme or unusual examples—often present combinations of characteristics that make them particularly worthy of further study. This strategy is used extensively in medical education, where profiles of individuals with puzzling and unusual symptoms are presented as compelling challenges for budding diagnosticians.

As HCI researchers often use case studies as tools for understanding the technology usage and needs of populations of potential users, these investigations often focus upon representative users and use cases, omitting extreme cases. As understandable as this strategy might be, a focus on general cases may miss out on some of the insights that might be gained from examining less familiar perspectives.

Geo-location services—tools that combine global positioning system (GPS) facilities with data and communication tools—have spawned numerous computing tools and services. Possibilities include facilities for finding nearby friends or restaurants; games; educational systems based on the location of items of interest in natural environments; and location-based data collection covering entire cities.

A case study based on extremes was used to explore some of the questions regarding perceptions of location and privacy (Troshynski et al., 2008). This investigation examined the habits and perceptions of a group of sex offenders who were required to have their locations tracked via GPS as part of their parole agreements. Building from theories that argue that marginalized groups may possess instructive insights into society, these researchers hoped to use this extreme population to reconsider HCI questions about location-based systems. Data collection involved semistructured focus group sessions with 10 parolees who were already participating in a pilot study on the use of GPS for parole supervision for sex offenders. Although several individuals participated, comments were analyzed as an undifferentiated whole, making this a single-case study of the group of parolees.

Analysis of the focus group data led to the identification of three main themes describing the impact of the system on the participants. The GPS systems structured their perception of space, making them acutely aware of how far they were from home and how close they may have come to forbidden locations such as schools and parks. The systems also constrained their time: the need to regularly charge batteries limited their ability to spend long periods of time away from convenient sources of electricity. The parolees' sense of their bodies was also changed, as the ankle-mounted GPS units both made certain clothing choices (such as short pants) impractical and effectively prohibited swimming, bathing, or other activities that might have exposed the unit to the possibility of water damage. The researchers used these insights to fuel a more general consideration of location-based interfaces in specific social and cultural contexts (Troshynski et al., 2008).

The value of these extreme cases lies in the distance between their perspectives and motivations and those of "typical" users of GPS-based computing systems. Generalization was not the goal of this study—it is hard to see how the concerns of a group of parolees who were required to use these systems might be applied to voluntary users of location-based systems for game playing or locating friends. Instead, the comments of this atypical user group provided a richer understanding that might not have emerged through investigation of the expected case.

7.4.3 DESCRIPTION

A description of a system and its impact can be of interest. In some cases, particularly those involving new design methodologies, the process behind the design may be the focus of a case study. In general, a single-case study describes a problem, the steps that were taken to understand it, the details of the eventual design, and the lessons learned that might be of more general interest. Case studies that describe design processes and results have been written for a wide variety of topics, including interfaces for people with Alzheimer's disease (Cohene et al., 2007) (see sidebar), fire alert services in South Africa (Davies et al., 2008), browsers for a collection of music written by a composer (Hochheiser, 2000), and mobile interfaces for sharing navigation information in cities (Bilandzic et al., 2008).

INTERFACES FOR PEOPLE WITH ALZHEIMER'S DISEASE

The process of developing a novel interface or interaction technique is often as interesting, if not more interesting, than the resulting product. This is particularly true for design efforts that tackle novel problems involving challenging contexts of use.

A University of Toronto project involving the design of an assistive technology tool for people affected by Alzheimer's disease provided the basis for an intriguing case study (Cohene et al., 2007). This project was based on a body of prior work that firmly established the importance of reminiscences for people with Alzheimer's disease. Specifically, the researchers were interested in developing multimedia "life histories" that people with Alzheimer's disease could use to recall and relive old memories. The case described the process of developing a system to be used by a 91-year-old woman named Laura.[1] The participation of Laura and her two daughters formed a crucial part of the study.

The initial phases of the study included exploratory efforts aimed at developing an understanding of the challenges faced by people with Alzheimer's disease and their families. Although the study was focused on developing a tool specifically for Laura, the researchers conducted a variety of inquiries aimed at providing greater understanding of the needs and abilities of individuals with Alzheimer's disease. The researchers conducted a modified ethnographic inquiry (see Chapter 9), interacting with groups of individuals engaged in recreational therapy activities. These observations provided a detailed understanding of the range of abilities and impairments of the participants, leading to a set of design principles. Discussions with caretakers and other experts formed the basis for a set of categories and themes that would assist with reminiscing.

Interviews with Laura's family members informed both the content of the life histories and an understanding of important needs and outcomes. Family members also completed a "family workbook" that contained storyboards describing stories that would be recounted with the tool to be developed.

---

[1] All names of participants in this study were changed to protect their privacy.

Photographs, home videos, and music were collected that formed the basis for the multimedia components of the tool. This data provided the basis for several generations of prototype, culminating in designs including multimedia DVDs to be controlled by a customized input device and an interactive photo album, with pages that could be displayed on a TV monitor. These descriptive elements in the case study give a detailed picture of how the research was conducted and how it informed the system design.

Elements of explanation and demonstration can be found in the discussion of how the prototypes were evaluated and refined. As with many HCI projects that examine new tools, this effort involved having the participant make frequent use of the tool over an extended period of time—in this case, eight times in 4 weeks.

This led to ideas for refining some designs, including modifying the design of the one-button remote control, while abandoning others, such as the interactive photo album, which was perceived to be too cognitively demanding. Follow-up interviews with family members confirmed initial hypotheses that the system would have multiple benefits for the participants, including providing perspective, sharing experiences, and communicating.

This project as a whole is an exploratory case study. As relatively little work has been done on user interfaces for people with Alzheimer's disease, the description of a successful process is valuable in and of itself. The design ideas presented raise interesting possibilities, but in many ways they raise more questions than they answer. The broad range of cognitive impairments experienced by people with Alzheimer's disease and the varying impacts that their condition has on family members makes generalization very hard: what works well for one individual and their family might not work well for others. Extending the applicability of this work—particularly by scaling the design process—was clearly a goal of the research team, as they describe further efforts involving additional participants and improving the process of designing life histories.

The intensive nature of the research—requiring substantial time commitments both from the individual with Alzheimer's disease and from family members who are dealing with the emotional strain of the decline of a family member—made the work extremely resource intensive. The elaboration of the design process and the completion of one specific design are important contributions, even if the resulting design does not generalize to other users.

The most broadly applicable results from this story lie in the lessons learned. The authors concluded that new design methods and principles were needed for working with individuals affected with Alzheimer's disease that active participation was more stimulating than passive, and that working with both the patients and their family members throughout the entire design process was necessary. Practical concerns included the resource-intensive nature of the research, the emotional commitment required of the family members, the need to make the approach practical for larger numbers of families, and the need for standards for evaluation (Cohene et al., 2007). Although drawn from this particular project, these insights might be extremely valuable to others interested in conducting related research.

7.4.4 DEMONSTRATION

Usually shorter and less in-depth than descriptive case studies, demonstrations are often found in papers describing new designs. Short anecdotes describing how one or more individuals successfully used a new tool to complete one or more appropriate tasks often complement usability studies, controlled experiments, and other data documenting the success of the design.

Demonstration case studies can play an important role in describing the success of a new design or tool, particularly when a controlled user study is inappropriate or impractical. This is often the case with a complete tool, which may have many elements and multiple metrics for evaluation. Demonstration case studies can also be appropriate in cases where the broad scope of the interface may preclude the use of a controlled study.

Demonstration case studies tend to follow a common pattern. The report generally starts with an introduction of the participants and their context of use. Other elements often found in the report include descriptions of how the participants used the system, problems they faced, strengths of the system design, and discussions of subjective responses. See the Interfaces for People with Quadriplegia sidebar for a discussion of such a case study.

INTERFACES FOR PEOPLE WITH QUADRIPLEGIA

Building interfaces for quadriplegic people is a significant challenge: without the use of their hands, fingers, or feet, these individuals may be restricted to using input devices that consist of a single action, such as blowing on a straw or pressing a single switch. Interfaces for such users are generally based on some form of scanning: a graphical window on the computer screen contains a grid of buttons that are scanned—highlighted in some predictable order—with each button being active for a given amount of time. When the desired button is highlighted, the user activates the switch to make a selection.

Steriadis and Constantinou (2003) include a demonstration case study as a partial validation of the proposed design of a new interface architecture. This paper presented widgets for single-switch input devices ("wifsids") that support a model of button selection appropriate for both discrete text input from the keyboard and continuous mouse movement. These widgets were used to build a set of applications that would run in Windows, supporting cursor movement, keyboard entry, selection of applications, macros for common functionality, and other features.

The case study described how the system was used by a 35-year-old man with amyotrophic lateral sclerosis (ALS), which left him bedridden and unable to speak. The paper describes how the participant decided to use a button between his knees to make selections, after having rejected other inputs as being difficult to use, cumbersome, or unattractive. The description of the participant's success in learning how to use the system, and in using it for communicating with family and the Internet, forms an important part of the description. Details of his use of the various components, along with initial difficulties and their resolutions, are also described (Steriadis and Constantinou, 2003).

This individual's success may not be generalizable: the system might not work so well for others. However, this is not the only evaluation found in the paper. An empirical study of how the typing rates of two additional quadriplegic users varied with word-prediction schemes formed the basis for a discussion of factors that might influence typing rate. Even though this study only involved two users, it provides some insight into the factors that influence success in using the tool to type text. The case study and the empirical study work together in a complementary fashion to demonstrate the strengths and limitations of the proposed system.

The four classes of case study are not mutually exclusive. Sara's case study has elements of both exploration and explanation. The Interfaces for People with Alzheimer's Disease sidebar describes a study involving elements of exploration, description, and demonstration.

7.5 TYPES OF CASE STUDY

7.5.1 INTRINSIC OR INSTRUMENTAL

Case studies are often conducted to shed light on a specific situation. You may be working with a client to design a new organizational website. A case study of the client's work processes, corporate organization, and information-sharing practices and procedures would inform your design process, but the results would be likely to apply only to that client. These *intrinsic* studies (Stake, 1995) describe cases that are of interest to a particular situation.

Case studies can also work towards developing a broader understanding. These *instrumental* case studies ask questions in the hope of generating insights that go beyond the case at hand. They become tools that lead to a broader understanding. Sara's case study involved the instrumental goal of identifying difficulties and workarounds that might be used by many others—not just Sara (Shinohara and Tenenberg, 2007).

Case studies can be both intrinsic and instrumental: it might be argued that Sara's case is both interesting in its own right (intrinsic) and aimed at broader understanding (instrumental).

7.5.2 SINGLE CASE OR MULTIPLE CASES

Although Sara's case study focused on one person's use of technology, case studies are certainly not limited to single cases. The use of multiple cases may initially seem to be a bit of a contradiction in terms, but there is nothing strange about doing case-study research with two or more cases.

To understand why you might use multiple cases when one might seem to do just as well, we must consider one of the important goals of many instrumental case studies: generalization. An in-depth discussion of one individual (such as Sara) is interesting, but the real value in a study of this sort lies in generating insights that can be applied to a broader class of design challenges. We might be pleased if Sara's case study led to some suggestions for the design of assistive devices that would help Sara with her daily challenges, but we would often like to go further. If the case study led to insights that apply to many blind people, any resulting designs might be useful to a much broader range of blind users.

If our goal is to generalize, we would ideally argue that our cases are somehow representative. They must be similar to the members of the broader group that is the focus of our generalization, at least in ways that are relevant to the study at hand. A single case may or may not be representative, and we may not have any way of evaluating whether or not any single case provides a basis for generalization. From the description of her tasks and challenges, we might infer that Sara is a reasonably representative blind college student, but we really can't say for sure. She may be more (or less) experienced with computers than other blind college students, more (or less) willing to try new technologies, and so on. Casting a broader net, we might wonder if insights gained from interviewing Sara can apply to blind people of different ages or education levels, such as working professionals or elementary school students.

Just as scientific experiments of all sorts rely upon replication to provide increased confidence in observed results, case studies can use multiple cases to provide critical support for confidence in the generality of any results. Suppose another college student had been interviewed, following the same protocol that was used with Sara. If the observations and insights gained from the two studies were similar, we might be more inclined to believe that these results were applicable to blind college students in general. This use of closely comparable cases to demonstrate consistency of results is known as *literal replication* (Yin, 2014).

The analogy between case studies and other scientific experiments can lead us to another useful form of multiple-case studies. Experimentation relies upon contrasts between situations that are similar but differ in specific, controlled ways. When these situations are created correctly, observed differences in experimental outcome can be attributed to the differences between the groups. Multiple-case studies might use cases with specific differences in much the same manner. Imagine an extension of Sara's study that involved a blind executive instead of another student. Differences between Sara and the executive in terms of how they use technology might be due to differences in their occupations.[2] The use of comparable cases to generate results that differ in ways that can be explained by differences between the cases is known as *theoretical replication* (Yin, 2014). The International Children's Digital Library sidebar describes a multiple-case study involving theoretical replication.

---

[2] Differences in age and economic resources might also play a role. Strictly controlling for differences is difficult with cases involving human participants.

THE INTERNATIONAL CHILDREN'S DIGITAL LIBRARY

The International Children's Digital Library (ICDL, http://www. childrenslibrary.org) is an online repository of thousands of books from around the world. Built "to help young people understand the value of tolerance and respect for diverse cultures, languages and ideas" (Druin et al., 2007), the ICDL provides interfaces specifically designed to support children in searching for and reading books. Search tools support strategies that children might use for finding books (such as the color of the cover, the types of character, or the length of the book) and several reader tools support a variety of reading strategies (Druin et al., 2007).

The ICDL's ambitious goals of serving a diverse group of children from all over the world presented a challenge and an opportunity. By studying how children in different countries with different economic and social backgrounds, used the ICDL, the research team hoped to gain a better understanding of how children in varied settings would interact with the ICDL. As both the interface and content are multilingual, they could examine the use of this single tool in diverse contexts, in order to understand how usage patterns differ across cultural boundaries.

The resulting multiple-case study involved students in four distinct geographical locations: Munich, Germany; Le Ceiba, Honduras; Wellington, New Zealand; and Chicago, USA. Three 8-year-old children participated in each location, along with parents, teachers, and administrators. Data collected over the course of 4 years included open-ended interviews with both children and adult participants, drawings that children made to illustrate their ideas about libraries, and book reviews that the children wrote. Grounded theory and content analysis approaches (see Chapter 11) were used to analyze the 152 interviews, 236 drawings, and 301 book reviews that were collected over the course of the study.

Although there were multiple participants at each site, data analysis focused on understanding how use patterns and responses differ across these varied circumstances. As the individual children were not the units of analysis, this case study can be seen as a holistic case, multiple-case study. The four groups can be seen as theoretical replications, with their varied backgrounds providing opportunities to examine how observed phenomena differ across cultures.

As differences between the groups were largely attributable to preexisting cultural differences, the results of this study demonstrate the likely outcome of theoretical replication. All children seemed to appreciate the digital library and the range of books that they read over time increased. Children in all four locations found books in languages that they did not know to be difficult or frustrating and they all liked the search tools but preferred to read physical books. They all valued libraries and children in all groups became more interested in learning about different cultures. Differences in responses may have been due to specific differences in circumstances. Compared to children

(Continued)

THE INTERNATIONAL CHILDREN'S DIGITAL LIBRARY—CONT'D

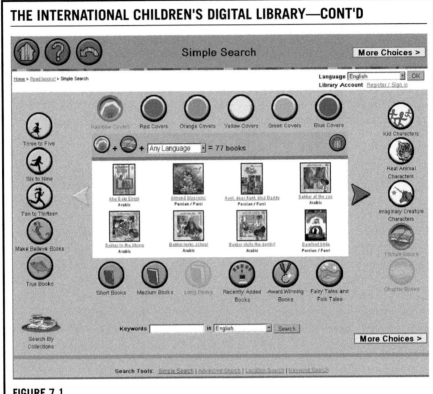

FIGURE 7.1

The search interface for the International Children's Digital Library provides young readers with search tools designed to meet their interests.

From the International Children's Library (http://www.childrenslibrary.org).

in the other countries, German children showed less increase in confidence in their ability to use technology effectively. However, the German children may have started out with higher levels of exposure to technology. Similarly, children in the United States—who live in a relatively homogenous environment—showed greater increase in interest in diverse cultures than children from the other, more diverse cultures (Figure 7.1) (Druin et al., 2007).

Increased confidence in the results may be a compelling argument for involving multiple cases in your studies. Multiple cases help to combat criticisms that you have chosen a single case that is unrepresentative. Any single case can be idiosyncratic, but multiple cases are much less likely to be unrepresentative in the same ways. "Cherry-picking" a single case to support hypotheses or justify a preexisting model might be possible, but this sort of bias—whether intentional or not—is less likely with multiple-case studies.

Despite the advantages of multiple-case studies, there may be some times when a single case design is the more—or only—appropriate option. If you are studying the use of a custom piece of software in a single workplace, you may be unable to find additional cases. Single-case designs are the only option in such cases (Yin, 2014). Cost—both in terms of financial and human resources—can also play a role in the decision to use a single-case design. Case studies can often be labor intensive, requiring extensive effort for preparation, data collection, and analysis. You may be unable to find the time needed for additional cases, as much as you might want to include them.

The goals of your study may play a role in determining whether you should use a single case or multiple cases. Multiple cases are most useful when you are interested in generalizing your results, but this may not be your goal. Some case studies may describe a unique case that cannot easily be compared to others, making a multiple-case study difficult, if not impossible. Other studies—such as Sara's—may be exploratory in nature, focusing on the generation of ideas and formulation of questions for future research (see Section 7.4.1). These exploratory case studies might lead to in-depth inquiries with broader populations, using surveys or other less expensive data collection approaches.

Although generalization may be appealing, extrapolating from a small set of cases to a larger population is not something that should be done lightly. Even if you do choose to use multiple cases, you should always be very cautious about any claims of generality. Some researchers feel that generalizing from case studies is always inappropriate—without a broad-based sample that can be shown to adequately represent a population, how can you conclude that any of your findings apply to all members of the larger group? Multiple cases can help you identify phenomena that might apply across larger groups, but you would need to conduct further research to truly justify claims of generality. By all means, look for these trends, and use multiple cases to show that they apply in multiple instances, but steer clear of any claims that imply that they will always apply.

7.5.3 EMBEDDED OR HOLISTIC

Even with only one participant, Sara's case study may be more complex than you might initially think. Although only one individual is involved, this case study discusses 12 tasks. Each of these tasks is a *unit of analysis*—a distinct subject of investigation. The inclusion of multiple units of analysis within a single case is referred to as an *embedded* case study, in contrast to *holistic* studies that address only one unit in each case (Yin, 2014).

This distinction arises at least in part from the nature of the questions being asked: as Sara uses multiple tools in different ways to address daily activities, any investigation of her use of technology should discuss these differences. A case study that did not address these differences might miss many interesting insights. Other examples of embedded designs might include academic departments in a university or designers on a product team.

Integration of the multiple units of analysis is an important aspect of embedded case study design. In Sara's case, insights from the various tasks were combined in a classification of challenges that she faced, including control, efficiency, portability, and interoperability. Just as these categories provide additional understanding of the individual tasks, individual units of analysis in an embedded design might be grouped or viewed from common perspectives.

The inclusion of multiple participants in a case does not necessarily imply an embedded case study. If participants are not discussed individually, with analyses identifying similarities and differences between them, they are not distinct units of analysis. In this case, the group is the unit of analysis in a holistic study. A study of virtual collaboration in a school in Finland provides an illustration (Lakkala et al., 2007). Although the class involved 14 students and seven teachers, the case study does not discuss students and teachers in any detail. Specific comments from both teachers and students are cited in the paper, but there is no attempt to discuss any of the participants as individuals, making this a single-case, holistic study. The sidebar on the International Children's Library presents an example of a case study involving a theoretical replication across four comparable groups, each of which is a single unit of analysis.

A paper discussing strategies for sustaining a "community computing infrastructure" provides an interesting example of an embedded case study (Farooq et al., 2007b). This single-case study examined an online community aimed at supporting professional development for teachers. Four "design interventions"—contact and bug forms, "needed features" group, task list, and help desk—were chosen as the units of analysis, due to their differences in terms of goals, primary mode of communication, participants, and implications for use. Separate discussions of each of these interventions complemented a general examination of how they worked together to support the continuing success of the community.

Although the distinction between holistic and embedded analysis might ideally be made before the study is conducted, the need for multiple units of analysis may not be clear until after data collection has started. A study of the use of a groupware tool in a corporate setting might start out as a holistic study of the tool's use in a given group, only to evolve with time to include embedded analyses of the differing tasks for which the tool would be used, the roles of the various members in the group, or the types of project for which it might be used.

7.6 RESEARCH QUESTIONS AND HYPOTHESES

As with almost any other form of research, a good case study is built on the foundations of a theoretical model. Although these theories might not be cleanly testable hypotheses that can be easily disproved, they can be used to describe what you are looking for, what you think you might find, and how you will use your data to support your theories.

Roughly speaking, there are four components of a case study design[3]:

- questions;
- hypotheses or propositions;
- units of analysis; and
- a data analysis plan.

Research *questions* describe the goals of your study—what you are interested in understanding.

Hypotheses or propositions are statements of what you expect to find. The *unit of analysis* defines the granularity of your study—what exactly you are focusing on. Are you studying an organization, a group of people, an individual, or individual activities? These questions will guide your data collection. The final component—a *data analysis plan*—is described in Section 7.8.

Just as in other forms of research, your research questions and hypotheses guide your efforts. You may be interested in understanding how users accomplish certain goals or tools, how the introduction of a new tool changes the workflows and patterns in an organization, or what a team needs from a new collaboration tool. Even if your case study is exploratory or descriptive, you should try to make your research questions and propositions explicit.

Taken together, your research questions and hypotheses form a preliminary model that will guide your development of the case study. By mapping out your interests and the range of concerns that you are trying to address, you will gain greater understanding of the criteria that you will use to choose your cases, the data sources that you might need to include, and how you will conduct your analysis. The approach of ignoring theory in favor of simply collecting data indiscriminately can be a recipe for failure (Yin, 2014).

In Sara's case study, the researchers were interested in understanding how a blind person might use a variety of assistive technologies to accomplish tasks and to recover from task failures using workarounds. These questions led to several propositions. The investigators expected to see common types of failures and workaround strategies. They also expected that the choice of implementing features in hardware or software might influence user interactions, including failures and responses to those failures.

A different set of research questions might have led the researchers to a very different case study. If, for example, a preliminary study had led them to believe that education or socioeconomic status might play an important role in determining how blind people use technology, they might have chosen a multiple-case design, including participants with backgrounds that differed in these relevant respects. They might also have asked a broader range of questions about background and included consideration about other aspects of their participants' lives.

---

[3] This list is based on Robert K. Yin's list of five components. His list divides the "data analysis plan" into two components: the logic linking the data to the propositions and the criteria for interpreting the findings (Yin, 2014).

A study of sociability in massive, multiplayer, online games provides another example of the important role of theory in case study design. In Ducheneaut et al. (2007), the researchers were interested in asking whether social spaces in these games acted as "third spaces," where players would socialize, just as coffee shops and other spaces support socializing in the real world. This question led them to choose a particular online game that provided strong support for social spaces, a data collection strategy involving active participation in these spaces in the game, and an analysis strategy that combined analysis of observations from their participation with quantitative analysis of activity in the game.

Once you have defined your questions and hypotheses, you can move on to consider other questions of case study design, including the type of case study, selection of cases, data collection, and data analysis.

7.7 CHOOSING CASES

Single-case studies may present little, if any, difficulty in case selection. Case studies often involve cases that are somehow unique or incomparable to others. Intrinsic case studies limit you to consideration of the specific instance of interest. Convenience can also be a factor—you may choose a specific case "because it's there." This is often the case when you are not particularly concerned about generalizing: when conducting an exploratory case study aimed at building initial understandings of a situation, any case might work (see Section 7.11). In all of these instances, selection is straightforward: you work with what you have available. Otherwise, you will want to put careful consideration into your criteria for selecting cases.

There are a few general guidelines that apply to almost any sort of case study. Like ethnographic investigations (Chapter 9), case studies require a great deal of time, careful preparation, and often close cooperation with one or more individuals or organizations. Given these challenges, the individuals, groups, organizations, or systems that you choose should be chosen carefully. You will want to try to identify case study participants who have an interest in committing some of their own resources to work with you to make the research successful. You should also try to maximize convenience, working with geographically convenient participants whenever possible.

Further considerations in your choice of cases will be driven by the details of your research design. If you are conducting an instrumental case study aimed at developing generalizable models of classes of users or contexts, you should aim for cases that are representative in the appropriate aspects. Although the analysis tools may be different, this is the same problem faced by quantitative user studies (see Chapter 2): if the participants in your study are sufficiently different from the group to which you are generalizing, your findings may not hold up, no matter how strong the analysis. Thus, if you are doing a case study to understand how technically unsophisticated users interact with antispyware and antivirus tools, you probably don't want to ask computer science undergraduates, who are likely to be more technically savvy than most users. The additional credibility that comes from having appropriate participants is referred to as *external validity* (Yin, 2014).

Multiple-case studies reduce concerns about external validity somewhat, as consistent findings across your cases can be used to counter the argument that you are describing some idiosyncrasy of your specific participants. However, these problems reappear if you are attempting theoretical replication—members of each group must both represent that group appropriately while differing from other groups in the appropriate dimensions.

Sara's case study provides an instructive example of case selection. When reading the paper, all we are told about Sara is that she is a blind college student. We are not given any other details about her age, background, or socioeconomic status. However, we can infer from the list of tasks—which includes activities such as organizing CDs, cooking, and receiving text messages by cell phone—that she is fairly active and self-reliant. In other words, as far as we know, she may be an appropriate participant for a study of the workaround strategies used by people who are blind. We might not be able to make generalizations that apply her results to other people, but that would be true of any single participant. Furthermore, as the study was described as descriptive and explanatory (Yin, 2014), the authors do not make any claims of generality.

Some case studies specifically seek out unusual, distinctive, or "edge" cases. When studying antispyware or antivirus tools, you might argue that computer science undergraduates are worth studying because you would look for an understanding of how their domain expertise helped them approach challenges that would stop less knowledgeable users. The Finnish study of virtual collaboration in a school setting was conducted in a school that was chosen specifically because "the pedagogical setting had several features that may be described as innovative" (Lakkala et al., 2007). See the Extreme Cases sidebar for a description of a case study that specifically sought out an atypical set of participants in order to get a fresh perspective on an established problem.

Some studies use *critical cases*—cases that are somehow particularly distinctive or notable with respect to the problem that is being considered (Flyvbjerg, 2006). For example, a case study examining the use of antivirus software by employees of a large company might focus on a firm that required all staff members to complete extensive training in the use of the tools in question. This required training makes the firm a strong candidate for success: if antivirus software isn't used there, it might not be used anywhere. Thus, the company becomes a critical case.

Still other strategies for identifying cases are possible. You might search for cases that are most or least likely to exhibit behavior that you are interested in investigating (Flyvbjerg, 2006).

If you find yourself trying to choose from a large pool of potential cases, consider expanding your research agenda to include a screening survey (Yin, 2011). A carefully constructed survey of potential participants can provide data that informs your selection process. Such surveys might assess both the fit between the participants and your criteria and the willingness of the participants to commit their time and energy to the success of the study. Ideally, screening surveys stand on their own as research results, providing insights into the larger group of re-spondents not selected for closer examination in your case study (Yin, 2011). See Chapter 5 for advice on conducting surveys.

7.8 DATA COLLECTION

Having defined your research questions, chosen the number of cases and the units of analysis, and determined whether your study is embedded or holistic, you are ready to plan your data collection. Specifically, you need to define the types of data you will collect and the specific procedures you will follow for collecting those data.

7.8.1 DATA SOURCES AND QUESTIONS

As described in Section 7.2, case studies often, if not always, rely on multiple data sources. Data sources for case studies in other fields include documentation, archival records, interviews, direct observation, participant observation (similar to ethnography), and physical artifacts (Yin, 2014). For HCI research, you may find yourself adapting and adding to this list as appropriate. If you are trying to understand some-one's use of existing computer tools, e-mail messages, web history logs, and related data sources may be considered archival. Logs of specific activities with applications of interest might be available or you might be able to use a variety of technical ap-proaches for collecting such data (see Chapter 12).

Your research questions and hypotheses will play a significant role in determin-ing which of the available data sources you will use. Documentation and archival records are likely to be most interesting if you want to understand past and current practices and use of existing software tools. Interviews are helpful for understand-ing perceptions, concerns, needs, and other user reactions. Direct observation can help you understand what people do in circumstances of interest, while participant observation can be a powerful tool for understanding complex organizational dynam-ics. For HCI researchers, artifacts can be used to provide valuable examples of how people bridge the gap between computer work and the rest of their lives. Classic examples include paper notes stuck to the edge of computer monitors.

Your choice of the types of data that you will collect should be guided by the goal of using multiple sources that address your questions from different perspectives. Sara's case study took this approach, combining interviews about early technology use, demonstrations of various physical and software artifacts, and speculation about desired designs.

By using your research goals to guide a careful selection of data sources and spe-cific questions, you will increase your chance of generating the multiple sources of evidence that form the backbone of data triangulation. A design that makes clear and explicit links between each of the data sources and your research questions will help you understand which questions are addressed by multiple data sources, and which are not. If you find that you have questions that are only represented in one of the data sources, you might want to rethink your design, adding additional data sources or questions.

7.8.2 COLLECTING DATA

Once you have identified your data sources, you need to develop protocols for how you will use each of them to collect data. For interviews, this will include the type of interview, questions, and an interview guide (see Chapter 8). Similar approaches can be used for examination of artifacts. Observations require you to specify the structure of the tasks that will be performed and the questions that will be asked. Each data source, in effect, becomes a mini-experiment within the larger case study, all tied to the common goals of the study as a whole.

You should also develop a protocol for the case study as a whole. In addition to the specific data sources and the procedures that you will use in examining each of these sources, the protocol includes important details that are needed to conduct the case study from start to finish. The case study protocol should start with an introduction, including the questions and hypotheses. It should continue with details of data collection procedures, including criteria for choosing cases, contact information for relevant individuals; and logistical plans for each case, including time requirements, materials, and other necessary preparations. Specific questions and methods for each of the data sources should be included in the protocol. Finally, the protocol should include an outline of the report that will be one of the products of the case study (Yin, 2014).

Although this may seem like an excessive amount of overhead, effort spent on careful development of a protocol is rarely wasted. The process of developing a clear and explicit explanation of your research plan will help clarify your thinking, leading to a better understanding of possible shortcomings and challenges that may arise during the study. Any problems that you identify can stimulate reconsideration and redesign, leading to a stronger research plan.

A draft outline of your report serves a similar purpose. Constructing a report before you collect any data may seem strange, but it's actually quite constructive. Many of the sections of your report are easy to enumerate: your report will always contain an introduction to the problem, a description of your questions and hypotheses; an explanation of your design and how it addresses those questions; informative presentations of data and analysis; and discussions of results. Within each of these components there is substantial room for adaptation to meet the needs of each project. An outline that is as specific as possible—even down to the level of describing charts, tables, and figures to be used for presentation of data and analysis—will help guide your design of the questions and methods that you will use to generate the necessary data.

A case study protocol can be a powerful tool for establishing reliability (Yin, 2014). If your protocol is sufficiently detailed, you should be able to use it to conduct directly comparable investigations of multiple cases—the protocol guarantees that differences in procedures are not the cause of differences in your observations or results. Ideally, a research protocol will be clear enough that it can be used by other researchers to replicate your results.

Consider running a pilot case study. Pilot tests will help you debug your research protocols, identifying questions that you may have initially omitted while potentially exposing flaws in your analysis plans. For some studies, a pilot may not be possible or desirable. If you have a unique case, this may not be possible. If your study is exploratory, you may find that a single case will provide you with sufficient data to generate an informative analysis.

7.9 ANALYSIS AND INTERPRETATION

As qualitative data is a key component of case study research, your analysis will use many of the techniques and strategies discussed in Chapter 11. You should start planning your data analysis early in the process, before you collect any data. Grounded theory, content analysis, and other techniques from Chapter 11 are commonly used to analyze case study data.

Perhaps the largest challenge in the analysis of case study data involves the limited range of data samples. Unlike controlled quantitative experiments, which use large numbers of participants to generate statistically significant results, case studies rely on a few samples, which may be idiosyncratic. This may present challenges if you are interested in building general models: how can you be confident that conclusions drawn from experience with your cases generalize to others?

To some extent, these validity concerns are inherent in case study research. No matter how carefully you choose your cases, collect your data, or conduct your analysis, your case study may lead to interpretations that are not valid or do not generalize to other cases. You should always keep in mind that case study results may not generalize. Even if yours seems to point to trends that hold in all cases, you should avoid assuming that those trends are truly general.

Careful attention to the strategies described in Chapter 11 can help increase the rigor of your analysis and confidence in your conclusion. Triangulation, documentation of chains of evidence, and consideration of rival theories are all appropriate tools for case study analysis.

Case study analysis generally proceeds in a bottom-up fashion, using techniques from grounded theory to code and categorize data (see Chapter 11). In Sara's case, the analysis might have involved examining all of her descriptions of previous interactions with technology, her current approaches and speculative desires for solving a specific task. Any conclusions that were supported by all three of these approaches might be seen as being reasonably valid. These analyses could then be used to form an integrated description of the unit of analysis—the specific task.

After analyzing individual units of interest, you are likely to want to push your analysis to help you understand larger trends that describe your case as a whole and (for multiple-case studies) can be used to support comparison of similar cases. The goal here is not necessarily to make everything agree: there may be fundamental differences between individual units of analysis or cases. That's fine. The point is to facilitate understanding of the differences and similarities between the individual elements.

The multiplicity of data sources used in case study research can support data source triangulation (Chapter 11). If you can use artifact, interview, and observation data together to provide a consistent interpretation of certain aspects of the case under examination, you will have a strong argument in favor of the validity of your interpretation.

Appropriate data displays can prove invaluable in this process. If you have multiple units of analysis that can be described in many ways, you may create a matrix display (Miles and Huberman, 1994) that lays out the data in a tabular format. With one unit of analysis per row and a specific aspect of the analysis in each column, these displays can easily be used to understand an individual unit (reading along a row) or to compare some aspect of each unit (reading down a column), see Table 7.1.

The relationship between the theory behind the case study design and the analysis of Sara's individual tasks provides an opportunity for the use of an important case study analysis technique—pattern matching. In this approach, case study observations can be matched to predictions from the theory behind the design. Matches between the observations and the theory provide support for the theory (Yin, 2014). The specific pattern that is being matched in Sara's study can be found in the researchers' discussion of their study: they initially believed that Sara would use a wide range of technological approaches and creative workarounds to solving problems, and that these practices would help provide a greater understanding of factors influencing the success or failure of tool designs. The description of each task in terms of the situation that led to the difficulty and the characteristics of the individual workarounds allowed each task to be matched directly to the theoretically proposed model.

A final level of analysis takes the comparisons between the units or cases and combines them to develop a model or framework that communicates the results of your case study and the over-arching themes that emerged from your analysis. As you analyze the individual pieces and their relationships, you may identify higher-level patterns, common concerns, or recurring ideas that may help explain, categorize, or organize your results. These explanations might cut across individual units of analysis or multiple cases, forming the basis of a case description (Yin, 2014), which might organize your case study into specific areas of interest. In Sara's case study, the researchers identified several criteria that technologies must meet to satisfy her needs, including efficiency, portability, distinguishability of similar items, and suitability for socially appropriate use in a sighted community (Shinohara and Tenenberg, 2007). As always, you should be very careful to consider rival explanations (see Chapter 11).

Although case studies may rely heavily on qualitative data, quantitative data is often vitally important. A study of massive, multiplayer, online games (Ducheneaut et al., 2007) used quantitative analysis to address questions left unresolved in the qualitative analysis. By defining measures of activity such as the number, frequency, and length of visits to social places, the researchers were able to conduct a quantitative analysis that provided a much richer description of the interaction dynamic than would have been possible with the qualitative data on its own.

7.10 WRITING UP THE STUDY

Documenting a case study can be challenging. More so than many other presentations of research results, case studies often read like descriptive discussions. Instead of presenting quantitative data or statistical results, you may find yourself trying to construct a narrative argument that uses the strength of the organization and writing to construct a convincing argument. In other words, your case study may live or die on the strength of your writing.

Starting your write-up early helps. Documenting your theory and your design in detail as soon as possible aids in clarifying your thinking; you have these artifacts to go back to. You do not want to be in the position of having to reconstruct these important details from memory or incomplete notes long after the fact.

You should make your theories, data, methodologies, analytic steps, and models as explicit as possible. Clear presentation of these important components help readers to understand where you have come from and how you got to any particular conclusions that you may have derived.

Presentation of data and analysis may take many forms. You might present summaries of your data followed by detailed analysis or you might intersperse data with interpretation. Case study reports often use analyses of individual observations or incidents to draw attention to noteworthy details. These analyses set the stage for discussions of broader themes that arise from the analysis. Case study data are usually presented in one of two forms—either thematically (Shinohara and Tenenberg, 2007) or chronologically (Farooq et al., 2007a). Chronological presentation is particularly useful for case studies that describe a project or process.

Story-telling is often an important component of a case study report. Carefully chosen anecdotes bring concrete details to your discussion, supporting your analytic results. These stories are particularly useful—and often required—in cases of direct interpretation (Stake, 1995). If you have chosen a specific incident as warranting detailed interpretation, you should relate all of the relevant details. Stories can also be used to introduce discussions of various components of your analysis. Short *vignettes* (Stake, 1995; Yin, 2011) that illustrate factors that you discuss in your analysis can make your subsequent analysis more concrete. These stories need not be narrative descriptions of specific incidents: direct quotes from interviews describing behaviors (Shinohara and Tenenberg, 2007) or individual perceptions (Troshynski et al., 2008) work very well in this regard.

A case study of the use of participatory design in support of a community organization developing a website (Farooq et al., 2007a) provides an example of a compelling and readable case study report. After introducing the problem and reviewing the literature, this report introduces the methodological approach of combining traditional participatory design methods with measures aimed at encouraging the learning that would need to happen for the project to continue to succeed after the research team ceased to be actively involved. The report continues by providing detailed background of the organization, including its context, goals, and staff resources. The data collection methods and analytic methods were then discussed. The case study data were discussed chronologically, with analysis interspersed, leading to a discussion of implications of the results. The resulting report has details that might be of interest to a wide range of users, including HCI researchers, technology experts, and community organizers.

When appropriate, your case study report should also discuss rival explanations. Having taken the time to consider alternative explanations for any of your analytic results, you should document the results of this effort. Introducing the rival theories and explaining why the available evidence better supports your conclusions can bolster the credibility of your report. If you do not find any evidence in favor of the alternatives say so (Yin, 2011, 2014).

Your write-up of your case study should reflect the limitations of case study research. Any discussions of observations that may apply to the community as a whole should be phrased so as to avoid claims of generality. If you make the same observation for several cases, you might say that your observation appears to apply to a broader population, but you should not claim that your conclusion is definitively general. You might also say that these recurring trends merit further investigation, implying the need for a more rigorously sampled study that would determine whether the findings were generally applicable. Proper attention to the validity of the claims that you are making will help defend you from critics who may feel that you are being overly broad in your interpretation.

Once you have written a draft of your report, you might consider letting your participants read it. This can be a valuable reality check—if your participants believe that you have the facts wrong, you may have a problem that needs to be revisited. If this happens, you may need to collect some more evidence to clarify the situation (Yin, 2014). Participants may also provide alternative viewpoints on the data, possibly including explanations or theories that might (or might not) complement yours. You may not agree with all of the comments that your participants make, particularly with regards to interpretation of the data, but you should do your best to be receptive to constructive criticisms from your participants. Having taken the time to work with you, they are likely to have some interest in helping make your work and your report as accurate as possible.

Case study write-ups often face the troubling question of anonymity. When you're dealing with an individual or a specific group, concerns about privacy are very real: particularly for unique cases, your write-up may be too revealing for comfort. In some cases, protocols for the protection of human research subjects (see Chapter 15) might require that you do not identify the participants in a research study. A good rule of thumb might be to be conservative—when in doubt, protect your participants.

7.11 INFORMAL CASE STUDIES

Although careful planning and design are never completely inappropriate in HCI research, there may be times when the construction of a fully fledged case study is overkill. You may be starting a completely new project, without any understanding of the application domain or the needs of the users. Or, you might be interested in getting some initial response to a proposed design for a new feature that you've designed for a software tool. Yet another possibility involves validation: can you collect some data to document the success of your completed design?

In situations like these, your goal is not to develop a general model or to construct a rigorous argument. Rather, you are more interested in feedback that will help you understand a new situation or a "sanity check" that will indicate whether a new idea is worth pursuing. Informal case studies with a small number (as few as one) of carefully chosen participants can be very valuable sources of feedback. Informal case studies are frequently used by HCI researchers to describe the successful use of a tool—see the Interfaces for people with quadriplegia sidebar for an example.

These case studies are "informal" in the sense that some of the guidelines and procedures might be relaxed in favor of expediency. As you're not looking to make broad, generally applicable claims, you do not need the rigorous planning and record-keeping that is necessary to establish chains of evidence. You might forego a theoretical background or defined analytical framework in favor of simple note-taking and observation.

Imagine a foray into designing a tool for an unfamiliar domain. You might consider running a fully fledged case study, asking several experts in the domain what they do, how they do it, and what they might want in a tool. The potential utility of this study might be significant, but you might need some initial background to plan the details. An informal case study with one potential user might help you gather the initial understanding that is necessary for designing the complete case study. Sometimes, you may find that limits on available resources (time and personnel) make it impossible for you to conduct a complete study. If this happens, informal case studies may be your best option for understanding the problem.

If you are looking for feedback on a proposed design or constructed interface, an informal case study can be an attractive alternative to user studies or observation sessions. Particularly if you can work with a participant who will use your tool on a problem that interests him or her, you can use an informal session to document an instance of the successful use of your tool in the intended domain. A negative result can be informative here as well: if it turns out that your design is fundamentally flawed, your single case can help you identify the error early, saving you the trouble of designing a more thorough summative evaluation.

Even if your case study is informal, your criteria for selecting participants should not be. Although the lesser time commitments of these shorter studies may make them more appealing to many participants, the relatively loose and informal nature may be troublesome to some. You probably don't want to do an informal, preliminary study of a proposed interface with a critical participant who won't be able to handle a few glitches along the way. People who have invested in the success of your project and willing to try out new ideas often make the best participants in informal case studies. It is not uncommon to rely upon such individuals for repeated sessions at different stages in a project: in such cases, these individuals become informants (see Chapters 8 and 9), providing a detailed understanding of the problem and regular feedback that (ideally) helps keep your project on track.

Although informal case studies may appear to be somewhat simpler than fully realized studies, you should still strive to be as rigorous as possible. An informal study conducted during an hour-long session can still involve multiple methods of data collection, a theoretical basis, and careful definition of the units of analysis. Although your data collection procedures might be relatively simple, you still want to keep careful notes and document your analysis appropriately.

Informal case studies trade scientific rigor for ease of data collection. By foregoing the use of multiple data sources, triangulation, and analytic techniques that give full-blown case studies scientific rigor, informal studies provide for the possibility of "quick-and-dirty" study and insights. Effective use of this approach and appropriate communication of results requires a clear understanding of the limits of this approach.

The example of Sara's use of technology provides a clear picture of the difference between formal and informal case studies. In studying Sara, the research team made multiple visits to Sara's home, using several techniques to examine technologies from differing perspectives. Building from a theoretical grounding in theories of interaction with devices in the home and the importance of failures and workarounds, the analysis of observations from these sessions led to a number of insights that point to potentially generalizable insights that might be addressed by designers of technologies for blind people (Shinohara and Tenenberg, 2007).

Imagine, instead, an informal case study of the same situation, involving a single, hour-long visit, using only observational techniques, and lacking a theoretical basis. This study might yield some interesting observations, but you would be hard pressed to gather the data that would inform the insights identified in the full case study. The abbreviated nature of the data collection session might limit your use of multiple sources, leaving you with less confidence in any particular result. As trends and themes that might arise during a longer session might not be apparent in the single visit, generalization of insights would be difficult, if not impossible. You might be able to use the session to generate some discussion that would be part of a longer report, but this informal case study would not stand very well on its own.

Reports of informal case studies should take these limitations into account. If your investigation is truly informal, you may wish to avoid the term "case study" altogether. This will help you avoid the possibility of creating a false impression of a rigorous study. Instead, you might talk about the lessons learned from observations of one or more individuals. Appropriately cautious statements about the significance of your observations and candid admission that more study is needed can help you avoid criticisms that the informality of your procedures does not justify the claims that you are making.

Informal case studies are often most effective as intermediate steps in larger research processes. This can be true of studies that are used as pilot investigations of user needs prior to more formal study with multiple cases or as initial investigations of a tool in use before conducting larger summative evaluations (Chapter 10). Descriptions of these case studies and how they influence the subsequent investigations can be valuable pieces of your eventual write-up.

7.12 SUMMARY

As every individual who uses computing tools does so in a unique context, with specific goals, backgrounds, and abilities, every use of a computer interface is, in some sense, an HCI case study. Close examination of these contextual factors can give researchers a rich, detailed understanding of the factors that influence system requirements and determine the success or failure of proposed designs. Unlike controlled experiments, which attempt to find general answers to fairly narrow questions, case studies are deep and narrow, focusing on thorough exploration of a small set of cases.

If your research leads you to a situation that seems to be in some sense notable or perhaps unique, you might find yourself considering a case study. Possibilities include studying a domain expert's information management techniques in order to inform the design of a new system; comparing two installations of a new collaborative tool in different contexts; or describing your use of a new participatory design technique in the development of a new tool. Regardless of the context, you should be clear about your goals, as they impact how you design and conduct your study. If you are interested in generalizing from your cases to make broader claims, you should be particularly careful about your research design and analysis, making sure that the data favor your arguments over alternative explanations. Open-ended explorations aimed at generating ideas and descriptions of a unique or unusual situation may not make any broader claims, but they will still benefit from a clearly thought-out design and analysis plan.

Case study research is harder than it may look. Although the small number of participants and the lack of quantitative analysis may be appealing, the studies present substantial analytical and logistical challenges. Selecting cases is often difficult, whether you are identifying the most promising participants from a large pool or worrying about the representativeness of the sole case that you have been able to find. Collecting multiple, corroborating pieces of data may be difficult and teasing interesting insights out of potentially messy and inconsistent data can be tricky. Scheduling the appropriate meetings and working around the needs of your participants can often be a real chore.

The case study's focus on deep, narrow investigation leads to inevitable concerns about validity. How can we learn anything general from the study of a small set—sometimes only having one member—of instances of a given phenomenon? With rigorous evaluation involving multiple participants and (very often) statistically analyzed quantitative results playing such a pivotal role in recent HCI research, it may be hard to convince some critical readers that case study research is worthwhile. "This study only includes one participant," they might say, "so how can we apply it to others?"

Case studies that make broad claims of generality are particularly likely to infuriate these critics, who may feel that any generalization from case studies is inappropriate. When conducting and describing case study research, always take care to remember the limits of this approach, and try to avoid making claims that cannot be sustained by a small number of cases.

Although concerns about validity and reliability are certainly appropriate, critics of case studies risk the loss of a valuable research tool. In digging deep into concrete situations, they can help researchers identify design particulars that are likely to go unnoticed by research in usability labs. In focusing on specific situations, they provide concrete illustrations of needs, motivations, and successes or failures. As explanatory tools, they take requirements from the abstract to the specific. Particularly when presented alongside complementary user studies that provide broader-based data, case studies can paint rich pictures that deepen our understanding of complex phenomena.

Case studies succeed when they build upon the fundamental human activity of learning through story-telling. If your case study can use the details of a specific situation to tell the story behind some HCI research question, it will succeed in its ultimate goal of increasing understanding and communicating that understanding to a broader audience.

DISCUSSION QUESTIONS

1. Case studies can be useful tools for exploring user requirements for software tools, but they present challenges: given a small number of cases, your results may not be generally applicable. Some user requirements from a case study might be easy to implement with minimal impact on a design—these might be included even if they are not of broad interest. Other requirements might require fundamental changes to system design. How can you be confident that you have gained a thorough, general understanding that is suitable for designing an application of broader interest? If additional cases are not available, how might you use other HCI research techniques to bolster your confidence in the results of your case study?

2. Case studies involve working closely with individuals who may have a substantial interest in the results of your work. This might lead some participants to put "spin" on their interactions with you, framing their activities and responses to questions to increase the likelihood of achieving their desired outcomes. How might you design your study and choose your data sources to account for this concern?

3. Although the case study of Sara's use of technology is a good example of case-study research, our discussion of it represents a different type of case study:

case study for educational purposes. Based on the discussion and analysis found in this chapter, how does an educational case study differ from a research case study? Consider questions such as the type of study, the number of cases, the data sources, and the analysis.

RESEARCH DESIGN EXERCISES

1. Sara's case study is an embedded, single-case study, with the individual tasks as units of analysis. Suppose you wanted to conduct a literal replication of this study with another blind person. Keeping in mind the potential differences in living arrangements, lifestyles, and personal habits that might distinguish Sara from other blind college students, describe the challenges that you might face in conducting this replication. If you could ask the authors of the paper about Sara for access to their notes and records, which items would be of particular interest? How would these challenges differ if you were to do a theoretical replication with another blind individual who was different from Sara in some potentially important regard, such as a retired person?

2. Case studies often focus on groups or organizations as their units of analysis. As specific details of group dynamics can influence the success or failure of software tools, these studies can be very helpful for understanding the use of tools for collaboration or other organizational goals. Design a case study aimed at understanding the information sharing and management processes of your research group. What would your underlying questions be? What hypotheses would you wish to explore? Describe your units of analyses, data sources, and analytic approach.

REFERENCES

Bilandzic, M., Foth, M., De Luca, A., 2008. CityFlocks: designing social navigation for urban mobile information systems. In: Proceedings of the 7th ACM Conference on Designing Interactive Systems. ACM, Cape Town.

Blythe, M., Monk, A., Park, J., 2002. Technology biographies: field study techniques for home use product development. In: CHI '02 Extended Abstracts on Human Factors in Computing Systems. ACM, Minneapolis, MN.

Cohene, T., Baecker, R., Marziali, E., Mindy, S., 2007. Memories of a life: a design case study for Alzheimer's disease. In: Lazar, J. (Ed.), Universal Usability: Designing Computer Interfaces for Diverse User Populations. John Wiley and Sons, London.

Davies, D.K., Vosloo, H.F., Vannan, S.S., Frost, P.E., 2008. Near real-time fire alert system in South Africa: from desktop to mobile service. In: Proceedings of the 7th ACM Conference on Designing Interactive Systems. ACM, Cape Town.

Druin, A., Weeks, A., Massey, S., Bederson, B.B., 2007. Children's interests and concerns when using the international children's digital library: a four-country case study. In: Proceedings of the 7th ACM/IEEE-CS Joint Conference on Digital Libraries. ACM, Vancouver, BC.

Ducheneaut, N., Moore, R., Nickell, E., 2007. Virtual "third places": a case study of sociability in massively multiplayer games. Computer Supported Cooperative Work 16 (1), 129–166.

Farooq, U., Ganoe, C.H., Xiao, L., Merkel, C.B., Rosson, M.B., Carroll, J.M., 2007a. Supporting community-based learning: case study of a geographical community organization designing its website. Behaviour & Information Technology 26 (1), 5–21.

Farooq, U., Schank, P., Harris, A., Fusco, J., Schlager, M., 2007b. Sustaining a community computing infrastructure for online teacher professional development: a case study of designing tapped in. Computer Supported Cooperative Work 16 (4), 397–429.

Flyvbjerg, B., 2006. Five misunderstandings about case-study research. Qualitative Inquiry 12 (2), 219–245.

Hochheiser, H., 2000. Browsers with changing parts: a catalog explorer for Philip Glass' website. In: Proceedings of the 3rd Conference on Designing Interactive Systems: Processes, Practices, Methods, and Techniques. ACM, New York, NY.

Lakkala, M., Ilomäki, L., Palonen, T., 2007. Implementing virtual collaborative inquiry practises in a middle-school context. Behaviour & Information Technology 26 (1), 37–53.

Miles, M.B., Huberman, A.M., 1994. Qualitative Data Analysis. Sage, Thousand Oaks, CA.

Naaman, M., Nair, R., Kaplun, V., 2008. Photos on the go: a mobile application case study. In: Proceeding of the Twenty-Sixth Annual SIGCHI Conference on Human Factors in Computing Systems. ACM, Florence.

Shinohara, K., Tenenberg, J., 2007. Observing Sara: a case study of a blind person's interactions with technology. In: Proceedings of the 9th International ACM SIGACCESS Conference on Computers and Accessibility. ACM, Tempe, AZ.

Stake, R.E., 1995. The Art of Case Study Research. Sage Publications, Thousand Oaks, CA.

Steriadis, C.E., Constantinou, P., 2003. Designing human-computer interfaces for quadriplegic people. ACM Transactions on Computer-Human Interaction 10 (2), 87–118.

Troshynski, E., Lee, C., Dourish, P., 2008. Accountabilities of presence: reframing location-based systems. In: Proceeding of the Twenty-Sixth Annual SIGCHI Conference on Human Factors in Computing Systems. ACM, Florence.

Yin, R.K., 2011. Applications of Case Study Research. Sage Publications, Thousand Oaks, CA.

Yin, R.K., 2014. Case Study Research: Design and Methods. Sage Publications, Thousand Oaks, CA.

Interviews and focus groups

8.1 INTRODUCTION

Direct feedback from interested individuals is fundamental to human-computer interaction (HCI) research. What should a new tool do? Ask the users. Does a proposed design do what it should do? If not, what should be changed or revised? Ask the users. As discussed in Chapter 5, surveys can be very useful in this regard, particularly for reaching large numbers of people easily. Unfortunately, surveys are somewhat limiting: respondents only answer questions that are asked, and open-ended questions that invite long, written responses are likely to go largely unanswered. As a result, surveys often end up being broad but not deep.

An alternative approach is to go deep but not broad. Direct conversations with fewer participants can provide perspectives and useful data that surveys might miss. Conversation and interaction with the right people can be both a hugely important source of insight and a significant challenge. What you ask, how you ask it, and who you ask can determine the difference between novel insight and wasted time. Just as with so many other topics in computing, garbage in leads to garbage out.

Direct discussions with concerned participants usually take one of two forms: *interviews* with individuals and *focus groups* involving multiple users at one time. Interviews and focus groups have different strengths and challenges: determining which approach you should use is perhaps the first key question to be answered. Other questions address structure and timing. How formal do you want to be? Conversations can range from free-form unstructured interviews to semistructured and fully structured interviews. When should you conduct your interviews or focus groups? As with other data collection approaches, interviews and focus groups can be used for both formative and summative purposes.

Having answered these questions, you're ready to face the big challenge—actually conducting interviews or convening focus groups. Successful use of these approaches is an art in itself, requiring significant conversational and observational skills. Moving conversation along, eliciting meaningful responses, revising questions based on interview responses, interpreting subtle cues, and interpreting detailed responses all require practice and experience.

This chapter discusses these issues, with an eye towards preparing you for designing and conducting interviews and focus groups. The challenges are real, but the value is there. If you don't listen to your users, you might miss some of the most important feedback that you can get.

Research Methods in Human-Computer Interaction. http://dx.doi.org/10.1016/B978-0-12-805390-4.00008-X

8.2 PROS AND CONS OF INTERVIEWS

The ability to "go deep" is perhaps the strongest argument in favor of interviewing. By asking questions that explore a wide range of concerns about a problem and giving interviewees the freedom to provide detailed responses, researchers can use interviews to gather data that would otherwise be very hard to capture. Given a chance to answer questions that encourage reflection and consideration, interviewees may go on at great length, generating ideas and sharing insights that would have been lost to surveys.

Like ethnography (Chapter 9) and other observational techniques, interviews can be open-ended and exploratory. Although almost all interviews have specific questions that must be asked, interviews can be extremely flexible. Based on interviewee responses, interviewers can choose to reorder questions or invent completely new lines of inquiry on the fly. Opportunistic interviewing—taking an interesting idea and running with it—can be particularly useful for increasing understanding.

The flip side of this compelling flexibility lies in the challenges of managing potentially unbounded discussions. Interviews are much more difficult to conduct than surveys. Interviewing is a skill that can take significant practice to develop. Furthermore, it's hard work. Sitting with one interviewee (or a dozen focus group participants) for an hour, listening carefully, taking notes, trying to decide which comments to pursue with further questions, and trying to understand nonverbal reactions all take substantial effort.

Higher effort requirements also limit interview-based studies to relatively small numbers of participants. Surveys can easily be sent to dozens, if not hundreds, of potential respondents who can complete them at their leisure. Interviews, however, are much more limiting. If each interview is one hour long, someone on your research staff team has to spend that hour with an interviewee. You're likely to find that your personnel resources are the limiting factor: don't be surprised if you find that you simply don't have the time to conduct all of the interviews that you were hoping for.

Analysis is also a major challenge. Transforming raw notes and recordings of open-ended responses to broad questions can take a great deal of time—as much as 10h for a single hour of audio recording (Robson, 2002). Deciding what is important and what is not—separating the good from the bad—can be a challenge.

Interviews share some inherent shortcomings with surveys. As both involve data collection that is separated from the task and context under consideration, they suffer from problems of recall. As participants report on their perceptions of needs or experiences, they are telling you what they remember. While this may provide some very useful data, it is, by definition, one step removed from reality. If you ask a software user which features they might need, the answers you get during an interview may be very different from the answers that same person might provide while sitting in front of a computer and actually using the tool in question.

To avoid these potential disconnects, you might consider combining your interviews with other techniques, such as observation—possibly during the interview session. These observations will help you understand the relationship between what interviewees say and what they do. As some researchers have suggested, "look at behavior, listen to perceptions" (Miller and Crabtree, 1999).

One study of the habits of users of in-car navigation systems used both road trips and interviews. During the rides, researchers observed drivers as they used the navigation systems to find their way. Detailed questions were asked after the drive in separate interviews, as responding in-depth while driving may have been too distracting. Observations from the ride, audio recordings, and the interviews were studied to understand how drivers used the navigation system (Leshed et al., 2008). Responses identified a variety of intriguing ways in which navigation systems influenced interviewees' responses to their environment: some participants described how the navigation system gave them the freedom to make mistakes and take wrong turns, and others discussed the benefits of reduced needs to pay attention to where they were going. Navigation systems also influenced interactions between passengers and drivers, with some passengers taking charge and using the navigation system and others assuming that the driver was doing so (Leshed et al., 2008).

8.3 APPLICATIONS OF INTERVIEWS IN HCI RESEARCH

HCI researchers use interviews and focus groups to help build an understanding of the needs, practices, concerns, preferences, and attitudes of the people who might interact with a current or future computer system. In their focus and breadth, interviews share strengths with several other research techniques. Like usability studies and surveys, interviews often include quantitative results. At the same time, interviews are subjective and more open-ended, often providing deeper insights similar to those associated with ethnographies and case studies.

HCI researchers can use interviews in almost any phase of a project, from initial exploration to requirements gathering, evaluation of prototypes, and summative evaluation of completed products.

8.3.1 INITIAL EXPLORATION

Imagine that you've just been asked to investigate new possibilities for helping people to manage digital artifacts of their lives (pictures and videos). You've got a strong feeling that the current tools are insufficient but you'd like to develop a better understanding of what people are doing and what they'd like to do. Ideally, this understanding would help you generate some ideas for developing a tool that will be the next great sensation.

When you're embarking on a new project involving the design of novel tools for unfamiliar users and needs, interviews and focus groups can be vital tools. You might sit down with various potential users to understand their goals and needs. What would they like to do with their pictures and videos? How do these artifacts play into their daily lives? Where and when are they most likely to reach for a picture or video? How do they use these records to tell stories about their lives? You might ask about existing technology practices, but your primary goal is to understand user needs and goals, so you might want to focus on asking high-level questions about types of functionality that are and aren't available, as opposed to specific details of design that may be troublesome.

Asking these broader questions in an interview or focus group can help you generate a deeper and more nuanced understanding of the problem. You might ask the following exploratory questions to understand how people use these media:

- What sort of recordings do you make of personal events? Pictures? Videos? Audio Recordings?
- How do you view these recordings? On a computer? On a TV?
- Where do you view them? Any particular rooms in the house? Outside the house?
- Who do you show them to? On what sort of occasions?
- How do you organize recordings?
- Do you ever make multiple records of a single event? How do you keep them together?
- Do you share these artifacts with friends or family? If so, how?
- Have you ever lost track of any particularly valuable photo or video?
- Do you edit photos or video?
- Do you distinguish between recordings that you've made and those that were made by family members or others?
- Have you found yourself interested in doing something with your recordings that your tools did not support? If so, what?

Note that interviews at this stage are not focused on specific questions of functionality and design. The goal is to understand the needs and challenges presented by a particular situation. Once those needs are well understood, you can move on to specific details that would lead to a concrete design.

Exploratory interviews share much in common with case studies (Chapter 7) and ethnography (Chapter 9), as they are all intended to provide an understanding of a complex and multifaceted situation. Interviews and focus groups have the advantage of being relatively easy and inexpensive to conduct: a series of four or five focus groups in different neighborhoods, each containing 5–10 individuals, could be used to collect a broad range of data in a matter of weeks, where case studies and ethnography might take months.

One study used this approach to understand why and when people replace cell phones, in the hopes of finding possibilities for designing phones and practices that would be more sustainable (Huang and Truong, 2008). Researchers combined web surveys with follow-on telephone interviews with a small number of participants. Analysis of over 700 items from the surveys and the interviews led to an understanding of why people replace phones (e.g., incentives to renew contracts or phone malfunctions) and what they do with old phones (give them to friends, donate to charities, hold on to them, or throw them out). These and other insights led to design suggestions, including the possibility of using contact lists to automatically identify friends who might need a new phone, modular designs that might allow for easy upgrading of appearance and features, and repurposing phones for other purposes, such as museum guides.

The Finding and Reminding and Green Living Interviews sidebars provide in-depth descriptions of two examples of the use of exploratory interviews for improving understanding of user needs, in the interest of building tools to meet these needs.

FINDING AND REMINDING

In the early 1980s, desktop information systems were relatively new and understanding of how people should organize information was incomplete at best. The desktop model (with files, folders, and other items that might be found on an office desk) was gaining popularity at this time. Thomas Malone, a researcher at Xerox's Palo Alto Research Center, noticed that although desktop interfaces claimed to mimic how people worked at their desks, this argument was not supported by research. None of the proposed desktop systems had any basis in research into how people actually organized information (Malone, 1983).

To address this shortcoming, Malone interviewed 10 workers in their offices. At the start of each interview, the interviewee would describe the layout of their office, indicating where information was stored and why. The interviewer did not ask any structured questions during this tour, but he did ask for clarifications. At the end of the interviews, some interviewees were asked to find documents (suggested by coworkers who believed that those documents would be in that office). All participants were asked the following set of questions about their practices:

1. How well organized would you say your office is on a scale from 1 to 5? [1 = not very well organized, 3 = about average, and 5 = very well organized]
2. What would you say are the biggest problems you have with the way your office is organized?
3. Do you keep lists of things to do?
4. Do you keep a calendar of appointments?
5. How often are you unable to find something you are looking for in your office? [Number of times per week or month]
6. How often do you forget to do something you were supposed to do? [Number of times per week or month]

The analysis of the data took several forms. Two participants—one with a "neat" office and another with a "messy" office—were described in detail to illustrate very different approaches. Malone divided participants into these categories based on his observations and used the answer to the question 1 as validation: the people he rated as "messy" all had low scores, while the "neat" people had high scores. Photographs were used to verify that the messy people had more piles.

(Continued)

FINDING AND REMINDING—CONT'D

Malone used his observation of the workers and their offices to note that people used structured, named *files* alongside unnamed, unorganized *piles*. This led him to suggest that information systems should support the creation of unnamed collections of information. Piles appeared to play the special role of *reminders* of work that had to be done: fully two-thirds of the piles were piles of things to do. Malone also noted that respondents often left information unclassified because they weren't quite sure how to organize it.

These observations led to several suggestions for better information environments. According to Malone, information systems should support the creation of hierarchies that would allow multiple classifications for any artifact. However, information systems should also allow for deferred classification— essentially giving the user the ability to create an electronic pile that might not be named until much later (if ever). Automatic classification—perhaps based on when information was accessed—might help as well. Powerful search facilities would be helpful, as would graphical aids for indicating the priority of various items on the to-do list.

More than 30 years later, Malone's investigation of information management practices are still relevant and several of his suggestions remain absent from desktop operating environments. His methods, questions, and analysis illustrate how well-conducted interviews can inform and guide HCI research.

GREEN LIVING INTERVIEWS

Environmental concerns have led to an interest in applying HCI techniques and practices to the development of tools and systems that encourage people to make environmentally responsible choices. To understand more concretely what this would mean, a group of researchers conducted a qualitative study with people in the United States who had made substantial commitment to the use of environmentally responsible systems or construction in their homes (Woodruff et al., 2008). These criteria were used because people who were willing to take the time and money to install solar panels or use salvaged materials to renovate their home were presumed to be deeply concerned about environmental matters. The researchers used green movements, green-home tours, and email lists to find appropriate participants, which led to a diverse group of 56 individuals living in 35 homes in several locations in California, New Mexico, and Oregon.

Home visits were used to conduct the bulk of the data collection. Each of the visits included a semistructured interview, a tour of the house, and other activities aimed at understanding user needs and perspectives, typically over the course of two to three hours. The visits were video recorded and photographed. These visits generated a substantial amount of data. Verbatim transcripts of all visits totaling around 3000 pages were analyzed by affinity clustering (Beyer and Holtzblatt, 1998). The roughly 5000 photos taken during the visit were analyzed as well.

This analysis led to a detailed understanding of participants' motivation, practices, and choices. Motivations ranged from concerns about stewardship of the earth to self-reliant tendencies and a desire to be sustainability trend-setters. Participants tended to be very thoughtful about their choices, which frequently involved an ongoing and gradual process. Many spoke of the continuing effort required to maintain the systems and tools that they used, comparing the effort to living on a ship. Participants were generally highly independent, valuing uniqueness, but they also saw a value in teaching and providing an example to others.

The research team used these perspectives to identify a number of implications for design in support of sustainable behavior. Detailed, "in-depth" learning opportunities, mentoring, and interactive tools that aid in the exploration of the impact of various alternatives might help people make decisions regarding the adoption of green tools. Social networking tools might also be used to help people establish appealing green identities. Noting that broader adoption of sustainable practices might require making these choices more approachable to a broader population, the authors suggest the development of tools that would support broader social change. Interactive technologies in support of digital democracy aimed at changing environmental policy, sharing and distribution of environmental data, and even construction of opportunities for social protest might prove constructive in this effort (Woodruff et al., 2008).

8.3.2 REQUIREMENTS GATHERING

During the process of gathering requirements for the design of a new tool, interviews can be invaluable for understanding user needs and concerns. Interviews conducted at this early stage in the process are likely to be fairly broad. What are the user's goals? How are they being met by current tools (if any are available)? What do users want to do that they are currently unable to do? What are the frustrations? Are the tasks associated with a given problem flexible enough to communicate with tools that solve different, but related problems?

Interviewing in search of requirements requires an appropriately broad and open-ended view of the possibilities. A focus on narrow questions or existing tools might be too limiting. Instead, you might want to ask broader questions about current—possibly noncomputer—practices, future goals, frustrations and concerns. You might even ask your participants to try to describe things that they'd like to do, regardless of the ideas' feasibility with current software: "If you could describe the perfect system for solving your problem, what would it look like?"

Returning to the example of managing digital artifacts (Section 8.3.1), suppose your initial interviews led to the idea of building a tool that would allow users to create digital scrapbooks combining photos, audio, video, text, and other multimedia. You would like your tool to support "one-stop shopping"—letting users do all of the necessary steps in one application without having to move data between multiple tools. To make this work effectively, you would need to understand the sorts of things people currently do to construct these scrapbooks, so that you might understand how to build a tool that would meet user needs.

Asking users how they lay out photos in a page-layout or web-page-creation system may be at too low a level of detail. In response to this question, an interviewee might talk about very specific tools for managing page content. As interesting and relevant as this may be—and it could be very interesting indeed—this line of inquiry might fail to uncover some insights that could be much more intriguing. If you instead were to ask the interviewee what he wanted to communicate with the scrapbooks and who the audience would be, you might get the inspiration for a new product or set of features aimed at completing similar tasks—insights that you would never have had with the simpler interview questions. The following list of questions might be asked to gather requirements for this scrapbook creation activity:

- What sort of scrapbook are you creating? Will it cover one event or many? Is it for family, friends, coworkers, or all of the above?
- How do you create traditional scrapbooks? What do you put into them? What do they look like? Can you show me a scrapbook that you've made?
- What sort of things do you want to put in the scrapbook? Pictures, music, movies, artwork? Anything else?
- How do you want to arrange things? Do you want to have individual pages like a traditional scrapbook, or should the layout be more open-ended, as if you were working on a large canvas?
- How would people read your scrapbook? Do you want them to have a set start-to-finish order or should readers be free to explore any way that they like?
- How many items would you want to put in a scrapbook?
- How and where would people read the scrapbook? Do you want to project it on a wall? Send it via email? View it on TV or on a phone? Post it on a web page?
- Do you want to give users tools to make comments and notes on your scrapbook?
- How would your scrapbook relate to others? Would you create links between scrapbooks posted on your own web pages or on social networking sites?

Note how little these questions have to do with the specific tools being used.

Although this approach to interviewing may help you get started, you may find that you need more information to truly understand user needs. Contextual inquiry—in-depth interviews involving demonstrations of how participants complete key tasks (see Section 8.5.2)—is a widely used technique for developing a deeper understanding of how work is done. Ethnographic techniques, including observation and participation in a group or workplace (see Chapter 9) can provide still richer insights.

Both contextual inquiry and ethnographic techniques have been used extensively by HCI researchers.

Low-level questions about how tasks are completed may be more appropriate if you are trying to improve interaction and process details for specific tools. You might ask how users accomplish various goals, which approaches they use (e.g., menu selections or keyboard shortcuts), what problems they face, which options work well, and which don't, and what sorts of functionality they'd like to add to their current software.

To really understand how someone uses current tools, you might ask them to demonstrate how they complete typical tasks. As they go about their tasks, you might ask questions aimed at helping you understand what they are doing and why. This approach may blur the line between interviewing and observation. Effectively, the tool acts as a "probe"—an external aid that encourages interviewees to provide more detail and explanation. The following list gives examples of questions relating to the use of available tools for the scrapbook example:

- Which tools do you use for scrapbook creation? What purpose do you use each of them for?
- What types of data do you use in your current tools for scrapbook creation?
- Do you have to make frequent use of multiple tools? Do you often move data between tools?
- How do you enter or organize the data values?
- Which calculations do you make? How do you make them?
- Can you preview your output?
- Do you print your scrapbooks on paper?
- What do your tools *not* do that you would like to be able to do?
- If you could change or improve this process, what would you do?
- Please show me how you create a scrapbook. Please explain which steps you take and why.

8.3.3 EVALUATION AND SUBJECTIVE REACTIONS

Interviews can also be very useful during the development process. As prototypes are developed, interviews can capture the reactions of various users. Early user feedback on information flow, location of controls, use of language, and other aspects can help designers validate their approach and identify areas in need of revision. Interviews at these stages focus on specific questions aimed at eliciting reactions to various design elements. Similarly, interviews can provide useful input for summative evaluations of completed products. A broader focus in such interviews may be productive, as the summative reactions to a completed tool can inform the process of designing the next revision. Interview questions for evaluating the design of proposed interfaces for the scrapbook tool may include:

- Do you find this interface easy to use?
- Do you understand the menus, icons, and language?

- Are you able to complete the comparisons that you want to do? If not, where do you have trouble?
- Are any parts of the interface particularly useful or helpful?
- How does this interface compare to your current tool?
- What (if anything) would you like to change about this tool?

Additional questions for understanding user reactions to interface designs might be based on existing usability questionnaires, such as the Questionnaire for User Interface Satisfaction (QUIS) (Chin et al., 1988); the System Usability Scale (Brooke, 1996); the User Metric for User Experience (UMUX) (Finstad, 2010); UMUX-Lite (James et al., 2013), or one of the others listed in Chapter 5.

The strengths and weaknesses of interviewing make it a strong complement to several other techniques. For understanding a problem during requirements gathering, a broad-based survey might be combined with a small number of in-depth interviews. Complementary questions in the two formats would allow researchers to combine a deep understanding of user needs and challenges (from the interviews) with an appreciation of how well those concerns generalize to a larger set of potential users.

For evaluation of an existing interface, you might combine usability tests or empirical studies aimed at understanding specific details of interface usability with interviews that ask about general reactions. These interviews can help you understand user perceptions, likes, and dislikes. This combination of results from different approaches can be informative and perplexing: don't be surprised if the usability or empirical studies are completely at odds with your interviews. This seemingly inconsistent state of affairs may arise if you're comparing two alternative designs: interviewees may prefer design A over design B, even though your studies indicated that design B was somehow superior (perhaps faster or less error prone) to A. These results present an opportunity for you to dig deeper in search of insights that might help you reconcile the contradiction. If you can find out why they preferred A, despite B's superior performance, you might use that information to develop a design C that combines the best elements of A and B.

8.4 WHO TO INTERVIEW

Who should you interview? When you are running usability studies, empirical tests, or observations, the question of participant selection starts from an obvious point: current or potential users of your proposed system or alternatives. If your interviews are aimed at trying to understand the pros and cons of specific features of a proposed interface, users might be appropriate interviewees. In either case, you might find that there are different categories of users who have differing views. Including representatives of each type of user will help ensure that you are not missing important perspectives. For investigations of broader concerns, such as system requirements or overall evaluation of system operation, a broader pool of interviewees drawn from all categories of *stakeholders* might be more informative.

A stakeholder is anyone who is affected by the use of a system. Relatively simple applications, such as games or Internet chat clients, might have only one type of user that you would want to interview. Then again, simplicity might be illusory—novice game players may have different perspectives from experts. Enterprise information systems, such as university course registration and management tools may have multiple types of users (or stakeholders), ranging from administrators who approve purchases of the tool and rely upon it for high-level reports, faculty who use it to manage course enrollment and grades, and students who must register for courses and pay tuition. In some cases, stakeholders may not be users at all: patients and their families may have valuable insights regarding hospital information systems, even if they never use them directly. For any reasonably complex system, you can expect that different groups of stakeholders will have very different perspectives on requirements, necessary functionality, and usability. Interviews with representatives of all of the stakeholder groups—or, at least, as many as possible—will provide a more complete picture of the situation.

Particularly when you are involved in an ongoing, long-term project with an organization or a group of users, you may find that there are certain individuals who are particularly good sources of information. These people may be particularly knowledgeable about how relevant work is done, they may play pivotal roles in the organization in question, or they may simply be unusually forthcoming. These individuals may play the role of *key informants*: individuals who are repeatedly called upon to provide important insights, usually over an extended period of time. Key informants can provide invaluable perspectives, if your interactions and relationship are well managed. Key informants must be selected carefully and their insights must be validated by external confirmation from other sources. A disgruntled employee with an axe to grind would not make a good key informant. Particularly in a workplace situation, you should take care not to abuse any information that might be used against the informant (Gilchrist and Williams, 1999). Working with key informants is closely related to—and, indeed, can be the first step in—ethnographic research, a topic discussed in detail in Chapter 9.

As with any other research, interviews should be conducted in a manner that respects the participants (see Chapter 14). For studies that involve populations of participants facing special needs or challenges, this may require extra care in planning and execution. Le Dantec and Edwards' study of the information practices of homeless people illustrates some of these challenges. Noting that simply looking for homeless people on the street could be problematic, they worked with outreach groups who provided feedback and acted as mediators between the researchers and the homeless interviewees. In consultation with caseworkers, they offered participants a choice of store gift cards or public transportation cards as incentives. Staff at the centers worked with the researchers to identify appropriate participants. Subjects were given disposable cameras and asked to take pictures of daily activities, places where they needed help, and things that they use. Subsequent interviews used the photos that the participants took to guide discussions about their use of phones, Internet, transportation, and other technology. The researchers found that their respondents made substantial use of voicemail and mobile phones, while relatively few used computers or the Internet. These observations formed the basis for a detailed discussion of the challenges of both meeting the needs of, and continuing to work with, this challenging population (Le Dantec and Edwards, 2008).

8.5 INTERVIEW STRATEGIES
8.5.1 HOW MUCH STRUCTURE?

Fully structured interviews use a rigid script to present questions in a well-defined order. Although some questions may be skipped, based on answers to previous questions, there is no room for asking questions out of order or for adding questions not found in the predefined interview script. You might think of a fully structured interview as a survey administered by a researcher, with some important differences. It's easier to answer an interview question than it is to write an answer to the same question in a survey. An interview question might yield an extensive answer to a question that would generate only a few words in a survey response.

Fully structured interviews also have the advantage of being relatively easy to analyze. If each subject is asked the same questions in the same order, and related topics are grouped together in the ordering, interviewees are likely to comment on similar topics at similar points. Analyzing these responses may be as easy as collecting all answers to each question in a single place.

The framework provided by a fully structured interview can be a curse as well as a blessing. In a fully structured interview, you must follow the script. If the interviewee makes some comments that you'd like to follow up or if you think of some unanticipated question that you'd like to ask, you're out of luck. Requests for clarification or additional questions are inappropriate, as they interfere with the primary motivation for using a fully structured interview: ensuring that each interviewee is asked the same questions.

If you want some room to ask for clarification, add questions, or follow interviewee comments wherever they may take you, a *semistructured* interview may be more appropriate. These discussions generally start with a set of questions, which may be similar (if not identical) to questions that might be used in a fully structured interview. However, in a semistructured interview, you can feel free to let the conversation go where it may. If your interviewee mentions something of interest, you can say "tell me more about that...." After she clarifies, you might inquire "how does this relate to..." or perhaps ask a question from further down on your list. Your goal should be to dig through the interviewee's comments, opportunistically looking for possibilities to gain additional insight and understanding.

Unstructured interviews take this idea to its logical extreme. An unstructured interview may simply be based on a list of topics or questions known as an interview guide (Robson, 2002). To conduct an unstructured interview, you would start off with an initial question for your interviewee, and then you would listen, letting the interviewee respond as she sees fit, discussing topics of her choosing. If conversation slows or stalls, you might introduce another topic or question from your interview guide. As the main benefit of using unstructured interviews lies in letting your interviewees focus on the topics and concerns that they find important, you should avoid imposing too much structure.

Semistructured and unstructured interviews open up the possibility of exploring topics in a depth and breadth that may be harder to achieve with fully structured interviews. As interviewee comments lead you to ask questions that you hadn't thought of and as they discuss issues that you had overlooked, your understanding of their concerns and perspectives will broaden in directions that you might have missed with a fully structured interview.

Of course, there is no such thing as a free lunch: interviews with less structure require more skill to conduct. When do you dig deeper in response to a comment? When do you back off and move on to something else? How do you keep interviewees on track or deal with those who answer in monosyllables? Effectively managing these challenges requires a fair amount of skill, which may come only with experience.

Less structure also means more challenges in interpretation. Semistructured or unstructured interviews may go all over the map, with related topics discussed in multiple places throughout the interview. You may need to collect comments made at very different points, searching through your notes, recordings, or transcripts, to find closely related topics.

These different types of interview can also be distinguished by considering who's in charge. As they are controlled largely by the interviewer, fully structured and semistructured interviews are often described as *respondent* interviews. In unstructured interviews, the interviewee's comments direct the course of the interview, with the interviewer following along and responding as necessary. As the interviewee is in control, these interviews are also described as *informant* or *nondirective* interviews. These names help remind us that the comments of the interviewee may be very structured, even if the interviewer does not impose any structure on the conversation: the perceived presence or absence of structure depends upon the viewpoint that is being considered (Robson, 2002).

How should you choose between these different styles? Fully structured interviews are most appropriate when you hope to compare responses across individuals. All interviewees are asked the same questions, so comparison should be straightforward. These comparisons are often most useful for evaluations aimed at understanding user responses to designs or systems.

Unstructured and semistructured interviews can be most appropriate when you are looking to dig deeper, in search of critical comments, design requirements, and other insights. These approaches can be particularly helpful when you are unfamiliar with a problem domain or set of users—when you don't even know which questions to ask. In these cases, semistructured or unstructured interviews give participants the chance to educate you. The understanding that you gain from their comments can help you understand their needs and, potentially, generate appropriate questions for subsequent structured interviews. Follow-up structured interviews can be particularly helpful for validating the results of your initial semistructured or unstructured attempts: if a second round of interviews elicits comments that are generally consistent with feedback from the first group, you might comfortably conclude that those comments apply generally to a broad range of users. The Green Living Interviews sidebar describes a research project that made extensive use of semistructured interviews and other complementary techniques to understand the practices of a very specific group of people, in the hopes of identifying possibilities for the design of new tools.

Greater ease of both conducting the interviews and analyzing the results makes fully structured interviews appropriate for your first effort. When all of your questions are explicitly spelled out, conducting an interview can be relatively straightforward. You simply ask a question, note the answer, and move on to the next question. Semistructured and unstructured interviews can require significantly more effort, as you will find yourself trying to decide when and how much to manage the interview process. When do you let the interviewee digress to seemingly unrelated topics? When should you let the interviewee talk and when should you direct the conversation? If you are working with someone who is not at all talkative, how can you get them to open up? Given these and other challenges, you might want to stay away from less-structured techniques until you've had some experience in interviewing.

8.5.2 FOCUSED AND CONTEXTUAL INTERVIEWS

Interviews in HCI research often revolve around the specific context of a problem or technology. We might be interested in how people use an existing system or how they solve a problem that might be addressed by software that has not yet been built. In circumstances such as these, an interview might go beyond simply asking questions; it might ask for demonstrations and more in-depth explorations. By asking interviewees to *demonstrate* how they solve a problem, instead of *explaining* how they do it, these interviews have the potential to illustrate aspects of the problem that might have been forgotten in a strictly verbal interview. Thomas Malone's classic work on office organization (see the Finding and Reminding sidebar) provides an example of this approach. To understand how people organize information, Malone asked people to show him around their offices, indicating where they store things (Malone, 1983). Hugh Beyer and Karen Holtzblatt expand upon this approach, providing a detailed inquiry model in their book on Contextual Design (Beyer and Holtzblatt, 1998) (see Contextual Inquiry sidebar).

CONTEXTUAL INQUIRY

Many HCI researchers and practitioners have found that simply asking people about their practices is not sufficient for developing a complete understanding of user requirements. If you ask someone who regularly makes scrapbooks how they go about doing it, they may share certain interesting details that demonstrate their *explicit* understanding—those parts of the process that they can think of and easily describe to you. If you watch that same person complete the task, you might find many *implicit* practices that are crucial for success, even if they aren't stated directly.

A popular exercise used in HCI and other computing classes provides a nice demonstration of the notion of implicit knowledge. The challenge involves sandwich construction. Students are asked to describe how to make a peanut butter and jelly sandwich, assuming one is given a loaf of bread and new jars of peanut butter and jelly. Participants invariably find that seemingly simple tasks—such as getting a knife full of peanut butter to be spread on the sandwich—are complicated by challenges that may not be remembered explicitly—in this case, removing the foil seal that might be found under the lid of the unopened jar of peanut butter (Davis and Rebelsky, 2007). If you limit your investigations to direct interviews, you might never come across interviewees who remember this crucial step. If you instead choose to observe someone in action, your first participant's attempts to remove the foil point to the need to include it in your process.

Contextual inquiry techniques for conducting interviews (Beyer and Holtzblatt, 1998) are specifically designed to uncover implicit knowledge about work processes. Contextual inquiry starts from observation at workplaces, with a focus on specific details rather than generalizations.

The simplest form of contextual inquiry is the contextual interview that consists primarily of a few hours of observation as the user completes his or her work. The goal is to form a partnership in search of a shared understanding of work. The preferred approach to this is to have the researcher and the interviewee work together in a manner similar to a master-apprentice relationship, with the participant describing what she is doing and why as she progresses through the various steps involved in completing her work. Researchers conducting contextual interviews are generally much more talkative than traditional apprentices, leading to a conversational partnership.

This collaboration extends into interpreting the data: the researcher begins to build a model of how the interviewee is working and asks if it reflects the user's understanding. If the interpretation is incorrect, the interviewee is likely to clarify: "No, that's not quite right." This discussion takes place in the context of a focus on the project as a whole, as opposed to any smaller components, such as the software that you might eventually design (Beyer and Holtzblatt, 1998).

(Continued)

CONTEXTUAL INQUIRY—CONT'D

Beyer and Holtzblatt's classic 1998 book presents a design approach that extends far beyond the interview. Their detailed and practical discussion details how analysis of interview results can be used to generate a series of informative graphical models describing key aspects of workflows under discussion. Flow models describe the sharing of information among individuals in a workplace; sequence models outline the steps in completing a task; artifact models collect the structure of information or other byproducts of work processes; cultural models describe the backgrounds and assumptions of the context in which the work is done; and physical models describe relevant physical and logistical constraints (Beyer and Holtzblatt, 1998). Explicit understanding of attitudes that users might have towards systems (cultural models) and of the environments in which a system is used (physical models) can be crucial for success.

In Beyer and Holtzblatt's model, individual interview sessions are analyzed in interpretation sessions, in which team members discuss each interview in detail. Notes from these sessions are organized into *affinity diagrams*— hierarchical groupings of structures and themes, built from the bottom up (Figure 8.1). Groupings are given names, and groups are brought into larger,

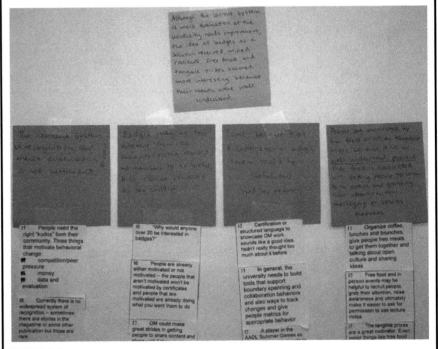

FIGURE 8.1

An affinity diagram, illustrating groupings of individual observations into higher level categories.

From https://www.flickr.com/photos/openmichigan/6266766746.

collective groups. Affinity diagrams are often constructed with sticky notes, using different colors to represent layers in the hierarchy (Beyer and Holtzblatt, 1998). Collecting notes from a series of contextual interviews into a single diagram leads to a "map" of the problem "terrain", with hierarchies providing guidance for understanding the relationships of various concerns that fall under the topics and subtopics. In the course of analyzing a large set of notes (perhaps around 1500), members of a research team can build a shared understanding of a challenging work process (Beyer and Holtzblatt, 1998).

Although the content of their 1998 book is still as relevant as ever, Holtzblatt and Beyer updated their models with a 2014 revision entitled *Contextual Design Evolved* (Holtzblatt and Beyer, 2014). Noting the importance of interface design for daily life activities conducted on mobile devices, this revised model adds new criteria including "Cool Concepts" designed to address factors relevant to this new class of applications, including accomplishment, connection and sensation (Holtzblatt and Beyer, 2014). This content, together with expanded examples and guidance on interview analysis methods, makes *Contextual Design Evolved* a must-read companion to the original book.

Other interviews aimed at understanding how technologies are currently used might include technology tours, which ask participants to show researchers how they use technology at home (Petersen and Baiilie, 2001) or other familiar space. Technology biographies build upon this approach, asking participants to discuss past uses of technology and to speculate about desirable future scenarios (Blythe et al., 2002).

One alternative perspective on interview strategies relies upon artifacts and context provided by the researcher, not by the subject. External aids aimed at eliciting feedback or reactions relevant to the subject at hand are known as "probes" (Gaver et al., 1999). As the goal of a probe is to promote engagement, it need not be technological: an interviewer interested in understanding user needs for organizing photos might ask interviewees to organize a small set of pictures on a table top. Observations of this process may prove to be significantly informative than a strictly verbal interview.

Software prototypes can also be used to focus interviews. Technology probes are simple prototypes that demonstrate new ideas (Hutchinson et al., 2003). Although they may be interesting as tools, technology probes are primarily designed to explore possibilities and understand needs and practices regarding technology use. A study of everyday technologies in family life used two forms of technology probe—a zoomable space for digital notes on a writable LCD tablet and a tool for capturing short, shareable videos—to understand how unfamiliar technologies might be used by family members (Hutchinson et al., 2003).

Interviews aimed at evaluating proposed designs for software tools often go one step further, asking users to comment on proposed interface designs, either on paper or as more-or-less functional prototypes. As prototypes become more fully functional, these interviews might even ask users to complete sample tasks. Although this feedback can be very useful—particularly early in the design process—such interviews must be conducted carefully. If participants are aware that they are evaluating a tool that you have designed, they may be overly favorable in their responses. When conducting an interview like this, you might want to discount favorable responses and give more credence to critical remarks.

8.6 INTERVIEWS VS FOCUS GROUPS

Interviewing is a powerful, but labor-intensive, data collection technique. To gather input from 20 individuals, an interviewer must meet with each person individually, perhaps for an hour or more. An attractive alternative might be to meet with several participants in *focus groups*. These group discussions provide a reasonably effective and inexpensive tool for easily gathering a broad range of opinions. Although opinions differ on optimal sizes, focus groups are generally not large. Some suggest between eight and 12 people (Robson, 2002), while others argue that smaller groups of five to seven participants might be more appropriate for an in-depth conversation (Krueger, 1994). A series of as many as five focus groups (Brown, 1999) could be used to engage up to 60 people in a few hours. Relying on a single focus group session is discouraged, as any single group could be unresponsive or unrepresentative. Two or more groups will increase your chances of success (Krueger, 1994).

The participation of several individuals in a focus group provides the possibility of a broad range of viewpoints and insights. Discussions can reveal similarities and differences between opinions. Limited doses of disagreement and debate can be very informative, as varying viewpoints can lead to a broader understanding than you would gain from a number of people who were in complete agreement. These conflicting perspectives might also lead you to new areas for further study (Brown, 1999). Perhaps you can develop a model or system that will handle all perspectives well.

The conversations that can arise in a focus group can help overcome many of the shortcomings of interviews. In a one-to-one setting the interviewer and interviewee are left to fend for themselves. If the interviewee is not talkative, or if an awkward dynamic stifles the discussion, the interview may fail. Group discussions support interactivity, with participants ideally balancing each other. Participants can encourage each other to speak up, either in support of or opposition to earlier statements. This highly dynamic situation can stimulate participants to raise issues that they might not have identified in one-to-one interviews.

As the rigidity of a fully structured interview is ill suited for group settings, focus groups are generally semistructured or unstructured. A fully structured focus group would require asking each question to each individual in order, without any room for interaction between participants. A fully structured focus group would essentially be equivalent to multiple individual interviews conducted simultaneously.

Interactive focus groups present researchers with several logistical and management challenges. As conversation takes time, focus groups might be limited to a relatively small number of questions—fewer than you would cover in comparable interviews. Conflicts may arise, particularly in focus groups involving controversial topics. Participants may be unwilling to discuss topics involving potentially sensitive information—perhaps relating to health care or finances—in a group setting. Individual interviews might be more appropriate for discussion of these topics.

Particularly talkative and opinionated participants can monopolize conversations, crowding out other viewpoints. If this happens, you will need to find a diplomatic way to ask chatterboxes to yield the floor. Simply cutting them off brusquely may give offense and discourage further participation. Disrespectful conduct can cause similar problems. When conducting a focus group, you must be careful to avoid power struggles or other confrontations with participants, as such battles can sabotage the whole process (Brown, 1999).

Group dynamics can impose certain limits on the extent to which you can generalize from focus group results. Although you'll know when people disagree strongly enough to speak up, you may not know how to interpret silence. Participants who sit quietly may agree with expressed opinions or they may simply be opting out of the conversation.

Extracting useful data from a focus group requires skillful facilitation. You need to manage personality conflicts, encourage participation from all participants, keep the conversation going, monitor the clock, and work through your list of questions, all the while collecting the data that is at the heart of your effort. With a roomful of participants to manage, this can be quite a challenge. Fortunately, this need not fall on only one person's shoulders. A focus group might have two moderators: someone who is skilled in running such groups can work alongside an HCI researcher who is familiar with the problem at hand (Brown, 1999). Together, these collaborators can work together to ensure successful data collection.

The selection of focus group participants can be an art in itself. Should your participants represent multiple backgrounds and perspectives, or would a more homogenous group be appropriate? What about familiarity—do you want participants who are unknown to each other or groups consisting of friends or colleagues? Participants in homogenous groups have common backgrounds and experiences that may help promote discussion and exchange, giving you viewpoints that represent this shared context. In some cases, you may not be able to find a broadly diverse group of participants. If you are developing a system for use by a narrowly defined group of experts—such as brain surgeons or HCI researchers—your groups are likely to be largely homogenous, at least in the relevant respects.[1] Homogenous groups have the disadvantage of narrowing the range of perspectives. For projects that aim to support

---

[1] There may be significant racial, ethnic, gender, and age diversity in any group of brain surgeons or HCI researchers. However, from the perspective of tools designed to support their professional activities, their shared training and experiences are likely to be much more important than any demographic diversity.

a broad range of users—for example, systems aimed at meeting the needs of all patrons in a large metropolitan library—broadly based focus groups representing multiple viewpoints may be more helpful. Groups that are too diverse may pose a different set of problems, as a lack of any common ground or shared perspectives may make conversation difficult (Krueger, 1994). In any case, participants in focus groups should have an interest in the topic at hand and they should be willing to participate constructively (Brown, 1999).

Focus groups may be inappropriate for addressing sensitive or controversial topics. Many participants may be reluctant to discuss deeply personal issues in a group setting. Controversial topics may lead to arguments and bitterness that could destroy the group's effectiveness (Krueger, 1994). Although such concerns may seem unrelated to much HCI work, group discussions can take on a life of their own, possibly bringing you unanticipated difficulties. If you have any concerns at hand about difficult issues, you may decide to use one-to-one interviews instead.

Although most focus groups are at least somewhat unstructured, structured focus group techniques can be useful for building group consensus on topics of common interest. The Nominal Group Technique (NGT) (Delbecq and Van de Ven, 1971) asks users to answer a specific question. Participants start by writing individual responses to the question, which are then provided to a moderator and discussed with the group. Participants then prioritize their "top 5" responses, and a ranked tally is generated to identify the most important consensus responses to the question at hand (Centers for Disease Control, 2006). An NGT inquiry into the information needs of home-care nurses and their unmet information needs in dealing with geriatric patients after hospital discharge asked participants "In your experience, what information-related problems have your elderly patients experienced that contributed to hospital readmissions?" Respondents identified 28 different needs in six different categories, including medication, disease/condition, nonmedication care, functional limitations, and communication problems (Romagnoli et al., 2013).

8.7 TYPES OF QUESTIONS

As seemingly small differences in the phrasing and form of interview questions can lead to big differences in responses, you should pay careful attention to what you ask your interviewees and how you ask the questions. Although writing these questions is more of an art than a science, there are some guidelines that should help you get started in the right direction.

One of the first considerations in the construction of any interview question involves the degree of structure. Structured, closed questions limit users to a small number of predefined choices. Examples include yes-no questions, multiple choice, true-false, and Likert-scale questions, asking for ratings on a scale of 3, 5, 7, or more possibilities (Robson, 2002). These questions have the advantage of being easy to analyze, as responses can be tabulated across all participants, and statistical methods can be used to describe the distribution of responses. However, giving your interviewees a small set of predefined responses might discourage elaboration and further comments. If you ask someone "Did you like the design of the home page?," they might just say "yes" or "no." However, if you ask "what do you think about this home page?," interviewees may be more inclined to elaborate, describing their reactions in more detail.

This second example—asking "what do you think about...?"—is an *open-ended* question. These questions ask for responses, opinions, or other feedback, without imposing any external constraints on the responses. This freedom invites the respondent to answer in depth, exploring any aspect of the issue that may be of interest. Such answers can often stimulate conversation and generate insights that closed questions might not reveal. Increased difficulty in analysis is the price that you pay for this insight. Instead of simply counting answers in different categories, you'll have to analyze the content of responses to open-ended questions, using techniques described in Section 8.10.

Knowing how you will analyze answers may help you determine which kind of question to ask. If you want to divide participants into groups, a closed question asking them which group they belong to is ideal. If you want to understand the relationship between education level and reactions to a proposed community information system, you might ask people to state their highest level of education completed. This would clearly establish your categories of interest. In other circumstances, you might find it useful to divide interviewees into those that have unfavorable, favorable, or neutral reactions to an existing system. In this case, a closed question with three choices would be more helpful than an open-ended question that might lead to a more ambiguous response.

If you're not quite sure how you're going to use the data, you might be better off starting with the least restrictive approach. If you're not sure how you intend to use interviewee age, you might prefer to ask for exact ages rather than ranges (such as 20–29, 30–39, etc.). This will preserve the option of reporting age statistics and aggregating them into ranges for a histogram. If you start by asking for the ranges, you can't switch to numeric values later.

Other forms of interview "questions" are tasks or exercises that ask participants to provide useful information, without presenting a question as such. You might ask users to complete a sentence: "The task that I would most like to be able to complete with my word processor is...." (Krueger, 1994). This may not be all that different from asking a direct question, but it does add some variety to the interview process. Another possibility involves *conceptual mapping*: asking participants to draw pictures or graphical layouts that describe their understanding of a situation. (Krueger, 1994) For a study of perceptions of websites, you might provide a list of 20 sites, asking interviewees to organize the list into groups of similar sites. In one study of user perceptions of web security, interviewees were asked to draw diagrams depicting their understanding of how secure web connections work. These pictures provided concise and informative illustrations of how users understood—and misunderstood—web security (Friedman et al., 2002) (see Figure 8.2).

Interview questions should be as simple as possible, without any technical terms or jargon. You don't want your questions to be puzzles that confuse your interviewees. Compound questions with multiple parts may cause problems for some participants

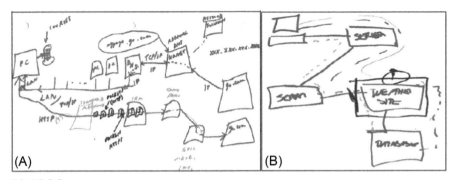

FIGURE 8.2

Interview participants were asked to draw a secure web connection: a secure web connection is (A) correctly depicted as protecting information transmitted from the PC to the web server and (B) incorrectly depicted as secure data storage.

From Friedman, B., Hurley, D., Howe, D.C., Felten, E., Nissenbaum, H., 2002. Users' conceptions of web security: a comparative study. CHI '02 Extended Abstracts on Human Factors in Computing Systems, Minneapolis, MN. ACM, pp. 746–747; https://doi.org/10.1145/506443.506510.

(Robson, 2002). If you find yourself writing such a question, break it up into multiple simpler questions. Complex comparative questions may be particularly challenging in this respect. Instead of asking "What were the strengths and weaknesses of the menu layout and the toolbar?," ask separate questions: "What did you think of the menu layout? What did you think of the toolbar? Which did you prefer?"

Your questions should be as unbiased and unjudgmental as possible. In particular, you should watch out for phrasing that might encourage your interviewee to give you the answer that they think you want to hear. This is another reason to prefer questions that ask "what do you think of…?" rather than "did you like…?" Particularly if you're talking about something that interviewees know you (or your team) have designed, asking if they like (or dislike) something or find it easy (or hard) to use, might influence responses. Questions that ask people "Why do you like this design?" (Robson, 2002) or "Don't you think this is hard to use?" are particularly troublesome in this regard. Some suggest avoiding questions with negative answers—simply ask "What did you think?" instead (Angrosino, 2005). You may find it hard to completely eliminate questions that have subtle potential for bias, but avoiding the worst pitfalls should not be too difficult.

You should construct questions that are appropriate for your audience. If your audience consists of well-educated professionals—similar to many HCI researchers—language that you are comfortable with may work well for your participants. Interviews or focus groups with participants with substantively different backgrounds from those of the researcher pose additional challenges—you have to learn to "speak their language." For example, interviews or focus groups involving young children may fare better if appropriately designed questions and options for answers are used. Instead of using a Likert scale for a closed question regarding subjective reaction to a system, you might consider using the "smileyometer" (a continuous and discrete rating scales based on a range from a deep frown to a broad smile), the "Fun Sorter" (a scale for ranking items in order of which was most fun), or the "Again-Again" scale, which asks children to indicate which activities they might like to repeat (Figure 8.3; Read and MacFarlane, 2006; Read et al., 2002). Although potentially useful, these tools might be difficult to use reliably

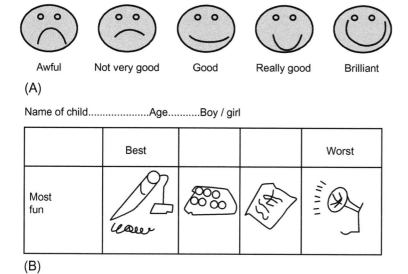

FIGURE 8.3

Questionnaire tools for assessing children's subjective responses to technology: (A) a smileyometer preference scale, (B) a Fun Sorter for relative preference between options, (C) an again-again scale for selecting which activities a child would like to repeat.

From Read, J.C., MacFarlane, S., 2006. Using the fun toolkit and other survey methods to gather opinions in child computer interaction. Proceedings of the 2006 Conference on Interaction Design and Children, Tampere, Finland. ACM, pp. 81–88; http://dx.doi.org/10.1145/1139073.1139096.

with younger children (Read and MacFarlane, 2006). In more complex cases, working with children or other groups with different backgrounds may require spending some time to understand the context before you design an interview—see Chapter 9 for background on ethnographic observations.

When your interview is less than fully structured, you may be generating questions on the spot, in response to specific interviewee comments. On-the-fly phrasing of questions that are clear, simple, and free from jargon and bias is an art requiring practice and experience. This may be another reason to stick with more structure until you gain some experience, but all is not lost: the informal give-and-take of semistructured and unstructured interviews gives you some room for rephrasing and revisiting questions as needed.

Human nature being what it is, interviewee responses may be inconsistent. This is to be expected. Including questions that are slightly redundant may help you assess the degree of consistency in responses, but you should probably decide in advance how you will handle any inconsistency. Possibilities include reporting inconsistencies and discounting responses from interviewees who appear to be particularly inconsistent. The Finding and Reminding sidebar in Section 8.3.1 discusses Thomas Malone's study of how people organize information in their offices—an example of a semistructured interview that generated some influential results.

8.8 CONDUCTING AN INTERVIEW

8.8.1 PREPARATION

With all of the details that must be addressed, appropriate planning and preparation is obviously important. Pilot-testing your interview—both with research colleagues and participants—is always a good idea. In addition to helping you find questions that are hard to understand, pilot testing can give you some idea of the potential length of an interview. If your pilot test runs past the two-hour mark, you may want to ask yourself if there is anything that you might trim. Although pilot testing may be harder for a focus group, it is not impossible. One approach might be to use your colleagues as pilot focus group participants. Other possibilities include asking experts familiar with focus groups to review your questions and other materials. You might also consider your first group to be the pilot: if it goes well, great. If not, you can revise it and remove the results from further consideration in your analysis (Krueger, 1994).

A clear and concise interview guide can help you remember which steps to take and when. Guides are particularly helpful for focus groups (Brown, 1999) and for any situation where more than one researcher is acting as an interviewer or moderator.

Proper preparation includes appropriate backups. Assume that your computer will crash, your recorder won't work, and the power will fail. Can you conduct your interview in the dark on paper? That might be a bit extreme, but extra batteries, paper, and perhaps even a backup recording device will prepare you for almost any contingency.

8.8.2 RECORDING THE RESPONSES

Having chosen the format of your interview, identified your participants, and written your questions, you are ready to plan the details of conducting the interview. Written notes and audio or video recordings all have advantages and disadvantages. You'll probably always want to have a notebook on hand. If you have an interviewing partner, she might take notes with the computer while you write your thoughts on paper, but it's probably too distracting for the primary interviewer to be typing on the computer during the course of the interview session. In any case, you should have a paper notebook available as a backup.

Written notes can be useful for recording interviewee responses and interviewer comments. Even if you are using audio or video recording devices for your main records of participant comments, you should use written notes to document nonverbal cues or concerns (Brown, 1999). Do your interviewees seem bored, anxious, or tired? This can be particularly important for focus groups: you'll want to note if you see body language cues indicating disagreement with the current speaker, general frustration, or lack of interest.

Simply writing down interviewee responses is likely to be most effective for simple, closed questions. Answers to open-ended questions and comments made in free-flowing unstructured interviews may be hard to capture adequately in writing. Transcribing spoken text in real time is a cognitive challenge. If you are busy trying to write down what your interviewee said a few seconds ago, you might miss an interesting comment. Participants may find it distracting as well, particularly if you are so focused on writing that you appear not to be paying attention to them.

You should strongly consider summarizing and possibly rewriting your notes as soon as possible after each interview. This will give you a chance to clarify any comments, add details that will help you remember the context, and clarify in other ways that increase the likelihood of extracting useful data from the record, even after a gap of months or years.

Audio and video recordings capture every word of an interview, at the potential cost of difficulty of transcription and interpretation. Turning a single hour of recorded discussion into text may take several hours (Robson, 2002) and substantially sized projects can generate massive amounts of content (see the Green Living Interviews sidebar in Section 8.3.1). Digital recorders make recording inexpensive and easy enough that you might decide to record interviews before committing to transcribing them, but such recordings may go unheard.

If you are going to record, the choice between audio and video can be important. Video recording is logistically harder, usually requiring a tripod and some maneuvering that might be challenging if you are in a tight space. Some interviewees may initially be uncomfortable with the video camera, but most forget about it within a few minutes. In many cases, the additional details captured by a video recording can be quite informative. Interviews with professionals aimed at understanding work in context would benefit from video recordings of workspaces and offices. You might even use a video camera to capture the use of a current software tool, but you should not count on using an inexpensive video camera to record screen output from a computer: such recordings generally don't work well. Screen-capture software operating directly on the computer would be a better bet. Audio recording is, of course, simpler and more straightforward. You might consider using audio recording along with still pictures from a digital camera. This will give you much of the benefit of video without the overhead.

Whatever approach you take to recording, you should be careful to respect the privacy and anonymity of your subjects. Written notes and recordings should be treated as identifying information which should be kept securely and treated as confidential.

You should have a consistent policy for dealing with comments made after you close your notebook or turn off the recording device. As you are wrapping up or even walking out by the door, some participants may make comments that are of interest. You can certainly pull your notebook back out or restart your audio recorder or camera, but you should deal with these comments consistently (Robson, 2002).

Paper notes, photos, and electronic recordings need not be the only records of your interview. If you ask users to complete a task on the computer, you might collect (with their permission) screen shots illustrating their tasks in progress. Any conceptual maps, drawings, or other outputs from tasks associated with your interview questions should be considered as part of the interview record and analyzed accordingly.

8.8.3 DURING THE INTERVIEW

8.8.3.1 Rapport

From the start of the interview, you should strive to help your interviewees feel comfortable and at ease. If you can convey the impression of being a professional, friendly, and likable person, your interviewees will be more inclined to trust you with honest and useful feedback. You may find that interviewees who are more at ease will be more candid with responses, providing useful input instead of telling you what they think you want to hear.

Steps that you take to make your interviewees feel more comfortable may have the added benefit of making the experience more enjoyable for you as well. This can be particularly important for projects involving a large number of interviews: if you dread the thought of conducting the next interview, it may not lead to much in the way of useful data.

Creating an environment that encourages open conversation is easier said than done. The first few minutes of an interview are crucial (Kvale, 2007): if you establish good rapport quickly, the rest might flow easily. To make the all-important good first impression, you should be friendly and supportive. Listen carefully, sincerely, and respectfully (Kvale, 2007): after all, you've invited the interviewee to participate—if you cannot be concerned enough to be interested, why should they? Be respectful, straightforward, clear, and nonthreatening (Robson, 2002). Judgmental responses are inappropriate. Cringing or frowning when you hear a response that you don't like won't encourage interviewees to share more with you. This is one area where some practice might help: you'll want to develop a poker face.

When you are conducting an interview or focus group, you are, to some extent, acting as a host. When appropriate, you might consider providing simple refreshments. A glass of water will help an interviewee or focus group participant feel comfortable enough to keep talking. Snacks may be nice, but should be chosen carefully to respect participants' cultural and dietary sensitivities. Loud, crunchy food is inadvisable, as it may distract participants and interfere with audio recordings (Barbour, 2007).

Finding some common ground of shared experience or perspective is a tried-and-true technique for building good relationships. Although this may be related to the topic of the interview, it need not necessarily be. If an interviewee comments on travel delays due to traffic or the need to leave early due to family obligations, you might respond with a short personal comment indicating your understanding of those challenges. Alternatively, you might include an initial interview question aimed at establishing some common ground. If it's at all relevant, you might consider asking interviewees to describe a notable technology failure: almost everyone will have a story to tell and you can commiserate with a story of your own. If you can focus this question on a specific technology relevant to your interview, so much the better.

As you work to establish rapport with your interviewees, be careful to avoid anything that gets too personal. As the interview is about you learning from the interviewee, you should be listening most of the time. Talking too much about your own experiences is inappropriate and may make some people uncomfortable. You might make brief comments about your own experiences or opinions whenever appropriate and then steer the conversation back to focusing on the interviewee.

8.8.3.2 The introduction

Most interviews or focus groups follow the same general outline. You should start with an introduction, telling the interviewees about the research and your goals. If appropriate, this would also be a good time to complete any paperwork, including (when necessary) the informed consent form required to document the interviewee's agreement to participate (Chapter 15). You should also tell participants if you are recording the session and how. For focus groups, you might use the introduction as an opportunity to encourage differing viewpoints (Krueger, 1994).

You might want to keep the introduction to your research brief. You should not go into too much detail regarding your goals and aims (Kvale, 2007), as a detailed description of your aims and goals might encourage your participants to provide answers that they think you would want to hear. This is particularly a concern if you're asking about reactions to a syste that you have built. You can provide more context after the session is over (see Section 8.8.3.5).

8.8.3.3 Getting down to business

The interview proper will start with relatively easy questions, useful for building trust and preparing the interviewee for harder questions. Risky questions come towards the end, perhaps followed by some simpler questions aimed at defusing any tension or anxiety. After your questions are complete, be sure to thank interviewees for their time (Robson, 2002).

During the interview, you must be on your best behavior. The first and most important rule is to remember that as the interviewer, your job is to *listen*. You are meeting with your interviewees to learn from them and you can't do that if you're doing all of the talking. After you introduce the interview and go over any administrative details, you should let the interviewee do most of the talking. You can certainly ask the questions, provide clarification if needed, and encourage further details, but that's about it—the interviewee should do the bulk of the talking. You'll have to give them time to speak—don't rush—and provide multiple opportunities to continue: "is there anything else you wanted to tell me?" or "take your time" are good ways to give your participants room to gather their thoughts without feeling pressured. Don't rush to move on to a new question until you are absolutely sure that the interviewee has finished answering the current question. Careful listening also involves paying attention to nonverbal cues: if the interviewee seems anxious or agitated, you may have interrupted her. If this happens, back up and give her a chance to continue.

Being adaptable and flexible is particularly important for semistructured or unstructured interviews. If you want to get the full benefits of ceding some control to your participants, you will have to be willing to go where they will lead you. This may mean reordering or eliminating certain questions and letting the conversation take some unexpected twists and turns. In some cases, you may be able to come back to those questions later, while other interviews may leave their original script and never return. As long as your interviewees don't go completely off-topic, you should try to follow them. If they digress into totally unrelated areas, you might want to gently nudge them back on track. Careful and early attention to conversational style can help you avoid irrelevant digressions. If you notice early on that you are talking with someone who is prone to wander off into unrelated topics, you can prepare yourself to repeatedly—but politely—interrupt and guide the conversation back on track.

Interviewees and focus group participants have their own need for clarity and continuity. You should take care to explain why you are asking each question, and how it relates both to the overall topic of the interview and to questions that you have previously asked. If participants aren't sure why you are asking a question, they might misunderstand it and provide an answer to what is, in effect, a different question.

Terminology, also introduces possibilities for misunderstanding. Provide definitions of any terms that might involve technical jargon or otherwise be unclear or ambiguous. If a participant introduces a term that may be problematic, ask for a clarification: "What exactly do you mean when you say…?" If the definition is not the one that you would tend to use, it's probably best to make a note of this difference and then to stick with it.

As the interview or focus group session progresses, you should try to distinguish between answers that the participants give because they are trying to please you and answers that genuinely reflect their opinions. The tendency of research participants to try to please researchers, particularly by providing information that would be perceived as confirming a hypothesis, is well known (Orne, 1962). If you hear participants saying uniformly positive things about a system that you developed or a model that you suggested, you might be a bit cautious about over-interpreting those responses.

As with all research involving human subjects, interviews must be conducted in a manner that respects the rights and concerns of the participants (see Chapter 15). Be sure to clearly explain to your interviewees that they can decline to answer any question. This is particularly important if you are discussing potentially sensitive topics. When they do decline to answer, simply note their lack of response and move on to the next question. Participants should have the chance to take breaks, particularly if the interview is long. Interviews and focus groups should be kept to a reasonable length—probably less than 2 hours (Brown, 1999).

Focus groups present additional challenges. Listening is still paramount, but you may want to jump in to keep conversation on track. Focus groups can go badly wrong in many different ways: discussions can digress; participants might talk at length to the exclusion of others; disagreements might arise; or you might simply have a group that doesn't get along well. If you see any signs of trouble, you can jump in, gently urging participants to stay on topic, let others speak, be polite, and so on. You might try to be particularly sensitive to participants who seem to be quietly observing without saying much. Although some quiet folks might not have anything to say, others might be intimidated. Particularly if your quieter participants appear to be agitated or uncomfortable, you might address them directly, offering an opportunity to speak: "Joan, is there anything you'd care to say about…?" Having asked this question, you must be ready to accept "no, thanks" as an answer.

8.8.3.4 Promoting discussion

What if you hold an interview (or focus group) and nobody talks? Spending an hour in a room with someone who responds in monosyllables is both unproductive and unenjoyable. You certainly can't force anyone to talk in any detail, but you might be able to encourage them. If your interview is fully structured you may not have much wiggle room, but you can add questions to semistructured and unstructured interviews, in the hopes of eliciting comments. If you are asking about user reaction to a given tool, you might rephrase the question in various different ways—do they use the tool at home or at work? Have they had problems at home or at work? Is the spreadsheet tool good for personal finances and for taxes? In some cases, overly general questions might discourage responses: if you dig deeper into specifics, you might remind your interviewee of some specific incident or need that is relevant.

Physical props, note cards, and other probes can also stimulate feedback. In Section 8.3.2, our sample exploratory questions included asking participants how they currently arrange items in scrapbooks. Instead of simply asking this question, you might give your interviewee a small pile of photos and ask him to arrange them as if he was constructing a scrapbook, explaining the process as he went. This use of probes can be particularly helpful for revealing attitudes and practices that your participants may not have fully articulated: even though your interviewee knows what he's doing and why, he may not have thought about it enough to put it into words. Probes also provide a potentially entertaining alternative to a steady stream of questions.

Some techniques for eliciting responses are specific to focus groups. If a participant's comment is followed by silence, you might specifically ask others to react: "does anyone have a different opinion?" A short pause can also provide an opening for someone who has been waiting for a chance to make a comment (Krueger, 1994).

8.8.3.5 Debriefing

Set aside some time at the end of the interview or focus group for wrapping up and debriefing. When you have finished covering the questions or topics on your list, you might ask participants if they have anything else to add and, for their reactions to participating in the interview or focus group (Kvale, 2007). This will provide an opportunity for the sharing of thoughts that did not seem to fit earlier in the conversation.

Once your participants have finished answering questions, you might want to provide details about your research goals and the purpose of the interview, without the risk of biasing their responses. This additional detail can help interviewees feel that their time has been well spent and satisfying. Your debriefing might also include a brief summary of what you have learned during the session. This summary gives participants an opportunity to correct any misunderstandings.

Consider turning off any recording devices before you begin the debriefing: if participants are aware that you are no longer recording, they may share some comments that they would not have made earlier (Kvale, 2007).

After you have thanked your interviewee or focus group participants, try to take a few minutes to gather your thoughts, summarize the results, and otherwise reflect upon the session (Kvale, 2007). Even if you have recorded the session and taken detailed notes, your initial reactions may include insights that will be difficult, if not impossible, to reconstruct even a few hours later.

8.9 ELECTRONICALLY MEDIATED INTERVIEWS AND FOCUS GROUPS

Modern communication technologies present the attractive option of conducting interviews and focus groups electronically. Online chat, conference calls, and one-to-one phone calls can all be used to communicate directly with participants from the comfort of your own office. You can even conduct interviews by email, sending questions and answers back and forth in an ongoing dialog. In some cases, electronically mediated interviews may be your only possibility. If you are working with domain experts who are geographically distant, face-to-face conversations may simply be too expensive to arrange. Even when face-to-face meetings are possible, cost considerations may lead you to choose the convenience of telephone or online interviews.

8.9.1 TELEPHONE

Telephone interviewing seems straightforward enough: simply pick up the phone, call, and talk. Focus groups require conference call support, but numerous commercial and freely available services can provide these services easily. However, it would be a mistake to assume that the ease of initiating communication means that the rest is smooth sailing. Before conducting phone interviews, you may want to consider a few concerns that make these interviews qualitatively different from face-to-face discussion.

Your first practical decision may involve recording. Inexpensive tools for recording telephone calls are readily available, but they should only be used as appropriate. There may be local or national laws that dictate appropriate behavior for recording phone calls: for example, you might need to inform participants and get their explicit consent.

The dynamics of a telephone interview are likely to be somewhat different from what they would be if you were talking to the same person face-to-face. Phone conversations lack the nonverbal cues that inform in-person conversations: you may not be able to tell if someone is bored, tired, or distracted. In fact, you probably won't have any information about what the other person is doing: you might be conducting a phone interview with someone who is cooking dinner, doing dishes, or attending to other distractions instead of paying attention to what you are saying.

That said, the lack of direct face-to-face contact may, in some situations, prove advantageous. Particularly if the conversation involves sensitive topics, interviewees may be willing to make some comments over the phone that they would not make in person.

Conference calls for focus groups pose different problems. When you have multiple unfamiliar people on a call, it's hard to keep track of who is speaking. Asking participants to state their name before each comment may work, but it quickly gets tedious. As anyone who's participated in a conference call knows, simply getting a chance to speak can often be a big challenge.

8.9.2 ONLINE

Computer-mediated interviews are generally conducted via email, instant-messaging, chat, or online conferencing tools. An email interview might involve an extended exchange of messages, as interviewers send questions and interviewees respond. Instant-message or online conferencing interviews and focus groups are closer in spirit to traditional face-to-face interviews, with questions and respondents coming in near real time.

Recruiting challenges in online interviewing include the usual problems associated with online research: you may or may not know who you are talking with (see Chapter 14). Identifying suitable participants for non-face-to-face interviews may require some extra effort in building relationships with potential interviewees and externally validating their identities and suitability for your work. However, respondents can also be anonymous, which may be useful if you are discussing illegal or otherwise undesirable activities.

Online interviews and focus groups are often easy to record. Email programs save both sent and received messages, and instant-messaging programs generally record transcripts of all comments. These running logs can be quite helpful for reviewing and interpreting the conversation, even while it is still in progress. For example, the interviewer can review the conversation to verify that all appropriate topics have been covered. Another possibility would be to use the respondents' previous comments to ask for further clarification: "Earlier, you said...." Reviewing these comments can also help the interviewer ask repetitive questions. At the close of a discussion, you might ask the interviewee to review the logs to see if there are any final comments that she would like to add to the conversation (Voida et al., 2004).

Contextual feedback in email and chat interviews may be even more impoverished than with telephone interviews, as these text-only exchanges lack both the visual feedback of face-to-face meetings and the audio information generally available on telephone calls. Many participants may be multitasking and perhaps carrying on other instant-messaging conversations during the course of an online interview (Voida et al., 2004). Text-based interviews via chat or email may lead to very different types of responses, as some respondents will be more formal than they might be in person. This is particularly the case for email, as some might take time to carefully organize thoughts. Different expectations of pacing may also influence the content and quality of responses. In a face-to-face conversation, we rarely pause for 30 s or one minute before responding to a question. Online chats, by contrast, frequently have delays of several minutes, and who among us hasn't let several days go by without responding to an email? This delay can be constructive in allowing for consideration of the question, but it might also contribute to distraction and half-hearted answers. Delays might indicate other potentially interesting behavior, including revision of initial responses. Many chat programs provide visual indicators of activity, such as a series of dots indicating that the person is typing. If a participant in an instant-messaging conversation provides a short answer after having been typing for quite some time, you might consider asking them to clarify their thinking (Voida et al., 2004).

Pacing in online interviews is also a challenge. Going too slowly might cause participants to lose focus and interest, but moving too quickly might prove unnerving. Expecting participants to respond to emailed interview questions within a matter of minutes is probably unrealistic. Online messaging need not always be instant. Given the breaks that seem to occur naturally in instant-messaging conversations, taking some time to rephrase a question or consider a response may be quite appropriate. On the other hand, cutting and pasting a question from an interview script into a messaging client may seem a bit too quick (Voida et al., 2004).

Online focus groups also lessen the presence of moderators—instead of being a powerful presence at the front of the room, the moderator is reduced to simply being another voice or line on the chat screen. This may reduce participant fear that the moderator may somehow disapprove of them or their comments (Walston and Lissitz, 2000).

In some studies, respondents using computer-based systems have reported a higher frequency of socially undesirable behavior, as compared to those participating in traditional surveys, possibly because responding directly to a computer (without the presence of a human) encourages more openness in responses (Walston and Lissitz, 2000). In comparison, in one study of behavior relating to HIV/AIDS in sub-Saharan Africa, interviews were administered using both paper and computers. In both cases, interviewers asked the questions to the interviewees and recorded the answers on the paper or computer. Analysis of the results indicated that participants who were interviewed with the computers were more likely to provide socially desirable answers regarding risky behaviors. Although more study would be needed to understand these responses, the researchers conjectured that interviewers who used computers may have appeared to have been either affluent or outsiders. Participants may simply have been trying to impress the interviewers (Cheng et al., 2008).

Online conferencing tools provide additional context that can narrow the gap between online and in-person interviews. The combination of real-time audio, which is obviously necessary for a conversational flow, and video, which can restore some of the visual cues associated with face-to-face conversation, can be almost as good as being there. As capabilities vary across service providers, you might want to experiment with multiple tools to find those that work best. Screen sharing and recording tools are often useful for conducting contextual inquiries online, as they allow detailed exploration of the participants' use of systems, with recordings capturing each interaction with the system. Other tools may provide remote mouse and keyboard input, allowing users to interact with software running on your computer. Although perhaps not as personal as in-person interviews, such approaches, like all electronically mediated interviewing techniques, can be a cost effective means of reaching a broader range of participants.

8.10 ANALYZING INTERVIEW DATA

Having conducted a series of interviews or focus groups, you'll find yourself faced with the daunting task of interpreting your data. Countless pages of written notes and hours of video or audio recordings pose a significant challenge—how do you make sense of it all? Your goal in analyzing interview data is to generate an accurate representation of interviewee responses. Usually, your analysis works towards a general, holistic understanding: the analysis of answers to individual questions are combined to form general models of user needs for a particular task, reactions to a proposed design, or other focus of the interview. This may not be possible—you may find that there are no consistent patterns. This is interesting as well.

Whichever techniques you choose to use, you should try to analyze your data as soon as possible. When the interview is fresh in your mind, you will be well-positioned to remember details and nuances that you may not have captured in your notes. As time passes, you will find it increasingly difficult to remember potentially important nonverbal cues or comments. Your notes will also become less useful over time, as hastily scribbled cryptic comments will be hard to interpret weeks or months later.

Effective analysis works to avoid bias and reliance on preconceived notions. The absence of "hard," numeric data makes interview responses and similar qualitative data sources particularly susceptible to biased manipulation. An emphasis on data points that confirm your favorite hypothesis, at the expense of comments that argue against it—a practice known as "cherry picking"—is just one of the possible biases in the analysis of results. Biased consideration of responses from specific participants, or classes of participants, can be a problem for focus group data. If your analysis pays disproportionate attention to female participants relative to male participants (or vice versa), any resulting interpretation will be somewhat distorted. Your analysis activities should always strive to be inclusive and data driven.

Additional information about the use of qualitative data analysis methods can be found in Chapter 11.

8.10.1 WHAT TO ANALYZE

Fully structured interviews consisting only of closed questions are the easiest to analyze. As all interviewees are asked the same questions and all answers are taken from a small set of possibilities, analysis is essentially a tabulation problem. You can tabulate the frequency of each answer and use straightforward statistical tests to determine when differences in response rates are meaningful (see Chapter 4). Quantitative results can also be used to group characteristics (see the Finding and Reminding sidebar in Section 8.3.1 for an example).

Analysis gets harder as your questions become more open-ended and the interview becomes less structured. Open-ended questions can be answered in a different way by each interviewee. Two participants might answer any given question in entirely different ways, creating the challenge of identifying the common ground. Unstructured or semistructured interviews introduce the additional complication of questions and topics arising at very different stages in different interviews. Analysis of these interviews may require tying together comments made at very different times under very different contexts.

Should your analysis be based on written notes or on audio or video recordings? Unlike written notes, recordings provide complete and unfiltered access to everything that an interviewee said or did, even months after the fact. This record can be used to reconstruct details, focus in on specific comments, and share user feedback with colleagues. The disadvantage, of course, is the expense and challenge of wading through hours of video or audio data. You can analyze recordings by listening to comments piece by piece, repeatedly replaying pieces of interest until you gain an understanding, but this can be a slow, often tedious process. Verbatim transcriptions translate these hours of discussions into pages of written text that might be more amenable to analysis and editing via software, but transcribing can also be an expensive and unappealing process. Although it may be possible to use automated speech recognition techniques to generate a transcript, these tools are subject to recognition errors that might limit the quality of the output.

Notes written during the interview have the advantage of being relatively compact and easy to work with. Your written notes may omit some interesting details, but it's likely that the comments you managed to get down on paper were among the most important made during the session. Even if you have to transcribe your handwritten notes into an electronic format, the amount of transcription required will be substantially less than that needed for a transcript of an audio recording of the same discussion.

These practical considerations play an important role in determining how you analyze the data. If time and money are particularly tight, you might be best served by an analysis of written records. Detailed examination of recordings is most appropriate for situations where you are interested in digging into the details as deep as possible and you are willing to commit the resources (time and money) to do this work.

8.10.2 **HOW TO ANALYZE**

After you decide whether to work from a recording (either directly or via a transcript) or interview notes, the next step is to decide how to approach the analysis. Interview analyses usually rely heavily on qualitative methods for coding data, either through emergent or a priori codes (Chapter 11). These methods attempt to find common structures and themes from qualitative data. In the case of interviews, your goal is to identify the important ideas that repeatedly arise during an interview.

One technique that is commonly used for analyzing interview data involves examination of the text of the interview for patterns of usage, including frequency of terms, cooccurrences, and other structural markers that may provide indications of the importance of various concepts and the relationships between them. This approach—known as *content analysis*—builds on the assumption that the structure of an interviewee's comments provides meaningful hints as to what he finds important and why (Robson, 2002). *Discourse analysis* goes beyond looking at discussions of words and contents to examine the structure of the conversation, in search of cues that might provide additional understanding (Preece et al., 2015). For example, do users say "we log out of the system when we are done" or do they say "the proper procedure is to log out when we are done"? The answer to this question might help you understand differences between what users actually do (the first option) and what IT managers might want them to do (the second option).

As interview and focus group research generally involves multiple participants, grouping of comments and resulting codes by participants can often prove useful as well, particularly if you can identify differences between participants that might be meaningful to the question at hand. You might find trends in responses that are associated with the age, educational level, and/or professional background of the participants. Even if response content does not correlate with demographic or other obvious variables, trends might indicate multiple "clusters" of users with similar perspectives. Counts of the frequency of mention of various terms, topics, or concerns (50% of participants over 65 years old expressed interest in the proposed design, while only 25% of those under 65 wanted to learn more…) might be one means of adding a quantitative perspective to otherwise qualitative interview data.

If these techniques sound too abstract and theoretical for your taste, you might want to try something simpler—an introductory approach is given in the Interview Analysis for Novices sidebar.

INTERVIEW ANALYSIS FOR NOVICES

Interview analysis can be somewhat intimidating. If you're feeling that you're in a bit over your head, don't panic. Although some analyses might best be done by an experienced collaborator, you don't need an advanced degree in the social sciences to get a basic understanding of interview data.

In school, many people have been taught to write notes on index cards—one idea per card—which can then be sorted and arranged as necessary. You can break responses to interview questions into individual thoughts or ideas, one per index card or one per line in a text document. Group lines with common ideas but don't restrict yourself to putting any idea into only one category. Feel free to place thoughts in multiple groups, as appropriate.

You might consider assigning categories to comments as they appear in the transcript. This can be done by annotating each line with a colored piece of text that names the category. Once you've done this, you can quickly search to find out all of the instances of a particular category. As the categories begin to grow, you may see connections between them. You can then put these categories into broader categories, forming a hierarchy of ideas.

How do you categorize each comment or concept? One approach would be to group things by the content words—nouns or verbs. You can use these words to understand the objects with which people work and the actions that they use with those objects. Organizing comments along these lines can help you understand the outlines of the problem domain.

As you dig through the interviews, you may begin to find relationships, information flows, sequences, or other patterns that repeatedly arise out of the comments. Pictures, sketches, outlines, or other representations of these interactions can help clarify your understanding.

Focus groups introduce the additional challenge of differing viewpoints. You might consider grouping comments by individual or by the individual's role. This might help you understand potentially important differences in perspectives.

In any case, if you are concerned about validity, enlist a colleague to work with you. You might each independently analyze the data and then compare your results, in the hopes of working towards a consensus analysis. Alternatively, you might work together, building agreement as you go along.

This informal analysis shares many characteristics with more rigorous established practices such as content analysis or discourse analysis. These approaches may differ in their level of attention to detail and their conformance to established practices but the goal is always the same: to help researchers move from an unordered and undifferentiated mess of interview data to a clear, structured understanding.

Informal techniques are often sufficient. If you are trying to build an initial understanding of a problem, gauge reaction to design proposals, or examine a problem without aspiring for generality and validity, this approach can be very productive. If you find that you need to add some rigor, you can always return to the data for a second, more rigorous analysis, perhaps with the help of a colleague with relevant experience.

Interviews and focus groups might also be examined for stories, responses, or comments that are particularly insightful, interesting, or otherwise important. Known as *critical-incident analysis*, this technique can be useful for identifying opportunities for digging deeper in search of useful information (Preece et al., 2015). In an interview, a critical incident might be a story that describes a notable failure of an existing system or a desired list of criteria for its replacement. As each critical incident becomes a case study—chosen not as a representative incident but rather as one that can provide useful information—techniques described in Chapter 7 can be applicable.

8.10.3 **VALIDITY**

Analyses based on the interpretation of texts often face questions of validity. Due to the necessarily subjective nature of the process of reading texts, any single analysis may be influenced in subtle (or not-so-subtle) ways by the viewpoints and biases of the individual analyst. If validity is a particular concern—as it might be when your goal is to make a general claim—you might want to have multiple researchers conduct independent analyses of your interviews. Ideally, their comments will be largely in agreement with each other. High value measures of *interrater reliability* can support your analysis (see Chapter 11).

Validity may not be a particular concern if your interviews are aimed at understanding user requirements. If you are working closely with users and customers, you will probably present your findings to them once your analysis is complete. If you have a good working relationship, they will let you know when your analysis has gone wrong. This feedback is very useful for refining your understanding.

8.10.4 **REPORTING RESULTS**

After you have conducted countless interviews and spent untold hours analyzing responses, you must report the results. Expectations vary among contexts; descriptions of a given set of results in an academic publication might differ significantly from how the same results would be presented in a corporate memo or presentation for a client. Despite these differences, some common principles apply.

Your presentation of interview results should be as clear and specific as possible. Tabulations of frequencies of responses can be used to give specific reports. Instead of saying "many users complained about...," say "seven out of 10 interviewees who responded complained about..." Replacing terms such as "many," "most," "often," "frequently," "rarely," and other vague quantifiers with concrete counts help users to understand not only the specific points but their relative importance.

You can also use respondent's words to make your reporting more concrete. Instead of paraphrasing or summarizing, use direct quotes. A small number of direct quotes illustrating interviewee sentiment can make your arguments much more concrete. This strategy can be particularly effective when coupled with frequency counts indicating widespread agreement with the quoted views.

If you do decide to quote users directly, you should be careful to do so in accordance with best practices for respecting human participants in research. Don't use participant names. If you have to repeatedly refer to an individual, use initials or a numeric code: S1, S2, etc. Don't use quotes that reveal any embarrassing or identifying details. You should always inform participants that their words may be used in research reports. This information should be explicitly included in the informed consent form (see Chapter 15). For questions that address particularly sensitive issues, you may wish to avoid quoting any interviewees directly.

8.11 SUMMARY

Interviews and focus groups present substantial challenges for HCI researchers and practitioners. Writing questions, identifying appropriate respondents, conducting interviews, and analyzing data all require considerable skill and experience. For those of us who come to HCI from a technical background, the social science techniques and strategies that are involved may seem unfamiliar and somewhat daunting.

Despite these concerns, interviews and focus groups are invaluable tools for HCI researchers and practitioners, providing data into user and stakeholder needs and perceptions that would be difficult, if not impossible to get using other techniques. It's that simple—if you want to know what people want or what they think, you must ask them. For researchers, this might mean in-depth conversations aimed at building models to explain how systems are used and why. For designers and builders of interfaces, interviews can help build understanding of needs and reactions to interfaces. If you want to know why your last design failed, you can start by interviewing the users.

The choice of one-to-one interviews or focus groups involves trade-offs in time, expediency, depth, and difficulty. Focus groups let you hear from many people at once but with less depth from any given individual. You should consider the trade-off between this loss of depth and the potentially fuller understanding that may arise from a conversation between participants having multiple perspectives. Unfortunately, there are no guarantees: this intriguing dynamic conversation might not materialize. As the moderator of a focus group, you have a very important role to play: this is where the difficulty comes in. Skillful moderation can keep conversation focused and inclusive, increasing your chances of getting good data.

Interviews and focus groups might best be conducted as complements to other data collection approaches. Empirical studies, usability tests, ethnographic investigations, and case studies are among the methods that might be used alongside interviews. You can use multiple, complementary tactics to confirm findings or identify potential disconnects. Perhaps users prefer one interface design over another, even though it is slower. Why is this? Well-formed interview questions might help you understand the reasons.

If you feel intimidated by these challenges, start small. A simple, fully structured interview with closed questions will help you get started. As you become more comfortable with writing questions, talking to interviewees, and analyzing data, you might move on to interviews with less structure and greater challenges. Don't be ashamed to bring in some outside help. A colleague who is knowledgeable and experienced in interviewing can be an invaluable aide.

DISCUSSION QUESTIONS

1. The trust required to successfully conduct an interview may be difficult to achieve under certain circumstances. If honest answers to difficult questions may have repercussions for your interviewees, they might be less than forthcoming. If you were interested in developing a tool that would encourage teens to pay for downloading music rather than illegally trading copyrighted songs, you might consider interviewing teens to understand their attitudes and practices. However, they may be reluctant to share information with you, for fear that their parents would learn of any inappropriate activity that they have been involved in. As parental consent is likely to be required for the participation of underage teens, these concerns are not necessarily invalid. How might you build trust with these teens? How might you evaluate their comments to determine whether they are being truthful?

2. The development of a tool to encourage teens to pay for downloaded music presents some challenges in data gathering. If teens are using home computers for potentially inappropriate activities, parents may feel that they have a legitimate interest and concern in what their children are doing. To better understand the problem, you might decide to interview parents as well as teens. Would you interview them separately or together? What sort of questions would you ask parents and how would they differ from questions that you might ask of teens? Would you use one-to-one interviews or focus groups? Why?

3. Interviews can become awkward if the interviewees start asking difficult questions about the research. Imagine you are interviewing hospital equipment repair technicians about their practices for recording their workflow, including repairs completed, time spent on each repair, and related tasks. What should you do if the workers' concern for their job security leads them to ask tough questions about why the data is being collected and what it will be used for? If you know that management is trying to collect data that might be used to raise expectations and workload or to reduce staff, what should you tell the technicians? How can you resolve your responsibility to the client (the management) who is paying the bills, while showing appropriate respect for the workers you are interviewing?

RESEARCH DESIGN EXERCISES

1. Design and conduct an interview. Chances are pretty good that most of the people you know have or use cell phones. They are also likely to have strong opinions about their likes and dislikes regarding phone interface design and features. Design an interview that you might use to understand what cell phone users would like to see in a new generation of phone. What sort of questions would you ask and why? How much structure would you want to have? Would you use any props or observations? Once you have this interview designed, try it on a friend, classmate, or colleague. What did this teach you about interviewing? Were there questions that you should have asked but didn't? What worked well, what didn't?

2. Revisit the cell phone usage interview from Exercise 1. What would be different if you were to collect this data via a focus group instead of interviews? Revise the questions to account for any differences between individuals, in terms of preferences, experiences, and needs. How might you foster discussion and deliberation between focus group participants?

3. Revisit the cell phone usage interview from Exercise 1, but try it online this time. Sign up for an account on an instant-messaging service (if you don't have one already), and ask a friend or classmate to be your interviewee. Ask the same questions that you asked before. How do the responses differ? Did you get as much information or less? Did you notice any differences in the amount of feedback or the quality of the responses? Which did you find most useful? Which did you prefer?

REFERENCES

Angrosino, M., 2005. Projects in Ethnographic Research. Waveland Press, Long Grove, IL.

Barbour, R., 2007. Doing Focus Group. Sage Publications, Thousand Oaks, CA.

Beyer, H., Holtzblatt, K., 1998. Contextual Design: Defining Customer-Centered Systems. Morgan Kaufmann, San Francisco, CA.

Blythe, M., Monk, A., Park, J., 2002. Technology biographies: field study techniques for home use product development. In: CHI '02 Extended Abstracts on Human Factors in Computing Systems. ACM, Minneapolis, MN, pp. 658–659.

Brooke, J., 1996. SUS: a "quick and dirty" usability scale. In: Jordan, P.W., Thomas, B., Weerdmeester, B.A., McClleland, A.L. (Eds.), Usability Evaluation in Industry. Taylor and Francis, London.

Brown, J.B., 1999. The use of focus groups in clinical research. In: Crabtree, B.F., Miller, W.L. (Eds.), Doing Qualitative Research. Sage Publications, Thousand Oaks, CA.

Centers for Disease Control (2006). Gaining Consensus Among Stakeholders Through the Nominal Group Technique. Evaluation Briefs. Retrieved March 15, 2017 from https://www.cdc.gov/healthyyouth/evaluation/pdf/brief7.pdf.

Cheng, K.G., Ernesto, F., Truong, K.N., 2008. Participant and Interviewer Attitudes Toward Handheld Computers in the Context of HIV/AIDS Programs in Sub-Saharan Africa. In: Proceeding of the Twenty-Sixth Annual SIGCHI Conference on Human Factors in Computing Systems. ACM, Florence, Italy, pp. 763–766.

Chin, J.P., Diehl, V.A., Normank, K.L., 1988. Development of an instrument measuring user satisfaction of the human-computer interface. In: Proceedings of the SIGCHI Conference on Human Factors in Computing Systems. ACM, Washington, DC, pp. 213–218.

Davis, J., Rebelsky, S.A., 2007. Food-first computer science: starting the first course right with PB & J. In: Proceedings of the 38th SIGCSE Technical Symposium on Computer Science Education. ACM, Covington, KY, pp. 372–376.

Delbecq, A.L., Van de Ven, A.H., 1971. A Group Process Model for Problem Identification and Program Planning. The Journal of Applied Behavioral Science 7 (4), 466–492.

Finstad, K., 2010. The usability metric for user experience. Interacting with Computers 22 (5), 323–327.

Friedman, B., Hurley, D., Howe, D.C., Felten, E., Nissenbaum, H., 2002. Users' conceptions of web security: a comparative study. In: CHI '02 Extended Abstracts on Human Factors in Computing Systems. ACM, Minneapolis, MN, pp. 746–747.

Gaver, B., Dunne, T., Pacenti, E., 1999. Design: cultural probes. Interactions 6 (1), 21–29.

Gilchrist, V.J., Williams, R.L., 1999. Key informant interviews. In: Crabtree, B.F., Miller, W.L. (Eds.), Doing Qualitative Research. Sage Publications, Thousand Oaks, CA.

Holtzblatt, K., Beyer, H., 2014. Contextual design: evolved. Synthesis Lectures on Human-Centered Informatics 7 (4), 1–91.

Huang, E.M., Truong, K.N., 2008. Breaking the disposable technology paradigm: opportunities for sustainable interaction design for mobile phones. In: Proceeding of the Twenty-Sixth Annual SIGCHI Conference on Human Factors in Computing Systems. ACM, Florence, Italy, pp. 323–332.

Hutchinson, H., Mackay, W., Westerlund, B., Bederson, B.B., Druin, A., Plaisant, C., et al., 2003. Technology probes: inspiring design for and with families. In: Proceedings of the SIGCHI Conference on Human Factors in Computing Systems. ACM, Ft. Lauderdale, FL, pp. 17–24.

James, R.L., Brian, S.U., Deborah, E.M., 2013. UMUX-LITE: when there's no time for the SUS. In: Proceedings of the SIGCHI Conference on Human Factors in Computing Systems. ACM, Paris, ISBN: 978-1-4503-1899-0, pp. 2099–2102.

Krueger, R.A., 1994. Focus Groups: A Practical Guide for Applied Research. Sage Publications, Thousand Oaks, CA.

Kvale, S., 2007. Doing Interviews. Sage Publications, Thousand Oaks, CA.

Le Dantec, C.A., Edwards, W.K., 2008. Designs on dignity: perceptions of technology among the homeless. In: Proceeding of the Twenty-Sixth Annual SIGCHI Conference on Human Factors in Computing Systems. ACM, Florence, Italy, pp. 627–636.

Leshed, G., Velden, T., Rieger, O., Kot, B., Sengers, P., 2008. In-car gps navigation: engagement with and disengagement from the environment. In: Proceeding of the Twenty-Sixth Annual SIGCHI Conference on Human Factors in Computing Systems. ACM, Florence, Italy, pp. 1675–1684.

Malone, T.W., 1983. How do people organize their desks? Implications for the design of office information systems. ACM Transactions on Information Systems 1 (1), 99–112.

Miller, W.L., Crabtree, B.F., 1999. Clinical research: a multimethod typology and qualitative roadmap. In: Crabtree, B.F., Miller, W.L. (Eds.), Doing Qualitative Research. Sage Publications, Thousand Oaks, CA.

Orne, M.T., 1962. On the social psychology of the psychological experiment: with particular reference to demand characteristics and their implications. The American Psychologist 17 (11), 776–783.

Petersen, M.G., Baiilie, L., 2001. Methodologies for designing future household technologies. In: Oikos 2001. Aarhus University Press.

Preece, J., Sharp, H., Yvonne, R., 2015. Interaction design: beyond human-computer interaction, fourth ed. John Wiley & Sons, Chichester.

Read, J.C., MacFarlane, S., 2006. Using the fun toolkit and other survey methods to gather opinions in child computer interaction. In: Proceedings of the 2006 Conference on Interaction Design and Children. ACM, Tampere, pp. 81–88.

Read, J., MacFarlane, S., Casey, C., 2002. Endurability, Engagement and Expectations: Measuring Children's Fun. Interaction Design and Children. Shaker Publishing, Eindhoven, Amsterdam, pp. 189–198.

Robson, C., 2002. Real World Research. Blackwell Publishing, Malden, MA.

Romagnoli, K.M., Handler, S.M., Ligons, F.M., Hochheiser, H., 2013. Home-care nurses' perceptions of unmet information needs and communication difficulties of older patients in the immediate post-hospital discharge period. BMJ Quality and Safety 22 (4), 324–332.

Voida, A., Mynatt, E.D., Erickson, T., Kellogg, W.A., 2004. Interviewing over instant messaging. In: CHI '04 Extended Abstracts on Human Factors in Computing Systems. ACM, Vienna, pp. 1344–1347.

Walston, J.T., Lissitz, R.W., 2000. Computer-mediated focus groups. Evaluation Review 24 (5), 457–483.

Woodruff, A., Hasbrouck, J., Augustin, S., 2008. A bright green perspective on sustainable choices. In: Proceeding of the Twenty-Sixth Annual SIGCHI Conference on Human Factors in Computing Systems. ACM, Florence, Italy, pp. 313–322.

Ethnography

9

9.1 INTRODUCTION

You've just been offered a fantastic opportunity to become involved in the design of an innovative new health-care information management system, to be used in hospital intensive-care units in a country that you've always wanted to visit. Your job is to design an integrated set of user interfaces, based on a detailed understanding of system requirements, organizational concerns, work practices, and a multitude of other relevant factors.

As soon as you accept the job, you realize that you've got a big problem: where to start? How should you go about developing an understanding of the situation that you will need to design these interfaces? You've never worked in a hospital—let alone an intensive-care unit—so you know almost nothing about how the people work, what information they need, how they want it displayed, and other factors that will be crucial elements of your designs.

This lack of background would be hard enough if the hospital was in your neighborhood, as you might be able to rely upon shared cultural background and perhaps even acquaintances to help you get started. However, you might find that the world of the hospital workers is very unfamiliar. If you haven't worked in that environment, the language, types of interactions, and values might effectively amount to a distinct subculture. Tackling these questions in a foreign country, with different social norms and work practices, seems much harder.

Whether in your home country or somewhere far from home, you should start by realizing that differences between cultures can be very important. An understanding of the ways that people work and interact is crucial for your success in designing the tool: assuming that your users are "just like you" might be a recipe for failure. How can you understand how people work and what they need from a computer system when you have almost no understanding of the context in which your designs will be used?

You might start by considering some of the other research techniques described in this book. Your first thought might be to consider surveying potential users. A survey containing questions about reactions to current information systems and hopes for future versions might help you build some initial understanding. Unfortunately, there are problems with this approach: not only do you not have much idea of which questions you should ask, you don't have much of an idea of how to ask them. You're also a bit concerned that your questions might fail to address certain key issues. Interviews might help, but they suffer from similar problems. Talking directly with potential users might be helpful, but is also prone to potential omission of important topics. Besides, you don't know if your questions would be culturally appropriate— you don't want to offend anyone.

Having reached this point, you might (perhaps not so reluctantly) conclude that you need to take a trip to observe workers in this environment in person. You decide to learn what you can about hospital workplace practices and general cultural background that will help you understand how things are done "over there." You talk to your clients to identify a hospital where you can observe potential future users working in the intensive-care unit. You ask them if they can introduce you to a trusted partner who can show you around. You talk to this person to get some basic understanding. You then observe the health-care workers in action and talk with some of them in detail. You might spend several days "shadowing" some of them, following them around as they attend to various tasks and concerns.

As you go through these various steps, you begin to understand how these professionals work and what they need. You use this understanding to begin working towards lists of requirements and elements of proposed designs. As time goes on, you'll discuss these artifacts with your potential users, looking to them to either approve your suggestions or to suggest revisions that might correct misperceptions. As your ideas become more fully developed, you travel to another hospital in a different city to determine whether or not your ideas are appropriate for this second group of users.

This combination of observation, interviews, and participation is known as *ethnography.* Ethnographic research projects use deep immersion and participation in a specific research context to develop an understanding that would not be achievable with other, more limited research approaches.

This added insight does not come without a substantial cost: ethnographic research can be very challenging. Participation in a specific context can help you understand how to build tools for that situation, but effective data collection requires well-developed skills in observation, conversation, and interpretation. Ethnographers must take significant care in deciding with whom they should be talking and how to reconcile contradictory data.

This chapter provides some background on ethnography and its use in human-computer interaction (HCI) research. We discuss the steps involved in an ethnographic research project: selecting groups to study, choosing a form of participation, making initial contact, building relationships within the group, iterative data collection and analysis, and reporting results.

We discuss the use of ethnography in a variety of HCI projects, including examples from homes, workplaces, schools, and online, with a goal of understanding when it is appropriate for HCI research and how it might best be conducted. Although one chapter in a textbook is obviously no substitute for years of ethnographic research experience, we hope to provide an introduction that helps you make the most of this powerful technique.

9.2 WHAT IS ETHNOGRAPHY?

One social scientist defined ethnography as "the art and science of describing a human group—its institutions, interpersonal behaviors, material productions, and beliefs" (Angrosino, 2007). At first reading, this definition may seem somewhat unsatisfactory. After all, many forms of research might be used to develop a description of a human group—we might do surveys, conduct interviews, observe activities, and use other approaches described in this book (and elsewhere). Later in this chapter, we see how these research methods are important parts of ethnographic studies. So, what's so special about ethnography?

Ethnography, as a research methodology, has its roots in anthropological studies of non-Western cultures. In attempting to develop deep understandings of unfamiliar civilizations, researchers found that limited interactions and observations were insufficient. Moving beyond these limits required stepping out of the role of dispassionate observer and engaging directly with people in their daily lives. Anthropologists spent years living and working in traditional villages and using this deeply embedded perspective to provide insights that would have been difficult, if not impossible, to get from other data collection methods. This form of participatory research evolved into what we currently call ethnography (Angrosino, 2007).

Ethnography is based in the notion that true understanding of complex human practices and contexts requires in-depth, engaged study. Individuals often describe what they do in a way that is not accurate. This may be due to a lack of awareness or understanding of what they are doing, or individuals may report more socially acceptable actions than their actual actions (Blomberg et al., 2007). In Section 9.1, we saw how some research methods were inadequate for developing an understanding of a thoroughly unfamiliar environment. The proposed solution was to become immersed in the problem, spending significant amounts of time in the working environment, talking with the medical staff, watching how things are done, and learning from being in the world that is being studied. A core belief in ethnography is that "to gain an understanding of a world that you know little about, you must encounter it firsthand" (Blomberg et al., 2007).

Participation—in some form—is a critical practice in ethnography. Although researchers may not realistically be able to act exactly as if they belong to the group being studied, they try to be as involved as practically and ethically possible. Anthropologists conducting ethnographic studies of traditional societies live in these communities for several years, using participation in the activities of daily life as a means of understanding the dynamics of the group being studied. Section 9.4.2 has a more in-depth discussion of possible types of participation in an ethnographic study. Qualitative methods that involve no participation or observation, such as content analysis and document analysis, are presented in Chapter 11. The focus of this chapter is on traditional ethnography research, which involves some level of observation or participation.

As a descriptive technique, ethnography is usually *inductive*, moving from raw data to the identification of patterns that regularly occur in the data and, often, on to general theories that explain the patterns. This inductive focus stands in direct contrast to hypothesis-driven research, which defines a narrowly controlled experiment to test well-defined alternative explanations or designs (Angrosino, 2007). There are no controls in ethnography—every case is unique.

Although ethnographies are similar to case studies (Chapter 7), there are some important differences. Like case studies, ethnographies rely on multiple types of data to confirm observations, a process known as triangulation (Angrosino, 2007). Ethnographies and case studies are both time intensive, personal, and largely based in the context being studied (Angrosino, 2007). The context often differentiates these research methods from methods such as surveys, experimental design, and other methods. In ethnography, context often is the main focus of understanding.

The primary difference between ethnography and case-study research lies in the use of theory. Case-study research is often based on hypotheses or propositions that guide the questions being asked. This theory-driven approach is subtly different from the inductive strategies used in ethnography.[1] Informally, you might think of an ethnographic study as being a very preliminary, exploratory case study.

Ethnographic research also differs from case studies and other qualitative research methods in the extent of the engagement with the group or situation being studied. The goal of ethnographic participation is to come as close as possible to achieving the rich perspective that comes from being part of the group being studied. Although this is rarely, if ever, possible (see Section 9.4.2), ethnographers tend to become deeply involved with the groups or situations that they are studying. Unlike case studies or other qualitative research projects that may use observations, interviews, and a similar range of data collection techniques in a relatively constrained manner over a short period of time, ethnographic research generally makes more fluid use of these techniques over a longer term, in close interaction with participants. In ethnographic research, the distinctions between "interaction," "interview," and "observation" are almost nonexistent, with all of these activities potentially occurring in the space of a few minutes. Of course, these somewhat arbitrary distinctions exist along a continuum with no clear boundaries: a long-term, highly interactive case study may be hard to distinguish from an ethnographic study.

One final note in defining ethnography: traditionally, the term "ethnography" has been used to define both the practice and the written outcome. Thus, ethnography is both a process and the outcome of that process. Like case studies, ethnographies are often narrative, telling the story behind the context being studied (Angrosino, 2007). Often, these stories strive to convey perspectives of the people being studied: giving "accounts of an event like community members do" has been described as an important ethnographic goal (Agar, 1980).

---

[1] The role of theory has been the subject of much debate in ethnographic circles. There are numerous theoretical perspectives on ethnography (Angrosino, 2007). Some viewpoints reject the notion of ethnography as a tool for developing theories, claiming that it is (or should be) merely descriptive. This perspective has generated substantial discussion (Shapiro, 1994; Sharrock and Randall, 2004).

9.3 ETHNOGRAPHY IN HCI

The description of ethnography as the practice of using some form of participation in a group to develop an understanding of the group is straight from social science research. Social science ethnographers spend time living in traditional villages, hanging out on inner-city street corners, and otherwise immersing themselves in unfamiliar settings to understand the dynamics of groups of interest.

As fascinating as this might sound, it may also seem a bit far removed from research into HCI. After all, HCI researchers are usually trying to understand how to build systems or how users interact with computers. How does this relate to the in-depth study of groups and why is participation useful and helpful?

The connection becomes clearer once we consider the use of modern computer systems. Even when we are sitting in front of a traditional computer, conducting seemingly familiar tasks such as word processing, we're not really computing so much as we are communicating. Much of our computing work that does not directly involve communication or collaboration (e-mail, instant messaging, online calendars, virtual worlds)—involves creating artifacts (documents, spreadsheets, presentations) that communicate ideas to others. Mobile and ubiquitous computing tools that make computing a more integrated part of daily life are even more focused on communication.

As soon as we start using computing technologies for communication and collaboration, we start forming groups. Whether these groups are "real" groups that have some physical existence outside the computing environment, such as schools (Wyeth, 2006), homes (Crabtree and Rodden, 2004; Taylor and Swan, 2005), and workplaces (Newman and Landay, 2000; Su and Mark, 2008), or are groups that would not exist without the technological intermediary, such as virtual worlds (Ducheneaut et al., 2007), they have their own norms and dynamics that are legitimate and important subjects of study.

But what does the HCI researcher hope to learn about these groups? Often, the goal is just understanding: How is a technology used? How do the features of the design influence how people use the system? HCI researchers can use ethnographic techniques of participating in the group to gain a detailed and nuanced understanding that other methods cannot provide.

Lucy Suchman's study of the users of an electronic help system on a photocopier is perhaps the most famous example of ethnography in HCI. Starting from a framework that describes all action as being a product of the context in which it is taken—a model known as *situated action*—Suchman observed users attempting to complete a photocopying task with the help of an expert system designed to help them identify problems and complete tasks correctly. Through analysis of videos and a framework designed to demonstrate the relevant features of the interactions between the humans and the expert system, Suchman developed a rich and detailed understanding of how differences between the human model of the copier and the expert system's model led to communication breakdowns and task failures (Suchman, 1987). This study remains influential both as a fascinating discussion of how problems in human-machine communication can arise and as an example of the utility of ethnography in HCI.

Often, the human, social, and organizational aspects of information systems development are the ones most critical to ensuring the success of a project (Harvey and Myers, 2002). Ethnography can help in providing an understanding of the context in which specific interfaces or systems are developed and implemented. While research methods such as experimental design focus on reducing research to a small number of hypotheses with findings that are easily generalizable to other projects, ethnography focuses on the opposite: understanding the context of individuals in groups, their processes and norms, at a specific point in time, without generalization as a goal (Harvey and Myers, 2002). In addition, ethnographic approaches can be especially good for designing technology out of a workplace context: "Designing for pleasure demands a different approach from designing for utility" (Gaver et al., 2004, p. 53).

In a study aimed at understanding the importance of communication to multitasking, researchers "shadowed" 19 workers at a large US corporation, noting all of the workers' activities at their desks and following them around wherever possible. The resulting 550 hours of data, including over 13,000 events, were analyzed and coded to understand how workers switch between tasks, interlocutors, and communication media. The finding that coordinating activities with multiple people was a stressful and difficult activity led the authors to suggest that communication systems might be designed to identify interruptions that might require significant coordination effort (Su and Mark, 2008). The detailed records of communication behavior collected in this study would have been difficult, if not impossible, to collect via other means: observing the workers' activities at their desks, analyzing e mail transcripts, or otherwise observing some subset of their activities would have given an incomplete picture of the activities and interactions between modes of communication.

The example of the hospital information system (see Section 9.1) illustrates the other primary goal of ethnography in HCI—to understand system requirements and user needs. Successful design of complex or novel interfaces for use in unfamiliar domains, requires researchers to build a detailed, multifaceted understanding of how the work is done, how users interact, how tools are used, what users need, what policies are in place, and other related questions. It comes down to understanding the context surrounding where the information system will be used and who will be using it.

As in the case of the hospital information system, interviews, surveys, and other simpler data collection techniques may not be up to the task. Ethnographic research puts developers into the thick of the situation, letting them observe and study the situation firsthand. Extending the hospital example, most computer developers would not know how hospitals typically refer to patients. In a typical database design, data about individual humans is often referred to by an ID number or their last and first name. However, in hospitals, patients are often referred to by bed number. In a typical database design, the ID does not represent anything physical or meaningful, but in a hospital situation there is a physical meaning (the bed number or location) behind the identifier. This is an important difference that might be uncovered using ethnographic techniques but otherwise would not be obvious to the average researcher or developer.

The use of ethnographic investigations for understanding the requirements for a computer system is closely related to a design philosophy known as *participatory design* (Schuler and Namioka, 1993). Starting from concerns about the impact of computer systems that are simply foisted on users without consideration of their needs and preferences, participatory design efforts involve users in every stage of design, from early discussions aimed at understanding problems, concerns, and needs, to brain-storming regarding design possibilities, evaluation of paper or other low-quality prototypes, and continued refinement of working systems. Although participatory design shares ethnography's interest in direct participation and engagement with the group being studied, the goal is generally different. Ethnography focuses on understanding people, their groups, their processes, their beliefs. Ethnography really focuses on understanding the problem. Participatory design is often the process of using ethnographic approaches with the end goal of designing a computer system. Participatory design can be seen as using ethnographic methods to understand the problem, and then intensely involving those same participants in building potential solutions to the problem. In ethnography, understanding the problem, the context, the culture, or the group interactions, is sufficient as a research study.

Participatory design as a development method is often used for systems development in three types of situations where a deep understanding of the situation is required. The first situation is where the user tasks are not well understood, such as the many different and complex tasks that teachers carry out in an average day (Carroll et al., 2000). The second situation is where the users themselves are not well-understood, such as people with cognitive impairment and memory loss (Wu et al., 2007). The third situation is where even minor errors in task completion can lead to catastrophic consequences, such as at a nuclear power plant or an aircraft carrier. While participatory design is ideal for developing all types of systems, it is very time and cost-intensive, and so participatory design is often used when the computer development projects are high risk, have a high likelihood of failure, and a high payoff for success. Most design projects cannot afford the time or cost involved in intensive ethnographic approaches.

That said, the delineations between some of these forms of research are often blurred, at best. Some self-described HCI "ethnographies" may involve theoretical propositions that make them seem more like case studies. Studies that aren't driven by a theoretical basis may make some use of ethnographic tools to build an understanding of contextual issues, without going into the detail associated with a full-blown ethnography. Projects involving the design of tools for domain experts—such as the hospital scenario described above—may involve techniques from ethnography, such as the shadowing of experts, while other similar efforts may seem more like participatory design than ethnography. No matter; the interest here lies in identifying appropriate research techniques and understanding how they might be used.

9.4 CONDUCTING ETHNOGRAPHIC RESEARCH

Ethnographic research can be extremely challenging. Ethnographic studies are usually conducted "in the wild," in homes, workplaces, educational settings, or other places where the "action" of interest takes place. As these studies often involve extended periods of interaction and observation, researchers may find themselves in unfamiliar environments for long periods of time. This time may be spent juggling between two complex and intertwined goals: understanding how to navigate the dynamics of these unfamiliar settings and conducting the observations that provide the data for subsequent analysis. This can be a challenge, to say the least.

Researchers are often advised to carefully consider how well suited they are for a given project before embarking on ethnographic projects (Agar, 1980; Angrosino, 2007). In some cases personal tastes and preferences may make participation in certain studies inadvisable: an otherwise highly capable HCI researcher who is uncomfortable with the sight of blood might not be a good choice for our hypothetical scenario of information systems in intensive-care units.

Other considerations involve differences in background. Researchers may be ethnically, culturally, or socio-economically different from members of the group being studied and these differences might prevent them from being complete participants. Subtler forms of bias are also a concern: as individuals with distinct perspectives, we pay more attention to some details than others, often in ways that we are unaware of. Ethnographers should strive to work past such biases to the greatest extent possible (Angrosino, 2007). Bias-awareness training, careful attention to methodology—including rigorous documentation of evidence—and the use of multiple researchers (Agar, 1980) are among the techniques that might be used to overcome the inevitable biases.

9.4.1 SELECTING A SITE OR GROUP OF INTEREST

Selecting a target of ethnographic research is in many ways similar to selecting cases for a case study (Section 7.7). You will want to find groups that are interesting, logistically workable, and committed to supporting the goals of the study.

Selection may not be an issue. HCI ethnographies conducted in the interest of understanding the requirements of a system for a specific customer may not have a great deal of latitude in the choice of site. If the intensive-care information system is to be used at a specific hospital, then that is where the research should be conducted.

In some cases, you may be interested in finding groups that are representative of similar instances, while in others you may wish to study extreme cases. These goals will influence your choice of site: if you want to understand how technologies are used in schools, you might look for sites that have average funding levels and representative student bodies to get a representative understanding. On the other hand, comparison of extremes—for example, well-funded suburban schools with poorly funded urban schools—might provide interesting contrasts.

There may be barriers to your involvement and participation in specific types of ethnographic site. For instance, health-care systems in many countries protect the data of patients receiving health-care services. You can't just walk in and start examining data and going along with teams of doctors or nurses. A similar problem occurs in schools. You can't just walk into a school and spend time in a classroom. If there is sensitive financial information, you can't just walk in and start taking part in discussions at an investment bank. Similarly, governmental and military installations often have sensitive data and discussions, so your presence may pose a challenge. For these situations, you may need to go through multiple stages of approval, including not only traditional institutional review board approval for research (see Chapter 15), but also certification, security and background checks, fingerprinting, sexual harassment training, and similar hurdles. You may be required to sign confidentiality agreements or other legal agreements. None of these should stop you from selecting a potential research site, but they are important considerations to be aware of.

In some cases, the selection of sites may be based on convenience—organizations, places, and people that you know well increase familiarity and comfort, which may make the research less daunting. Familiarity is not without its own hazards, however, as you might find that foreknowledge limits your objectivity.

If you are faced with the good fortune of having several potentially viable candidate groups to choose from, you might want to do a bit of preliminary work to inform your choice. Your interactions with the individuals in a group may provide some indication as to whether that group is a good candidate for your research. You'll always need to work to build a relationship with the members of groups that you study, but you might be more inclined to work with a group that seems welcoming and encouraging, rather than a group that seems hostile or uninterested.

Some groups, or group members, may have very good reasons for being wary about participating in an ethnographic study. They may be legitimately concerned about your research agenda, as the questions you ask, the conclusions you draw, and the reports that you write might have a very real impact on them. Consider a study of the work habits of repair technicians. You might be interested in building an understanding of technicians' work habits, in the hopes of designing tools that will help them more effectively share information. If, however, a candidate group perceives this system as an attempt to "de-skill" their work, threatening their employment stability or autonomy, they may be reluctant to participate. You may have to work to build trust to convince group members that participation in your project will not be something that they will regret.

You should also consider the practical impact of your research on the group that you are studying. If you are going to be spending a great deal of time in someone's home, school, or workplace, you might be in the way. Questions that you might ask in order to help your understanding might distract from the goals of the people that you're working with. One rule of thumb might be to try to make sure that the benefits outweigh the costs for your participants: they should get something worthwhile out of the time that they commit to helping your research (Angrosino, 2007). If you're studying work practices in order to understand the requirements for a new system—as in our hospital example—the benefits to the participants might be clear: you'll be able to build a system that will support their work. If the benefits are less immediate, you might consider trying to find some way to compensate participants.

9.4.2 PARTICIPATING: CHOOSING A ROLE

Participation is a critical part of ethnography. Realizing that there are limits in what can be learned by observing from the outside, ethnographers strive to be involved in the situations that they are studying. Participation removes the need for intermediaries. Instead of relying upon members of a group to describe situations of interest, a participant-researcher can experience it first hand, relying upon their own powers of observation to understand the situation. Direct experiences of phenomena of interest can provide a richness of data that is almost impossible to get from any other research approach.

Having decided to participate, you must decide exactly what this means. You might be tempted to try to join the group—to become a member in order to study the group. This form of participation evokes images of anthropologists living in traditional villages. By sleeping, eating, and working with residents of the village, and becoming—as much as possible—part of their community, a researcher learns "from the inside." These *complete participants* (Gold, 1958) may learn a great deal, but at great expense, often involving years of fieldwork. Even if you are able to make this effort, you may run the risk of losing the ability to be a detached observer, as your identity as a member of the group may overwhelm your training as a researcher. Known as "going native" (Gold, 1958), this reaction may impair your ability to continue your research.

Some ethnographers have pushed complete participation to its logical limits, concealing their identity as researchers in order to make their membership in the group appear more authentic. This strategy has the advantage of easing access to the group: if you don't present yourself as a researcher, you don't have to explain your work or deal with concerns of group members. This strategy can be particularly appropriate in public or near-public settings where you generally would not be asked to justify your presence or behavior (Lofland et al., 2006).

Private settings pose more of a challenge for such "covert" research, as concealing your identity may mean deceiving group members as to the reasons for your participation. Even when conducted in the interest of fidelity of research, it is often considered unethical for researchers to intentionally misrepresent the goals of their research. Deceptions about a researcher's identity are also considered unethical if they are conducted in order to get access to a group or context that they would not otherwise be able to join (Angrosino, 2007). Thus, creating an avatar for participation in a virtual world (Ducheneaut et al., 2007) does not raise an ethical concern because membership in these worlds is not constrained and interactions are not intended to be private. However, falsely claiming to be a resident of a neighborhood in order to join a residents-only discussion group might be considered inappropriate. These concerns notwithstanding, some researchers have used covert participation in situations where they believed that it was the only way that they could gain access to the group (Lofland et al., 2006).

Pragmatic considerations can also limit the practicality of complete participation. Let's return to the hospital information system that we described earlier. You might be able to spend a great deal of time watching intensive-care nurses and physicians up close, and you might learn a great deal about how medical care is given in the ICU, but you probably shouldn't be involved directly in patient care. Even if you are a trained and licensed medical professional, it is not at all clear if you could be working effectively both as an HCI researcher and as a caregiver at the same time.

The opposite extreme—minimal participation—addresses some of these concerns while raising different issues. The *complete observer* (Gold, 1958) observes without interacting directly, limiting participation to simply "being there" as events of interest transpire. Complete observers remain detached from the subjects of their observation—they rarely worry about "going native." However, they do so at the cost of losing out on a wealth of information. If a complete observer sees something of interest that she does not understand, she does not ask a group member for clarification: she simply does her best to interpret what she sees. As a result, complete observers may at times misinterpret the particular details or significance of events (Gold, 1958).

Usability testing (Chapter 10) is a research method that uses primarily observation, and not participation, in understanding what challenges users are having with an interface. However, usability testing is generally a short-term data collection method, only focusing on a few individuals (generally not working together) and generally not focused on groups, human dynamics, or context (Siegel and Dray, 2005). Furthermore, usability testing generally has the goal of simply finding and fixing flaws in an interface, not understanding any higher-level research questions. Usability testing tends to come into the picture after an interface feature (or multiple potential interface features) has already been developed. Like participatory design, usability testing is focused on the end product of design, although participatory design is an entire design lifecycle approach, whereas usability testing is one late-stage activity. Ethnography is an approach to understanding the problem, whereas usability testing is often a method for evaluating potential solutions (Siegel and Dray, 2005).

Most ethnographic projects in HCI avoid the extremes of complete participation and observation, opting for an intermediate approach. Some ethnographers become temporary members of the group that they are studying, with all participants fully informed as to the nature of their participation. Possibilities include combining some degree of participation with observation. These researchers might generally disclose their role as researchers and then get more or less involved in group activities, sometimes participating, other times observing. One common approach is to "shadow" group members—following them around as they go about their business, asking questions as needed for clarification and interpretation.

These roles form a continuum of possible research approaches (see Figure 9.1). Researchers may adopt multiple, evolving roles throughout the course of a single project. One common approach is to begin research as a complete observer, using initial findings to create questions and goals for more in-depth participation (Gold, 1958).

Given both the difficulty of truly becoming a member of a group and the possibilities of misinterpretation associated with observation from outside the group, you might be tempted to observe a culture that you are already a member of. This approach has some appealing aspects. If you are part of a group, you already have access to group members, existing relationships, and trust. You also probably have some curiosity about how the group works and why it works this way (Lofland et al., 2006). Together, these factors give you a real head start. You may have to do a good

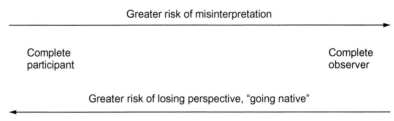

FIGURE 9.1

The spectrum of roles for ethnographic researchers.

Data from Gold, R., 1958. Roles in sociological field observations. Social Forces 36 (3), 217–223.

deal less preliminary work to build the groundwork for a study. You understand context and background that would be unclear to a newcomer, and group members might be less hesitant to respond to your questions. Even if you are open, and have disclosed that you are doing research, this may be seen with less skepticism.

If you find yourself intrigued by the ease of working with a group of which you are already a member, you would be well advised to reconsider this strategy as an automatic first choice. Your participation in a group may lead to bias and preinformed opinions—even worse than the complete participant who has "gone native," you *are* native. You may have deeply ingrained habits, opinions, and preferences of which you are not aware. Furthermore, you lack the fresh perspective associated with learning about a new topic and problem domain.

These concerns aside, group membership may, on occasions, lead to the identification of interesting opportunities for research: see the Ethnographic Research of Your Own Community sidebar for one example.

ETHNOGRAPHIC RESEARCH OF YOUR OWN COMMUNITY

In an ideal research world, you study groups or communities simply because they are interesting and in need of better understanding. In the reality of HCI research, you are often asked to study a specific group of people or work environment because:

- there are problems which need to be understood or improved upon, and you have relevant experience;
- there are problems or interesting research questions that you are aware of in a group of which you are already a member, and you could help to understand and address those problems.

Sometimes, you stumble across great ethnographic studies accidentally. In 1998, Jenny Preece, an HCI researcher, tore her anterior cruciate ligament (ACL) in her knee. She joined an online community called Bob's ACL Bulletin board to learn more about her injury, along with various treatments. She became a member of the group and later found the level of empathic support to be fascinating.

> She decided to do ethnographically informed research to learn more about the people of the online community, what they communicated about, and how they communicated (Preece, 1998). She was not a strict observer, since she was already a member of the community. She could understand, more than a strict observer could, what it meant to have a torn ACL. The founder of the bulletin board, Bob Wilmot, was aware of her research and helped answer her questions.
>
> In contrast, when her student Diane Maloney-Krichmar, continued to study the same community years later, she was a strict observer, not a participant in any form. As Maloney-Krichmar noted in her paper, to participate in the community fully would require faking the fact that she had the ACL knee injury, which she could not do, because doing so might also taint the findings of the research study, since she would be lying to community members and unable to take a full part in the discussions (Maloney-Krichmar and Preece, 2005).

Many of the previous examples focus on ethnography in physical locations, with face-to-face contact where researchers are physically present. Online research presents opportunities for ethnographic research that transcend these roles. The complete participant role in traditional ethnographic research is predicated on the notion that participation requires presence: to be a member of the group, you must be physically with the members of that group, interacting with them face-to-face. This proximity leads to many of the challenges of highly participative research, requiring researchers to be (at least passably) good actors and encouraging the connections that might cause some to "go native." More information about doing ethnographic research in online settings is in Section 9.5.5.

9.4.3 BUILDING RELATIONSHIPS

Ideally, every ethnographer would be warmly welcomed into the group that they are interested in studying. Members of the group would honestly and openly share secrets, discuss issues, and provide fair and unbiased assessments of how things work.

Unfortunately, this ideal may be realized only rarely. Even if there is nominal buy-in from someone associated from the group, that doesn't mean that all group members are interested or enthusiastic. Subjects of ethnographic research may be outwardly hostile or simply indifferent to the project. Workplace ethnographies may raise concerns among workers that the research may be used against them: "Maybe they're going to use this study to figure out how to eliminate my job."

Conducting ethnographic research would be very difficult indeed if you were working with people who didn't like, trust, or respect you. Careful attention to some fairly common-sense principles can help you define yourself as someone with whom folks in the group will want to work with. Trying to be helpful—being a participant instead of a burden—can help engender good will, if you follow through on your promises. If you're not acting as a complete participant, you should take time to explain to someone why you're there, what you hope to learn, and what you hope to do with that knowledge. You should also respect the needs and goals of the individuals you are speaking with: your need for research data should not trump their need for privacy, job security, or other things (Angrosino, 2007). Making people feel threatened is probably not the right way to get good research data.

It is important to try to understand the conventions and norms that are shared by members of the groups that you study (Agar, 1980). Even if you're working with groups of people who are culturally and socio-economically similar to you, they may have very different habits, expectations, values, or jargon. Understanding these cultural factors may not be easy to do, but it's worth the effort. You don't want to say something that offends someone in the group and you don't want to be misinterpreted. Slang and jargon are particularly challenging in this regard. You may think that you know the meaning of a slang term in your particular context, but you'd be well advised to make sure that your understanding is correct (Agar, 1980).

9.4.4 MAKING CONTACT

Many ethnographic efforts start with discussions with a small number of individuals. Even if you are introduced to all members of the group from the outset, you can't start talking to them all at once—it's simply not possible. In some cases, particularly if the group of interest is not completely defined, your initial contacts may help you meet others.

Your initial contacts play a very important role. Well-chosen contacts can help you orient yourself to the ways and workings of the environment that you will be studying. Particularly if they are well respected, they can help smooth the way, convincing others who trust them that you are "OK."

Because your first contacts will influence your perceptions of and interactions with other group members, you should carefully consider who you choose to work closely with at first. Experienced researchers have noted that the first people to talk to ethnographers often fall into one of two categories: *stranger-handlers* and *deviants* (Agar, 1980).

Stranger-handlers are people who make it their business to work with people who are new to the group. They introduce you to others, show you around, and appear to be very helpful. They might also show you a particularly slanted view, emphasizing details that they want you to know about while omitting others that they want to leave hidden. If there are factions within the group, a stranger-handler might encourage you to associate with his faction, possibly alienating members of other subgroups. As outcasts who may not be well respected, a deviant might try to use you to gain attention, to validate their otherwise under-appreciated role in the group, or to denigrate their enemies. As your goal is to gain a broad understanding of the group, you should beware of such people.

Unfortunately, you may not know that you're dealing with a deviant or a stranger-handler until it is too late. You may want to rely upon your initial feel for each individual—do they seem trustworthy? Do you "click" with them? If so, they may be good bets. If, however, they seem to be providing you with selective information, bad-mouthing others, or trying to manipulate your efforts, you might want to watch out.

The people who you choose to work closely with should also be those who can provide good information. Someone who knows few people, doesn't get along with others, doesn't explain things well, or is unobservant is unlikely to be a good informant (Agar, 1980) and you probably want to avoid such people.

Even if you find an initial informant—or set of informants—who is trustworthy, seemingly unbiased, and well respected by a broad spectrum of the group, you might be well advised to avoid becoming too closely associated with any group members. You don't want the appearance of close ties with anyone to impair your ability to work with other group members (Agar, 1980; Angrosino, 2007). This may be easier said than done.

Whoever you choose to work with, you should remember that these informants are not necessarily telling you the truth. This is not to say that they're lying—they're simply giving you their viewpoint. The notion of truth in describing human interactions is more than a bit troublesome. Your job is to use your initial informants to help you derive questions, build theories, and plan further investigation. As we see below, you will use subsequent interactions with other group members to help provide a broader perspective.

Participating in a group can be difficult—you may find that you don't like the people that you are working with, that you don't have access to the information that you need, or that you are inappropriately identifying with the subjects of your research. You may also find that you have to work to maintain relationships. A variety of strategies, including presenting yourself as nonthreatening and acting as if you are somewhat incompetent and need to be taught about the group that you are studying (Lofland et al., 2006), can help you convince participants that you are someone to be trusted.

9.4.5 INTERVIEWING, OBSERVING, ANALYZING, REPEATING, AND THEORIZING

Ethnographic researchers have developed a variety of theoretical frameworks to inform their investigations (Angrosino, 2007). Many of these frameworks provide perspectives on how groups function and how meaning is constructed out of human relationships. As you go about your ethnographic research, you should always remember that your job is to create an interpretation of the potentially biased, incomplete, and somewhat contradictory data points that you collect from talking with and observing members of the group. The result may not be "the truth" about this group, but ideally it provides some understanding and explanation of how the group functions.

Like case studies (Chapter 7), ethnographic studies rely upon multiple data collection techniques to gain a broad perspective, with the hope of *triangulating*—using corroborating evidence from multiple perspectives to increase confidence in the validity of conclusions that are drawn. As with case-study research, ethnographic studies rely on interviews, case studies, and documents or other artifacts as their primary sources of data.

Interviews in ethnography serve many purposes. Unlike traditional interviews (see Chapter 8), in which a researcher has a single meeting with a study participant for a limited period of time, an ethnographic interview is often part of a longer, ongoing relationship. In the early stages of a study, interviews may be informal discussions aimed at building trust and understanding broad parameters. As you may not know what you're looking for at first, your early interviews are likely to be very open-ended and unstructured (Angrosino, 2007). In fact, these informal interviews may not even feel like interviews. You might be asking questions as people show you around, discussing issues of concern as you interact with group members, and otherwise participating in seemingly ordinary interactions. Although these conversations might not feel like interviews, they can be useful data collection techniques. A commonly used technique in ethnographic interviews involves presenting participants with items—known as "probes"—designed to provoke reaction and spark conversation (See Chapter 8 for a discussion of probes).

The goal of these informal interviews is generally to get people talking. As they say more about the environment that you're studying, your informants increase the breadth and depth of your understanding. Appropriately asked questions can be very useful in this regard. If they describe an interesting situation, you might ask how often it occurs. Leading questions present a viewpoint that invites either agreement or dissent: "Is this tool really that hard to use?" Other questions might invite comparisons, contrasts, or detailed explanation (Agar, 1980). The challenge of planning questions like these in the course of ongoing conversation may seem substantial, but you might find that your curiosity as a researcher takes you a long way. If a comment piques your interest, find a respectful way to ask for more detail.

Not all of your interviews will be completely informal. More structured techniques, such as life histories (Agar, 1980) (see the Design for Alzheimer's Disease sidebar in Chapter 7) and time diaries (Chapter 6), can be informative components of ethnographic studies. As your data collection and analysis leads you to build a deeper understanding of the group that you're studying, you may find it useful to conduct slightly more formal interviews with group members with whom you've not previously interacted. These discussions can help you validate models or conclusions derived from earlier interactions with other informants.

Observation is easier than it sounds. Just stand back and watch, right? If only it were that simple. Unfortunately, several factors work against us. As much as we might like to think that we're objective observers, we're not. By necessity, we filter what we see and hear, and interpret our observations through the lenses of our own history, experience, expertise, and bias. The goal of ethnographic observation is to shed this baggage, in the hopes of seeing things with "new" eyes, perhaps as a stranger would (Angrosino, 2007). Of course, this is easier said than done, particularly if you are in a situation that is somewhat familiar. A clear distinction between observation and interpretation might be helpful in this regard (Angrosino, 2007). If you only record what you see ("the user opened the help facility and searched for several different terms"), you run less risk of misinterpreting or injecting bias than you do if you interpret what you see as it happens ("the user became frustrated when she was not able to find help with the feature"). You might try to regularly challenge yourself to broaden the scope of your observation: ask yourself, "is there anything I'm missing? Is there anything that I think doesn't look interesting?" If you force yourself to examine all aspects of a complex situation, you may get a broader, less biased picture of what is going on. That said, it is worth noting that observation is a skill that might require significant practice to develop.

Taking appropriate notes from ethnographic observations—and, to a lesser extent, informal interviews—is a daunting challenge. You might be advised to record relevant details such as time, place, identities of people present (perhaps anonymized to protect their privacy), and descriptions of the context, behaviors, and interactions, and include word-for-word transcriptions of conversations (Angrosino, 2007). Although such information would undoubtedly convey a detailed picture of the situation that you have observed, there are significant practical problems involved with overly detailed notes. You will soon become overwhelmed, as the quantity of data will quickly become enormous. Furthermore, it's virtually impossible to record that much data and to observe at the same time: as you take notes, you simply miss out on what is happening (Agar, 1980). Audio or video recordings can help, but analysis of these records can be a tedious, time-consuming chore in itself.

Deciding what is interesting enough to include in your notes, and understanding how to describe it, may become somewhat easier once you have passed the initial stages of your work. When you first start out, you may not have much idea of what is interesting: you're in an unfamiliar context and everything is fair game. As you begin to build some understanding, you may work your way towards an understanding of what is interesting and what is not. Once you have this baseline, you might think of your field notes as recording observations that describe familiar events in terms of patterns that you've identified, while noting unfamiliar events that may be worthy of consideration. You might also make note of questions that arise: if you see something that you don't understand, it may be an appropriate subject for future investigation (Agar, 1980).

Timing is also a challenge in recording notes from observations and informal interviews. You might try to be prepared to record observations at all times, but you never really know when something interesting is going to happen. You might hear an interesting discussion or witness a relevant interaction just when you least expected it. In this case, the best that you can do might be to remember as much as possible and write notes as soon as possible. This is, of course, a highly fallible process, as you are likely to forget important details and misremember others (Agar, 1980). You would be well advised to seek out additional validating evidence for any observations that are recorded long after the fact.

Documents, archives, and artifacts can also be useful sources of information. Records that describe past activities: pictures, letters, e mails, deliverable documents, and even tools; can provide information about how a group works and what the dynamics are like. An ethnographic study of a software engineering group might investigate process documents, e-mail exchanges over the course of one or more projects, papers, and presentations generated during the course of the work in order to understand how that group works. These archival data sources have the advantage of being relatively static and impersonal—you can take your time reading old e-mails and you don't risk asking an inappropriate question. At the same time, these materials may be incomplete, biased, or error-prone (Angrosino, 2007).

Having collected data from interviews, observations, and archives, your next step is to analyze it. Data analysis generally combines qualitative and quantitative analysis techniques. This chapter focuses on collecting data using ethnographic methods, but Chapter 11 helps you take your various observations and group them into categories and frameworks that help you understand and explain the situation. Quantitative techniques help you ask questions about the frequency or prevalence of certain behaviors. These analyses are very useful for moving your understanding from the general ("this happened frequently") to the specific ("this happened in 79% of cases").

Analysis in ethnographic research is often a precursor to further data collection. As you examine your data points to identify patterns, you may find other questions arising. In some cases, you may be uncertain about the interpretation of an event or a comment—you may wish to ask someone for clarification or simply for confirmation that your interpretation is correct. Other data points may open up entirely new lines of questioning. Observations from a community event, such as a meeting or public gathering, may lead to multiple questions that you might ask at a subsequent interview—whether formal or informal—with someone who was present (Agar, 1980). This iterative process can continue for multiple rounds (Figure 9.2), until you run out of resources (time and money) or have learned all that you're going to learn.

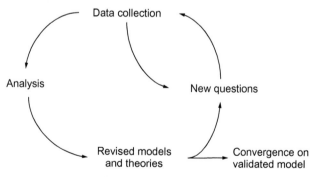

FIGURE 9.2

The iterative process of ethnographic research.

Although many ethnographers strive to develop models and theories that place their observations in some sort of theoretical model or framework, this approach is not universally shared. Some researchers reject theories and models, claiming that ethnographers should simply describe what they see, without building models that may reflect researcher or procedural biases as much as (if not more than) they reflect the phenomena being studied. Others reject this viewpoint, arguing that researcher participation in deciding what should be observed and how it should be analyzed inevitably leads to bias (Shapiro, 1994; Sharrock and Randall, 2004). Of course, if the goal of your ethnographic research is to understand requirements for a system that will be built, you will probably find yourself building a model of some sort.

If you decide to use your ethnographic research to develop models, you should strive to develop robust explanations and descriptions that are based on all of your data. As you analyze the data, you should try to make sure that you are not "cherry-picking" the data. If there are observations that are not consistent with your model, then you should consider revising your model or looking for other potential models. If you seek out, but do not find, data points that disagree with your model, you can be more confident of the correctness of the model.

Because all ethnography is inherently interpretive and qualitative, there are often legitimate questions as to why one model is better than the other. Comparison with alternative models can also help in understanding the strengths and weaknesses of your model, because you could potentially argue that your model fits the data better than other alternative interpretations.

Other measures that you might take to improve the validity of your findings include the use of multiple informants and multiple observers. Multiple informants help you avoid the distortions that might occur from talking to only one member of the group. Interacting with members who differ in background, perspective, experience, or demographic factors such as age, gender, and ethnicity, can help you understand the diversity of perspectives. Having another colleague (or two or three) study the group can minimize the impact of biases of any individual researcher. If your colleagues come to the same conclusions as you, despite having interviewed different people or observed different events, you can have increased confidence in those results. Just as with informants, diversity of observers can be a useful strategy. (Angrosino, 2007).

9.4.6 REPORTING RESULTS

Ethnographic reports are similar to case study reports (Chapter 7). You want to describe your goals and methods, along with a justification of the specific groups—how were they chosen and why? You should describe your methods of data collection and analysis, along with presentation of raw data and analytical results. Matrices, charts, and figures can be very helpful, particularly for analyses involving quantitative data. Another important similarity with case study reports involves discussion of rival explanations: if you've considered and rejected alternative models because your preferred models were better suited, say so, and explain.

Like case studies, ethnographic reports tell a story. You should consider interesting incidents and include direct quotes where appropriate.

Ethnography also often involves consultation with participants. When appropriate, you might consider sharing your report with group members before it is published. This gives them a chance to understand what you've done and why, thus increasing the chances that they have positive feelings about the experience. Your informants can also provide important reality checks—if they think you've misinterpreted important (or perhaps not-so-important) details, they'll let you know. This sharing of draft reports may not be appropriate in some circumstances, including (but not limited to) studies that involved complete participation (participants who weren't aware of the research might be somewhat upset at seeing the report) and situations in which participants might be interested in "slanting" the contents of the report to meet their (real or perceived) interests.

Finally, like case studies, ethnographic research reports often raise questions of privacy and confidentiality. When possible, consider anonymizing location details. The hospital study discussed at the beginning of the chapter might be described as occurring in a "large urban hospital," instead of providing the hospital name. Uniquely identifying details might be suppressed or used only with permission of the groups and individuals involved.

9.5 SOME EXAMPLES

Ethnographic methods have a rich history in the social sciences. However, they have only recently come to the forefront in the area of HCI. A number of studies have utilized ethnography methods to understand the context of technology usage. Most often, these ethnographic studies take place in homes, workplaces, educational settings, and virtual settings. While ethnographic research is not limited to those four types of setting, they are the ones that seem to garner the most attention and examination in the HCI world. Studies of mobile devices have also started to come to the forefront.

9.5.1 HOME SETTINGS

One important area of technology usage is people's homes. To separate out and examine the technology in a sterile lab would be to miss the rich context of home usage. One specific series of ethnographic studies of homes and technology use in different countries provides a baseline for understanding the challenges (Bell et al., 2005). The bottom line is that country, culture, and religion have a great impact on how technology is used in homes. While not specifically an article on ethnography, Chavan et al. (2009) report on examples of home technology products that failed because designers didn't understand the context of usage. For instance, in southern India, clothes washing machine sales were awful for Whirlpool, because traditional southern Indian clothes, using very thin fabrics, were often getting caught and shredded in the washing machines.

There are also, in many cases, gender issues to understand. In many countries, even though women put in an equal amount of work in the workplace, women also perform a majority of domestic household tasks (Blythe and Monk, 2002; Rode et al., 2004; Bell et al., 2005). In one ethnographic study, it was noted that while men may not do an equal share of the household work, they often feel guilty about this (Blythe and Monk, 2002). This ethnography study noted that many domestic technologies are esthetically designed with a gender inclination to them (often, towards women) and posed the question as to whether household technologies should be designed with more of a male focus (Blythe and Monk, 2002).

In another ethnographic study of domestic (home) use of technology, a "felt board" was used to help model daily home life (Rode et al., 2004). The board had different sections for different rooms in the house. Users were asked to place felt icons representing appliances in appropriate rooms, and to identify if they programmed these devices in advance (although the term programming wasn't used). The fuzzy felt board was used to help understand patterns of usage, after participants provided a tour of where the devices were in the home (Rode et al., 2004).

Another ethnographic study examined the use of cleaning products by older individuals (Wyche, 2005). The goal was to better understand the challenges that older individuals face in trying to use cleaning products in their homes, to inspire some potentially useful designs for new cleaning technologies. The researcher observed 20 individuals, between the ages of 69 and 91, in their homes to learn what types of cleaning product and technology they use, where they store them, and which ones are very hard to use. The researcher then presented ideas for some potential technology solutions to these challenges (Wyche, 2005).

9.5.2 WORK SETTINGS

Ethnographic methods are often used to examine the context of technology usage in the workplace. For instance, ethnographic methods were used to understand how insurance claims adjusters do their job in the workplace. Researchers observed the entire process of claims handling, with a special focus on fraudulent claims (Ormerod et al., 2003). A number of process barriers were discovered, such as poor documentation and communication, and claims adjusters were discovered to use a number of heuristics and alternative explanations to discover fraud. This ethnographic research of how claims adjusters work was then used to help develop a new software tool for detecting insurance fraud.

Ethnographic methods were also used in studying a highways department from a state government. The goal was to understand the process of designing and building a bridge, so that an electronic-document management system could be built (Suchman, 2000a,b). One of the challenges was in understanding how electronic documents and paper documents were used. It was discovered that it was important to design connections between the electronic and paper documents, and then determine who needed access to the electronic documents, since paper documents have limited access based on physical location but electronic documents don't have that limitation.

Health-care settings are also of interest to ethnographers. Pedersen and Wolff (2008) documented ethnographic research in two physical therapy clinics in the USA, to understand how small health operations work. They had originally wanted to observe at general health-care clinics (and they had done previous interviews with 10 small health-care clinics), but had problems getting access to observe at these sites. Therefore, physical therapy, in which a lot of patient treatment occurs in a semi-public gym space, seemed like a good compromise (Pedersen and Wolff, 2008). Ethnographic observations helped in understanding work practices and challenges the physical therapy clinics might face as they moved towards full electronic medical records. Similarly, Balka et al. (2008) documented ethnographic studies in Canada and Austria, where again, the goal was to better understand medical work practices, to assist in the development of a new health information system. The study looked at various departments within a hospital, such as emergency departments, oncology, and neurosurgery (Balka et al., 2008).

While office settings are obviously the most common setting, ethnographic methods are even more useful in nonoffice-based work settings. For instance, one ethnographic study examined the potential use of technology in a vineyard setting. Specifically, the researchers wanted to understand the potential use of sensors across a vineyard (Brooke and Burrell, 2003). The researchers became participant-observers, working in vineyards, helping with harvesting, and assisting with grape crushing. The researchers were better able to understand how sensors could be used, to monitor microclimates (combination of sunlight, rain, temperature), which could then predict the chances of grape disease. This, in turn, could provide useful information on which areas of the vineyard needed more attention, labor, chemicals, and different harvesting times.

9.5.3 EDUCATIONAL SETTINGS

Ethnographic methods can be especially useful for understanding the complex context of school settings. For instance, ethnographic methods were used in understanding how children (typically between 4 and 6years old) spend play times in a kindergarten (Wyeth, 2006). In the daily schedule of a kindergartener, there is both structured group time and "loosely structured, self-structured, free time activities." The free-play activities themselves could be divided into three categories: calm activities, play, and artistic interactions. This increased understanding of how young children play in classroom settings may hint at some potential possibilities for technology in early childhood settings. For instance, technology for young children may need to be more flexible, allowing for creativity and discovery, and not be separate from but, rather, work in tandem with the other activities going on in the classroom.

The importance of understanding the context increases when doing a cross-cultural study of educational settings. For instance, Druin et al. used a number of methods, including ethnographic observation in the classroom, to understand how children in different cultures used the International Children's Digital Library, how their reading patterns changed over time, and how their reading patterns influenced communication with others, interest in other cultures, and attitudes towards technology and libraries (Druin et al., 2007).

Ethnographic methods for use in education are not limited to young children. Becvar and Hollan (2007) used ethnographic methods to better understand how dental hygiene students learn. The dental hygiene students were in postsecondary education and, after completing their academic program, had to pass both state and national certification exams. The researchers observed the tools and technologies used by students, the activities and circumstances that occurred, and how the students studied and practiced, both at the university and at their homes (Becvar and Hollan, 2007). The goal of this ethnographic research was to understand how dental hygiene students learn, with the eventual goal of designing instructional technology to assist students in their instructional program.

9.5.4 ETHNOGRAPHIES OF MOBILE AND UBIQUITOUS SYSTEMS

In taking computing beyond the desktop, mobile and ubiquitous systems create context-sensitive environments where computing is part of some other, larger opportunity, instead of a primary focus of its own. Understanding how people make use of these systems while traveling, meeting with friends, or going about their daily lives presents intriguing challenges for ethnographers.

A study of the use of in-car global positioning systems (GPS) used ethnographic techniques to understand how the tools changed perceptions of the larger environment and of the tasks of driving and navigating. To address these questions, a team of researchers went along for several rides—some planned and some conducted specifically for research purposes—with GPS users and, in some cases, additional passengers. Data from these rides—which lasted between 1 and 3 hours—included hundreds of pages of notes and transcriptions. Analysis of this data indicated that the GPS systems led users to be both less engaged (they didn't have to worry so much about seeing turns and landmarks) and more engaged (they were able to learn about parks and other attractions that were nearby but not visible from the road) with the surrounding environment (Leshed et al., 2008).

Ethnographic studies can be useful for understanding how technology use changes over time. A study of iPhone users used ethnographic techniques to understand how perceptions of the device changed over the course of several weeks. Six participants were recruited on the basis of their expressed interest in purchasing an iPhone. One week before purchasing the phone, each participant wrote a narrative describing their expectations and completed a survey indicating the importance of each expectation. After purchasing their phones, participants listed activities related to the phone, estimated the time spent, picked important experiences, and rated the product relative to each specific situation. Findings were used to build a model that described the use of the iPhone as a sequence from anticipation of using it, to orientation to features, incorporation of the device into everyday life, and then to identification with the phone as an important part of their lives (Karapano et al., 2009).

Ethnographic investigations of ubiquitous computing have required some HCI researchers to go into some unexpected places. One project examined the navigation needs of firefighters, in the hopes of identifying opportunities for developing ubiquitous systems that would help firefighters find their way out of hazardous, smoke-filled environments. The research team developed a series of simulations—conducting research in actual fires being, of course, too dangerous—aimed at exploring how a tool might work. Members of the research team then donned firefighting gear and joined in a simulation involving navigational activities commonly used by firefighters. Observations from their participation, and from observing firefighters in other simulations, helped the researchers understand how firefighters use improvisation and collaboration to navigate while fighting fires (Denef et al., 2008).

9.5.5 **VIRTUAL ETHNOGRAPHY**

Most of the examples discussed thus far in this chapter involve "real-world" ethnographies—studies of groups and communities situated in familiar, physical settings. This is not an inherent limitation in the technique—ethnography does not always mean a researcher being present physically to observe the group or community. The growth of countless online communities supporting many different types of interaction presents the possibility of "virtual ethnography."

The term "virtual ethnography" has been used to describe different things, such as using web cams or videos (Blomberg et al., 2007). However, this in no way involves participation and, furthermore, there is a high likelihood of missing a lot of contextual information as people may act differently for the camera, shut off the camera at times, or avoid the area with the camera. If the researcher is not in the context, this leads to a poorer quality of data collection and understanding. However, when ethnographic methods are used to research a community that is strictly virtual or online, there is less likelihood of missing anything, as the "there" is only online. If participation is the goal, if being in the context is the goal, researchers can "be" in a virtual community and experience it as everyone else is experiencing it.

The virtual nature of these communities presents some opportunities and challenges for ethnographic researchers. Online identity is much more fluid and controllable than it is in the real world. In many online groups, message boards, and virtual worlds, users can control exactly what others know about us and how they see us. This can be very convenient for ethnographic study, as researchers can easily define themselves as complete participants (with some limitations), without having to face the challenge of playing those roles in frequent face-to-face relationships. Furthermore, researchers might find that maintaining scientific objectivity is relatively easy when all interaction with the subjects of study are conducted through the mediation of a computer screen.

The tenuous nature of links between online identities presents some interesting possibilities for ethnographers. As many online communities require little, if any, direct link between a virtual identity and a real person, conducting an ethnographic study without revealing one's identity as a researcher is a very real possibility. Furthermore, the transient and artificial notion of participation in these virtual worlds makes complete participation a very real possibility. Before embarking on any study of this sort, you might want to consider what circumstances merit revealing your identity as a researcher. For example, you might decide to "out" yourself to an individual or a larger group if you feel that other participants are becoming suspicious of your motives.

The construction of multiple identities presents further intriguing opportunities. As many virtual communities allow users to create multiple online identities, virtual ethnographers might use multiple online manifestations to examine community responses to different types of behavior or even to create situations that might be the focus of studies. For example, a researcher conducting a virtual ethnography might start an argument between two online identities that she controls as a means of studying how other participants would react.

Of course, this multiplicity of identities cuts both ways as well. Virtual ethnographers may face greater challenges in evaluating the honesty of the people with whom they are interacting. Barring external confirmation—such as verifiable real-world interactions—it may be hard to confirm the claimed identities of online interlocutors.

As virtual environments run the gamut from simple text-based forums to social networks and online worlds, the types of ethnography that may be conducted will also change. Fully graphical environments, such as Second Life, present opportunities for observing group interaction, physical positioning, and other visual cues that are not generally available in text-only environments. Although these cues may make ethnographies of graphical virtual worlds seem more "real" than other virtual ethnographies, it is important to note that the questions of identity don't ever disappear.

In Section 9.4.2, the Ethnographic Research of Your Own Community sidebar presented information about the ethnographic research done into online empathic support communities. The example given was of an online support community for people with a torn ACL (Maloney-Krichmar and Preece, 2005). Ethnographic methods have also been used to examine multiplayer virtual worlds. For instance, Ducheneaut and Moore used ethnographic methods to research the Star Wars Galaxies multiperson online role-playing game. The two researchers each created a character (one a combat-oriented character, the other an entertainer) and logged in for a minimum of 4 hours per week for 3 months. They later created two additional characters and tried to encourage other role-playing individuals in the Star Wars Galaxies to communicate with their characters (Ducheneaut and Moore, 2004). Specifically, they spent time in locations collecting data on the frequency and type of visitors, types of interaction, and related factors that could be used to characterize the social activity in these places (Ducheneaut et al., 2007). As complete participants, they were able to participate in genuine interactions, without having to reveal themselves as researchers or to maintain the pretense of being "real" group members.

Of course, many online communities have face-to-face components and this is where the dividing line between virtual and physical can become very complex. The Researching Online Dating sidebar discusses the situation of research into online dating communities. In these communities, the interaction starts out virtual but has the stated goal of moving towards face-to-face meetings.

RESEARCHING ONLINE DATING

One of the more fascinating topics being addressed by HCI researchers in recent times is the topic of online dating. Individuals go online to various sites (such as http://www.eharmony.com), providing photos and descriptions of their interests in the hopes that they might meet people for dates or relationships. With millions of subscribers of various ages, these sites represent an interesting area for HCI research. Although a number of approaches have been used to study online dating sites, ethnography has not been the primary approach. This raises an interesting question—can ethnography be applied to online dating?

At first this might seem like a research focus on individuals but online dating communities are groups with group norms, accepted practices, and shared group communication tools (such as chat rooms). These online groups differ primarily from work groups in terms of the goal of the interaction (dating, not work), the goal of the presentation (to look attractive and interesting, rather than to present information), and the transient population of members in the group (people join and leave the online dating community very rapidly). An example of a group norm and practice is that if you e-mail someone and they do not respond, it is considered totally inappropriate to e-mail them a second time.

Hancock et al. (2007) took the approach of recruiting people who were already involved in online dating, to determine the accuracy of their online dating profiles. A self-selected group responded to their recruitment advertisement. The researcher team met with these 80 participants, who presented copies of their online dating profiles (Hancock et al., 2007). Participants were asked to rate the accuracy of their profiles with regard to height, weight, and age. Only 18% of participants had inaccurate age information in their profile but 48% of participants had inaccurate height information and 59% of participants had inaccurate weight information in their online profile. An analysis of the participants' perception of profile accuracy showed that most participants were aware when their profile information was not accurate and were aware that this could be potentially deceptive.

Fiore and Donath (2005) examined how people in online dating communities tend to communicate with other people who have similar interests and preferences. The researchers were able to broker an agreement with a dating site to access profiles, statistics, and e-mails (Fiore and Donath, 2005). It is unclear in the paper if users were aware that their profile information was shared with researchers, although it is unlikely (since the researchers did analysis on over 236,000 messages sent from over 29,000 users to over 51,000 users). An analysis of 110,000 conversations (messages between a unique pair of users), found that 78% were single messages that were not responded to by the recipient. Users were more likely to contact other users who had similar characteristics (such as "wants children," smoking, educational level, and religion) and responses to those initial contacts were even more highly correlated to the presence of similar characteristics. Note that "user" is a more appropriate term than "participant," since these users did not choose to participate in the research.

Lee and Bruckman (2007) examined the use of general purpose social networking sites (such as MySpace and Facebook) for dating. They interviewed 12 people who had used Friendster or MySpace for dating (Lee and Bruckman, 2007), recruited through public postings (e.g. on Craigslist) and word of mouth. Although some of the interviews were in person and some were conducted by phone, all of the participants allowed the researchers to examine their social networking profiles. Participants described the credibility provided by contacts within the social networks as an advantage in meeting potential dates, as friends would be likely to challenge or respond negatively to misrepresentation. Participants specifically found the set of "top friends" useful for providing credible information. The number of friends, types of comment left by friends, and types of picture posted also provided useful details about potential dates. Participants who began dating people met on a social networking site also commented that the site could provide useful feedback on their relationship status, through their rank on their new partner's "top friends" list.

Fiore et al. (2008) tried to identify online dating features most strongly associated with assessments of the attractiveness of potential dates. They used a random selection of 25 male and 25 female profiles from the Yahoo! Personals website, five each from different cities in the USA (Fiore et al., 2008), constructing four different versions of each profile: picture, free text, fixed-choice answers, and full profile, which includes all three sections. A group primarily made up of university students evaluated the various profile components for attractiveness. The researchers found that the photo had the greatest impact on perceptions of attractiveness, but the free text also greatly influenced perceptions of attractiveness. The fixed-question responses did not impact on perceptions of attractiveness, except in cases where they were used to evaluate "deal-breakers," such as smoking.

Although the complex phenomena and group dynamics of online dating might make ethnography seem an appealing research method, there are a number of troubling ethical and logistical questions. If you were to research online dating communities, would you be a true participant? Would the emotion of meeting and dating these people cause you to lose your sense of objectivity? Furthermore, is it ethical to go on a date acting as if a long-term relationship was the main goal, when it is a research exercise? Would that be misleading? If you were to notify people that you are doing research, would that lead to loss of credibility or access into the community? If you were to not notify people about your research, wouldn't that be unethical? Would it even be possible to be a complete observer, watching from the sidelines?

(Continued)

RESEARCHING ONLINE DATING—CONT'D

How would that work? Note that in two of the research studies above, profiles or data were taken from online dating sites and used in research studies, without the express permission of the owners (although the terms and conditions of site usage would allow it). Although these people were not research subjects, their online profiles were involved. Clearly, if ethnographic methods were used and researchers went out on dates with unsuspecting research participants, this would be a far more serious ethical concern. This leads to an important question: how can you do ethnographic research and collect accurate data, while participants are aware of your research? For further discussion of the ethical issues associated with online dating research projects, see Section 1.5.2.4.1.

If a community has both a physical and a virtual component, both might be good candidates for ethnographic research. For instance, Ploderer, Howard, and Thomas (Ploderer et al., 2008) were interested in researching the community of bodybuilders, people who are passionate about staying fit, building muscle, and taking part in bodybuilding competitions. The researchers used ethnographic methods in both the physical community and the online community. They went to seven bodybuilding gyms to observe and also attended two bodybuilding competitions. In addition, the BodySpace social networking website has over 160,000 people interested in bodybuilding. The researchers created a profile and for 4 months, participated with and observed the members of the community and communicated with various community members (Ploderer et al., 2008).

9.6 SUMMARY

Ethnographic methods are very useful in understanding the context of technology usage. By examining the human, social, and organizational contexts of technology, a deeper understanding of who these users are can be developed. In ethnographic traditions, a better understanding of a group of people and their traditions and processes is itself a noble and worthwhile goal. However, in the HCI community, ethnography is often used as a first step, to understand a group of users, their problems, challenges, norms, and processes, with the eventual goal of building some type of technology for them or with them. Currently, ethnographic research methods are used most often in home settings, work settings, educational settings, and online. However, new approaches to ethnographic research are being developed to study, for example, how people use ubiquitous computing in real-world settings anywhere, such as the street, the subway, or a park, for activities including role-playing games, geocaching, and education (Crabtree et al., 2006).

DISCUSSION QUESTIONS

1. Ethnographic research has been described as inductive. What does that mean?

2. Is generalization a goal of ethnographic research?

3. How is participatory design similar to ethnographic research? How is it different?

4. What are three potential challenges in finding a group to study?

5. What are the four most common settings for doing ethnographic research in human-computer interaction?

6. Participating in a group implies changing it. In the most obvious sense, the group has one more member after the ethnographer joins it. More subtly, the addition of a new member might alter the dynamics of communication and interaction between group members. How does the role that the ethnographer plays influence the extent of the changes that his presence might bring? Can you suggest any approaches that ethnographers might use to minimize the impact of their presence upon groups being studied?

7. Some people might think that the ultimate form of participant research would be to conduct an ethnographic study of a group of which one was already a member. For researchers, this might mean studying research groups, academic departments, corporate teams, or professional societies. What concerns would you have about the appropriateness and validity of such research?

8. Go back and reread the Researching Online Dating sidebar. How could ethnographic methods be used in researching online dating communities? How could you study the community in a way that is both ethical and did not greatly influence how people would act towards you?

9. Workplace ethnographies present specific challenges in navigating the often complicated interactions between employees at differing levels of authority and responsibility. If you are hired by management, workers may feel that they have nothing to gain by participating in your study, and potentially a great deal to lose, in terms of job security or responsibility. To make matters worse, you may not know all of the motivations behind the study: management might, in fact, be hoping to use the results of your work to build systems that change how work is done. Finally, you may be given an initial goal and problem description that is too narrow or inappropriately focused. Given all of these challenges, what strategies might you use to work with both employees and management to build the trust and participation necessary for conducting a methodologically sound study?

10. Working closely with research participants raises questions of trust regarding material that should or should not be included in a study. Particularly when working closely with an individual in a home or workplace setting, you may

see or hear things that might be both very interesting and potentially sensitive. Examples include comments about a coworker's (or manager's) incompetence or discussion of children hiding certain behavior from parents. Although these observations may be intriguing, fear of repercussions may lead you to be wary of reporting them. How might you deal with this conflict between research fidelity and the trust of your participants?

RESEARCH DESIGN EXERCISES

1. Imagine an ethnographic study of how college students use technology to work on group projects. How would you go about designing such a study? You might say that you will pick a class that involves group work, but this is only the beginning—which courses would you consider? Which types of student? Which roles would be appropriate? What sort of data would you collect? How would your answer depend upon your status? In other words, would a college student conducting this study use the same approach as a professor?

2. Conduct a mini-ethnography. Working in a team of two or three, observe a group of people. You might observe students waiting outside a class on campus, families at a playground, friends at a coffee shop, meetings of a student group, or some other similar activity. (As this won't be a formal study, you probably shouldn't interview participants or use other data collection methods, but you can watch and listen in public places.) Write down your observations individually and try to describe what you have seen and learned. Once all group members have done this, meet and discuss your findings. Can you combine your observations and individual models to build a consensus model? Build a model that incorporates all of your conclusions and discusses differences in your findings.

REFERENCES

Agar, M., 1980. The Professional Stranger. Academic Press, Inc., New York.

Angrosino, M., 2007. Doing Ethnographic and Observational Research. Sage, London, England.

Balka, E., Bjorn, P., Wagner, I., 2008. Steps toward a typology for health informatics. In: Proceedings of the 2008 ACM Conference on Computer Supported Cooperative Work. ACM, San Diego, CA, USA, pp. 515–524.

Becvar, L.A., Hollan, J.D., 2007. Transparency and technology appropriation: social impacts of a video blogging system in dental hygiene clinical instruction. In: Proceedings of the 2007 International ACM Conference on Supporting Group Work. ACM, Sanibel Island, FL, USA, pp. 311–320.

Bell, G., Blythe, M., Sengers, P., 2005. Making by making strange: defamiliarization and the design of domestic technologies. ACM Transactions on Computer-Human Interaction 12 (2), 149–173.

Blomberg, J., Burrell, M., Guest, G., 2007. An ethnographic approach to design. In: Julie, A.J., Andrew, S. (Eds.), The Human-Computer Interaction Handbook. L. Erlbaum Associates Inc, pp. 965–986.

Blythe, M., Monk, A., 2002. Notes towards an ethnography of domestic technology. In: 4th Conference on Designing Interactive Systems: Processes, Practices, Methods, and Techniques. ACM, London, England.

Brooke, T., Burrell, J., 2003. From ethnography to design in a vineyard. In: Proceedings of the 2003 Conference on Designing for User Experiences. ACM, San Francisco, CA, pp. 1–4.

Carroll, J.M., Chin, G., Rosson, M.B., Neale, D.C., 2000. The development of cooperation: five years of participatory design in the virtual school. In: Proceedings of the 3rd Conference on Designing Interactive Systems: Processes, Practices, Methods, and Techniques. ACM, New York City, NY, USA, pp. 239–251.

Chavan, A.L., Gorney, D., Prabhu, B., Arora, S., 2009. The washing machine that ate my sari—mistakes in cross-cultural design. Interactions 16 (1), 26–31.

Crabtree, A., Benford, S., Greenhalgh, C., Tennent, P., Chalmers, M., Brown, B., 2006. Supporting ethnographic studies of ubiquitous computing in the wild. In: 6th Conference On Designing Interactive Systems. ACM, University Park, PA, USA.

Crabtree, A., Rodden, T., 2004. Domestic routines and design for the home. Computer Supported Cooperative Work 13 (2), 191–220.

Denef, S., Ramirez, L., Dyrks, T., Stevens, G., 2008. Handy navigation in ever-changing spaces: an ethnographic study of firefighting practices. In: Proceedings of the 7th ACM Conference On Designing Interactive Systems. ACM, Cape Town, South Africa.

Druin, A., Weeks, A., Massey, S., Bederson, B.B., 2007. Children's interests and concerns when using the international children's digital library: a four-country case study. In: Proceedings of the 7th ACM/IEEE-CS Joint Conference On Digital Libraries. ACM, Vancouver, BC, Canada, pp. 167–176.

Ducheneaut, N., Moore, R., Nickell, E., 2007. Virtual "Third Places": a case study of sociability in massively multiplayer games. Computer Supported Cooperative Work 16 (1), 129–166.

Ducheneaut, N., Moore, R.J., 2004. The social side of gaming: a study of interaction patterns in a massively multiplayer online game. In: Proceedings of the 2004 ACM Conference on Computer Supported Cooperative Work. ACM, Chicago, IL, USA, pp. 360–369.

Fiore, A.T., Donath, J.S., 2005. Homophily in online dating: when do you like someone like yourself? In: CHI'05 Extended Abstracts on Human Factors in Computing Systems. ACM, Portland, OR, USA, pp. 1371–1374.

Fiore, A.T., Taylor, L.S., Mendelsohn, G.A., Hearst, M., 2008. Assessing attractiveness in online dating profiles. In: Proceedings of the SIGCHI Conference on Human Factors in Computing Systems. ACM, Florence, Italy, pp. 797–806.

Gaver, W.W., Boucher, A., Pennington, S., Walker, B., 2004. Cultural probes and the value of uncertainty. Interactions 11 (5), 53–56.

Gold, R., 1958. Roles in sociological field observations. Social Forces 36 (3), 217–223.

Hancock, J.T., Toma, C., Ellison, N., 2007. The truth about lying in online dating profiles. In: Proceedings of the SIGCHI Conference on Human Factors in Computing Systems. ACM, San Jose, CA, USA, pp. 449–452.

Harvey, L., Myers, M., 2002. Scholarship and practice: the contribution of ethnographic research methods to bridging the gap. In: Myers, M., Aison, D. (Eds.), Qualitative Research in Information Systems: A Reader. Sage Publications, London, pp. 169–180.

Karapano, E., Zimmerman, J., Forlizzi, J., Martens, J.-B., 2009. User experience over time: an initial framework. In: Proceedings of the 27th International Conference On Human Factors In Computing Systems. ACM, Boston, MA, USA.

Lee, A.Y., Bruckman, A.S., 2007. Judging you by the company you keep: dating on social networking sites. In: Proceedings of the 2007 International ACM Conference on Supporting Group Work. ACM, Sanibel Island, FL, USA, pp. 371–378.

Leshed, G., Velden, T., Rieger, O., Kot, B., Sengers, P., 2008. In-car gps navigation: engagement with and disengagement from the environment. In: SIGCHI Conference on Human Factors in Computing Systems. ACM, Florence, Italy.

Lofland, J., Snow, D.A., Anderson, L., Lofland, L.H., 2006. Analyzing Social Situations: A Guide to Qualitative Observation and Analysis. Wadsworth/Thomson Learning, Belmont, CA.

Maloney-Krichmar, D., Preece, J., 2005. A multilevel analysis of sociability, usability, and community dynamics in an online health community. ACM Transactions on Computer-Human Interaction 12 (2), 201–232.

Newman, M.W., Landay, A., 2000. Sitemaps, storyboards, and specifications: a sketch of Web site design practice. In: 3rd Conference On Designing Interactive Systems: Processes, Practices, Methods, and Techniques. ACM, New York City, NY, USA.

Ormerod, T., Morley, N., Ball, L., Langley, C., Spenser, C., 2003. Using ethnography to design a mass detection tool (MDT) for the early discovery of insurance fraud. In: CHI'03 Extended Abstracts on Human Factors in Computing Systems. ACM, Ft. Lauderdale, FL, USA.

Pedersen, E.R., Wolff, G., 2008. Paper interface to electronic medical records: a case of usage-driven technology appropriation. In: Proceedings of the 7th ACM Conference On Designing Interactive Systems. ACM, Cape Town, South Africa, pp. 40–49.

Ploderer, B., Howard, S., Thomas, P., 2008. Being online, living offline: the influence of social ties over the appropriation of social network sites. In: Proceedings of the 2008 ACM Conference on Computer Supported Cooperative Work. ACM, San Diego, CA, USA, pp. 333–342.

Preece, J., 1998. Empathic communities: reaching out across the Web. Interactions 5 (2), 32–43.

Rode, J., Toye, E., Blackwell, A., 2004. The fuzzy felt ethnography—understanding the programming patterns of domestic appliances. Personal and Ubiquitous Computing 8 (3–4), 161–176.

Schuler, D., Namioka, A. (Eds.), 1993. Participatory Design: Principles and Practices. Lawrence Erlbaum Associates, Hillsdale, NJ.

Shapiro, D., 1994. The limits of ethnography: combining social sciences for CSCW. In: Proceedings of the 1994 ACM Conference on Computer Supported Cooperative Work. ACM, Chapel Hill, NC, United States.

Sharrock, W., Randall, D., 2004. Ethnography, ethnomethodology and the problem of generalisation in design. European Journal of Information Systems 13 (3), 186–194.

Siegel, D., Dray, S., 2005. Avoiding the next schism: ethnography and usability. Interactions 12 (2), 58–61.

Su, N.M., Mark, G., 2008. Communication chains and multitasking. In: SIGCHI Conference on Human Factors in Computing Systems. ACM, Florence, Italy.

Suchman, L., 2000a. Embodied practices of engineering work. Mind, Culture, and Activity 7 (1–2), 4–18.

Suchman, L., 2000b. Organizing alignment: a case of bridge-building. Organization 7 (2), 311–327.

Suchman, L.A., 1987. Plans and Situated Action: The Problem of Human-Machine Communication. Cambridge University Press, Cambridge.

Taylor, A.S., Swan, L., 2005. Artful systems in the home. In: SIGCHI conference on Human factors in computing systems. ACM, Portland, OR, USA.

Wu, M., Baecker, R., Richards, B., 2007. Designing a cognitive aid for and with people who have anterograde amnesia. In: Lazar, J. (Ed.), Universal Usability: Designing Computer Interfaces for Diverse User Populations. John Wiley & Sons, Chichester, UK, pp. 317–356.

Wyche, S.P., 2005. Designing speculative household cleaning products for older adults. In: Proceedings of the 2005 Conference on Designing for User Experience. AIGA: American Institute of Graphic Arts, San Francisco, CA, USA, pp. 49.

Wyeth, P., 2006. Ethnography in the kindergarten: examining children's play experiences. In: SIGCHI Conference on Human Factors in Computing Systems. ACM, Montréal, Québec, Canada.

Usability testing

10

10.1 INTRODUCTION

Usability testing is often known as "user research." Often, in usability testing, we're not researching the user, we're researching the interface. We're trying to figure out how to make a specific interface better. However, user research is also a broader term that may include elements of design and development, such as personas, user profiles, card sorting, and competitive research that generally might not be considered "research" by those who consider themselves researchers (Kuniavsky, 2003). Furthermore, usability testing as a research method (utilizing representative users and representative tasks) can be used to learn more about how people interact with interfaces, even when the goal is not fixing the interface, but instead learning more about users and interactions. So, in usability testing, maybe we *are* researching the user?

10.2 WHAT IS USABILITY TESTING?

Usability testing, in general, involves representative users attempting representative tasks in representative environments, on early prototypes or working versions of computer interfaces (Lewis, 2006). If that sounds like a very broad definition, it is meant to be that way. The world of usability testing includes:

- testing prototypes that have only been built on paper (known as paper prototypes);
- testing screen mock-ups or wireframes which have no functionality
- testing screen layouts which have partial functionality
- testing prototypes that look complete but have a human behind the scenes responding (known as the "Wizard of Oz" technique);
- testing working versions of software before it is officially released;
- testing software that has already been implemented in existing systems.

The interfaces being usability tested are typically screen layouts for desktop, laptop, or tablet computers, as well as smart phones and other mobile devices. Usability testing can also be done to evaluate physical interaction with devices. Mobile devices frequently need usability testing, since the interaction approaches (such as multi-touch screens) are newer, more content is stuffed into a smaller screen size, and it can

Research Methods in Human-Computer Interaction. http://dx.doi.org/10.1016/B978-0-12-805390-4.00010-8

be easy to activate features by accident (e.g. holding the smartphone in your hand and hitting a button; or making a call, putting the phone up to your face, and accidentally selecting a feature).

All of these approaches to usability testing have one basic goal: to improve the quality of an interface by finding flaws-areas of the interface that need improvement. While usability testing should discover interface flaws that cause problems for users, at the same time, we want to discover what is working well with an interface design, so that we make sure to keep those features in place! What's an interface flaw? It is some aspect, some component, some widget of the interface that is confusing, misleading, or generally suboptimal. It is not about style or color preferences. Someone may prefer dark blue text instead of black text, on a white background and that's fine. It becomes a usability problem only when you have white, yellow, orange, or red text on a white background, all of which are hard for the eye to perceive. When we talk about usability testing, we are talking about discovering interface flaws that cause problems for a majority of people. Figure 10.1 gives an example of an interface that has a major flaw. The screen shot shows the process of checking in online for an airline flight. Once you enter your information, the website asks if you would like to upgrade your seat to the class called "economy plus." Typically, most individuals would not want to upgrade. However, the user's eye naturally goes to the large yellow arrow

FIGURE 10.1

An airline check-in screen with at least one clear usability flaw.

Source: www.ua2go.com.

on the right, which would seem to continue to the next screen. In reality, clicking the yellow arrow causes the user to upgrade their seat. To continue without an upgrade, the user needs to click on the textual link on the left, which is small (in comparison to the arrow) and not obvious. This is a confusing and potentially misleading interface flaw (whether it was intentionally misleading is a question that we will not address). This is a very minor flaw to change. However, it will have a major improvement on user interaction and performance.

The range of usability testing is quite broad. Usability testing can involve hundreds of users, have a number of controls, and use a true experimental design. Usability testing can also involve a researcher sitting down next to three users, watching them go through the interface, and then taking basic notes on where the problems are. While both of these exercises can be called usability testing, it is more likely that the former would be considered research and would be published. Usability testing can involve hypothesis testing, tight controls, control groups, and a large enough number of participants to determine statistically significant differences. However, that's not the way that most usability testing happens (Rubin and Chisnell, 2008). Why? In industry, the extra time needed to plan controls and do random assignments, and the high number of participants needed, are often a barrier to entry (Rubin and Chisnell, 2008). If the choice is that you must do all of those or nothing at all, businesses often choose to do nothing. Therefore, more flexible, easier, and quicker methods are often used. Where does usability testing end and research begin? It's an unclear, fuzzy line and the distinction is not all that important.

10.3 HOW DOES USABILITY TESTING RELATE TO "TRADITIONAL" RESEARCH?

Usability testing can be considered a close cousin of traditional research methods, and is often known as "user research." In reality, the approaches utilized in usability testing are often the same as those used in classic research. Metrics utilized in usability testing include measurement of task performance and time performance, similar to experimental design. Methods utilized as part of usability testing include surveys to measure user satisfaction. Observation techniques, from ethnography, are often utilized in usability testing. Key logging and clickstream analysis (see Chapters 12 and 13) can be utilized in usability testing. As discussed in other chapters of this book (primarily Chapters 12 and 13), there are many automated data collection methods that could be used for usability testing. In usability testing, the rights that participants have are the same as in any other type of research. The names of the participants must remain anonymous, participants must be informed of their rights and sign some type of informed consent form, and participants have the right to leave the research at any time, just as in traditional research.

However, usability testing often has different end goals. Usability testing is primarily an industrial approach to improving user interfaces. As an industrial approach, there is little concern for using only one research method or having strict controls. In fact, Wixon goes as far as to say that usability testing has more in common with engineering than traditional research (Wixon, 2003). Wixon's assertion is that usability testing, like engineering, is involved in building a successful product, in the shortest amount of time, using the fewest resources, with the fewest risks, while optimizing trade-offs. Often in industry, schedule and resource issues, rather than theoretical discussions of methodology, drive the development process (Wixon, 2003). One practice that is somewhat accepted in usability testing is to modify the interface after every user test, when major flaws are discovered, to help immediately eliminate the flaws and improve the interface. Making immediate changes to the interface allows for those changes to be evaluated during the next user test, which can help ensure that no new interface problems have been introduced in making the changes (Wixon, 2003). While this may not happen due to time constraints, it is an acceptable practice. Clearly, this practice would be considered unacceptable in experimental design, where the goal would be to ensure that all users in a group have the same treatment. And since usability testing is an industrial, practical approach, it is also important to note that not all interface flaws discovered during usability testing are fixed. Very often, the list of interface flaws discovered is prioritized and only the most serious problems are fixed.

By now, it should be clear that the goal of usability testing is to be practical and have a major impact. Since the goal is often to improve interfaces and have an important impact on the financial bottom line of a company, many companies don't publish their usability test findings, as they consider it confidential and a part of their competitive advantage. There are, however, a number of documented cases of usability testing that we have included in this chapter.

There are some similarities and some differences between usability testing, and the ethnography and participatory design methods discussed in chapter 9. Ethnography is more focused on understanding people, their groups, their processes, and their beliefs. Often, ethnographic methods are used as part of a systems development method called *participatory design* (again, discussed in detail in Chapter 9). The end goal of ethnography is simply understanding a group, an organization, or a problem, whereas the end goal of participatory design is building a computer system. Usability testing follows a similar pattern, with an end goal of improved interface design in a specific system. In fact, participatory design includes the stages of both ethnographic observation (in the user's situational context) and usability testing. Development methods or lifecycles, such as participatory design, the systems development lifecycle, the web development lifecycle, or community-centered design, can be thought of as recipes, with the individual activities, such as ethnographic observation and usability testing, as the ingredients in those recipes. The methods used in usability testing borrow most closely from experimental design and ethnography. Table 10.1 provides a comparison of classical research methods (such as experimental design and ethnography) and usability testing. Again, it is important to note that while many of the same approaches from classical research can be utilized in usability testing, they are often implemented differently, with different end goals.

To make things a bit more confusing, there is also research about usability testing! That is, research exists on evaluating which usability testing methods are

Table 10.1 Differences Between Classical Research and Usability Testing

Classical Research Source	Classical Research Description	Usability Testing Description
Experimental design	Isolate and understand specific phenomena, with the goal of generalization to other problems	Find and fix flaws in a specific interface, no goal of generalization
Experimental design	A larger number of participants is required	A small number of participants can be utilized
Ethnography	Observe to understand the context of people, groups, and organizations	Observe to understand where in the interface users are having problems
Ethnography	Deep participatory embedding of the researcher in the community is often encouraged	Researcher participation is not encouraged, except when an intervention is needed to help the user get "unstuck" (with strict protocols for doing so)
Ethnography	Longer-term research method	Short-term research method
Ethnography and experimental design	Used to understand problems or answer research questions	Used in systems and interface development
Ethnography and experimental design	Used in earlier stages, often separate from (or only partially related to) the interface development process	Can take place as early as paper prototypes, where there is more potential impact on the interface, but often takes place in later stages, after interfaces (or prototype versions of interfaces) have been developed, with less potential impact on the interface
Ethnography and experimental design	Used for understanding problems	Used for evaluating solutions

most effective. For instance, in the debate on how many participants you need (see Section 10.5.3), the focus is not on improving specific interfaces, but on understanding and improving the usability methods themselves. But that isn't usability testing, that's research on how to do usability testing and that's a whole different topic!

10.4 TYPES OF USABILITY TESTING OR USABILITY INSPECTIONS

There are many different types of usability testing. A more general term, "usability engineering," has sometimes been used to describe any process or activity that aims to improve the ease of use of an interface. Under this heading, and sometimes under the heading of usability testing, there are three distinct categories: expert-based testing, automated testing, and user-based testing.

An expert-based test involves interface experts in using a number of different structured methods for finding interface flaws. An automated test is a software program that applies a series of guidelines (developed by the experts) to an interface and determines where the interface doesn't meet the guidelines. A user-based test involves representative users performing representative tasks (at various stages in the development process). While user-based tests are the majority focus of usability evaluation, expert-based tests and automated tests are sometimes used in human-computer interaction (HCI) practice.

As multimethod research approaches gain strength, we expect to see a greater appearance of expert and automated usability testing. Note that expert and automated usability tests are sometimes known as *usability inspections,* and *usability testing* is reserved for user-based testing. Whole books have been written about each type of usability testing, so this chapter provides only a summary of each type. Since the primary interest in HCI research is users and collecting data from users, this chapter primarily focuses on user-based testing. First, we briefly discuss expert-based testing and automated testing.

10.4.1 EXPERT-BASED TESTING

Expert-based tests are essentially structured inspections by interface experts. The people who developed the prototype interface being evaluated should not be involved with the expert review, as that may bias the results. People who are unfamiliar with the interface should carry out the expert reviews. Expert-based tests are often used in conjunction with user-based tests, but the expert-based tests always come first. Interface experts are experts in interfaces but they are typically not experts in the tasks to be performed within a certain interface. Conversely, representative users are typically experts in performing the tasks but are not experts in interface design. Often a certain portion of interface functionality can be understood and improved without a deep understanding of the tasks, but other portions of the interface can only be examined with a deep understanding of the tasks involved.

Interface experts first use a structured inspection to attempt to uncover some of the more obvious interface flaws, such as confusing wording, inconsistent or misleading layouts, and color inconsistency. If possible, suggested improvements to the interface from the expert review should be made before user-based usability testing occurs. This timeline allows the experts to find the obvious interface flaws and get them fixed; the users can then find the deeper, more granular, and task-related interface flaws which may not be obvious to the interface experts (Lazar, 2006). If there are many interface flaws and no expert has reviewed the interface, the users may be distracted by the major interface flaws and may be unable to help the developers by identifying the more granular, task-based flaws.

There are a number of different types of expert review, also known as expert inspections or usability inspections. The most common expert reviews are the heuristic review, the consistency inspection, and the cognitive walkthrough. In a heuristic review, an expert takes a set of heuristics (rules of thumb) and compares the heuristics to the interface in question. Heuristics are short sets of usually no more than 10 interface rules. To be truly effective, the expert must be very familiar with the heuristics and have previous experience in interpreting them. Lazar provides a list of various sets of heuristics for different types of websites (Lazar, 2006) but the best-known set of broad interface heuristics is probably Shneiderman's 8 Golden Rules of Interface Design (see Table 10.2).

Table 10.2 Shneiderman's 8 Golden Rules of Interface Design

Strive for consistency
Cater to universal usability
Offer informative feedback
Design dialogs to yield closure
Prevent errors
Permit easy reversal of actions
Support internal locus of control
Reduce short-term memory load
(Shneiderman et al., 2017)

In a consistency inspection, one or more experts review a series of screens or web pages for issues of consistency in layout, color, terminology, or language. Sometimes, an organization has a specific set of style guidelines (for colors and typefaces) and a consistency inspection can check for overall consistency with those style guidelines.

A cognitive walkthrough is an expert review method in which interface experts simulate users, "walking through" a series of tasks. The experts must have experience with general interface design and a good understanding of who the users are and what tasks they are expected to perform in the interface that is being evaluated. Because of the exploratory nature of a cognitive walkthrough, it can give an understanding of how users might interact with an interface the first time that they attempt to use it (Hollingsed and Novick, 2007). Both high-frequency tasks and rarely occurring but important tasks (such as error recovery) should be included in a cognitive walkthrough (Shneiderman et al., 2017). Because it is task-based, rather than rule-based for experts, it is still somewhat controversial, as some people feel that it is not as productive as user-based testing.

Not as popular as the previous three methods, but still occurring often, is the guidelines review, in which an expert compares a set of interfaces to a previously written set of interface guidelines. While this sounds like a heuristic review, the main difference is that a guidelines review uses a large set of guidelines (usually 10–200). Heuristic reviews take place more often because they are easier and take less time. However, guideline reviews are more thorough. Probably one of the best-known sets of guidelines is the Web Content Accessibility Guidelines (WCAG, currently in version 2.0), created by the World Wide Web Consortium (http://www.w3.org/WAI). These guideline documents provide guidance on making website content accessible for people with disabilities. Internationally, most laws that deal with accessible web content were written based on the WCAG. The Web Accessibility Initiative also has guidelines related to authoring tool accessibility, user agent accessibility, and rich Internet application accessibility. These guidelines, while being commonly used, can be overwhelming in scope and so the Web Accessibility Initiative also offers shorter versions of the guidelines documents (such as checkpoints and quick tips) which can be considered as heuristics. Other commonly used guidelines include the operating systems interface guidelines documents from Apple and Microsoft, the research-based web design and usability guidelines from the US government and the KDE or GNOME interface guidelines. In addition, firms such as the Nielsen Norman Group have large numbers of specialized guideline sets that are available for a price.

Other types of expert review, such as the formal usability inspection and the pluralistic walkthrough, are not as common (Hollingsed and Novick, 2007). If you are interested in different types of expert review, you should read the classic book on expert reviews (Nielsen and Mack, 1994) or recent HCI papers about expert review methods. However, since expert-based reviews really don't involve users, we won't go into any more details on this topic.

10.4.2 AUTOMATED USABILITY TESTING

An automated usability test is a software application that inspects a series of interfaces to assess the level of usability. Often, this works by using a set of interface guidelines (described in Section 10.4.1) and having the software compare the guidelines to the interfaces. A summary report is then provided by the automated usability testing application. Automated usability testing applications are often used when a large number of interfaces need to be examined and little time is available to do human-based reviews. The major strength is that these applications can read through code very quickly, looking for usability problems that can be picked up. These applications typically have features to either offer advice about how the code should be fixed or actually fix the code. However, the major weakness is that many aspects of usability cannot be discovered by automated means, such as appropriate wording, labels, and layout. And most automated tools are designed only to test web interfaces. For instance, an application can determine if a web page has alternative code for a graphic (important for accessibility, and a requirement under the WCAG 2.0), by examining to determine the existence of an <alt> attribute in an <img> tag. However, an application cannot determine if that alternative text is clear and useful (e.g. "picture here" would not be an appropriate text but it would meet the requirements of the automated usability testing application). In many situations like that, manual checks are required. A manual check is when one of these applications notes that because of the presence of certain interface features, a human inspection is required to determine if a guideline is complied with (e.g. if a form has proper labels).

Automated usability testing applications are good at measuring certain statistics, such as the number of fonts used, the average font size, the average size of clickable buttons, the deepest level of menus, and the average loading time of graphics (Au et al., 2008). These are useful metrics, but they do not ascertain how users interact with those interfaces, only how well these interfaces comply with some guidelines. Automated tools can also help with determining a high-level view of thousands of web pages, for example, within an organization, to determine how many are meeting certainly basic usability requirements. For instance, Lazar et al. (2017) utilized automated accessibility testing tools to examine which US federal agencies had accessibility features present on a large portion of their web sites (not whether a specific web page was fully compliant or not). Automated tools are good for tasks such as that, determining the presence of features and getting a high-level overview. A large number of tools exist for automated accessibility testing, including standalone applications such as Deque WorldSpace, Cryptzone ComplianceSherriff, and SSB Accessibility Management Platform, as well as free web-based tools such as A-Checker, WAVE, and Functional Accessibility Evaluator, all of which check interfaces for compliance with the WCAG 2.0 guidelines. A classic article about the concepts behind automated usability testing can be found in the ACM Computing Surveys (Ivory and Hearst, 2001).

10.5 THE PROCESS OF USER-BASED TESTING

User-based testing is what most people mean when they refer to usability testing. Mostly, it means a group of representative users attempting a set of representative tasks. This can take place very early in development, during development, or very late in development. It is better to start doing user-based testing earlier rather than later, when the results can influence the design more and when costs to make changes are much lower. Ideally, user-based testing would take place during all stages of development, but that is not always possible. Why do we do usability testing? As much as designers try to build interfaces that match the needs of the users, the designers are not users and even the users themselves sometimes cannot clearly identify their interface needs. So interface prototypes, at various stages, need to be tested by users. Note that users are testing interfaces, but users are not being tested. This is an important distinction. Furthermore, some authors even go so far as to say that the developers who create an interface design should not be the ones who moderate a usability test (Rubin and Chisnell, 2008). If you create an interface, you are likely to be supportive of that interface, feel that you have time invested in it, and may not be as open to user suggestions. From a strict experimental point of view, the interface developer shouldn't moderate a usability test or interact with the participants (although the developer can observe the testing to learn what aspects of their design aren't working well). However, since perfect design isn't the goal of usability testing, there are situations where the interface developer serves double duty and moderates the usability test.

10.5.1 FORMATIVE AND SUMMATIVE USABILITY TESTING

Usability testing that takes place early in development tends to be exploratory and to test early design concepts. Sometimes, this is known as formative testing and may include wireframes or paper prototypes, also known as low-fidelity prototypes (Dumas and Fox, 2007). This type of usability testing is often more informal, with more communication between test moderators and participants (Rubin and Chisnell, 2008). In early exploratory testing, there is more of a focus on how the user perceives an interface component rather than on how well the user completes a task (Rubin and Chisnell, 2008). Paper prototypes are especially useful, because they are low cost and multiple designs can be quickly presented and evaluated by participants. In addition, because paper prototypes involve little development time, designers and developers tend not to become committed to a specific design early on. And users may feel more comfortable giving feedback or criticizing the interface when they see that not much work has been done yet on the interface. With fully functional prototypes, users may be hesitant to criticize, since they feel that the system is already finished and their feedback won't matter that much. More information on paper prototyping can be found in Snyder (2003).

Usability testing that takes place when there is a more formal prototype ready, when high-level design choices have already been made, is known as a summative test. The goal is to evaluate the effectiveness of specific design choices. These mostly functional prototypes are also known as high-fidelity prototypes (Dumas and Fox, 2007).

Finally, a usability test sometimes takes place right before an interface is released to the general user population. In this type of test, known as a validation test, the new interface is compared to a set of benchmarks for other interfaces. The goal is to ensure that, for instance, 90% of users can complete each task within 1 minute (if that statistic is an important benchmark). Validation testing is far less common than formative or summative testing.

It is important to note that there are variations in how usability testing is structured, regardless of the type of usability test or the stage of interface development. So in general, the data collected in a validation test or summative test will tend to be much more quantitative, and less focused on users "thinking aloud." More formative testing, on earlier prototypes, will tend to be more thinking aloud and qualitative data. But none of these are 100% definite. With well-developed paper prototypes, you theoretically could measure task performance quantitatively, and you could utilize the thinking aloud protocol when an interface is fully developed. The key thing to remember is that, the more that users "think aloud" and speak, the more that their cognitive flow will be interrupted, and the longer time a task will take to complete (Hertzum, 2016; Van Den Haak et al., 2003). It is also important to remember that, at first, individual children participants involved in usability testing may not feel comfortable criticizing an interface out loud (Hourcade, 2007), but pairs of children doing usability testing may be more effective (Als et al., 2005). Usability testing is flexible and needs to be structured around the activities that are most likely to result in actual changes in the interface being evaluated.

Different authors use different definitions for these terms. For instance, we have used the definitions from Rubin and Chisnell. West and Lehman, however, define formative tests as those that find specific interface problems to fix and summative tests as those that have a goal of benchmarking an interface's usability to other similar interfaces (West and Lehman, 2006). Sauro and Lewis (2012) have a similar view, describing any type of usability test to find and fix usability problems as formative, and describe summative only as metrics for describing usability.

The one thing that most authors agree on is that earlier, formative usability tests tend to focus more on qualitative feedback, moderator observation, and problem discovery, whereas summative usability tests tend to focus more on task-level measurements, metrics, and quantitative measurements (Lewis, 2006). The "Usability Testing of the Kodak Website" sidebar gives an example of formative and summative usability testing.

USABILITY TESTING OF THE KODAK WEBSITE

The Eastman Kodak Company is one of the world's largest manufacturers and marketers of imaging products. Both formative and summative usability testing took place on the Kodak website.

Formative testing took place on a paper prototype of the new home page design, specifically the links and groups. Twenty participants were given 30 tasks and were asked to identify the homepage link most likely to lead to the information that would complete that task. Participants were then asked to describe what type of content they expected to find behind each homepage link. Finally, participants were given descriptions of what actually was behind each home page link, and were asked to rate how well the label matched the actual content.

Later, summative testing with 33 participants took place on a working prototype of the new home page and all top-level pages on the site. A list of 22 tasks was developed, but each participant was given only 10 information-seeking tasks to complete. Some tasks were attempted by all 33 participants, while other tasks were attempted by only 11 participants. All links were functional, although not all visual design elements on the pages were complete. Each participant was given a maximum of 3 minutes to complete each task. Task completion for individual tasks ranged from 100% to 9% in the allotted 3 minutes. Based on the results of the usability testing, changes were made to the pages, including removing images along the left side of the page, adding longer descriptors to more of the links, and labeling major chunks of information (Lazar, 2006).

Whether a usability test is formative, summative, or validation can influence how formal or informal the usability test is. At one end of the spectrum is a formal approach to usability testing, which parallels experimental design. This form of usability testing can involve specific research questions, research design (between-subject design or within-subject design), and multiple interfaces to test. If you are using inferential statistics, hypotheses, a control group, large numbers of subjects, and strict controls on user recruitment, usability testing may, in fact, become experimental design. The only difference would be that experimental design is looking for statistically significant differences between groups to learn some research truth, whereas usability testing is looking for ways to identify usability flaws and improve specific interfaces.

10.5.2 STAGES OF USABILITY TESTING

Usability testing is not something that just happens. It requires a lot of advance planning. Different authors on the topic describe different steps, but the reality is that there are a lot of advance planning steps involved. See Table 10.3 for examples of the stages of usability testing from two different authors.

Table 10.3 Stages of Usability Testing From Different Authors

Stages of Usability Testing	
(Rubin and Chisnell, 2008)	(Lazar, 2006)
Develop the test plan	Select representative users
Setup the test environment	Select the setting
Find and select participants	Decide what tasks users should perform
Prepare test materials	Decide what type of data to collect
Conduct the test sessions	Before the test session (informed consent, etc.)
Debrief the participants	During the test session
Analyze data and observations	Debriefing after the session
Report findings and recommendations	Summarize results and suggest improvements

There are a number of stages of usability testing that seem very similar to experimental design (see Chapter 3). Often, a usability expert, taking the role of the usability moderator, manages the process. For more detailed information about moderator roles, we suggest that you consult Dumas and Loring (2008). The moderator should determine which users would be appropriate, representative participants to take part in the usability testing. If the typical users of the new interface system are nurses at a hospital, it is inappropriate (and probably unethical) to use undergraduate students in business to perform the usability testing (although nursing students might be appropriate, depending on the level of domain knowledge and job experience required). If appropriate user-centered design methods have been utilized, there should be existing user personas and task scenarios that can help guide you in this process. Some of the most common criteria for determining representativeness of users, include age, gender, education, job responsibility and or/domain expertise, technical experience (in general), and experience with specific software or hardware devices (Tullis and Albert, 2008).

Once you have figured out who the representative, appropriate users are, the next goal is to try and recruit them. Again, this is very similar to experimental design. For instance, users expect to be paid for their participation in usability testing, just as they expect to be paid for their participation in an experimental study. However, recruitment in usability testing is generally seen to be more flexible than in experimental design, and samples of convenience are common and appropriate (Tullis and Albert, 2008). While it is very important that the recruited participants accurately represent the target user population, it is less relevant how you recruit those users. Unless you are dealing with multiple user populations across cultures, countries, or languages (in which case you may want to do usability testing at each site), it can be satisfactory, for instance, to recruit users from only one or two companies or in only one geographic area.

10.5.3 HOW MANY USERS ARE SUFFICIENT?

One of the most common questions when planning usability testing is "how many users do I need to have?" It's also a bit of a hotbed of discussion in the HCI community, and a consensus has not emerged over time. If you were doing a strict experimental design, the types of research design and the statistical tests that you run would dictate the minimum number of participants required. However, usability testing has different goals and different requirements.

Many people say that five users is sufficient, and that five users will find approximately 80% of usability problems in an interface (Virzi, 1992). This has become an often-quoted number in HCI, but many other researchers disagree with the assertion. The major challenge in determining the right number of users, is that you don't know in advance how many interface flaws exist, so any estimate of how many users are needed to find a certain percentage of interface flaws is based on the assumption that you know how many flaws exist, which you probably don't. Other research studies have found that five users are not sufficient to discover and identify a majority of usability flaws (Lindgaard and Chattratichart, 2007; Spool and Schroeder, 2001). In a classic paper, Nielsen and Landauer, who in earlier work had asserted the number five, expressed that the appropriate number depends on the size of the project, with seven users being optimal in a small project and 15 users being optimal in a medium-to-large project (Nielsen and Landauer, 1993). However, in that same paper, they indicated that the highest ratio of benefits to costs is when you have 3.2 users doing usability testing (Nielsen and Landauer, 1993). In an analysis of existing research on the topic, Hwang and Salvendy (2010) suggest that 10 ± 2 is the optimal number of users for usability testing, although more recent work by Schmettow (2012) suggests that even 10 users is not enough to discover 80% of the usability problems.

Lewis says that all authors could theoretically be right about the appropriate number of users, as it depends on how accurate they need to be, what their problem discovery goals are, and how many participants are available (Lewis, 2006). Even if five users are enough, what happens when you have multiple user groups taking part in usability testing. Do you need five users from each group? Lindgaard and Chattratichart (2007) take a different approach: they assert that the number of usability flaws found depends more on the design and scope of the tasks, rather than on the number of users.

By now, "five participants in usability evaluation" is part of the HCI lore, in the same way that "7 ± 2 menu items" is part of the HCI lore. We are told that we should organize our menu items and menu bars into chunks of five to nine items, based on classic psychological research literature (Miller, 1956). However, this is misleading: the 7 ± 2 limitation in short-term memory applies to recall, not recognition, and most interface design (including menus) is recognition, where we see or hear an icon or item and think, "oh yes, that's what I wanted" (Preece et al., 2002 explained this well, although their explanation hasn't appeared in later editions of their book). However, "five participants" and "7 ± 2 menu items" remain part of the HCI folklore, even when there is real debate about their validity.

The reality is that most usability testing will never uncover all, or even most, of the usability flaws. And even if all of the flaws were uncovered, most of them will never be fixed. Instead, the goal should be to find the major flaws, the flaws that will cause most problems, and get them fixed. From an industry point of view, the exercise of finding flaws, without the consideration of whether they can be fixed, is not of value (Wixon, 2003). It simply would not make sense to expend all of the available "usability time" in a development lifecycle on finding flaws, rather than balancing time between finding flaws and fixing flaws. It may be useful to examine the effectiveness of various usability testing methods. But in industry, usability testing logistics are often driven not by what should or needs to be done, but instead, on how much time is left in the development process, how much money has been set aside by management for usability testing, and how many users are available and willing to participate. For instance, in usability testing on the website of the American Speech-Language-Hearing Association, the usability engineer identified 16 different user populations for the website. But after the prototype of the new website was built, the budget only allowed for usability testing with school-based, speech-language pathologists, the largest group of users for the website (Lazar, 2006). So instead of saying, "how many users must you have?," maybe the correct question is "how many users can we afford?," "how many users can we get?" or "how many users do we have time for?"

10.5.4 LOCATIONS FOR USABILITY TESTING

Usability testing can take place anywhere. It can take place in a fixed laboratory, a workplace, a user's home, over the phone, or over the web. The location may be determined by what locations are available or where participants are, as well as what type of data you want to collect. None of the types of location are superior to any others. You should use whatever works for your specific usability testing project.

The most traditional setting for usability testing is a two-room setup. The user sits in one room and works on the tasks on a computer. Microphones and cameras record what the user is doing and output from the user's computer screen is also recorded. In the other room, the test moderators, and other stakeholders, sit and watch what the user is doing during the test. The moderators' room generally has a number of computer screens and monitors and the recording equipment, so all appropriate data can be recorded. In addition, the moderators' room often has a one-way mirror so that the moderators can directly observe what the user is doing, but the user cannot see into the moderators' room (see Figure 10.2). If a one-way mirror is not possible (either due to structural concerns or the moderators' room being located elsewhere in the building), a large image projected on to a wall is sufficient for the same purpose.

FIGURE 10.2

A formal usability laboratory with a one-way mirror.

Source: Photo by Elizabeth Buie for UserWorks, Inc., a usability consulting firm located in Silver Spring, MD,
www.userworks.com.

While a formal usability laboratory is typically used for desktop or laptop computer applications, with minor modifications to the camera angles and mounting, a formal laboratory can also be utilized for usability testing of hand-held and mobile devices. For instance, one solution utilized for videotaping interactions on a mobile device is a document camera, which is often available in a classroom or presentation room. Readers are suggested to reference (Schusteritsch et al., 2007) on different types of camera mountings and logistics for usability testing of hand-held devices.

Figures 10.3 and 10.4 show two examples of formal, fixed usability labs. One lab layout is located at a university, where there is only one participant room. The other lab layout is from the US Census Bureau, where three participant rooms are connected to one evaluation room. It is important to note that while it is very good to have a formal usability laboratory, and the willingness to spend money and commit space may speak about the importance of usability to an organization, having a fixed usability laboratory is NOT necessary for usability testing.

Another possible location for usability testing is in the user's workplace or home. This may help in recruiting users, because it's less of a hassle for the users

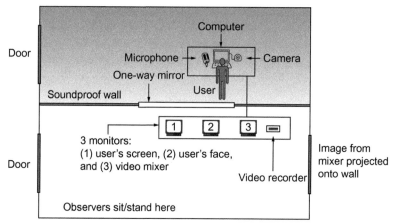

FIGURE 10.3

Potential layout for a single-participant usability lab.

From Lazar, J., 2006. Web Usability: A User-Centered Design Approach. Addison-Wesley, Boston.

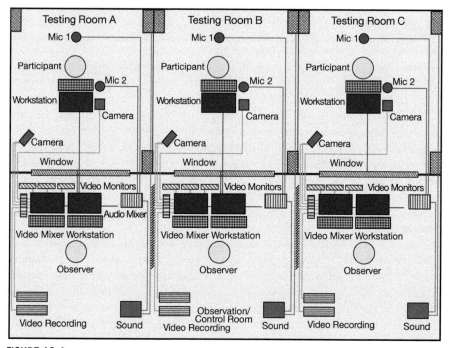

FIGURE 10.4

Potential layouts for a multiuser usability lab.

From US Census Bureau.

than having to go to a usability laboratory or a central location. Visiting users in their workplace or home may also be easier if you are working with users with disabilities, for whom transportation is often a challenge (see Chapter 16). In many ways, the user's workplace or home setting is ideal for usability testing. The user is exposed to customary space, noise, and attention limitations while testing the interface. The user may feel most comfortable in their normal environment, using their own technology, which again, may enhance their performance. In fact, testing in the user's natural setting goes along with the ideals of ethnography (see Chapter 9). For the user, it's the easiest and most natural form of usability testing. However, for the usability testing moderator, it can be the most challenging.

First of all, a lot of travel may be needed to visit each user. Secondly, a decision needs to be made: do you install the software or interface on the user's computer (which is more natural but may involve technical problems) or do you bring a laptop with the software or interface installed on it (which is technically easier but it's not the computer that the user is familiar with, so you may get some conflicting results). Chapter 16 provides an in-depth discussion of this decision. If you are usability testing a mobile device, you typically bring the device along. Thirdly, how are you going to record data? There are different approaches, all with benefits and drawbacks. If you observe the users by sitting beside them, this may make them feel uncomfortable and they may act differently. You can use a number of technical approaches, but they take some time to set up before you begin the session. For instance, you could use data logging (where user keystrokes are recorded), record audio or send screen output to another local computer. If you have the equipment, or the budget to rent equipment, you could use a portable usability laboratory. A portable usability laboratory includes the same equipment (cameras, microphones, digital recording devices, etc.) as a fixed usability laboratory, but in a portable case, with very long wires (or a wireless signal). The idea is that, when you get to the user's home or workplace, you set up the equipment so that it essentially mirrors the setup in a fixed lab, so that a camera and a microphone are trained on the user and screen capture is in place. You then find a location near the user (not next to the user, or where the user feels your presence, or where you can physically see the user) but where the equipment wires are long enough to reach (or wireless signals can help with this). You can both record audio/video and watch a live feed and take notes. This may be ideal from a research point of view, since you get rich data capture and recording and the user is in their most comfortable and familiar setting, but the downside is that portable usability equipment is very expensive, takes a long time to set up, and there are often technical problems. If you are usability testing a mobile device, how do you accurately observe or record user actions on a device that may be too small to watch, unless you are standing right behind the user? If they are continuously moving the device around their own environment (as most people do), how do you observe or record data, aside from data logging (Schusteritsch et al., 2007)?

Sometimes, it is not feasible to do usability testing in a centralized location at a usability lab or in a user's workplace or home. It could be that the representative user population is not within easy traveling distance of the usability evaluators or moderators. Or there could be other logistical factors that limit the ability to do face-to-face usability testing. For instance, it could be appropriate to do remote usability testing with individuals with disabilities for whom transportation might be a problem (see Chapter 16). When an interface will be deployed in multiple countries, it is necessary to have users from all of the countries test the interface but it may not be possible for the evaluators to visit all the countries (Dray and Siegel, 2004). For doing usability testing involving children, the familiarity with the testing location is only one of the potential logistical concerns (also including topics such as how to get consent for children to participate). For those who are doing usability testing involving children, it is suggested to consult a thorough guide to children and HCI, such as Fails et al. (2012) or Hourcade (2007).

Remote usability testing is typically where users are separated from the evaluators by space, time, or both (Andreasen et al., 2007). Video, audio, and network connections allow evaluators to monitor users, including streaming output from the user's screen and clickstream data. While this used to be done using videoconferencing and private networks (Dray and Siegel, 2004), now, it is just as likely that a web-based remote usability testing tool (such as UserZoom) is utilized for remote testing. One of the challenges with remote testing is the difficulty (with synchronous videoconferencing) or impossibility (with many web-based usability testing tools which offer limited video and audio) of picking up nonverbal and interpersonal cues. Also with asynchronous remote testing, it is hard (or impossible) to provide instructions when things "go wrong," you can't ask any probing questions, and you often miss the context of what was happening. To offset these drawbacks, there are many benefits of remote usability testing, such as easy access to more potential participants (since you are not geographically limited), and easy collection and analysis of clickstream data (which can easily be turned into graphs and heatmaps).

Remote usability testing, on the whole, works better for summative testing, when you are more interested in quantitative metrics, than for formative testing, where you tend to be more interested in the qualitative observations (Dray and Siegel, 2004). In addition, synchronous remote usability testing, where the evaluators are observing the users in different locations at the same time using videostreaming, may be more effective than asynchronous testing, where the evaluator observes at a later time (Andreasen et al., 2007). While remote usability testing can be technically very challenging and small problems can delay testing (since moderators aren't there to address any technical problems), it can be a very useful technique in the toolbox of the usability evaluator. Table 10.4 displays benefits and drawbacks of remote usability testing.

Finding an appropriate place to do usability testing, and recruiting a sufficient number of representative users, is always an ongoing challenge. The next two sidebars describe how two of the leading technical companies, Google and Yahoo, use innovative approaches for recruitment of participants for usability testing.

Table 10.4 Benefits and Drawbacks of Remote Usability Testing

Benefit	Drawback
Easy access to a greater number of participants	Difficult or impossible to pick up nonverbal and interpersonal cues
Participants have more flexibility in participating in a usability test on their own schedule, and researchers can run multiple usability tests at the same time	Hard (or impossible) to provide instructions when things "go wrong"
	Researchers can't ask any probing questions based on what occurs
Easy collection and analysis of clickstream data	Researchers often miss the context of what was happening
Works better for summative testing, when you are collecting quantitative metrics	

USER NIGHTS AT YAHOO! (WRITTEN BY GARY MOULTON)

Yahoo is unique in combining its UX Researchers and Accessibility specialists to form an organization called User Experience Research and Accessibility (UXRA). UXRA partners with product groups throughout the development life cycle to gather, analyze, and present observations from user research when teams are gathering requirements, have a fully developed idea, and are working on a new mobile app or Web property. Yahoo is unique in combining Accessibility specialists with traditional User Experience Researchers. They work closely together with individuals that identify themselves as having a disability to observe and quantify user interactions with, and validate the compatibility of, mobile apps and Web properties with popular assistive technologies (e.g. screen readers, alternate input devices, etc.).

Yahoo's UXRA uses a wide variety of qualitative and quantitative research tools and methodologies for providing research throughout the development lifecycle. One of the unique methods is called "User Night" where up to 100 external users are paired individually with members of a particular Yahoo product team, who are called "Yahoos." Yahoos are briefed in advance and provided a script and coaching to run their own study with their participant. For up to an hour, they have conversations about the use of their product and observe real-world use on the participants' own devices (phones and/or laptops). After the event, team members share key findings in large group settings, and findings from these sessions are aggregated and fed back to the entire team. This process enables rapid, larger-scale feedback than is possible to be obtained in a single-day, five-user, traditional usability study. These events create unique empathy among product team members for real users, their issues as well as joys, in using the product that they spend each day building.

(Continued)

USER NIGHTS AT YAHOO!—CONT'D

Yahoo conducts several User Nights per quarter, each focused on a particular product or product feature, like Yahoo Search, Yahoo Finance, or Yahoo Fantasy Sports. The product manager (PM) will partner with their embedded UX researcher to determine the goals of the event (e.g. user reaction to a Yahoo product or feature), the number, and demographics of the participants and outline the tasks users will be asked to complete during User Night.

The UXRA researcher works with the project manager before the User Night to create a script based on the task list. The scripts are very detailed and comprehensive including methods of setting user expectations, "do's and don'ts," reminders for the Yahoos conducting 1:1 interactions, and the step-by-step way in which the specific tasks are to be conducted. An accessibility specialist will also be consulted to determine if assistive technology users will need to be recruited. The featured product and the specific tasks to be covered must not have any significant accessibility issues (i.e., a screen reader user should be able to successfully complete the tasks) when individuals with disabilities will be recruited.

Following this initial meeting, those in UXRA tasked with recruiting begin to solicit users for participation. Recruiting is accomplished using multiple methods including emailing a list of individuals who have volunteered to be included in Yahoo's User Night database and making targeted calls to individual users. Some User Nights require a higher percentage of users who have used Yahoo products previously and others require those who have never used a Yahoo product or participated in a previous User Night. The number of participants recruited for a User Night averages from 50 to 100 depending on the study.

To encourage participation, User Nights are held in the evening from about 7:00 to 9:00pm. Upon arrival, users register, sign NDAs (nondisclosure agreements) and are feted with "heavy" hors d'oeuvres or a light dinner. This serves several practical purposes: it ensures everyone is on time and ready when the study begins, socializes, and relaxes nervous participants, and provides time to prepare Yahoo product teams for their 1:1 interactions and coach them on best practices for observation.

One hour before the start of a Yahoo User Night, the UXRA researcher and PM conduct an orientation meeting with the Yahoos who will help facilitate the user testing. They review the User Night agenda and schedule (welcome, dinner, pairing with users, making observations, note-taking, debriefing, etc.), review the script and answer any last-minute questions. Due to the large number of product developers at Yahoo, User Night is often as new to the Yahoo product developers as it is to the user, so this employee orientation time is crucial in making the night successful and enjoyable.

User Night "officially" begins when a Yahoo is matched with a user. Yahoo's IT department provides all the equipment (e.g. smartphones or laptop computers) when a user's own device can't be used—typically due to using prerelease software that they're not allowed to install on their own devices. Yahoos conducting the session with the user are advised to mostly "watch and listen" and note any feedback or suggestions users provide for improving the product experience as they guide their assigned user through the script. This makes up the bulk of the time spent at User Night and lasts approximately 1 hour. These interactions become so engaging it's often difficult to bring the night to a close, but the night must come to an end.

When the dust settles, and the users have left, the most critical part of User Night takes place. All of the Yahoos remain to conduct a debriefing with the UX researcher, accessibility specialist, and PM to discuss what was learned. Commonly experienced issues and observations quickly rise to the surface, but it is also important to capture the odd, curious and unusual observations, and feedback as these provide opportunities for further investigation in the future. A report recording, prioritizing, and analyzing all these findings is later created and shared with the entire product team such that those who were not able to participate in the User Night can also benefit from what was observed.

Yahoo's User Night is a unique and innovative methodology to observe and interact with a large number of users in a very short time period, gather immediate, impactful feedback, and provide product groups with prioritized and actionable improvements that can be used to make Yahoo products, services, and technology more usable and accessible. It has proven to energize product teams, encourage deeper consideration of end users during design, and result in the delivery of improved products faster into market, with higher quality and greater customer satisfaction.

THE GOOGLE RESEARCH VAN (WRITTEN BY LAURA GRANKA)

The research van is the newest method in Google's User Experience (UX) toolkit, aiming to overcome some limitations of traditional lab-based UX research. We created the van to help improve Google's user research studies by enabling more participant diversity, agile recruiting, and flexibility when planning and executing research.

At Google, we do much of our research in UX labs at our headquarters in Mountain View, CA, and at our other major locations, like New York City, NY and Seattle, WA. As with all methods, research in physical onsite labs has its limitations, and in our case, we were growing increasingly concerned about participant diversity—namely routinely doing research with people willing and able to participate in our *onsite* research studies.

(Continued)

THE GOOGLE RESEARCH VAN—CONT'D

Broader User Population. We created the van (Figure 10.5) as a response to a key challenge we face doing research on Google premises—user sample. The population in any one geographical area is not always representative of the attitudes and behaviors we'd see in the broader US or international population. We want to reduce as much bias as possible in our product development process, and research with a representative user base is one way to achieve that.

Nimble Recruiting. By driving to locations like malls, community centers, and parks, we can reach users during the natural course of their day without a time-consuming recruitment and scheduling process for us and them. The van presence serves as natural recruitment: individuals who were previously unaware of user studies can walk right up to the van to participate in research. We are also able to reach users who otherwise cannot come to a lab either due to time constraints, accessibility, or other factors, including the many people who are unaware that they can sign up to be contacted for user research. Once we arrive and park our research van, we can invite people passing by, to participate in research studies within minutes.

Nimble Research. Another challenge is the nature of the research itself. In traditional lab research, we recruit and schedule users to participate, sometimes weeks in advance, and ask them to take time out of their day. This process of recruiting and scheduling users can be time consuming; a potentially heavy cost in an industry with quick turnaround and iteration. If participants fail to show up, we lose valuable data and time, and either have to move forward with limited insights or go through the recruiting process again to make up for it.

FIGURE 10.5

The Google user research van.

About the Research Van

The research van is equipped like most other standard usability labs, with an audio and video recording to capture both user reactions and interactions with their mobile device. Considering that research in the field and using a vehicle could add additional stress, the van was designed to be as easy to use as possible. A one button record covers end-to-end and simple default settings allow for easy set up. The cameras capture two key angles: the interactions on the device and the participant's facial and body language. A third video feed includes an HDMI input for the highest resolution view of the device's screen. The researcher can choose to record a full screen of any, or a combination of two in picture-in-picture. A small preview monitor behind the participant allows the moderator to see if the device has gone off camera view and adjusts as necessary, and a large monitor behind the participant allows the note taker to see the video feed clearly for taking notes. The van has enough seats to accommodate the standard moderator, participant, and note taker, as well as two additional stakeholders for product team involvement.

About the Research Tour

We launched the research van with a 6-week cross country research tour in 2016. We went to 10 cities across a range of regions in the US and a variety of locations such as rural towns, college towns, and metropolitan hubs. We were able to meet with people who had never before seen a physical Google presence, much less the opportunity to directly interact with us. In larger cities, we even had the opportunity to talk with tourists from across the country and world. Over 300 people participated in our lab studies inside the van, and we also conducted video interviews and surveys with over 500 participants outside the van. While the research we conducted on our cross country tour was immensely impactful and useful for our product development teams, we can achieve these benefits even closer to home. We can leverage the van by driving to new locations and towns just 1–3 hours outside of Google headquarters, as these regions will also help us reach a much different participant population.

The research van has opened up a world of opportunities for our research practice in reaching a broader user population, increasing flexibility in recruiting, and agility in conducting research. The success of the research van helped us establish new models for recruiting and sourcing as well as brainstorming new standards for our traditional labs. We're excited to see the interest from other areas in Google as well as practitioners industry-wide and we hope to spread the method. We look forward to what more we can do with the research van as a core research infrastructure product and how it can influence research across Google and the industry.

10.5.5 **TASK LISTS**

Creating the task list can be one of the most challenging parts of creating a usability test. Unless the usability testing is very exploratory, formative, and takes place with very early stage prototypes (possibly on paper), it is likely that a task list will be needed. A task list is used so that when users go through an interface, they are goal-directed. Tasks need to be clear and unambiguous and not need further, additional explanation. While a background scenario may be presented at the beginning of the task list, just to set the participant in the context of the tasks, the task list should not require the participant to ask additional questions about the tasks. The tasks should typically have one clear answer or one clear solution where users know that they have completed the task. Tasks should relate to the key features of the interface, tasks should not be requests for information that the user could know regardless of whether they used the interface (or items that would primarily be found using a web search engine such as Google or Bing). For instance, it would not be appropriate to ask participants to use the interface to find out when Victoria was Queen of England or who won the World Cup in Football in 2012. Participants might already know the answers to these tasks and would not need to use the specific interface. The tasks should clearly require participants to utilize the interface.

Tasks are often chosen based on a number of factors (Dumas and Fox, 2007). For instance, it is important to have tasks that are performed often and are central to the goal that users want to accomplish. In addition, tasks that are critical, such as logging into an account or checking out on an e-commerce site, even if not frequent, should be included. If there are sections of an interface where there are existing questions about usability problems, they could be a focus of some of the tasks. In addition, sometimes, task lists try to be all-inclusive. For instance, if users can utilize menus, shortcuts, or a command line to reach material, some usability moderators design tasks that use all three approaches.

Typically, the task scenarios and the tasks themselves are representative, however they do not utilize any of the user's real data or personal information. Usability testing an interface typically does not involve any of the user's real financial, health, or contact information. Often, test accounts (also known as "dummy" accounts) are created on e-mail servers and transactional servers, so that, as a part of the testing, users will not need to use their own accounts or enter any personal information. These test accounts will be utilized only for the purpose of testing. Even fake identities may be used in usability testing, for instance, when filling out an online form as a part of the usability test; users will be given a fake name, such as "John Smith."

It is important to note a few things about the use of test accounts and fake names. First of all, do not ask users to actually create the fake identities or test accounts, as it will be a waste of time. Have these accounts and fake names already prepared for users. Second, be aware that, while test accounts and fake identities are often utilized in usability testing, there are situations where it could be a violation of law to submit fake information. So, for instance, Wentz et al. noted that, when submitting data to government emergency agencies, even as a part of usability testing of their interfaces, you may not submit fake information, without the express approval of and collaboration with the government agency (Wentz et al., 2014). Third, people with cognitive disabilities may find it confusing to use test accounts or fake names (see Chapter 16 for more information).

Generally, while the moderators may need to have information about how old the users are, their level of education, and their home address (for example, to mail payment for participation), this information is not used as a part of the testing tasks. Furthermore, if a task involves purchasing an item on an e-commerce site, participants should not be required to use their own credit or debit card. Rather, a separate credit card should be provided for their use, so that participants are not charged, and they do not need to provide any personal data. Zazelenchuk et al. (2008) describe how users' real personal data could potentially be used to get a more realistic usability test for financial interfaces, where users are familiar with their own data, emotionally engaged by their own data, and have no trouble understanding the meaning of it. While this may be more realistic from a testing point of view, there are many challenges and logistical concerns to using actual user data, regarding permission to use the data, disposal of the data, and permission from the users themselves. Zazelenchuk et al. even noted that when participants were asked to bring their own financial data to a usability testing session, a number of participants dropped out; to compensate and recruit more people, participants had to be paid a higher amount of money for the extra work and concern. Furthermore, if the usability testing needs to be approved by some sort of institutional review board (see Chapter 15), it is possible that this type of usability testing plan would be rejected. This would be especially likely if the usability testing involved user health care information, as many countries have specific laws relating to the privacy and security of health care information.

When creating the task list, it is important to provide direction on how to navigate the task list itself. Must participants go through tasks in the order listed? Can they skip tasks or start at the last task? Do certain tasks require that other tasks be completed first? How should participants respond if they get stuck and are unable to complete one task? Should they skip that task and move onto the next task? Is there a time limit per task? Is there an overall time limit for the usability testing session? While there might be research reasons for having a time limit per task or per session, there might also be practical reasons. For instance, the supervisor at the workplace may have said that participants can spend no more than 30 minutes on this outside activity or the moderators may only have use of the usability lab space (or another space) for a limited amount of time.

The moderators also need to decide, in advance, whether interventions will be allowed. Interventions are when there is an interface barrier that users are presented with, which does not allow the participant to continue in the interface. The moderator can intervene, if the user gets totally stuck and indicates that they are unable to move on. For instance, if a login screen or an introductory screen is very hard to use, users may not be able to access the rest of the web site or application. If the moderator helps the user move onto the next step, it is still possible to get useful feedback. Interventions specific to people with disabilities and accessibility are described in

Chapter 16. Generally, if researchers do not intervene, this means that the data collection is over, and that would be a missed opportunity to learn more about other aspects of an interface or other aspects of data collection. An intervention is when a researcher helps the participant move forward by providing advice or suggesting a action. Before beginning any usability testing, a researcher should have a clear decision on whether any interventions will be allowed, under what circumstances, how they will be documented, and how this will be accounted for in reporting the results. Typically, the researchers (moderators) don't get involved with providing advice to users, and interventions are not a frequent methodological occurrence. However, the benefit of interventions is that they allow for the maximal amount of feedback about what aspects of the interface need improvement. The details of the intervention should be clearly noted in any data results or write up (Dumas and Fox, 2007)

10.5.6 MEASUREMENT

There are many different types of data that can be collected during usability testing. The three most common quantitative measurements are task performance, time performance, and user satisfaction. Task performance or correctness means how many tasks were correctly completed (and the related metrics of how many tasks were attempted but not successfully completed). Time performance means how long each task took to successfully complete (and the related metrics of how long people spent on incorrect tasks before they gave up). User satisfaction is often measured by a standardized, validated survey tool. See Section 5.8 for a list of standard survey tools for measuring satisfaction.

While these are the three most common quantitative measurements in usability testing, there are many other metrics that could be useful. For instance, additional metrics might include the number of errors, average time to recover from an error, time spent using the help feature, and number of visits to the search feature or index. Depending on the purpose of the usability testing, additional specific metrics might be useful. For instance, if you have redesigned the search engine on a website and the usability testing tasks are focused on the search engine, then an important metric might be something like the average number of search engine responses clicked on, or the average search ranking of the choice that provided the solution. If you utilize key logging, there are many metrics that can be easily analyzed, such as the time spent on specific web pages, the number of web pages viewed, mouse movements, typing speed (Atterer and Schmidt, 2007). See Chapter 12 for information on key logging. Eye tracking used to be prohibitively expensive, but as costs have come down, eye tracking has become more prevalent for usability testing. For more information about eye tracking, see Chapter 13.

In usability testing, especially formative usability testing (on early-stage designs), qualitative data is often just as important as quantitative data. For instance, users are often encouraged to "think aloud" as they are going through the interface (known as the "thinking aloud" protocol). This is more common in formative usability testing than in summative usability testing (when users may be expected to focus more on task completion). When users state their feelings, their frustrations, and their progress out loud, there is often very useful feedback. For instance, a user may say things such as "Where is the menu choice? I would expect it to be right there" or "I certainly would not purchase anything from this website. It looks so unprofessional." Even younger users can make useful comments during a usability session (see the Leescircus sidebar). It is important to be aware that how comfortable someone may feel about speaking aloud during the tasks may be culturally influenced, and therefore people from some cultures may not feel comfortable expressing their concerns immediately (Shi and Clemmensen, 2008). Also, the more that users talk, the more their task or time performance data may be influenced (Dumas and Loring, 2008). The more they talk, the longer their task times will be (Dumas and Loring, 2008). If you want both true user comments and very accurate task and time performance data, it is possible to run a reflection session, also known as an interpretation session or a retrospective session, after the tasks are performed. In an interpretation session, the users watch raw video of themselves immediately after attempting a series of tasks; working with the evaluators, they interpret the problems they encountered and where they feel that the major interface flaws are (Frokjaer and Hornbæk, 2005). In more traditional research with larger numbers of participants, the goal might be to categorize the qualitative comments using content analysis and look for patterns. With usability testing, we're trying to use these comments to help improve the interface. Certainly, there is an even more important message for researchers if you hear the same comment multiple times, but the strength of even one comment is important.

USABILITY TESTING OF THE SOFTWARE LEESCIRCUS

Usability testing took place for an educational software package called *Leescircus*, designed for 6- and 7-year-old children in the Netherlands. One example of a typical task was to match pictures that rhyme. A total of 70 Dutch children (32 girls and 38 boys), aged 6 or 7, took part in the usability testing. Most of the children had previous experience with computers and some had previous experience with the program. The children were asked to find problems with this version of the software. There were four sets of eight or nine tasks and each child performed only one set of tasks. Usability evaluators observed the children while they were performing the tasks. The children were encouraged to speak their comments aloud while using the software. The time period was limited to 30 minutes, as it was expected that the attention span of the children wouldn't last much longer. Although only 28 children did make comments out loud, the novice students (with less computer experience) tended to make more comments than the experts. Usability findings included the need to enlarge the clickable objects, clarify the meaning of icons, and improve consistency (so that it was clear whether an icon could or could not be clicked) (Donker and Reitsma, 2004). This case study shows that children, too, can provide feedback using the "think aloud" protocol during a usability test, although not all will feel comfortable enough to speak up during the usability test

10.5.7 THE USABILITY TESTING SESSION

Before the testing session is scheduled, it is important to contact the participants, remind them about the upcoming session, and confirm the location, regardless of where the usability testing session will take place. Make sure to leave extra time in your schedule, since the participants may show up late, or take longer than expected. Immediately before the session starts, confirm that all computers, recording devices, and other technologies are working properly.

Remember that while the goals of usability testing may be different from classical research like experimental design or ethnography, the protection of human subjects are exactly the same. Just as in any type of research, participants must be given notice of their rights, agree if they are to be video- or audio-recorded, and be allowed to leave at any time. At no point can participants be held against their will, or punished in any way. Unless the participants have specifically given permission to do so, their participation must remain anonymous—at no point can their participation be identified to the outside world. Their data must be protected as in any other type of research method.

It is important to let the participants know if there are any time constraints, either on the session as a whole, or for completing specific tasks. For more information about human subjects protections and IRB forms, see Chapter 15. In usability testing, when new interfaces are being tested, these interfaces might be confidential company information. So participants may also be asked to sign some type of confidentiality agreement, in which they agree not to release or discuss any details of this new interface product (Dumas and Loring, 2008). Finally, it should be clarified before the testing session begins whether participants will receive payment at the end of the session or if a check (or a gift card or something similar) will be mailed to their home. It should also be made clear to the participants that even if they cannot complete the session or feel the need to end the session early, as is common practice, they will still be paid for their participation.

As noted previously, usability testing is about finding flaws that can be fixed, not about having a perfect methodology. One practice that is common in usability testing is to modify the interface after every user test, to help immediately improve the interface flaws discovered; those changes are then evaluated during the next user test (Wixon, 2003). If changes aren't made immediately after each user, changes may be made to the interface after a few users, and then a second round of usability testing is held, using the same tasks, to see if the performance improves and if the changes improved the interface. See the "Usability Testing at Fidelity Investments" sidebar for an example of this practice. Making changes after each user, while an interface is still under development, is commonplace in usability testing. A newer approach to usability testing is A/B testing, where minor tweaks are made in interfaces that are already in daily use. So, for websites that are visited by thousands of users a day, users may receive versions that have slight differences in color, layout, terminology, or other changes that might not be noticeable to the user, with data collected about patterns of usage. After data is collected over perhaps a few weeks, the interface changes that are deemed to be successful, increasing traffic, increasing sales, and reducing costs are permanently rolled out.

USABILITY TESTING AT FIDELITY INVESTMENTS

Usability testing took place at Fidelity Investments, evaluating the prototype of an interface to manage individual benefits, including company benefits, retirement savings, and pensions. A total of 27 participants tested the first prototype (this included both younger and older users, which would be expected for this type of interface). Each participant was given 15 tasks to complete, such as switching retirement money from one plan to another and determining what pension benefits would amount to if the individual retired at 65 years old. Task success rates were 64.2% for users under 55 years old and 44.8% for users aged 55 years or older.

Based on the usability testing of the first prototype, changes were made to the interface, including improved terminology, making links consistently obvious, adding more instruction for detailed table data, adding more titles, and removing false window bottoms and mouseover-based navigation tabs.

Usability testing then took place with the second interface prototype and a new set of 22 participants took part. The new participants had the same profile of age and computer experience as the participants in the first round of testing. The participants in the second round of usability testing were given the same 15 tasks as participants in the first round of testing, with a few minor wording changes due to the updated interface. With the new interface prototype, task success rates improved to 80.6% for users under age 55 and 58.2% for users aged 55 years and older (Chadwick-Dias et al., 2003).

Unlike in other traditional research, in usability testing, it is considered a standard practice to tell participants before they start that they are not being tested. Rather, the participants are testing the interface. Their feedback is important. They are the experts and have the right to criticize the interface. Users are not being tested. You may need to remind them of that fact multiple times.

Note that during the testing session, there are two "tracks" of data collection. One track is the quantitative metrics, such as task and time performance. Moderators may be timing the tasks, data logging may be keeping track, or video recording may be used for later review. The second track is the qualitative data. Sometimes, participants are very talkative and provide a verbal track of what they are doing. If the participants are not very talkative, and if thinking aloud is the methodological goal, moderators should try to encourage them to share more of how they are feeling. However, these reminders should not be often, since the more that the moderator interrupts the user, the more the user feels watched, the more the user's cognitive flow is interrupted, and the more that the user's behavior may deviate from normal. The thinking aloud protocol is more common in formative usability testing than in summative usability testing, since, if quantitative metrics are considered very important by the stakeholders of that interface, the more the participant stops to talk, the more that their task time is interrupted. So while it is acceptable for the users to stop every now and then to describe what they are doing, if the user talks continuously for 10 minutes, clearly, the task performance time is of questionable use.

Since usability testing is a practical approach to solving problems, hybrid approaches are often used. In a reflection or interpretation session, users, immediately after completing a series of tasks, review the raw video with the usability moderators, and help interpret the interface problems (Frokjaer and Hornbæk, 2005). Even without a formal interpretation session, users often make comments about the interface during the debriefing which follows the usability testing session. Without being prompted, users often make comments out loud during the usability testing session. All feedback from users is important data!

In addition, qualitative data, in terms of observation by moderators, is very important. Moderators can often tell a lot about how participants are managing an interface even when the participant is not saying anything. Participants may sigh or grunt and their facial expressions may tell a story of frustration. It is possible to see frustration or anger in the facial expressions of participants. In fact, certain muscle movements in the face are clear signs of stress (Hazlett, 2006). Even without complex interpretation, it is very probable that, if a user keeps moving towards the screen or squinting, the icons or fonts on the screen may be a bit too small.

10.5.8 MAKING SENSE OF THE DATA

Analyzing data from usability testing is similar to analyzing data from any other type of research. However, the goal of the analysis is different. Since usability testing often uses fewer participants, inferential statistics often are not possible; but simple descriptive statistics are possible. With traditional research, the goal is to write up the results in a paper, publish it in a journal, conference proceedings, or book, and help influence future research and design. With usability testing, the goal is often to write up the results and help influence the design of the specific interface that was tested. Sometimes, a presentation about the results is made to a group of developers or managers who have the power to ensure that the interface is changed. The usability testing report (or presentation) should be oriented towards the goal of improving the specific interface and to those who will read it: interface designers, software engineers, project managers, and other managers involved in software development.

The usability test may have uncovered many different interface flaws that should be addressed. However, due to time concerns, not all of these flaws will be improved upon. So while the report should identify all flaws discovered during usability testing, the report should also prioritize which ones are most important to fix. For each flaw identified, the report should describe the problem, present the data from the usability test, identify the priority of the flaw, suggest a fix, and also estimate the time for the fix. Sometimes, data from usability testing can point to which flaws caused users to lose the most time or be unable to complete their tasks and which flaws were easily overcome by users. It is not always clear how to improve every single flaw. Sometimes, you may improve upon one flaw but introduce other problems. An experienced usability moderator may use their expertise to determine which flaws should be prioritized, which flaws are not as problematic, and how to make improvements which do not introduce new problems.

Rubin and Chisnell (2008) suggest splitting the report into three sections:

- why you did usability testing and how you prepared;
- what happened during the testing; and
- the implications and recommendations.

While typical research publications need to be thorough and detailed, if usability testing reports are going to management, they should be short and to the point. If certain aspects of the interface worked well, it might be useful to note that in the report as well. When interface flaws are fixed and changes are made, new flaws can be introduced into the interface. So it can be helpful to note the interface components that worked well and should not be changed.

It is important to note that you should never include names or identifying information for the participants who took part in the usability testing (Dumas and Loring, 2008). If all participants are from within a specific organization, even giving a combination of age, gender, and job title could be the equivalent of identifying someone. When in doubt, provide only the average age of participants, the number of each gender who took part, and basic job titles. You never want to identify who took part in the usability testing, so it's a good idea to refer to the participants as Participant #1, Participant #2, and so on. You never know to whom and where your usability reporting results will be sent to, so make sure you would be comfortable with that fact.

10.6 OTHER VARIATIONS ON USABILITY TESTING

This chapter has presented traditional ways of doing usability testing. But, since usability testing is all about being practical and about changing methods to fit the needs that you have in a project, of course, there are new and different approaches to usability testing. If you read the proceedings of any well-established HCI conference, you can find new approaches, new hybrids, combining multiple methods, that could potentially be used in certain types of usability engineering activities. Two of the more well-known approaches are "technology probes" and "Wizard-of-Oz testing."

Technology probes wouldn't technically be considered usability testing, but they are certainly closer to usability testing than traditional research. A technology probe is similar to a cultural probe (described in Chapter 8). However, a cultural probe has the goal of generally learning more about people, their groups, and their lifestyles. Technology probes involve putting a technology into a real-world setting. Technology probes combine the social science goal of collecting information about people in a real-world setting, the engineering goal of evaluating a new technology, and the design goal of creating new ideas for potential technologies (Hutchinson et al., 2003). A technology is installed in a real-world setting to see how it is used and then reflection on these experiences gives feedback on who the users are and what types of technology could be successfully used in these settings by these users. The technologies themselves are not the interfaces being tested for usability. Technology probes have been used to understand how family members communicate and share images (Hutchinson et al., 2003) and how people in a relationship show public affection (O'Brian and Mueller, 2006). The focus in a technology probe isn't the probe itself but, rather, what can be learned about the people taking part and what technologies they could potentially use.

A Wizard-of-Oz[11] method is essentially a simulation of functionality that doesn't exist yet in an interface application. The user perceives that they are interacting with the actual interface and system. In reality, the user is interacting with another human being that is providing the responses to the user (Dahlback et al., 1993; Gould et al., 1983). Wizard-of-Oz methods can be used when the functionality has not been built due to cost concerns and when the technology doesn't exist, to test potential future interfaces (White and Lutters, 2003). In addition, due to the low time and cost involved, the method may also be helpful in determining feasibility and testing concepts prior to any real systems development (White and Lutters, 2003). Because there can sometimes be a time delay before the "wizard" responds, it can be helpful to have a set of precompiled responses that can quickly be accessed, which helps to improve the realism of the simulation (since participants typically don't know that the functionality isn't being provided by the computer system). The Wizard-of-Oz method has been used in evaluating motion-based computer games for children (Höysniemi et al., 2004), spoken dialog systems in driving vehicle simulators (Hu et al., 2007), and speech recognition systems (Sinha et al., 2001).

10.7 **SUMMARY**

Usability testing is often known more generally as "user research." Usability testing, typically involves representative users attempting representative tasks in representative environments, on early prototypes or working versions of computer interfaces, with the goal of improving the quality of an interface by finding flaws, areas of the interface that need improvement. In reality, the approaches utilized in usability testing are often the same as those used in classic research. Metrics utilized in usability testing include measurement of task performance and time performance, similar to experimental design, but usability testing often has different end goals. The goal is not to create research that can be generalized to other projects, but rather, to discover specific flaws so that a specific interface can be improved. As an example, making immediate changes to the interface allows for those changes to be evaluated during the next user test, which is considered acceptable in usability testing, but would be considered unacceptable in experimental design. While expert reviews and automated usability testing do help improve interfaces, typically they are not considered HCI research and/or user research, since they do not involve representative

---

[1] The name comes from the man behind the curtain in the movie *The Wizard of Oz*.

users in the research. Usability testing can involve many different stages of interface development: paper prototypes, wireframes, partially working, or fully functional prototypes. The specific details of the usability testing, such as the stage of prototype development, location of testing, level of formality, task list, number of participants, and the metrics used, will be determined by the budget, timeline, and logistics of the interface development project. The goal is to coordinate closely with the developers of the interface so that the interface problems discovered, will actually translate into changes being made in the interface in a timely manner. Usability testing is focused on practical usage in industry. Professional groups, such as the Usability Experience Professionals Association (www.uxpa.org), provide useful information for practitioners and researchers.

DISCUSSION QUESTIONS

1. Name two ways in which usability testing is similar to experimental design and two ways in which it is different from experimental design.

2. What business factors tend to drive the scope of usability testing?

3. Which should come first, a user-based test or an expert-based test and why?

4. What is a manual check in an automated usability test?

5. What is the difference between a formative usability test and a summative usability test?

6. From a practical point of view, what business factors tend to determine how many participants take part in usability testing?

7. What are the three qualities of a good task in a task list?

8. Why might it be challenging to utilize the user's personal data in a usability test?

9. What are the three most common quantitative measurements in a usability test?

10. What is the "thinking aloud" protocol and is it used more in formative or summative testing?

11. What is a reflection session?

12. What three things do you need to remind participants about before they begin a usability test?

13. Why should you not give any identification information about participants in the final usability testing report?

14. What are two good reasons for using a Wizard-of-Oz approach to testing?

15. How does a technology probe differ from a cultural probe?

RESEARCH DESIGN EXERCISE

Imagine that you are planning a user-based usability test to evaluate a new interface that allows people to track online their medical information, such as blood tests, diagnostics, annual check-ups, and patient visits. Since many governments have set the goal to move to full electronic patient records in the next few years, this is an important project. Doctors will also use this application but, for this exercise, we're focused on patients. Where might you want to recruit potential participants? Would you utilize real patient data in the usability testing? What might five representative tasks be? Since privacy and security of medical data is important, how would you include tasks that assess how comfortable people are with the privacy and security of their data? Where should these usability tests take place? What type of setting would be most authentic and appropriate? How might you compare the usability of this interface with other interfaces for similar tasks? What specific steps might you take to make participants feel more at ease?

REFERENCES

Andreasen, M., Nielsen, H., Schroder, S., Stage, J., 2007. What happened to remote usability testing? An empirical study of three methods. In: Proceedings of the ACM Conference on Human Factors in Computing Systems, pp. 1405–1414.

Atterer, R., Schmidt, A., 2007. Tracking the interaction of users with AJAX applications for usability testing. In: Proceedings of the ACM Conference on Human Factors in Computing Systems, pp. 1347–1350.

Als, B., Jensen, J., Skov, M., 2005. Comparison of think-aloud and constructive interaction in usability testing with children. In: Proceedings of the 2005 Conference on Interaction Design and Children, pp. 9–16.

Au, F., Baker, S., Warren, I., Dobbie, G., 2008. Automated usability testing framework. In: Proceedings of the 9th Australasian User Interface Conference, pp. 55–64.

Chadwick-Dias, A., McNulty, M., Tullis, T., 2003. Web usability and age: how design changes can improve performance. In: Proceedings of the ACM Conference on Universal Usability, pp. 30–37.

Dahlback, N., Jonsson, A., Ahrenberg, L., 1993. Wizard of Oz studies: why and how. In: Proceedings of the ACM International Conference on Intelligent User Interfaces (IUI), pp. 193–200.

Donker, A., Reitsma, P., 2004. Usability testing with young children. In: Proceedings of the Interaction Design and Children Conference, pp. 43–48.

Dray, S., Siegel, D., 2004. Remote possibilities?: International usability testing at a distance. Interactions 11 (2), 10–17.

Dumas, J., Fox, J., 2007. Usability testing: current practice and future directions. In: Sears, A., Jacko, J. (Eds.), The Human Computer Interaction Handbook. second ed. Lawrence Erlbaum Associates, New York, pp. 1129–1149.

Dumas, J., Loring, B., 2008. Moderating Usability Tests: Principles and Practices for Interacting. Morgan Kaufmann Publishers, Amsterdam.

Fails, J.A., Guha, M.L., Druin, A., 2012. Methods and techniques for involving children in the design of new technology for children. Foundations and Trends in Human-Computer Interaction 6 (2), 85–166.

Frokjaer, E., Hornbæk, K., 2005. Cooperative usability testing: complementing usability tests with user-supported interpretation sessions. In: Proceedings of the ACM Conference on Human Factors in Computing Systems, pp. 1383–1386.

Gould, J., Conti, J., Hovanyecz, T., 1983. Composing letters with a simulated listening typewriter. Communications of the ACM 26 (4), 295–308.

Hazlett, R., 2006. Measuring emotional valence during interactive experiences: boys at video game play. In: Proceedings of the ACM Conference on Human Factors in Computing Systems, pp. 1023–1026.

Hertzum, M., 2016. A usability test is not an interview. Interactions 23 (2), 82–84.

Hollingsed, T., Novick, D., 2007. Usability inspection methods after 15 years of research and practice. In: Proceedings of the ACM Conference on Design of Communication, pp. 249–255.

Hourcade, J.P., 2007. Interaction design and children. Foundations and Trends in Human-Computer Interaction 1 (4), 277–392.

Höysniemi, J., Hämäläinen, P., Turkki, L., 2004. Wizard of Oz prototyping of computer vision based action games for children. In: Proceedings of the 2004 Conference on Interaction Design and Children, pp. 27–34.

Hu, J., Winterboer, A., Nass, C., et al., 2007. Context & usability testing: user-modeled information presentation in easy and difficult driving conditions. In: Proceedings of the ACM Conference on Human Factors in Computing Systems, pp. 1343–1346.

Hutchinson, H., Mackay, W., Westerlund, B., et al., 2003. Technology probes: inspiring design for and with families. In: Proceedings of the ACM Conference on Human Factors in Computing Systems, pp. 17–24.

Hwang, W., Salvendy, G., 2010. Number of people required for usability evaluation: the 10 ± 2 rule. Communications of the ACM 53 (5), 130–133.

Ivory, M., Hearst, M., 2001. The state of the art in automating usability evaluation of user interfaces. ACM Computing Surveys 33 (4), 470–516.

Kuniavsky, M., 2003. Observing the User Experience: A Practitioner's Guide to User Research. Morgan Kaufmann Publishers, San Francisco.

Lazar, J., Williams, V., Gunderson, J., Foltz, T., 2017. Investigating the potential of a dashboard for monitoring U.S. federal website accessibility. In: Proceedings of the 2017 Hawaii International Conference on System Sciences (HICSS), pp. 2428–2437.

Lazar, J., 2006. Web Usability: A User-Centered Design Approach. Addison-Wesley, Boston.

Lewis, J., 2006. Sample sizes for usability tests: mostly math, not magic. Interactions 13 (6), 29–33.

Lindgaard, G., Chattratichart, J., 2007. Usability testing: what have we overlooked? In: Proceedings of the ACM Conference on Human Factors in Computing Systems, pp. 1415–1424.

Miller, G., 1956. The magical number seven, plus or minus two: some limits on our capacity for processing information. Psychological Review 63 (2), 81–96.

Nielsen, J., Landauer, T., 1993. A mathematical model of the finding of usability problems. In: Proceedings of the ACM Conference on Human Factors in Computing Systems, pp. 206–213.

Nielsen, J., Mack, R. (Eds.), 1994. Usability Inspection Methods. John Wiley & Sons, New York.

O'Brian, S., Mueller, F., 2006. Holding hands over a distance: technology probes in an intimate, mobile context. In: Proceedings of the 2006 OZCHI Conference, pp. 293–296.

Preece, J., Rogers, Y., Sharp, H., 2002. Interaction Design: Beyond Human-Computer Interaction. John Wiley & Sons, New York.

Rubin, J., Chisnell, D., 2008. Handbook of Usability Testing, 2nd. ed. Wiley Publishing, Indianapolis.

Sauro, J., Lewis, J.R., 2012. Quantifying the user experience: practical statistics for user research. Elsevier, Amsterdam.

Schmettow, M., 2012. Sample size in usability studies. Communications of the ACM 55 (4), 64–70.

Schusteritsch, R., Wei, C., LaRosa, M., 2007. Towards the perfect infrastructure for usability testing on mobile devices. In: Proceedings of the ACM Conference on Human Factors in Computing Systems, pp. 1839–1844.

Shi, Q., Clemmensen, T., 2008. Communication patterns and usability problem finding in cross-cultural thinking aloud usability testing. In: Proceedings of the ACM Conference on Human Factors in Computing Systems, pp. 2811–2816.

Shneiderman, B., Plaisant, C., Cohen, M., Jacobs, S., Elmqvist, N., Diakopoulos, N., 2017. Designing the user interface: strategies for effective human-computer interaction, sixth ed. Addison-Wesley, Boston, MA.

Sinha, A., Klemmer, S., Chen, J., et al., 2001. SUEDE: iterative, informal prototyping for speech interfaces. In: Proceedings of the ACM Conference on Human Factors in Computing Systems, pp. 203–204.

Snyder, C., 2003. Paper prototyping: the fast and easy way to design and refine user interfaces. Morgan Kaufmann Publishers, San Francisco.

Spool, J., Schroeder, W., 2001. Testing web sites: five users is nowhere enough. In: Proceedings of the ACM Conference on Human Factors in Computing Systems, pp. 285–286.

Tullis, T., Albert, W., 2008. Measuring the user experience: collecting, analyzing, and presenting usability metrics. Morgan Kaufmann, Amsterdam.

Van Den Haak, M., De Jong, M., Jan Schellens, P., 2003. Retrospective vs. concurrent think-aloud protocols: testing the usability of an online library catalogue. Behaviour & Information Technology 22 (5), 339–351.

Virzi, R., 1992. Refining the test phase of usability evaluation: how many subjects is enough? Human Factors 34 (4), 457–468.

Wentz, B., Lazar, J., Stein, M., Gbenro, O., Holandez, E., Ramsey, A., 2014. Danger, danger! Evaluating the accessibility of web-based emergency alert sign-ups in the northeastern United States. Government Information Quarterly 31 (3), 488–497.

West, R., Lehman, K., 2006. Automated summative usability studies: an empirical evaluation. In: Proceedings of the ACM Conference on Human Factors in Computing Systems, pp. 631–639.

White, K., Lutters, W., 2003. Behind the curtain: lessons learned from a Wizard of Oz field experiment. SIGGROUP Bulletin 24 (3), 129–135.

Wixon, D., 2003. Evaluating usability methods: why the current literature fails the practitioner. Interactions 10 (4), 28–34.

Zazelenchuk, T., Sortland, K., Genov, A., Sazegari, S., Keavney, M., 2008. Using participants' real data in usability testing: lessons learned. In: Proceedings of the ACM Conference on Human Factors in Computing Systems, pp. 2229–2236.

Analyzing qualitative data 11

11.1 INTRODUCTION

In Chapter 4, we discussed how to use significance tests to study quantitative data and measures such as speed, error rate, distance, adoption rate, and rankings. The well-defined nature of quantitative measures makes them appealing options for many studies. When we can clearly specify our measures of interest and how they are to be measured, research methods and analytic procedures can be clearly defined, making study design reasonably straightforward. Of course, complications may arise, but we don't need to worry about the definition of the underlying units used to measure task completion times.

Our discussions of case studies, interviews, and ethnography introduce markedly different kinds of data associated with research questions and analysis methods that are not quite so clear-cut. Rather than searching for numerical measurements, these qualitative studies attempt to study texts, observations, video, and artifacts to understand complex situations. Analysis of these data often raises challenges that rarely raise with quantitative data, as we struggle to interpret ambiguous comments and understand complex situations. To make matters worse, we don't even know what the "truth" is—as multiple researchers might (and often do) have different perspectives on the same situation.

Acknowledging these challenges, social science researchers have developed research methods designed to increase rigor and validity in analyzing qualitative data. Qualitative methods do not aim to eliminate subjectivity—instead, they accept that subjectivity is inherent to process of interpreting qualitative data, and they strive to show that interpretations are developed methodically to be consistent with all available data, and representative of multiple perspectives.

In this chapter, we present an introduction to qualitative research, discussing techniques for ensuring high-quality analysis of qualitative data that is both *reliable* and *valid.* We introduce the process of *coding,* which assigns labels to observations from text or other qualitative data forms. We specifically focus on grounded theory (Glaser and Strauss, 1967), the starting point for many qualitative analyses. The use of content analysis to extract categories from diverse "texts" is described, along with a discussion of the analysis of two very important forms of qualitative data: text and multimedia. In order to control the impact of subjective interpretation, a commonly accepted coding procedure should be adopted and

Research Methods in Human-Computer Interaction. http://dx.doi.org/10.1016/B978-0-12-805390-4.00011-X

299

statistical methods used to evaluate the validity and reliability of the coding completed by human coders. The general strategy discussed in this chapter is just one of the many approaches available for analyzing text and other qualitative information. Substantially different strategies may be used for different disciplines, such as literature or art.

11.2 GOALS AND STAGES OF QUALITATIVE ANALYSIS

The goal of qualitative analysis is to turn the unstructured data found in texts and other artifacts into a detailed description about the important aspects of the situation or problem under consideration. This description can take many forms, including textual narratives, graphical diagrams, and summary tables. These items can often be combined to provide the range of perspectives needed for understanding the underlying complexity.

According to Corbin and Strauss (Corbin and Strauss, 2014), qualitative data analysis consists of three stages. We start with a data set containing information about our problem of interest. For example, the problem can be related to challenges faced by or unique needs of a specific group of users (i.e., people with visual disabilities, senior citizens, children, etc.). It can focus on a specific technology such as a gesture-based input method, a photo sharing application, or 3D printing. The problem can also examine the interaction behavior in a specific context, such as text entry on a small screen while the user is constantly walking. Via analysis, we hope to identify major themes and ideas that describe the context, activities, and other perspectives that define the problem. In the second stage, we drill down into each component to find relevant descriptive properties and dimensions. In many cases, we need to understand not only the nature of each component, but also how they relate to each other. In the third stage, we use the knowledge we gained from studying each individual component to better understand the original substance and make inferences about that substance.

For example, we might analyze chat logs to study the online behavior of Internet users. Reading these logs, we might notice that three factors, namely personality, education, and computer-related experience, are repeatedly found to influence users' online behavior. We continue to study each of those three factors and how they relate to each other. We study the literature in psychology and sociology to understand the types of personality, how an individual forms and develops a specific personality, and how a specific type of personality affects an individual's social behavior. Once we have a thorough understanding of the three factors, we can tie the knowledge back to the original texts and examine how each of the components affects a user's online behavior. Specifically, we might use our literature review to identify specific personality or educational behaviors that might influence online behaviors, This application of experience and contextual knowledge is critical for the appropriate interpretation of qualitative data and the entire knowledge discovery process.

11.3 CONTENT ANALYSIS

Widely used in vastly different domains, *content analysis* refers to the process of developing a representative description of text or other unstructured input. Stemler (2001) summarized previous work (i.e., Berelson, 1952) and stated that content analysis is a systematic, replicable technique for compressing many words of text into fewer content categories based on explicit rules of coding. A broader definition proposed by Holsti (1969) allows for other types of information, defining content analysis as "any technique for making inferences by objectively and systematically identifying specified characteristics of messages" (p. 14). According to this definition, content analysis not only applies to textual information, but also to multimedia materials, such as drawings, music, and videos.

Content analysis is normally in-depth analysis that searches for theoretical interpretations that may generate new knowledge. As described by Corbin and Strauss (Corbin and Strauss, 2014), this type of analysis "presents description that embodies well-constructed themes/categories, development of context, and explanations of process or change over time" (p. 51). Although many people think content analysis is a qualitative research method, both quantitative and qualitative techniques can be used in the process of content analysis (Neuendorf, 2002).

11.3.1 WHAT IS CONTENT?

The target of content analysis usually covers two categories: media content and audience content. Media content can be any material in printed publications (e.g., books, journals, magazines, newspapers, and brochures), broadcast programs (e.g., TV or radio programs), websites (e.g., news websites, web portals, personal websites, or blogs), or any other types of recording (e.g., photos, films, or music).

Audience content is feedback directly or indirectly collected from an audience group. Audience content can be collected through a variety of methods such as surveys, questionnaires, interviews, focus groups, diaries, and observations. Traditionally, information collected via those methods is text based. In the HCI field, researchers and practitioners frequently collect both text-based information and multimedia-based information from the participants. Text or multimedia information used for content analysis can be collected through a variety of methods listed in Table 11.1. For more detailed information on each of those data collection methods, please refer to Chapters 5–9.

11.3.2 QUESTIONS TO CONSIDER BEFORE CONTENT ANALYSIS

Before you start analyzing the data, you need to consider several questions that can help frame the scope of the content analysis as well as the specific techniques that should be used for the analysis (Krippendorff, 1980).

First, you need to have a clear definition for the data set that is going to be analyzed. In some studies the definition of the data set is very straightforward. For example, if

Table 11.1 Major Categories of Content

Category	Subcategory	Examples
Media content	Publications	Books, journals, newspapers, brochures
	Broadcasting	TV programs, radio programs
	Websites	News, web portals, organizational websites, blogs
	Others	Films, music, photos
Audience content	Text	Notes from interviews, focus groups, or observations or diaries or surveys, text posts on social media
	Multimedia	Video- or audio-recording of interviews, focus groups, observations, or user studies, pictures or video recordings posted on social media

you interview 10 mobile device users on their daily usage of the device, your interview notes would be the data set that you are going to analyze. In other cases, the definition of the data set may not be that straightforward and special consideration is needed to select the appropriate content or messages that should be included in the data set. Suppose you want to study the development of interpersonal trust among members of an online community. The public messages that the community members leave on the bulletin board may contain valuable information. The messages that the community members exchange privately through applications such as Instant Messaging or email would also be useful. In this case, you need to consider the scope of your data set: Do you want to study the public messages only, the private messages only, or both? The answer to this question depends on both your research question and the practical issues of your study. If your research question is focused on the impact of the general community atmosphere and the sense of community on trust development, you may want to limit the data set to the public messages because they are the most relevant to your research question. In some cases, you may have to stick to the public messages because you have no access to the messages that are exchanged privately among the community members. You may also restrict the data set to messages posted during a specific time period. Overall, the scope of your data set may affect the key words or categories that you are going to use during the content analysis.

Once a clear definition of the data set is specified, you should study the data closely and remove any data that do not meet the criteria of the definition. In the online community study example, if you decide to study the public messages posted in 2015, then all of the private messages and any public messages from earlier or later years must be abandoned. If those messages remain in the data set and are analyzed, the data set is polluted and the results may be biased or misleading.

Content analysis studies should also clearly define the population from which the data set is drawn. This seems to be straightforward but many issues may be encountered in practice. In the online community study example, the term "community members" may raise some questions. How do you define community members? Do community members include all the people who have visited the online community website? If the answer to this question is "yes," it means you are interested in examining not only those visitors who have posted messages, but also the people who have visited the website but have never posted a message (lurkers). If your data set only consists of the public messages, then the data comes from a subset of your population (those who have contributed by posting messages) and, therefore, it is not representative of the overall population. In this case, it may be more appropriate to restrict the target population of your study to those people who have posted messages. Examination of the data might reveal a wide range in the number of messages posted by participants. Some people might visit and post messages on a daily basis. Some people might only post one or two messages through the entire year. Do you count those extremely infrequent visitors as community members? If so, there may be concerns over whether the small number of postings from those visitors' limits the accuracy of the depiction of their opinions or behavior. Other factors that should be considered when defining the population include, but are not limited to, age, gender, profession, education, and domain experience.

Thirdly, you need to know the specific context of the data. Data analysis out of context is meaningless and highly biased. Any words, terms, and claims need to be interpreted in the specific context from which they are extracted. Consideration of the context is an iterative process, occurring at multiple levels throughout analysis. Before data analysis, you need to have a clear understanding of the higher-level context of your data set. For example, if you are studying the end-user's attitude toward security procedures in the organizational environment, you need to be aware that the type of business or profession may have a notable impact on the topic. An employee of a government agency who has access to classified information works in a very different environment from a staff of an entertainment facility. The government worker may have to go through security training on a regular basis while the staff working in the entertainment industry may have no security-related training. Therefore, the specific context of their work has great impact on the data that they provide. If you analyze their input without considering the context, it is like comparing apples with pears and the results are tainted. During the data analysis process, you need to consider lower-level context, such as the phrase, sentence, or paragraph. We discuss the interpretation of low-level context in Section 11.4.2.

11.4 ANALYZING TEXT CONTENT
11.4.1 CODING SCHEMES

Analyzing text content involves assigning categories and descriptors to blocks of text, a process called "coding." A common misunderstanding is that coding is nothing more than paraphrasing the text and counting the number of key words in the text. Actually, coding is much more than paraphrasing and key word counts. As stated by Corbin and Strauss (Corbin and Strauss, 2014), coding "involves interacting with data, making comparisons between data, and so on, and in doing so, deriving concepts to stand for those data, then developing those concepts in terms of their properties and dimensions." A set of well-developed procedures for analyzing text content has been widely accepted in the social sciences and related fields. Because qualitative research is more vulnerable to bias than quantitative research, it is particularly important to follow the standard procedure to ensure the quality of the analysis and the robustness of the results.

Solid qualitative analysis depends on accurately identified concepts that later serve as "categories for which data are sought and in which data are grouped" (Blumer, 1969). The concepts and categories are also a means of establishing relations (e.g., correlation, causal relationships, etc.) between different entities. Identifying the coding categories can be a very daunting task for inexperienced researchers. The coding categories may come from several sources: an existing theoretical framework, the researcher's interpretation (research-denoted concepts), and original terms provided by the participants (in vivo codes).

There are two different approaches to analyzing the data: *emergent* coding and *a priori* coding. *Emergent* coding refers to the qualitative analyses conducted without any theory or model that might guide your analysis—you simply start by noting interesting concepts or ideas and continually refine those ideas until you are able to form a coherent model that captures the important details. *A priori* coding involves the use of an established theory or hypothesis to guide the selection of coding categories. These categories might come from previously published work in related areas, or from your own prior investigations of the topic at hand.

To illustrate the difference between these coding approaches, consider the earlier example of the study of online communities. Some studies might be based on the theory participants in the communities adopted various roles that defined the manner and content of their posts. These studies would use a priori coding, with codes selected to identify roles and their application. Other studies might be interested in understanding conversational dynamics more broadly, without any particular starting point. These studies would use emergent codes. Some studies might use a mixture of both methods.

The choice between emergent and a priori coding is often not straightforward. Existing theories and codes have the advantage of being somewhat simpler to use, at the potential costs of broader insight that might come from the more open-ended analysis associated with open coding.

11.4.1.1 Grounded theory and emergent coding

If you are working on a new topic that has very limited literature to build on, you may not be able to find established theories that allow you to develop the coding categories in advance. In this case, the emergent coding approach, based on the notion of *grounded theory,* is appropriate. Grounded theory was first proposed by Glaser and Strauss (Glaser and Strauss, 1967), who described a qualitative research method that seeks to develop theory that is "grounded in data systematically gathered and analyzed" (Myers, 2013). Grounded theory is an inductive research method that is fundamentally different from the traditional experimental research methods described in Chapters 2 and 3. As demonstrated in Figure 11.1, when conducting experimental research, we normally start from a preformed theory, typically in the form of one or more hypotheses, we then conduct experiments to collect data and use the data to prove the theory. In contrast, grounded theory starts from a set of empirical observations or data and we aim to develop a well-grounded theory from the data. During the process of theory development, multiple rounds of data collection and analysis may be conducted to allow the underlying theory to fully emerge from the data (Myers, 1997; Corbin and Strauss, 2014). Therefore, some researchers refer to the theory generated using this method as the "reverse-engineered" hypothesis.

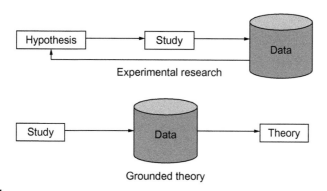

FIGURE 11.1

Experimental research compared with grounded theory.

Grounded theory can be applied to a variety of research methods discussed in this book such as ethnography (Chapter 9), case studies (Chapter 7), and interviews (Chapter 8). The major difference between qualitative research strategies that are mainly descriptive or exploratory and grounded theory is its emphasis on theory development from continuous interplay between data collection and data analysis.

Because grounded theory does not start from a preformed concept or hypothesis, but from a set of data, it is important for researchers to start the research process without any preconceived theoretical ideas so that the concepts and theory truly emerge from the data. The key to conducting successful grounded theory research is to be creative and have an open mind (Myers, 2013). Since grounded theory was first proposed in 1967, opinions on how to conduct research using grounded theory have diverged (Glaser, 1992; Strauss, 1987; Corbin and Strauss, 2014). The founders disagree on whether grounded theory can be formalized into a set of clear guidelines and procedures. Glaser believes that procedures are far too restrictive and may contradict the very basis of this method: creativity and an open mind. Even with the public disagreement, the procedures and guidelines proposed by Strauss and Corbin have been widely used in the field of social science, probably partly due to the fact that the procedure makes grounded theory more tangible and easier to implement.

We briefly introduce the procedures of grounded theory according to Corbin and Strauss (Corbin and Strauss, 2014).

The grounded theory method generally consists of four stages:

- open coding;
- development of concepts;
- grouping concepts into categories;
- formation of a theory.

In the open coding stage, we analyze the text and identify any interesting phenomena in the data. Normally each unique phenomenon is given a distinctive name or code. Given a piece of text to analyze, you would read through, trying to identify the patterns, opinions, behaviors, or other issues that sound interesting. Since you are not constrained by preestablished theories, frameworks, or concepts, you are open to all possibilities that reside in the data.

During this process, you need to find terms to describe the interesting instances that emerge from the data. Sometimes the participants may provide terms that describes the instances or key elements so vividly or accurately that you can borrow the term directly. Coding categories generated in this manner are called *in vivo* code. In vivo coding can help ensure that the concepts stay as close as possible to the participants' own words. These types of codes are largely adopted when using the grounded theory method. In one survey that the authors conducted on computer usage by children with Down syndrome, we borrowed many terms (e.g., curriculum integration) directly from parents' response and used them as low-level themes (Feng et al., 2010).

When the original text does not contain a key term to describe the instance of interest, the researcher will need to find an appropriate term to describe the instance. Those terms are called "researcher-denoted concepts." For example, if you read the following descriptions in the data, you may use the term "frustration" to describe the underlying theme of both responses:

My son just sits there and sobs when the computer does not do what he wants.
He becomes irritated and keeps pushing the Enter button when the web page loads slowly.

In the second stage, collections of codes that describe similar contents are grouped together to form higher level "concepts," which can then be grouped to form "categories" (the third stage). Definitions of the concepts and categories are often constructed during this phase of the analysis. The identification and definition of relationships between these concepts—a process often referred to as "axial coding" (Preece et al., 2015; Corbin and Strauss, 2014) is often a key step in this process. As analysis continues, we are constantly searching for and refining the conceptual construct that may explain the relationships between the concepts and categories (Glaser, 1978).

Although this description implies a linear process with well-defined phases, analyses might not be quite so clear-cut. The identification of new codes through open coding, the grouping of these codes into categories, and the definition of relationships between these codes is a complex process involving the evolving construction of an understanding of the data. Iterative review of the data is often a key part of the process, as identification of new codes and categories might lead you to rereview documents from the perspective of codes identified in later documents. This rereview might also suggest multiple categorizations or types of relations between codes.

In the last stage, theory formulation, we aim at creating inferential and predictive statements about the phenomena recorded in the data. More specifically, we develop explicit causal connections or correlations between the concepts and categories identified in the previous stages. This process might be followed by *selective coding,* in which previously coded data might be revisited from the context of the emerging theory. Of course, further iteration and identification of open codes or axial codes is also possible.

A study of the issues involved in building information technology support for palliative care provides an instructive example of the use of emergent coding and grounded theory. Noting that palliative care differs significantly from other forms of medical care in a focus on the individual needs of each patient, Kuziemsky and colleagues conducted a grounded theory analysis of multiple data sources, including 50 hours of interviews with seven professionals (nurses, physicians, and counselors), patient charts, and research literature. Figure 11.2 provides an example of open and axial codes used in this analysis. This coding process was used to form a more detailed map of relationships between factors important to palliative care (Kuziemsky et al., 2007).

While conducting research using grounded theory, it is important to fully understand the advantages and limitations of this research method. Grounded theory obviously has a number of advantages. First, it provides a systematic approach to analyzing qualitative, mostly text-based data, which is impossible using the traditional experimental approach. Second, compared to the other qualitative research methods, grounded theory allows researchers to generate theory out of qualitative data that can be backed up by ample evidence as demonstrated in the thorough coding. This is one of the major attractions of the grounded theory and even novice users found the procedure intuitive to follow. Third, grounded theory encourages researchers to study the data early on and formulate and refine the theory through constant interplay between data collection and analysis (Myers, 2013).

On the other hand, the advantages of grounded theory can become disadvantages at times. It is not uncommon for novices to find themselves overwhelmed during the coding stage. The emphasis on detailed and thorough coding can cause researchers to be buried in details and feel lost in the data, making it difficult to identify the higher-level concepts and themes that are critical for theory formulation. In addition, theories developed using this method may be hard to evaluate. Unlike the traditional experimental approach in which the hypothesis is clearly supported or rejected by quantitative data collected through well-controlled, replicable experiments, grounded theory starts from textual information and undergoes multiple rounds of data collection and coding before the theory fully emerges from the data. The evaluation of the outcome depends on measures that are less direct, such as the chain of evidence between the

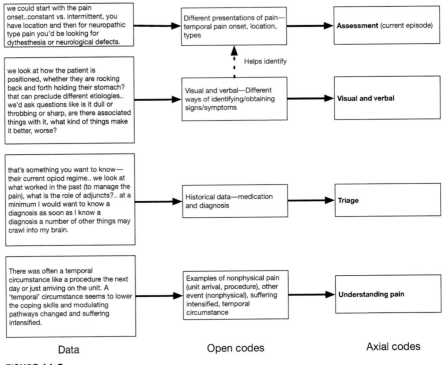

FIGURE 11.2

Example open and axial codes from a grounded theory analysis of issues relating to palliative care pain management. Note that the axial codes both abstract multiple open codes into more general categories and also (in the case of the arrow labelled "helps identify") describe relationships between the codes.

Adapted from Kuziemsky, C.E., et al., 2007. A grounded theory guided approach to palliative care systems design. International Journal of Medical Informatics 76, S141–S148.

finding and the data, the number of instances in the data that support the specific concept, and the familiarity of the researcher with the related topic. Lastly, the findings of the grounded theory approach may be influenced by the researchers' preconceived opinions and, therefore, may be subject to biases. In order to avoid these issues from happening, researchers should always keep in mind the key of this approach: being creative and open minded; listening to the data. When there is a gap between the concept and the data, additional data need to be collected to fill in the gap and tighten the linkage between the concept and the data. Due to these limitations, some researchers prefer to use grounded theory just as a coding technique, not as a theory generation method. For a detailed exploration of these and many other issues relating to the use of grounded theory in qualitative analysis, see "The SAGE Handbook of Grounded Theory" (Bryant and Charmaz, 2007) and Corbin and Strauss' classic text *Basics of Qualitative Research: Techniques and Procedures for Developing Grounded Theory* (Corbin and Strauss, 2014).

11.4.1.2 A priori coding and theoretical frameworks

Theoretical frameworks are commonly used in multiple stages of qualitative research (Corbin and Strauss, 2014). In the research design stage, theoretical frameworks can help you frame the research questions, decide on the specific research approach to adopt (i.e., survey, interview, focus group, etc.), and identify the concepts and questions to be included in each approach. When analyzing text information, theoretical frameworks can help you identify the major categories and items that need to be coded and explain the findings of your research. Therefore, at the beginning of a research project, it is important to study the research literature and find out whether there is any theoretical framework related to the research topic that you are investigating.

For example, suppose you interview a number of senior citizens to examine the major difficulties that they experience when using computers. One question you would like to answer is the underlying cause of those difficulties. You know a large proportion of the difficulties can be attributed to the gradual decline of human capabilities. According to well-established literature, human capabilities can be grouped into three major categories: cognitive, physical, and perceptual abilities. You can use those three types of capability as the high-level categories of your coding scheme and try to group the participants' responses in each of those three categories.

In the HCI field, theoretical frameworks are also called taxonomies. Numerous taxonomies have been developed to help guide research and understand the data collected through various user studies. One example of the earlier taxonomies proposed is about the types of task that users conduct (Norman, 1991). By grouping tasks into categories, such as "structured and unstructured" or "regular and intermittent," and summarizing the different nature and requirements of each type of task, researchers and designers can study the interaction in a consistent way and make easier connections between different aspects of the result. For a comprehensive discussion on task analysis, see (Courage et al., 2007). Another widely cited taxonomy in the HCI field groups human errors into mistakes and slips (Norman, 2013). Slips can be further categorized into capture errors, description errors, data-driven errors, associative-activation errors, loss-of-activation errors, and mode errors. Each type of slip has different causes, and different design techniques can be used to help prevent, detect, and recover from those errors. Well-studied and validated taxonomies can provide great insights for identifying the potential categories to be included for coding.

In both emergent coding and a priori coding, different coding techniques may be adopted depending on the nature of the data and the study context. Examples include magnitude coding, in which codes are associated with qualitative or quantitative assessments of the strength or frequency of the concept; process coding, which uses gerunds ("-ing" verbs) to identify actions; and a variety of affective coding methods focused on emotions and values. Saldaña (Saldaña, 2012) provides an in-depth catalog of different coding approaches and methodologies.

11.4.1.3 Building a code structure

After the key coding items are identified, they can be organized and presented in a code list (also called a "nomenclature" or a "codebook"). A nomenclature is a list of numbered categories intended to represent the full array of possible responses to a specific question (Lyberg and Kasprzyk, 1997). For studies using theoretical frameworks, the codes will come from the categories and concepts identified by the theory. Emergent coding, however, means that the codes are not identified in advance—the list will emerge as new concepts of interest are found in the source material. A code list is normally built into a hierarchical structure, containing multiple levels, each level representing concepts with increasing amounts of detail. Building a code structure is not an easy task. It requires both extensive knowledge of the existing theories and literature and a deep understanding of the data collected. Many times, the analyst needs to make compromises between the theoretical framework and the practical aspects of the study.

Figure 11.3 demonstrates an example of a code structure generated by Feng et al. (2010) when investigating computer usage behaviors by children with Down syndrome. The researchers adopted a mixture of emergent coding and a priori coding

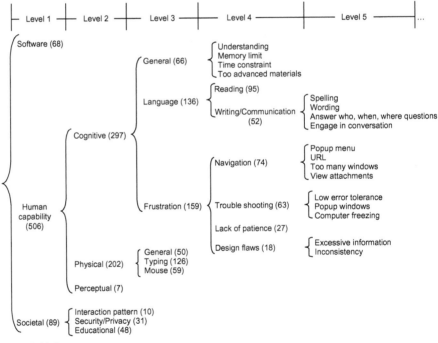

FIGURE 11.3

Example code structure using both emergent coding and a priori coding about difficulties experienced by children with Down syndrome when using computers or computer-related devices (Numbers in parentheses represent the number of children whose parents reported the particular type of difficulty. Some parents reported in more than one subcategories so the numbers do not necessarily add up to the total number in the parent category.)

Excerpted from Feng, J., et al., 2010. Computer usage by children with down syndrome: challenges and future research. ACM Transactions on Accessible Computing 2 (3), 32. Copyright ACM.

when trying to identify the key concepts and categories. Most of the code items at level three, four, and five were identified through emergent coding, and so were the three categories listed under "Societal difficulties." In contrast, the three categories under "Human capabilities" were derived from existing theory from psychology and behavioral science.

11.4.2 CODING THE TEXT

When the data set is not large, which is typically true for interviews, focus groups, or observations, it is recommended to read the text from beginning to end before starting to do any coding. During the first round of reading, you may find interesting issues and feel the urge to write among the text or in the margins. Those activities should wait until you start the coding. The purpose of this first round of reading is to immerse you into the life and experience of the participants and get a general, unbiased idea of the data set before focusing on any specific aspects. After this first read-through, you should be ready to dive in and start coding.

Inexperienced coders may find it difficult to identify anything interesting (or anything that is worth being coded) in the data, especially when the coding category is not established and they are doing open coding to identify coding categories or themes. Other coders may experience the other end of the scale: they may feel that the data is so rich that they need to code almost every word or phrase. Eventually they may be overwhelmed by the large number of coding items that they are trying to document. They may be distracted by the less important or even trivial coding items and fail to identify the most interesting or informative patterns in the data. In order to avoid both situations, we recommend the following steps for coding:

1. Look for specific items.
2. Ask questions constantly about the data.
3. Making comparisons constantly at various levels.

We'll discuss these steps in the following sections.

11.4.2.1 Look for key items

While coding the data, specific types of "statements" are more likely to carry valuable information. A partial list of such statements is given in Table 11.2. In fact, these categories might prove useful as codes on their own!

Objectives deliver important information. A user's computer usage behavior and interaction style is largely affected by the objectives that they want to achieve. If a user uses a specific application just for entertainment, it may be unrealistic to expect the user to devote a substantial amount of time to learning how to use the application. It would be totally different if the application is a critical tool at work.

Words, phrases, and sentences that describe actions are also important. They tell you what the users do with the specific application or technique. They also tell you what functions are frequently used and what are less frequently used. Once you detect an action code in the data, you can follow up on that and examine whether the user

Table 11.2 Some Examples of Statements to Look for While Coding

Statement	Examples
Objectives	Use computers for educational purposes
Actions	Enter a password, chat online
Outcomes	Success or failure, whether the objective is achieved
Consequences	Files unintentionally deleted, a specific application abandoned
Causes	Limited memory, dated equipment
Contexts	User is computer savvy, user works with classified information
Strategies	Avoid specific tasks, multimodal interaction

described the outcome of the action. Was the action successfully completed? Did the action completely fail? Was the action partially completed? Whenever an action is not completely successful, you may want to pursue the consequences or costs of the unsuccessful action: Is the consequence highly detrimental? Does it cause the user to lose several days of work? Does it prevent the user from completing some tasks on time? Is it a minor nuisance or is it so frustrating that the user decides to abandon the action?

Causes are also associated with failed actions. Whenever an action completely or partially fails, it is worth pursuing the causes of the failure. Does the failure trace back to the user or the application? If it is caused by the user, what kinds of capability are involved? Is it due to cognitive overload? Is it due to lack of attention? Is it due to physical or perceptual limitations? Or is it due to the interaction between two or more of those factors. Statements about the context of the interaction or usage are also important. Different types of user may report different satisfaction levels for the same application with similar performance measures because the comparison context is drastically different (Sears et al., 2001). Finally, descriptions of interaction styles and strategies are also valuable information that is hard to examine during empirical lab-based studies.

11.4.2.2 Ask questions about the data

A good way to help detect interesting patterns and connections in data is to constantly ask questions about the data. In Section 11.4.2.1, we listed a series of questions that you can ask once you identify an interesting action in the data. Those questions can be related to the specific action, its outcome, and its consequence, as well as the causes of failed actions. Most of those questions are practical questions that may help you identify interaction challenges and design flaws.

Corbin and Strauss (Corbin and Strauss, 2014) discussed the art of asking questions in a larger context with the primary objective of theory development. They proposed four types of questions and two of them are particularly important during the analysis phase: sensitizing questions and theoretical questions. Sensitizing questions help coders better understand the meaning of the data: What is happening here? What did the user click? How did the user reach the specific web page? Theoretical questions help the researchers make connections between concepts and categories: What is the relationship between two factors? How does the interaction change over time?

11.4.2.3 Making comparisons of data

Both during the coding process and the stage afterwards to interpret the results, you are encouraged to make comparisons at multiple levels. First, you can compare instances under different coding categories. For example, if you are investigating the difficulties that older people experience when using computers, you can compare the frequency with which each capability (physical, cognitive, perceptual) is reported. You can also compare the degree of impact between different capabilities.

Second, you can compare the results between different participant groups. You may find that the capabilities and computer usage behaviors vary substantially among the users. You can further investigate this diversity via different dimensions: Is the diversity related to age, educational background, or community and family support? To answer these questions, you need to subdivide the data set and compare the results among subsets.

Third, you can compare the findings in your data to previously reported literature. Do your findings align with the existing literature or is it contradictory? If your findings differ from existing literature, can you explain why? Is the existing literature incorrect? Or is the difference caused by a different context? Sometimes the need to compare your findings with a related population or tasks may facilitate you to conduct additional studies to collect more data. For example, if you observe some interesting computer usage behavior in children with autism, you may want to conduct the same study for neurotypical children to investigate whether there is a difference between the neurotypical children and children with Autism.

11.4.2.4 Recording the codes

When you find an item in the content that you wish to describe with a code, you should note exactly what you are coding and which codes you are assigning. The "what" should provide enough detail to unambiguously identify the relevant content—you might quote specific paragraphs, sentences, or phrases from a textual document or identify start and end points for time intervals in an audio recording. The code(s) that you are assigning will come from your list of codes. Note that coders often find that they want to describe a given item with multiple codes.

A variety of strategies can be used to record codes. One low-tech approach might involve marking up text with comment and highlighting tools from a word processor. Another possibility might be to use a spreadsheet with columns for the identification of the item being coded and for the codes being assigned.

A number of commercial and academic software packages provide dedicated support for text analysis, including tools for creating codebooks, coding documents, and searching and querying for material associated with given codes. Other tools support automated text content analysis via features for searching, counting, sorting, and conducting basic statistics. Examples of commonly used text analysis software include SAS (https://www.sas.com), GATE (the General Architecture for Text Engineering) (https://gate.ac.uk), and Carrot2 (http://project.carrot2.org).

11.4.2.5 Iterating and refining

Qualitative coding leads to the construction of an evolving conceptual framework. As you examine raw data and assign codes to elements of that data, you are in effect organizing the components and constructing an understanding that will grow and change as you continue. For emergent coding efforts, the addition of new codes is the emergence of your understanding. However, even theoretically informed efforts may find that a deeper appreciation of the data leads to the realization that the initial framework is not quite adequate or correct. If this happens, you may wish to add codes to your codebook, and to reconsider previously coded material in the light of these new codes. This iterative extension of the codebook and rereview of material can be time consuming, but it does reflect the evolving nature of your understanding.

11.4.3 ENSURING HIGH-QUALITY ANALYSIS

Qualitative data analysis is not objective. During the data-coding process, a human researcher makes a series of decisions regarding the interpretation of individual observations: Which category does this item belong in? Are these items really members of the same group or should they be separated? No matter how expert the judgment of the individual making these decisions, the possibility of some conscious or unconscious bias exists. Given the inherent fallibility of human researchers, how can we increase our confidence in the results of qualitative analysis? More specifically, how can we make our qualitative analysis *valid* and *reliable*?

Before we can answer that question, we must be clear on what we mean by these terms. In terms of qualitative research, *validity* means that we use well-established and well-documented procedures to increase the accuracy of findings (Creswell, 2013). More strictly speaking, validity examines the degree to which an instrument measures what it is intended to measure (Wrench et al., 2013). *Reliability* refers to the consistency of results (Creswell, 2013): if different researchers working on a common data set come to similar conclusions, those conclusions are said to be reliable.

Ensuring reliability and validity of qualitative HCI research is a challenge. For additional guidance on improving the rigor of your qualitative research—and, indeed, on all aspects of qualitative HCI—see the monograph *Qualitative HCI Research: Going Behind the Scenes* (Blandford et al., 2016).

11.4.3.1 Validity

Validity is a very important concept in qualitative HCI research in that it measures the accuracy of the findings we derive from a study. There are three primary approaches to validity: face validity, criterion validity, and construct validity (Cronbach and Meehl, 1955; Wrench et al., 2013).

Face validity is also called content validity. It is a subjective validity criterion that usually requires a human researcher to examine the content of the data to assess whether on its "face" it appears to be related to what the researcher intends to measure. Due to its high subjectivity, face validity is more susceptible to bias and is a weaker criterion compared to construct validity and criterion validity. Although face validity should be viewed with a critical eye, it can serve as a helpful technique to detect suspicious data in the findings that need further investigation (Blandford et al., 2016).

Criterion validity tries to assess how accurate a new measure can predict a previously validated concept or criterion. For example, if we developed a new tool for measuring workload, we might want participants to complete a set of tasks, using the new tool to measure the participants' workload. We also ask the participants to complete the well-established NASA Task Load Index (NASA-TLX) to assess their perceived workload. We can then calculate the correlation between the two measures to find out how the new tool can effectively predict the NASA-TLX results. A higher correlation coefficient would suggest higher criterion validity. There are three subtypes of criterion validity, namely predictive validity, concurrent validity, and retrospective validity. For more details regarding each subtype—see Chapter 9 "Reliability and Validity" in Wrench et al. (2013).

Construct or factorial validity is usually adopted when a researcher believes that no valid criterion is available for the research topic under investigation. Construct validity is a validity test of a theoretical construct and examines "What constructs account for variance in test performance?" (Cronbach and Meehl, 1955). In Section 11.4.1.1 we discussed the development of potential theoretical constructs using the grounded theory approach. The last stage of the grounded theory method is the formation of a theory. The theory construct derived from a study needs to be validated through construct validity. From the technical perspective, construct or factorial validity is based on the statistical technique of "factor analysis" that allows researchers to identify the groups of items or factors in a measurement instrument. In a recent study, Suh and her colleagues developed a model for user burden that consists of six constructs and, on top of the model, a User Burden Scale. They used both criterion validity and construct validity to measure the efficacy of the model and the scale (Suh et al., 2016).

In HCI research, establishing validity implies constructing a multifaceted argument in favor of your interpretation of the data. If you can show that your interpretation is firmly grounded in the data, you go a long way towards establishing validity. The first step in this process is often the construction of a database (Yin, 2014) that includes all the materials that you collect and create during the course of the study, including notes, documents, photos, and tables. Procedures and products of your analysis, including summaries, explanations, and tabular presentations of data can be included in the database as well.

If your raw data is well organized in your database, you can trace the analytic results back to the raw data, verifying that relevant details behind the cases and the circumstances of data collection are similar enough to warrant comparisons between observations. This linkage forms a chain of evidence, indicating how the data supports your conclusions (Yin, 2014). Analytic results and descriptions of this chain of evidence can be included in your database, providing a roadmap for further analysis.

A database can also provide increased reliability. If you decide to repeat your experiment, clear documentation of the procedures is crucial and careful repetition of both the original protocol and the analytic steps can be a convincing approach for documenting the consistency of the approaches.

Well-documented data and procedures are necessary, but not sufficient for establishing validity. A very real validity concern involves the question of the confidence that you might have in any given interpretive result. If you can only find one piece of evidence for a given conclusion, you might be somewhat wary. However, if you begin to see multiple, independent pieces of data that all point in a common direction, your confidence in the resulting conclusion might increase. The use of multiple data sources to support an interpretation is known as data source *triangulation* (Stake, 1995). The data sources may be different instances of the same type of data (for example, multiple participants in interview research) or completely different sources of data (for example, observation and time diaries).

Interpretations that account for all—or as much as possible—of the observed data are easier to defend as being valid. It may be very tempting to stress observations that support your pet theory, while downplaying those that may be more consistent with alternative explanations. Although some amount of subjectivity in your analysis is unavoidable, you should try to minimize your bias as much as possible by giving every data point the attention and scrutiny it deserves, and keeping an open mind for alternative explanations that may explain your observations as well as (or better than) your pet theories.

You might even develop some alternative explanations as you go along. These alternatives provide a useful reality check: if you are constantly re-evaluating both your theory and some possible alternatives to see which best match the data, you know when your theory starts to look less compelling (Yin, 2014). This may not be a bad thing—rival explanations that you might never find if you cherry-picked your data to fit your theory may actually be more interesting than your original theory. Whichever explanations best match your data, you can always present them alongside the less successful alternatives. A discussion that shows not only how a given model fits the data but how it is a better fit than plausible alternatives can be particularly compelling.

Well-documented analyses, triangulation, and consideration of alternative explanations are recommended practices for increasing analytic validity, but they have their limits. As qualitative studies are interpretations of complex datasets, they do not claim to have any single, "right" answer. Different observers (or participants) may have different interpretations of the same set of raw data, each of which may be equally valid. Returning to the study of palliative care depicted in Figure 11.2, we might imagine alternative interpretations of the raw data that might have been equally valid: comments about temporal onset of pain and events might have been described by a code "event sequences," triage and assessment might have been combined into a single code, etc. Researchers working on qualitative data should take appropriate measures to ensure validity, all the while understanding that their interpretation is not definitive.

11.4.3.2 Reliability

The ambiguous data that is the focus of content analysis exemplifies many of the reliability challenges presented by qualitative data analysis. The same word may have different meanings in different contexts. Different terms or expressions may suggest the same meaning. The data may be even more ambiguous when it comes to the interpretation of body language, facial expression, gestures, or art work. The same people may interpret the same gesture differently after viewing it at different times. In many studies, the data set is very large and multiple coders may code different subsets of the data. Due to the nature of content analysis, it is more vulnerable to biases and inconsistencies than the traditional quantitative approach. Therefore, it is particularly important to follow specific procedures during the coding process and use various measures to evaluate the quality of the coding. The ultimate goal of reliability control is to ensure that different people code the same text in the same way (Weber, 1990).

Reliability checks span two dimensions: stability and reproducibility. Stability is also called *intracoder reliability*. It examines whether the same coder rates the data in the same way throughout the coding process. In other words, if the coder is asked to code the same data multiple times, is the coding consistent time after time? If the coder produces codes that shows 50% in category A, 30% in category B, and 20% in category C the first time; then 20% in category A, 20% in category B, and 60% in category C the second time, the coding is inconsistent and the intracoder reliability is very low.

In the context of content analysis, intercoder reliability is widely adopted to measure reproducibility. It examines whether different coders code the same data in a consistent way. In other words, if two or more coders are asked to code the same data, is their coding consistent? In this case, if one coder produces codes that shows 50% in category A, 30% in category B, and 20% in category C; while the other coder produces codes that show 20% in category A, 20% in category B, and 60% in category C, then the coding is inconsistent and the intercoder reliability is very low.

A further step in demonstrating reliability might use multiple coders specifically chosen for differences in background or theoretical perspectives, leading to a theoretical triangulation (Stake, 1995). If individuals with substantially different intellectual frameworks arrive at similar conclusions, those results may be seen as being very reliable.

In order to achieve reliable coding both from the same coder and among multiple coders, it is critical to develop a set of explicit coding instructions at the beginning of the coding process. All of the coders need to be trained so that they fully understand the instructions and every single coding item. The coders then test code some data. The coded data is examined and reliability measures are calculated. If the desired reliability level is achieved, the coders can start the formal coding. If the desired reliability level is not achieved, measures must be taken to improve reliability. These measures might include retraining and recoding the data used in the test coding. Alternatively, the coders might use a discussion of disagreements to determine how coding should be conducted, and revise the codebook and coding instructions to reflect the new consensus. After the formal coding process starts, it is important to conduct reliability checks frequently so that inconsistent coding can be detected as early as possible.

One of the commonly used reliability measures is the percentage of agreement among coders, calculated according to the following equation:

$$\%agreement = \frac{\text{the number of cases coded the same way by multiple coders}}{\text{the total number of cases}}$$

When analyzing a survey on software and technology for children with autism, Putnam and Chong (2008) coded the data independently and reported a 94% agreement between the two coders, which is quite a satisfactory level. However, the percentage agreement approach does have a limitation: it does not account for the fact that several coders would agree with each other for a certain percentage of cases even when they just code the data by chance. Depending on the specific feature of the coding, that percentage may be quite substantial.

To address this limitation, you can adopt other measures such as Cohen's Kappa (Cohen, 1960), which rates interrater reliability on a scale from 0 to 1, with 0 meaning that the cases that are coded the same are completely by chance and 1 meaning perfect reliability. Kappa is calculated by the following equation:

$$K = \frac{P_a - P_c}{1 - P_c}$$

where P_a represents the percentage of cases on which the coders agree and P_c represents the percentage of agreed cases when the data is coded by chance.

Suppose we conduct a survey of senior citizens and ask them to describe the primary causes of the difficulties that they encounter when using computers. We identify three major categories of causes: difficulties due to physical capabilities, difficulties due to cognitive capabilities, and difficulties due to perceptual capabilities. Two coders code the data independently. Their coding results are summarized in an agreement matrix as illustrated in Table 11.3. The diagonal line from top left shows the percentages of cases on which the coders agreed. For example, the number of cases that both coders coded under the "physical difficulty" category accounts for 26% of the total number of cases. The other cells contain the cases on which the two coders disagreed (i.e., 7% of the cases were coded under "physical difficulties" by the first coder and under "cognitive difficulties" by the second coder). The "marginal

Table 11.3 The Distribution of Coded Items Under Each Category by Two Coders (Agreement Matrix)

		Coder 2			
		Physical	**Cognitive**	**Perceptual**	**Marginal total**
	Physical	0.26 (0.14)	0.07 (0.08)	0.04 (0.15)	0.37
Coder 1	Cognitive	0.04 (0.07)	0.12 (0.04)	0.01 (0.07)	0.17
	Perceptual	0.09 (0.18)	0.02 (0.10)	0.35 (0.18)	0.46
	Marginal total	0.39	0.21	0.40	1.00

totals" are calculated by adding up the values in each row or column. The "marginal total" values always add up to one. The value in parentheses in each cell represents the expected percentage agreement when the data is coded by chance, calculated by multiplying the marginal totals of the corresponding row and column (i.e., the expected percentage agreement for (physical, physical) is $0.37 \times 0.39 = 0.14$).

Based on the data provided by Table 11.3, we can compute the value of P_a as:

$$P_a = 0.26 + 0.12 + 0.35 = 0.73$$

The value of P_c is computed by adding the expected percentage agreement (in parentheses on the diagonal):

$$P_c = 0.14 + 0.04 + 0.18 = 0.36$$

Therefore,

$$K = \frac{0.73 - 0.36}{1 - 0.36} = 0.58$$

A well-accepted interpretation of Cohen's Kappa is that a value above 0.60 indicates satisfactory reliability. Table 11.4 summarizes a more detailed interpretation of Cohen's Kappa (Landis and Koch, 1977; Altman, 1991). When the value of Kappa is below 0.60, the reliability of the analysis is questionable.

Table 11.4 Interpretation of Cohen's Kappa

Interpretation	Kappa range
Poor or slight agreement	$K \leq 0.20$
Fair agreement	$0.20 < K \leq 0.40$
Moderate agreement	$0.40 < K \leq 0.60$
Satisfactory agreement	$0.60 < K \leq 0.80$
Near-perfect agreement	$K > 0.80$

In addition to the percentage agreement and Cohen's Kappa, there are several other coefficients that measure coder agreement, such as Osgood's coefficient (also named CR) proposed by Osgood (1959) and the S coefficient proposed by Bennett et al. (1954). Hallgren (2012) provided a more detailed tutorial on Cohen's Kappa and related measures. For detailed discussions of the differences among the agreement measures, see Krippendorff (2004) or Artstein and Poesio (2008).

The process of achieving high interrater reliability often involves multiple iterations, as low initial reliability might lead to changes in codebooks and/or instructions. Once acceptable reliability has been achieved on a subset of the data, coders are presumed to be reliable and can proceed independently without further checks. Whenever possible, having multiple coders review all documents at a high-level of reliability is preferred, but in some cases resource limitations may require multiple coding of only a subset of the data.

11.4.3.3 Subjective versus objective coders

You should be aware of the advantages and disadvantages of using subjective or objective coders and their impact on coding reliability. When the coders are the same people who developed the coding scheme, and in many cases they also design the study and collect the data, they are called *subjective* or *inside* coders. When the coders are not involved in the design of the study, the data collection, or the development of the coding scheme, they are called *objective* or *outside* coders.

There are pros and cons of both approaches. Because subjective coders are usually the researchers themselves, they know the literature well and have substantial knowledge and expertise in the related topic. That knowledge and specialty can help them understand the terms and concepts provided by participants and detect the underlying themes in the text. They also require minimal training since they developed the coding scheme themselves. However, the fact that they have already worked so closely with the data becomes a disadvantage during the actual coding. The preacquired knowledge may constrain their abilities to think beyond the established concepts in their mind. Sometimes they may form hidden meanings of the coding without being aware of it. The consequence is that the reliability reported by subjective coders may be inflated (Krippendorff, 1980).

On the contrary, objective coders usually do not have preacquired knowledge of the subject and, therefore, may be more open to potential instances in the data. The reliability reported by objective coders is less likely to be inflated. However, their lack of domain knowledge and expertise may also hinder their ability to accurately understand the data and detect interesting instances. In addition, objective coders usually need a substantial amount of training and the entire process can be very costly.

In practice, it is very common for studies to use subjective coders for content analysis and this approach is usually considered acceptable as long as the appropriate procedure is followed and reported, along with the reliability measures.

11.5 ANALYZING MULTIMEDIA CONTENT

Multimedia data has become prevalent in our daily life thanks to the rapid advances in affordable portable electronic devices and storage technologies. Researchers can collect a large quantity of image, audio, and video data at fairly low cost. Multimedia information such as screen shots, cursor movement tracks, facial expressions, gestures, pictures, sound, and videos provide researchers an amazingly rich pool of data to study how users interact with computers or computer-related devices.

Multimedia information also presents substantial challenges for data analysis. In order to find interesting patterns in the interactions, the image, audio, and video data need to be coded for specific instances (i.e., a specific gesture, event, or sound). Without the support of automated tools, the researcher would have to manually go through hours of audio or video recordings to identify and code the instances of specific interest. This process can be extremely time-consuming, tedious, and in many cases, impractical.

The basic guidelines for analyzing text content also apply to multimedia content. Before you start analyzing the data, you need to study the literature and think about the scope, context, and objective of your study. You need to identify the key instances that you want to describe or annotate. After the analysis, you need to evaluate the reliability of the annotation. If a manual annotation approach is adopted, it may be a good idea to select a subset of the entire data set for analysis due to high labor cost. For example, Peltonen et al. (2008) picked eight days of data from a study that lasted for 1 month. They first automatically partitioned the video footage into small "sessions," then manually coded the information in which they were interested (the duration of interaction, the number of active users, and the number of passive bystanders).

Another application domain related to multimedia content analysis is the online search of media content. There is a huge amount of images, videos, and audios on the web. Users frequently go online to search for images, videos, or audio materials. Currently, most multimedia search is completed by text-based retrieval, which means that the multimedia materials have to be annotated or labeled with appropriate text. So far, annotation can be accomplished through three approaches: manual annotation, partially automated annotation, and completely automated annotation.

Considering the huge amount of information that needs to be annotated, the manual approach is extremely labor intensive. In addition, it can also be affected by the coder's subjective interpretation. The completely automated approach is less labor intensive. However, due to the substantial semantic gap between the low-level features that we can currently automatically extract and the high-level concepts that are of real interest to the user, existing automatic annotation applications are highly error prone (i.e., many images that have nothing to do with cats may be annotated with "cat" using this automatic annotation). A more recent development in this field is the partially automated approach. Human coders manually annotate a subset of the multimedia data. Then the manually coded data is used to train the application to establish the connection between the low-level features and the high-level concept. Once a concept detector is established, the detector can be used to automatically annotate the rest of the data (Rui and Qi, 2007). The same approach can be applied to images and video and audio clips.

The techniques for multimedia content analysis are built on top of multiple domains including image processing, computer vision, pattern recognition and graphics. One of the commonly adopted approaches used by all those fields is machine learning. The specific algorithms or techniques of multimedia content analysis are still seeing dramatic advances. For more detailed information on those topics, see publications in the related fields (Hanjalic et al., 2006; Sebe et al., 2007; Divakaran, 2009; Ohm, 2016). The specific applications that are particularly interesting to the HCI field include action recognition and motion tracking (Zhu et al., 2006; Vondrak et al., 2012), body tracking (Li et al., 2006), face recognition, facial expression analysis (Wu et al., 2006; Wolf et al., 2016), gesture recognition (Argyros and Lourakis, 2006), object classification and tracking (Dedeoğlu et al., 2006; Guo et al., 2015), and voice activity detection (Xue et al., 2006). A substantial number of studies have focused on automatic annotation and management of images.

In addition to the automatic annotation applications, a number of other tools have been developed to facilitate the process of multimedia content analysis. Dragicevic et al. (2008) developed a direct manipulation video player that allows a video analyst to directly drag and move the object of interest in the video to specific locations along their visual trajectory. Wilhelm et al. (2004) developed a mobile media metadata framework that enables image annotation on a mobile phone as soon as a picture is taken. The unique feature of this system is that it guesses the content of the picture for the purpose of reducing the amount of text entry needed during the annotation. Kandel et al. (2008) proposed the PhotoSpread system, which allows users to organize and analyze photos and images via an easy-to-use spreadsheet with direct manipulation functions. Applications that support content visualization for easy data sharing and analysis have also been developed (Cristani et al., 2008). The ChronoViz tool supports playback and review of multiple, synchronized streams of multimedia data (Fouse et al., 2011).

Techniques for automatic annotation still need substantial advancements in order to achieve reliable coding. The applications to facilitate manual coding have shown promising results but improvements are also needed to improve the usability and reliability of those systems.

11.6 SUMMARY

Text, multimedia, and other qualitative data are important sources of information for HCI researchers and practitioners. The procedure and techniques commonly used to analyze qualitative data are quite different from those applied to the analysis of quantitative data. Probably the most unique characteristic of content analysis is that it involves human coding. The absence of numeric data and direct measures makes qualitative data analysis more susceptible to biased interpretation or subjective manipulation. Therefore, it is critical to adopt well established procedures and techniques to ensure high-quality analysis that is both valid and reliable. Although there is disagreement regarding its implementation process and guidelines, grounded theory is widely used for qualitative data analysis. The major difference between grounded theory and other qualitative research strategies is its emphasis on theory development in continuous interplay between data collection and data analysis.

When analyzing text content, we need to develop a set of coding categories that accurately summarizes the data or describes the underlying relationships or patterns buried in the data. Depending on the specific context of the research question, a priori coding or emergent coding may be used to generate the coding categories. In order to produce high-quality coding, multiple coders are usually recommended to code the data. During the coding process, the coders should constantly look for statements likely to carry valuable information, ask questions about the data, and make comparisons at various levels. Reliability control measures such as Cohen's Kappa should be calculated and evaluated throughout the coding process. Cohen's Kappa at or above 0.60 indicates satisfactory intercoder reliability.

The basic guidelines for analyzing text content also apply to multimedia content. Due to the special nature of multimedia data, the analysis can be much more labor-intensive than for text data if a completely manual annotation procedure is adopted. In order to address that challenge, a number of techniques have been developed to assist the annotation of multimedia data. To date, the completely automated annotation techniques are highly error prone. Applications to facilitate manual coding have shown promising results and may serve as a useful tool for analyzing multimedia data.

DISCUSSION QUESTIONS

1. What is the goal of qualitative analysis?

2. What are the stages of qualitative analysis?

3. What is content analysis?

4. What are the major types of content?

5. What do you need to consider before starting content analysis?

6. What is the difference between a priori coding and emergent coding?

7. What is grounded theory?

8. How does grounded theory differ from the traditional empirical research approach?

9. What are the four stages of grounded theory?

10. What is in vivo code?

11. What are the advantages and limitations of grounded theory?

12. What are the benefits of using theoretical frameworks when coding qualitative data?

13. What is a nomenclature/code book?

14. What is the procedure for analyzing text information?

15. What are the key items to look for while coding?

16. What is the meaning of 'validity' in qualitative analysis?

17. What is the meaning of 'reliability' in qualitative analysis?

18. What are the three primary types of validity in qualitative analysis?

19. What can you do to improve the validity of the findings of a HCI study?

20. Why do you need to conduct reliability checking during and after the coding process?

21. What is "stability" in the context of a reliability check?

22. What is "reproducibility" in the context of a reliability check?

23. What is the formula for computing Cohen's Kappa?

24. How do you interpret a specific value of Cohen's Kappa?

25. What is the difference between intracoder reliability and intercoder reliability?

26. What is the advantage and disadvantage of using a subjective coder?

27. What is the advantage and disadvantage of using an objective coder?

28. Why is analyzing multimedia content difficult?

29. How does the partially automated annotation method work?

RESEARCH DESIGN EXERCISE

You interview 50 children between the ages of 8 and 15 to study their computer usage behavior. During the data analysis, you find that the objective of using computers can be grouped into three categories: educational, communication, and entertainment. Two coders independently code the data and the agreement of their coding regarding computer usage objective is summarized in Table 11.5. Answer the following questions based on the agreement table:

1. Develop an agreement matrix. (Hint: You need to compute marginal totals for each row and column and the expected percentage agreement for each cell.)

2. Calculate Cohen's Kappa.

3. Discuss the result and determine whether the coding is reliable.

Table 11.5 Children's Computer Usage Objectives Coding Agreement

		Coder 2		
		Education	**Communication**	**Entertainment**
	Education	0.49	0.05	0.02
Coder 1	Communication	0.03	0.11	0.01
	Entertainment	0.04	0.02	0.23

REFERENCES

Altman, D.G., 1991. Practical Statistics for Medical Research. Chapman and Hall, London, England.

Argyros, A.A., Lourakis, M.I.A., 2006. Vision-based interpretation of hand gestures for remote control of a computer mouse. In: Huang, T.S., Sebe, N., Lew, M.S., et al. (Eds.), Computer Vision in Human-Computer Interaction: ECCV 2006 Workshop on HCI, Graz, Austria, May 13. Proceedings. Springer Berlin Heidelberg, Berlin, Heidelberg, pp. 40–51.

Artstein, R., Poesio, M., 2008. Inter-coder agreement for computational linguistics. Computational Linguistics 34 (4), 555–596.

Bennett, E.M., et al., 1954. Communications through limited-response questioning. Public Opinion Quarterly 18 (3), 303–308.

Berelson, B., 1952. Content Analysis in Communication Research. Free Press, Glencoe, IL.

Blandford, A., et al., 2016. Qualitative HCI research: going behind the scenes. Synthesis Lectures on Human-Centered Informatics 9 (1), 1–115.

Blumer, H., 1969. Symbolic Interactionism: Perspective and Method. Prentice-Hall, Englewood Cliffs, NJ.

Bryant, A., Charmaz, K., 2007. The SAGE Handbook of Grounded Theory. Sage Publications, Los Angeles, CA.

Cohen, J., 1960. A coefficient of agreement for nominal scales. Educational and Psychological Measurement 20 (1), 37–46.

Corbin, J., Strauss, A.L., 2014. Basics of Qualitative Research: Techniques and Procedures for Developing Grounded Theory, fourth ed. Sage Publications, Los Angeles, CA.

Courage, C., et al., 2007. Task analysis. In: Sears, A., Jacko, J. (Eds.), The Human Computer Interaction Handbook: Fundamentals, Evolving Technologies, and Emerging Applications. Lawrence Erlbaum Associates, New York.

Creswell, J.W., 2013. Research Design: Qualitative, Quantitative, and Mixed Methods Approaches. Sage Publications, Thousand Oaks, CA.

Cristani, M., et al., 2008. Content visualization and management of geo-located image databases. In: CHI'08 Extended Abstracts on Human Factors in Computing Systems. ACM, Florence, Italy, pp. 2823–2828.

Cronbach, L., Meehl, P., 1955. Construct validity in psychological tests. Psychological Bulletin 52, 22.

Dedeoğlu, Y., et al., 2006. Silhouette-based method for object classification and human action recognition in video. In: Huang, T.S., Sebe, N., Lew, M.S., et al. (Eds.), Computer Vision in Human-Computer Interaction: ECCV 2006 Workshop on HCI, Graz, Austria, May 13. Proceedings. Springer Berlin Heidelberg, Berlin, Heidelberg, pp. 64–77.

Divakaran, A., 2009. Multimedial Content Analysis: Theories and Applications. Springer.

Dragicevic, P., et al., 2008. Video browsing by direct manipulation. In: Proceedings of the SIGCHI Conference on Human Factors in Computing Systems. ACM, Florence, Italy, pp. 237–246.

Feng, J., et al., 2010. Computer usage by children with down syndrome: challenges and future research. ACM Transactions on Accessible Computing 2 (3), 32.

Fouse, A., et al., 2011. ChronoViz: a system for supporting navigation of time-coded data. In: CHI'11 Extended Abstracts on Human Factors in Computing Systems. ACM, Vancouver, BC, Canada, pp. 299–304.

Glaser, B.G., 1978. Theoretical Sensitivity: Advances in the Methodology of Grounded Theory. Sociology Press, Mill Valley, CA.

Glaser, B.G., 1992. Emergence vs. Forcing Basics of Grounded Theory Analysis. Sociology Press, Mill Valley, CA.

Glaser, B.G., Strauss, A.L., 1967. The Discovery of Grounded Theory: Strategies for Qualitative Research. Aldine, Chicago.

Guo, H., Wang, J., Xu, M., Zha, Z., Lu, H., 2015. Learning multi-view deep features for small object retrieval in surveillance scenarios. In: Proceedings of the 23rd ACM International Conference on Multimedia, pp. 859–862.

Hallgren, K.A., 2012. Computing inter-rater reliability for observational data: an overview and tutorial. Tutorial in Quantitative Methods for Psychology 8 (1), 23–34.

Hanjalic, A., et al., 2006. Multimedia content analysis, management and retrieval. In: Proceedings of the International Society for Optical Engineering (SPIE), pp. 6073.

Holsti, R., 1969. Content Analysis for the Social Sciences and Humanities. Addison-Wesley, Reading, MA.

Kandel, S., et al., 2008. Photospread: a spreadsheet for managing photos. In: Proceedings of the SIGCHI Conference on Human Factors in Computing Systems. ACM, Florence, Italy, pp. 1749–1758.

Krippendorff, K., 1980. Content Analysis: An Introduction to its Methodology. Sage Publications, Newbury Park, CA.

Krippendorff, K., 2004. Reliability in content analysis. Human Communication Research 30 (3), 411–433.

Kuziemsky, C.E., et al., 2007. A grounded theory guided approach to palliative care systems design. International Journal of Medical Informatics 76, S141–S148.

Landis, J.R., Koch, G.G., 1977. The measurement of observer agreement for categorical data. Biometrics 33 (1), 159–174.

Li, Y., et al., 2006. Robust head tracking with particles based on multiple cues fusion. In: Huang, T.S., Sebe, N., Lew, M.S., et al. (Eds.), Computer Vision in Human-Computer Interaction: ECCV 2006 Workshop on HCI, Graz, Austria, May 13. Proceedings. Springer Berlin Heidelberg, Berlin, Heidelberg, pp. 29–39.

Lyberg, L., Kasprzyk, D., 1997. Some aspects of post-survey processing. In: Lyberg, L., Blemer, P., Collins, M., et al. (Eds.), Suvery Measurement and Process Quality. John Wiley and Sons, New York.

Myers, M.D., 1997. Qualitative research in information systems. MIS Quarterly 21 (2), 241–242.

Myers, M.D., 2013. Qualitative Research in Business and Management, second ed. Sage Publications, Los Angeles, CA.

Neuendorf, K., 2002. The Content Analysis Guidebook. Sage Publications, Thousand Oaks, CA.

Norman, D., 2013. The Design of Everyday Things: Revised and Expanded Edition. Basic Books, New York, NY.

Norman, K.L., 1991. Models of the mind and machine: information flow and control between humans and computers. In: Marshall, C.Y. (Ed.), Advances in Computers. vol. 32. Elsevier, pp. 201–254.

Ohm, J., 2016. Multimedia Content Analysis. Springer.

Osgood, E.E., 1959. The representational model and relevant research. Trends in Content Analysis. I. de Sola Pool. University of Illinois Press, Urbana, IL.

Peltonen, P., et al., 2008. It's Mine, Don't Touch!: interactions at a large multi-touch display in a city centre. In: Proceedings of the SIGCHI Conference on Human Factors in Computing Systems. ACM, Florence, Italy, pp. 1285–1294.

Preece, J., et al., 2015. Interaction Design: Beyond Human-Computer Interaction. John Wiley & Sons, Ltd., West Sussex, UK.

Putnam, C., Chong, L., 2008. Software and technologies designed for people with autism: what do users want? In: Proceedings of the 10th International ACM SIGACCESS Conference on Computers and Accessibility. ACM, Halifax, Nova Scotia, Canada, pp. 3–10.

Rui, Y., Qi, G.-J., 2007. Learning concepts by modeling relationships. In: Sebe, N., Liu, Y., Zhuang, Y., Huang, T.S., et al. (Eds.), Multimedia Content Analysis and Mining: International Workshop, MCAM 2007, Weihai, China, June 30–July 1. Proceedings. Springer Berlin Heidelberg, Berlin, Heidelberg, pp. 5–13.

Saldaña, J., 2012. The Coding Manual for Qualitative Researchers. SAGE Publication, Thousand Oaks, CA.

Sears, A., et al., 2001. Productivity, satisfaction, and interaction strategies of individuals with spinal cord injuries and traditional users interacting with speech recognition software. Universal Access in the Information Society 1 (1), 4–15.

Sebe, N., et al., (Eds.), 2007. Multimedia content analysis and mining. In: Proceedings of the Multimedia Content Analysis and Mining International Workshop MCAM 2007. Lecture Notes in Computer Science.

Stake, R.E., 1995. The Art of Case Study Research. Sage Publications, Thousand Oaks, CA.

Stemler, S., 2001. An overview of content analysis. Practical Assessment, Research & Evaluation 7 (17), 137–146.

Strauss, A.L., 1987. Qualitative Analysis for Social Scientists. Cambridge University Press, Cambridge.

Suh, H., et al., 2016. Developing and validating the user burden scale: a tool for assessing user burden in computing systems. In: The ACM Conference on Human Factors in Computing Systems (CHI). ACM, San Jose, pp. 3988–3999.

Vondrak, M., Sigal, L., Hodgins, J., Jenkins, O., 2012. Video-based 3D motion capture through biped control. ACM Transactions on Graphics (TOG) – Proceedings of ACM SIGGRAPH. 31 (4), Article 27.

Weber, R.P., 1990. Basics of Qualitative Research: Grounded Theory Procedures and Techniques. Sage Publications, Newbury Park, CA.

Wilhelm, A., et al., 2004. Photo annotation on a camera phone. In: CHI'04 Extended Abstracts on Human Factors in Computing Systems. ACM, Vienna, Austria, pp. 1403–1406.

Wolf, K., Abdelrahman, Y., Landwehr, M., Ward, G., Schmidt, A., 2016. How to browse through my large video data: face recognition & prioritizing for lifelog video. In: Proceedings of the 15th International Conference on Mobile and Ubiquitous Multimedia, pp. 169–173.

Wrench, J., et al., 2013. Quantitative Research Methods. Oxford University Press, New York.

Wu, Q., et al., 2006. EigenExpress approach in recognition of facial expression using GPU. In: Huang, T.S., Sebe, N., Lew, M.S., et al. (Eds.), Computer Vision in Human-Computer Interaction: ECCV 2006 Workshop on HCI, Graz, Austria, May 13. Proceedings. Springer Berlin Heidelberg, Berlin, Heidelberg, pp. 12–21.

Xue, W., et al., 2006. Voice activity detection using wavelet-based multiresolution spectrum and support vector machines and audio mixing algorithm. In: Huang, T.S., Sebe, N., Lew, M.S., et al. (Eds.), Computer Vision in Human-Computer Interaction: ECCV 2006 Workshop on HCI, Graz, Austria, May 13. Proceedings. Springer Berlin Heidelberg, Berlin, Heidelberg, pp. 78–88.

Yin, R.K., 2014. Case Study Research: Design and Methods, fifth ed. Sage, Thousand Oaks, CA.

Zhu, G., et al., 2006. Action recognition in broadcast tennis video using optical flow and support vector machine. In: Huang, T.S., Sebe, N., Lew, M.S., et al. (Eds.), Computer Vision in Human-Computer Interaction: ECCV 2006 Workshop on HCI, Graz, Austria, May 13. Proceedings. Springer Berlin Heidelberg, Berlin, Heidelberg, pp. 89–98.

Automated data collection methods

12

12.1 INTRODUCTION

Data are the building blocks of research. As the recorded output of research efforts, data are the raw materials that must be processed, analyzed, and interpreted to provide answers to research questions. Data collection is therefore a critical phase in any research effort.

Data collection is also often one of the most challenging aspects of research. Timing user task completion with a stopwatch, furiously writing notes describing user interactions with software systems, coding notes from ethnographic observations, and many other tasks are laborious, time consuming, and often—as a result—error-prone.

Fortunately, human-computer interaction (HCI) researchers can use the computers that are the subject of our research as powerful data collection tools. Software tools can be used to collect vast amounts of user interaction data, often with little or no direct effort on the part of the researcher administering the study. Interaction logging software tracking keystrokes and mouse clicks, special-purpose instrumented software designed to track use of specific features in tools, web site access logs, and home-grown customized tools for tracking what users do and when can simplify data collection, increase consistency, and decrease error.

Approaches to automated data collection can generally be placed on a spectrum of ease of use and flexibility (Figure 12.1). Existing software tools such as website access log analyzers can often be easily used or adapted for research purposes, but capabilities might be limited. System observation and logging software may be somewhat more powerful, but installation and configuration issues can be challenging. Custom-built or modified software can be crafted to meet the precise research needs, but the development effort can be substantial.

All of these automated methods for computerized data collection are capable of producing voluminous data sets. This can pose a substantial problem for researchers: while generating data is easy, deciding which data to collect and how best to analyze that data can be challenging. Although many projects involving automated data collection (including data collected from human subjects—see Chapter 13) follow a familiar arc of planning, data collection, cleaning, analysis, and iteration to refine methods and techniques, details vary between projects due to technological differences in data acquisition methods and analytic differences associated with varying research questions. Some of these issues will be discussed here and in Chapter 13,

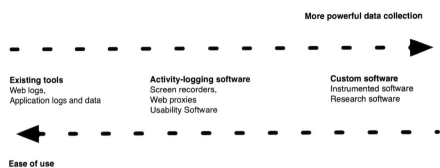

Ease of use
FIGURE 12.1

Computerized data collection systems present a trade-off between power and ease of implementation and use.

but you may need to digger deeper in the literature to find similar work for more specific guidance on appropriate data granularity, data cleaning, and analytic techniques.

In this chapter, we focus on log and data capture. This is certainly not the full story of the use of automated data capture in HCI. Newer technologies such as smartphones and a huge variety of inexpensive sensors provide rich troves of data suitable for understanding how we interact with computers in a wide variety of environments. These applications will be discussed in Chapter 13 on Human Data collection and Chapter 14 on online and ubiquitous HCI research.

12.2 EXISTING TOOLS

Many commonly used software tools collect and store data that can be used in HCI research. These tools have the obvious appeal of relative simplicity: although some effort may be required for analysis, data collection tools may be readily available. For some widely analyzed data sources—such as web server logs—commercial and freely available tools can provide substantial assistance in interpretation.

These advantages do not come without a cost. Using unmodified, commodity software is likely to limit you to data that is collected by default. If your research questions require additional data, you may be out of luck. This is often not a real barrier—many successful research projects have been based on analysis of data from available software. A sound strategy might be to start with these tools, pushing them to see how far they can take your research efforts and moving toward more complex measures if needed.

12.2.1 WEB LOGS

Web servers, email servers, and database servers all generate log files that store records of requests and activity. As a sequential listing of all of the requests made to a server, a log file provides a record of how the server has been used and when. This detailed information can be useful for evaluating system performance, debugging problems, and recovering from crashes.

Web logs have also proven to be a potent tool in HCI research. Given a website and a log file, researchers can often analyze entries to determine where users went and when. When combined with an understanding of the architecture of a site, this information can be used to assess the usability of a site. Timing data in web logs also presents opportunities for empirical studies. Although log data is not perfect, and often presents analytic challenges, appropriate analysis can often yield useful insights.

12.2.1.1 Web log contents

Although web servers can be configured to store a variety of data fields along with each request, most log files store data that can identify a request and its source. Some log files also contain fields that are generally less useful. The useful data includes:

- *Host*: The Internet protocol address of the remote computer that made the request. As many people access the Internet via networks that use firewalls or proxy hosts that forward requests from internal machines, a host address might not correspond directly to a specific user's computer.
- *Timestamp*: When the request occurred, usually including a date and a time code. Times may be given relative to Greenwich Mean Time.
- *Request:* The HTTP request sent by the client to the server. The request has several fields that may be of interest:
  - *HTTP Method*: The type of request being made—usually "GET" or "POST" (Fielding and Reschke, 2014).
  - *Resource*: The file, script, or other resource requested from the server.
  - *Protocol:* The version of the HTTP protocol used.
- *Status Code:* A numeric response from the server, indicating success (200–299), redirection (300–399), client error (400–499), or server error (500–599) (Fielding and Reschke, 2014).

Several other potentially useful fields may be available:

- *Size*: The size—in number of bytes—of the item returned to the client.
- *Referrer*: The web page that "referred" the client to the requested resource. If a user on http://yourhost/index.html clicks on the "search.html" link, the request indicates that "http://yourhost/index" was the referrer. Some requests, such as those that come via an address typed in to a browser, do not arrive via a link and have a dash ("-") in the referrer field.
- *User Agent:* The make and model of the web browser that made the request. As this is self-reported, it may or may not be accurate.

Figures 12.2 and 12.3 give some example log entries.

Most web servers use the common log format (World Wide Web Consortium, 1995) or similar formats as the basis for formatting log files. Customization facilities provided by most web services allow for the inclusion of specific fields. This can be very useful for adapting your logs to fit the needs of each project. If you are running a study involving users who are particularly sensitive to privacy concerns, you might configure your server to remove the client IP number from the log files. Similar

10.55.10.14 - - [13/Jul/2007:13:42:10 -0400] "GET /homepage/classes/spring07/686/index.html HTTP/1.1"
200 8623

10.55.10.14 - - [13/Jul/2007:13:48:32 -0400] "GET /homepage/classes/spring07/686/schedule.html
HTTP/1.1" 200 16095

10.55.10.14 - - [13/Jul/2007:13:48:33 -0400] "GET /homepage/classes/spring07/686/readings.html
HTTP/1.1" 200 14652

FIGURE 12.2

Log file entries, containing host IP address, timestamp, request, status code, and number
of bytes.

10.55.10.14 %t "GET /homepage/classes/spring07/686/readings.html HTTP/1.1" 200 14652
"http://10.55.10.128/homepage/classes/spring07/686/schedule.html" "Mozilla/5.0 (X11; U; Linux i686; en-
US; rv:1.8) Gecko/20051202 Fedora/1.5-0.fc4 Firefox/1.5"

FIGURE 12.3

A detailed version of the last entry from Figure 12.2, including the referrer and the user
agent.

changes can be made regarding the recording of the referrer, the user agent, or other
fields. For many studies, it may be useful to create a special-purpose log in parallel
with a traditional access log. The customized log file provides the information needed
for your study, without interfering with access logs that might be used for ongoing
website maintenance. Customized log file formats may require customization of the
web server software or of the log analysis tools, but this is generally not hard to do.

Most web servers generate error logs in addition to access logs. The list of requests that generated server errors can be useful for identifying problems with a site
design, such as links to nonexistent pages or resources. Check your server documentation for details.

As web logs can become quite voluminous, proper care and handling is very important. Numerous software tools extract information from log files for static reports
or interactive analysis: several approaches to this analysis are described in this chapter.

Logs from publicly accessible sites may include regular and repeated visits from
web robots, tools used by search engines and other tools to retrieve web pages, follow
links, and analyze web content. Before using the logs of your publicly accessible site
for research purposes, you might consider using the robot exclusion protocol (Koster,
2007) to discourage these automated tools. This protocol is very straightforward: all
you need to do is to place one simple file in the root directory of your server. Polite
bots will not make further requests once they see this file. As a result, the proportion
of your log entries generated by these crawlers will be reduced, leaving you with
more of the good stuff—visits from human users. As this step may have the (possibly
undesirable) effect of reducing your site's visibility to search engines, you may wish
to exclude robots for short periods of time while you collect data. Once your data
collection is complete, you can disable your robot exclusion measures, thus allowing
search engines to index your site and maintain your visibility.

Note that web requests—and therefore web logs—are not limited solely to recording clicks in web browsers. Many web sites provide Application Programming

Interfaces (APIs), often following the Representational State Transfer (REST) conventions (Fielding and Taylor, 2002). Essentially, REST (and similar) APIs define structured web requests to return data suitable for extraction and manipulation by third-party web sites and other programs. As these APIs can be used to provide data to mobile apps and stand-alone desktop programs—as well as web pages—any such accesses will be included in web logs, and can therefore be analyzed to track usage patterns.

12.2.1.2 *Web usability/design research*

By telling us which pages were accessed and when, web access logs can provide valuable information for usability evaluations and understanding of usage patterns. Relatively simple page access counts tell us which pages are accessed frequently, and which are not. When coupled with an understanding of page layout information, this can help identify opportunities for improving usability. Aggregate counts of timestamps, referrers, and user agents can be used to understand when a site is being used, how people are getting to links within a site (external referrers are particularly interesting in this regard), and which browsers they are using—all potentially useful information in the context of evaluating a site design. Interactive visualizations of this data at multiple granularities—particularly when coordinated with views of the site—can provide guidance for improving site design (Hochheiser and Shneiderman, 2001). For example, if important areas of the site are infrequently accessed, links might be moved to more prominent locations or be made more visually distinctive. Postmodification analysis can be used to evaluate the success (or lack thereof) of such measures.

Web access logs also provide the intriguing possibility of extracting information about the actions of specific users as they navigate a website. This information can be very useful for understanding which path users take through a site and where they might run into problems.

As each entry in an access log can contain an Internet address, a timestamp, the requested URL, the referring URL, and a user agent, we might be tempted to combine this information with knowledge of a site's layout to infer the path of specific users through a site. If we see that an access to "index.html" is soon followed by a request for "help.html," with both requests originating from the same network address, we might think that these requests came from the same user. Matching user agents and an entry indicating that the referrer page for the "index.html" page was the "help.html" page might increase our confidence in this theory. Judiciously used web cookies can provide additional useful information.

Unfortunately, things are not necessarily that simple. Firewalls and other network address schemes may make requests that come from multiple users appear as if they all come from the same machine. Web browsers can easily be configured to provide misleading information for the user agent fields and referrer fields. Web redirects may create misleading requests, appearing as if a user intended to visit a site, when they had no such interest. Cookies may be disabled by some users and browsers.

Despite the problems, access logs can be used to generate useful models of user paths (Pirolli and Pitkow, 1999). Augmenting these records with additional information including keywords extracted from visited web pages or URLs and page view time can provide increased accuracy in characterizing user sessions (Heer and Chi, 2002).

As a stand-alone tool, web log analysis is limited by a lack of contextual knowledge about user goals and actions. Even if we are able to extract individual user paths from log files, these paths do not tell us how the path taken relates to the user's goals. In some cases, we might be able to make educated guesses: a path consisting of repeated cycling between "help" and "search" pages is most likely an indication of a task not successfully completed. Other session paths may be more ambiguous: long intervals between page requests might indicate that the user was carefully reading web content, but they can also arise from distractions and other activity not related to the website under consideration. Additional information, such as direct observation through controlled studies or interviews, may be necessary to provide appropriate context (Hochheiser and Shneiderman, 2001).

Complex web applications can be designed to generate and store additional data that may be useful for understanding user activity. Database-driven websites can track views of various pages, along with other actions such as user comments, blog posts, or searches. Web applications that store this additional data are very similar to "instrumented" applications—programs designed to capture detailed records of user interactions and other relevant activities (Section 12.4.1).

The analysis of web log information presents some privacy challenges that must be handled appropriately. IP numbers that identify computers can be used to track web requests to a specific computer, which may be used by a single person. Analyses that track blog posts, comments, purchases, or other activity associated with a user login can also be used to collect a great deal of potentially sensitive information. Before collecting any such data, you should make sure that your websites have privacy policies and other information explaining the data that you are collecting and how you will use it. Additional steps that you might take to protect user privacy include taking careful control of the logs and other repositories of this data, reporting information only in aggregate form (instead of in a form that could identify individuals), and destroying the data when your analysis is complete. As these privacy questions may raise concerns regarding informed consent and appropriate treatment of research participants, some web log analyses might require approval from your institutional review board (see Chapter 15).

Web server logs have been the subject of many research studies over the years. The development of visualization tools to interpret these logs has been a recurring theme since the 1990s and continuing on to more recent work (Pirolli and Pitkow, 1999; Hochheiser and Shneiderman, 2001; Malik and Koh, 2016). Web search logs, particularly from search engines, have proven to be a particularly fruitful data source for studying how users conduct searches and interpret results (White, 2013; White and Hassan, 2014), particularly for specific tasks such as searching for medical information (White and Horvitz, 2009). For more on the use of web search logs to study user behavior, see Chapter 14. As is often the case, web log analysis studies often use multiple complementary datasets to confirm and complement log data. A study of the social network Google+ combined log analysis with surveys and interviews to understand how users choose to share different types of content with different people on the network (Kairam et al., 2012).

12.2.1.3 Empirical studies

Empirical studies of task performance times require some means of capturing timing data. Although hand-held stopwatches can do this job admirably, software that measures and records elapsed times between starting events and task completion is usually more reliable and easier to work with. As described later in this chapter, this approach has been used extensively in special-purpose software built specifically for HCI studies.

For experimental tasks involving selections that can be presented as links on web pages, web servers and their logs present an ideal platform for gathering empirical task performance data. In this model a web server is run on the same machine that is used to perform the experimental tasks. This eliminates any delays associated with requesting materials over a network connection. The selection of a link from a starting page indicates the beginning of the task, with subsequent link selections indicating intermediate steps. Eventually, a link indicating successful task completion is selected. The elapsed interval between the selection of the start and completion links is the task completion time, with access records of intermediate requests indicating steps that were taken to complete the task and the elapsed time for each subtask.

This method is not without drawbacks. Extraction of the relevant information from logs may require manual interpretation or implementation of special-purpose log analysis software. Timestamps in server log files time events by the second, so this approach is not suitable for studies that require finer task-time resolution.

Web browser caches may cause additional problems. These caches store local copies of pages that have been recently accessed. If a user requests a page that is in the cache, the browser returns the copy that has been stored locally, instead of making a new request from the web server. This may cause problems if you are trying to track every user request, as requests for cached pages might not generate web server log entries.[1] You may want to turn off caching facilities before using a particular browser to run an experiment.

One helpful strategy for keeping data clean and clear is to start each session with an empty log file. After the session is complete, the file can be moved to a separate directory containing all of the data for the given subject. This simplifies analysis and prevents any problem associated with disentangling multiple participants from a longer log file.

In practice, these drawbacks usually do not create serious problems. The "Simultaneous vs. Sequential Menus" sidebar describes a study that used server logs to compare alternative web menu designs.

---

[1] Then again, they might. It all depends on the server configuration. However, it is best to be defensive about such matters: assume that they will not and take appropriate steps.

SIMULTANEOUS VS. SEQUENTIAL MENUS

Computer interfaces may be designed to present choices in a hierarchical, sequential manner, even if the items in the menu are not necessarily hierarchical. A restaurant selection tool for a city might allow users to select a neighborhood, followed by a price range, and finally a type of cuisine, but this is not the only possibility order. A simultaneous menu scheme would allow selections to be made in each of these three criteria at any time.

A comparison of the strictly sequential menu approach versus the simultaneous menu approach used a locally hosted web server to present alternative menu structures for the same underlying data set (Hochheiser and Shneiderman, 2000): US Census Bureau economic data for counties in the state

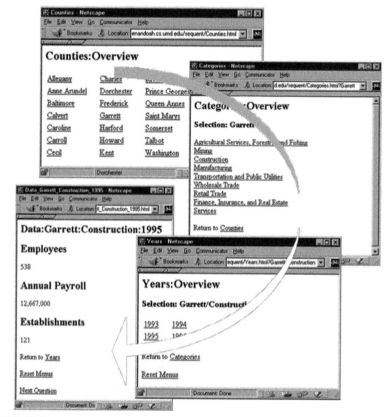

FIGURE 12.4

Sequential menus: users choose first from counties, then from categories, and finally from years, in order to get to a detail page.

From Hochheiser, H., Shneiderman, B., 2000. Performance benefits of simultaneous over sequential menus as task complexity increases. International Journal of Human–Computer Interaction 12 (2), 173–192.

of Maryland. A sequential menu allowed users to select a county, followed by a business category, and then a year (Figure 12.4). Simultaneous menus allowed for selection in any one of these criteria at any time, with detail displays showing data based on values for the three attributes selected (Figure 12.5). Each task in each menu structure began with the selection of a "start" link, and ended with the selection of a link that led to the correct answer.

Pages were presented on web pages, loaded onto a single machine, and accessed directly from that machine to minimize network delays. All menu selections were implemented as standard web links and captured in a standard log files. Logs were analyzed to extract the difference in time between the event signifying the start of the task and the corresponding event indicating task completion, using timestamps from log file entries.

This study found that sequential menus fared well for simple tasks, but simultaneous menus were preferable for more complex tasks (Hochheiser and Shneiderman, 2000).

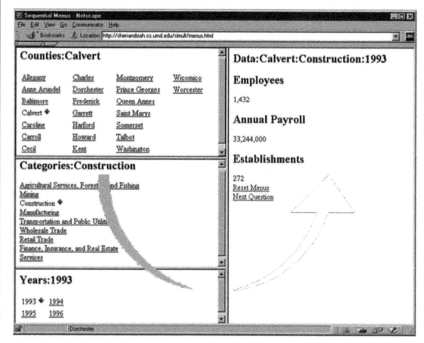

FIGURE 12.5

Simultaneous menus: once a user has selected a value for each of the three variables, details are shown on the right.

From Hochheiser, H., Shneiderman, B., 2000. Performance benefits of simultaneous over sequential menus as task complexity increases. International Journal of Human–Computer Interaction 12 (2), 173–192.

12.2.2 STORED APPLICATION DATA

As we use computers, we leave traces that provide valuable information about how we interact with applications and store and manage information. The tools that we use collect substantial data trails that implicitly and explicitly describe user activities. Examples include (but are not limited to):

- File systems: The files and folders that we create and use present a model of how we organize information. Do we separate work activities from home? Do we have many folders, each containing a small number of files, or only a few folders, each with many files?
- Graphical user interface (GUI) desktops: Some people have dozens of icons on their desktops, while others have only a few. Does this say anything about their organizational preferences?
- Email programs: Many people use an email "inbox" as a todo list, reminding them of tasks that must be completed. Some users make extensive use of filing and filtering capabilities, while others leave all messages in one folder.
- Web bookmarks can also be more or less organized.
- Social networking tools such as Facebook or LinkedIn provide detailed perspectives on how people connect to each other and why.

Each of these domains (and others) can be (and have been) studied to understand usage patterns and to potentially inform new designs. This research is a form of HCI archeology—digging through artifacts to understand complex behavior patterns.

There are attractive aspects to using existing data that is stored by tools that users work with on a daily basis. Interference with the user's work or habits is minimal. Users do not have to participate in experimental sessions to be part of the study and no training is necessary.

The generality of this approach is limited by the tools involved and the data that they collect. The example tools given earlier (file explorers, email clients, web browser bookmark tools, GUI desktops, etc.) all provide tools that can be used to manipulate and maintain organizations of information. As a result, they can be used to identify which structures exist, which categories' items might be placed in, etc. As more transient activities—such as selections of menu items—are generally not recorded, this approach is not well suited for the study of specific implementations. Instead, this approach to data analysis is best suited for the study of long-term patterns of ongoing tasks such as those described earlier.

As the analyses may involve exploration of potentially sensitive matters such as email messages, file system content, and web bookmarks, investigators using these approaches should be sensitive to privacy concerns. In addition to properly informing participants of the privacy risk (see Chapter 15), researchers should exercise discretion when examining potentially sensitive data. Investigations should be limited to only the data that is strictly necessary. An exploration of email communication patterns might reduce privacy risks by examining message headers, instead of message bodies. If this is not sufficient, anonymizing the content to simply indicates that A had an email conversation with B can provide further privacy protection.

A final limitation of this approach involves the challenge of extracting data. Converting these computational artifacts from their native form to a representation suitable for analysis can be challenging. You may need to write special-purpose software to extract data from these tools. In some cases, this may require interpreting (or reverse engineering) nonstandard file formats.

Although log files and implicitly stored data may prove useful for the analysis of many important tasks and activities, these approaches have some very real limitations. These tools are often limited in the granularity of the data that are collected. A web log that provides detailed information about the paths followed by various users in the course of completing some tasks does not contain any information about the users' activities while they were on a given site. Similarly, an email client may provide information regarding the structure of nested mailboxes, but information about intermediate states—such as the names of mailboxes that were created and later deleted—may not be captured.

Numerous studies have looked at email use from a variety of perspectives, including understanding how users "refind" old emails (Whittaker et al., 2011), using content to personalize search results (Teevan et al., 2005), and understanding how batching and work practices influence productivity and stress associated with email (Mark et al., 2016).

12.3 ACTIVITY-LOGGING SOFTWARE

Software tools for logging and recording user activity can provide rich data for usability studies. Tools that capture mouse actions (movements and clicks), keystrokes, and other interactions can help us identify common sequences, understand actions used to complete tasks, and often to gather information about transitions between different tools. Unlike the web server logs described earlier, these data collection tools can be applied to many different applications, providing the possibility of insight into the use of email, office productivity tools, and core operating system features.

These tools generally fall into two main categories: proxies and interaction recording tools. Proxies intercept user actions and record appropriate data points before passing the actions on to the original software (Figure 12.6). Data returned from the application can also be intercepted and modified before being returned to the user. Both user interaction data and application response data can be stored in a log file.

Interaction recording tools generally capture screen video and potentially microphone audio, providing a record of what happened and when. The resulting video and audio streams provide context and details not possible with simple proxies, allowing us to know not just that the user was working with a word processor, for example, but what she was typing and often why. Some usability tools use a combination of recording tools and proxies to capture both raw events and video, providing a rich mix that puts recorded actions in context.

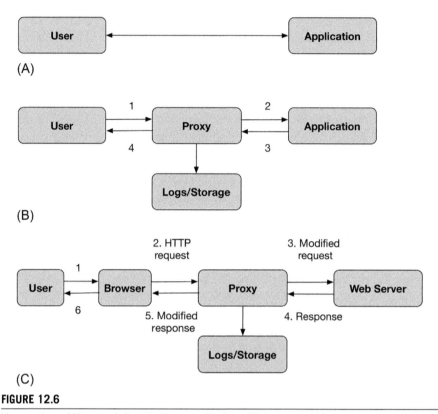

FIGURE 12.6

User actions: (A) passed directly to an application, (B) intercepted by a proxy, and (C) managed through a web proxy.

Proxies and interaction tools lie in between web logs and custom software in terms of flexibility and utility. Although they capture more data and can be more flexible than web logs and existing software (Section 12.2.2), they require more work in configuration. However, the tools described in this section are significantly less challenging than custom software.

12.3.1 WEB PROXIES AND INTERACTION LOGGERS

Web proxies were initially designed as tools for optimizing web browsing: users in an organization would forward all of their web requests to a specified proxy server, which would store copies of requested sites in a local cache. If an outgoing request asked for a page that was in the cache, the proxy server would simply return the contents of the cache entry, thus saving the cost of making a new request to the remote server and processing the response.

Web proxies for HCI research involve a more general approach to this model. In essence, the proxy becomes an intermediary that receives all web requests from a group of users, retrieves the requested materials, and returns them to the users. As all requests from a group of users are handled by the proxy server, it can collect complete session data for all users. This provides a broader picture of user activities than standard server logs, which only contain records for requests from a single site.

Web proxies can intercept (and modify) user requests before sending them on to the server. Proxies can also modify the responses from the remote servers before the resulting web pages are displayed by the client software. Specifically, pages can be modified to include content necessary for the collection of additional interaction data (Atterer et al., 2006).

The first step in using a web proxy—for any purpose, including HCI research—is selecting an appropriate computing environment. As the computational demands of handling web requests for a large group of users can be substantial, you probably want to dedicate resources (computers, disk space, and network bandwidth) specifically for this purpose. If your proxy server is not able to process web requests quickly and efficiently, users will notice delays in their web browsing. This may cause some users to change their browsing habits, while others may simply refuse to use the proxy server. Ideally, the proxy server should not impose any performance penalties on end users.

Many open-source shareware, and commercial proxy servers are available for all major computing platforms. The Squid proxy server (http://www.squid-cache.org) is widely used on Linux and Unix systems. The popular Apache web server (http://httpd.apache.org) can also be configured to act as a proxy server. The choice of platform and software is likely to be dictated by your specific computing needs.

Once installed, proxy software must be appropriately configured and secured. You need to consider who may use your proxy server—you can limit access to users only from certain Internet domains or numbers—which sites you will allow access to, and what sorts of information you might want to store in the logs. As configuration options differ widely from one proxy package to the next, you should carefully study your software documentation and related resources.

Web browsers must be configured to use general-purpose web proxies. The configuration process tells the browser to contact the appropriate proxy host for all web requests. The most straightforward approach is to specify the proxy server settings directly in a web browser configuration dialog (Figure 12.7), but this requires manual configuration of every browser. Alternatives include proxies at the level of the Internet gateway or router—many organizations and companies use proxies or similar intermediate processors to filter web content, for purposes such as blocking adult content. This approach might be possible in some organizations, but would likely require working with your IT support teams.

Once the proxy server and web browser have been configured, users can continue to browse the web as before. Web requests are handled transparently by the proxy server and noted in the log files (Figure 12.8).

The resulting log files contain information on all sites visited by all users of the proxy. This is a major difference between proxy servers and web logs (Section 12.2.1). Whereas web logs maintain access requests for a single site, proxy servers track all

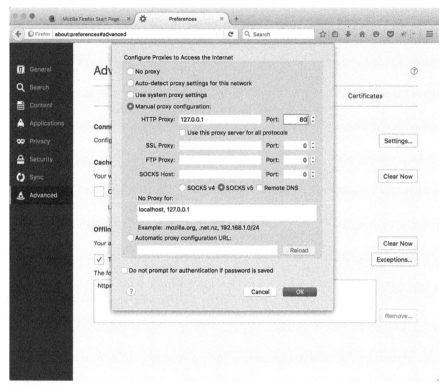

FIGURE 12.7

Firefox proxy configuration dialog for the web browser: the computer at address 127.0.0.1 will act as a proxy server on port 80.

- 127.0.0.1 - - [26/Sep/2007:10:22:19 -0400] "GET http://triton.towson.edu/~hhochhei/ HTTP/1.1" 304 -
- 127.0.0.1 - - [26/Sep/2007:10:22:19 -0400] "GET http://triton.towson.edu/~hhochhei/hhstyle.css HTTP/1.1" 304 -
- 127.0.0.1 - - [26/Sep/2007:10:22:19 -0400] "GET http://triton.towson.edu/~hhochhei/hh.jpg HTTP/1.1" 304 -
- 127.0.0.1 - - [26/Sep/2007:10:22:19 -0400] "GET http://triton.towson.edu/~hhochhei/towson-header.gif HTTP/1.1" 304 -
- 127.0.0.1 - - [26/Sep/2007:10:22:19 -0400] "GET http://triton.towson.edu/~hhochhei/arrow.gif HTTP/1.1" 304 –

FIGURE 12.8

Log entries from a proxy server. Note that each request contains a full URL for a web resource, as opposed to a local path, as in Figure 12.2.

requests from all users—capturing information on the use of many web sites not controlled by the team managing the proxy and collecting the data. Since proxy access is configured through the browsers or routers, users might not even be aware that the proxy use—or the data collection—is happening.

Although this information can be used to provide a rich picture of user browsing habits over time, care and discretion should be used when studying this data. As users may forget that they are using a proxy that logs their requests, they might visit sites that are potentially embarrassing or inappropriate. Records of this sort should be treated carefully, including detailed and clear explanations in any consent forms. Possible approaches for avoiding embarrassment include anonymization of users or websites.

Logging of web requests is only the tip of the proxy iceberg. Several researchers have made extensive—and creative—use of web proxies to collect web usage data. WebQuilt (Hong et al., 2001) was a proxy server specifically designed to aid in the collection of usability data. WebQuilt combines logging facilities with an engine for transforming log file entries into inferred user actions, a tool for aggregating log files into graph structures, and visualization components for the display of graphs displaying user paths through a site.

Unlike general-purpose web proxies, WebQuilt was designed to be used to collect data on a site-specific basis. To run a usability test for a given website, the experimenter asked users to visit a URL specifically designed to support proxy-based access to the site under investigation. The WebQuilt proxy handled all requests for the site, including the modification of page content to route subsequent requests for that site through the proxy. As a result, WebQuilt did not require any configuration of the browser software.

Proxy servers can be quite powerful, but they present numerous technical challenges. Installing, configuring, and managing a proxy server can be difficult. Your proxy server must have the processing power and network bandwidth for effective operation. If your study involves only a small set of users for a short time frame, a single machine might be sufficient. Large-scale studies involving multiple users for extended time periods might need a more robust solution, involving many machines and more bandwidth. Cutting corners on proxy capabilities might jeopardize your study: if users find that the proxy is too slow for effective web use, they might temporarily or permanently stop using the proxy, effectively removing their data from your study.

Instrumentation software can often provide an attractive alternative to proxies. MouseTracks (Arroyo et al., 2006), UsaProxy (Atterer et al., 2006), and other similar systems (Kiciman and Livshits, 2010; Carta et al., 2011a,b; Huang et al., 2011, 2012) modified pages with JavaScript code that recorded low-level interaction data including mouse movements. This data was sent to the server for logging and visualization. Similar approaches have also been used to track touch interactions on mobile devices (Buschek et al., 2015). Although somewhat less flexible than JavaScript, which can be delivered solely from the server hosting relevant web pages, browser plugins can also be used to record detailed user interactions (Guo and Agichtein, 2009).

Selection of appropriate tools for tracking web interactions will likely require tradeoffs between expressive power and complexity. Proxies are relatively easy to configure. An organizational proxy can transparently collect and log access information for multiple web sites, without requiring any changes to those sites. Capture of more fine-grained data, through JavaScript, plugins, or any of the research idea tools discussed earlier, will require additional programming and configuration, possibly including changes to the sites under question. Although potentially labor-intensive, these changes may provide access to otherwise unavailable data regarding user interactions with your sites.

12.3.2 KEYSTROKE AND ACTIVITY LOGGERS

Modern GUI windowing systems that support multitasking and concurrent use of multiple related tools present intriguing possibilities for HCI research. How often do users change applications? How many tasks do people work on at any given time? How long do users generally work within any given window before switching to another? What fraction of time is spent on overhead such as resizing windows, moving windows, or adjusting system controls? Answering these and other related questions requires data collected at the level of the operating environment.

Activity-logging software runs invisibly in the background, recording mouse movements, keyboard input, and windowing systems' interactions including window movement, resizing, opening, and closing. These tools act as proxies for user interaction events, recording events as they happen, before they are passed along to applications or the operating environment. Keyloggers are a special subclass of activity-logging software, focusing only on keyboard input. Activity-logging software has achieved a fair amount of notoriety in recent years, as these tools have been used as "spyware," to surreptitiously record user interactions in the hopes of stealing passwords, finding evidence of criminal behavior, or collecting evidence of spousal infidelity.

Commercial activity-logging products are often marketed as being tools for employers and parents to track inappropriate computer use by employees and children, respectively. Although some of these tools might be appropriate for data collection for research purposes, some antispyware programs may defeat or remove activity loggers. You may want to test the logging software on relevant computers and disable antispyware measures before trying to use these tools to collect data.

The disruption and recovery tracker (DART) (Iqbal and Horvitz, 2007) logged window positions and sizes, window actions, user activities, and alerts from various systems. DART's design presents an example of the responsible use of these tools for conducting legitimate research while remaining sensitive to privacy concerns. Keyboard logging was limited to a subset of possible choices, including menu shortcuts and some punctuation, and only a portion of each window title was collected. The resulting data therefore did not include file names, email addresses or subject lines, or web page titles. The analysis of more than 2200 hours of activity data collected from the main computers of 27 people over a two-week period generated numerous insights into time lost due to email or instant-messaging alerts, and how users respond to and recover from those interruptions (Iqbal and Horvitz, 2007). Logging studies can also be used to collect data on effective use of devices, as in a study that captured mouse movements of adults with disabilities as they completed everyday computer tasks, in the hopes of building tools that might adapt to better suit the needs of these users (Hurst et al., 2013).

Mobile devices present additional possibilities for activity tracking, providing not only the opportunity to record which keys and controls were activated and when, but also detailed information regarding users' geographic location. HCI researchers have used logs of user location to predict short-term motion of individuals in crowds in a city environment (Fan et al., 2015), to infer movement characteristics associated with depression (Canzian and Musolesi, 2015), and undoubtedly for countless other interesting questions. See Chapter 14 for further discussion of the possible uses of mobile and ubiquitous computing for tracking user activity.

12.3.3 INTERACTION RECORDING TOOLS

Think-aloud studies and contextual inquiries involving direct observation and recording of user activities can be invaluable means of identifying and understanding usability problems, but they can also be a challenge to interpret. Recording what goes on as a user executes a series of actions to complete a complex task can be time consuming and error-prone, and subsequent discussions of the activity details and motivating context can be hard to capture. Similarly, although studies of log files can indicate what happened and when, the why of the observed interactions is often harder to gauge.

Screen capture and audio recording tools can provide invaluable assistance in these situations. Full-screen video with mouse pointers and accompanying audio can provide rich detail suitable for detailed analysis down to the mouse click. Audio can capture user comments vital for interpreting outcomes of think-aloud studies or other usability inquiries. Screen capture can also be very useful for exploring the use of computational tools as work as being conducted, as unobtrusive recording might capture interactions with greater realism than possible in lab settings. This approach has been used to study contexts including work in law offices (Cangiano and Hollan, 2009) and the use of electronic medical records during patient visits with physicians (see the "LAB-IN-A-BOX" sidebar, Chapter 13).

Recording tools generally come in one of two flavors. Commodity tools adopted for research provide a simple and cost-effective, yet limited solution. Screen recorders generally used to capture demonstrations will capture some or all of the screen, along with audio, providing a video in a standard format such as MP4. Some real-time web conferencing services include similar recording facilities, providing an excellent option for studies involving users in remote locations.

For more functionality at a likely higher cost, many researchers choose to use dedicated usability study software packages. These tools augment basic screen and audio capture with linked and integrated loggers for mouse and keyboard action, often with additional data streams including webcam images of the users at work.

Although potentially expensive and requiring some effort in configuration and management, tools in this class—led by TechSmith's Morae software—have been widely adopted by HCI researchers.

12.4 CUSTOM SOFTWARE

Modern computing applications are complex: word processors, spreadsheets, email programs, and web browsers may have dozens, if not hundreds of toolbar buttons and menu items. Which of these items are used and which are not? How would modifications to the interface change usage patterns for various functions? These questions are of interest both to researchers, who might be interested in understanding the efficacy of various strategies for grouping and rearranging controls for complex operations, and for product developers interested in comparing the effectiveness of proposed interface changes.

There are several approaches to collecting detailed data on the usage of complex interfaces. User observations, interviews, video recordings, and other strategies described elsewhere in this book can and have been used effectively for these purposes. However, these approaches are all laborious and expensive, requiring many hours spent observing users, asking questions, or coding events on videotape.

In many cases, a more attractive alternative is to have the software collect data on its own usage. A program designed for this sort of data collection would store every important user action—menu choices, toolbar button selections, key presses, and more, in a log file or database. Storage of these events in chronological order, including a timestamp, would provide a complete history of which options were selected and when. Analysis of this data might help developers understand which commands are used frequently, rarely, or usually in close combination with other commands (such as "cut" followed by "paste").

12.4.1 INSTRUMENTED SOFTWARE

The practice of adding measurement and recording tools to software is known as *instrumenting*. Constructing instrumented software may require a fair amount of technical expertise, as code for handling user interactions must be substantially modified. For many commercial or "closed source" software products, this level of access to the source code may be available only to the vendor or the developer of the product. However, macro and extension facilities in some products have been successfully used to write instrumentation code for interface evaluation purposes. A third possibility involves open-source software. Researchers interested in studying the usage of the interfaces of open-source projects might produce their own, instrumented versions of popular programs for use in research data collection. Detailed versions of each of these approaches are described in the Instrumented Software for HCI Data Collection sidebar.

INSTRUMENTED SOFTWARE FOR HCI DATA COLLECTION

Instrumented software has been used to collect usage data in support of widely used commercial products, research prototypes, and open-source tools. These examples are representative of some of the possibilities.

Microsoft Office 2003

Microsoft's Customer Experience Improvement Program let users opt in to having usage data collected anonymously. Data collected includes menu selections, keyboard shortcuts, and artifacts of user customization, including the number of mail folders and any modifications or customizations. This broad-ranging data collection was open ended, rather than hypothesis driven: "In short, we collect anything we think might be interesting and useful as long as it doesn't compromise a user's privacy" (Harris, 2005).

The large data set (over 13 billion user sessions) provided substantial insight that informed the redesign of the Office interface for the Office 2007 release (Harris, 2005). Even though the Paste command—the most popular, with more than 11% of all command usage in Word—was frequently accessed via shortcuts, the Paste button was the most frequently clicked button on the toolbar. This led Microsoft's UI team to place the Paste button prominently in the revised interface for Word (Harris, 2006).

This study also confirmed that Word users frequently use a small subset of features while rarely using other features (McGrenere and Moore, 2000). The top five commands in Word accounted for more than 32% of all command usage, with frequencies declining quickly after the top 10 (Harris, 2006).

Personalized Versions of Application Interfaces

Noting the potential difficulties associated with complex interfaces for desktop applications, McGrenere et al. set out to investigate the possible utility of a simplified user interface containing only items selected by the user. Using the scripting tools in Microsoft Word 2000, they built an extension to Word that would allow users to work with this simplified interface. Tools for adding items to their personalized interface were included, along with a control that could be used to switch between the simplified interface and the full interface as desired. In a field study with 20 users, this software was installed along with a logging tool for capturing usage and a program that would upload usage logs to an Internet server. Usage data collected included histograms of function usage frequency. This data indicated that only a small number of commands were used very frequently and that the users added almost all of those commands to their personalized interfaces. A series of questionnaires indicated that users preferred the personalized interfaces in terms of navigation and ease of learning (McGrenere et al., 2002).

(Continued)

INSTRUMENTED SOFTWARE FOR HCI DATA COLLECTION—CONT'D

Instrumenting Open-Source Software

As few commercial products offer customization tools comparable to those found in Microsoft Office, instrumentation of open-source software has proven to be a fruitful alternative. One study of web navigation patterns used an instrumented version of the Firefox web browser to collect data on the use of browser features such as the "back" button, history views, and bookmarks. This relatively small study (25 users) combined instrumented software with web proxies in order to identify new patterns in web browser feature usage and browsing behavior, some of which may have been related to the rise in tabbed browsing and other relatively new browser features (Obendorf et al., 2007).

Ingimp provides an example of broader use of instrumented open-source software for HCI data collection. Short for "instrumented GIMP," ingimp was an instrumented version of the Gnu Image Manipulation Program, a powerful open-source tool for photo editing and image processing. Created by a group from the University of Waterloo, ingimp was widely publicized in the hope of motivating users to participate in the study.

Ingimp collected a variety of data, including usage timing, the number of windows and layers open at a time, command usage, and task-switching details. Instrumenting GIMP to collect this data required modifying the open-source program to record appropriate events and transmit them to a central server. Interaction data is transmitted at the end of each session. If the software crashes before a log is transmitted, the incomplete log is detected and sent to the server when the program is next used.

The ingimp instrumentation approach involved several privacy protection measures. Although mouse events and key press events are recorded, specific details—which key was pressed or where the mouse was moved—are not recorded. A dialog box on startup provides users with the option of disabling event logging for the current session. As GIMP is an open-source project, the developers of ingimp made all the source code available. Knowledgeable users can investigate "patches"—descriptions of the differences between the original GIMP and ingimp. These differences reveal where the logging code has been added and what details it logs. Although few (if any) users are likely to take the trouble to do this, this does represent a thorough attempt at full disclosure.

Ingimp's developers used this information to improve the usability of GIMP and other free or open-source software tools (Terry et al., 2008).

Whichever approach you select for implementing data collection instruments, you should think carefully about the data that you are collecting. Although you may be tempted to collect as much data as possible, doing so may not be beneficial. Instrumenting every possible interaction in a complex application may require a great deal of effort, and as the amount of data collected may increase with the extent and granularity of the instrumentation, you might consider exactly what you need to capture. In some cases, individual mouse movements and key strokes might be needed, while other studies might need only higher-level user actions, such as selection of the "paste" operation. Careful attention to the relationship between your experimental hypotheses—what do you hope to learn?—and the data collected may help increase your chances of success. Another successful strategy involves associating each recorded action with one or more categories, allowing ease of processing and filtering by criteria appropriate to an analysis. This approach might allow comparison of keyboard and mouse-movement records to higher-level task indicators.

12.4.2 RESEARCH SOFTWARE

Another class of custom software tools for automatic data collection involves software that is explicitly created for the sole purpose of running an experiment. These tools generally present users with a series of tasks to be completed and record data regarding task completion time, errors, and whatever other data may be necessary. The Fitts' Law, Children, and Mouse Control sidebar discusses an example of a custom software package developed for a study of how well young children use computer mice. Researchers interested in studying how well young children use a mouse built a tool that tracked task completion time as well as the trajectory of mouse movements in tasks that involved moving between two targets. This study found that younger children were much less accurate mouse users than adults (Hourcade et al., 2004).

FITTS' LAW, CHILDREN, AND MOUSE CONTROL

Full-size computer keyboards, keypads on phone and small devices, mice, trackballs, jog wheels, and joysticks are familiar controls for computers and other electronic devices, but familiarity does not necessarily imply understanding. How do we use these tools? How efficient are we? What sort of mistakes do we make? What are the factors that determine task completion time, accuracy, and error rate? Although researchers—in cognitive psychology and more recently in HCI—have been asking these and similar questions for more than 50 years, detailed study of the human use of these devices can still lead us to valuable insights.

Target selection is an important task in this area. Given multiple targets that a user might want to select—keys on a keyboard or buttons on a graphical user interface—what determines how quickly and accurately a user can move from one to another? Studies of target selection performance guide the size and selection of graphical icons, placement of buttons on a cell-phone keypad, and many other aspects of interface design.

(Continued)

FITTS' LAW, CHILDREN, AND MOUSE CONTROL—CONT'D

Paul M. Fitts conducted pioneering experiments in this area in the 1950s, leading to the development of Fitts' law, a frequently cited result in HCI research.[2] Originally intended as investigations of the theoretical limits of human performance in performing tasks of differing amplitudes of movement, Fitts' experiments involved asking participants to move between two targets separated by a distance. Fitts found that the information content of the task was determined by the distance between the targets and the inverse of the width of the targets (Fitts, 1954). This result was later generalized to expressive movement time as being a function of the logarithm of the ratio of the movement amplitude to the target width (MacKenzie, 1992).

Fitts' law tells us that as the distance between targets increases, or the size of the targets decreases, the time required to move between them increases. This has a certain intuitive appeal: it is harder to reach small targets than it is to reach larger targets, just as we can cover short distances more quickly than we can cover long distances. As much of our interaction with computers involves target selection, Fitts' law can help us understand the impact of design decisions regarding the placement and sizing of icons on a screen or keys on a keyboard.

Fitts' law is important enough to have spawned follow-on works, with researchers examining a wide variety of variations on the original task (MacKenzie, 1992; MacKenzie and Buxton, 1992). Extensions and novel applications of have confirmed the relevance of Fitts' law to the use of mobile devices while walking (Lin et al., 2007); developed models for "two-thumb" text entry on small keyboards (Clarkson et al., 2007); proposed extensions for nonrectangular targets (Grossman et al., 2007); explored implications for novel input modalities including multitouch devices (Nguyen et al., 2014) and flexible displays (Burstyn et al., 2016); added an extra dimension for virtual reality and 3D displays (Lubos et al., 2014; Teather and Stuerzlinger, 2014; Janzen et al., 2016); and even extended Fitts' law to foot input for under-desk devices (Velloso et al., 2015).

Juan-Pablo Hourcade and his colleagues at the University of Maryland faced this problem in the course of their work with young children. Faced with 5-year-old children who had difficulty clicking on computer icons, they set out to understand how preschool children differed from young adults in their ability to complete target-selection tasks (Hourcade et al., 2004). Although several researchers had conducted Fitts' law research with young children, none had specifically addressed the question of whether performance differences justified the effort required to build interfaces specifically for this class of young users.

---

[2] Authors of books on HCI research are contractually obligated to refer to Fitts' law at least once.

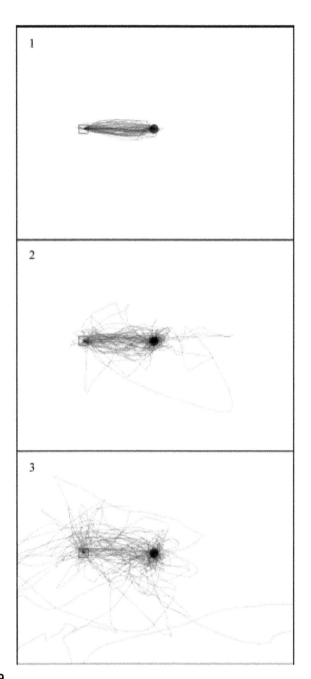

FIGURE 12.9

Aggregate mouse controls for all users show striking differences in the paths covered by different groups: (1) adults, (2) 5-year olds, and (3) 4-year olds (Hourcade et al., 2004).

From Hourcade, J.P., Bederson, B.B., Druin, A., Guimbretière, F., 2004. Differences in pointing task performance between preschool children and adults using mice. ACM Transactions on Computer-Human Interaction 11 (4), 357–386.

(Continued)

FITTS' LAW, CHILDREN, AND MOUSE CONTROL—CONT'D

Their study involved 13 4-year-old children, 13 5-year-old children, and 13 adults (between 19 and 22 years old). Participants were asked to move the mouse from a home area to a target to the right. Targets had three diameters—16, 32, or 64 pixels—with three distances between start and target—128, 256, or 512 pixels. Participants completed 45 tasks in roughly 15 minutes—about the limit of the attention span of 4- to 5-year-old children. Data collected measured accuracy (did they press the button inside the target), time, and measures of reentry (leaving and reentering the target). Software developed for conducting the experiments also collected mouse motion data sufficient for reconstructing mouse movement paths.

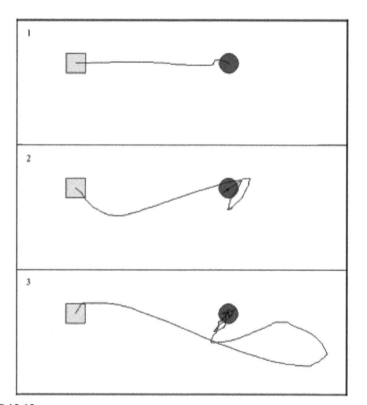

FIGURE 12.10

Typical paths illustrate greater reentry rates for children: (1) adult, (2) 5-year-old, and (3) 4-year-old (Hourcade et al., 2004).

From Hourcade, J.P., Bederson, B.B., Druin, A., Guimbretière, F., 2004. Differences in pointing task performance between preschool children and adults using mice. ACM Transactions on Computer-Human Interaction 11 (4), 357–386.

> Comparison of the data from children and adults generated several important insights. Children were slower and less accurate than adults. Children also tended to hover over targets, reentering much more frequently than adults. Hourcade and colleagues found that while Fitts' law does apply to children, the model is more accurate for adults.
>
> Mouse motion paths (or "trails") provide striking illustrations of the differences between children and adults. While adults move accurately and quickly between targets, 5-year-old children went far afield, often overshooting targets. Four-year-old children were even worse, moving all over the screen (Figure 12.9). Children were also much more likely to repeatedly enter, leave, and reenter targets (Figure 12.10).

Based on these differences in performance profiles, Hourcade et al. suggested several possible approaches to designing interfaces for young children. Possible solutions include larger icons, smaller mice, expanding targets, slower or accelerated mouse movement, and constrained motion between selections (using directional arrows and a selection button) (Hourcade et al., 2004).

12.5 HYBRID DATA COLLECTION METHODS

If one source of HCI data is good, then two must be better. Multiple channels of data collection can be combined to overcome the shortcomings of any one approach. Logging user interactions with a word processor may be a good start toward understanding how various controls are used, but log files provide little, if any, contextual information that might prove invaluable for interpretation and analysis. Video recordings or direct observation of users at work can help researchers understand users' goals, frustrations, state of mind, and satisfaction (or lack thereof) with the system being used. Taken together, these data sources provide a much more detailed and complete picture of user activity than either would on its own.

Combining outputs from log files and video sessions may require specialized software support. Ideally, we might want to identify an event in a log file and jump right to the video recording that displays what the user was doing at that moment. HCI researchers have developed tools that provide this synchronized access (Hammontree et al., 1992; Crabtree et al., 2006; Fouse et al., 2011). These features may also be available in professional tools for usability studies, such as the interaction recording tools discussed in Section 12.3.3.

Similar approaches can be used for evaluation of web-based systems. Web log files and web proxies are limited in their ability to capture details of user interactions—and possibly in their ability to identify distinct users. However, they are relatively easy to configure and deploy. An instrumented web browser can provide vastly greater detail regarding specific user events, but it requires installation of unfamiliar software on end-user computers, potentially limiting the number of participants. One way to resolve this dilemma is to use both approaches in the same study. Specifically, data would be collected through both proxies and instrumented browsers (Obendorf et al., 2007). Although this approach might be more expensive and time consuming than either approach used independently, the resulting data may be of higher quality.

Another form of hybrid might combine automated data capture and analysis with observation or other qualitative approaches (Chapter 11). As mentioned, log files from web activities or instrumented software are limited in their ability to describe the context of work. It is often difficult to go from the fine-grained detail of individual actions in a log file to a broader understanding of a user's goals and motivations. If we combine log data with active observation by a human researcher, we stand a better chance of understanding not just what the user was doing, but why she was doing it. The observer might sit behind the subject, watching her activities and making notes in real time, creating a log of observations that can be synchronized with the events in the server log. Alternatively, video recordings allow for annotation and observation at some later time. Log analysis studies involving remote users or those not involved in a formal study (see the discussion of "A/B" testing in Chapter 14) might be accompanied by an optional survey at the end of a session, asking users to complete questions relating to their satisfaction with the system (see Chapter 5 for more discussion of surveys). In any case, appropriate software can be used to view individual user events alongside observer annotations and content, thus providing a more detailed and informative picture than either source would give on its own. Combinations of multiple log approaches with observer annotations can provide even greater detail.

12.6 DATA MANAGEMENT AND ANALYSIS
12.6.1 HANDLING STORED DATA

Whenever you write or modify software to track user activities, you need to decide how to manage the data. Two approaches are commonly used: log files and databases. Log files are plain text files that indicate what happened, when it happened, and other details—such as the user ID—that might help when interpreting data. Log files are easy to write, but may require additional tools for interpretation. The comments from Section 12.2 are generally applicable to any application logs, with one important exception. As commonly available software tools that parse and interpret standard web log formats may not be immediately applicable to logs that you might develop for your software, you may need to dig in and develop custom tools for parsing these log files.

Databases can be very useful for storing user activity information. Carefully designed relational databases can be used to store each action of interest in one or more database tables, along with all other relevant information. Powerful query languages, such as SQL, can then be used to develop flexible queries and reports for interpretation of the data. This approach may be most useful when working with an application that already connects to a relational database. When your tool uses a relational database to store application data, additional user activity information can often be added without much effort. This is often the case for database-driven web applications. If, however, your tool does not interact with a database, developing tools to parse log files might be easier than adding a database to the application.

12.6.2 ANALYZING LOG FILES

Having collected some log files, you will want to do something with them. Although log files for web servers, proxies, keystroke trackers, and custom-instrumented software might all have different formats and contents, the general approach toward instrumentation is roughly the same: in each case, you have one line in the file for each event of interest. Each line is likely to have some text indicating the time and date of the event (otherwise known as the timestamp), a description of what happened (such as the URL that was requested), and other related details.

How you proceed in your analysis is largely determined by your goals. If you are simply interested in trying to count certain events—for example, how many people pressed the Print button—you might be able to read through the file, classifying each event into one or more counters of various types. A single event in a log file might be classified according to the page that was requested, the day of the week, the time of day, and the type of web browser that made the request.

Reading through the file to extract the various pieces of information known about each event is an example of a common computing practice known as *parsing*. Often written in scripting languages, such as Perl and Python, log-file-parsing programs read one line at a time, breaking the entry for each event into constituent pieces and then updating data structures that keep counts and statistics of different types of event, as needed. Once the parser has read all of the relevant events and tallied up the numbers, results can be displayed graphically or in tabular form.

Countless programs for parsing and analyzing web log data have been developed since the web first came onto the scene in the 1990s. These tools range from freely available, open-source (but still highly functional) offerings to high-end commercial products, providing a variety of ways to slice-and-dice data. Many of these tools work on data from proxy servers as well.

For publicly available websites, many operators rely on the detailed querying and visualization tools provided by Google Analytics. Using a small bit of code inserted to every page on the site, Google Analytics collects data and sends it to Google, where it is stored for analysis via Google's tools. Google Analytics is a popular and powerful tool for understanding website usage patterns, but as it is not intended for supporting usability studies, you might want to try a test run before using it for a full study. Furthermore, as Analytics only works on public sites, it is not appropriate for studies using locally hosted material.

Data from nonweb applications might prove a bit more challenging to analyze. Keystroke loggers and activity loggers may come with their own log-parsing and analysis packages, but you are likely to be on your own if you write software instrumentation to collect data. One approach in this case might be to design your log files to match the formats used by web servers. This mimicry would make your data amenable to analysis by web-log analysis tools. Another possibility is to create parsing and analysis software: if you can instrument your user interface to collect interaction information, you will probably find this to be a reasonably manageable task.

More sophisticated questions might require fancier footwork. One common goal is to study the sequence of events. Do users click Print before Save more frequently than they click Save before Print? Similar challenges are found when trying to infer the structure of interaction from web logs, leading to a variety of strategies that have been used to pick out user "sessions" (Heer and Chi, 2002).

Another approach might be to visualize log files. Highly interactive visualizations might show each event in a log file as a point on the screen, while providing tools for filtering and displaying data based on different criteria. As with other approaches for analyzing log files, visualization has been most widely used for web logs. WebQuilt (Hong et al., 2001) displays pages and links between them as nodes and links in a graph. Links are drawn as arrows, with thicker arrows indicating more heavily used links and shading indicating the amount of time spent on a page before selection of a link (Figure 12.11A). Users can zoom into a node to directly examine the page in question (Figure 12.11B).

Other visualizations include the use of two-dimensional "starfield" displays for viewing individual requests by date, time, and other attributes (Hochheiser and Shneiderman, 2001) and finer-grained visualizations of mouse events on individual pages (Arroyo et al., 2006; Atterer et al., 2006).

As with any other analysis, understanding your goals and planning your data acquisition and analysis appropriately is key to effective use of these detailed logs. Ben-Naim et al. describe the use of log analysis for an adaptive learning program, including an explicit list of the questions involved and a description of the approaches used to answer those questions (Ben-Naim et al., 2008). Appropriate storage of log data can also facilitate analysis, with some researchers using business-oriented online analytical processing (OLAP) tools to drill down into relevant details (Mavrikis et al., 2015).

Data mining and machine learning techniques can be well suited for the extracting patterns from log files. Relatively simple techniques such as association rules (Agrawal et al., 1993) might be used to determine patterns of frequently cooccurring accesses—for example, "sitemap" and "search" page accesses might frequently be associated with clicks on a "contact us" page. Data mining approaches have been used to inform site design and usage characterization from a variety of perspectives, including personalization of content (Srivastava et al., 2000; Eirinaki and Vazirgiannis, 2003) with results familiar to any web users who have seen web pages including advertisements matching search terms that they have recently used. Clustering techniques might also be used to develop models useful for clustering users into groups based on their usage patterns or predicting desirable outcomes such as purchases. Although fascinating, and also relevant to the processing of physiological data (Chapter 13) and ubiquitous computing data (Chapter 14), data mining is largely beyond the scope of this book—for more information, see one of the many online courses or textbooks on machine learning and data mining.

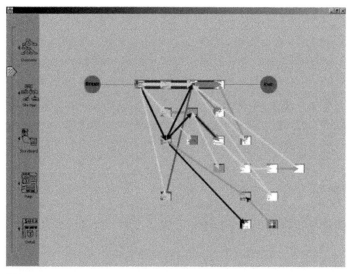

(A)

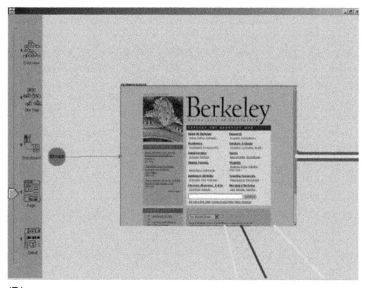

(B)

FIGURE 12.11

WebQuilt visualizations of log file data: (A) visualization of paths between two endpoints and (B) a page in context (Hong et al., 2001).

From Hong, J.I., Heer, J., Waterson, S., Landay, J.A., 2001. WebQuilt: a proxy-based approach to remote web usability testing. ACM Transactions on Information Systems 19 (3), 263–285. Copyright ACM.

12.7 AUTOMATED INTERFACE EVALUATION

If using computers to collect data for HCI research is good, why not go further? Perhaps we can build software that automatically tests and evaluates user interfaces, generating data on usability issues or potential task performance times.

Automated inspection methods involve the analysis of aspects of user interfaces including layout, content, and language, in order to determine how well they conform to design guidelines (Ivory and Hearst, 2001). Generally, these tools provide reports indicating the extent to which an interface complies (or fails to comply) with guidelines. These reports can help designers understand where users might run into problems, and how an interface might be improved. The evaluations provided by these tools are generally based on empirical evidence, accepted design practices, and other accumulated experience. Automated inspection tools have been widely used in assessing the accessibility of websites. These tools examine web pages in search of images without explanatory text (<alt> tags), embedded scripts that might not be interpretable by screen readers, lack of navigation support, and other problems that may cause difficulties for users with disabilities. Dozens of web accessibility evaluation tools—ranging from free websites to expensive commercial software—have been developed. See Chapter 10 for more information.

Although these tools may provide some useful advice, the utility of any particular tool may be limited by the validity and scope of the underlying guidelines: analyses that are based on broad, well-supported guidelines are likely to be more appropriate than those that examine a narrower range of concerns. The use of multiple inspection methods to test interfaces from varying perspectives might be helpful. Ideally, these tools should be seen as companions to—not replacements for—traditional design reviews and user testing.

A variety of approaches to automated testing have been explored. Systems that focus on the use of modeling or simulation to predict task performance times and other quantitative and qualitative characteristics of interface usage are appealing, but they may be difficult to construct and limited in utility (Ivory and Hearst, 2001). Other efforts the use of modeling techniques that carry through the design and development phase into support for automated testing (Humayoun et al., 2012; Wollner et al., 2015).

12.8 CHALLENGES OF COMPUTERIZED DATA COLLECTION

Automated software for HCI data collection has many advantages. The use of software to record user interaction events along with timestamps can ease data collection for structured experiments, simplifying work that previously would have been done with a stopwatch and paper records. Logs from web servers and other activity tracking tools document interaction events in unstructured, "natural" activities with far less difficulty than earlier techniques of observing or videotaping users.

However, effective use of these tools requires addressing several important challenges. As with any method for data collection, automated methods work best if their use is carefully considered in the context of the specific situation that is being studied and the research questions that are being asked. Before collecting data—or designing a system to collect data—you should ask yourself what you hope to learn from your research and how the data that you collect will help you answer those questions. Collecting too much data, too little data, or the wrong data will not be particularly helpful.

Computer use can be considered over a wide range of time scales, with vastly different interpretations. At one end of the spectrum, individual keyboard and mouse interactions can take place as frequently as 10 times per second. At the other extreme, repeated uses of information resources and tools in the context of ongoing projects may occur over the course of years (Hilbert and Redmiles, 2000). Successful experiments must be designed to collect data that is appropriate for the questions being asked. If you want to understand usage patterns that occur over months and years, you probably do not want to collect every mouse event and key click; the volume of data will be simply overwhelming. Similarly, understanding dynamics of menu choices with specific applications requires more detailed information than simply which applications were used and when.

The amount of data collected is generally referred to as the granularity or resolution of the data. Fine-grained, high-resolution data involves every possible user interaction event; coarse-grained, low-resolution data contains fewer events, perhaps involving specific menu items, selection of specific buttons, or interaction with specific dialog boxes.

The specificity of the questions that you are asking may help determine the granularity of data that you need to collect. Many experiments involve structured questions regarding closed tasks on specific interfaces: which version of a web-based menu layout is better? To support these studies, automated data collection tools must collect data indicating which links are clicked, and when (see the Simultaneous vs Sequential Menus sidebar for an example). Web server logs are very well suited for such studies.

Open-ended studies aimed at understanding patterns of user interactions may pose greater challenges. To study how someone works with a word processor, we may need to determine which functions are used and when. Activity loggers that track individual mouse movements and key presses may help us understand some user actions, but they do not record structured, higher-order details that may be necessary to help understand how these individual actions come together to involve the completion of meaningful tasks. Put another way, if we want to understand sequences of important operations in word-processing tasks, we do not necessarily want a list of keystrokes and mouse clicks. Instead, we would like to know that the user formatted text, inserted a table, and then viewed a print preview. Still higher-level concepts are even harder to track: how do we know when a user has completed a task?

Researchers have tried a variety of approaches for inferring higher-level tasks from low-level interaction events. Generally, these approaches involve combining domain knowledge of both the software being studied and user behavior to identify patterns that would be representative of defined tasks (Hammontree et al., 1992; Ivory and Hearst, 2001). These inferential efforts face many challenges. For example, applications that provide multiple methods for accessing given functionality (such as both a menu choice and a toolbar button for Print) may generate log files that contain all of these methods. However, log entry analysis approaches may not recognize these multiple paths as leading to a common goal. Establishing appropriate contextual information may also be difficult: log file entries that indicate a button was pressed are less informative than those that indicate which button was pressed (Hilbert and Redmiles, 2000).

Analysis challenges are particularly pronounced in the analysis of web server logs, which may contain interleaved requests from dozens of different users. Statistical analyses and visualization tools have been used to try to identify individual user sessions from log files (Pirolli and Pitkow, 1999; Hochheiser and Shneiderman, 2001; Heer and Chi, 2002), but these tools are imperfect at best. If a web browser coming from a given Internet address accesses a page on your site and then accesses a second page 10 minutes later, does that count as one session or two? Your log file cannot tell you if the user was reading the page between those two requests or if she was talking on the telephone. Those requests may not have come from the same person—for all you know, it is a shared computer in a library or classroom that is used by dozens of individuals on any given day.

Custom-built or instrumented software may alleviate some data-granularity problems by providing you with complete control over the data that is collected, at the expense of the time and effort required to develop the data collection tools. If you are willing and able to commit the resources necessary for software customization, you can configure the software to capture all of the data that you think might be interesting: nothing more, nothing less.

Unfortunately, matters are rarely so clean-cut. There may be a vast difference between what you think you need before you start large-scale data collection and what you may wish you had collected once you begin analyzing the data. The expense of running experiments—particularly those that involve substantial effort in participant recruitment—creates a tendency toward collecting as much data as possible. "It's easy to collect this information," the thinking goes, "so we may as well. After all, storage is inexpensive, and these details may prove useful later on."

Although there is a certain logic to the defensive approach of collecting as much data as possible, there are some limits to this approach. As anyone who has sifted through megabytes of event logs can tell you, collecting lots of data may simply leave you with lots of uninformative data junk to sift through. Even with software tools, the identification of meaningful patterns (as opposed to random coincidences) can be difficult. Lower resolution data may be somewhat easier to analyze.

If your data collection tools can clearly distinguish between coarse-grained and fine-grained events, you might be able to have your cake and eat it too. Data collection tools might mark each event with an indication of the level of granularity that lets you fine-tune your analysis—looking only at high-level events, such as menu selections; only at low-level events, such as mouse movements; or perhaps some hybrid approach that examines low-level events that precede or follow interesting high-level events.

As with any HCI research, proper attention to pilot testing can be important. Pilot testing of both the data collection and data analysis pieces of the experiment can help you verify that the data you are collecting actually tells you what you want it to. Analyzing the pilot data may help you verify that you are collecting data of the appropriate granularity.

All of the approaches to automatic data collection raise potential security concerns. Logs of web browser activity can say a good deal about a person browsing the web. This information might be used to infer sensitive or embarrassing details about a person's habits, interests, or medical concerns. Although the potential harm from the logs of any single website may be relatively minimal, proxy servers can be configured to capture all of the interactions with every website visited by a given computer. Indirect (and sometimes nonexistent) links between people and computers make matters even worse in this regard. Web logs track the identity (in terms of the IP number) of the computer that makes each request. A number in a web server log may correspond to the computer on your desk, but this does not mean that you were the person that was at the computer when the browser visited embarrassing websites.

Activity loggers and keystroke loggers make matters even worse. By tracking every input action, these tools collect enough data to reconstruct documents, emails, calendars, and other damaging evidence. These tools have been surreptitiously used in criminal investigations and divorce proceedings. Regardless of your views on the appropriateness of using secretive software to spy on family members, you should take care to ensure that your data collection tools do not gather data that others would find sensitive, damaging, or otherwise private. Some approaches include customizing your tools to avoid potentially problematic data, such as specific keys that are pressed (as opposed to simply noting that a key was pressed) and window titles (which may contain document titles).

12.9 SUMMARY

Automated data collection systems give researchers the ability to easily collect detailed user interaction information. Appropriately configured software tools can be used to replace labor-intensive approaches such as manual observation or coding of events on video. The result is a qualitative, as well as quantitative difference: not only can more data be collected, but the increased ease of data collection allows researchers to conduct experiments that otherwise would be too difficult or expensive. These strengths make automated data collection a clear first choice for many HCI research efforts.

There are three broad categories of question that might benefit from automated methods of data collection:

- Retrospective analyses of information management behavior: These studies look at artifacts of computer use, including location of documents, email folders, and other structures created during the course of using and managing information, in order to understand how people use these tools.
- Controlled experiments: Web server logs and completely customized software can be used to collect timing and related data for experiments. As web logs contain entries for each link selection event, they are most useful for cases involving the study of selection of web links. With proper design, web links can be used to model menu layouts and related topics. Fully customized software may be needed if additional data (such as mouse movements) is required, but hybrids may be useful. For example, JavaScript embedded in a web page might be used to record mouse movements and translate those movements into events stored in a log file alongside the basic server logs.
- Usability studies and other explorations of how users work with tools: Web server logs, proxy server logs, keystroke loggers, and activity loggers record user interaction events with one or more websites, applications, or operating environments. The interactions can be used to examine which features of a tool a user used and when. With appropriate analysis, this data can be used to find interaction problems and identify opportunities for usability improvements.

Successful use of any of these approaches requires careful consideration of the appropriate granularity of data to be collected and the tools to be used for data analysis. As with other data collection approaches, the key is to precisely identify the data that is needed and collect only that data.

Tools that collect data on user activities have potential privacy implications. This is particularly important when the goal is to study how users work with tools to complete real tasks: providing artificial tasks in the hopes of reducing privacy concerns may decrease the realism of the data. Experiments involving this set of data should be carefully designed, in consultation with appropriate institutional review boards (see Chapter 15), to avoid violations of participant privacy and trust.

DISCUSSION QUESTIONS

1. Online spreadsheets, word processors, and other office productivity tools blur the line between websites and traditional software. In doing so, they provide both opportunities and challenges for HCI researchers. As the software infrastructure for online tools resides completely on the hosting server, researchers can easily modify and redeploy interfaces without having to update individual computers. As with traditional web interfaces, requests for content from the server can be logged and resulting files can be analyzed. However, as client-side interactions (usually executed through JavaScript code)

do not generate server requests, additional data recording measures may be necessary. What other challenges or opportunities can you see in such dynamic applications? Pick an online word processor, spreadsheet, or presentation tool: how would you design a system to study its usability?

2. A hybrid system for automated computer data collection might involve a combination of web server logs—ideally from a proxy that would track all of a participant's interactions—and one or more software packages instrumented to collect data of interest. What would be the pros and cons of such a system relative to a full-scale activity logger that would track all user interactions?

3. Legitimate concerns about user privacy have led some researchers to be very cautious about the data that they collect with keyboard or activity loggers. This appropriate concern for user privacy does not come without a cost: in throwing away details such as document titles, destination addresses for emails, and specifics of visited web pages, researchers lose information that might have been used to develop a more nuanced understanding of the underlying activity. For example, was the user sending email to colleagues at work, or at home? Can you think of ways to configure logging software to collect certain attributes of document titles, email headers, and related information in a manner that might prove useful for research purposes while still being respectful of user privacy? What effect might greater notification—perhaps telling participants that you might record sensitive information—have on your experiments?

4. The Fitts' Law, Children, and Mouse Control sidebar provides an example of experiments that used mouse motion data to study how children differed from adults in their use of mice. Although 3- to 5-year-old children do not make much of use keyboards, slightly older children might begin to type. How would you study differences between children and adults in terms of their use of keyboards? What sort of data would you collect and how would you interpret it? How would this differ if you were considering smaller keyboards such as those used on some cell phones?

RESEARCH DESIGN EXERCISES

1. Experiment with web server logs and log analysis on your desktop.

   (a) Start by getting or generating a web server log file. You might ask computing support people in your school or company for some web log data. Log files can be *very* large: you probably only want a small snapshot. If your school or department gets a good deal of web traffic, you should be able to get a few megabytes of log data. Be forewarned, some network administrators may not like the idea of handing out this information. You may have to convince them that you will use it responsibly. Alternatively, you can install a web server and run it. If your computer does not have a web server installed, the Apache web server (http://httpd.apache.org) is available for most major platforms. Download the server, install it, and configure it. The server configuration file (httpd.conf) will have entries that indicate where log files can be found. Once you get the server running, build a few web pages with links between them and access them.

(b) Examine the log files to determine what they can tell you about pages that were accessed, when they were accessed, and other related details.

(c) Find an open source web log analysis tool and use it to analyze the log files.

(d) For a further challenge, try to configure and use a web proxy server, such as Squid (www.squid-cache.org).

2. Use implicitly collected information data from your computer to conduct an investigation of information management patterns. Start with folders and subfolders for documents: Do you have all of your documents in one folder or do you have many subfolders? How many documents in each folder? How many subfolders in each subfolder? What is the maximum "depth" of your subfolders? How many documents do you have on your desktop? Collect similar information for your email: How many items are in the inbox? How many folders? Repeat this analysis with a friend's data. Can you draw any conclusions about data management habits and practices?

3. Try to find and use a keyboard logger or general activity tracker. Install the program on your computer and use it to accomplish some tasks. Find and examine the log files: what do they tell you about how you used the program? Can you relate the contents of the log files to the tasks that you performed with the program?

4. Some simple excursions into collecting data on keyboard and mouse usage can be conducted without writing custom software.

(a) For keyboard usage, carefully remove the backspace and arrow keys from your keyboard. Disconnect your mouse as well. Ask someone to type a paragraph of text into a word processor and time their response. As your participant will be unable to delete any mistakes or use the arrow keys to move to a different part of the text, you will get a record of exactly which keys were pressed. You can use this data to collect error rates.

(b) Mouse usage can be measured with a drawing program. Draw two circles on opposite sides of the screen. Select the "pencil" tool and ask the user to hold down the mouse while moving back and forth several times between the two targets. As long as the mouse is held down, this will lead to a set of trails similar to those found in Figures 12.10 and 12.11. Time the results. If you vary the distances between the targets and the size of the targets, you can run a Fitts' law study.

REFERENCES

Agrawal, R., Imieliński, T., Swami, A., 1993. Mining association rules between sets of items in large databases. In: Proceedings of the 1993 ACM SIGMOD International Conference on Management of Data. ACM, Washington, D.C., pp. 207–216.

Arroyo, E., Selker, T., Wei, W., 2006. Usability tool for analysis of web designs using mouse tracks. In: Extended Abstracts, ACM Conference on Human Factors in Computing Systems. ACM Press, New York, pp. 484–489.

Atterer, R., Wnuk, M., Schmidt, A., 2006. Knowing the user's every move: user activity tracking for website usability evaluation and implicit interaction. In: Proceedings of the 15th International Conference on World Wide Web, Edinburgh, Scotland. ACM Press, New York.

Ben-Naim, D., Marcus, N., Bain, M., 2008. Visualization and analysis of student interactions in an exploratory learning environment. In: Proceedings of the 1st International Workshop on Intelligent Support for Exploratory Environments (Part of ECTEL 2008).

Burstyn, J., Carrascal, J.P., Vertegaal, R., 2016. Fitts' law and the effects of input mapping and stiffness on flexible display interactions. In: Proceedings of the 2016 CHI Conference on Human Factors in Computing Systems, Santa Clara, CA, USA. ACM, New York, pp. 3649–3658.

Buschek, D., Auch, A., Alt, F., 2015. A toolkit for analysis and prediction of touch targeting behaviour on mobile websites. In: Proceedings of the 7th ACM SIGCHI Symposium on Engineering Interactive Computing Systems, Duisburg, Germany. ACM, New York, pp. 54–63.

Cangiano, G.R., Hollan, J.D., 2009. Capturing and restoring the context of everyday work: a case study at a law office. In: Kurosu, M. (Ed.), Human Centered Design: First International Conference, HCD 2009, Held as Part of HCI International 2009, San Diego, CA, USA, July 19–24, 2009 Proceedings. Springer, Berlin, pp. 945–954.

Canzian, L., Musolesi, M., 2015. Trajectories of depression: unobtrusive monitoring of depressive states by means of smartphone mobility traces analysis. In: Proceedings of the 2015 ACM International Joint Conference on Pervasive and Ubiquitous Computing, Osaka, Japan. ACM, New York, pp. 1293–1304.

Carta, T., Paternò, F., de Santana, V.F., 2011a. Web usability probe: a tool for supporting remote usability evaluation of web sites. In: Campos, P., Graham, N., Jorge, J., et al. (Eds.), Human-Computer Interaction—INTERACT 2011: 13th IFIP TC 13 International Conference, Lisbon, Portugal, September 5–9, 2011, Proceedings, Part IV. Heidelberg, Berlin, pp. 349–357.

Carta, T., Paternò, F., Santana, V., 2011b. Support for remote usability evaluation of web mobile applications. In: Proceedings of the 29th ACM International Conference on Design of Communication, Pisa, Italy. ACM, New York, pp. 129–136.

Clarkson, E., Lyons, K., Clawson, J., Starner, T., 2007. Revisiting and validating a model of two-thumb text entry. In: Proceedings of the SIGCHI Conference on Human Factors in Computing Systems, San Jose, CA, USA. ACM, New York, pp. 163–166.

Crabtree, A., Benford, S., Greenhalgh, C., Tennent, P., Chalmers, M., Brown, B., 2006. Supporting ethnographic studies of ubiquitous computing in the wild. In: ACM Conference on Designing Interactive Systems, University Park, PA, USA. ACM Press, New York.

Eirinaki, M., Vazirgiannis, M., 2003. Web mining for web personalization. ACM Transactions on Internet Technology 3 (1), 1–27.

Fan, Z., Song, X., Shibasaki, R., Adachi, R., 2015. CityMomentum: an online approach for crowd behavior prediction at a citywide level. In: Proceedings of the 2015 ACM International Joint Conference on Pervasive and Ubiquitous Computing, Osaka, Japan. ACM, New York, pp. 559–569.

Fielding, R., Reschke, J. (Eds.), 2014. Hypertext Transfer Protocol (HTTP/1.1): Semantics and Content. Retrieved from https://tools.ietf.org/html/rfc7231 (3.17.2017).

Fielding, R.T., Taylor, R.N., 2002. Principled design of the modern Web architecture. ACM Transactions on Internet Technology 2 (2), 115–150.

Fitts, P.M., 1954. The information capacity of the human motor system in controlling the amplitude of movement. Journal of Experimental Psychology 47 (6), 381–391.

Fouse, A., Weibel, N., Hutchins, E., Hollan, J.D., 2011. ChronoViz: a system for supporting navigation of time-coded data. In: CHI'11 Extended Abstracts on Human Factors in Computing Systems, Vancouver, BC, Canada. ACM, New York, pp. 299–304.

Grossman, T., Kong, N., Balakrishnan, R., 2007. Modeling pointing at targets of arbitrary shapes. In: Proceedings of the SIGCHI Conference on Human Factors in Computing Systems, San Jose, CA, USA. ACM, New York, pp. 463–472.

Guo, Q., Agichtein, E., 2009. Beyond session segmentation: predicting changes in search intent with client-side user interactions. In: Proceedings of the 32nd International ACM SIGIR Conference on Research and Development in Information Retrieval, Boston, MA, USA. ACM, New York, pp. 636–637.

Hammontree, M.L., Hendrickson, J.J., Hensley, B.W., 1992. Integrated data capture and analysis tools for research and testing on graphical user interfaces. In: Proceedings of the SIGCHI Conference on Human Factors in Computing Systems, Monterey, CA, United States. ACM Press, New York, pp. 431–432.

Harris, J., 2005. Inside Deep Thought (Why the UI, Part 6). Jensen Harris: An Office User Interface Blog. Retrieved from http://blogs.msdn.com/jensenh/archive/2005/10/31/487247.aspx (07.01.17).

Harris, J., 2006. No Distaste for Paste (Why the UI, Part 7). Jensen Harris: An Office User Interface Blog. Retrieved from http://blogs.msdn.com/jensenh/archive/2006/04/07/570798.aspx (07.01.17).

Heer, J., Chi, E.H., 2002. Separating the swarm: categorization methods for user sessions on the web. In: ACM Conference on Human Factors in Computing Systems, Minneapolis, MN, USA. ACM Press, New York, pp. 243–250.

Hilbert, D.M., Redmiles, D.F., 2000. Extracting usability information from user interface events. ACM Computing Surveys 32, 384–421.

Hochheiser, H., Shneiderman, B., 2000. Performance benefits of simultaneous over sequential menus as task complexity increases. International Journal of Human–Computer Interaction 12 (2), 173–192.

Hochheiser, H., Shneiderman, B., 2001. Using interactive visualizations of www log data to characterize access patterns and inform site design. Journal of the American Society for Information Science and Technology 52 (4), 331–343.

Hong, J.I., Heer, J., Waterson, S., Landay, J.A., 2001. WebQuilt: a proxy-based approach to remote web usability testing. ACM Transactions on Information Systems 19 (3), 263–285.

Hourcade, J.P., Bederson, B.B., Druin, A., Guimbretière, F., 2004. Differences in pointing task performance between preschool children and adults using mice. ACM Transactions on Computer-Human Interaction 11 (4), 357–386.

Huang, J., White, R.W., Buscher, G., Wang, K., 2012. Improving searcher models using mouse cursor activity. In: Proceedings of the 35th International ACM SIGIR Conference on Research and Development in Information Retrieval, Portland, OR, USA. ACM, New York, pp. 195–204.

Huang, J., White, R.W., Dumais, S., 2011. No clicks, no problem: using cursor movements to understand and improve search. In: Proceedings of the SIGCHI Conference on Human Factors in Computing Systems, Vancouver, BC, Canada. ACM, New York, pp. 1225–1234.

Humayoun, S.R., Dubinsky, Y., Catarci, T., Nazarov, E., Israel, A., 2012. A model-based approach to ongoing product evaluation. In: Proceedings of the International Working Conference on Advanced Visual Interfaces, Capri Island, Italy. ACM, New York, pp. 596–603.

Hurst, A., Hudson, S.E., Mankoff, J., Trewin, S., 2013. Distinguishing users by pointing performance in laboratory and real-world tasks. ACM Transactions on Accessible Computing 5 (2), 1–27.

Iqbal, S.T., Horvitz, E., 2007. Disruption and recovery of computing tasks: field study, analysis, and directions. In: Proceedings of the SIGCHI Conference on Human Factors in Computing Systems, San Jose, CA, USA. ACM Press, New York, pp. 677–686.

Ivory, M.Y., Hearst, M.A., 2001. The state of the art in automating usability evaluation of user interfaces. ACM Computing Surveys 33 (4), 470–516.

Janzen, I., Rajendran, V.K., Booth, K.S., 2016. Modeling the impact of depth on pointing performance. In: Proceedings of the 2016 CHI Conference on Human Factors in Computing Systems, Santa Clara, CA, USA. ACM, New York, pp. 188–199.

Kairam, S., Brzozowski, M., Huffaker, D., Chi, E., 2012. Talking in circles: selective sharing in Google+. In: Proceedings of the SIGCHI Conference on Human Factors in Computing Systems, Austin, TX, USA. ACM, New York, pp. 1065–1074.

Kiciman, E., Livshits, B., 2010. AjaxScope: a platform for remotely monitoring the client-side behavior of web 2.0 applications. ACM Transactions on the Web 4 (4), 1–52.

Koster, M., 2007. Robots Exclusion. Retrieved from http://www.robotstxt.org/ (07.01.17).

Lin, M., Goldman, R., Price, K.J., Sears, A., Jacko, J., 2007. How do people tap when walking? An empirical investigation of nomadic data entry. International Journal of Human–Computer Studies 65 (9), 759–769.

Lubos, P., Bruder, G., Steinicke, F., 2014. Are 4 hands better than 2?: bimanual interaction for quadmanual user interfaces. In: Proceedings of the 2nd ACM Symposium on Spatial User Interaction Honolulu, HI, USA. ACM, New York, pp. 123–126.

MacKenzie, I.S., 1992. Fitts' law as a research and design tool in human-computer interaction. Human–Computer Interaction 7 (1), 91–139.

MacKenzie, I.S., Buxton, W., 1992. Extending Fitts' law to two-dimensional tasks. In: Proceedings of the SIGCHI Conference on Human Factors in Computing Systems, Monterey, CA, United States. ACM, New York, pp. 219–226.

Malik, S., Koh, E., 2016. High-volume hypothesis testing for large-scale web log analysis. In: Proceedings of the 2016 CHI Conference Extended Abstracts on Human Factors in Computing Systems, Santa Clara, CA, USA. ACM, New York, pp. 1583–1590.

Mark, G., Iqbal, T.S., Czerwinski, M., Johns, P., Sano, A., Lutchyn, Y., 2016. Email duration, batching and self-interruption: patterns of email use on productivity and stress. In: Proceedings of the 2016 CHI Conference on Human Factors in Computing Systems, Santa Clara, CA, USA. ACM, New York, pp. 1717–1728.

Mavrikis, M., Zhu, Z., Gutierrez-Santos, S., Poulovassilis, A., 2015. Visualisation and analysis of students' interaction data in exploratory earning environments. In: Proceedings of the 24th International Conference on World Wide Web, Florence, Italy. ACM, New York, pp. 1419–1424.

McGrenere, J., Moore, G., 2000. Are we all in the same "Bloat"? In: Proceedings of Graphics Interface, pp. 187–196.

McGrenere, J., Baecker, R.M., Booth, K.S., 2002. An evaluation of a multiple interface design solution for bloated software. In: Proceedings of the SIGCHI Conference on Human Factors in Computing Systems, Minneapolis, MN, USA. ACM Press, New York.

Nguyen, E., Modak, T., Dias, E., Yu, Y., Huang, L., 2014. Fitnamo: using bodydata to encourage exercise through Google glass™. In: CHI'14 Extended Abstracts on Human Factors in Computing Systems, Toronto, Ontario, Canada. ACM, New York, pp. 239–244.

Obendorf, H., Weinreich, H., Herder, E., Mayer, M., 2007. Web page revisitation revisited: implications of a long-term click-stream study of browser usage. In: Proceedings of the SIGCHI Conference on Human Factors in Computing Systems, San Jose, CA, USA. ACM Press, New York, pp. 597–606.

Pirolli, P., Pitkow, J., 1999. Distributions of surfers' paths through the World Wide Web: empirical characterizations. World Wide Web 2 (1), 29–45.

Srivastava, J., Cooley, R., Deshpande, M., Tanw, P.-N., 2000. Web usage mining: discovery and applications of usage patterns from Web data. SIGKDD Explorations Newsletter 1 (2), 12–23.

Teather, R.J., Stuerzlinger, W., 2014. Visual aids in 3D point selection experiments. In: Proceedings of the 2nd ACM Symposium on Spatial User Interaction, Honolulu, HI, USA. ACM, New York, pp. 127–136.

Teevan, J., Dumais, S.T., Horvitz, E., 2005. Personalizing search via automated analysis of interests and activities. In: Proceedings of the 28th Annual International ACM SIGIR Conference on Research and Development in Information Retrieval, Salvador, Brazil. ACM, New York, pp. 449–456.

Terry, M., Kay, M., Van Vugt, B., Slack, B., Park, T., 2008. Ingimp: introducing instrumentation to an end-user open source application. In: Proceeding of the Twenty-Sixth Annual SIGCHI Conference on Human Factors in Computing Systems, Florence, Italy. ACM, New York, pp. 607–616.

Velloso, E., Alexander, J., Bulling, A., Gellersen, H., 2015. Interactions under the desk: a characterisation of foot movements for input in a seated position. In: Abascal, J., Barbosa, S., Fetter, M., et al. (Eds.), Human-Computer Interaction—INTERACT 2015: 15th IFIP TC 13 International Conference, Bamberg, Germany, September 14–18, 2015, Proceedings, Part I, Cham. Springer, New York, pp. 384–401.

White, R., 2013. Beliefs and biases in web search. In: Proceedings of the 36th International ACM SIGIR Conference on Research and Development in Information Retrieval, Dublin, Ireland. ACM, New York, pp. 3–12.

White, R.W., Hassan, A., 2014. Content Bias in Online Health Search. ACM Transactions on the Web 8 (4), 1–33.

White, R.W., Horvitz, E., 2009. Cyberchondria: studies of the escalation of medical concerns in Web search. ACM Transactions on Information Systems 27 (4), 1–37.

Whittaker, S., Matthews, T., Cerruti, J., Badenes, H., Tang, J., 2011. Am I wasting my time organizing email? A study of email refinding. In: Proceedings of the SIGCHI Conference on Human Factors in Computing Systems, Vancouver, BC, Canada. ACM, New York, pp. 3449–3458.

Wollner, P.K.A., Langdon, P.M., Clarkson, P.J., 2015. Integrating a cognitive modelling framework into the design process of touchscreen user interfaces. In: Marcus, A. (Ed.), Design, User Experience, and Usability: Users and Interactions: 4th International Conference, DUXU 2015, Held as Part of HCI International 2015, Los Angeles, CA, USA, August 2–7, 2015, Proceedings, Part II. Springer, Cham, pp. 473–484.

World Wide Web Consortium, 1995. Logging Control in W3C httpd. Retrieved from http://www.w3.org/Daemon/User/Config/Logging.html (29.11.15).

Measuring the human

13

13.1 INTRODUCTION

As the study of human-computer interaction (HCI) is all about understanding how users interact with computer and information systems, it is obvious that participation of those users is vital to our research. Previous chapters have outlined how we might involve participants in surveys, case studies, interviews, usability studies, and empirical studies, leading to both quantitative and qualitative data that provide vital insights. However, these chapters barely scratch the surface of the rich and varied data that human participants can provide for research studies.

This chapter broadens the focus, describing the numerous ways that the bodies of research participants can act as data-generating devices, providing us with measures of attention, emotional response, and brain activity. A wide variety of physical and emotional measurements can help us gain significant insight into the way that users work with our interfaces. Although we always, of course, strive to treat participants with the respect and dignity that they deserve (Chapter 15), they can also be treasure troves of detailed information that may otherwise be hard—if not impossible—to acquire. This makes familiarity with human data collection an important skill for any HCI researcher.

Automated human data collection techniques cover a range of complexity, cost, and invasiveness. Some of the simplest techniques involve data from familiar input devices, such as mice and keyboards. These familiar tools can help us understand how people navigate in graphical environments and provide textual input. More complicated approaches include eye-tracking tools for studying patterns in eye movements, galvanic skin response, and blood-volume and heart-rate measurements for the study of physical and emotional responses. At the high end, functional magnetic resonance imaging (fMRI) tools can be used to examine how different parts of the brain react and interact in various circumstances.

Although many of these techniques involve expensive equipment and may require training that is beyond the reach of many HCI researchers, they present intriguing possibilities for gaining understanding that would otherwise be elusive. Eye-tracking tools that tell us where people are looking on a screen can help us understand visual processes involved in navigating lists of options. Skin response or cardiovascular monitors can provide insight into a user's level of arousal or frustration. The rich, detailed information about user activities and responses provided by these tools can help extend our understanding of human use of computer interfaces.

Research Methods in Human-Computer Interaction. http://dx.doi.org/10.1016/B978-0-12-805390-4.00013-3

This chapter discusses a variety of options, with an eye toward cost-benefit trade-offs: as some tools are clearly more difficult and expensive than others, we strive to use the simplest and least expensive tools suitable for a given job.

13.2 EYE TRACKING
13.2.1 BACKGROUND

Countless traditional HCI studies used—and continue to use—measurements of mouse or keyboard interactions in an attempt to see how users control computers. This approach can be very useful, but it paints a necessarily incomplete picture, as simply knowing which keys were pressed and where the mouse was moved does not help us understand what's going on—where were they looking? Which aspects of the system drew their attention?

Eye-tracking systems can help us begin to answer these questions. Using cameras or other sensors, these systems continuously track the orientation of the fovea—the center of the field of vision. This information can be used to identify where the user is looking, which is in turn assumed to be the center of their attention. Although perhaps overly simplistic, this simplified model provides the basis for all eye-tracking work (Duchowski, 2007). Generally, eye-tracking systems will use transform raw data regarding gaze direction into a series of coordinates mapping direction into (x, y) coordinates on the display being viewed. These coordinates can then be further transformed into trails identifying where the user looked and when (Figure 13.1), providing information that can help us understand how user attention relates to task completion, and possibly how aspects of the interface command attention and influence whether or not tasks are completed successfully and how long they take.

Technologies and applications have progressed significantly since the first use of eye tracking in the early 20th century (Jacob and Karn, 2003). Modern systems use sensors based on the desktop or on head-mounted devices to track the reflection of infrared light from the cornea or retina (Jacob and Karn, 2003; Kumar, 2006). Eye-tracking devices have become increasingly inexpensive, with highly functional commercial systems now available for less than $200. Open-source university-developed systems costing less than $100 have shown performance comparable to more expensive commercial systems (Agustin et al., 2010; Johansen et al., 2011). The advent of low-cost cameras and other inexpensive hardware have reduced the costs of eye trackers (Kumar, 2006), although inexpensive systems may lack collect data at a lower frequency than higher-end alternatives. Systems are often hard to use, requiring calibration for each user and inconvenience such as head-mounted devices or restrictions on the range of movement allowed to the user (Jacob and Karn, 2003).

Interpretation of eye movements is a nontrivial challenge, due to the constant motion of our eyes. Rapid motions known as *saccades* last anywhere from 10 to 100 ms (Duchowski, 2007). These movements are used to reposition the eyes to a new viewpoint (Duchowski, 2007)—perhaps in anticipation of a new task or in response to some stimulus. These transitions lead to *fixation*—focus on a new area of interest. However, fixation does not mean lack of motion—even when focused on a target; eyes will continue to move in small *microsaccades*, which are essentially random noise (Duchowski, 2007). Following a moving target (as in a video game) leads to a final class of eye movements known as *smooth pursuits*.

Sophisticated software uses the geometry of the eye and the related optics to filter out the noise and to identify saccades and fixations, providing highly accurate measures of where the user is looking at any given time. The first step in this process is generally to remove noise, often by ignoring measurements that are not plausible given the operating characteristics of the eye tracker. De-noised movements are then separated into saccades and fixations through one of two approaches. *Dwell-time* methods look for periods of little or no variance in eye position. Low-variance intervals lasting for more than some minimal amount of time are classified as fixations, with other intervals classified as saccades. *Velocity-based* methods take the opposite approach, classifying saccades as intervals when eye-movement velocity exceeds a given threshold. Experience from prior literature can be used to select appropriate parameters for fixation intervals, saccade velocity, and other thresholds (Duchowski, 2007). Although custom implementations are always possible, many users will adopt saccade and fixation detection approaches, along with corresponding thresholds, directly from software tools provided with eye-tracking hardware.

Identifying eye-movement features is only the first step in an eye-tracking study. As where the user's eyes are looking and what they are looking at on the screen are both important (Jacob and Karn, 2003), appropriate use of eye-tracking data often requires mapping eye-gaze data to screen coordinates (Duchowski, 2007), and then integrating that data with information regarding the contents of the screen display at each time point and any additional interaction about mouse and keyboard interaction. Software tools that automatically synchronize these data streams can simplify the data interpretation process (Crowe and Narayanan, 2000). Systems that can overlay "trails" indicating the path of a user's gaze onto screen shots can be particularly useful (Figure 13.1). As data analysis tools are often tied to specific hardware platforms, eye-gaze research studies should be carefully designed and controlled (Duchowski, 2007), so as to minimize the risk of artifacts in data collection and interpretation that might influence interpretation and results.

13.2.2 APPLICATIONS

When interpretation and analysis challenges are handled appropriately, eye-gaze data can present researchers with intriguing possibilities. If we can understand how users move their eyes when completing various interface tasks, we might gain some insight into where attention is focused and how choices are made. This additional data can take us beyond the relatively uninformative traces of mouse and keyboard events, filling in the holes: just where did the user look before she moved her mouse from one menu to the next? Which portions of a web page initially attract user attention?

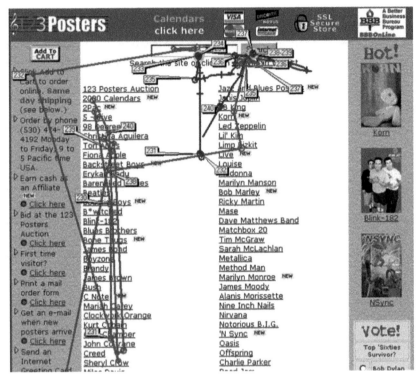

FIGURE 13.1

A web page annotated with eye-tracking data: lines indicating gaze paths link fixation points annotated with time stamps, providing a trail for a series of interactions.

From Card, S.K., Pirolli, P., Van Der Wege, M.M., Morrison, J.B., Reeder, R.W., Schraedley, P., Boshart, J., 2001. Information scent as a driver of Web behavior graphs: results of a protocol analysis method for Web usability. In: Proceedings of the SIGCHI conference on Human factors in computing systems, Seattle, Washington, United States. ACM. © ACM.

These possibilities have led to the application of eye tracking in many domains, both as new forms of computer input and as the basis for research projects aimed at using eye movements as a source of data for studying HCIs (Jacob and Karn, 2003; Kumar, 2006). Eye tracking has been widely used as an assistive technology for people with quadriplegia and others who are unable to use motor functions to operate a mouse, keyboard, or other adaptive input device (Hornof et al., 2004; Barreto et al., 2008). The use of gaze control for pointing and selecting objects—eye gaze as complementing (Zhai et al., 1999; Bieg, 2009) or replacing (Jacob and Karn, 2003; Murata, 2006; Kumar et al., 2007) mice—has been suggested by many researchers, leading to a variety of proposed designs. Others have explored taking eye tracking one step further, using gaze as an input or control signal. One study of immersive, collaborative environments used eye trackers to make virtual avatars "look" where users in virtual environments were looking (Steptoe et al., 2008). Other studies have used eye-gaze history data to help users monitor semiautonomous agents, using visual cues from prior gaze information to highlight where users should look for a monitoring task (Taylor, 2015). Eye-tracking systems have also been developed for GUI interface control including pointing and clicking (Kumar et al., 2007), window selection (Fono and Vertegaal, 2005), multimodal interfaces (Stellmach and Dachselt, 2013; Pfeuffer et al., 2016), and for remote collaboration (Higuch et al., 2016).

Researchers have used eye tracking to study user behavior with a wide range of computer interfaces. Web browsing and navigation have been particularly well-studied in this regard. In a pair of studies, researchers at Microsoft used an eye-tracking system to examine the impact of factors such as the placement of a target link in a list of results and the length of the contextual text snippet that accompanies the results (Cutrell and Guan, 2007; Guan and Cutrell, 2007). In study of placement, users were observed to be more likely to look at links early in a list than later and to spend more time looking at the earlier links (Guan and Cutrell, 2007). Consideration of the length of text summaries led to interesting results: when looking for a specific link, users tended to focus on more search results as the summaries got longer. This effect was less notable for open-ended "informational" tasks that were not focused on a specific goal. The researcher speculated that this difference was due to the relevance of the summaries in each case: summaries that were useful in the informational task were distractions that obscured the specific link name in the other tasks (Cutrell and Guan, 2007). Other studies have examined patterns in eye movements as users interact with websites, moving both within individual pages and across multiple pages (Card et al., 2001; Goldberg et al., 2002; Buscher et al., 2009).

Other experiments have used eye tracking to understand the progression of eye focus during menu selection tasks. One study found that eye-focus patterns in tasks involving reading menu items differed significantly from selecting items. Although users fixated on each item when reading menus, they tended to use sequences of eye movements in a given direction—known as "sweeps"—when performing selection tasks (Aaltonen et al., 1998). Eye tracking has also been used to study differences in how user attention differs for alternative visualizations of hierarchical structures (Pirolli et al., 2000), and to build document summaries based on eye-gaze data describing areas that were the focus of user attention (Xu et al., 2009).

Given the complexity of eye tracking, some researchers might be tempted to look for other measurements that might provide hints as to where a user's attention is focused. For GUI-based systems, mouse position and movement might be seen as a proxy for eye gaze, as we might tend to look where the pointer goes as we move the mouse. A strong correlation between mouse movement and gaze might completely eliminate the need for eye tracking in some GUI-based contexts. Alas, the reality is somewhat more complicated. A number of studies have attempted to track the relationship between gaze and mouse movement, developing algorithms for using mouse position to predict gaze (Chen et al., 2001; Bieg et al., 2010; Huang et al., 2012; Diaz et al., 2013; Navalpakkam et al., 2013), although the nature of the relationship might be somewhat task dependent (Liebling and Dumais, 2014).

Of course, studies that use eye tracking, mouse movements, or other measurements as proxies for attention run into all of the usual problems associated with indirect measurements. Before undertaking such a study, consider triangulation approaches such as postfact review of screen video with participants, asking them to describe what they were thinking while they were interacting with the system. This "retrospective think-aloud" approach (Bowers and Snyder, 1990) might be preferable to real-time feedback, which might distract users from the task at hand. Interestingly, eye-tracking analyses have been used to validate retrospective think-aloud (Guan et al., 2006).

Although eye tracking has been successfully used for both top-down, hypothesis-driven experiments and bottom-up exploratory work (Jacob and Karn, 2003), appropriate experimental design may increase the odds of success. Exploratory analysis offers the possibility of generating novel, unexpected insights, at the potential cost of open-ended searching for illusive needles in haystacks of data. Hypothesis-driven experiments constrain the analysis needed, helping avoid fruitless searches down blind alleys.

A narrow focus can also help simplify exploratory work. A study of the effectiveness of browser feedback for secure websites used eye tracking to study the use of security indicators, including the secure web protocol indicator ("https://"), lock or key icons, and security certificates (Whalen and Inkpen, 2005). Focusing on these areas, researchers learned that users often looked at the lock icon on the browser window before or after looking at the HTTPS header in the web location bar. Eye tracking also identified potential confusion due to browser designs, as some users looked at the lower left-hand corner of the browser (where the lock is on Netscape/Mozilla browsers) rather than the lower right-hand corner (where it could be found on the Internet Explorer browser used in the study) (Whalen and Inkpen, 2005).

Eye tracking can also be a vitally useful tool for understanding complex and cognitively challenging workflows and tasks (see the "Measuring Workload" sidebar), as demonstrated by explorations of the use of eye tracking in studying electronic medical records (EMRs) and other clinical information tools. Examples include the use of eye tracking to improve EMR design, through investigations of the detrimental impact of layout clutter on task performance (Moacdieh and Sarter, 2015) and in conjunction with retrospective think-aloud, to understand information search and access patterns during the use of EMRs (Wright et al., 2013). Other studies have investigated the use of eye tracking to identify the skill levels of EMR users (Kocejko et al., 2015); to understand EMR workflow (Doberne et al., 2015; Mazur et al., 2016) and visual search patterns (Fong et al., 2016); to explore how EMRs are used during patient visits (Rick et al., 2015) and particularly the impact that they might have on communication between patients and physicians (Montague and Asan, 2014); and to examine how emergency physicians interpret test results (Nielsona et al., 2013). Comparable studies with consumers of health information have examined understand how audiences read and interpret health information, including antialcohol messages (Brown and Richardson, 2012) and public safety guidelines (Bass et al., 2016). An eye-tracking study of reading patterns for users of a health discussion found that gaze patterns differ between user seeking information regarding their own health, as compared to those seeking for information about someone else's symptoms

(Pian et al., 2016). Eye tracking has also been used extensively to understand visual processes involved in interpreting complex biomedical data, such as cardiovascular data from electrocardiograms (Bond et al., 2015) and medical imaging, including virtual pathology slides (Krupinski et al., 2006), cranial scans (Venjakob et al., 2016), and other volumetric imaging (Venjakob and Mello-Thoms, 2015).

Beyond traditional desktop environments, eye tracking presents myriad opportunities for augmented reality, particularly as lower-cost devices such become available as commodity hardware. Sensors mounted on eyeglasses and headsets can track gaze direction as users work in specialized environments or carry on day-to-day activities, presenting opportunities for input, object recognition, and control. As a relatively low-cost commodity system capable of gaze-tracking, Google Glass inspired significant interest, leading to the development of novel software approaches for data collection and analysis (Jalaliniya et al., 2015). Although Glass was not a commercial success, and has since been discontinued, the increased of goggles for virtual reality and augmented availability seems almost inevitable—commercial successes may be just around the corner. Additional examples of the use of Google Glass in HCI research can be found in Chapter 14.

Alternative approaches leverage the power of smartphones to enable mobile eye tracking. Commercially available eye-tracking goggles have been combined with smartphone software to map eye-gaze coordinates to locations on a wearer's smartphone screen (Paletta et al., 2014). Of course, the logical conclusion would be to use the smartphone camera to do the eye tracking. Kyle Krafka and colleagues presented such a system, based on data models collected from over 1450 people and trained via a convolutional neural network, in a 2016 paper (Krafka et al., 2016).

MEASURING WORKLOAD

Workload is the effort associated with completing a task. As much of user interaction design aims to develop tools that are easy to use, HCI researchers and designers are often interested in assessing workload. Understanding when and where a tool makes mental demands on users can help us identify opportunities for improvement through redesign.

Unfortunately, workload can be very difficult to assess, as our mental processes are not easily observed. To work around this limitation, researchers have expended significant effort developing surveys such as the Subjective Workaround Assessment Technique (SWAT) (Reid and Nygren, 1988), and the NASA Task Load Index, or NASA-TLX (Hart and Staveland, 1988; Hart, 2006). The NASA-TLX is the most widely used of these instruments, having been used in hundreds of studies. The TLX scale includes six questions assessing mental demand, physical demand, temporal demand, performance, effort, and frustration level, along with a protocol for assessing the relative importance of these six measures to each specific task.

(Continued)

MEASURING WORKLOAD—CONT'D

Despite their wide acceptance, these instruments suffer from the same shortcomings as other surveys. Asking users to rate the workload after they have completed a task relies on fallible human memory, leading to potentially inconsistent assessments that fail to account for much of the nuanced workload requirements inherent in many complex tasks.

These shortcomings have led to the development of a variety of approaches for using physiological sensors to measure workload. One possible approach involves the use of eye-gaze tracking to measure pupil diameter, which has been shown to increase with stress or frustration (Barreto et al., 2008; Klingner et al., 2008; Jiang et al., 2014). Links between pupil dilation and mental load have been used to explore user interactions in contexts such as web content, where relevant content has been associated with larger pupil dilation than less relevant content, indicating that more mental effort is involved when content is pertinent (Gwizdka and Zhang, 2015). Other efforts have looked at the use of microsaccades and saccadic intrusions—deviations from a gaze point followed by a short fixation and then a return to the original point—to derive similar measures (Tokuda et al., 2009, 2011).

Other physiological measures—many of which are discussed in this chapter—have also been used to assess workload. One 2010 study investigated the utility of several simultaneous measures, including an eye tracker, an electrocardiogram armband, a wireless electroencephalogram headset, and a heart-rate monitor, along with NASA-TLX ratings, to determine which combination of signals best measured workload. The average of the heat flux (as measured by the armband) and the variability of the electrocardiogram provided the highest classification accuracy (Haapalainen et al., 2010), suggesting that combinations of measurements may be useful in measuring complex phenomena such as workload. Alternative approaches to assessing workload through physiological signals, including more direct measures of brain activity, are discussed later in the chapter.

13.3 MOTION AND POSITION TRACKING

If the study of the motions of our eyes can provide insights into attention, workload, and other important processes, what else can we learn from the human body? Human bodies are constantly moving: even when we are "sitting still," our torsos move slightly with each breath. Movements of our hands, arms, heads, torsos, and even legs and feet can be measured by multiple types of sensors, providing useful opportunities for studying and changing how we interact with computers.

13.3.1 **MUSCULAR AND SKELETAL POSITION SENSING**

The Wii remote, introduced by Nintendo in 2005, introduced a new era of consumer electronics capable of sensor position and motion. Using a combination of accelerometers and optical sensing, the Wii remote provides multiple degrees of freedom, allowing natural inputs for games such as tennis and bowling. In addition to commercial success, the Wii was quickly adopted by HCI researchers who explored the possibility of enhancing the range of applications to include possibilities such as gesture recognition (Schlömer et al., 2008), and studied the use and adoption of the new games, particularly in social contexts (Voida and Greenberg, 2009).

Although the Wii might have been the first notable commercial success, HCI researchers have been working with novel sensing devices for years. Early published HCI work with accelerometers predates the Wii by several years (Levin and Yarin, 1999). The use of accelerometers in HCI research exploded with the advent of ubiquitous availability in smartphones. Applications have included sensing posture to help stroke survivors (Arteaga et al., 2008), identifying repetitive and troublesome behavior from students with autism spectrum disorder (Albinali et al., 2009), fall detection (Fudickar et al., 2012; Ren et al., 2012; Mehner et al., 2013), and even detecting bad driving (Singh et al., 2013). Smartphone accelerometers have also been used as mouse-like input devices (Yun et al., 2015) and for gesture recognition (Kim et al., 2016).

Moving beyond accelerometers in smartphones, recent years have seen an explosion in the availability of wrist-worn sensors. Although wrist-watch heart-rate monitors have been available for years, the current generation of fitness sensors go much further, adding the capability to track steps, sleep, floor-climbing, and energy usage, in combination with integrated smartphone functionality. Although concerns about the accuracy of some measurements may limit the utility of these devices for some purposes (Kaewkannate and Kim, 2016; Wallen et al., 2016), feedback provided by these tools may help users understand and increase the efficacy of their habits. The challenge of understanding how these tools are used over time can be significant, as technical challenges, nuanced user behavior often involving multiple devices, accuracy, inappropriate mental models, and other challenges complicate effective use of the tools and interpretation of resulting data (Harrison et al., 2014; Rooksby et al., 2014; Yang et al., 2015). As these devices continue to grow in capability and popularity, further research will undoubtedly continue to ask how these monitoring capabilities can be used more effectively. For example, one study of physical activity monitors found that customized plans that encouraged users to reflect on exercise strategies were more effective than automatically constructed plans (Lee et al., 2015).

Smartwatches such as the Apple Watch provide wrist-worn easy access to a wider range of smartphone facilities than those provided by fitness sensors. These watches have been used to develop approaches for sensing gestures made by fingers (Xu et al., 2015; Wen et al., 2016; Porzi et al., 2013; Ogata and Imai, 2015). The 2016 example of the Apple Watch presents more opportunities for HCI researchers, particularly as new tools are developed to explore the use of the watch as an unobtrusive computing device in everyday settings (Bernaerts et al., 2014; Quintana et al., 2016). Exercise and fitness sensors provide similar capabilities—see Chapter 14 for additional discussion of these sensors.

Microsoft's Kinect takes a different approach to sensing position and motion. Like the Wii remote, Kinect comes out of the gaming world—in this case, Microsoft's Xbox. Kinect includes a depth sensor, cameras, and microphones capable of capture body motion in 3D, and recognizing faces and voices (Zhang, 2012). Kinect sensors have been used in a wide range of contexts, including for assessing posture and movement (Clark et al., 2012; Dutta, 2012), observing audience responses to interactive displays (Shi and Alt, 2016), providing feedback to speakers giving public presentations (Tanveer et al., 2016), interacting with large displays (Zhang, 2015), and, of course, playing games, both for entertainment (Marshall et al., 2016; Tang et al., 2015) and for rehabilitation (Huang et al., 2015; Wang et al., 2014; Muñoz et al., 2014). Data complexity can make analysis of Kinect interactions somewhat challenging as several types of analyses are needed to extract objects, human activities, gestures, and even surroundings from Kinect data (Han et al., 2013). Toolkits such as Kinect Analysis (Nebeling et al., 2015) might simplify this analysis, but proper design and interpretation will always be a key component of any study using Kinect or similar data. For a discussion of the challenges involved in using Kinect data in natural (non-lab) settings, see the LAB-IN-A-BOX sidebar below.

The Wii, smartphone accelerometers, smart watches, fitness monitors, and Kinect all provide examples of consumer technologies used in HCI research. These commodity tools provide researchers with commercial-quality, ready-to-use hardware and software that can be readily integrated into research, without requiring any of the engineering work required to collect data using home-grown or assembled components. For further discussion of smart watches and fitness trackers, see Chapter 14.

The need to transcend the limitations of commercial tools has inspired countless tinkerers and experimenters to develop and adapt novel motion and position sensing tools to both collect input from users and to measure activity. The accessibility community has been developing novel interfaces enabling users with reduced motor capacity to control computers since at the 1970s (Meiselwitz et al., 2010). Other recent efforts have involved the development of any number of innovative sensors. Fiber optics (Dunne et al., 2006b), flexible sensors (Demmans et al., 2007), and sensors mounted on chairs (Mutlu et al., 2007) have been used to assess posture. Foam sensors stitched into clothing can detect both respiration and shoulder and arm movements (Dunne et al., 2006a). Wheel rotation sensors' on wheelchairs can be used to collect motion data suitable for classification of different types of activity (Ding et al., 2011). One study published in 2015 explored the use of a system for detecting magnetic radiation from electrical devices. Using an array of sensors worn on a wristband, this system collects and classifies data, identifying electrical devices used by the wearer (Wang et al., 2015). Although the initial design is often somewhat cumbersome, these early prototypes pave the way for future refinements that may themselves lead to commercial innovations. Other efforts might suggest novel uses of existing technology to collect otherwise unavailable data, such as the use of commercial Doppler radar devices to sense sleep patterns without placing sensors on the body (Rahman et al., 2015).

These custom sensing approaches might require help from engineers and signal-processing efforts not necessarily found in HCI research teams, but the broad possibilities for innovation and insight can often be well worth the effort.

Motion and position-sensing devices have many potential applications in HCI research, from assessing everyday activity such as posture, to studying activity while using a system, to forming the basis for new input modalities. Although custom-designed sensors will likely be the approach of choice to those with the engineering capability who are truly interested in pushing the envelope, the availability of cheaper and smaller sensors places these tools within the reach of many HCI researchers.

13.3.2 MOTION TRACKING FOR LARGE DISPLAYS AND VIRTUAL ENVIRONMENTS

Some forms of HCI inherently require users to move around in space. Users of wall-sized displays routinely move from one side to another, or up and down, just as teachers in a classroom move to different parts of the room. Users of virtual environments turn their heads, walk around, and move their hands to grasp objects. Collecting data that will help understand patterns of motion—where do users move, how do they move, and when do they do it?—requires data collection tools and techniques beyond those used with desktop systems.

Motion-tracking tools using cameras and markers worn by study participants can track motion through a large space. As the participant moves through space, the cameras use the marker to create a record of where the participant went and when. One study used this approach to examine activity in the course of using a wall-sized display (24 monitors, arranged as 8 columns of 3 monitors each, see Figure 13.2) to search and explore real-estate data. Researchers were interested to see whether users would move around more (physical navigation) or use zooming and panning mechanisms (virtual navigation).

Participants wore a hat with sensors for the motion-tracking system (Figure 13.3), which recorded their activity. Different display widths—ranging from one column to all eight columns—were used to study the effect of the width of the display. Participants generally used virtual navigation less and physical navigation more with wider displays. They also preferred physical navigation (Ball et al., 2007).

Researchers have used sensors that directly measure the position and orientation of various body parts to answer questions about movement and activity in immersive virtual environments. In one study, participants used a head-mounted display and a 3D mouse to interact with an immersive environment. Sensors monitored the position of the head, arms, legs, or other appropriate body parts. This approach provided insights into user activity in a variety of applications of virtual environments, including the diagnosis of attention deficit hyperactivity disorder (ADHD) and neurological rehabilitation of stroke patients (Shahabi et al., 2007).

FIGURE 13.2

A portion of the wall-sized display used in the navigation study.

From Ball, R., North, C., Bowman, D.A., 2007. Move to improve: promoting physical navigation to increase
user performance with large displays. In: Proceedings of the SIGCHI Conference on Human Factors in
Computing Systems, San Jose, California, USA. ACM. © ACM.

FIGURE 13.3

A hat mounted with head-tracking sensors for the study of navigation with wall-sized
displays.

From Ball, R., North, C., Bowman, D.A., 2007. Move to improve: promoting physical navigation to increase
user performance with large displays. In: Proceedings of the SIGCHI Conference on Human Factors in
Computing Systems, San Jose, California, USA. ACM. © ACM.

13.4 PHYSIOLOGICAL TOOLS

Our bodies are intricate devices, with numerous interrelated systems that change their behavior as we are excited, frustrated, or otherwise aroused. Each cell in our body is part of an electrical system, with voltage levels that differ across cell membranes and change under the right conditions (Stern et al., 2001). Blood flow, heart rate, rate of breathing, and electrical conductivity of various parts of the body are just a few of the measures that have been studied in an attempt to better understand these responses. The combination of these physiological measures with more traditional study of task performance and subjective responses is known as *psychophysiology* (Wastell and Newman, 1996).

Psychophysiology brings the possibility of using concrete measurements of the state of the human body to accompany assessments captured through surveys or observations. Imagine a study of user frustration levels with a series of alternative interface designs. You might start by asking participants to complete a series of tasks with each interface. After they complete the tasks, you could ask the users to complete one or more questionnaires aimed at understanding frustration levels. You might even ask them which features of the designs were more or less frustrating.

Even though this might be a fine design for your study, it misses some potentially important and interesting information. For example, when were the users most frustrated? Were they frustrated on the same task for each interface or did some designs cause less frustration on some tasks and more frustration on others? Postfact questionnaires are simply too coarse-grained to address these questions. The retrospective nature of questionnaires means that you are relying on the participants' fallible and incomplete memories to get your results.

Suppose your careful and thorough reading of the appropriate literature tells you that increases in frustration lead to increases in heart rate. With some sensors, recording equipment, and appropriate training in their use, you could change your experiment to monitor heart rate during task completion time. Appropriate tools for synchronizing the physiological data with other data that you collect during the tasks—such as task completion time or fine-grained records of all activities—will let you see exactly what the participant was doing when he became most frustrated. Correlating this information with feedback from the subjective questionnaire will provide you with a much fuller picture than you would have been able to get from only the task performance data and subjective responses.

13.4.1 PHYSIOLOGICAL DATA

Appropriate use of physiological data for research requires an understanding of the types of data that can be collected, the tools required for data collection, and the ways in which these data sources respond to various stimuli. Skin conductivity, blood flow, and respiration rate (to name a few examples) are very different measures, each presenting a variety of challenges in terms of both collection and interpretation.

Approaches to collecting data from various parts of the body require different classes of sensor for measuring responses. Broadly speaking, these sensors fall into two classes: electrodes, which directly record electrical signals, and transducers, which convert mechanical or physical measurements into an electrical form (Stern et al., 2001). In both cases, the resulting analog signals are converted to digital form by an analog-to-digital converter and stored on computers for filtering and analysis.

Complex physiological responses to different stimuli can make interpretation a challenge: there is no single, monolithic interpretation of these signals. Although measurements of heart rate, electric conductance of skin, respiration, or brain activity may be well-defined in terms of the underlying mechanical or biological activity, the meaning of those phenomena may be much harder to interpret. If an activity causes a person's heart rate to increase and changes activation patterns of different areas in their brain, is that because the task was hard? Establishing links between these physiological methods and concepts of interest to HCI researchers is often difficult. Understanding the limits of any particular measurements, and any debates over the interpretation of those measurements, is critical for conducting reliable and valid research with physiological data. Although some of these issues are discussed later, careful researchers will dive into more recent work in these rapidly evolving areas before rushing into conduct studies.

The sources of physiological data that have been used in HCI research can be classified according to the type of signal involved, the location on the body, and the kinds of sensors required (see Table 13.1). The range of data sources and their applications are likely to continue to expand as researchers find creative applications for new and evolving technologies.

Table 13.1 Types of Physiological Data Used in HCI Research

Data Source	Technique	Signal Type	Possible Locations	Sensors
Electrodermal activity	Galvanic skin response (GSR) (Scheirer et al., 2002; Mandryk and Inkpen, 2004)	Electrical	Fingers, toes	Surface electrodes
Cardiovascular data	Blood-volume pressure (Scheirer et al., 2002)	Light absorption	Finger	Surface electrodes
	Electrocardiography (Mandryk and Inkpen, 2004)	Electrical	Chest, abdomen	Surface electrodes
Respiration	Chest contraction and expansion (Mandryk and Inkpen, 2004)	Physical	Thorax	Stress sensor
Muscular and skeletal positioning	Pressure or position sensing (Brady et al., 2005; Dunne et al., 2006a,b; Dunne and Smyth, 2007)	Physical or electrical	Varied	Pressure sensor, fiber optics, others
Muscle tension	Electromyography (Mandryk and Inkpen, 2004)	Electrical	Jaw, face	Surface electrodes
Brain activity	Electroencephalography (Lee and Tan, 2006)	Electrical	Head	Electrodes in helmet
	Evoked responses (Stern et al., 2001)	Electrical	Head	Surface electrodes

13.4.1.1 *Electrodermal activity or galvanic skin response*

As many science-museum exhibits demonstrate, human bodies can act as conductors for electricity. Glands in our hands and feet produce sweat in response to emotional and cognitive stimuli. The salty sweat increases conductivity, allowing more electricity to flow (Stern et al., 2001; Mandryk and Inkpen, 2004). Conductivity is a measure of how well electricity flows through a substance: higher conductivity means a greater flow of electricity. Electrodermal activity is the measurement of the flow of electricity through the skin. Electrodermal systems use a pair of electrodes on the skin—usually connected to fingers—to measure the conductivity between two points (Figure 13.4). Research efforts have linked conductance level to arousal, cognitive activity (Mandryk and Inkpen, 2004), and frustration (Scheirer et al., 2002). Some studies have established differences in the magnitudes of changes associated with different emotions. For example, fear leads to smaller increases in skin conductance than sadness (Cacioppo et al., 2000).

13.4.1.2 *Cardiovascular signals*

Anyone who has ridden a roller coaster or watched a suspenseful movie has first-hand knowledge of how the heart responds to stimuli. Increased heart rate is one part of a complex set of reactions that may involve changes in the variability of the heart rate, blood pressure, and blood-volume pressure (BVP) (Scheirer et al., 2002). Heart-rate variability has been used to measure mental effort and stress (Wastell and Newman, 1996; Rowe et al., 1998; Mandryk and Inkpen, 2004) as well as emotional responses including fear, happiness, and anger (Cacioppo et al., 2000).

FIGURE 13.4

Thought technology's skin conductance sensor attaches to two fingers or toes to measure galvanic skin response (GSR).

From http://www.thoughttechnology.com/sciencedivision/pages/products/skinconduct.html (accessed 04.06.16)

Commonly used techniques for measuring cardiovascular activity include BVP monitoring and electrocardiography (EKG). BVP sensors worn on fingers measure changes in reflect light associated with changes in blood volume in finger capillaries. These measurements can be used as indirect measures of anxiety and other emotional responses such as that have been found to be correlated with blood. Heart-rate variability information can also be inferred from BVP data (Scheirer et al., 2002). Electrocardiography measures the electrical current that causes the heart to pump. Using sensors placed on different places on the body, EKG can measure heart rate, the interval between heartbeats, and heart-rate variability (Mandryk and Inkpen, 2004).

13.4.1.3 Respiration

Just as certain stimuli can make our hearts beat faster, changes in mood can affect our breathing. Arousal may make us breathe faster and some emotions can cause irregular breathing (Mandryk and Inkpen, 2004). Respiratory measures are strongly linked to cardiovascular activity (Stern et al., 2001).

A relatively straightforward approach to measuring respiration involves tracking the expansion and contraction of the chest cavity. Sensors that can measure how far and how rapidly the chest moves with each breath can be attached to the thorax (Stern et al., 2001; Mandryk and Inkpen, 2004) and even integrated into clothing (Brady et al., 2005).

13.4.1.4 Muscle tension

The contraction of muscles creates electrical signals that can be detected through electrodes placed on the muscle of interest, a technique known as electromyography (EMG). Measurements on the jaw can reveal tensions associated with a clenched jaw. Sensors on eyebrows or cheeks can detect muscle movements associated with frowns or smiles, respectively. Mildly positive emotions lead to lower EMG readings over the eyebrow and mildly higher activity over the cheek, relative to mildly negative emotions. Reactions to specific emotional moods including sadness, fear, and happiness have been studied as well, with less clear results (Cacioppo et al., 2000). EMG has also been used as an input modality: one project investigated the use of an EMG armband as a means of unobtrusively controlling a digital media player (Costanza et al., 2007).

13.4.1.5 Brain activity

Numerous techniques for directly and indirectly measuring brain activity have been developed. Brain-imaging techniques provide detailed displays, but expensive equipment and required medical expertise have limited their use in HCI research. Indirect measures that use changes in electrical signals on the head to measure brain activity provide less detail, but they are significantly easier to work with.

Electroencephalography (EEG) involves the use of electrodes distributed across the scalp to measure brain activity in the cerebral cortex. Typically, this involves placing a cap containing 128–256 electrodes on a participant's scalp (Figure 13.5). These electrodes are used to measure electrical activity in various locations,

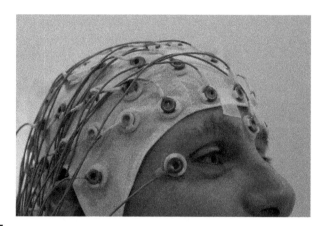

FIGURE 13.5

An electroencephalography (EEG) recording cap.

From https://commons.wikimedia.org/wiki/File:EEG_Recording_Cap.jpg.

with differences between locations or relative to some average baseline used as indicators of various types of activity (Stern et al., 2001). Evoked response measurements involve measurements of differentials between electrodes in two locations (perhaps earlobe and scalp), in response to auditory or visual responses (Stern et al., 2001).

Functional near-infrared spectroscopy (fNIRS) uses the reflectivity characteristics of the skull, scalp, and brain to measure mental activity. Near-infrared light can travel 2–3 cm into the brain before being either absorbed or reflected. Wavelengths that are reflected by hemoglobin can be used to measure mental activity (Izzetoglu et al., 2004; Hirshfeld et al., 2007). An fNIRS measurement system generally includes light sources and detectors mounted on a flexible headband.

Preliminary applications to HCI research have examined the ability of fNIRS to measure mental effort. An examination of the mental effort involved in solving rotating cube puzzles found that fNIRS measured distinguishable differences when comparing tasks with a graphical cube on a screen to tasks involving a physical cube. fNIRS was able to distinguish between tasks at three different levels of difficulty, with better-than-random accuracy (Hirshfeld et al., 2007). The application of fNIRS to a military command-and-control task found that fNIRS could be used to predict workload (Izzetoglu et al., 2004). The results from these studies were interpreted as demonstrating the utility of fNIRS for HCI research. fNIRS has subsequently been used in a number of HCI studies, addressing topics such as the impact of think-aloud protocols (Pike et al., 2014) and web-form layout (Lukanov et al., 2016) on mental workload; evaluating information visualization systems (Peck et al., 2013); and even as a form of input (Solovey et al., 2012; Afergan, 2014).

Functional magnetic resonance imaging (fMRI) has also been used in HCI research. fMRI works by tracking blood flow through the brain: as blood will flow to areas of the brain involved in relevant cognitive processes, locations associated with particular classes of problems can be identified. One study used fMRI to observe an emotional response to emoticons, even when regions of the brain associated with face recognition were inactive, indicating that participants did not recognize the emoticons as faces (Yuasa et al., 2006). Other HCI studies have applied fMRI to study the effect of multiple exposure to security warnings (Anderson et al., 2015), the extent to which participants feel that they are "present" in virtual reality (Clemente et al., 2014); mental loads associated with 3D motion and interactivity in virtual reality (Sjölie et al., 2010); perception of the quality of design (Lee et al., 2009), processes involved in learning new tools (Kitamura et al., 2003) and information search processes (Mostafa and Gwizdka, 2016); and validation of think-aloud protocols (Durning et al., 2013), among others.

Measurements of brain activity present tantalizing prospects for HCI research, presenting the possibility of getting "under the hood" and gaining otherwise unavailable understanding of mental states and cognitive processes. However, these techniques are not without their drawbacks. Although EEGs may be used reasonably inexpensively, fMRI research requires often expensive access to complex machinery. Data are often quite noisy, and interpretation can be challenging. Collaboration with neuroscientists trained in these techniques is often a winning strategy for HCI studies.

13.5 DATA COLLECTION, ANALYSIS, AND INTERPRETATION

Whether eye tracking; motion and posture sensing; or one of the several types of physiological data discussed earlier, studies measuring human activity will generally follow the same set of steps as any other study: designing, configuring, and testing data collection approaches; analyzing captured data; and interpreting the results. Despite these similarities to other studies, studies using the techniques described in this chapter present their own specific challenges at each of these stages (Figure 13.6)

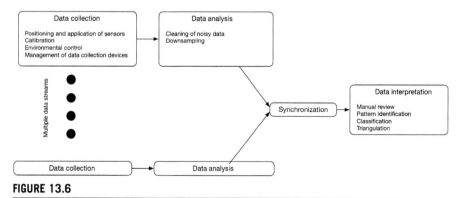

FIGURE 13.6

Stages and challenges in research studies involving collection of data from the human body.

13.5.1 DATA COLLECTION

Physiological data collection presents some challenges that are not generally encountered in more traditional HCI research. To make use of the data sources that literally measure the body, researchers must be in direct physical contact with their subjects. For galvanic skin response or blood-volume measurements, this may be as simple as placing an electrode on a finger tip. Surface electrodes (for EKG or EMG) and chest-mounted sensors (for respiration measurements) are substantially more complicated. These electrodes must be attached carefully in the appropriate position to ensure high-quality recording of the desired data.

Measurements based on body-mounted sensors involving pressure (Brady et al., 2005) or skeletal positioning (Dunne et al., 2006b) present a different set of challenges. As these approaches are relatively new and the technology is rapidly evolving, off-the-shelf tools with clear guidance may be few and far between. You may need to familiarize yourself with the pros and cons of a variety of sensors before conducting this sort of work. Before using any of these tools for measuring physiological data, you should make sure that you have appropriate training in their use. Partnering with an experienced health professional is an attractive means of ensuring correct use of sensors and other—probably expensive—equipment.

Although electrodes and sensors are not physically invasive, they may cause some discomfort and unease for some participants in your study. You may want to take extra care to be sensitive to participant's concerns, particularly involving the placement and attachment of electrodes. Some researchers suggest that electrodes should be attached only by someone of the same gender as the participant, in order to reduce anxiety and embarrassment (Stern et al., 2001). As some participants may become uncomfortable, your informed consent forms (Chapter 15) should be particularly explicit regarding potential risks. Take extra care to observe the participants' moods: when faced with a particularly distressed subject, you may wish to remind them that they can withdraw if they are uncomfortable. In addition to being considerate, this approach may save you from difficulties in data interpretation: if a participant's anxiety levels are high due to concern about the experiment, it may be difficult or impossible to identify anxiety responses caused by your stimuli.

These logistical challenges are even greater for more invasive techniques that require the involvement of a trained expert. Although surface electrodes are widely used in EMG measurements, needles placed in muscles are a possible alternative for many applications (Raez et al., 2006). Although the needles are safe, they must be used correctly, making them a strictly "don't try this at home" proposition. HCI researchers have shied away from this approach (Mandryk and Inkpen, 2004); unless your team has an experienced EMG professional, you would be well-advised to do so as well.

Even if you are not using needles or electrodes, more prosaic restrictions might apply. Eye-tracking devices might require that users be seated within an optimal distance range from the monitor, wired sensors might have limited ranges, and external distractions must be controlled to minimize confounding stimuli that might distract users and add unwanted cognitive load.

If you want to use physiological data to identify arousal, frustration, or other responses to specific interactions with a computer, you need to be able to synchronize changes in physiology with user actions. Plainly speaking, if you know that the variability in a user's heart rate increased at a certain point in time, you won't be able to interpret that change unless you know what the user was doing at the time. You are likely to be keeping a textual log of user actions, tracking mouse movements, key presses, and related information about the state of the application. Your physiological data would similarly be recorded via software that would create fine-grained records containing multiple measurements per second.

The first measurement challenge involves fine-grained measurements. Whereas physiological data are essentially continuous, tracking of events on the computer may not be. Fine-grained timing information may require using system clocks which operate on the order of milliseconds. Recording the number of internal clock "ticks" between events is one way to get high-resolution event data (Scheirer et al., 2002). Due to processing or hardware requirements, physiological data might be captured on one computer while tasks are completed on another. This arrangement presents the challenge of managing a fairly complex experimental setup. Besides the two computers (one for the application and one for data collection), you have sensors, analog-to-digital converters for converting the physiological signals into a form suitable for storage on the computer, potentially modified input devices, and possibly other equipment for audio and video recording (Figure 13.7).

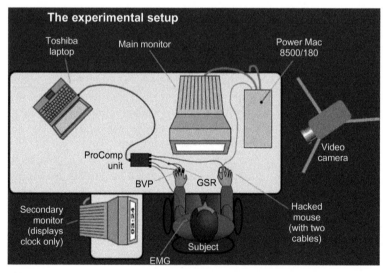

FIGURE 13.7

A complex experimental setup: physiological signals are collected by the ProComp analog-to-digital converter and stored on the laptop; the mouse is modified to simultaneously send control events to the computer and pulses to the analog-to-digital converter.

From Scheirer, J., Fernandez, R., Klein, J., Picard, R.W., 2002. Frustrating the user on purpose: a step toward building an affective computer. Interacting with Computers 14, 93–118. © Elsevier.

Data collection challenges often lead researchers to choose to conduct physiological studies in the comfort and convenience of the lab. Working in surroundings that are well-lit, well-organized and well-stocked with all needed supplies is a good strategy for minimizing the uncertainty associated with these data collection techniques. However, lab studies have their limits. The idealized settings may not reflect "real-world" situations where technologies might be used, leading to results that may be somewhat artificial. This disconnect between the environment of the study and the environment of use is described as reducing the *ecological validity* of the study. For studies addressing how interfaces are used in practice, lab settings might simply be unable to capture all of the richness of real usage environments. See the "LAB-IN-A-BOX" sidebar for a description of a suite of tools developed to address these challenges.

13.5.2 DATA ANALYSIS

Like other naturally occurring signals, eye-tracking data, motion detection systems, and physiological measurements are all very noisy, containing artifacts and variability that can make interpretation difficult. EMG signals, for example, suffer from significant amounts of distortion and random noise from other muscles (Raez et al., 2006). Tonic activity levels measure physiological responses in the absence of specific responses. These "baseline" measurements can differ significantly from one individual to the next and sometimes within individuals, due to factors such as headaches. Furthermore, the magnitude of response to a specific condition may be influenced by the tonic levels of a given signal: the response to any given stimulus might be lesser for a heart that is already beating quickly. Habituation is another concern: the magnitude of response to a stimulus decreases after repeated presentation (Stern et al., 2001). This can present a challenge for both experimental design and data interpretation. Eye-tracking and motion detection systems face similar challenges in distinguishing between intentional actions including saccades, pursuits, and fixations and seemingly random noise (microsaccades) (Duchowski, 2007). Appropriate use of software tools accompanying eye-tracking hardware can help address these difficulties.

Although a wide variety of methods has been proposed for extracting the signal from the surrounding noise (Raez et al., 2006), their use might require additional expertise: without a basis in a solid understanding, the application of signal-processing tools to noisy data streams can become a case of "garbage-in, garbage-out."

Once you have extracted the signal in your physiological data from the noise, your next challenge is to determine the granularity of the data that you will analyze. Some experiments call for relatively coarse data: if you are interested in comparing average responses for various testing conditions, you can just process data as it arrives, without worrying about specific correspondences between physiological data points and events in the computer interface. In cases where you want more detail, you might find that capturing *all* of the data available from your sensors is overwhelming. Some form of downsampling (capturing one out of every *n* data points instead of all data points) can often provide a useful means of reducing data volume without sacrificing fidelity or accuracy (Rick et al., 2015).

If you are trying to link physiological responses to specific actions or events, you may face the stream of integrating data streams that are collected separately—perhaps even on different computers. Although your application data may be fine-grained logs of individual events, physiological data streams may not have access to that information. If all data collection is done on one computer, the timestamp might be used with both data streams. When physiological data is captured on a separate computer, some clever engineering might be necessary. One set of experimenters used a modified mouse to solve this problem: in addition to sending control signals to the computer running the application, the mouse had a second wire that sent a pulse to the computer collecting physiological data. These pulses were used to synchronize the two streams (Scheirer et al., 2002).

Appropriate use of tools and validated approaches can simplify matters somewhat. Many eye-tracking systems will come with associated software that will collect and analyze data, potentially sparing you from the need to clean noisy data streams and identify fixations. Ideally, such tools will provide access to raw data along with summarized data, providing you with the means to conduct your own detailed analyses as needed.

13.5.3 DATA INTERPRETATION

Given multiple streams of complex, synchronized data involving one or more physiological signals and interactions with one or more computer programs, potentially alongside complementary data including survey data and audio/video recording, how can this data be interpreted?

One initial possibility is manual review. Particularly in earlier stages of interpretation, looking at the signals to find examples of any anomalies, episodes of interactions that might be informative, or other similar items of interest can often be a good way to decide where to explore in more details. Tools that facilitate comparison and alignment of multiple data streams can be very helpful in this regard. ChronoViz (Fouse et al., 2011) provides features for alignment and side-by-side review of multiple temporal data streams, allowing users to, for example, review synchronized displays of screen-capture video alongside physiological measurements. The "LAB-IN-A-BOX" sidebar discusses the use of the ChronoViz tool to analyze complex, synchronized data streams.

Identification of specific items or actions is often a first step. For example, you might be interested in seeing how often the user in an eye-tracking study looks in a certain region of the screen. When criteria are clearly and objectively defined, the identification of relevant intervals or incidents is generally straightforward.

Data granularity can also influence analysis and interpretation. For simple comparisons involving overall responses to differing conditions, averages might be sufficient (Mandryk and Inkpen, 2004). More complex analyses might attempt to model and classify episodes of emotional reaction (Scheirer et al., 2002), potentially using machine learning techniques to automatically identify actions and reactions with high degrees of confidence. Such classification methods may require manual identification of desired outputs, to be used as training sets for supervised learning.

A final interpretive challenge lies in the difficulty of understanding physiological signals. Even if you have a clear difference in some measure that seems to come in response to a specific event, interpreting that measure may prove challenging. You may be tempted to classify a response as specific emotional state—happiness, sadness, disgust, fear, or other examples—but data for many measures is inconclusive (Cacioppo et al., 2000). Although triangulation through the use of multiple signals can be a promising approach, there is no guarantee that any combination of responses will be sufficient. Mixed or incomplete measures are a very real possibility: some stimuli may lead to a response in one measure, with no change in another (Stern et al., 2001).

Physiological data presents tantalizing possibilities for researchers. Although the challenges of collecting and interpreting data from these sources are considerable, the possibility of identifying fine-grained, real-time responses to interfaces is often hard to resist. Before committing your valuable human and financial resources to such an effort, you may want to ask yourself if there is an easier way to observe the phenomena of interest. You may legitimately decide that your study of user frustration requires fine-grained detail about specific events, making post-test questionnaires insufficiently detailed. Before concluding that physiological data measures are required to identify incidences of frustration in real-time, you should consider using simpler methods such as videotapes, observations, think-aloud protocols, or time diaries. You may find that simpler methods get the job done with much less headache and expense. For a more detailed discussion of the use of eye tracking and physiological data into HCI design and evaluation, see Bergstrom and Schall's practical book *Eye Tracking in User Experience Design* (Bergstrom and Schall, 2014).

LAB-IN-A-BOX

Studies involving human data collection can be particularly challenging when they involve either realistic locations or collection and correlation of multiple data streams. Combining these two challenges can make matters even more interesting, leading often to innovative techniques. Nadir Weibel and colleagues struggled with these questions as they developed a multimodal set of data collection and analysis techniques to examine a complex and multifaceted set of HCIs: the use of electronic medical records (EMRs) by physicians during outpatient medical visits.

Although the use of electronic medical records has expanded substantially in recent years, the impact of this change on medical care is far from well understood. Although researchers have known for quite some time that

(Continued)

LAB-IN-A-BOX—CONT'D

physicians see EMRs as bringing changes in documentation, communication, and work processes, along with concerns about data quality (Embi et al., 2004), understanding the dynamics of *how* these records impact care is more challenging. A 2016 literature review found that although some studies found that although EMR use involved a range of both positive and negative communication behaviors, there was no conclusive evidence of any negative impact on patient perceptions of satisfaction or communication with physicians (Alkureishi et al., 2016).

Although these results suggest that in-depth studies of the use of EMRs during patient visits are needed to understand specific behaviors and to separate negative from positive impacts, conducting such studies presents several challenges. Lab-based simulations are likely too artificial, lacking the open-ended challenges associated with medical practice. Some researchers have resorted to video and audio recordings providing data capture from multiple perspectives (Asan and Montague, 2014). This approach is informative, but limited, as these captures might be able to identify where users are looking and how they are interacting, but details of interactions with the EMR will not be recorded, leaving researchers with the challenge of inferring how the details of the computer use might impact communication with patients.

Noting these difficulties, Nadir Weibel and colleagues developed a data and analysis infrastructure known as LAB-IN-A-BOX, designed to capture multiple streams of data detailing the dynamics of interactions between the physician, the patient, and the computer during medical visits. LAB-IN-A-BOX combines directional audio through a microphone array; eye tracking; full-room video, screen capture, mouse movements, mouse clicks, and other computer interactions through Techsmith Morae usability software (https://www.techsmith.com/morae.html); and Kinect for Windows to measure orientation of the user's body (Weibel et al., 2014). Realizing that using this device in physician examination rooms would require a great deal of flexibility in transportation and installation, Weibel and colleagues configured a hard plastic rolling case to hold all of the equipment, wiring, and connectors, enabling setup and data collection in 10 minutes or less (Weibel et al., 2014) (Figure 13.8).

To address the challenge of analyzing the various data streams, Weibel and colleagues started with a synchronization algorithm that aligns audio and video components. Kinect data is segmented to differentiate (when possible) between the clinician, the patient, and objects in the room such as chairs— all problems that would not be faced in an idealized lab environment with only one participant and no furniture. This data is then further processed to determine where the physician is looking at any given time, and to identify any gestures. Directional audio is processed to distinguish physician speech from patient speech. Mouse, keyboard, and other computer activities also are

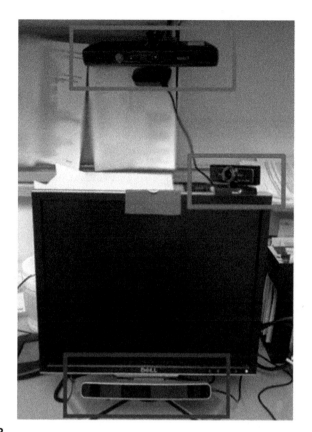

FIGURE 13.8

LAB-IN-A-BOX components: three sensors are installed around the monitor used by the physician: a Kinect sensor at the top, a digital webcam right above the monitor, and a remote eye tracker below the monitor (Weibel et al., 2014).

From Weibel, N., Rick, S., Emmenegger, C., Ashfaq, S., Calvitti, A., Agha, Z., 2014. LAB-IN-A-BOX: semi-automatic tracking of activity in the medical office. Personal and Ubiquitous Computing 19, 317–334.

analyzed to identify when the computer is being used and, through screen capture, what the user is doing. The resulting data streams can be viewed using the ChronoViz analysis tool (Fouse et al., 2011) (Figure 13.9). Noting the utility of using this data to develop deeper understandings than would be available from either lab-based studies or traditional ethnography, the LAB-IN-A-BOX team described this approach as "Computational Ethnography" (Zheng et al., 2015).

(Continued)

LAB-IN-A-BOX—CONT'D

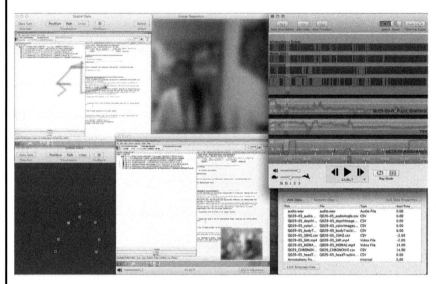

FIGURE 13.9

LAB-IN-A-BOX data: a series of ChronoViz displays of data captured during a patient visit. Counter-clockwise from upper-left: visualization of the eye-gaze path; body joints from Kinect; Morae video with mouse and room video; synchronization display of the various data sets; a ChronoViz window showing mouse clicks, window events, keystrokes, and pupil data from the eye tracker; and blurred room video (Weibel et al., 2014).

From Weibel, N., Rick, S., Emmenegger, C., Ashfaq, S., Calvitti, A., Agha, Z., 2014.
LAB-IN-A-BOX: semi-automatic tracking of activity in the medical office.
Personal and Ubiquitous Computing 19, 317–334.

13.6 **EXAMPLES**

Despite the challenges, numerous HCI researchers have used physiological data to observe user interactions in ways that would not otherwise be possible. An examination of some of these studies indicates the common theme of using these techniques to record real-time observations of a task in progress, as opposed to subjective, post-test response.

A study of cognitive load and multimodal interfaces used three different traffic control interfaces with three different task complexity levels to investigate the possibility of using galvanic skin response (GSR) to measure cognitive load. Participants used gesture-based, speech-based, or multimodal (speech and gesture) interfaces to complete tasks. Initial analysis of data from five participants indicated that average response levels were lowest for the multimodal interface, followed by speech and then gesture interfaces. For all three interfaces, the total response increased with task complexity. This was interpreted as providing evidence for the utility of using GSR to indicate cognitive loads. Analysis of specific recordings found GSR peaks to be correlated with stressful or frustrating events, with responses decreasing over time. Peaks were also correlated with major events that were thought to be cognitively challenging, including reading instructions and competing tasks (Shi et al., 2007).

Another study used both galvanic skin response (GSR) and blood-volume pressure (BVP) to measure user frustration in an explicit attempt to develop methods for using multiple sensing technologies. The experimental design involved a game with several puzzles. Participants were told that the experimenters were interested in how brightly colored graphics would influence physiological variables in an online game. Unbeknown to the participants, the game software was rigged to randomly introduce episodes of unresponsiveness. As participants were being timed and had been offered a reward if they had the fastest task completion times, these delays would presumably cause frustration.[1] BVP and GSR responses were used to develop models that could distinguish between frustrating and nonfrustrating states (Scheirer et al., 2002).

Interaction with computer games is a natural topic for physiological data. As anyone who has played video games knows, players can become excited while driving race cars, hunting aliens, or playing basketball on the computer. However, the fast-paced nature of these games limits the applicability of many techniques. Intrusive data collection techniques, such as "think-aloud" descriptions, interfere with the game-playing experience and posttest questionnaires fail to recapture all of the nuances of the playing experience (Mandryk and Inkpen, 2004).

One study used various physiological data sources—GSR, EKG, cardiovascular rate, respiration rate, and facial EMG—to measure responses to computer games played against a computer and against a friend. Starting from the premise that the physiological data would provide objective measures that would be correlated to players' subjective reports of experiences with video games, the researchers hypothesized that preferences and physiological responses would differ when comparing playing against a computer to playing against a friend. Specifically, they hypothesized that participants would prefer playing against friends, GSR and EMG values would be higher (due to increased competition), and that differences between GSR readings in the two conditions would correspond to subjective ratings (Mandryk and Inkpen, 2004).

To test these hypotheses, they asked participants to play a hockey video game, against the computer and against a friend. Participants were recruited in pairs of friends, so each person knew their opponent. The hypotheses were generally

---

[1] This experimental design is an example of deception (see Chapter 15). At the end of each session, participant debriefing explained the true purpose of the experiment. Participants were offered the opportunity to withdraw their data after the debriefing (Scheirer et al., 2002).

confirmed: participants found playing against a friend to be more exciting, and most had higher GSR and facial EMG levels when playing with a friend. Cardiovascular and respiratory measures did not show any differences. Investigation of specific incidents also revealed differences—participants had a greater response to a fight when playing a friend. Examination of the relationship between GSR, fun, and frustration revealed a positive correlation with fun and a negative correlation with frustration (Mandryk and Inkpen, 2004). The use of multiple coordinated sensors to measure frustration in game playing continues to be an active area of research, with more recent papers exploring topics such as the impact of system delays (Taylor et al., 2015).

EEGs have been also used by HCI researchers to develop brain-computer interfaces that use measurable brain activity to control computers (Millán, 2003). Machine-learning algorithms applied to EEG signals have been used to distinguish between different types of activity. Similar to the study of cooperative gaming described earlier (Mandryk and Inkpen, 2004), one study found that EEG signals could be used to distinguish between resting states, solo game play, and playing against an expert player (Lee and Tan, 2006). Other HCI applications involving EEG signals include identifying images of interest from a large set (Mathan et al., 2006) and measurement of memory and cognitive load in a military command-and-control environment (Berka et al., 2004).

Electromyography has been used to measure a variety of emotional responses to computer interfaces. One study of web surfing tasks found strong correlations between facial EMG measures of frustration and incorrectly completed tasks or home pages that required greater effort to navigate (Hazlett, 2003). Similar studies used EMG to measure emotional responses to videos describing new software features, tension in using media-player software (Hazlett and Benedek, 2006), and task difficulty or frustration in word processing (Branco et al., 2005). An experiment involving boys playing racing games on the Microsoft Xbox established the validity of facial EMG for distinguishing between positive and negative events (Hazlett, 2006). Combinations of multiple physiological measures, including EMG, have also been used to study emotional responses (Mahlke et al., 2006).

A broad body of work has explored the use of body sensing in a variety of healthcare domains, including assessment of disability, rehabilitation, and in use by clinicians. Several of these applications have been discussed in this chapter; for a more in-depth discussion, see "Body Tracking in Healthcare" in O'Hara et al. (2016).

13.7 SUMMARY

Many HCI questions involve digging deeper than the level of individual tasks. Instead of simply asking whether a task was completed correctly or how quickly it was completed, these efforts hope to understand what happened during the completion of the task. Such questions may involve examination of what the user is doing (which keys they are pressing, where they are moving the mouse, where they are looking) and how they are reacting (are they happy, sad, frustrated, or excited)?

Traditional measurement and observation techniques can be used to address these questions, but they are limited in their applicability. Even the most careful observations and video recording are very limited in determining which keys a user presses and how quickly they are pressed. Observation and video tape present similar limitations for tracking mouse movements or eye gazes. Inferring emotional states is similarly challenging: we may be able to identify excitement simply by watching someone playing a video game, but more subtle responses such as frustration may not be apparent. Asking users after the fact provides some detail, but questionnaires or interviews are limited to details that the participant remembers after the fact, making fine-grained data collection difficult, if not impossible.

Automated data collection approaches provide data that are unavailable through these more traditional approaches. For studies of mice and keyboard usage, actions that are intrinsically part of user tasks can be recorded for further analysis. Relatively simple data collection software can collect data tracking exactly what the user did (mouse press, mouse movement, key press) and when she did it. This information can be used to describe accuracy, identify problems in task completion, and classify task completion into periods of activity and inactivity. Combinations of multiple input devices—such as keyboard and mouse—can provide richer details.

Other interesting sources of human data may require a larger investment, potentially in analysis and possibly in equipment. Costs of eye-tracking systems have decreased significantly, but data analysis and interpretation can be a challenge. These concerns are even more pronounced for physiological measurements, which require equipping participants with electrodes, sensors, gauges, headbands, even helmets, or even more complex machinery. Interpreting the resulting noisy data is another challenge that requires substantial experience in signal processing.

You might want to start with simpler, less expensive techniques before you commit to the expense and difficulty associated with eye-tracking or physiological approaches. You might try simpler measures such as observation, video recording, or interviews, to see if they can be used to generate the insights that you need. Another approach would be to find proxies: although you might be tempted to use eye gaze to track a user's attention, tracking mouse movements might be a workable alternative. Eye tracking and galvanic skin response are tools that (perhaps with a little help from appropriate experts) many HCI researchers should be able to adopt for their own work.

For some research problems, the temptation of fine-grained physiological data using neuroimaging or other advanced techniques may be too great to resist. If you find yourself faced with such a question, be sure to work with experts: the assistance of collaborators who are familiar with both the equipment and the data interpretation challenges will be crucial to your success.

DISCUSSION QUESTIONS

1. Physiological data measurement tools present an interesting dilemma for researchers. Electrodes, helmets, chest-mounted sensors, and other tools used to measure these signals may be unfamiliar to many participants in research studies. Particularly for head-mounted equipment, the unfamiliarity and potential discomfort associated with these data collection tools may cause some individuals to become nervous, upset, or otherwise ill at ease. These responses might create a problem for studies aimed at understanding emotional responses to computer tasks. How would you go about distinguishing between measurable physiological responses that result from the use of unfamiliar, and potentially uncomfortable, monitoring hardware from responses to the task in question? How might factors such as the length of the experimental session and characteristics of the tasks complicate the challenge of distinguishing between these types of reactions?

2. Collaborative systems have the potential for generating a wide range of emotional reactions. When two or more people use a single computer system to work together on a problem of common interest (known as "colocated, synchronous collaboration"), some tasks may cause conflict, tension, excitement, or a variety of other emotional reactions. System behavior can also influence user reactions, as technical glitches and encouraging or discouraging feedback may lead to feelings of frustration. Technical concerns are even greater for collaboration between users at different locations ("distributed collaboration"), as network latencies, dropped connections, and slow responses are just a few of the problems that might be encountered. How would you go about measuring these emotional responses? Discuss the advantages and disadvantages of physiological data in this context, as opposed to self-reports, observation, or video recording. How might you use physiological data to study frustration in distributed collaboration?

RESEARCH DESIGN EXERCISE

Commonly available, inexpensive heart-rate monitors used for monitoring exercise might be usable for measuring physiological responses to computer use. Use one of these monitors to measure your pulse while you do a variety of computer tasks. First, measure your pulse while you are relaxed. Then, try some increasingly demanding and stressful tasks. You might try performing a simple task, such as completing an email message, a more complex task involving an advanced tool, such as a photo editor, a mentally challenging task, such as a math puzzle, and a fast-paced, exciting video game. How does your pulse change with each of these activities? As the act of pausing to read the display of the monitor may change your activity level, you might want to ask a friend to do the measurement and take notes.

REFERENCES

Aaltonen, A., Hyrskykari, A., Räihä, K.-J., 1998. 101 spots, or how do users read menus? In: Proceedings of the SIGCHI Conference on Human Factors in Computing Systems, Los Angeles, California, United States. ACM Press/Addison-Wesley Publishing Co., New York, pp. 132–139.

Afergan, D., 2014. Using brain-computer interfaces for implicit input. In: Proceedings of the Adjunct Publication of the 27th Annual ACM Symposium on User Interface Software and Technology, Honolulu, Hawaii, USA. ACM, New York, pp. 13–16.

Agustin, J.S., Skovsgaard, H., Mollenbach, E., Barret, M., Tall, M., Hansen, D.W., Hansen, J.P., 2010. Evaluation of a low-cost open-source gaze tracker. In: Proceedings of the 2010 Symposium on Eye-Tracking Research and Applications, Austin, Texas. ACM, New York, ISBN: 978-1-60558-994-7, pp. 77–80.

Albinali, F., Goodwin, M.S., Intille, S.S., 2009. Recognizing stereotypical motor movements in the laboratory and classroom: a case study with children on the autism spectrum. In: Proceedings of the 11th International Conference on Ubiquitous Computing, Orlando, Florida, USA. ACM, New York, pp. 71–80.

Alkureishi, M.A., Lee, W.W., Lyons, M., Press, V.G., Imam, S., Nkansah-Amankra, A., Werner, D., Arora, V.M., 2016. Impact of electronic medical record use on the patient-doctor relationship and communication: a systematic review. Journal of General Internal Medicine 31 (5), 548–560.

Anderson, B.B., Kirwan, C.B., Jenkins, J.L., Eargle, D., Howard, S., Vance, A., 2015. How polymorphic warnings reduce habituation in the brain: insights from an fMRI study. In: Proceedings of the 33rd Annual ACM Conference on Human Factors in Computing Systems, Seoul, Republic of Korea. ACM, New York, pp. 2883–2892.

Arteaga, S., Chevalier, J., Coile, A., Hill, A.W., Sali, S., Sudhakhrisnan, S., Kurniawan, S.H., 2008. Low-cost accelerometry-based posture monitoring system for stroke survivors. In: Proceedings of the 10th International ACM SIGACCESS Conference on Computers and Accessibility, Halifax, Nova Scotia, Canada. ACM, New York, pp. 243–244.

Asan, O., Montague, E., 2014. Technology-mediated information sharing between patients and clinicians in primary care encounters. Behaviour & Information Technology 33 (3), 259–270.

Ball, R., North, C.N., Bowman, D.A., 2007. Move to improve: promoting physical navigation to increase user performance with large displays. In: Proceedings of the SIGCHI Conference on Human Factors in Computing Systems, San Jose, California, USA. ACM, New York, pp. 191–200.

Barreto, A., Gao, Y., Adjouadi, M., 2008. Pupil diameter measurements: untapped potential to enhance computer interaction for eye tracker users? In: Proceedings of the 10th International ACM SIGACCESS Conference on Computers and Accessibility, Halifax, Nova Scotia, Canada. ACM, New York, pp. 269–270.

Bass, S.B., Gordon, T.F., Gordon, R., Parvanta, C., 2016. Using eye tracking and gaze pattern analysis to test a "dirty bomb" decision aid in a pilot RCT in urban adults with limited literacy. BMC Medical Informatics and Decision Making 16 (1), 1–13.

Bergstrom, J.R., Schall, A., 2014. Eye Tracking in User Experience Design. Morgan Kaufmann, Amsterdam.

Berka, C., Levendowski, D.J., Cvetinovic, M.M., Petrovic, M.M., Davis, G., Lumicao, M.N., Zivkovic, V.T., Popovic, M.V., Olmstead, R., 2004. Real-time analysis of EEG indexes of alertness, cognition, and memory acquired with a wireless EEG headset. International Journal of Human–Computer Interaction 17 (2), 151–170.

Bernaerts, Y., Druwé, M., Steensels, S., Vermeulen, J., Schöning, J., 2014. The office smartwatch: development and design of a smartwatch app to digitally augment interactions in an office environment. In: Proceedings of the 2014 Companion Publication on Designing Interactive Systems, Vancouver, BC, Canada. ACM, New York, pp. 41–44.

Bieg, H.-J., 2009. Gaze-augmented manual interaction. In: Proceedings of the 27th International Conference Extended Abstracts on Human Factors in Computing Systems, Boston, MA, USA. ACM, New York, pp. 3121–3124.

Bieg, H.-J., Chuang, L.L., Fleming, R.W., Reiterer, H., Bülthoff, H.H., Bieg, H.-J., Chuang, L.L., Fleming, R.W., Reiterer, H., Bülthoff, H.H., 2010. Eye and pointer coordination in search and selection tasks. In: Proceedings of the 2010 Symposium on Eye-Tracking Research and Applications, Austin, Texas. ACM, New York, pp. 89–92.

Bond, R.R., Kligfield, P.D., Zhu, T., Finlay, D.D., Drew, B., Guldenring, D., Breen, C., Clifford, G.D., Wagner, G.S., 2015. Novel approach to documenting expert ECG interpretation using eye tracking technology: a historical and biographical representation of the late Dr Rory Childers in action. Journal of Electrocardiology 48, 43–44.

Bowers, V.A., Snyder, H.L., 1990. Concurrent versus retrospective verbal protocol for comparing window usability. Proceedings of the Human Factors and Ergonomics Society Annual Meeting 34 (17), 1270–1274.

Brady, S., Dunne, L.E., Tynan, R., Diamond, D., Smyth, B., O'Hare, G., 2005. Garment-based monitoring of respiration rate using a foam pressure sensor. In: Proceedings of the Ninth IEEE International Symposium on Wearable Computers. IEEE Computer Society, Los Alamitos, pp. 214–215.

Branco, P., Firth, P., Miguel, E.L., Bonato, P., 2005. Faces of emotion in human-computer interaction. In: CHI '05 Extended Abstracts on Human Factors in Computing Systems, Portland, OR, USA. ACM, New York, pp. 1236–1239.

Brown, S.L., Richardson, M., 2012. The effect of distressing imagery on attention to and persuasiveness of an anti-alcohol message: a gaze-tracking approach. Health Education & Behavior 39, 8–17.

Buscher, G., Cutrell, E., Morriss, M.R., 2009. What do you see when you're surfing?: using eye tracking to predict salient regions of web pages. In: Proceedings of the 27th International Conference on Human Factors in Computing Systems, Boston, MA, USA. ACM, New York, pp. 21–30.

Cacioppo, J.T., Bernston, G.G., Larsen, J.T., Poehlmann, K.M., Ito, T.A., 2000. The psychophysiology of emotion. In: Lewis, M., Haviland-Jones, J.M. (Eds.), Handbook of Emotions. The Guilford Press, New York, pp. 173–191.

Card, S.K., Pirolli, P., Van Der Wege, M., Morrison, J.B., Reeder, R.W., Schraedley, P.K., Boshart, J., 2001. Information scent as a driver of Web behavior graphs: results of a protocol analysis method for Web usability. In: Proceedings of the SIGCHI Conference on Human Factors in Computing Systems, Seattle, Washington, United States. ACM, New York, pp. 498–505.

Chen, M.C., Anderson, J.R., Sohn, M.H., 2001. What can a mouse cursor tell us more?: correlation of eye/mouse movements on web browsing. In: CHI '01 Extended Abstracts on Human Factors in Computing Systems, Seattle, Washington. ACM, New York, pp. 281–282.

Clark, R.A., Pua, Y.-H., Fortin, K., Ritchie, C., Webster, K.E., Denehy, L., Bryant, A.L., 2012. Validity of the Microsoft Kinect for assessment of postural control. Gait & Posture 36 (3), 372–377.

Clemente, M., Rey, B., Rodríguez-Pujadas, A., Barros-Loscertales, A., Baños, R.M., Botella, C., Alcañiz, M., Ávila, C., 2014. An fMRI study to analyze neural correlates of presence during virtual reality experiences. Interacting with Computers 26 (3), 269–284.

Costanza, E., Inverso, S.A., Allen, R., Maes, P., 2007. Intimate interfaces in action: assessing the usability and subtlety of EMG-based motionless gestures. In: Proceedings of the SIGCHI Conference on Human Factors in Computing Systems, San Jose, California, USA. ACM, New York, pp. 29–36.

Crowe, E.C., Narayanan, N.H., 2000. Comparing interfaces based on what users watch and do. In: Proceedings of the 2000 Symposium on Eye Tracking Research & Applications, Palm Beach Gardens, Florida, United States. ACM, New York.

Cutrell, E., Guan, Z., 2007. What are you looking for?: an eye-tracking study of information usage in web search. In: Proceedings of the SIGCHI Conference on Human Factors in Computing Systems, San Jose, California, USA. ACM, New York, pp. 407–416.

Demmans, C., Subramanian, S., Titus, J., 2007. Posture monitoring and improvement for laptop use. In: CHI '07 Extended Abstracts on Human Factors in Computing Systems, San Jose, CA, USA. ACM, New York, pp. 2357–2362.

Diaz, F., White, R., Buscher, G., Liebling, D., 2013. Robust models of mouse movement on dynamic web search results pages. In: Proceedings of the 22nd ACM International Conference on Information & Knowledge Management, San Francisco, California, USA. ACM, New York, pp. 1451–1460.

Ding, D., Hiremath, S., Chung, Y., Cooper, R., 2011. Detection of wheelchair user activities using wearable sensors. In: Stephanidis, C. (Ed.), Universal Access in Human-Computer Interaction, Context Diversity: 6th International Conference, UAHCI 2011, Held as Part of HCI International 2011, Orlando, FL, USA, July 9–14, 2011, Part III. Springer, Berlin, pp. 145–152.

Doberne, J.W., He, Z., Mohan, V., Gold, J.A., Marquard, J., Chiang, M.F., 2015. Using high-fidelity simulation and eye tracking to characterize EHR workflow patterns among hospital physicians. In: AMIA Annual Symposium Proceedings 2015. pp. 1881–1889.

Duchowski, A., 2007. Eye-Tracking Methodology: Theory and Practice. Springer, New York.

Dunne, L.E., Smyth, B., 2007. Psychophysical elements of wearability. In: Proceedings of the SIGCHI Conference on Human factors in Computing Systems, San Jose, California, USA. ACM, New York, pp. 299–302.

Dunne, L.E., Brady, S., Tynan, R., Lau, K., Smyth, B., Diamond, D., O'Hare, G.M.P., 2006a. Garment-based body sensing using foam sensors. In: Proceedings of the 7th Australasian User Interface Conference, Volume 50. Hobart, Australia. Australian Computer Society, Darlinghurst, pp. 165–171.

Dunne, L.E., Walsh, P., Smyth, B., Caulfield, B., 2006b. Design and Evaluation of a Wearable Optical Sensor for Monitoring Seated Spinal Posture. In: 10th IEEE International Symposium on Wearable Computers, Montreux, Switzerland, IEEE, pp. 65–68.

Durning, S.J., Artino, A.R., Beckman, T.J., Graner, J., van der Vleuten, C., Holmboe, E., Schuwirth, L., 2013. Does the think-aloud protocol reflect thinking? Exploring functional neuroimaging differences with thinking (answering multiple choice questions) versus thinking aloud. Medical Teacher 35 (9), 720–726.

Dutta, T., 2012. Evaluation of the Kinect™ sensor for 3-D kinematic measurement in the workplace. Applied Ergonomics 43 (4), 645–649.

Embi, P.J., Yackel, T.R., Logan, J.R., Bowen, J.L., Cooney, T.G., Gorman, P.N., 2004. Impacts of computerized physician documentation in a teaching hospital: perceptions of faculty and resident physicians. Journal of the American Medical Informatics Association 11 (4), 300–309.

Fong, A., Hoffman, D.J., Zachary Hettinger, A., Fairbanks, R.J., Bisantz, A.M., 2016. Identifying visual search patterns in eye gaze data; gaining insights into physician visual workflow. Journal of the American Medical Informatics Association 23 (6), 1180–1184.

Fono, D., Vertegaal, R., 2005. EyeWindows: evaluation of eye-controlled zooming windows for focus selection. In: Proceedings of the SIGCHI Conference on Human Factors in Computing Systems, Portland, Oregon, USA. ACM, New York, pp. 151–160.

Fouse, A., Weibel, N., Hutchins, E., Hollan, J.D., 2011. ChronoViz: a system for supporting navigation of time-coded data. In: CHI '11 Extended Abstracts on Human Factors in Computing Systems, Vancouver, BC, Canada. ACM, New York, pp. 299–304.

Fudickar, S., Karth, C., Mahr, P., Schnor, B., 2012. Fall-detection simulator for accelerometers with in-hardware preprocessing. In: Proceedings of the 5th International Conference on PErvasive Technologies Related to Assistive Environments, Heraklion, Crete, Greece. ACM, New York, pp. 1–7.

Goldberg, J.H., Stimson, M.J., Lewenstein, M., Scott, N., Wichansky, A.M., 2002. Eye tracking in web search tasks: design implications. In: Proceedings of the 2002 Symposium on Eye Tracking Research & Applications, New Orleans, Louisiana. ACM, New York, pp. 51–58.

Guan, Z., Cutrell, E., 2007. An eye tracking study of the effect of target rank on web search. In: Proceedings of the SIGCHI Conference on Human Factors in Computing Systems, San Jose, California, USA. ACM, New York, pp. 417–420.

Guan, Z., Lee, S., Cuddihy, E., Ramey, J., 2006. The validity of the stimulated retrospective think-aloud method as measured by eye tracking. In: Proceedings of the SIGCHI Conference on Human Factors in Computing Systems, Montreal, Quebec, Canada. ACM, New York, pp. 1253–1262.

Gwizdka, J., Zhang, Y., 2015. Differences in eye-tracking measures between visits and revisits to relevant and irrelevant web pages. In: Proceedings of the 38th International ACM SIGIR Conference on Research and Development in Information Retrieval, Santiago, Chile. ACM, New York, pp. 811–814.

Haapalainen, E., Kim, S., Forlizzi, J.F., Dey, A.K., 2010. Psycho-physiological measures for assessing cognitive load. In: Proceedings of the 12th ACM International Conference on Ubiquitous computing, Copenhagen, Denmark. ACM, New York, pp. 301–310.

Han, J., Shao, L., Xu, D., Shotton, J., 2013. Enhanced computer vision with microsoft Kinect sensor: a review. IEEE Transactions on Cybernetics 43 (5), 1318–1334.

Harrison, D., Marshall, P., Berthouze, N., Bird, J., 2014. Tracking physical activity: problems related to running longitudinal studies with commercial devices. In: Proceedings of the 2014 ACM International Joint Conference on Pervasive and Ubiquitous Computing: Adjunct Publication, Seattle, Washington. ACM, New York, pp. 699–702.

Hart, S.G., 2006. Nasa-Task Load Index (NASA-TLX); 20 years later. Proceedings of the Human Factors and Ergonomics Society Annual Meeting 50 (9), 904–908.

Hart, S.G., Staveland, L.E., 1988. Development of NASA-TLX (Task Load Index): results of empirical and theoretical research. In: Peter, A.H., Najmedin, M. (Eds.), Advances in Psychology, vol. 52. North-Holland, Amsterdam, pp. 139–183.

Hazlett, R., 2003. Measurement of user frustration: a biologic approach. In: CHI '03 Extended Abstracts on Human Factors In Computing Systems, Ft. Lauderdale, Florida, USA. ACM, New York, pp. 734–735.

Hazlett, R., 2006. Measuring emotional valence during interactive experiences: boys at video game play. In: Proceedings of the SIGCHI Conference on Human Factors in Computing Systems, Montréal, Québec, Canada. ACM, New York, pp. 1023–1026.

Hazlett, R.L., Benedek, J., 2006. Measuring emotional valence to understand the user's experience of software. International Journal of Human–Computer Studies 65 (4), 306–314.

Higuch, K., Yonetani, R., Sato, Y., 2016. Can eye help you?: effects of visualizing eye fixations on remote collaboration scenarios for physical tasks. In: Proceedings of the 2016 CHI Conference on Human Factors in Computing Systems, Santa Clara, California, USA. ACM, New York, pp. 5180–5190.

Hirshfeld, L.M., Girouard, A., Solovey, E.T., Jacob, R., Sassaroli, J.K.A., Tong, Y., Fantini, S., 2007. Human-computer interaction and brain measurement using functional near-infrared spectroscopy (poster paper). In: ACM Symposium on User Interface Software and Technology (UIST).

Hornof, A., Cavender, A., Hoselton, R., 2004. Eyedraw: a system for drawing pictures with eye movements. In: Proceedings of the 6th International ACM SIGACCESS Conference on Computers and Accessibility, Atlanta, GA, USA. ACM, New York, pp. 86–93.

Huang, J., White, R., Buscher, G., 2012. User see, user point: gaze and cursor alignment in web search. In: Proceedings of the SIGCHI Conference on Human Factors in Computing Systems, Austin, Texas, USA. ACM, New York, pp. 1341–1350.

Huang, L.-L., Chen, M.-H., Wang, C.-H., Lee, C.-F., 2015. Developing a digital game for domestic stroke patients' upper extremity rehabilitation—design and usability assessment. In: Antona, M., Stephanidis, C. (Eds.), Universal Access in Human-Computer Interaction. Access to Learning, Health and Well-Being: 9th International Conference, UAHCI 2015, Held as Part of HCI International 2015, Los Angeles, CA, USA, August 2–7, 2015, Part III. Springer International Publishing, Cham, pp. 454–461.

Izzetoglu, K., Bunce, S., Onaral, B., Pourrezaei, K., Chance, B., 2004. Functional optical brain imaging using near-infrared during cognitive tasks. International Journal of Human–Computer Interaction 17 (2), 211–231.

Jacob, R.J.K., Karn, K.S., 2003. Commentary on section 4. Eye tracking in human-computer interaction and usability research: ready to deliver the promises. In: Hyona, J., Radach, R., Deubel, H. (Eds.), The Mind's Eyes: Cognitive and Applied Aspects of Eye Movements. Elsevier Science, Oxford.

Jalaliniya, S., Mardanbegi, D., Sintos, I., Garcia, D.G., 2015. EyeDroid: an open source mobile gaze tracker on Android for eyewear computers. In: Adjunct Proceedings of the 2015 ACM International Joint Conference on Pervasive and Ubiquitous Computing and Proceedings of the 2015 ACM International Symposium on Wearable Computers, Osaka, Japan. ACM, New York, pp. 873–879.

Jiang, X., Atkins, M.S., Tien, G., Bednarik, R., Zheng, B., 2014. Pupil responses during discrete goal-directed movements. In: Proceedings of the SIGCHI Conference on Human Factors in Computing Systems, Toronto, Ontario, Canada. ACM, New York, pp. 2075–2084.

Johansen, S.A., Agustin, J.S., Skovsgaard, H., Hansen, J.P., Tall, M., 2011. Low cost vs. high-end eye tracking for usability testing. In: CHI '11 Extended Abstracts on Human Factors in Computing Systems, Vancouver, BC, Canada. ACM, New York, ISBN: 978-1-4503-0268-5, pp. 1177–1182.

Kaewkannate, K., Kim, S., 2016. A comparison of wearable fitness devices. BMC Public Health 16 (1), 1–16.

Kim, J.-W., Kim, H.-J., Nam, T.-J., 2016. M. Gesture: an acceleration-based gesture authoring system on multiple handheld and wearable devices. In: Proceedings of the 2016 CHI Conference on Human Factors in Computing Systems, Santa Clara, California, USA. ACM, New York, pp. 2307–2318.

Kitamura, Y., Yamaguchi, Y., Hiroshi, I., Kishino, F., Kawato, M., 2003. Things happening in the brain while humans learn to use new tools. In: Proceedings of the SIGCHI Conference on Human Factors in Computing Systems, Ft. Lauderdale, Florida, USA. ACM, New York, pp. 417–424.

Klingner, J., Kumar, R., Hanrahan, P., 2008. Measuring the task-evoked pupillary response with a remote eye tracker. In: Proceedings of the 2008 Symposium on Eye Tracking Research & Applications, Savannah, Georgia. ACM, New York, pp. 69–72.

Kocejko, T., Goforth, K., Moidu, K., Wtorek, J., 2015. Visual attention distribution based assessment of user's skill in electronic medical record navigation. Journal of Medical Imaging and Health Informatics 5, 951–958.

Krafka, K., Khosla, A., Kellnhofer, P., Kannan, H., Bhandarkar, S., Matusik, W., Torralba, A., 2016. Eye tracking for everyone. In: IEEE Conference on Computer Vision and Pattern Recognition (CVPR).

Krupinski, E.A., Tillack, A.A., Richter, L., Henderson, J.T., Bhattacharyya, A.K., Scott, K.M., Graham, A.R., Descour, M.R., Davis, J.R., Weinstein, R.S., 2006. Eye-movement study and human performance using telepathology virtual slides: implications for medical education and differences with experience. Human Pathology 37, 1543–1556.

Kumar, M., 2006. Reducing the Cost of Eye Tracking Systems. Stanford University Computer Science Technical Report.

Kumar, M., Paepcke, A., Winograd, T., 2007. EyePoint: practical pointing and selection using gaze and keyboard. In: Proceedings of the SIGCHI Conference on Human Factors in Computing Systems, San Jose, California, USA. ACM, New York, pp. 421–430.

Lee, J.C., Tan, D.S., 2006. Using a low-cost electroencephalograph for task classification in HCI research. In: Proceedings of the 19th Annual ACM Symposium on User Interface Software and Technology, Montreux, Switzerland. ACM, New York, pp. 81–90.

Lee, H., Lee, J., Seo, S., 2009. Brain response to good and bad design. In: Jacko, J.A. (Ed.), Human-Computer Interaction. New Trends: 13th International Conference, HCI International 2009, San Diego, CA, USA, July 19–24, 2009, Part I. Springer, Berlin, Heidelberg, pp. 111–120.

Lee, M.K., Kim, J., Forlizzi, J., Kiesler, S., 2015. Personalization revisited: a reflective approach helps people better personalize health services and motivates them to increase physical activity. In: Proceedings of the 2015 ACM International Joint Conference on Pervasive and Ubiquitous Computing, Osaka, Japan. ACM, New York, pp. 743–754.

Levin, G., Yarin, P., 1999. Bringing sketching tools to keychain computers with an acceleration-based interface. In: CHI '99 Extended Abstracts on Human Factors in Computing Systems, Pittsburgh, Pennsylvania. ACM, New York, pp. 268–269.

Liebling, D.J., Dumais, S.T., 2014. Gaze and mouse coordination in everyday work. In: Proceedings of the 2014 ACM International Joint Conference on Pervasive and Ubiquitous Computing Adjunct Publication, UbiComp '14 Adjunct, New York, NY, USA. ACM Press, New York, pp. 1141–1150.

Lukanov, K., Maior, H.A., Wilson, M.L., 2016. Using fNIRS in usability testing: understanding the effect of web form layout on mental workload. In: Proceedings of the 2016 CHI Conference on Human Factors in Computing Systems, Santa Clara, California, USA. ACM, New York, pp. 4011–4016.

Mahlke, S., Minge, M., Thüring, M., 2006. Measuring multiple components of emotions in interactive contexts. In: CHI '06 Extended Abstracts on Human Factors in Computing Systems, Montréal, Québec, Canada. ACM, New York, pp. 1061–1066.

Mandryk, R.L., Inkpen, K., 2004. Physiological indicators for the evaluation of co-located collaborative play. In: Proceedings of the 2004 ACM Conference on Computer Supported Cooperative Work, Chicago, Illinois, USA. ACM, New York, pp. 102–111.

Marshall, J., Linehan, C., Hazzard, A., 2016. Designing brutal multiplayer video games. In: Proceedings of the 2016 CHI Conference on Human Factors in Computing Systems, Santa Clara, California, USA. ACM, New York, pp. 2669–2680.

Mathan, S., Whitlow, S., Erdogmus, D., Pavel, M., Ververs, P., Dorneich, M., 2006. Neurophysiologically driven image triage: a pilot study. In: CHI '06 Extended Abstracts on Human Factors in Computing Systems, Montréal, Québec, Canada. ACM, New York, pp. 1085–1090.

Mazur, L.M., Mosaly, P.R., Moore, C., Comitz, E., Yu, F., Falchook, A.D., Eblan, M.J., Hoyle, L.M., Tracton, G., Chera, B.S., Marks, L.B., 2016. Toward a better understanding of task demands, workload, and performance during physician-computer interactions. Journal of the American Medical Informatics Association 23 (6), 1113–1120.

Mehner, S., Klauck, R., Koenig, H., 2013. Location-independent fall detection with smartphone. In: Proceedings of the 6th International Conference on Pervaise Technologies Related to Assistive Environments, Rhodes, Greece. ACM, New York, pp. 1–8.

Meiselwitz, G., Wentz, B., Lazar, J., 2010. Universal usability: past, present, and future. Foundations and Trends in Human-Computer Interaction 3 (4), 213–333.

Millán, J.D.R., 2003. Adaptive brain interfaces. Communications of the ACM 46 (3), 74–80.

Moacdieh, N., Sarter, N., 2015. Clutter in electronic medical records: examining its performance and attentional costs using eye tracking. Human Factors 57, 591–606.

Montague, E., Asan, O., 2014. Dynamic modeling of patient and physician eye gaze to understand the effects of electronic health records on doctor-patient communication and attention. International Journal of Medical Informatics 83 (3), 225–234.

Mostafa, J., Gwizdka, J., 2016. Deepening the role of the user: neuro-physiological evidence as a basis for studying and improving search. In: Proceedings of the 2016 ACM on Conference on Human Information Interaction and Retrieval, Carrboro, North Carolina, USA. ACM, New York, pp. 63–70.

Muñoz, J.E., Chavarriaga, R., Lopez, D.S., 2014. Application of hybrid BCI and exergames for balance rehabilitation after stroke. In: Proceedings of the 11th Conference on Advances in Computer Entertainment Technology, Funchal, Portugal. ACM, New York, pp. 1–4.

Murata, A., 2006. Eye-gaze input versus mouse: cursor control as a function of age. International Journal of Human–Computer Interaction 21 (1), 1–14.

Mutlu, B., Krause, A., Forlizzi, J., Guestrin, C., Hodgins, J., 2007. Robust, low-cost, non-intrusive sensing and recognition of seated postures. In: Proceedings of the 20th Annual ACM Symposium on User Interface Software and Technology, Newport, Rhode Island, USA. ACM, New York, pp. 149–158.

Navalpakkam, V., Jentzsch, L., Sayres, R., Ravi, S., Ahmed, A., Smola, A., 2013. Measurement and modeling of eye-mouse behavior in the presence of nonlinear page layouts. In: Proceedings of the 22nd International Conference on World Wide Web, Rio de Janeiro, Brazil, May 13–17. ACM, New York, pp. 953–964.

Nebeling, M., Ott, D., Norrie, M.C., 2015. Kinect analysis: a system for recording, analysing and sharing multimodal interaction elicitation studies. In: Proceedings of the 7th ACM SIGCHI Symposium on Engineering Interactive Computing Systems, Duisburg, Germany. ACM, New York, pp. 142–151.

Nielsona, J.A., Mamidala, R.N., Khan, J., 2013. In-situ eye-tracking of emergency physician result review. Studies in Health Technology and Informatics 192, 1156.

Ogata, M., Imai, M., 2015. SkinWatch: skin gesture interaction for smart watch. In: Proceedings of the 6th Augmented Human International Conference, Singapore, Singapore. ACM, New York, pp. 21–24.

O'Hara, K., Morrison, C., Sellen, A., Bianchi-Berthouze, N., Craig, C., 2016. Body tracking in healthcare. Synthesis Lectures on Assistive, Rehabilitative, and Health-Preserving Technologies 5 (1), 1–151.

Paletta, L., Neuschmied, H., Schwarz, M., Lodron, G., Pszeida, M., Ladstätter, S., Luley, P., 2014. Smartphone eye tracking toolbox: accurate gaze recovery on mobile displays. In: Proceedings of the Symposium on Eye Tracking Research and Applications, Safety Harbor, Florida. ACM, New York, pp. 367–368.

Peck, E.M.M., Yuksel, B.F., Ottley, A., Jacob, R.J.K., Chang, R., 2013. Using fNIRS brain sensing to evaluate information visualization interfaces. In: Proceedings of the SIGCHI Conference on Human Factors in Computing Systems, Paris, France. ACM, New York, pp. 473–482.

Pfeuffer, K., Alexander, J., Gellersen, H., 2016. Partially-indirect bimanual input with gaze, pen, and touch for pan, zoom, and ink interaction. In: Proceedings of the 2016 CHI Conference on Human Factors in Computing Systems, Santa Clara, California, USA. ACM, New York, pp. 2845–2856.

Pian, W., Khoo, S.G.C., Chang, Y.-K., 2016. The criteria people use in relevance decisions on health information: an analysis of user eye movements when browsing a health discussion forum. Journal of Medical Internet Research 18 (6), e136.

Pike, M.F., Maior, H.A., Porcheron, M., Sharples, S.C., Wilson, M.L., 2014. Measuring the effect of think aloud protocols on workload using fNIRS. In: Proceedings of the SIGCHI Conference on Human Factors in Computing Systems, Toronto, Ontario, Canada. ACM, New York, pp. 3807–3816.

Pirolli, P., Card, S.K., Van Der Wege, M.M., 2000. The effect of information scent on searching information: visualizations of large tree structures. In: Proceedings of the Working Conference on Advanced Visual Interfaces, Palermo, Italy. ACM, New York, pp. 161–172.

Porzi, L., Messelodi, S., Modena, C.M., Ricci, E., 2013. A smart watch-based gesture recognition system for assisting people with visual impairments. In: Proceedings of the 3rd ACM International Workshop on Interactive Multimedia on Mobile & Portable Devices, Barcelona, Spain. ACM, New York, pp. 19–24.

Quintana, R., Quintana, C., Madeira, C., Slotta, J.D., 2016. Keeping watch: exploring wearable technology designs for K-12 teachers. In: Proceedings of the 2016 CHI Conference Extended Abstracts on Human Factors in Computing Systems, Santa Clara, California, USA. ACM, New York, pp. 2272–2278.

Raez, M.B.I., Hussain, M.S., Mohd-Yasin, F., 2006. Techniques of EMG signal analysis: detection, processing, classification and applications. Biological Procedures Online 8.

Rahman, T., Adams, A.T., Ravichandran, R.V., Zhang, M., Patel, S.N., Kientz, J.A., Choudhury, T., 2015. DoppleSleep: a contactless unobtrusive sleep sensing system using short-range Doppler radar. In: Proceedings of the 2015 ACM International Joint Conference on Pervasive and Ubiquitous Computing, Osaka, Japan. ACM, New York, pp. 39–50.

Reid, G.B., Nygren, T.E., 1988. The subjective workload assessment technique: a scaling procedure for measuring mental workload. In: Peter, A.H., Najmedin, M. (Eds.), Advances in Psychology. North-Holland, Amsterdam, pp. 185–218.

Ren, L., Zhang, Q., Shi, W., 2012. Low-power fall detection in home-based environments. In: Proceedings of the 2nd ACM International Workshop on Pervasive Wireless Healthcare, Hilton Head, South Carolina, USA. ACM, New York, pp. 39–44.

Rick, S., Calvitti, A., Agha, Z., Weibel, N., 2015. Eyes on the clinic: accelerating meaningful interface analysis through unobtrusive eye tracking. In: 9th International Conference on Pervasive Computing Technologies for Healthcare, pp. 213–216.

Rooksby, J., Rost, M., Morrison, A., Chalmers, M.C., 2014. Personal tracking as lived informatics. In: Proceedings of the 32nd Annual ACM Conference on Human Factors in Computing Systems, Toronto, Ontario, Canada. ACM, New York, pp. 1163–1172.

Rowe, D.W., Sibert, J., Irwin, D., 1998. Heart rate variability: indicator of user state as an aid to human-computer interaction. In: Proceedings of the SIGCHI Conference on Human Factors in Computing Systems, Los Angeles, California, United States. ACM Press/Addison-Wesley Publishing Co., New York, pp. 480–487.

Scheirer, J., Fernandez, R., Klein, J., Picard, R.W., 2002. Frustrating the user on purpose: a step toward building an affective computer. Interacting with Computers 14, 93–118.

Schlömer, T., Poppinga, B., Henze, N., Bolll, S., 2008. Gesture recognition with a Wii controller. In: Proceedings of the 2nd International Conference on Tangible and Embedded Interaction, Bonn, Germany. ACM, New York, pp. 11–14.

Shahabi, C., Kiyoung, Y., Hyunjin, Y., Rizzo, A.A., McLaughlin, M., Marsh, T., Minyoung, M., 2007. Immersidata analysis: four case studies. Computer 40 (7), 45–52.

Shi, J., Alt, F., 2016. The anonymous audience analyzer: visualizing audience behavior in public space. In: Proceedings of the 2016 CHI Conference Extended Abstracts on Human Factors in Computing Systems, Santa Clara, California, USA. ACM, New York, pp. 3766–3769.

Shi, Y., Ruiz, N., Taib, R., Choi, E., Chen, F., 2007. Galvanic skin response (GSR) as an index of cognitive load. In: CHI '07 Extended Abstracts on Human Factors in Computing Systems, San Jose, CA, USA. ACM, New York, pp. 2651–2656.

Singh, P., Juneja, N., Kapoor, S., 2013. Using mobile phone sensors to detect driving behavior. In: Proceedings of the 3rd ACM Symposium on Computing for Development, Bangalore, India. ACM, New York, pp. 1–2.

Sjölie, D., Bodin, K., Elgh, E., Eriksson, J., Janlert, L.-E., Nyberg, L., 2010. Effects of interactivity and 3D-motion on mental rotation brain activity in an immersive virtual environment. In: Proceedings of the SIGCHI Conference on Human Factors in Computing Systems, Atlanta, Georgia, USA. ACM, New York, pp. 869–878.

Solovey, E., Schermerhorn, P., Scheutz, M., Sassaroli, A., Fantini, S., Jacob, R., 2012. Brainput: enhancing interactive systems with streaming fNIRS brain input. In: Proceedings of the SIGCHI Conference on Human Factors in Computing Systems, Austin, Texas, USA. ACM, New York, pp. 2193–2202.

Stellmach, S., Dachselt, R., 2013. Still looking: investigating seamless gaze-supported selection, positioning, and manipulation of distant targets. In: Proceedings of the SIGCHI Conference on Human Factors in Computing Systems, Paris, France. ACM, New York, pp. 285–294.

Steptoe, W., Wolff, R., Murgia, A., Guimaraes, E., Rae, J., Sharkey, P., Roberts, D., Steed, A., 2008. Eye-tracking for avatar eye-gaze and interactional analysis in immersive collaborative virtual environments. In: Proceedings of the ACM 2008 Conference on Computer Supported Cooperative Work, San Diego, CA, USA. ACM, New York, pp. 197–200.

Stern, R.M., Ray, W.J., Quigley, K.S., 2001. Psychophysiological Recording. Oxford University Press, Oxford.

Tang, T.Y., Winoto, P., Wang, Y.F., 2015. Alone together: a multiplayer augmented reality online ball passing game. In: Proceedings of the 18th ACM Conference Companion on Computer Supported Cooperative Work & Social Computing, Vancouver, BC, Canada. ACM, New York, pp. 37–40.

Tanveer, M.I., Zhao, R., Chen, K., Tiet, Z., Hoque, M.E., 2016. AutoManner: An Automated Interface for Making Public Speakers Aware of Their Mannerisms. In: Proceedings of the 21st International Conference on Intelligent User Interfaces, Sonoma, California, USA. ACM, New York, pp. 385–396.

Taylor, P., 2015. EyeFrame: real-time memory aid improves human multitasking via domain-general eye tracking procedures. Frontiers in ICT 2.

Taylor, B., Dey, A., Siewiorek, D., Smailagic, A., 2015. Using physiological sensors to detect levels of user frustration induced by system delays. In: Proceedings of the 2015 ACM International Joint Conference on Pervasive and Ubiquitous Computing, Osaka, Japan. ACM, New York, pp. 517–528.

Tokuda, S., Palmer, E., Merkle, E., Chaparro, A., 2009. Using saccadic intrusions to quantify mental workload. Proceedings of the Human Factors and Ergonomics Society Annual Meeting 53 (12), 809–813.

Tokuda, S., Obinata, G., Palmer, E., Chaparro, A., 2011. Estimation of mental workload using saccadic eye movements in a free-viewing task. In: 2011 Annual International Conference of the IEEE Engineering in Medicine and Biology Society.

Venjakob, A.C., Mello-Thoms, C.R., 2015. Review of prospects and challenges of eye tracking in volumetric imaging. Journal of Medical Imaging 3 (1), 011002.

Venjakob, A.C., Marnitz, T., Phillips, P., Mello-Thoms, C.R., 2016. Image size influences visual search and perception of hemorrhages when reading cranial CT: an eye-tracking study. Human Factors: The Journal of the Human Factors and Ergonomics Society 58 (3), 441–451.

Voida, A., Greenberg, S., 2009. Wii all play: the console game as a computational meeting place. In: Proceedings of the 27th International Conference on Human Factors in Computing Systems, Boston, MA, USA. ACM, New York, pp. 1559–1568.

Wallen, M.P., Gomersall, S.R., Keating, S.E., Wisløff, U., Coombes, J.S., 2016. Accuracy of heart rate watches: implications for weight management. PLoS ONE 11 (5), e0154420.

Wang, Y.-X., Lo, L.-Y., Hu, M.-C., 2014. Eat as much as you can: a Kinect-based facial rehabilitation game based on mouth and tongue movements. In: Proceedings of the 22nd ACM International Conference on Multimedia, Orlando, Florida, USA. ACM, New York, pp. 743–744.

Wang, E.J., Lee, T.-J., Mariakakis, A., Goel, M., Gupta, S., Patel, S.N., 2015. MagnifiSense: inferring device interaction using wrist-worn passive magneto-inductive sensors. In: Proceedings of the 2015 ACM International Joint Conference on Pervasive and Ubiquitous Computing, Osaka, Japan. ACM, New York, pp. 15–26.

Wastell, D.G., Newman, M., 1996. Stress, control and computer system design: a psycho-physiological field study. Behaviour & Information Technology 15, 183–192.

Weibel, N., Rick, S., Emmenegger, C., Ashfaq, S., Calvitti, A., Agha, Z., 2014. LAB-IN-A-BOX: semi-automatic tracking of activity in the medical office. Personal and Ubiquitous Computing 19, 317–334.

Wen, H., Rojas, J.R., Dey, A.K., 2016. Serendipity: finger gesture recognition using an off-the-shelf smartwatch. In: Proceedings of the 2016 CHI Conference on Human Factors in Computing Systems, Santa Clara, California, USA. ACM, New York, pp. 3847–3851.

Whalen, T., Inkpen, K.M., 2005. Gathering evidence: use of visual security cues in web browsers. In: Proceedings of Graphics Interface 2005, Victoria, BC. Canadian Human-Computer Communications Society.

Wright, M.C., Dunbar, S., Moretti, E.W., Schroeder, R.A., Taekman, J., Segall, N., 2013. Eye-tracking and retrospective verbal protocol to support information systems design. Proceedings of the International Symposium on Human Factors and Ergonomics in Health Care 2, pp. 30–37.

Xu, S., Jiang, H., Lau, F., 2009. User-oriented document summarization through vision-based eye-tracking. In: Proceedings of the 13th International Conference on Intelligent User Interfaces, Sanibel Island, Florida, USA. ACM, New York, pp. 7–16.

Xu, C., Pathak, P.H., Mohapatra, P., 2015. Finger-writing with smartwatch: a case for finger and hand gesture recognition using smartwatch. In: Proceedings of the 16th International Workshop on Mobile Computing Systems and Applications, Santa Fe, New Mexico, USA. ACM, New York, pp. 9–14.

Yang, R., Shin, E., Newman, M.W., Ackerman, M.S., 2015. When fitness trackers don't 'fit': end-user difficulties in the assessment of personal tracking device accuracy. In: Proceedings of the 2015 ACM International Joint Conference on Pervasive and Ubiquitous Computing, Osaka, Japan. ACM, New York, pp. 623–634.

Yuasa, M., Saito, K., Mukawa, N., 2006. Emoticons convey emotions without cognition of faces: an fMRI study. In: CHI '06 Extended Abstracts on Human Factors in Computing Systems, Montréal, Québec, Canada. ACM, New York, pp. 1565–1570.

Yun, S., Chen, Y.-C., Qiu, L., 2015. Turning a mobile device into a mouse in the air. In: Proceedings of the 13th Annual International Conference on Mobile Systems, Applications, and Services, Florence, Italy. ACM, New York, pp. 15–29.

Zhai, S., Morimoto, C., Ihde, S., 1999. Manual and gaze input cascaded (MAGIC) pointing. In: SIGCHI Conference on Human Factors in Computing Systems, Pittsburgh, PA, USA. ACM, New York, pp. 246–253.

Zhang, Z., 2012. Microsoft Kinect sensor and its effect. IEEE MultiMedia 19 (2), 4–10.

Zhang, Z., 2015. Vision-enhanced immersive interaction and remote collaboration with large touch displays. In: Proceedings of the 23rd ACM International Conference on Multimedia, Brisbane, Australia. ACM, New York, pp. 3–4.

Zheng, K., Hanauer, D.A., Weibel, N., Agha, Z., 2015. Computational ethnography: automated and unobtrusive means for collecting data in situ for human-computer interaction evaluation studies. In: Patel, L.V., Kannampallil, G.T., Kaufman, R.D. (Eds.), Cognitive Informatics for Biomedicine: Human Computer Interaction in Healthcare. Springer International Publishing, Cham, pp. 111–140.

Online and ubiquitous HCI research

14

14.1 INTRODUCTION

Where and how do humans interact with computers? Much of the early work in human-computer interaction (HCI) research—and, indeed, some of the content in this book—focused on traditional computers—monitors and keyboards on desks, perhaps with mice or other input devices by their side. However, that is far from the whole story. As important as traditional computing has been and continues to be, much of how we interact with computers has moved from beyond the desktop onto the Internet and beyond. Social media, crowdsourcing, connected devices, and the "Internet of Things" all present interesting opportunities across the spectrum of human-computer interaction research—from understanding needs to evaluating systems and then studying how those systems are used.

This chapter attempts to tie together areas of work that might at first seem disjoint. *Online research* discusses techniques for conducting remote usability studies and other internet-enabled research, including studies of social media and online communities (online surveys are covered in Chapter 5). *Human computation* discusses the use of online tools that ask large numbers of users to perform small tasks—an approach that has proven very useful for many HCI studies. *Sensors and Ubiquitous computing* expands upon the cell phones and fitness monitoring devices described in Chapter 13, to include the widespread use of inexpensive sensors to measure aspects of the world around us, providing augmented depictions of daily life and everyday environments.

Although these topics may seem very different, they share the common thread of investigating computer use outside of traditional contexts and goals. Online studies and ubiquitous computing research investigate the role of computing in social and everyday environments that would not have been possible in the early days of HCI research in the 1980s. Similarly, human computation studies envision novel approaches of the power of connected communities of people to solve otherwise difficult problems. We will discuss some examples of these new forms of computing, and how they might inform and extend the possibilities of your HCI research.

14.2 ONLINE RESEARCH

Finding the right way to engage and interact with potential participants is a constant struggle for HCI researchers. Offering a small cash payment and perhaps some free food to nearby undergraduates may help to some extent, but such convenience samples raise concerns about validity and generalizability. Finding users who may represent a broad range of ages, skills, and backgrounds may require getting out of the lab to engage with a broader range of participants. These challenges become even more profound for studies requiring specialized populations, such as highly trained domain specialists or users with particular disabilities, who might be both hard to identify and hard to get to the lab, due to their busy schedules and other constraints. Like many of our colleagues, we all have had the experience of struggling to find times to meet with those hard-to-engage participants, traveling around our cities to conduct studies in participants' homes, and otherwise worrying about our ability to find the right folks to finish our studies.

Although certainly no panacea, the Internet can help. Beyond the obvious approach of using message boards and mailing lists to recruit participants, HCI researchers have found various types of online studies to be appealing and effective. Although not without their pitfalls, online research studies can, when designed correctly, help HCI researchers extend their reach and complete studies with less difficulty and expense. The unique challenges, pitfalls, and opportunities of online research should be considered carefully before starting any studies.

Moving beyond simply conducting traditional studies online, this section also looks at online activity as the focus of HCI research studies. These studies—which are inherently "online research"—explore the dynamics of social interactions conducted online to understand how message boards, social media, and other tools enable social interaction and the spread of ideas.

14.2.1 OBSERVATIONAL ONLINE STUDIES

The classic HCI investigation involves watching a participant as they use a computer. Contextual inquiries; think-aloud and other usability studies; and empirical comparisons certainly differ in their design, content, and execution, but they share a common core: a participant in the study sits at the computer using a tool to complete a task, while one or more researchers watch, take notes, and record data. Being in the same room provides many advantages, as researchers are able to establish rapport with participants and build trust necessary for constructive conversations. Physical colocation also helps observant researchers learn from watching their participants, noting body language that might suggest discomfort, impatience, or other reactions to the tool or task at hand. Despite these benefits, in-person studies are also inherently limiting, as two (or more) people must find their way to the same location.

Noting these difficulties, HCI researchers have developed strategies for using Internet technologies to conduct usability studies remotely. Although web-based conferencing tools (also discussed in Section 12.3.3) may still seem relatively novel—and are still often difficult to use—the use of these tools for usability studies is at least 20 years old (Hartson et al., 1996). Web conferencing tools capable of remote screen-sharing (either one window at a time or full-screen) and integrated audio via voice-over IP or telephone, provide a basis for conversations between researcher and participant, both looking at the same screen content. Some tools go further, providing webcam video for participants, recording capabilities, and even remote mouse/keyboard control, providing one participant in the conversation to (with permission) control their interlocutor's computer.

Given these features, it is quite possible to conduct contextual inquiry and think-aloud studies online. Contextual inquiries are perhaps easiest: your participant can share his or her screen, start their work, and you can sit back and watch, asking questions as needed. The click-by-click view of the tool at hand will provide a detailed picture of how individual actions are taken to complete tasks, and answers to questions should help you understand the work. Think-aloud studies that use traditional desktop software are slightly more challenging, as your participants will probably not have your software installed on their computers. Thus, web applications are particularly well suited for remote think-aloud studies, as users can access your web site from their computer, just as they would if the tool were deployed on a production server. Alternatively, you might be able to send your participants an installable version of the software that they might run locally. If this is not possible, remote mouse and keyboard capabilities might help users control the software on your machine. In any case, once these details are worked out the study can proceed much like any other think-aloud.

Choosing the correct tools for this sort of work is critical. Beyond basic screen-sharing and integrated audio, functionality for recording sessions is invaluable. The ability to replay and review sessions will augment your memory and free you up to focus on the participants' comments and actions, rather than on note-taking. Webcam video can be a great way to see the participants' facial expression and body language, restoring some of the fidelity lost when the participant is not in the room with the re-searcher. However, this value is limited—many tools provide only webcam or screen sharing, but not both simultaneously. Remote mouse keyboard/control can be very helpful, but only if it works well. If you are planning on using this remote control facility, do not forget that your computer will be unavailable to you while the par-ticipant is controlling things—you will not be able to use your own machine to take notes. A second computer might be needed. Do your due diligence before relying on one of these tools to conduct your study—compare features, use free trials to see how well services really work, and try multiple pilot sessions.

Other technical challenges associated with online observational studies include firewalls and desktop configurations. Some users may work in institutions that might be unfriendly to the use of these tools, potentially blocking access. Network poli-cies at your own institution may be a difficulty as well, as firewall exceptions might be needed to place your web application on a system that is visible to the outside world. Web conferencing tools might require the installation of plugins on the par-ticipants' computers, a process that might be difficult or impossible in some working environments. For these reasons, you might also ask each participant to conduct a "test-drive" before your main session. If you only have a limited amount of time for each participant, you do not want to spend too much of it working on software configuration.

Even if all of the technology works perfectly, you should be prepared for a different experience when conducting online observational studies. The lack of physical presence will make it harder to gauge participants' reactions, and even to know how intently they are focusing on the task (Dray and Siegel, 2004). More bluntly, you might have no way of knowing when users are surfing the web as opposed to attending to your questions. You might also find that contextual inquiries are somewhat limited: webcams might do a great job of showing faces, but they will not help you see anything that does not involve computer work, such as filing papers or reviewing printed material. Finally, do not forget that any plans to record sessions should be approved by your institutional review board or equivalent (see Chapter 15).

Online studies are not limited simply to web-conferencing systems. HCI researchers have experimented with other techniques designed to address shortcomings of both in-person and online studies. One effort found that 3D virtual world simulation of a usability lab provided some advantages over a web-conferencing-based usability study (Madathil and Greenstein, 2011). Webcam-based eye trackers (see Chapter 13) have also been used to remotely collect low-level interaction data as needed for usability studies (Chynał and Szymański, 2011). Alternatively, you might consider simpler, more low-tech approaches. Online reporting of critical usability incidents and posting of usability problems to online forums have been shown to be effective for identifying usability problems, although at a lower rate than in-person usability tests (Andreasen et al., 2007; Bruun et al., 2009). Such studies also have the advantage of being potentially asynchronous—you might ask participants to complete tasks at their convenience, reporting usability problems as appropriate. As is often the case with usability studies and expert reviews, providing specific predefined tasks may help participants identify more usability problems (Bruun and Stage, 2012).

Remote online usability studies can be useful for recruiting and including hard-to-find participants, such as individuals with disabilities who might have some difficulty in making the trip to a usability lab. Although this approach has been shown to have some potential utility, technologies should be chosen carefully to fit the needs of target populations (Petrie et al., 2006) (see Chapter 16 for further discussion of HCI research involving people with disabilities). Remote studies also provide for the possibility of software enhancements for people with specific disabilities, such as sign-language facilities for use by deaf participants (Schnepp and Shiver, 2011).

14.2.2 ONLINE DATA COLLECTION

Online HCI techniques are not limited to usability and think-aloud studies. Online surveys have become very familiar—see Chapter 5 for a discussion of the ins and outs of conducting online surveys. Chapter 12 discusses two useful online research techniques: the use of instrumented software to collect user interaction data and the use of web logs to study how web sites are used.

Web log analysis can be particularly useful for comparison of alternative web site designs or interactions. "A/B" testing is a widely used approach for comparing alternative designs for active web sites. In an A/B test a server is configured to randomly select one of two alternatives—the "A" and "B" designs to be presented whenever a visitor comes to a site. Given enough visits, data can be collected to see which users complete specified tasks more quickly or with fewer errors. Such tests might also add quick surveys asking users for their impression of a site. By using functioning web sites to gather data on many users who had come to a site, these A/B tests enable rapid collection of usability data, without the need to conduct a formal usability test.

Building on this approach, it is also possible to conduct empirical studies online. Just as web logs might be used to extract event and therefore task completion times in web-based studies run on a local server, an appropriately structured site might enable easy extraction of task completion times, results, etc. You can also create appropriate components of the web site to collect informed consent (with approval of your IRB, see Chapter 15), demographic information, and other needed details. Such an installation has the advantage of allowing participants to enroll in a study without your participation—they can just go to the URL in question and follow the directions.

Any timing data collected from either A/B testing or online empirical studies runs the risk of being confounded by network latencies or problems. If a network problem slows the communication between participants' computers and your servers, task completion times may be slowed, but you would not have any way of knowing that that had happened. Larger numbers of participants might help with this problem, as extreme values in latency will be more clearly identified as outliers.

Validity of online versus lab-based studies may be a concern. One study of the utility of online versus lab-based studies for empirical evaluation of search interfaces found that online and lab-based studies produced comparable results (Kelly and Gyllstrom, 2011). To ensure similar generalization to your problems of interest, you might consider pairing a small in-person study with a larger online study. Similarities in the results will increase confidence in the online data, but discrepancies might indicate some difficulties in translation (Meyer and Bederson, 1998).

A/B testing has been used extensively by companies with prominent Internet business activity, as Amazon, Microsoft, and other familiar web companies are well aware of the importance in small changes in design and task completion. For sites serving millions of users, an increase of even 1% on ad views or completed sales can mean significant increases in revenue. The importance of A/B testing has led to significant methodological interest, from practical guidance from web usability guru Jakob Nielsen (Nielsen, 2005, 2012, 2014) to papers on the design of A/B studies (Kharitonov et al., 2015) and the investigation of novel statistical analysis techniques (Deng et al., 2013, 2014; Deng, 2015). Ron Kohavi and colleagues at Microsoft have published extensively in this area, including a survey presenting a broad overview of the topic (Kohavi et al., 2009) and papers discussing some of the pitfalls and lessons learned from Microsoft's extensive A/B testing (Crook et al., 2009; Kohavi et al., 2012, 2013).

A/B testing is also limited by the coarse-grain nature of the data. Knowing which elements are clicked on which pages can be useful, but additional data might be needed to know where and how those pages command user attention. Eye-tracking techniques (Chapter 13) and additional software tools such as proxies and JavaScript libraries (Chapter 12) can provide finer-grain detail when necessary.

14.2.3 **ONLINE ACTIVITY**

The rich stores of data created through our online lives provide tantalizing HCI research possibilities. Exploration of online content and activity can provide deep insight into how people communicate, create communities, learn, and interact online, including how ideas develop and spread, and what we might learn from information dissemination patterns. Although the techniques are very similar to others discussed earlier in this book—including both qualitative content analysis (Chapter 11) and statistical review of automatically captured interaction data and human physiological signals (Chapters 12 and 13)—the domain is qualitatively different, in that analysis of online activity effectively involves the emergence of community and collective behavior.

14.2.3.1 Online communities

Computers have been used for online communities since the early 1980s, with the early USENET discussion groups on the ARPANET (Leug and Fisher, 2003) leading to online bulletin boards where home computer users with dial-up modems could interact. The growth of the Internet in the 1990s led to the emergence of countless bulletin boards for communities of interest, providing researchers with an opportunity to study communication and patterns, community growth, and related dynamics.

Analyses of these communities often combine qualitative and quantitative methods. Qualitative methods might include thematic content analysis (see Chapter 11), aimed at extracting common themes and types of interactions, perhaps guided by some theory. These studies will typically involve reading through large numbers of posts, coding contents for types of concerns, types of posts (questions, answers, guidance, emotional support), and for conversational structure (introduction of new members, arguments over controversial topics, resolutions of disputes, etc.). Although time-consuming, these techniques offer the possibility of immersion in the community under consideration, providing rich context that might enable deep understanding.

As online community content is often, if not exclusively, found in the form of online text, it is particularly well suited for automated analysis and quantitative investigation of patterns of interest, including how and when certain terms or types of discourse are used. Forum content and posts can generally be downloaded, although with varying levels of difficulty, depending on the underlying software platform. Communities built on open platforms might provide programming libraries known as Application Programming Interfaces (APIs) capable of extracting data. Using these libraries, software developers might develop custom programs to gather and collate data needed to address research questions of interest. Barring such facilities, researchers might need to resort to parsing HTML content. Once message content is available, it can be analyzed via textual analysis approaches, including building distributions of words or phrases used in different contexts. These data might then be stored in a database and analyzed for frequency of occurrence, sequences, or other patterns of interest. For a slightly more nuanced approach, natural-language processing techniques might be applied to posts to distinguish between, for example, cases where someone is discussing their own current concerns as opposed to those faced in the past, or experienced by a family member (Harkema et al., 2009). As with other triangulation approaches, these techniques might work best hand in hand, with qualitative insights suggesting patterns that might be quantified and quantitative identification of frequent behaviors driving new theories for qualitative exploration.

Diane Maloney-Krichmar and Jenny Preece's in-depth study of an online forum for people with knee injuries provides a rich example of the use of both qualitative and quantitative methods to understand the dynamics of a complex online community. Using a four-phase research plan, Maloney-Krichmar and Preece combined preliminary observation with usability analysis, detailed quantitative analysis of 1 week's worth of messages, and interviews with members of the site. Results included characterization of site features supporting sociability; membership patterns encouraging the health of the community, including identifiable subgroups; task and individual roles assumed by members; distribution of discussion length, including the number of messages in each thread; and characterization of the role of group participation in members' lives (Maloney-Krichmar and Preece, 2005). This detailed picture provides an example of the possibilities of applying ethnographic techniques to online communities.

HCI researchers have studied a wide range of online communities. Analyses of content and interviews with participants were used to develop detailed descriptions of a 2015 "protest" in the Reddit online community, during which volunteer moderators protested changes in company policy and staff (Centivany and Glushko, 2016; Matias, 2016). A study of contributions to a repository of projects developed using the online programming tool Scratch used review of published user profiles and comments on projects to explore the diversity of participants in the community (Richard and Kafai, 2016).

Online communities can be useful research resources even if you are not willing (or able) to undertake a detailed ethnographic analysis of a specific group's dynamics. As shared resources for individuals with common interests, these communities can often be valuable tools for recruiting participants for studies of factors surrounding community goals. One study of the dynamics of conflict in free and open-source software development conducted a survey involving participants in the software development site GitHub, home to many open-source projects (Filippova and Cho, 2016). Other studies might involve communities spanning multiple sites. A study of the credibility of medical "crowdfunding" requests (using online sites to solicit contributions to offset medical expenses) examined Reddit discussions regarding campaigns posted on other sites. Like other studies discussed earlier, this investigation combined content analysis of postings with participant interviews (Kim et al., 2016a).

14.2.3.2 Following trends: Social media and online interaction data

What can we learn from behavior on the online sites that seem to occupy so much of our collective attention? Moving beyond the closed confines of online communities, broader studies of both content and patterns of online activity can tell us a great deal about how people interact, how ideas spread, and what meaning might be attributed to those patterns.

Studies of online activity can be classified into three broad categories, distinguished by data source. *Social media* studies explore participation in familiar sites such as Twitter and Facebook to understand how these tools can be used to find and share information. In this context, we use the term "social media" to refer to general-purpose sites supporting individually selected lists of "friends" or "contacts," as opposed to interest-specific communities described in Section 14.2.3.1. Examples include studies of how people use social media to meet information needs (Menefee et al., 2016), and examinations of the impact of social media on dissemination of information from research conferences (Winandy et al., 2016). *Web search* studies examine queries submitted to general Internet search engines, looking for behaviors common to many web users, such as searching for information about flu outbreaks (Ginsberg et al., 2009) and other health conditions (White et al., 2013; Paparrizos et al., 2016). Examinations of *blogs, wikis, and other user-generated content* explore how users interact in creating and sharing information on the web, including video blogs (Huh et al., 2014), Wikipedia editing (Viégas et al., 2004, 2007a,b; Kittur and Kraut, 2008), and online reviews (Hedegaard and Simonsen, 2013, 2014), to name a few. Boundaries between these categories are fuzzy, and many of these goals can be met by multiple sources of interaction data.

Identification of appropriate data sources, and of the means of accessing that data, is often the first step in conducting studies of online interactions. Designing a study to investigate the use of "social media" in examining a topic of interest is a reasonable start, but details are important—which social media sites will you consider? Which content types? Various sources will differ significantly in their willingness to share data and in the tools available to access any data that is openly available. Open-source sites like Wikipedia might allow access to data that might be considered proprietary by for-profit search engines. Some social media sites such as Facebook (https://developers.facebook.com/docs/graph-api) and Twitter (https://dev.twitter.com/overview/documentation) sites provide API access suitable for querying data sets, while others may require the use of more manual tools to "screen-scrape" data off of web pages. However, the mere presence of an API might not be sufficient—APIs that limit the quantity or range of content that can be retrieved might not be sufficient for some tasks.

An examination of selected papers provides a sampling of some of the approaches researchers have used to access social media interaction data. Small-scale studies—such as examining the impact and diffusion of social media content for a specific issue among a small community—can be conducted relatively easily. Organizers of a 2011 health research conference established social media presences on Facebook,

Twitter, Flickr, and other sites and tracked the utilization and dissemination of content over time as a means of examining the impact of their efforts (Winandy et al., 2016). Such focused efforts have the advantage of generally being feasible with information available to account holders on these sites. Other, similarly small studies, can be conducted through standard interactions, as in a study of YouTube video blogs for illness support: researchers manually searched YouTube to identify videos of interest and reviewed transcripts and comments on those videos to see how they were used for social support (Huh et al., 2014)

For larger studies, APIs provided by vendors are often the most effective means of capturing data. Twitter APIs have been used to access data for many studies, including investigation of spammers' social networks (Yang et al., 2012), extraction of sporting event summaries from Tweets (Nichols et al., 2012), and understanding the spread of information during times of social upheaval (Starbird and Palen, 2012). Twitter data has been used to explore patterns of discussion during emergency situations (Cassa et al., 2013), smoking behavior (Myslín et al., 2013), and many other health-related topics. Facebook has also been the subject of significant research interest, including studies of strengths of relationships (Xiang et al., 2010), relationships between social network use and well-being (Burke et al., 2010), and information diffusion (Bakshy et al., 2012) to name just a few. However, as for-profit businesses, Twitter and Facebook consider their data to be valuable, making only a subset available through APIs, with access to larger data sets possibly available for a fee (Finley, 2014). Twitter has also made limited access to their archives of historical content available to researchers through a data grant program (Kirkorian, 2014). Largely as a result of restrictions on data availability, this research is often conducted by researchers employed by the social networking sites being studied (Xiang et al., 2010; Burke et al., 2010; Bakshy et al., 2012).

Bulk datasets often make good data sources for studies of interaction patterns. Studies of Wikipedia trends have relied on bulk data downloads providing snapshots of site content at specific points in time (Viégas et al., 2007b)—such datasets can be invaluable when available, but the volume of content can also be daunting. Sampling of a smaller subset, either randomly, by time, or by content, can be an appropriate means of identifying a more manageable dataset. The Enron corpus, a database of several hundred thousand email messages from the failed energy company, provides an uncommon view into the electronic communications in a large company. This dataset has been analyzed in dozens of studies, addressing questions such as the identification of words and phrases used to indicate power relations in the corporate structure (Gilbert, 2012).

As with social network data, search engine research is perhaps most easily conducted by scientists working in the research labs of prominent search engine firms like Google (Ginsberg et al., 2009) and Microsoft (Huang et al., 2011, 2012; White and Horvitz, 2009; White, 2013; White et al., 2013; White and Hassan, 2014). See the "Google Flu" Sidebar for a discussion of the promises and challenges of log analysis, as illustrated by the high profile case of Google's Flu prediction analysis.

GOOGLE FLU

The history of Google's flu trend analysis tools (https://www.google.org/flutrends/about/) illustrates some of the potential value—and some of the pitfalls—in examining search data. Google's team analyzed a large corpus of search queries combined with geographical information identifying the location from which each query was issued. Noting a strong correlation between flu-related queries and clinicians' visits potentially related to flu, they were able to accurately predict which regions in the United States were experiencing flu outbreaks (Ginsberg et al., 2009). The excitement generated by these results was soon tempered by further experience demonstrating the trickiness of relating web search activity to online reality. A 2011 investigation of the performance of Google Flu Trends during the 2009 H1N1 influenza pandemic found that search behavior changed during the pandemic, as users searched for terms for influenza and related complications (Cook et al., 2011), and the estimates for the 2013 flu season varied radically from those issued by the Centers for Disease Control (Butler, 2013). A 2014 commentary reviewed related results and suggested that search data might be most useful when combined with other existing data sources (Lazer et al., 2014). This commentary also raised an important concern relevant to other studies of web search trends: as search engines are based on proprietary algorithms subject to regular revision, results may not be reliable or replicable (Lazer et al., 2014). Unsurprisingly, the exploration of twitter data for tracking flu epidemics has also been an area of active research (Allen et al., 2016; Santillana et al., 2015).

Despite concerns regarding the validity of predictions generated by Google Flu Trends, search logs continue to be a rich source of data for researchers interested in studying the implications of health-related terms. Some of this work attempts to validate Flu Trends, using other relevant indicators, such as flu-related visits to emergency departments (Klembczyk et al., 2016) as comparison points. A South Korean effort used social media (Twitter and blog) efforts to identify potential starting points in a subsequent examination of search terms for flu-related concepts (Woo et al., 2016), providing an example of the utility of combining multiple sources of online behavior data. Other efforts include flu tracking using only Twitter data (Allen et al., 2016; Santillana et al., 2015), and the use of search logs to identify possible adverse interactions between two drugs (White et al., 2013), to study the increasing severity of concern when searching for medical content (known as "Cyberchondria") (White and Horvitz, 2009), or to identify symptoms that might be early indicators of cancers (Paparrizos et al., 2016). Related studies have used search data to explore biases in the search for health-related information (White, 2013; White and Hassan, 2014).

If your data source is either inaccessible due to business concerns, lack of an open API, or unacceptable costs, you might consider reframing your study to match what can be accomplished within your means. Substituting smaller scale studies or qualitative research for broad examinations into usage patterns might be one approach. One study used a set of interviews with Facebook users to understand how the content, layout, and functionality of the site influenced communication of health information (Menefee et al., 2016). Although smaller qualitative studies lack the broad appeal of the analysis of millions of posts, they might be more economical to complete.

If you are lucky enough to get your hands on a large dataset relevant to your interests, you might use a variety of techniques, depending on your interests and goals. Be prepared to spend some time on data cleaning and extraction, potentially taking textual representations of tweets, posts, or other data and formatting them in a normalized pattern suitable for querying or text searching (Baeza-Yates and Riberio-Neto, 2011). Once the data is ready for analysis, you may use any of a range of techniques. Possibilities include natural-language processing approaches that try to extract key concepts and relationships from free text (Hedegaard and Simonsen, 2013), and information retrieval techniques (Baeza-Yates and Riberio-Neto, 2011) to model similarities between documents and common concepts and terms. Other approaches have used descriptive statistics tracking types of activities and relationships (Kittur and Kraut, 2008), relative frequencies of different types of events (White et al., 2013), and any number of other techniques as appropriate. For social media analysis, you might build networks indicating relationships between individuals, topics, and other items of interest. Graph algorithms might be used to find network members who are "hubs"—outliers in terms of number of connections or presence on important paths (Scott, 2013). The Social Media Research Foundation (http://www.smrfoundation.org) has developed a tool known as NodeXL, which supports the development of networks, calculation of centrality measures, and visualization, all through spreadsheet data (Bonsignore et al., 2009; Hansen and Shneiderman, 2010).

In a refrain that should be familiar to readers who have made it this far, any of these data sources can be augmented by appropriate analysis with related data collected through different modalities. Examples include the use of surveys to understand user practices and beliefs with regard to searches for health information (White, 2013) and the use of instrumented web pages (Chapter 12) (Huang et al., 2012) or eye tracking (Chapter 13) (Huang et al., 2011) to capture fine-grain data correlated with search engine interactions. Approaches like these also open search engine interaction research to those who are not directly working with the relevant companies, as logging toolkits and eye-tracking experiments might be conducted in usability labs lacking access to large volumes of search interaction logs.

14.2.4 ONLINE RESEARCH DESIGN CHALLENGES

14.2.4.1 Appropriate topics for online research

Although it may seem somewhat obvious to note that online research will involve working with participants who are online, this helps point us toward the insight that online HCI research may be most appropriate for studies about the tools that people use online and the uses that they make of those tools. Participants in online studies will probably be working with web browsers, chat tools, and related online software as they read instructions, provide informed consent, perform tasks, and otherwise complete your experimental protocol. Research that works within this realm may be most successful.

Specifically, studies involving web applications or online tools are particularly well suited for online research. If you are running the web site on your own servers, web logs (Chapter 12) can provide useful feedback regarding timing, tasks, and errors. Conversely, studies of other application software, mobile devices, or novel interaction devices may be harder to do online: data collection is likely to be more difficult, incompatibilities between software versions may pop up, etc.

That is not to say that online studies of web site designs are easy. Good design practice certainly calls for cross-platform testing, but there is no guarantee that you will not run into versioning and compatibility problems, even with seemingly straightforward web pages.

14.2.4.2 Recruiting

By opening your research up to the Internet, you provide yourself with access to a much larger pool of participants. Recruiting can be easier, as emails to appropriate lists and postings on various web sites can go a long way toward identifying potential subjects. As online research generally involves the use of a web site or other online software, participants do not need to be local. Self-driven web site or study tools allow participants to complete tasks at their leisure, eliminating the need for scheduling.

Just as the use of undergraduates as study participants introduces a bias that may not be appropriate for some studies, online recruitment limits your subject pool to a particular segment of the larger population: Internet users who are interested enough to participate. This may mean that you might not attract relatively inexperienced individuals or participants who limit their time online to relatively focused activities. Whether or not this poses a problem depends on the specifics of the study in question.

In some cases, online research can give you access to pools of participants that otherwise would have been unavailable. This is particularly true for people with disabilities, who may find traveling to a researcher lab to be logistically unfeasible (Petrie et al., 2006), and domain experts, who may be hard to find in sufficient numbers in some locales (Brush et al., 2004). See Chapter 16 for more details on HCI research involving people with disabilities. Collaborative research involving distant partners can also be substantially aided by online tools for communicating and gathering data.

One important difference between online and in-person research is the potentially complete anonymity of participants in online studies. When you meet a participant face-to-face, you can usually make a pretty good guess about their age, gender, and other demographic characteristics. The lack of face-to-face contact with online participants makes verification of such details harder—you have no way of verifying that your participants are male or female, old or young. This presents some recruiting challenges, particularly if your research requires participants who meet certain demographic constraints such as age or gender. If your only contact is via email or other electronic means, you may not be able to verify that the person with whom you are communicating is who he or she is claiming to be. Online studies that do not require the participants to reveal their true identity (relying instead on email addresses or screen names) are highly vulnerable to deception. Certain incentives, such as offering to enter participants in a draw for a desirable prize, might compound this problem. For example, a survey aimed at a specific demographic group might draw multiple responses from one individual, who might use multiple email addresses to appear as if inquiries were coming from different people. Possible approaches for avoiding such problems include eliminating incentives; requiring proof of demographic status (age, gender, disability, etc.) for participation; and initial phone or in-person contact in order to provide some verification of identity. Since payment or other delivery of incentives often requires knowing a participant's name and address, verification of identity is often not an added burden.

14.2.4.3 Study design

Surveys (Lazar and Preece, 1999) (Chapter 5), usability evaluations (Brush et al., 2004; Petrie et al., 2006), and ethnographic studies of support groups (Maloney-Krichmar and Preece, 2005) have all been successfully completed online. Examples of online usability studies have shown that both synchronous studies with domain experts (Brush et al., 2004) and asynchronous studies with users with disabilities (Petrie et al., 2006) have yielded results comparable to those that were found in traditional usability studies. Perhaps due to difficulties in sampling and controls, online empirical studies of task performance are less common. One study of the influence of informal "sketch-like" interfaces on drawing behavior used an online study as a means of confirming the results of a smaller, traditional study. Results from the 221 subjects in the online study were highly consistent with the results from the 18 subjects in the traditional, controlled study in the lab. The agreement between the two sets of results provides a more convincing argument than the lab study on its own (Meyer and Bederson, 1998).

Opinions differ on the appropriateness of online research for different types of data collection. The lack of controls on the participant population might be seen as a difficulty for some controlled, empirical studies. Others have argued that as online research does not allow for detailed user observation, it is more appropriate for quantitative approaches (Petrie et al., 2006). In the absence of any clear guidelines, it is certainly appropriate to design studies carefully and to clearly describe and document the reasoning behind any designs that are adopted. When possible, hybrid approaches involving both in-person and online research may provide additional data and avoid some of the downsides associated with each approach.

Online studies involving surveys, self-selected visits to web sites, crowdsourcing, or other approaches that do not require synchronous interactions with researchers might be subject to frequent dropouts, as users decide to start a task and then stop half-way through. Study designs should anticipate such dropouts and consider how they might be reported. If you are looking at task completion success rate, it is probably appropriate to include all participants who started the task. If you are looking at task completion times, you might want to focus only on those who completed the tasks. Providing numbers for those who started tasks, those who completed tasks, and indicating which groups were considered for which analyses is probably most appropriate.

14.2.4.4 Ethical concerns

Although the usual guidelines regarding protection of participants apply to online research, numerous confounding factors can create some interesting and challenging dilemmas.

Studies of online communities must consider questions of privacy and online consent. What is the expectation of privacy when participants in an online forum post messages publicly? Are such messages fair game for researchers? Is informed consent required before messages can be used? What if the site is only accessible to users who register and login? These questions have generated debate, discussions, and some guidelines (Bruckman, 2002; Frankel and Siang, 1999), but specific issues vary from case to case. Researchers are urged to be particularly careful when exploring communities describing sensitive topics such as health. The trust needed for participants to share stories of challenging personal times such as illnesses may lead some users to forget that they are effectively participating in a public forum where materials may be read by many individuals. Lurking in such communities or posing as a member may not be seen as appropriate behavior. Before doing so, you might consider talking to the organization or individuals responsible for the site and introducing your study to the group. Creating communities specifically for research purposes can be a successful—if not always practical—alternative (Bruckman, 2002).

Informed consent and debriefing for online studies can also be tricky. Providing important information for either of these tasks via online text may not be sufficient. In-person studies provide the possibility of direct feedback: experimenters know if participants have any questions or if there is any postexperiment distress. These factors are much harder to gauge online (Azar, 2000). Although one study indicated that comprehension of informed consent forms online may be comparable to comprehension of forms on paper, poor recall in both cases illustrates the general challenge of constructing effective consent forms (Varnhagen et al., 2005). These issues may be even thornier for studies conducted retrospectively, through API access to posted data or other methods allowed under web site terms of service. Although such studies are not inappropriate, and may not require consent, it is still best to tread carefully. When possible, provide clear and easily understandable descriptions of research goals and implications. In any case, these studies should not be undertaken without careful attention to appropriate rules for protection of human research participants. Detailed discussions of human subject protections can be found in Chapter 15.

The considerable challenges and headache associated with deceptive online research provide a strong argument against this sort of approach. If you find yourself tempted to try this sort of study, consider a lab-based study instead. You may still use deception in this case but the use of prior informed consent can help you avoid many difficult questions.

As with any HCI research, online research can be particularly challenging if there is potential harm involved or when dealing with special cases, such as research involving children. Technical measures such as encryption of transmitted data may be useful for privacy protection and for verifying parental consent in the case of minors (Kraut et al., 2004). Laws such as the Children's Online Privacy Protection Act of 1998 (COPPA) in the United States may limit the amount of information that can be collected from minors. Researchers working in these areas should construct study materials carefully; consult with appropriate authorities responsible for human research participant protection (known as Institutional Review Boards in the United States—see Chapter 15) and external experts to review proposed procedures; and use traditional studies as opposed to online studies when appropriate (Kraut et al., 2004).

14.3 HUMAN COMPUTATION
14.3.1 INTRODUCTION TO HUMAN COMPUTATION

What can people do more effectively than computers? Despite the frustrations associated with seemingly endless bugs and glitches, most people who use computers frequently would probably agree that computers do many jobs more quickly and more accurately than humans (if you ever talk to someone who disagrees, see what happens if you ask them to give up their smartphone or laptop). However, there are some areas where humans continue—at least for the time being—to outperform computers. Tasks requiring detailed interpretation of complex inputs are a prime example. Despite recent improvements in computer vision, natural-language processing, and other fields of artificial intelligence, software systems often struggle to identify objects in digital images or to interpret written text, even when such tasks are straightforward for many humans.

Given these differing—and often complementary—strengths of both humans and computers, many observers have argued for the use of computers to augment human cognition (Shneiderman, 2002). This line of inquiry dates back to the prehistory of HCI, in speculative designs such as Vannevar Bush's Memex (Bush, 1945) and Douglas Englebart's work on augmenting human intellect (Engelbart, 1962), which led to the famous 1968 demos of the first computer mouse, early graphical user interface, and word processor.

Human Computation takes the opposite approach. Given a task that might be hard for a computer but relatively easy for a human, a human computation strategy might ask multiple humans to complete small pieces of that task. For example, consider a computer vision algorithm for identifying numerals in digital photographs. A machine learning tool for such a task might be challenged by the range of sizes, fonts, and colors of numerals found on building, signs, and elsewhere in images, even when a human could read those numbers very easily. A human computation task might ask multiple participants to interpret a large set of images, thus providing a large collection of labeled images. Resulting labels might be used to train improved machine learning for classifying similar images, or to develop a search tool for identifying images matching specified descriptions. These tasks that require human—as opposed to computer—cognition are often referred to as *Human Intelligence Tasks*. When such tasks are explicitly organized with the goal of efficiently finding an accurate solution for a computational problem, the resulting system might be called a *human computation system* (Law and Ahn, 2011). See the "CAPTCHA and reCAPTCHA" sidebars for the story of the most familiar human computation tasks.

CAPTCHA AND reCAPTCHA

CAPTCHA—the Completely Automated Public Turing test to tell Computers and Humans Apart—is perhaps the most familiar example of human computation. The term CAPTCHA was developed by Luis von Ahn and colleagues, who proposed the use of a problem that is hard for computers but easy for humans as a web site security measure, suitable for distinguishing between human visitors to a site and automated scripts pretending to be humans (Ahn et al., 2003). The original task—deciphering letters in a word distorted so as to defeat computer vision programs—has since spawned numerous variations familiar to users of many web sites.

A closely related line of research explored related ideas, originally in the realm of image annotation. Annotations in the form of image labels are required to support image search, as computer vision tools may not be sufficiently powerful to identify image content matching terms of interest. However, these labels are not easy to come by, as they must be generated by humans who must interpret the images and provide descriptions. Noting these problems, Luis von Ahn and Laura Dabbish suggested a simple and intriguing solution: turn it into a game. The ESP game presents two players with an image, asking them both to provide a label describing the image. The players are challenged to come up with an agreed-upon description, getting points for each agreement, with large bonuses for surpassing a certain goal in a given time period. The need for agreement creates the challenge that makes the game enjoyable, while increasing the quality of the labels, as two participants are unlikely to agree upon an inaccurate description. Additional labels can be generated for each image through the use of "taboo" words: once a first pair of partners labels an image, subsequent partners will be asked to find a label without using any of the previously used words (Ahn and Dabbish, 2004). The ESP game introduced the notion of "Games with a purpose"—tools that hide useful work under the guise of a challenging and enjoyable game (Ahn and Dabbish, 2008). Just as Tom Sawyer turned the work of painting a fence from a chore into a pleasure, games with a purpose turn image labeling and other tedious tasks into a bit of fun.

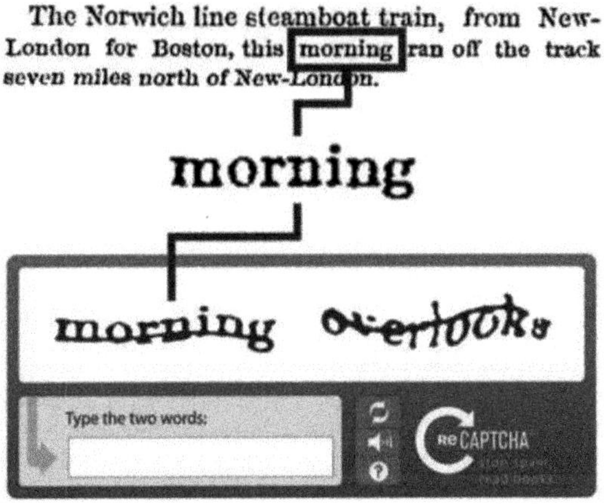

FIGURE 14.1

reCAPTCHA: (A) The original reCAPTCHA asked users to type in words that could not be recognized via optical-character recognition. A sample of text that might have been recognized is shown, along with a depiction of how the text might be distorted before being presented to the user. (B) More recent reCAPTCHA tasks involve image classification, such as choosing images from a set that match a specified criteria—in this case, images containing fireworks.

(A) From von Ahn, L., Maurer, B., McMillen, C., Abraham, D., Blum, M., 2008. ReCAPTCHA: humanbased character recognition via web security measures. Science 321, 1465–1468; (B) From https://www.google.com/recaptcha/api2/demo (accessed April 8, 2017).

(Continued)

CAPTCHA AND reCAPTCHA—CONT'D

Subsequent work merged CAPTCHA's goal of using human intelligence tasks as security with the ESP games notion of using these tasks to accomplish useful work, leading to the reCAPTCHA tool (von Ahn et al., 2008). reCAPTCHA was designed to solve the problem of digitizing text that had proven challenging for optical-character recognition (OCR) systems. reCAPTCHA provides users with images including text that has proven difficult for computer vision systems to interpret. Specifically, the original reCAPTCHA asked users to decipher words that have each failed to be consistently recognized by two different OCR programs. Each time a reCAPTCHA is used, the user is asked to interpret images containing two words: one for which the interpretation is known, and another which has not yet been classified. If the user provides a correct answer for the known word, the answer for the other word is assumed to be correct. Each word is presented to multiple users, and words can be promoted to become known words if sufficient accurate human guesses are provided. All words are distorted in an attempt to defeat computer vision programs (Figure 14.1A) (von Ahn et al., 2008). reCAPTCHA has been used on many web sites to provide the security that motivated the design of the original CAPTCHA, primarily verification of user registration and login on web sites. reCAPTCHA was purchased by Google in 2009 (Zlatos, 2009), with subsequent evolution of the tool including variants for labeling images (Figure 14.1B) and predictive tools capable of identifying users as human based on interactions with the widget, without the need for image labeling (Shet, 2014).

reCAPTCHA's use of images highlights a key design challenge. The image-labeling tasks in the ESP game were purely entertainment on the part of the users. CAPTCHAs, on the other hand, are often used on sites that might be the sole route for users to access functionality needed for personal or professional purposes. As a result, accessibility becomes a key concern, as some users—particularly those with low vision or blindness—might struggle with some of the images used in tools like reCAPTCHA. This problem is magnified by the nature of the tools—by definition, the images used in reCAPTCHA are those that have been in some ways hard to process. reCAPTCHA has always had an audio option, which has generally asked users to type a sequence of spoken digits. Alternative CAPTCHA tests have been the subject of multiple research efforts (Sauer et al., 2010; Davidson et al., 2014).

Although reCAPTCHA is likely the most familiar human computation task, the notion of using games to motivate participation has been used in many different domains. Online games have been particularly successful in scientific fields, with the Fold.It game (http://fold.it) harnessing the power of multiple users to generate high-quality protein models (Khatib et al., 2011; Eiben et al., 2012) and bioinformatics games at http://www.genegames.org challenging users to complete tasks such as curating gene-disease associations (Good et al., 2012).

Despite the success of games with a purpose and related tools, not all tasks in need of human input are easily converted into small subtasks amenable to competition or collaboration between participants. Longer, more complex tasks may take more time to complete and require additional training or expertise. *Crowdsourcing studies*[1] use online platforms to collect data from participants over the web, usually through the use of web software designed to enroll participants, provide training, and complete relevant tasks.

Crowdsourced research studies can be (roughly) divided into two key groupings. Studies involving *systems based on crowdsourced data* explore applications of user-contributed data to develop novel solutions to challenging problems. Like CAPTCHA and other human computation tasks described earlier, these studies are all focused around some task(s) that humans can do better than computers. Examples include annotating research reports to identify discussions of potentially harmful drug-drug interactions (Hochheiser et al., 2016), extracting relationships between texts and tables in written reports (Kong et al., 2014); delivering crowd-based emotional support in online interventions for depression (Morris et al., 2015); translating text (Hu et al., 2014); prototyping user interface designs (Lasecki et al., 2015); and using real-time crowd interpretation of cell phone images to help blind people identify nearby objects (Bigham et al., 2010; Lasecki et al., 2014), to name just a few of many.

A second, crowdsourced model involves *crowdsourced HCI experiments*: web-based studies involving large numbers of participants in more or less traditional empirical evaluations of interfaces or visualizations. As the goal of these studies is to evaluate how humans use a tool to accomplish a task, they are not necessarily strictly human computation: some studies in this category may include tasks that might, in fact, be done by computers. However, other elements are similar, in that large numbers of people will be asked to complete tasks, through an online infrastructure supporting with recruitment, enrollment, and data collection. Examples of crowdsourced experiments have been used in studies evaluating visualization designs (Heer and Bostock, 2010; Abdul-Rahman et al., 2014; Micallef et al., 2012), mobile applications (Zhang et al., 2016), and even (via a creative proxy) haptic interfaces (Schneider et al., 2016).

14.3.2 CONDUCTING HUMAN COMPUTATION STUDIES

Using crowdsourcing services to inexpensively identify and enroll a large pool of study participants might appear to be a very appealing prospect. However, matters are (perhaps unsurprisingly) not quite that simple, as previous work has identified concerns that might impact the quality of the data collected. Consideration of these concerns, and of recommendations originating in these earlier studies, can help you design tasks and use task performance data to ensure that your experiments generate the high-quality data that you need to move your research.

---

[1] Not to be confused with crowdsourcing content, which refers to the process of combining the efforts of multiple authors and editors to write articles such as those found on Wikipedia.

To understand the challenges, we might compare crowdsourced studies to traditional studies. Familiar lab-based studies use advertisements and word of mouth to spread the word, often offering a small honorarium to encourage interest. Participants come to the lab, spend some amount of time—perhaps an hour or two—and are given payment upon completion of their participation. Although this approach often leads to maddening difficulties in recruiting sufficient numbers of participants, it offers several advantages. Perhaps most importantly, individuals who express interest in such studies can usually be depended upon to complete the studies appropriately and in good faith. Enticements of $20 or even $50 might be sufficient to encourage some people to participate in studies that do not interest them, but it is generally not worth the bother to participate without taking the study seriously. Although we have not evaluated the question empirically, our experience has been that most people who agree to join in lab studies do so honestly and with every intention of working with the researcher to meet the goals of the study.

Direct interaction with participants is a second, closely related, benefit. When someone sits down in your lab to participate in a study, you will be able to talk with them and to observe their work as they complete the tasks at hand. These interactions provide valuable "sanity check" information, allowing you to form impressions of each individual's task performance and motivations, and specifically to avoid participants who might not be taking your tasks seriously. You certainly do not want to rush to discard data from someone who is goofing off—including the data and raising the concern in a discussion would be much more appropriate—but having observed this behavior might help you understand results, particularly if you identify participants with bad behavior that might have led to unexpected results in your data.

There are many appealing aspects to the use of human computation in HCI research. A properly constructed human computation study can be constructed in software, deployed on a web site (often using dedicated software services, as discussed later), and advertised to large numbers of potential workers at reasonably low cost. Participant enrollment, completion of consent forms, administration of the study, and data collection can be largely automated, thus eliminating the need for tedious work that has afflicted many graduate and undergraduate student workers. Online human computation studies can also enroll many more participants than comparable traditional studies, providing greater statistical power. The user base may be large and diverse, involving a broader range of education levels, ethnicities, and backgrounds than you would likely get in a lab (Kittur and Kraut, 2008).

Of course, the reality is somewhat more complicated. As with any other type of HCI study, human computation experiments require careful selection of participants and tasks. You will also need an appropriate software infrastructure, capable of handling all of the enrollment and screening processes conducted to enroll participants; and the presentation of tasks and collection of data necessary for the study itself. Human computation studies must be carefully designed to ensure high-quality responses: although tasks involving intrinsic motivation such as entertainment, intellectual curiosity, or accessing a desired resource might motivate participants to perform honestly and accurately, users who are paid for their answers (as is often the case) might be in it for the money. The nature of the small tasks might encourage users to emphasize speed over accuracy, rushing through tasks to collect as much payment as possible, without any regard for the quality of the answers provided (Kittur and Kraut, 2008).

14.3.2.1 Software infrastructure

Human computation studies need not have extensive or complex software infrastructure. Studies can easily be run through homegrown or customized web applications, together with logging software capable of tracking the details and time of any given interaction. One productive approach for such tools might be to build a database-driven web application capable of storing appropriate demographic background information associated with each participant, along with details of each action and task completed. You might even add an administrative component capable of managing and enrolling prospective participants. These homegrown applications are generally not terribly difficult to construct, particularly if you have a web-based implementation of the key tasks under consideration, or were planning on building one anyway. For some tasks—particularly those involving collection of fine-grained detail or requiring complex interactions—the freedom associated with constructing your own application may be necessary to get the job done.

Commercial crowdsourcing services provide an attractive alternative to homegrown software. These commercial offerings provide platforms for creating tasks, including providing training materials, presenting task components, and collecting task results, with tools designed to minimize—if not eliminate—the need to do any programming. Perhaps even more importantly, they also offer access to registered workers who have expressed interest in completing small tasks in exchange for *micropayments*. This infrastructure significantly simplifies recruitment of participants—once you publish your tasks registered users can find them on the site and get to work. These tools can facilitate enrolling users, managing payments, and even prescreening users to verify eligibility in terms of demographic requirements (gender, age, etc.) or background knowledge (Paolacci et al., 2010), thus eliminating many of the headaches of study design. Although Amazon's Mechanical Turk (http://www.mturk.com) is by far the crowdsourcing tool most used in published human-computer interaction studies, other systems such as CrowdFlower also appear in the literature (Kucherbaev et al., 2016).

Although details obviously differ across platforms, construction of studies is generally straightforward. Tasks and instructions can be created via tools provided by the sites, with custom HTML and JavaScript programming as needed, particularly for more complex tasks. Some platforms also allow tasks that load contents of external web sites (McInnis and Leshed, 2016), providing more control to task designers. Software development APIs often provide additional flexibility, at the cost of some amount of programming (Amazon, 2016; CrowdFlower, 2016).

A number of research efforts have extended the Mechanical Turk software toolkits to better support crowdsourced studies of web interface usability (Nebeling et al.,

2012, 2013); to enable synchronous and longitudinal studies (Mao et al., 2012); to use Turk workers to plan the contents of tasks to be completed by subsequent workers (Anand et al., 2011); and to simplify the construction of tasks (Greg et al., 2010), potentially including components for predicting and evaluating confidence level and costs (Barowy et al., 2016).

The infrastructure provided by Mechanical Turk and similar crowdsourcing platforms provides many advantages over "roll-your-own" designs. As any experienced HCI researcher knows well, the challenges of recruiting, enrolling, and consenting participants can consume substantial amounts of time. Even if you are able to build your own web application to do the trick, you might find that leveraging these platforms—particularly with one of the add-on libraries—might simplify your life considerably. These advantages aside, commercial crowdsourcing tools have potential downsides. Financially, payment for microtasks might be more expensive than the gifts or small payments traditionally made to study participants. Be sure to estimate your costs before you embark on a study. Technical challenges may arise—integration of complex, preexisting web applications with APIs provided by the crowd worker platforms might be a complex task. Consider a preliminary study to prove the concept and test the tasks thoroughly before starting a study. If the commercial platform does not work out, you might want to fall back on homegrown tools. In any case, you will still have to deal with the selection of which tasks you want users to complete and how you might design the tasks to ensure high-quality responses.

14.3.2.2 Tasks and study design

Law and von Ahn present a framework for developing appropriate tasks for human computation studies (Law and Ahn, 2011). Tasks can be seen as containing three main elements: introductory description, clear definitions of success criteria, and incentives (financial for Mechanical Turk and other systems, entertainment for games, access to services for CAPTCHA). Each task will involve multiple design decisions, including which *information* is presented to encourage completion of tasks without bias; tradeoffs in *granularity* between the value of the result and the time required to complete; whether tasks are completed individually or collaboratively; which incentives are offered, and how quality is ensured (Law and Ahn, 2011). For an in-depth discussion of these and related issues, Law and von Ahn's in-depth discussion (Law and Ahn, 2011) is highly recommended. An alternative model is presented by Alexander Quinn and Benjamin Bederson, who developed a multidimensional classification taxonomy. The Quinn-Bederson model describes human computation systems in terms of motivations for participation, quality control measures, techniques for aggregating responses, required human skills, orders and workflows for processing tasks, and the cardinality of tasks to requests (how many users are mapped to each task) (Quinn and Bederson, 2011).

Concerns over quality control have led to a variety of approaches in task design to attempt to ensure high-quality results from crowdsourcing studies (Table 14.1).

Table 14.1 Quality Control Measures for Crowdsourcing Studies

Strategy	Proposed Approach
Question design	Include questions with known answers (Kittur et al., 2008)
	Make accurate answers easy to provide (Kittur et al., 2008)
Study design	Develop predictive models based on question types to determine how many responses are needed to ensure high-quality answers for each question type (Barowy et al., 2016)
	Use micro-diversions or other distracters to offset declines in response quality as users get bored or tired (Dai et al., 2015)
Task performance data analysis	Look for patterns indicating answers that might have been faked or rushed, including repeated free text or questions answered too quickly (Kittur et al., 2008)
	Use task completion metadata to develop predictive models of individual workers (Ipeirotis et al., 2010) and tasks (Rzeszotarski and Kittur, 2011; Zhu et al., 2012)

Anniket Kittur, Ed Chi, and Bongwun Suh (Kittur et al., 2008) made three suggestions for designing high-quality crowdsourcing tasks. (1) Each task should include questions with known answers that can be easily checked. Asking participants to count the number of images in the page, or to answer a simple question based on the text in the page, can help determine if they are answering seriously or simply rushing through. (2) Accurate answers should be no harder to provide than rushed, inaccurate answers. For example, a task asking users to summarize a site might be easily subverted by short one-word answers, but an explicit requirement that users provide a certain number of keywords to describe content might be easier to fill out accurately. (3) Look for other ways to find low-quality answers, such as by identifying tasks that are completed too quickly or have answers repeated across multiple tasks (Kittur et al., 2008). Having multiple users complete each task and using agreement on results as a measure of quality—just as described earlier for CAPTCHA—is another possibility, but redundancy can be expensive (Ipeirotis et al., 2010). Alternatively, models of the complexity of different response types (checkboxes, radio boxes, free text) can be used to predict the number of responses needed to arrive at high-quality levels with high confidence (Barowy et al., 2016). "Micro-diversions"—games or other entertaining distractions designed to disrupt the monotony of performing multiple repeated tasks over long periods of time—might also help improve response quality (Dai et al., 2015).

Other studies have used task completion metadata to develop predictive models suitable for identifying invalid answers. Noting that Mechanical Turk collects detailed data on each task, including measures of start and end time, Zhu and colleagues built predictive models based on initial estimates of task performance and data from actual tasks. They then used these models to classify subsequent responses as either valid or invalid (Zhu et al., 2012). Other efforts have explored building models of individual workers (Ipeirotis et al., 2010) and using JavaScript web-page instrumenting techniques (Chapter 12) to collect mouse and keyboard usage data sufficient for building "task fingerprints" capable of predicting performance (Rzeszotarski and Kittur, 2011).

Successful design of a crowdsourced study does not end with the design of individual tasks. Although some studies—particularly studies involving online evaluation of user interface designs—may be based on large numbers of workers completing very similar tasks, more complex control structures have been used in crowdsourcing studies to decompose large problems, to introduce feedback—whereby responses to some questions will influence the content of subsequent question, or to influence workflows. Edith Law and Luis von Ahn provide a summary of different workflow strategies in their in-depth review of human computation (Law and Ahn, 2011).

14.3.2.3 Pros and cons of crowdsourced studies

Easy to create, potentially inexpensive, and backed by services that simplify recruitment and enrollment of participants, crowdsourced studies can be very appealing. Other potential advantages include potentially decreased bias and increased validity, as participants who do not interact directly with researchers or even know that they are participating in an experiment might be less susceptible to implicit or explicit pressures (Paolacci et al., 2010). Although the use of services like Mechanical Turk does remove some knowledge about participants (Kittur et al., 2008), some have argued that Turk users may be demographically similar to broader populations (Paolacci et al., 2010). Technical questions might influence the validity of task completion times from crowdsourced experiments, as network delays might impact task completion times (see Chapter 12). Finally, the lack of direct interaction with participants eliminates the possibility of gaining any insight from direct observation of task completion. Pairing studies—as discussed earlier—provides one possible means of avoiding this lack of feedback. A small lab study might give you the insight associated with direct interaction with users, while a companion human computation study will help you enroll larger numbers of participants.

Before jumping into studies using systems like Mechanical Turk, you should take care to ensure that your software components are implemented and tested correctly, and that you understand the social dynamics of the workers. Online forums for mechanical Turk users, including Turkopticon (https://turkopticon.ucsd.edu) (Irani and Silberman, 2013) and Turker Nation (http://turkernation.com), provide workers with the opportunity to discuss interesting tasks, problems with task requestors, and other topics of interest to workers trying to earn money through Mechanical Turk. These groups can provide valuable resources and feedback to researchers using human computation in their work. Brian McInnis and Gilly Leshed described how interactions with these groups proved particularly useful when software errors prevented tasks from working correctly, and workers from being paid. Interactions with the participant community helped resolve the issues and provide fair payment, thus avoiding the unfortunate outcome of a failed experiment leading to ill will (McInnis and Leshed, 2016). It may not be possible to identify all problems in advance, but working with the community of users to build trust and promote fairness may be an important strategy for successful human computation studies.

14.3.3 FUTURE OF HUMAN COMPUTATION

Human computation has many promising applications. A 2014 workshop of the Computing Community Consortium of the Computing Research Association outlined numerous possibilities for the use of human computation to meet pressing social needs, including social support for people in need; combining training with problem solving to improve the process of interpreting radiology images; to collect river-level information and serve as an early warning for possible floods; and others (Michelucci et al., 2015). As our engagement with our devices continues to occupy much of our time and attention, attempts to channel this fascination in socially meaningful ways are likely to continue to be a growing part of the landscape.

HCI research efforts have explored possible extensions to crowd source models, designed to increase the utility of crowdsourced work. Possibilities include changing task structures to include "handoffs" between workers, thus possibly increasing the quality of the resulting work (Embiricos et al., 2014); using algorithmic approaches to plan task workflow (Weld, 2015); exploring the impact of task ordering on speed and mental demand during the completion of a sequence of small tasks (Cai et al., 2016); and using new models to encourage participation, including leveraging participant curiosity (Law et al., 2016), providing entertaining "micro-diversions" to improve productivity of workers conducting many tasks (Dai et al., 2015), or using "twitch" microtasks capable of being completed very quickly to lower barriers to involvement (Vaish et al., 2014). Other efforts have explored paying crowd workers to be ready to respond quickly, thus enabling real-time crowdsourcing (Bernstein et al., 2011), applying algorithmic approaches to identify when tasks should be reassigned because original workers have abandoned them (Kucherbaev et al., 2016), and using models of increased error tolerance to increase the rate at which large tasks can be completed (Krishna et al., 2016).

Another promising line of research asks a slightly different question—"how can crowdsourced workers help with familiar, knowledge-intensive tasks?" As complex tasks, writing papers, drawing figures and diagrams, and analyzing budgets require significant cognitive effort and attention to detail, crowdsourced workers might help writers, designers, and analysts with on-demand suggestions for improving the quality of their work. These possibilities drove the development of Soylent, a set of tools for using human computation to improve the writing process. Developed as extensions to Microsoft Word, Soylent provides writers with the ability to request human computation assistance in shortening texts, grammar and spell-checking, and other tasks not easily accomplished via existing word processing tools (Bernstein et al., 2015). Although the possibilities of using human computation assistance to assist with these familiar tasks may be intriguing, further work will likely be needed to understand when, where, and for whom such models are appropriate. For more news on developments in Human Computation, see the web site of the Human Computation Institute (http://humancomputation.org).

14.4 SENSORS AND UBIQUITOUS COMPUTING

Taking advantage of advances in miniaturization of components, reduced power requirements, and advances in abilities to sense and distribute information without physical connections through electrical or data networks, engineers have developed approaches that revolutionize our ability to collect data. Originally discussed in the context of the RFID tags that can be used to sense uniquely identified objects through radio frequencies, the "Internet of Things" (Ashton, 2009) has become a familiar means of describing a landscape where data collection, sensing, and computing are all around us, and often invisibly hidden in unobtrusive devices. Although the smartphones and fitness monitors described in Chapter 13 are perhaps the most familiar, they are only the beginning. Sensors embedded in clothes or eyeglasses have arrived in commercial products, and Internet-connected thermostats, security alarms, and security cameras help concerned homeowners keep an eye on things while they are away. Low-cost development platforms including Arduino and Raspberry PI provide tinkerers with the tools to design their own ubiquitous data collection tools.

Broadly speaking, HCI researchers engage in two types of research with these sensors. From a system-building point of view, needs assessment through qualitative research is generally needed to understand what should be built and how it should work. Once systems are deployed, analysis of interaction data (using techniques from Chapters 12 and 13) will generally be combined with ethnography (Chapter 9), case studies (Chapter 7), and other qualitative approaches (Chapter 11) to understand how the tools worked in practice. A discussion of some example systems and their techniques and methods will help us appreciate some of the challenges and how they have been addressed. Table 14.2 provides an overview summary of types of sensor/ubiquitous research, research methods, and challenges.

Table 14.2 Overview of Study Types, Research Methods, and Challenges of HCI Research Involving Sensors and Ubiquitous Computing

Study Types	Methods	Challenges
• Alternative input • Sensors and monitoring • Mobile devices • Wearables	• Diaries • Interviews • Field studies • Usage log analysis • Ethnography • Participatory design	• Data transfer • Data storage • Data processing • Engineering and configuration of sensors and networking

14.4.1 HISTORY AND EXAMPLES

The origins of ubiquitous computing are generally traced back to Marc Weiser's 1991 article "The Computer for the 21st century" (Weiser, 1991). Writing as chief technologist of the Xerox Palo Alto Research Labs—home of pioneering work in early graphical user interfaces—Weiser imagined a future working environment with active badges, computational devices, and pads and tabs linked by networks of wired and wireless transceivers. Perhaps more importantly, Weiser urged the notion of "embodied virtuality"—taking computing from the workstations of the time and embedding it in numerous, ubiquitous devices. Coming at a time when sensors and wireless communication were beginning to be sufficiently small, powerful, and inexpensive to enable this computing infrastructure (Weiser, 1991). Weiser's vision inspired researchers to create the field of Ubiquitous computing, led by the flagship UbiComp conference since 2001. A 2011 study of research and co-citation in ubiquitous computing identified almost 6000 papers published between 1995 and 2009 (Zhao and Wang, 2011)—a number that has undoubtedly grown steadily since (Figure 14.2). Although a full review of these varied research areas is beyond the scope of this section, description of some selected research efforts will identify recurrent trends and related research methods.

FIGURE 14.2

A map of keywords from titles and abstracts *(triangles)* and other noun phrases *(circles)* found in a collection of almost 6000 ubiquitous computing research articles published between 1995 and 2009.

From Zhao, R., Wang, J., 2011. Visualizing the research on pervasive and ubiquitous computing.
Scientometrics 86 (3), 593–612.

Alternative input devices were an early focus of ubiquitous computing research. Noting the short comings of mouse and keyboard input, these projects explored various physical devices, complete with associated electronics, that might be used to control software applications. The *Tangible Bits* effort described several possible mechanisms including an arm-mounted LED screen, a horizontal back-projected computing "surface," and physical icons—known as "phicons"—that might be used to represent and manipulate items in the display (Ishii and Ullmer, 1997).

Sensors and monitoring tools have been developed to use computing to address challenges associated with everyday lives. Noting the difficulties that many families face in dealing with aging relatives who may want to remain in their own homes despite increased frailty and need for support, Elizabeth Mynatt and colleagues developed the digital family portrait, which would use sensors distributed throughout the house of an older person to collect data associated with successful completion of activities of daily life. These readings would be collected electronically and distributed via the Internet to a computerized picture frame in the home of the younger family member. A border on the screen would display icons that might vary in size and intensity to indicate recent activity levels and trends, assuring the younger caretaker that their older relative was safely up and about, while maintaining privacy for the older person (Figure 14.3) (Mynatt et al., 2001; Rowan and Mynatt, 2005). Similar concerns about the well-being of older people have led to designs combining motion sensing data from smartphones with Microsoft Kinect motion sensing (see Chapter 13) and social media feeds to identify activities in the home and related variations in mood (Ghose et al., 2013). Other studies have been more purely formative, such as a contextual interview study that asked older adults about objects of

FIGURE 14.3

A digital family portrait, with a picture of an older relative surrounded by butterfly icons scaled to indicate relative levels of activity. Levels for the current day are represented with new icons added hourly, while the previous 27 days are summarized with one icon per day.

From Rowan, J., Mynatt, E.D., 2005. Digital family portrait field trial: support for aging in place. In: Proceedings of the SIGCHI Conference on Human Factors in Computing Systems. ACM, Portland, OR, pp. 521–530.

importance, in the hopes of developing technologies that might promote social interaction. Results of these interviews indicated that many valued devices were routinely used in social interaction, even though they were not specifically communication devices (Vaisutis et al., 2014).

Other efforts have explored the possibility of widespread data collection through mobile devices. The "Smart Citizen Kit" provides Arduino-based hardware, including sensors, battery, and WiFi, suitable for collecting environmental data that can be shared, aggregated, and used for community planning (Diez and Posada, 2013). Noting that data from these sensors often provide data that is hard to interpret, the Physikit project augmented the smart citizen kit with physical ambient displays (inspired, in part by Tangible Bits (Ishii and Ullmer, 1997)) using light, movement, buzzing, or air motion to display data trends (Houben et al., 2016).

From a research (but not commercial) perspective, it is hard to talk about ubiquitous computing without mentioning wearables such as Google Glass. Growing out of a long line of research on wearable computing, Glass was the first broadly available head-mounted display for everyday use. Although not commercially successful, Glass had an impact on the research world. Researchers have applied Glass to challenges such as object recognition (Chen et al., 2015) and gaze recognition (Kangas et al., 2014), with applications including assistive help for people with Parkinson's disease (McNaney et al., 2014), supporting hands-free computer use in laboratory settings (Hu et al., 2015), physics education (Weppner et al., 2014a), logging of activity (Weppner et al., 2014b), and encouraging exercise (Nguyen et al., 2014; Sörös et al., 2013). One prototype system combined Google Glass with an EEG headset (Chapter 13) to support home control, allowing users to combine gaze at an object along with a thought about a desired outcome to complete tasks such as adjusting a thermostat (Simoens et al., 2014). Google Glass may not have been a commercial success, but these and related efforts suggest that some future product might find its niche.

14.4.2 UBIQUITOUS COMPUTING RESEARCH METHODS

Ubiquitous computing research might be technologically innovative, but the research methods involved are often somewhat familiar, using methods described throughout this book. Given the importance of the embedded nature of these tools, qualitative case studies and other examinations of the use of the tools in context may be more prominent than empirical studies, and methods chosen will also vary with the project. Input device research might include some empirical or usability studies, but the novelty of the tools and related tasks often require design explorations with little or no evaluation to simply explore possibilities (Ishii and Ullmer, 1997). In another example, a project involving the development of digital family portraits used preliminary interviews to assess needs for a proposed tool. This formative work was followed by field studies combining use of the tool in participants' homes with ongoing diary and interview studies. These later studies provided detailed insight into how one family made use of the tools (Mynatt et al., 2001; Rowan and Mynatt, 2005).

The importance of contextual factors and the novelty of the technologies involved make up-front qualitative investigations vitally important, as misunderstandings of contexts and how tools might be used can often compromise the goals of the system. Interviews with users, particularly when conducted in context (Vaisutis et al., 2014; Mynatt et al., 2001; Rowan and Mynatt, 2005) can identify key requirements and guide design. Similarly, field studies are often vital for understanding impacts of the tools in context (Houben et al., 2016), particularly in terms of the many privacy and control concerns associated with unobtrusive sensors and monitors that might capture activities that some individuals might not want recorded (Mynatt et al., 2001; Rowan and Mynatt, 2005; Kärkkäinen et al., 2010). Despite the strengths of these field studies, they remain expensive and challenging, leading some to look for alternative approaches such as scale models useful for inexpensively demonstrating and exploring possibilities (Chatzigiannakis et al., 2014).

Other efforts have explored the use of more quantitative versions of diaries. One exploration looked at the frequencies and locations of interactions with all things in the home—whether digital or not—during intervals lasting several hours. Histograms indicating the frequency of use of various objects, along with maps describing locations, provide detailed understanding of interactions with objects that might conceivably be integrated into an Internet of Things (Crabtree et al., 2006). Similar approaches to studying the use of everyday, noncomputer onjects and how those uses might inform the Internet of Things have led to the development of "object-oriented ethnography"—the study of how objects interact with our lives and how this understanding might inform the design of devices augmented with computing capabilities (Nansen et al., 2014).

Design sessions, similar to those used in participatory design, can also be useful for developing ideas. One effort examined devices, interactions, and roles to develop a set of graphical building blocks describing roles of individuals and devices in various ubiquitous computing scenarios, using these blocks to both convey elements of design and to identify difficulties with proposed designs (Kim et al., 2016b). Although the development of methods of this sort quickly becomes its own research project involving multiple iterations and revisions, the results can often be very informative.

Sensor data presents its own challenges. Inexpensive sensors for detecting motion and sound might be available commercially, either as "ready-to-deploy" products or as components suitable for assembly or control via Arduino or Raspberry PI hardware (Diez and Posada, 2013). Transferring data from sensors to remote servers, through wireless or USB connections will be a requirement. You will also need a plan for storing or processing sensor data, which can be quite voluminous. A willingness to tinker and to consider outrageous ideas can be helpful in tackling these projects, as unexpected approaches can often be quite helpful. In response to the potential expense and complexity of sensors used in projects like digital family portraits, one study found that microphones taped to pipes in a basement could inexpensively and accurately identify the use of bathrooms (sinks, showers, and toilets) and kitchen appliances (Fogarty et al., 2006).

Like physiological data discussed in Chapter 13, sensor-based ubiquitous computing also requires thoughtful planning and careful analysis including preprocessing, filtering, detection of specific types of signals, classification of activities, and storage and management of data—possibly both raw and processed and related patterns. Researchers have proposed a variety of processing pipelines (Ghose et al., 2013), data monitoring tools (Bannach et al., 2010), reference datasets (Reiss and Stricker, 2012), data integration strategies (Schuldhaus et al., 2014), and database architectures, including the use of so-called NoSQL databases (Zeni et al., 2014), to address these challenges. Details of these components will generally be dependent upon sensor capabilities, requirements for data storage, and the specific questions being asked.

Triangulated coordination of data collection and interpretation can often be highly informative. A study of movement throughout places in the home illustrates the potential for coordination of automated data collection with qualitative data—in this case, interviews (Aipperspach et al., 2006). To understand the patterns of activity in homes, researchers placed location sensors at various points throughout several homes. These sensors captured where people were, when they were there, and for how long. Mathematical models were used to combine individual events in the log files into meaningful aggregates that identified "places"—locations of significant activity in the home. The models were evaluated by comparing the automatically identified places with the results of interviews with the participants. Interviews with the participants had the added advantage of providing context to explain some of the results of the models. In one case, models identified a "place" that included both a kitchen table and a living room couch. Interviews with the residents of this particular home indicated that this data was collected during the course of a birthday party, when they were continually moving between the kitchen and the living room, acting as if the two locations were part of one larger space (Aipperspach et al., 2006). Automated methods that focused only on the contents of the activity logs would not have had access to this more nuanced explanation of resident activity.

14.5 SUMMARY

As the growth of the Internet and the availability of low-cost sensors led information and computing into ubiquitous and familiar roles pervading all aspects of everyday life, it seems only natural that these technologies would play key roles in HCI research. Remote usability studies simplify the process of conducting usability studies while providing access to larger scales of data. Human computation systems have opened the door to an entirely new type of data collection, harnessing the power of networks to engage many individuals in completing small tasks providing insight unavailable through computational tools. Sensor-based systems allow for the easy collection of new types of data in volumes not previously imaginable.

Online activity also provides a rich source of data for close examination of complex interactions and communication patterns. Examination of online discussions and interactions can tell us a great deal about the dynamics of group conversation and the spread of key ideas.

Online and ubiquitous HCI research will likely continue to be shaped by—and to shape—emerging tools and technological approaches. Improved conferencing tools with richer integration of simultaneous screen-sharing and webcam feedback will likely enable richer and more informative online research studies, while new social applications will enable novel interaction patterns, promote further study, and suggest further innovations in the next generation of tools and applications. Comparable advances in sensors and ubiquitous tools will facilitate the collection of richer, higher-resolution, and higher-fidelity data.

As the scope of online HCI research increases, ethical concerns associated with frequent and often unobserved data collection will expand as well. Although the comparison of alternative web site designs via A/B testing may be relatively benign, integrated analyses of social media interactions, health data collected by wearable devices, and other ubiquitous sensor data may identify insights not possible from any single dataset, possibly revealing sensitive information that some participants might prefer to leave undiscussed.

DISCUSSION QUESTIONS

1. The earlier discussion of remote usability testing cited a lack of direct feedback from participants as a possible drawback. For in-person studies, careful observation of facial expression and body language during usability tests might help researchers identify moments of frustration or other emotional responses. These cues might not be available in synchronous remote usability studies, as some web conferencing tools might have limited video feedback through webcams, while others support only screen sharing. However, there might be some advantages to the lack of direct feedback. For example, in some cases, participants might be willing to be more frank in providing direct feedback if they do not have to see the facial expressions of the person administering the experiment. Are there other types of studies or questions that might provide better feedback if conducted remotely (as opposed to in-person)? How might you evaluate the suitability of different questions for remote versus in-person usability studies?

2. Ubiquitous mobile social computing through smartphones blurs lines between "traditional" social networks and sensor-based ubiquitous computing. From location-based apps used for identifying friends who might be physically nearby to the Pokemon Go game that challenged users to explore and find Pokemon characters on city streets and in natural environments, these apps present the possibility of capturing and studying very rich datasets. What are some of the challenges associated with studying datasets that might combine geographical locations, social media posts, and detailed interactions with

custom apps? Are there additional ethical dilemmas associated with the combination of these various data types?

3. Many crowdsourcing user studies might be seen as generalizations of remote usability studies, conducted through a software platform built to support participant recruitment. However, incentives might differ: in traditional lab studies, participants might be offered some money or a gift for participating, but crowdsourcing workers are generally paid by the task. Does this approach raise any concerns regarding the ethical treatment of research participants?

RESEARCH DESIGN EXERCISE

The combination of human computation and ubiquitous computing raises some interesting and challenging opportunities for HCI research. Imagine a novel application of the intersection of these techniques designed to help with a distinctly ancient and noncomputerized human activity: gardening. Specifically, a gardening support network might use online fora (or is it flora?) for members to exchange information and tips about cultivation of various plants in different climes. Participants might use ubiquitous computing tools to capture photos of plants, to measure activity in watering, and to track time spent working on the garden. Finally, human computation elements might be used to verify the identity of unfamiliar plants or blights or other infections that might harm plants: images collected from an individual's garden might be sent to a community of workers who might theorize about the identity of the plant in question, with a majority vote summarizing the consensus of the community. Speculate as to how you might go about constructing and studying this complex ecosystem. What design issues and challenges do you see? How might issues such as differing levels of expertise and experience be accounted for in the design? How might users distinguish between good advice and bad? How can users be enticed to participate in the interpretation of provided images? How might you evaluate the success of the various components of this system?

REFERENCES

Abdul-Rahman, A., Proctor, K.J., Duffy, B., Chen, M., 2014. Repeated measures design in crowdsourcing-based experiments for visualization. In: Proceedings of the Fifth Workshop on Beyond Time and Errors: Novel Evaluation Methods for Visualization. ACM, Paris, pp. 95–102.

Ahn, L.v., Dabbish, L., 2004. Labeling images with a computer game. In: Proceedings of the SIGCHI Conference on Human Factors in Computing Systems. ACM, Vienna, pp. 319–326.

Ahn, L.v., Dabbish, L., 2008. Designing games with a purpose. Communications of the ACM 51 (8), 58–67.

Ahn, L.V., Blum, M., Hopper, N.J., Langford, J., 2003. CAPTCHA: using hard AI problems for security. In: Proceedings of the 22nd International Conference on Theory and Applications of Cryptographic Techniques. Springer-Verlag, Warsaw, pp. 294–311.

Aipperspach, R., Rattenbury, T., Woodruff, A., Canny, J., 2006, September. A quantitative method for revealing and comparing places in the home. In: International Conference on Ubiquitous Computing. Springer Berlin Heidelberg, pp. 1–18.

Allen, C., Tsou, M.H., Aslam, A., Nagel, A., Gawron, J.M., 2016. Applying GIS and machine learning methods to twitter data for multiscale surveillance of influenza. PLoS One 11 (7), e0157734.

Amazon, 2016. Amazon Mechanical Turk Documentation. Retrieved August 30, 2016, from https://aws.amazon.com/documentation/mturk/.

Anand, P.K., Matthew, C., Bjoern, H., 2011. Turkomatic: automatic recursive task and workflow design for mechanical Turk. In: CHI '11 Extended Abstracts on Human Factors in Computing Systems. ACM, Vancouver, BC, pp. 2053–2058.

Andreasen, M.S., Neilsen, H.V., Schrøder, S.O., Stage, J., 2007. What happened to remote usability testing?: an empirical study of three methods. In: Proceedings of the SIGCHI Conference on Human Factors in Computing Systems. ACM, San Jose, CA, pp. 1405–1414.

Ashton, K., 2009. That 'Internet of Things' thing. RFID Journal. http://www.rfidjournal.com/articles/view?4986 (accessed March 19, 2017).

Azar, B., 2000. Online experiments: ethically fair or foul? Monitor on Psychology 31 (4), 50–51.

Baeza-Yates, R., Riberio-Neto, B., 2011. Modern Information Retrieval: The Concepts and Technology Behind Search. Addison-Wesley-Longman, Reading, MA.

Bakshy, E., Rosenn, I., Marlow, C., Adamic, L., 2012. The role of social networks in information diffusion. In: Proceedings of the 21st International Conference on World Wide Web. ACM, Lyon, pp. 519–528.

Bannach, D., Kunze, K., Weppner, J., Lukowicz, P., 2010. Integrated tool chain for recording and handling large, multimodal context recognition data sets. In: Proceedings of the 12th ACM International Conference Adjunct Papers on Ubiquitous Computing—Adjunct. ACM, Copenhagen, pp. 357–358.

Barowy, D.W., Curtsinger, C., Berger, E., McGregor, A., 2016. AutoMan: a platform for integrating human-based and digital computation. Communications of the ACM 59 (6), 102–109.

Bernstein, M.S., Brandt, J., Miller, R.C., Karger, D.R., 2011. Crowds in two seconds: enabling realtime crowd-powered interfaces. In: Proceedings of the 24th Annual ACM Symposium on User Interface Software and Technology. ACM, Santa Barbara, CA, pp. 33–42.

Bernstein, M.S., Little, G., Miller, R.C., Hartmann, B., Ackerman, M.S., Karger, D.R., Crowell, D., Panovich, K., 2015. Soylent: a word processor with a crowd inside. Communications of the ACM 58 (8), 85–94.

Bigham, J.P., Jayant, C., Ji, H., Little, G., Miller, R.C., Miller, R., Miller, A., Tatarowicz, B., White, S., White, T., Yeh, T., Miller, R., 2010. VizWiz: nearly real-time answers to visual questions. In: Proceedings of the 23rd Annual ACM Symposium on User Interface Software and Technology. ACM, New York, NY, pp. 333–342.

Bonsignore, E.M., Dunne, C., Rotman, D., Smith, M., Capone, T., Hansen, D.L., Shneiderman, B., 2009. First steps to Netviz Nirvana: evaluating social network analysis with NodeXL. In: International Conference on Computational Science and Engineering, CSE '09, pp. 332–339.

Bruckman, A.s., 2002. Ethical Guidelines for Research Online. Retrieved March 19, 2017, from http://www.cc.gatech.edu/~asb/ethics/.

Brush, A.J., Ames, M., Davis, J., 2004. A comparison of synchronous remote and local usability studies for an expert interface. Extended Abstracts, ACM Conference on Human Factors in Computing Systems, ACM Press, Vienna, pp. 1179–1182.

Bruun, A., Stage, J., 2012. The effect of task assignments and instruction types on remote asynchronous usability testing. In: Proceedings of the SIGCHI Conference on Human Factors in Computing Systems. ACM, Austin, TX, pp. 2117–2126.

Bruun, A., Gull, P., Hofmeister, L., Stage, J., 2009. Let your users do the testing: a comparison of three remote asynchronous usability testing methods. In: Proceedings of the SIGCHI Conference on Human Factors in Computing Systems. ACM, Boston, MA, pp. 1619–1628.

Burke, M., Marlow, C., Lento, T., 2010. Social network activity and social well-being. In: Proceedings of the SIGCHI Conference on Human Factors in Computing Systems. ACM, Atlanta, GA, pp. 1909–1912.

Bush, V., 1945. As we may think. The atlantic monthly 176 (1), 101–108.

Butler, D., 2013. When Google got flu wrong. Nature 494, 155–156.

Cai, C.J., Iqbal, S.T., Teevan, J., 2016. Chain reactions: the impact of order on microtask chains. In: Proceedings of the 2016 CHI Conference on Human Factors in Computing Systems. ACM, Santa Clara, CA, pp. 3143–3154.

Cassa, C.A., Chunara, R., Mandl, K., Brownstein, J.S., 2013. Twitter as a sentinel in emergency situations: lessons from the Boston marathon explosions. PLos Currents Disasters. Edition 1. http://dx.doi.org/10.1371/currents.dis.ad70cd1c8bc585e9470046cde334ee4b.

Centivany, A., Glushko, B., 2016. "Popcorn tastes good": participatory policymaking and Reddit's. In: Proceedings of the 2016 CHI Conference on Human Factors in Computing Systems. ACM, Santa Clara, CA, pp. 1126–1137.

Chatzigiannakis, I., Drude, J.P., Hasemann, H., Kröller, A., 2014. Developing smart homes using the internet of things: how to demonstrate your system. In: Streitz, N., Markopoulos, P. (Eds.), Distributed, Ambient, and Pervasive Interactions: Second International Conference, DAPI 2014, Held as Part of HCI International 2014, Heraklion, Crete, Greece, June 22–27, 2014. Springer International Publishing, pp. 415–426.

Chen, T.Y.-H., Ravindranath, L., Deng, S., Bahl, P., Balakrishnan, H., 2015. Glimpse: continuous, real-time object recognition on mobile devices. In: Proceedings of the 13th ACM Conference on Embedded Networked Sensor Systems. ACM, Seoul, pp. 155–168.

Chynał, P., Szymański, J.M., 2011. Remote Usability Testing Using Eyetracking. In: Campos, P., Graham, N., Jorge, J., et al. (Eds.), Human-Computer Interaction—INTERACT 2011: 13th IFIP TC 13 International Conference, Lisbon, Portugal, September 5–9, 2011, Part 1. Springer, Berlin, Heidelberg, pp. 356–361.

Cook, S., Conrad, C., Fowlkes, A.L., Mohebbi, M.H., 2011. Assessing Google flu trends performance in the United States during the 2009 influenza virus A (H1N1) pandemic. PLoS One 6 (8), e23610.

Crabtree, A., Benford, S., Greenhalgh, C., Tennent, P., Chalmers, M., Brown, B., 2006. Supporting ethnographic studies of ubiquitous computing in the wild. In: ACM Conference on Designing Interactive Systems. ACM Press, University Park, PA, pp. 60–69.

Crook, T., Frasca, B., Kohavi, R., Longbotham, R., 2009. Seven pitfalls to avoid when running controlled experiments on the web. In: Proceedings of the 15th ACM SIGKDD International Conference on Knowledge Discovery and Data Mining. ACM, Paris, pp. 1105–1114.

CrowdFlower, 2016. API | CrowdFlower. Retrieved August 30, 2016, 2016, from https://www.crowdflower.com/docs-api/

Dai, P., Rzeszotarski, J.M., Paritosh, P., Chi, E.H., 2015. And now for something completely different: improving crowdsourcing workflows with micro-diversions. In: Proceedings of the 18th ACM Conference on Computer Supported Cooperative Work and Social Computing. ACM, Vancouver, BC, pp. 628–638.

Davidson, M., Renaud, K., Li, S., 2014. jCAPTCHA: accessible human validation. In: Miesenberger, K., Fels, D., Archambault, D., Peñáz, P., Zagler, W. (Eds.), Computers Helping People with Special Needs: 14th International Conference, ICCHP 2014, Paris, France, July 9–11, 2014, Part I. Springer International Publishing, pp. 129–136.

Deng, A., 2015. Objective Bayesian two sample hypothesis testing for online controlled experiments. In: Proceedings of the 24th International Conference on World Wide Web. ACM, Florence, p. 913.

Deng, A., Xu, Y., Kohavi, R., Walker, T., 2013. Improving the sensitivity of online controlled experiments by utilizing pre-experiment data. In: Proceedings of the Sixth ACM International Conference on Web Search and Data Mining. ACM, Rome, pp. 123–132.

Deng, A., Li, T., Guo, Y., 2014. Statistical inference in two-stage online controlled experiments with treatment selection and validation. In: Proceedings of the 23rd International Conference on World Wide Web. ACM, Seoul, Korea, pp. 609–618.

Diez, T., Posada, A., 2013. The fab and the smart city: the use of machines and technology for the city production by its citizens. In: Proceedings of the 7th International Conference on Tangible, Embedded and Embodied Interaction. ACM, Barcelona, pp. 447–454.

Dray, S., Siegel, D., 2004. Remote possibilities?: international usability testing at a distance. Interactions 11 (2), 10–17.

Eiben, C.B., Siegel, J.B., Bale, J.B., Cooper, S., Khatib, F., Shen, B.W., Players, F., Stoddard, B.L., Popovic, Z., Baker, D., 2012. Increased Diels-Alderase activity through backbone remodeling guided by Foldit players. Nature Biotechnology 30 (2), 190–192.

Embiricos, A., Rahmati, N., Zhu, N., Bernstein, M.S., 2014. Structured handoffs in expert crowdsourcing improve communication and work output. In: Proceedings of the Adjunct Publication of the 27th Annual ACM Symposium on User Interface Software and Technology. ACM, Honolulu, Hawaii, pp. 99–100.

Engelbart, D.C., 1962. Augmenting Human Intellect: A Conceptual Framework. SRI Summary Report.

Filippova, A., Cho, H., 2016. The effects and antecedents of conflict in free and open source software development. In: Proceedings of the 19th ACM Conference on Computer-Supported Cooperative Work & Social Computing. ACM, San Francisco, CA, pp. 705–716.

Finley, K., 2014. Twitter Opens Its Enormous Archives to Data-Hungry Academics. Wired. Retrieved August 20, 2016, from http://www.wired.com/2014/02/twitter-promises-share-secrets-academia/.

Fogarty, J., Au, C., Hudson, S.E., 2006. Sensing from the basement: a feasibility study of unobtrusive and low-cost home activity recognition. In: Proceedings of the 19th Annual ACM Symposium on User Interface Software and Technology. ACM, Montreux, pp. 91–100.

Frankel, M.S., Siang, S., 1999. Ethical and Legal Aspects of Human Subjects Research on the Internet. American Association for the Advancement of Science.

Ghose, A., Sinha, P., Bhaumik, C., Sinha, A., Agrawal, A., Choudhury, A.D., 2013. UbiHeld: ubiquitous healthcare monitoring system for elderly and chronic patients. In: Proceedings of the 2013 ACM Conference on Pervasive and Ubiquitous Computing Adjunct Publication. ACM, Zurich, pp. 1255–1264.

Gilbert, E., 2012. Phrases that signal workplace hierarchy. In: Proceedings of the ACM 2012 Conference on Computer Supported Cooperative Work. ACM, Seattle, WA, pp. 1037–1046.

Ginsberg, J., Mohebbi, M.H., Patel, R.S., Brammer, L., Smolinski, M.S., Brilliant, L., 2009. Detecting influenza epidemics using search engine query data. Nature 457 (7232), 1012–1014.

Good, B.M., Loguercio, S., Nanis, M., Su, A.I., 2012. Genegames.org: high-throughput access to biological knowledge and reasoning through online games. In: IEEE Second International Conference on Healthcare Informatics, Imaging and Systems Biology (HISB), p. 145.

Greg, L., Lydia, B.C., Max, G., Robert, C.M., 2010. TurKit: human computation algorithms on mechanical Turk. In: Proceedings of the 23nd Annual ACM Symposium on User Interface Software and Technology. ACM, New York, NY, ISBN: 978-1-4503-0271-5, pp. 57–66.

Hansen, D., Shneiderman, B., 2010. Analyzing social media networks with NodeXL: insights from a connected world. Morgan Kaufmann, Burlington, MA.

Harkema, H., Dowling, J.N., Thornblade, T., Chapman, W.W., 2009. ConText: an algorithm for determining negation, experiencer, and temporal status from clinical reports. Journal of Biomedical Informatics 42 (5), 839–851.

Hartson, H.R., Castillo, J.C., Kelso, J., Neale, W.C., 1996. Remote evaluation: the network as an extension of the usability laboratory. In: Proceedings of the SIGCHI Conference on Human Factors in Computing Systems. ACM, Vancouver, BC, pp. 228–235.

Hedegaard, S., Simonsen, J.G., 2013. Extracting usability and user experience information from online user reviews. In: Proceedings of the SIGCHI Conference on Human Factors in Computing Systems. ACM, Paris, pp. 2089–2098.

Hedegaard, S., Simonsen, J.G., 2014. Mining until it hurts: automatic extraction of usability issues from online reviews compared to traditional usability evaluation. In: Proceedings of the 8th Nordic Conference on Human-Computer Interaction: Fun, Fast, Foundational. ACM, Helsinki, pp. 157–166.

Heer, J., Bostock, M., 2010. Crowdsourcing graphical perception: using mechanical Turk to assess visualization design. In: Proceedings of the SIGCHI Conference on Human Factors in Computing Systems. ACM, Atlanta, GA, pp. 203–212.

Hochheiser, H., Ning, Y., Hernandez, A., Horn, J.R., Jacobson, R., Boyce, R.D., 2016. Using nonexperts for annotating pharmacokinetic drug-drug interaction mentions in product labeling: a feasibility study. JMIR Research Protocols 5 (2), e40.

Houben, S., Golsteijn, C., Gallacher, S., Johnson, R., Bakker, S., Marquardt, N., Capra, L., Rogers, Y., 2016. Physikit: data engagement through physical ambient visualizations in the home. In: Proceedings of the 2016 CHI Conference on Human Factors in Computing Systems. ACM, Santa Clara, CA, pp. 1608–1619.

Hu, C., Resnik, P., Bederson, B.B., 2014. Crowdsourced monolingual translation. ACM Transactions on Computer-Human Interaction 21 (4), 1–35.

Hu, G., Chen, L., Okerlund, J., Shaer, O., 2015. Exploring the use of Google Glass in Wet Laboratories. In: Proceedings of the 33rd Annual ACM Conference Extended Abstracts on Human Factors in Computing Systems. ACM, Seoul, pp. 2103–2108.

Huang, J., White, R.W., Dumais, S., 2011. No clicks, no problem: using cursor movements to understand and improve search. In: Proceedings of the SIGCHI Conference on Human Factors in Computing Systems. ACM, Vancouver, BC, pp. 1225–1234.

Huang, J., White, R.W., Buscher, G., Wang, K., 2012. Improving searcher models using mouse cursor activity. In: Proceedings of the 35th International ACM SIGIR Conference on Research and Development in Information Retrieval. ACM, Portland, OR, pp. 195–204.

Huh, J., Liu, L.S., Neogi, T., Inkpen, K., Pratt, W., 2014. Health vlogs as social support for chronic illness management. ACM Transactions on Computer-Human Interaction 21 (4), 23:1–23:31.

Ipeirotis, P.G., Provost, F., Wang, J., 2010. Quality management on amazon mechanical Turk. In: Proceedings of the ACM SIGKDD Workshop on Human Computation. ACM, Washington, DC, pp. 64–67.

Irani, L.C., Silberman, M.S., 2013. Turkopticon: interrupting worker invisibility in amazon mechanical Turk. In: Proceedings of the SIGCHI Conference on Human Factors in Computing Systems. ACM, Paris, ISBN: 978-1-4503-1899-0, pp. 611–620.

Ishii, H., Ullmer, B., 1997. Tangible bits: towards seamless interfaces between people, bits and atoms. In: Proceedings of the ACM SIGCHI Conference on Human Factors in Computing Systems. ACM, Atlanta, GA, pp. 234–241.

Kangas, J., Akkil, D., Rantala, J., Isokoski, P., Majaranta, I., Raisamo, R., 2014. Using gaze gestures with haptic feedback on glasses. In: Proceedings of the 8th Nordic Conference on Human-Computer Interaction: Fun, Fast, Foundational. ACM, Helsinki, pp. 1047–1050.

Kärkkäinen, T., Vaittinen, T., Väänänen-Vainio-Mattila, K., 2010. I don't mind being logged, but want to remain in control: a field study of mobile activity and context logging. In: Proceedings of the SIGCHI Conference on Human Factors in Computing Systems. ACM, Atlanta, GA, pp. 163–172.

Kelly, D., Gyllstrom, K., 2011. An examination of two delivery modes for interactive search system experiments: remote and laboratory. In: Proceedings of the SIGCHI Conference on Human Factors in Computing Systems. ACM, Vancouver, BC, pp. 1531–1540.

Kharitonov, E., Vorobev, A., Macdonald, C., Serdyukov, P., Ounis, I., 2015. Sequential testing for early stopping of online experiments. In: Proceedings of the 38th International ACM SIGIR Conference on Research and Development in Information Retrieval. ACM, Santiago, Chile, pp. 473–482.

Khatib, F., DiMaio, F., Cooper, S., Kazmierczyk, M., Gilski, M., Krzywda, S., Zabranska, H., Pichova, I., Thompson, J., Popović, Z., Jaskolski, M., Baker, D., 2011. Crystal structure of a monomeric retroviral protease solved by protein folding game players. Nature Structural & Molecular Biology 18 (10), 1175–1177.

Kim, J.G., Kong, H.K., Karahalios, K., Fu, W.-T., Hong, H., 2016a. The power of collective endorsements: credibility factors in medical crowdfunding campaigns. In: Proceedings of the 2016 CHI Conference on Human Factors in Computing Systems. ACM, Santa Clara, CA, pp. 4538–4549.

Kim, Y., Kim, H., Bae, S.-H., Lee, S., Kim, C.-J., 2016b. Building blocks for designing future multi-device interaction. In: Proceedings of the 2016 CHI Conference Extended Abstracts on Human Factors in Computing Systems. ACM, Santa Clara, CA, pp. 2548–2554.

Kirkorian, R., 2014. Introducing Twitter Data Grants. Retrieved August 20, 2016, from https://blog.twitter.com/2014/introducing-twitter-data-grants.

Kittur, A., Kraut, R.E., 2008. Harnessing the wisdom of crowds in Wikipedia: quality through coordination. In: Proceedings of the ACM Conference on Computer Supported Cooperative Work. ACM, San Diego, CA, pp. 37–46.

Kittur, A., Chi, E.H., Suh, B., 2008. Crowdsourcing user studies with mechanical Turk. In: Proceedings of the SIGCHI Conference on Human Factors in Computing Systems. ACM, Florence, pp. 453–456.

Klembczyk, J.J., Jalalpour, M., Levin, S., Washington, R.E., Pines, J.M., Rothman, R.E., Dugas, A.F., 2016. Google Flu trends spatial variability validated against emergency department influenza-related visits. Journal of Medical Internet Research 18 (6), e175.

Kohavi, R., Longbotham, R., Sommerfield, D., Henne, R.M., 2009. Controlled experiments on the web: survey and practical guide. Data Mining and Knowledge Discovery 18 (1), 140–181.

Kohavi, R., Deng, A., Frasca, B., Longbotham, R., Walker, T., Xu, Y., 2012. Trustworthy online controlled experiments: five puzzling outcomes explained. In: Proceedings of the 18th ACM SIGKDD International Conference on Knowledge Discovery and Data Mining. ACM, Beijing, pp. 786–794.

Kohavi, R., Deng, A., Frasca, B., Walker, T., Xu, Y., Pohlmann, N., 2013. Online controlled experiments at large scale. In: Proceedings of the 19th ACM SIGKDD International Conference on Knowledge Discovery and Data Mining. ACM, Chicago, IL, pp. 1168–1176.

Kong, N., Hearst, M.A., Agrawala, M., 2014. Extracting references between text and charts via crowdsourcing. In: Proceedings of the SIGCHI Conference on Human Factors in Computing Systems. ACM, Toronto, ON, pp. 31–40.

Kraut, R., Olson, J., Banaji, M., Bruckman, A., Cohen, J., Couper, M., 2004. Psychological research online: report of board of scientific affairs' advisory group on the conduct of research on the internet. The American Psychologist 59 (2), 105–117.

Krishna, R.A., Hata, K., Chen, S., Kravitz, J., Shamma, D.A., Fei-Fei, L., Bernstein, M.S., 2016. Embracing error to enable rapid crowdsourcing. In: Proceedings of the 2016 CHI Conference on Human Factors in Computing Systems. ACM, Santa Clara, CA, pp. 3167–3179.

Kucherbaev, P., Daniel, F., Tranquillini, S., Marchese, M., 2016. ReLauncher: crowdsourcing micro-tasks runtime controller. In: Proceedings of the 19th ACM Conference on Computer-Supported Cooperative Work & Social Computing. ACM, San Francisco, CA, pp. 1609–1614.

Lasecki, W.S., Zhong, Y., Bigham, J.P., 2014. Increasing the bandwidth of crowdsourced visual question answering to better support blind users. In: Proceedings of the 16th International ACM SIGACCESS Conference on Computers & Accessibility. ACM, Rochester, NY, pp. 263–264.

Lasecki, W.S., Kim, J., Rafter, N., Sen, O., Bigham, J.P., Bernstein, M.S., 2015. Apparition: crowdsourced user interfaces that come to life as you sketch them. In: Proceedings of the 33rd Annual ACM Conference on Human Factors in Computing Systems. ACM, Seoul, pp. 1925–1934.

Law, E., Ahn, L.V., 2011. Human computation. Synthesis Lectures on Artificial Intelligence and Machine Learning 5 (3), 1–121.

Law, E., Yin, M., Goh, J., Chen, K., Terry, M.A., Gajos, K.Z., 2016. Curiosity killed the Cat, but makes crowdwork better. In: Proceedings of the 2016 CHI Conference on Human Factors in Computing Systems. ACM, Santa Clara, CA, pp. 4098–4110.

Lazar, J., Preece, J., 1999. Designing and implementing web-based surveys. Journal of Computer Information Systems 39 (4), 63–67.

Lazer, D., Kennedy, R., King, G., Vespignani, A., 2014. The parable of Google flu: traps in big data analysis. Science 343 (6176), 1203–1205.

Leug, C., Fisher, D., 2003. From Usenet to CoWebs: Interacting With Social Information Spaces. Springer, London.

Madathil, K.C., Greenstein, J.S., 2011. Synchronous remote usability testing: a new approach facilitated by virtual worlds. In: Proceedings of the SIGCHI Conference on Human Factors in Computing Systems. ACM, Vancouver, BC, pp. 2225–2234.

Maloney-Krichmar, D., Preece, J., 2005. A multilevel analysis of sociability, usability, and community dynamics in an online health community. ACM Transactions on Computer-Human Interaction 12 (2), 201–232.

Mao, A., Chen, Y., Gajos, K.Z., Parkes, D.C., Procaccia, A.D., Zhang, H., 2012. TurkServer: enabling synchronous and longitudinal online experiments. In: Fourth Workshop on Human Computation (HCOMP 2012).

Matias, J.N., 2016. Going dark: social factors in collective action against platform operators in the reddit blackout. In: Proceedings of the 2016 CHI Conference on Human Factors in Computing Systems. ACM, Santa Clara, CA, pp. 1138–1151.

McInnis, B., Leshed, G., 2016. Running user studies with crowd workers. Interactions 23 (5), 50–53.

McNaney, R., Vines, J., Roggen, D., Balaam, M., Zhang, P., Poliakov, I., Olivier, P., 2014. Exploring the acceptability of Google glass as an everyday assistive device for people with Parkinson's. In: Proceedings of the SIGCHI Conference on Human Factors in Computing Systems. ACM, Toronto, ON, pp. 2551–2554.

Menefee, H.K., Thompson, M.J., Guterbock, T.M., Williams, I.C., Valdez, R.S., 2016. Mechanisms of communicating health information through Facebook: implications for consumer health information technology design. Journal of Medical Internet Research 18 (8), e218.

Meyer, J., Bederson, B., 1998. Does a Sketchy Appearance Influence Drawing Behavior? Human Computer Interaction Lab Tech Report. University of Maryland. Retrieved March 20, 2017 from http://hcil2.cs.umd.edu/trs/98-12/98-12.pdf.

Micallef, L., Dragicevic, P., Fekete, J.D., 2012. Assessing the effect of visualizations on Bayesian reasoning through crowdsourcing. IEEE Transactions on Visualization and Computer Graphics 18 (12), 2536–2545.

Michelucci, P., Shanley, L., Dickinson, J., Hirsh, H., 2015. A U.S. Research Roadmap for Human Computation. Computing Community Consortium Technical Report. Available at https://arxiv.org/ftp/arxiv/papers/1505/1505.07096.pdf (accessed April 8, 2017).

Morris, R.R., Schueller, S.M., Picard, R.W., 2015. Efficacy of a web-based, crowdsourced peer-to-peer cognitive reappraisal platform for depression: randomized controlled trial. Journal of Medical Internet Research 17 (3), e72.

Mynatt, E.D., Rowan, J., Craighill, S., Jacobs, A., 2001. Digital family portraits: supporting peace of mind for extended family members. In: Proceedings of the SIGCHI Conference on Human Factors in Computing Systems. ACM, Seattle, WA, pp. 333–340.

Myslín, M., Zhu, S.-H., Chapman, W., Conway, M., 2013. Using twitter to examine smoking behavior and perceptions of emerging tobacco products. Journal of Medical Internet Research 15 (8), e174.

Nansen, B., Ryn, L.v., Vetere, F., Robertson, T., Brereton, M., Dourish, P., 2014. An internet of social things. In: Proceedings of the 26th Australian Computer-Human Interaction Conference on Designing Futures: The Future of Design. ACM, Sydney, NSW, pp. 87–96.

Nebeling, M., Speicher, M., Grossniklaus, M., Norrie, M.C., 2012. Crowdsourced web site evaluation with crowdstudy. In: Proceedings of the 12th International Conference on Web Engineering. Springer-Verlag, Berlin, pp. 494–497.

Nebeling, M., Speicher, M., Norrie, M.C., 2013. CrowdStudy: general toolkit for crowdsourced evaluation of web interfaces. In: Proceedings of the 5th ACM SIGCHI Symposium on Engineering Interactive Computing Systems. ACM, London, pp. 255–264.

Nguyen, E., Modak, T., Dias, E., Yu, Y., Huang, L., 2014. Fitnamo: using bodydata to encourage exercise through Google glass. In: CHI '14 Extended Abstracts on Human Factors in Computing Systems. ACM, Toronto, Ontario, Canada, pp. 239–244.

Nichols, J., Mahmud, J., Drews, C., 2012. Summarizing sporting events using twitter. In: Proceedings of the 2012 ACM International Conference on Intelligent User Interfaces. ACM, Lisbon, pp. 189–198.

Nielsen, J., 2005. Putting A/B Testing in Its Place. Retrieved July 18, 2016, from https://www.nngroup.com/articles/putting-ab-testing-in-its-place/.

Nielsen, J., 2012. A/B Testing, Usability Engineering, Radical Innovation: What Pays Best? Retrieved July 18, 2016, from https://www.nngroup.com/articles/ab-testing-usability-engineering/.

Nielsen, J., 2014. Define Stronger A/B Test Variations Through UX Research. Retrieved July 18, 2016, from https://www.nngroup.com/articles/ab-testing-and-ux-research/.

Paolacci, G., Chandler, J., Ipeirotis, P.G., 2010. Running experiments on Amazon Mechanical Turk. Judgment and Decision making 5 (5), 411–419.

Paparrizos, J., White, R.W., Horvitz, E., 2016. Screening for pancreatic adenocarcinoma using signals from web search logs: feasibility study and results. Journal of Oncology Practice 12 (8), 737–744.

Petrie, H., Hamilton, F., King, N., Pavan, P., 2006, April. Remote usability evaluations with disabled people. In Proceedings of the SIGCHI conference on Human Factors in computing systems, ACM, pp. 1133–1141.

Quinn, A.J., Bederson, B.B., 2011. Human computation: a survey and taxonomy of a growing field. In: Proceedings of the SIGCHI Conference on Human Factors in Computing Systems. ACM, Vancouver, BC, pp. 1403–1412.

Reiss, A., Stricker, D., 2012. Creating and benchmarking a new dataset for physical activity monitoring. In: Proceedings of the 5th International Conference on Pervasive Technologies Related to Assistive Environments. ACM, Heraklion, Crete, pp. 1–8.

Richard, G.T., Kafai, Y.B., 2016. Blind spots in youth DIY programming: examining diversity in creators, content, and comments within the scratch online community. In: Proceedings of the 2016 CHI Conference on Human Factors in Computing Systems. ACM, Santa Clara, CA, pp. 1473–1485.

Rowan, J., Mynatt, E.D., 2005. Digital family portrait field trial: support for aging in place. In: Proceedings of the SIGCHI Conference on Human Factors in Computing Systems. ACM, Portland, OR, pp. 521–530.

Rzeszotarski, J.M., Kittur, A., 2011. Instrumenting the crowd: using implicit behavioral measures to predict task performance. In: Proceedings of the 24th Annual ACM Symposium on User Interface Software and Technology. ACM, Santa Barbara, CA, pp. 13–22.

Santillana, M., Nguyen, A.T., Dredze, M., Paul, M.J., Nsoesie, E.O., Brownstein, J.S., 2015. Combining search, social media, and traditional data sources to improve influenza surveillance. PLoS Computational Biology 11 (10), e1004513.

Sauer, G., Lazar, J., Hochheiser, H., Feng, J., 2010. Towards a universally usable human interaction proof: evaluation of task completion strategies. ACM Transactions on Accessible Computing 2 (4), 1–32.

Schneider, O.S., Seifi, H., Kashani, S., Chun, M., MacLean, K.E., 2016. HapTurk: crowdsourcing affective ratings of vibrotactile icons. In: Proceedings of the 2016 CHI Conference on Human Factors in Computing Systems. ACM, Santa Clara, CA, pp. 3248–3260.

Schnepp, J., Shiver, B., 2011. Improving deaf accessibility in remote usability testing. In: The Proceedings of the 13th International ACM SIGACCESS Conference on Computers and Accessibility. ACM, Dundee, Scotland, pp. 255–256.

Schuldhaus, D., Leutheuser, H., Eskofier, B.M., 2014. Towards big data for activity recognition: a novel database fusion strategy. In: Proceedings of the 9th International Conference on Body Area Networks. ICST (Institute for Computer Sciences, Social-Informatics and Telecommunications Engineering), London, pp. 97–103.

Scott, J., 2013. Social Network Analysis. Sage Publications, Ltd., London.

Shet, V., 2014. Are you a robot? Introducing "No CAPTCHA reCAPTCHA". Google Security Blog. Retrieved August 24, 2016, from https://security.googleblog.com/2014/12/are-you-robot-introducing-no-captcha.html.

Shneiderman, B., 2002. Leonardo's Laptop: Human Needs and the New Computing Technologies. MIT Press, Cambridge, MA.

Simoens, P., Coninck, E.D., Vervust, T., Wijmeersch, J.-F.V., Ingelbinck, T., Verbelen, T., Beeck, M.O.d., Dhoedt, B., 2014. Vision: smart home control with head-mounted sensors for vision and brain activity. In: Proceedings of the Fifth International Workshop on Mobile Cloud Computing and Services. ACM, Bretton Woods, NH, pp. 29–33.

Sörös, G., Daiber, F., Weller, T., 2013. Cyclo: a personal bike coach through the glass. In: SIGGRAPH Asia, Symposium on Mobile Graphics and Interactive Applications. ACM, Hong Kong, pp. 1–4.

Starbird, K., Palen, L., 2012. (How) will the revolution be retweeted?: information diffusion and the 2011 Egyptian uprising. In: Proceedings of the ACM 2012 Conference on Computer Supported Cooperative Work. ACM, Seattle, WA, pp. 7–16.

Vaish, R., Wyngarden, K., Chen, J., Cheung, B., Bernstein, M.S., 2014. Twitch crowdsourcing: crowd contributions in short bursts of time. In: Proceedings of the SIGCHI Conference on Human Factors in Computing Systems. ACM, Toronto, ON, pp. 3645–3654.

Vaisutis, K., Brereton, M., Robertson, T., Vetere, F., Durick, J., Nansen, B., Buys, L., 2014. Invisible connections: investigating older people's emotions and social relations around objects. In: Proceedings of the 32nd Annual ACM Conference on Human Factors in Computing Systems. ACM, Toronto, ON, pp. 1937–1940.

Varnhagen, C.K., Gushta, M., Daniels, J., Peters, T.C., Parmar, N., Law, D., Hirsch, R., Takach, B.S., Johnson, T., 2005. How informed is online informed consent? Ethics & Behavior 15 (1), 37–48.

Viégas, F.B., Wattenberg, M., Dave, K., 2004. Studying cooperation and conflict between authors with *history flow* visualizations. In: Proceedings of the SIGCHI Conference on Human Factors in Computing Systems. ACM, Vienna, pp. 575–582.

Viégas, F.B., Wattenberg, M., Kriss, J., Ham, F.V., 2007a. Talk before you type: coordination in Wikipedia. In: 40th Annual Hawaii International Conference on System Sciences, 2007, HICSS 2007, pp. 1–10.

Viégas, F.B., Wattenberg, M., McKeon, M.M., 2007b. The hidden order of Wikipedia. In: Schuler, D. (Ed.), Online Communities and Social Computing: Second International Conference, OCSC 2007, Held as Part of HCI International 2007, Beijing, China, July 22–27, 2007. Springer, Berlin, Heidelberg, pp. 445–454.

von Ahn, L., Maurer, B., McMillen, C., Abraham, D., Blum, M., 2008. ReCAPTCHA: human-based character recognition via web security measures. Science 321, 1465–1468.

Weiser, M., 1991. The computer for the 21st century. Scientific american 265 (3), 94–104.

Weld, D.S., 2015. Intelligent control of crowdsourcing. In: Proceedings of the 20th International Conference on Intelligent User Interfaces. ACM, Atlanta, GA, pp. 1–2.

Weppner, J., Hirth, M., Kuhn, J., Lukowicz, P., 2014a. Physics education with Google glass gPhysics experiment app. In: Proceedings of the 2014 ACM International Joint Conference on Pervasive and Ubiquitous Computing: Adjunct Publication. ACM, Seattle, WA, pp. 279–282.

Weppner, J., Poxrucker, A., Lukowicz, P., Ishimaru, S., Kunze, K., Kise, K., 2014b. In: Proceedings of the 2014 ACM International Joint Conference on Pervasive and Ubiquitous Computing: Adjunct Publication. ACM, Seattle, WA, pp. 283–286.

White, R., 2013. Beliefs and biases in web search. In: Proceedings of the 36th International ACM SIGIR Conference on Research and Development in Information Retrieval. ACM, Dublin, pp. 3–12.

White, R.W., Hassan, A., 2014. Content bias in online health search. ACM Transactions on the Web 8 (4), 1–33.

White, R.W., Horvitz, E., 2009. Cyberchondria: studies of the escalation of medical concerns in Web search. ACM Transactions on Information Systems 27 (4), 1–37.

White, R.W., Tatonetti, N.P., Shah, N.H., Altman, R.B., Horvitz, E., 2013. Web-scale pharmacovigilance: listening to signals from the crowd. Journal of the American Medical Informatics Association 20 (3), 404–408.

Winandy, M., Kostkova, P., de Quincey, E., St. Louis, C., Szomszor, M., 2016. Follow #eHealth 2011: measuring the role and effectiveness of online and social media in increasing the outreach of a scientific conference. Journal of Medical Internet Research 18 (7), e191.

Woo, H., Cho, Y., Shim, E., Lee, J.-K., Lee, C.-G., Kim, S.H., 2016. Estimating influenza outbreaks using both search engine query data and social media data in South Korea. Journal of Medical Internet Research 18 (7), e177.

Xiang, R., Neville, J., Rogati, M., 2010. Modeling relationship strength in online social networks. In: Proceedings of the 19th International Conference on World wide Web. ACM, Raleigh, NC, pp. 981–990.

Yang, C., Harkreader, R., Zhang, J., Shin, S., Gu, G., 2012. Analyzing spammers' social networks for fun and profit: a case study of cyber criminal ecosystem on twitter. In: Proceedings of the 21st International Conference on World Wide Web. ACM, Lyon, pp. 71–80.

Zeni, M., Zaihrayeu, I., Giunchiglia, F., 2014. Multi-device activity logging. In: Proceedings of the ACM International Joint Conference on Pervasive and Ubiquitous Computing: Adjunct Publication. ACM, Seattle, WA, pp. 299–302.

Zhang, X., Chen, Z., Fang, C., Liu, Z., 2016. Guiding the crowds for android testing. In: Proceedings of the 38th International Conference on Software Engineering Companion. ACM, Austin, TX, pp. 752–753.

Zhao, R., Wang, J., 2011. Visualizing the research on pervasive and ubiquitous computing. Scientometrics 86 (3), 593–612.

Zhu, S., Kane, S.K., Feng, J., Sears, A., 2012. A crowdsourcing quality control model for tasks distributed in parallel. In: CHI '12 extended abstracts on human factors in computing systems. ACM, Austin, TX, ISBN: 978-1-4503-1016-1, pp. 2501–2506.

Zlatos, B., 2009. Google Purchases Carnegie Mellon University Spin-Off ReCaptcha. Pittsburgh Tribune-Review.

Working with human subjects

15

15.1 INTRODUCTION

Research into human-computer interaction (HCI) almost invariably involves the participation of human subjects. Whether you are running a focus group, leading a collaborative design process, running a controlled study, or conducting an ethnographic investigation, you need to engage people in your work.

Although this may sound simple, it isn't. As anyone who has done so can tell you, working with human subjects involves many challenges. Finding the right subjects is often difficult and time consuming, especially for evaluation of systems designed for specific populations or situations.

The real fun can begin when the subjects are ready to begin participating in your study. Research ethics require that participants must be treated fairly and with respect. This means that they must be provided with information about the nature of the study, which they can use to make a meaningful decision as to whether or not they really want to be involved. This notion of *informed consent* is a critical component of modern research on human subjects.

Although some of the details may differ, the general challenges involved in finding and informing research subjects apply to any form of research involving human participants, regardless of the type of person involved. The additional challenges that online research presents in each of these areas are described in Section 15.3 and in Chapter 16. Although different research communities may have a preference for one or the other, this chapter uses the terms subject and participant interchangeably.

15.2 IDENTIFYING POTENTIAL PARTICIPANTS

You've just built a novel two-handed interface for an architectural modeling tool. Your design allows users to use one device in their dominant hand to draw lines while a second device can be used to pan and zoom, allowing easier and more fluid construction of lines and boundaries. Having implemented a prototype supporting these capabilities, you'd like to run some usability tests to see how well your ideas work in practice. This leaves you with a problem: who should participate in your study? There are plenty of potential users with two hands, but having the physical ability to manipulate your tool is just a start. People without the appropriate training and experience will be unable to tell you if your tool succeeds in its primary goal—supporting the work

Research Methods in Human-Computer Interaction. http://dx.doi.org/10.1016/B978-0-12-805390-4.00015-7

of an architect. Narrowing your pool of potential participants to architects would be your next logical step, but even this limitation may not be fine-grained enough. Are you willing to accept architecture students? This might help if there is a school of architecture nearby, but students may lack real-world experience. This might lead you to insist upon professional architects, who may be hard to find. HCI researchers are familiar with these and related challenges in finding appropriate study participants.

In the early days, in the late 1970s and early 1980s, many of the participants in HCI research were workers in corporate computing environments. This population of relatively early users was professionally motivated to participate in studies aimed at improving the systems that they used. As computer use spread more broadly into society and academic groups became active centers of HCI research, students became available (often just walking down the hall) and easily motivated (via cash or food) pools of participants. Countless studies involving computer science or psychology undergraduates have been published over the years.

So, what's wrong with recruiting undergraduate students—or other easily found subjects—in HCI research? Often, nothing. If you are interested in evaluating interfaces intended for use by undergraduate students, this approach is perfect. However, tests that draw on a homogeneous, nonrepresentative group of participants may be open to criticism: results may not apply to users from a different demographic group. Even if a specific menu arrangement in a word-processing program works well for (predominantly young, male) computer science students, it may not work well for retired women. In a case like this, the mismatch may simply limit the extent to which you can claim that your study answers the problem.

The number of participants is another crucial factor. Different forms of research require different numbers of participants. Studies with too few participants may not yield generalizable results, while studies with too many participants are unnecessarily expensive and time consuming.

15.2.1 WHICH SUBJECTS?

In selecting participants, you should strive to find people with *personal attributes* and *goals* appropriate for your study. By personal attributes, we mean demographic, educational, vocational, and avocational details. Some studies may simply need computer users, while others need participants of a certain gender, age range, education level, professional background, or any combination of these characteristics.

Each individual's goals, background, and motivations may play a role in determining how appropriate they are for your study. Insufficiently interested subjects may be unlikely to contribute constructively, no matter how well they match your other criteria. Even with the right physical attributes, an architect who is strongly opposed to the use of computers for modeling would probably not make a good subject for studying the architectural tool described above. On the other hand, some studies might benefit from the perspective of less-motivated participants, who might be more critical and less forgiving of shortcomings than enthusiasts. The participation of these less-motivated users can be particularly useful when studying tools that may be used by a broad range of users in nonvoluntary circumstances, such as mandatory workplace timesheet reports. Unmotivated users can also be useful for studies aimed at understanding the factors that might influence reluctance to adopt new technology.

Expertise is always an important consideration: study participants should have expertise that is comparable to that of the expected users. We usually define expertise in terms of two largely separable dimensions: computer expertise and domain expertise—knowledge of the problems, systems, goals, and tools used in a specific line of work. If you are testing a tool that is built for highly trained professionals who rarely use complex computer applications, you'll be looking for users who may be computer novices, even though they have significant domain expertise. In other cases, you might be looking for sophisticated computer users who are using a new type of software for an unfamiliar task: computer experts but domain novices. Any differences in expertise between your target population and the participants in your study may lead to results that are hard to interpret.

Interfaces that are intended for use by a broad audience present relatively little difficulty in terms of user characteristics. General-purpose desktop computing tools and interfaces on widely used communications devices are likely to be used by many motivated users, so study participants do not need to meet many specific criteria and can often (but not always) be similar to each other.

The need for appropriate participants becomes more apparent with tools that are designed for specific populations. Children and adults have vastly different cognitive and physical abilities, which directly influence their ability to act as useful study participants. Similarly, cultural differences between users may play a significant role in task performance for communication systems. Whenever possible, studies of tools designed for specific ages, genders, social backgrounds, and physical or cognitive abilities should involve participants who fit the appropriate category. Asking college students to evaluate a tool designed for elderly users would almost certainly be inappropriate. Ethnographic studies (Chapter 9) of specific users and situations are also sensitive to the appropriateness of the participants. If study participants are not the intended users of a system, you can only make limited claims about the utility of the system for the intended population.

Systems designed for domain experts can be particularly challenging in this regard. As the construction of tools for highly specialized tasks requires a detailed understanding of domain-specific work practices, there is a natural tendency to use techniques such as participatory design to involve users in system design. This inclusion may lead to valuable insights, but domain experts who were involved in the design of a tool may have biases in favor of the resulting design, making them inappropriate candidates for subsequent usability tests or other summative evaluations.

Differences between users can also be an important part of study design. Investigations of potential gender differences in organizing certain forms of information would require both male and female participants. Similarly, an experiment exploring the role of user motivation in understanding the effectiveness of a given interface design may need participants who are highly motivated, as well as those who are not at all motivated.

Additional care is necessary when study designs require multiple groups that differ in some dimension. Ideally, the groups would differ in the relevant attribute but be comparable in all others. Any other differences would be possible confounding variables—factors that could be responsible for observed differences. In the study of gender differences in information management, the male and female groups should be comparable in terms of education, age, income, professional experience, and as many other factors as possible. If the women were significantly younger than the men, it might be hard to determine whether any performance differences were due to age or gender: further experimentation may be necessary.

Although these issues may be most important for controlled experiments, the identification of an appropriately general group of participants is always a challenge. Appropriate recruiting methods can help, but there are no guarantees. Despite your best efforts to find a representative population, you always face the possibility that your group of participants is insufficiently representative in a way that was unanticipated. As this bias is always possible, it is best to explicitly state what steps you have taken to account for potentially confounding variables and to be cautious when making claims about your results.

15.2.2 HOW MANY SUBJECTS?

Determining the number of participants to involve in a research study is a trade-off between the information gained in the study and the cost of conducting it. Studies with a very large number of participants—say, tens of thousands—probably involve many people of different ages, educational backgrounds, and computer experience. Any outcome that you see consistently from this population may therefore not be something that can be explained away by the specific characteristics of the individual participants: it is likely to be a "real" effect. Huge studies like this are particularly helpful for controlled experiments in search of statistically significant results. Even subtle differences can be statistically significant if the populations are sufficiently large.

Unfortunately, large studies are difficult and expensive to run, involving substantial costs for recruiting, enrolling, conducting the study, and managing data. If the participants are not at your workplace, there may be travel involved, and many studies pay people for their time. If your study allows you to involve many people at once—perhaps 20 people in a roomful of computers—you may be able to achieve some efficiencies in terms of the time involved. However, research that involves one-on-one interactions between a researcher and a participant may have costs that grow linearly with the number of participants.

At the other extreme, a study with one individual has very real limitations. This study would be relatively inexpensive, but also very limited. Because this study would not have a range of users with different characteristics, any results would run the risk of telling you more about the participant than they did about the research question at hand. If you're conducting an ethnographic study (Chapter 9) with one person, you may learn a great deal about how that person performs certain types of work, but you have no idea about how representative the person's habits are: you may get unlucky and find someone who is completely unlike colleagues in the field. As studies with few participants rarely, if ever, produce statistically significant results, the conclusions that you can draw from these small studies are extremely limited.

Controlled experiments or empirical studies require a sample group of participants large enough to produce statistically significant results. The research design (the number of independent variables, within or between subjects) will play a role as well. Experiments involving larger numbers of independent variables and between-subjects (as opposed to within-subjects) experiments can require more participants (see Chapter 3). Limitations on resources can often lead researchers to substitute the feasible experiment—the design that requires fewer participants—for the experiment they'd prefer to be doing. In some cases, statistical techniques can be used to determine the minimum number of subjects necessary for a result of a given significance (Chapter 3). Usually, you want at least 15–20 participants: smaller studies may miss potentially interesting results.

The inclusion of more participants gives you more statistical power. As each participant comes with costs in terms of time, energy, and money, there are always good arguments in favor of limiting the size of the study. However, larger populations—ranging from several dozen to several hundred participants—offer the possibility of stronger statistical significance or the identification of subtle effects that would not be significant in smaller populations.

Statisticians have developed a range of techniques for determining the number of participants necessary for establishing statistically significant effects with differing degrees of confidence: Cook and Campbell (1979) is a classic text in this area. These techniques can help you understand how many participants you need *before* your study starts, thus minimizing the chances for painful problems further down the line.

By contrast, case studies and ethnographic studies (Chapters 7 and 9) can often be conducted with a small number of users. If your goal is to gather requirements from domain experts, in-depth discussions with two or three motivated individuals may provide a wealth of data. The length of the session also plays a role here: ethnographic observations generally take more time per participant—and therefore place more demands upon the participants—than controlled experiments.

Usability studies can also be successfully conducted with a small set of participants. These studies may use a combination of expert reviewers equipped with guidelines and heuristics, followed by user-based testing, to identify potential usability problems with proposed interface designs (Chapter 10). Although early work in this area was interpreted to mean that studies involving as few as five participants might be sufficient for finding 2/3 of usability problems (Nielsen and Molich, 1990), this claim has been the subject of significant debate, with more recent work suggesting that significantly more participants might be necessary for effective coverage (Hwang and Salvendy, 2010; Schmettow, 2012). User skills and background can play an important role in determining the number of evaluators needed: as evaluators with experience both in usability and in the problem domain can be more effective, fewer numbers of so-called "double experts" may be needed (Nielsen, 1992). Of course, these highly skilled participants can be incredibly hard to find and enroll.

The nature of the participants required for your study often plays a role in this decision. Studies that involve systems for general use by a broad range of users should be able to attract a suitably large pool of participants, even if hundreds of people are needed. On the other hand, research aimed at studying very specific populations may need to rely on substantially smaller pools of participants: there simply aren't tens of thousands of potential participants for the study of a tool for space shuttle astronauts. Studies of domain experts often face challenges in this regard.

Finding a suitably large participant pool can be particularly challenging for research involving people with disabilities (see Chapter 16 for more information). In addition to being an often-overlooked segment of society, people with disabilities often face significant challenges in transportation, making trips to research labs difficult. Studies with these users are often smaller, tending towards observational case studies with two or three users (Steriadis and Constantinou, 2003), rather than controlled experiments, see Chapter 16 for more details.

The time required for each participant is another important factor. Studies that require a single session of limited length (perhaps a few hours) can enroll larger numbers of participants than ethnographic observations that may involve several days or controlled experiments that require multiple sessions conducted over a period of weeks. As the time required from each participant—both in terms of direct involvement and the elapsed interval from start to finish—increases, it becomes more difficult to recruit and retain people who are willing to commit to that level of involvement.

How many participants should your study have? You should start by using your design as a guide. Ethnographies and case studies can be successfully completed with as few as two or three people. Numbers vary wildly for controlled experiments: although studies with as few as 12 users are not uncommon in HCI, results with 20 or more users are more convincing. From that base, you might expand to involve as many subjects as you can reasonably afford to include. You should then add a few more for pilot tests, replacements for participants who drop out, and a margin for error. Investigation of related work in the research literature can help in this regard: basing your population on a population used in similar prior work can be a good strategy. If there is no clearly related work, you might be able to use a smaller population, and perhaps an experimental methodology isn't the most appropriate method to start with (see Chapter 1 for more information).

15.2.3 RECRUITING PARTICIPANTS

Once you have determined *who* your participants are and *how many* you need, you must find them and convince them to participate.

If you work for a large corporation that frequently performs user studies, you may be able to draw upon the expertise of a dedicated group that maintains rosters of people interested in user studies and generates participant pools for research. Those who don't have such resources available (i.e., most of the professionals who conduct HCI studies) generally must do their own legwork.

The characteristics of your desired participants play an important role in determining how you will go about finding them. If you have relatively few constraints, recruiting is relatively simple. Advertisements and flyers on your college, university, or corporate bulletin boards (both physical and electronic) can entice users. However, this must be done carefully: if you wish to get participants with a wide range of ages and education by recruiting on a university campus, you should be careful to explicitly recruit faculty and staff, as well as students. Notices in local newspapers and on community-oriented websites can be useful for recruiting an even broader group of participants.

More specific requirements are likely to require more focused recruiting efforts. Increased specificity in advertisements is a starting point: you might specifically indicate that you are looking for female college students. Community groups, professional organizations, and similar groups can be helpful for finding people with other, more specific characteristics. Many of these groups will be willing to pass along messages to members, particularly if the research may be of interest to them. If you can find a group of people that meet your specific needs, it may help to go to them. If you can give a short presentation at a meeting and make yourself available for questions later, you may encourage otherwise reluctant people to participate. Email lists and online groups can be helpful in this regard as well, but these tools should be used carefully: sending out messages that don't comply with the policies of the posted group or lists is inappropriate. Sending unsolicited email messages directly to individuals is almost certainly a bad idea. Although an email message that comes from a trusted mailing list might be well received, the same message sent directly by an individual might be seen as annoying junk email.

Focused ethnography and long-term case studies require fewer subjects, but the effort involved in enrolling each participant may be greater. These projects may require building cooperative arrangements with companies, schools, other organizations, and individuals in order to identify appropriate subjects. Many academic researchers address these challenges by bringing in outside organizations as collaborators. In addition to creating a formal agreement, collaboration can also provide funds that support the efforts of the cooperating organizations.

Incentives can often motivate people to participate. Many undergraduates have been lured into research sessions by promises of cash or pizza. If you can pay your subjects for their time, do so. Gifts can be more appropriate for some participants—particularly children. If you don't have enough funds to pay all participants, you can offer to enter them in a raffle for a desirable prize. Compensation can also be a motivator that can elicit desired behavior: in one study on interruption, researchers asked participants to both complete a memory task and respond to interrupting signals. In order to entice participants to complete both tasks, extra payment was given to the subjects with the best performance (Gluck et al., 2007). Incentives for organizations that assist in recruiting can also be useful. In addition to the research collaborations described above, you might pay groups as consultants (see the Menu Task Performance Studies with Blind Users sidebar for an example).

Although financial and other incentives are routinely used to encourage participation in research studies, it is certainly appropriate to consider the potential impact that prospects of financial gain might have on participant behavior. Researchers have long known that participants may examine "demand characteristics "—trying to provide responses that they think will please the researcher (Orne, 1962). Although careful researchers will always be on the lookout for opportunities to reduce potential sources of bias, when working with incentives it might be particularly important to stress to participants that they will be rewarded regardless of the answers they give.

MENU TASK PERFORMANCE STUDIES WITH BLIND USERS

Task performance with hierarchical menus has been the subject of many studies over the years, leading to a general consensus that menus with many choices at each of a few levels (broad, shallow trees) lead to faster task completion than menus with a few choices at each of many levels (narrow, deep structures), see Chapter 1. As these studies have generally been conducted with sighted users, who could rely upon a visual scan to quickly identify items in a long list, we were interested if these results would hold for blind users who rely upon the serial presentation of items by screen readers. To address this question, we designed a study based on an early experiment that looked at breadth versus depth in web-based choices from an encyclopedia (Larson and Czerwinski, 1998).

Experimental studies involving blind people can be particularly challenging to run. As blind people often face challenges in transportation, asking users to come to our university offices would be inconvenient. We also knew that we wanted a particular population: experienced users of a particular screen-reader package, who did not have any residual vision.

For this research project, we collaborated with the National Federation of the Blind (NFB), who helped identify potential participants and provided us with access to space in their offices, where we were able to run the study. NFB was paid as a consultant on the project and study participants were compensated as well. Due to the specific nature of the participants, compensation was significantly higher than is customary for similar studies. With NFB's help, we were able to recruit a sufficient number of qualified participants, and we found that, like sighted individuals, our blind participants fared better with broad, shallow menu structures (Hochheiser and Lazar, 2010).

Compensation should be commensurate with the amount of time requested and the type of participants involved. Busy professionals may command a higher fee than students or children. For longer ethnographic or case studies, particularly with domain experts, direct payment for study participation is unlikely to account for the value of their time. In these cases, finding ways to pay experts as consultants may be the best approach. For formative studies aimed at capturing requirements for systems to be used by domain experts, the ability to use the software being developed in their daily work might be a powerful enticement.

Special populations may require creative incentives and accommodations. If you are working with children, you might give them small toys as gifts for participating (cash compensation for accompanying parents is probably always welcome). Elderly people or others without easy access to transportation may be interested in participating but may be unable to make the trip to your lab or office. You might consider trying to conduct your study in participants' homes, community centers, or other locations that would be easy for interested participants to travel to.

Some studies may have additional requirements that require screening of interested participants to determine whether or not they meet important criteria. For example, tools designed for novices should probably not be evaluated by people who work professionally with similar interfaces. Initial questions and interviews with potential subjects can be important tools for ensuring that an individual is appropriate for your study. Specific questions about education, age, experience, and other important attributes can be asked to verify that there is indeed a good match. If you take this approach, you might also consider asking whether they are willing to be contacted in the future for subsequent studies. People who agree to future contact can form the basis for a home-grown database of study participants. Maintaining such a database may involve a fair amount of work, but it can be potentially very useful if you plan to run many studies.

Your database of potential subjects can be an important safety net in the event of difficulties along the way. You may start out with 15 (or 20, 30, or 60) participants with confirmed appointments, only to find that several cancel at the last minute or simply fail to show up. Other problems associated with participant characteristics may force you to dig deeper for a wider range of ages, skills, or backgrounds. If the participants in your study of a general-purpose tool for managing personal photos are all men between 35 and 40 years old (or women over 60), you might have a hard time arguing that your results are indeed generalizable. It's easy to argue that better planning and participant screening might help with this problem, but such details are often not obvious from the beginning. If you're faced with this dilemma, your best option might be to dig deeper into your list, inviting more participants to form a larger (and hopefully more representative) study.

Experiments that involve multiple experimental conditions may require reanomizing participants into roughly equal-sized groups. If you are comparing performance across user attributes—such as age or gender—your groups must differ in the relevant attributes, while remaining as comparable as possible for other characteristics. If your potential pool of participants is large, you need to select participants in a manner that minimizes any potential bias in selection: selecting the first names from a list that is sorted by gender may get you a group of subjects that is entirely male or female. See Chapter 4 for more discussion of these and related issues in population sampling.

15.3 CARE AND HANDLING OF RESEARCH PARTICIPANTS

Studies with human participants put researchers in a privileged position. As "scientific experts", researchers have expertise, experience, and contextual knowledge that make them well equipped to understand the reasons for conducting the experiment and the potential costs and benefits involved in participation in a study. Potential participants may lack some or all of this relevant background.

Research studies should be designed to protect participants. Informed consent—the notion that research participants should be provided with the information needed to make a meaningful decision as to whether or not they will participate—is the cornerstone of this protection. Academic and industrial organizations that conduct research with human subjects generally rely on institutional review boards (IRBs) to review proposed research for any possible risks and to guarantee that appropriate procedures for informed consent are being followed.

15.3.1 RISKS AND CONCERNS OF RESEARCH PARTICIPANTS

Participation in a research study involves multiple agreements between the participant and the researcher. The participant agrees to perform certain tasks as needed by the experiment and the experimenter frequently agrees to provide some incentive or compensation to the participant. Perhaps more importantly, experimenters agree to conduct responsible research that protects participants' rights, health, privacy, and safety.

Risks to participants are often most pronounced in medical research, where investigation of new drugs, devices, and procedures can lead to health risks, particularly when things don't work as intended (or hoped). However, physical harm is not necessarily the only relevant concern. Famous psychology experiments have shown how research that places people in uncomfortable situations can cause significant emotional distress (see the Milgram's Experiment and Stanford Prison Experiment sidebars). Although some HCI experiments might raise these concerns, most of the studies in our field are low risk. Some studies may lead to fatigue (from mouse movements) or eye strain, but these risks are minor. Regardless of the level of risk involved, researchers must treat human participants with dignity and respect.

MILGRAM'S EXPERIMENT

Perhaps the most famous example of deception in psychology research, Stanley Milgram's obedience experiment illustrates one possible extreme associated with research on human subjects.

In this study, subjects were told that they were participating in a study of the effect of punishment on learning. They were asked to administer tests to another subject—a "learner"—who would have to identify a word that had previously been associated with a stimulus word. Subjects were told that they had to administer an electric shock to the learner if incorrect answers were given and that the voltage of the shock should be increased after each incorrect answer. Shocks were described as being "extremely painful," but incapable of causing permanent damage (Milgram, 1963).

This description was an elaborate deception aimed at concealing the true goal of the experiment: a study of the limits of obedience. As the "learner" was in fact a colleague of the experimenter's, no actual shocks were administered. However, the subject did receive a mild shock to provide evidence of the authenticity of the equipment and the learner acted as if shocks had been applied. The experimenter participated actively in the deception, urging subjects to continue with the experiment even when they expressed reluctance.

The results of the study were intriguing: of 40 participants, all continued giving shocks until after the point where the "learner" kicked on the wall and stopped responding to the test questions. Most (26 out of 40) of the participants administered the maximum level of shock—two steps beyond "Danger: Severe Shock." Participation caused discomfort including nervous laughter, embarrassment, and seizures for several subjects.

This experiment would not have worked without deception: had the subjects known that they were not actually administering potentially painful shocks, they presumably would have been even less reluctant to participate. The deception created a scenario in which obedience had a real cost, in terms of the distress associated with inflicting harm on a fellow human being.

Milgram's experiment would not be considered appropriate human subjects research in most current research environments. The extreme nature of the psychological distress involved in these experiments and the strong reactions experienced by some of the participants raise serious questions as to whether such research can ever be conducted responsibly (Milgram, 1963).

Virtual environments provide interesting possibilities for subsequent investigations of similar phenomena without raising the ethical concerns associated with Milgram's experiment as originally executed. In a "virtual reprise" of those experiments, subjects were asked to administer shocks to a female virtual human in an immersive environment. The use of a computer-generated character eliminated the need for deceit, thus removing some of the possible ethical objections. Although participants knew that they were interacting with a computer-generated avatar, they responded to the situation as if they were working with a real person, particularly if they could see the avatar (as opposed to communicating via a text chat interface) (Slater et al., 2006).

THE STANFORD PRISON EXPERIMENT

Many interesting and important questions about human behavior in difficult situations can only be examined by conducting studies that expose participants to the risk of significant psychological distress. As interesting as these questions may be, the risks are substantial enough to make this research effectively off limits.

The Stanford prison experiment, conducted by Philip Zimbardo and his colleagues during the summer of 1971, provides an example of both the risks and insight potentially associated with research that exposes participants to significant emotional distress. In order to examine the social forces associated with prisons, the researchers divided a group of Stanford undergraduates (all males) into "guards" and "prisoners." Prisoners were arrested at their homes, blindfolded, placed in uniforms, and incarcerated in a makeshift prison constructed in the basement of Stanford's psychology building. Guards were not given training—they were simply told to do what was necessary to maintain order.

The researchers and participants were all surprised by their responses. Both guards and prisoners completely fell into their roles. Guards humiliated prisoners, using tactics such as awaking prisoners throughout the night for "counts" and placing people in solitary confinement to establish their authority and prevent rebellion. Prisoners temporarily lost their personal identity, thinking of themselves only by their prisoner number. They were passive, depressed, and helpless. One prisoner suffered significant stress, including crying and rage. Both the guards and the researchers responded like real prison staff, believing that he was faking. Dr. Zimbardo—the professor in charge of the experiment—found himself acting like a prison warden, bristling at concerns for the well-being of the prisoners—who were, after all, innocent bystanders. Originally planned for 2 weeks, the study was terminated after six days, out of concern for the participants (Haney et al., 1973; Zimbardo, 2008b).

The observation that seemingly ordinary people would quickly assume the role of sadistic prison guards raises serious questions about the role of context in determining human behavior. Although we would all like to think that we would not behave abusively in such contexts, the Stanford Prison Experiment raises the concern that environment and expectations can play a huge role in encouraging seemingly inhuman behavior. This lesson continues to have significant relevance, through explorations including Kyle Alvarez' 2015 film *The Stanford Prison Experiment* and Philip Zimbardo's outspoken commentary on the behavior of guards at the Abu Ghraib prison in Iraq (Zimbardo, 2008a,b).

The Stanford prison experiment also provides a cautionary tale regarding the evolution of research ethics. Despite the known potential for harm, this study was approved by Stanford's Human Subjects Review Board, participants signed an informed consent form, and a 1973 review from the American Psychological Association determined that the study had been consistent with existing ethical guidelines (Zimbardo, 2008b). Changing views on responsible research—influenced at least in part by this—have led to a much more conservative view of appropriate research. Philip Zimbardo publicly apologized for his role in the study (Zimbardo, 2008b) and the establishment of beneficence—maximizing of benefits while minimizing harm (The National Commission for the Protection of Human Subjects of Biomedical and Behavioral Research, 1979)—argued for research that would strive to avoid the harms seen in the prison experiment. It is hard to imagine a study with this degree of potential harm being approved by any modern IRB.

Specific definitions of the responsibilities of researchers grew out of concerns about inappropriate medical procedures conducted during the mid-20th century (see the Informed Consent: Origins and Controversies sidebar). In 1979, the National Commission for the Protection of Human Subjects of Biomedical and Behavioral Research published the Belmont Report (The National Commission for the Protection of Human Subjects of Biomedical and Behavioral Research, 1979). This document established three principles for the treatment of research participants: respect for persons, beneficence, and justice. Respect for persons involves allowing individuals to make independent and autonomous decisions regarding their participation in research. Researchers must allow participants to make judgments and must provide the information necessary for making those judgments. Special consideration must be given in cases of illness or disability that may limit an individual's ability to make independent decisions. Beneficence refers to the need to minimize possible harm while maximizing possible benefits. Justice requires that neither the burdens of participating in research nor the benefits of the research should be limited to certain populations, particularly when some groups of people may be easily manipulated (The National Commission for the Protection of Human Subjects of Biomedical and Behavioral Research, 1979). These principles form the basis for informed consent.

INFORMED CONSENT: ORIGINS AND CONTROVERSIES

Famous (or infamous) medical research experiments conducted during the mid-20th century led to the development of modern concepts of informed consent and appropriate treatment of research participants. Nazi Germany's use of concentration camp prisoners in often brutal and barbaric medical experiments led to the Nuremberg code, which established some of the principles behind informed consent.

(Continued)

INFORMED CONSENT: ORIGINS AND CONTROVERSIES—CONT'D

The US Public Health Service Syphilis Study at Tuskegee involved hundreds of black men with syphilis over 40 years. Although they were told that they were being treated, no treatment was in fact given, and efforts were actively made to prevent participants from getting treatment (Centers for Disease Control and Prevention, 2007). Several other studies in the US involving administration of drugs or treatment without consent were conducted in the US after the end of World War II (Pellegrino, 1997). More recently, drug trials conducted by Western companies in countries such as India have raised concerns about the nature of informed consent across such cultural and financial divides (Sharma, 2005).

The costs associated with these studies are not limited to the substantial harm inflicted upon the subjects. These unethical experiments reflect poorly on science and scientists in general, harming public trust and increasing reluctance to participate. One study of both white and black residents of Detroit found that black residents were more likely to have heard of the Tuskegee experiments. They were also more likely to be distrustful of researchers and less likely to participate in research (Jones, 1993; Shavers et al., 2000).

15.3.2 PROTECTING PRIVACY

Participants should also be assured that their privacy will be protected. Researchers should obtain consent for the collection and storage of personal information; limit the information collected to that which is necessary; identify the uses that will be made of any information; limit the use, disclosure, and retention of the information; securely protect any information; disclose policies and procedures; provide a means for addressing concerns regarding compliance with information practices; and be accountable for those practices. Patrick provides a set of more than 30 questions suitable for addressing adequacy of practices in each of these areas (Patrick, 2007b).

The use of photography and video or audio recording presents special challenges regarding the privacy of participants. Photos, videos, and audio recordings can be very useful tools for illustrating the use of an interface, but they can also unambiguously identify individuals as having participated in a research project. There are several steps that you should take in any project before you start the shutters snapping or cameras rolling. You should clearly tell participants what you are recording and why. If you are going to consider using images of participants in any publications or reports, participants should be fully informed of this possibility. These practices should be mentioned in your informed consent forms (Section 15.3.4) and discussed with participants. If you are video recording, you might consider recording a portion of the discussion, taking care to include footage of the participants explicitly agreeing to be video recorded. You should plan your photos or videos carefully: if you are really interested in what is going on with the interface, take pictures and video of the inputs and display—not the faces of the participants. You might be able to shoot over the users' shoulders to get a fuller view without identifying your participants. Similarly, audio recordings captured for potential distribution should minimize use of the participant's voices—record the voices of the research staff if necessary.

Although data minimization may limit risks to participant privacy, the associated loss of detail may not be acceptable in some circumstances. Studies of the clinical use of electronic medical records have used audio, video, screen capture, and related techniques to collect rich records of the technical and interpersonal aspects of the use of these tools in practice (Asan and Montague, 2013; Weibel et al., 2015). Given the particularly sensitive nature of medical data, such records should be made carefully, protected through encryption and appropriate security, and only used by authorized research staff members.

More generally, data storage and backup choices should also consider participant privacy. Research data storage should preserve both privacy and availability of data, particularly given increased mandates for data sharing. Storage on local hard drives or on digital media stored in locked file cabinets can often be best for protecting privacy, with somewhat reduced availability. Although cloud-based services may offer easier data sharing, privacy protections may be weaker. However, cloud providers are increasingly offering services with higher levels of security and access control. If you have any concerns, check with your IRB or research office.

Appropriate choices in dissemination—particularly in publishing—can also help protect participant's privacy. If you must show people in action, you might consider using image-manipulation techniques, such as blurring or black bars over the eyes to hide the identity of the participants. Pictures or videos of the research staff might be more appropriate for distribution. Finally, you might provide an alternative for participants who are concerned about their privacy: you might not need video or audio recordings of every individual in your study. Case studies and interviews with participants might take care to ensure that descriptions, quotes, and other details are presented in a manner that removes all materials that might jeopardize participants' well-being, health, and livelihood.

15.3.3 INSTITUTIONAL REVIEW BOARDS

Universities, hospitals, corporations, and other organizations that conduct research often have standing committees that review and approve projects involving human subjects. These IRBs examine proposed studies for appropriate practices, procedures, goals, and disclosures. By conducting this review prior to the start of research with human subjects, IRBs protect all of the groups and individuals that may be affected by the research. Participants are protected by examination of proposed research for any elements that may be manipulative, coercive, or otherwise abusive. Proposals that contain any such elements should not be approved by IRBs. Researchers and institutions benefit from the knowledge that the proposed research has been reviewed for issues that may cause embarrassment or legal liability. Although this review is certainly not foolproof, it generally works well in practice.

IRB review and approval for proposed research generally begins when a researcher submits materials relating to proposed research. A description of the proposed research, draft informed consent forms, instructions to be provided to users, questionnaires, and materials to be used during the course of the research are some of the items that might be required. Upon receipt of these materials, the IRB will review them for completeness and content. The board may approve the research, request additional information, require revision of materials, or take other steps as appropriate.

As research cannot begin until the IRB approval is complete, it is generally best to start this process early. Some research funding agencies will not release any funds until appropriate IRB approvals have been obtained. As each IRB has its own rules, it is important that researchers understand and follow the appropriate procedures for their institution. Many IRBs have websites that describe policies and provide relevant forms. It is a good idea to familiarize yourself with this material. Although some boards consider applications on a rolling basis, others have scheduled meetings, with published submission deadlines for consideration at each meeting. Attention to detail is particularly important for boards that meet on a set schedule: if your IRB meets bi-monthly, minor omissions in a proposed package may lead to a 2-month delay in acquiring the necessary approval.

Some IRBs—particularly those at large research institutions with affiliated medical schools—may spend much of their time focusing on drug or treatment studies. If your IRB falls into this category, board members may not be aware of the techniques used in HCI research (and described in this book). You may have to spend some time and effort explaining ethnography, research based on online data sources, or other techniques that they are not familiar with. If you run into this sort of challenge, you should stress the widespread application of these techniques, and the existing body of research from groups such as the Association of Internet Researchers (http://www.aoir.org) or the Ethnographic Praxis in Industry Conference (EPIC, https://www.epicpeople.org/). It's best to approach such discussions from a collegial, not confrontational, perspective.

IRB policies for US government and government-funded institutions (including almost all universities and colleges in the United States) are dictated by the Federal Policy for Protection of Human Research Subjects, otherwise known as the *Common Rule* (45 CFR, part 46) (Department of Health and Human Services, 2009). The Common Rule describes requirements for institutional review, including categories of studies that can be given expedited review or exempt from review altogether. Studies that both involve "minimal risk," and fall into one of nine specified categories can be candidates for expedited review. Although most of these categories are specific to biomedical research, categories involving collection of data from recordings made for research purposes and research involving group characteristics or behavior are directly of interest to HCI studies. Similarly, studies involving educational strategies; test surveys, interviews, or observations of public behavior; and studies of existing data or research data can be considered exempt from full IRB review (Department of Health and Human Services, 2009). Generally, institutions will have specific sets of forms for studies that require full IRB review, expedited review, or exemptions, with expedited review often quicker than full review. Studies that qualify as exempt must still be reviewed by IRB staff, who will then provide documentation indicating that the study is, in fact, exempt.

Although the paperwork required by some IRBs may feel like a nuisance, you should consider your IRB as an ally. By insisting upon procedures, IRBs protect researchers and institutions from problems associated with research that goes wrong. IRBs can also provide helpful feedback in situations that may raise questions. Some projects may blur the lines between participating in the research and acting as a collaborative partner. For example, projects involving participatory design may involve ethnographic observation of users in the workplace. Is informed consent necessary in this case? Although the conservative approach of requiring informed consent is unlikely to be inappropriate, discussing this question with a member of your IRB might provide insight into your institution's policies regarding such research. Many IRBs require researchers to take training courses before conducting any studies involving human subjects research. These courses may not seem exciting, but they can provide valuable information that might prove helpful when you are preparing informed consent materials.

Organizations that infrequently engage in human subjects research may not have an established IRB. This may be particularly true for small companies that run occasional user studies. If you find yourself in such a situation, it may be helpful to discuss matters with appropriate professionals in your organization, including community relations staff and legal counsel. IRBs from nearby research institutions may be willing to provide feedback as well. The use of informed consent forms and proper procedures is always appropriate, even in the absence of a formal review from an IRB.

Researchers and regulators share a common interest in optimizing IRB review requirements and procedures. In the US, a 2011 Advanced Notice of Proposed Rule-Making (ANPRM) suggested significant changes to IRB procedures, including the creation of an "IRB of record" provision that would allow one review for all participants in a multi-institution study, as opposed to separate review for all institutions, as is the current process. Other changes proposed in this ANPRM include changes to methods for determining risk, new categories of studies designed to minimize review requirements for low-risk studies, and revised rules for determining when informed consent is not required, among others (Cohen and Lynch, 2014). Further discussion of these issues included a "request for information" regarding the use of single IRB review for multi-institution studies funded by the National Institutes of Health (National Institutes of Health, 2014). A Sep. 2015 notice in the US Federal Register revived the federal review proposals with a Notice of Proposed Rule-Making (NPRM) in response to the 2011 ANPRM. The proposed rules retain many of the changes that might facilitate HCI research, including the single IRB proposal and the possibility of defining "certain types of social and behavioral research conducted with competent adults" as exempt from IRB review (Federal Register, 2015). There is widespread agreement that some reform of these rules is needed. However, the complexity of the regulations and the 4-year gap between the ANPRM and the NPRM suggest that acceptance of these proposals and implementation of any changes may be a gradual process (Schrag, 2015; Cohen and Lynch, 2014). A Jun. 2016 report issued by the US National Academies, raised multiple concerns about the proposed rule-making, suggesting that it be withdrawn and that a national commission on human subjects research be established (National Academies of Sciences, 2016).

15.3.4 INFORMED CONSENT

The notion of informed consent has two parts. "Informed" means that study participants must understand the reason for conducting the study, the procedures that are involved, potential risks, and how they can get more information about the study. Without this information, participants do not have the information necessary to make a truly meaningful decision as to whether or not they wish to participate. If potential participants are not told that the use of a specific virtual-reality environment can occasionally cause nausea, particularly sensitive individuals may agree to participate without being aware that they might be subjecting themselves to an unpleasant experience. For these reasons, researchers should strive to clearly provide information that is relevant and necessary for appropriate decision-making. Truly informing potential participants means that the information must be provided in a manner that is comprehensible. The reason for the study, the procedures being used, and other details should be provided in a manner that is clear, accessible, and free from professional jargon.

The second, equally important notion is "consent": participation in research studies should be entirely voluntary and free from any implied or implicit coercion. Potential participants should not be given any reason to believe that a decision not to participate will lead to repercussions or retaliation, whether in the form of punishment by employers; withholding of medication or the use of a system; or disapproval from the researcher. Researchers in academic settings should be very careful about giving students credit for coursework in exchange for their participation in studies: if an alternative means of earning the credit are not provided, some students may feel that their grades will suffer if they decline to participate. In such circumstances, participation would be coerced, not consensual.

In most cases, researchers provide participants with an informed consent document that contains several sections (Office for Human Research Protections, 1998):

- *Institution and Researcher Identification:* Who is responsible for the research? Specifically, which individuals and institutions are conducting the study?
- *Contact Information:* Who should participants contact if they have questions or concerns? This section should contain names and contact information for the researchers in charge of the study, as well as for representatives of the IRB or other appropriate body.
- *Title and Purpose*: Why is the study being done?
- *Description of Procedures:* What will be asked of participants? For HCI studies, this probably involves using one or more interface variants, discussing goals and needs, commenting on design proposals, and other related tasks.

- *Duration:* How long will each participant be involved in the study? This should tell the user how much time will be involved. If there are multiple sessions, the number of sessions, the length of each session, and the elapsed interval required should all be specified.
- *Risks:* What risks might be involved in participation? Medical trials may involve the risks of unknown drug side-effects, but the risks are generally less severe in HCI studies. Fatigue, boredom, and perhaps slight discomfort due to repetitive motion are possible risks for studies involving desktop computers. Virtual-reality systems may involve some risk of nausea or disorientation. Studies involving mobile devices, computers in cars, or other interfaces in nontraditional settings may involve additional health or safety risks. Evaluation of the potential distractions caused by computing devices in cars should probably not be conducted in cars driving on public roads! Other interfaces involving social interactions may pose emotional risks, if tasks or content may prove upsetting to participants (see Milgram's Experiment sidebar). The privacy risks of photography and video or audio recording are discussed above; projects involving online conferencing or ongoing use of online chat systems may present similar concerns. Experimenters should, of course, design studies to minimize all risks. Any remaining risks should be described in detail in informed consent forms and then discussed honestly and thoroughly with study participants.
- *Benefits:* What are the benefits of participation? Some researchers may provide participants with ongoing access to software that is being evaluated. In other cases, financial or material compensation is the main benefit.
- *Alternatives to Participation:* What other options are available? For most HCI studies common alternatives include simply not participating, opting out of the study at any point in time, and continuing to use the software that was being used before the study.
- *Confidentiality:* Participants' privacy should be respected. This section of the form generally includes comments indicating that personally identifying information will not be used or published in any way. Confidentiality is a particularly important issue for HCI research involving observation of user behavior such as search or information use activity. Web search, email organization, and other activities may reveal sensitive personal information that could compromise confidentiality. Proper protection of participant privacy involves limiting the use, disclosure, and retention of data; taking appropriate measures to protect data, including encryption and secure storage; openly describing policies and practices; providing avenues for challenging compliance with data protection procedures; and providing for training and related measures to ensure accountability (Patrick, 2007b).
- *Costs/Additional Expenses:* Are there any financial expenses or other costs associated with participation? Although such costs may not be inappropriate, they may discourage some users from participating. If you are going to ask participants to make costly trips to travel to your location, to purchase software

for their computer, or to spend significant amounts of time entering data into diaries, you need to make sure that they are aware of these costs.

- *Participant's Rights:* This section should make three important points:
  - Participation is voluntary.
  - Participants can choose to stop participating at any time, without penalty. The informed consent form should describe what will be done with data for participants who withdraw.
  - Participants have the right to be informed of any new information that will affect their participation in the study.
- *Supplemental Information:* Where should participants go for further information? This section should list resources that can be used for additional information, including (but not limited to) descriptions of the research program and institutional policies and procedures for research involving human subjects.
- *Signature:* Participants should sign a copy of the consent form. The signature should be accompanied by a statement indicating that the participant:
  - has volunteered to participate;
  - has been informed about the tasks and procedures;
  - has had a chance to ask questions and had questions answered;
  - is aware that he/she can withdraw at any time;
  - consented prior to participation in the study (Shneiderman et al., 2016).

The researcher should provide a copy of the consent form to each participant for reference, while retaining the signed copies as documentation of the consent.

Construction of an informed consent document can be a useful step in ensuring that your research meets accepted ethical standards. If you have accounted for the risks, benefits, alternatives, and confidentiality measures associated with your project, the relevant sections of the document should be relatively straightforward to be put together. Similarly, difficulty in construction of these sections may indicate the need to rethink proposed practices in procedures.

Writing clear, concise informed documents is not trivial. One study of informed consent forms for medical research studies found that users preferred simpler statements written at a seventh-grade level (as opposed to at a college graduate level) but the simpler statements did not lead to greater comprehension (Davis et al., 1998). Pilot testing of the consent forms, either as part of a pilot test for an experiment or via reviews by potential participants or collaborators can help identify confusing language or areas that may need clarification. A sample informed consent form is given in Figure 15.1.

Informed consent requires affirmative agreement from an individual who is capable of understanding the implications of agreeing to participation in the research. Research involving participants who are not able to interpret informed consent forms may require additional measures. Requirements and procedures regarding assent for children's participation in research are described in Section 15.3.6.3, while issues relating to participants with disabilities are discussed in Chapter 16.

Local or national legislation may place additional constraints on the content of an informed consent document. In the United States, federal regulations prohibit

INFORMED CONSENT FORM

Evaluating Menu Selection Task Performance

PRINCIPAL INVESTIGATOR: A. Researcher

Department of Computer and Information Sciences

Research University Phone: 555-555-5555

Email: researcher@research.edu

Purpose of the Study: The goal of this study is to understand how computer interfaces might be customized to best suit the needs of users. Participants will be asked to use a menu interface to find items in various multilevel hierarchy designs. Task completion times and subjective responses will be used to determine which (if any) design is most suitable for these users.

Procedures: Participation in this study will involve two phases. In the first phase, you will be asked to use a web browser to make selections from a menu of choices, in order to locate a specified entry. You will be given the opportunity to try a sample task, and then you will be asked to complete multiple tasks with different menu structures. This study should take about one hour to complete.

After you have completed the experimental tasks, we may ask you some questions about the various interfaces. These questions will be designed to help us understand which (if any) of the interfaces you preferred, and why. We may also ask some general questions about your habits and practices with respect to computer use.

Risks/Discomfort: You may become fatigued during the course of your participation in the study. You will be given several opportunities to rest, and additional breaks are also possible. There are no other risks associated with participation in the study. Should completion of either the task or the interview become distressing to you, it will be terminated immediately.

Benefits: It is hoped that the results of this study will be useful for the development of guidelines for the design of user interfaces that will help people use computers more effectively.

Alternatives to Participation: Participation in this study is voluntary. You are free to withdraw or discontinue participation at any time.

Cost and Compensation: Participation in this study will involve no cost to you. You will be paid for your participation.

FIGURE 15.1

Informed consent form.

language in informed consent forms that would waive legal rights or absolve researchers of legal responsibility. The use of informed consent forms—even those that are approved by IRBs (see Section 15.3.3) should not be seen as a green light to move forward with research that may otherwise raise questions regarding respect for the rights and concerns of participants.

Evolution of the research landscape often spurs innovation in informed consent practices. Complexity is often a challenge for studies that may involve some risk to participant privacy, as long consent forms laden with technical information may be difficult to understand. Concerns about the complexity of detailed consent form for research projects involving genetic studies of biological samples have led to the development of simplified consent forms (Beskow et al., 2010) and studies of comprehensible phrasing for relevant content (Beskow et al., 2015). HCI researchers tackling deceptive studies have struggled with similar challenges (see Section 15.3.6.1). The growth of ubiquitous computing research, with many studies of contextualized computer and device use or interaction in use in homes, schools, and other public places has led some to suggest that consent should be more nuanced and contextualized than a simple blanket agreement to the terms of a research study (Luger and Rodden, 2013a,b).

15.3.5 RESPECTING PARTICIPANTS

The Belmont report describes respect for persons in terms of ensuring that participants are able to make independent and informed decisions about their involvement in research studies. Although this is perhaps most directly applied through the informed consent process described above, truly respecting participants requires consideration of their needs, concerns, and values throughout all aspects of designing the study, conducting the research, and publishing the results.

15.3.5.1 Study design

The experiments conducted by Milgram and Zimbardo arguably arose at least in part because their interest in their research question overshadowed concerns that they may have had about the impact that the research would have on the participants. Although these studies would clearly be considered unethical by current standards, controversies regarding the impact of research on participants still rage. Examination of these debates can shed some light on the challenges raised by some HCI research projects.

A newsworthy study published in July 2014 by researchers from Cornell University and Facebook (Kramer et al., 2014) provides a textbook example of how these concerns might arise in modern HCI research. In order to understand the impact of "emotional contagion", these researchers worked with Facebook to manipulate the presentation of items on users' news feeds. Over the course of 1 week in Jan. 2012, researchers adjusted news feeds, decreasing either the amount of positive or negative emotional content, as determined by the inclusion of words previously shown to be correlated with measures of well-being. Examining news feeds for a large (almost 700,000) group of Facebook users, they found that reductions in positive posts appearing on a users' feed were associated with reductions in positive content in that individuals postings, with comparable effects for reductions in negative content (Kramer et al., 2014).

The Facebook paper raised a firestorm of research ethics controversy immediately upon completion. An "Editorial Expression of Concern" (Verma, 2014) published alongside the paper noted the major concern: the research was conducted without explicit informed consent from participants. The study was consistent with Facebook's data use policies, which describe creation of an account as implicit agreement to participate in research. Furthermore, Cornell University's IRB determined that the study was not under their jurisdiction, as it was conducted by Facebook. As a result, participants were not informed of their participation, which the editor considered to be "not fully consistent with informed consent" (Verma, 2014). Reports of user concern quickly spread throughout the new media (Goel, 2014), as users complained that they may have been manipulated without their knowledge or consent. Subsequent soul-searching in the academic literature (Fiske and Hauser, 2014; Puschmann and Bozdag, 2014; Ross, 2014) examined the implications for evolving research ethics in the age of social media.

Many issues raised by the Facebook study are thorny questions that are not easily resolved. Should Facebook have informed users and obtained consent? Would that have biased results, as users might have been more sensitized to positive or negative content in posts? Would a design involving consent with some amount of deception (see 15.3.6.1) have been more appropriate?

The participation of Facebook as a corporate sponsor of research complicates matters further. As acknowledged in the paper, and in the Editor's expression of concern, Facebook is a private company and therefore not subject to the requirements of the Common Rule (Verma, 2014). This raises the interesting question of corporate ethics and conflicts of interest—specifically, what are the obligations of corporations that conduct human subjects research that are not subject to external regulation? How, if at all, did the Facebook study differ from the widely used techniques of showing different web site designs to different sets of users to determine which is preferred (so-called "A/B testing"? (Merritt et al., 2010)).

Discussions of corporate research behavior are likely to continue and evolve for the foreseeable future. Not long after the publication of the Facebook paper, online dating site OkCupid published a blog post describing the many ways that they have experimented with manipulations of content, in the hopes of understanding how participants respond to postings describing potential dates (Rudder, 2014). In contrast with Facebook's effort, these experiments did not involve academic researchers as partners, and were not published in a scientific journal. Do these differences change our perceptions of the ethical implications of the work, or our interpretations of the results?

These questions do not have simple answers, but they do illustrate concerns that most researchers would be well advised to consider carefully. Corporations such as Facebook and OkCupid may be able to weather the publicity associated with these potentially controversial research studies, but many academic researchers—specifically, those working with public funds in public in university settings—might want to think twice before conducting studies that might lead participants to feel as if they had not been treated appropriately.

Perhaps an application of the golden rule to study design might be appropriate. Before conducting a study, you might ask how you might feel if asked to participate, or, as in the Facebook study, you later found that your actions might have been part of the study without your knowledge. If you decide that you might not be comfortable, others might have the same reaction, and you might consider revising your study design.

15.3.5.2 Practical issues

Participants are crucial to our studies—without them, HCI research would be all but impossible. We should make every effort to treat participants in a manner that reflects this importance. Compensation for time and effort is certainly helpful, but researchers should also take concrete steps to make participation convenient and enjoyable. Comfortable surroundings may put participants at ease. Ample opportunities for rest or bathroom breaks should be provided, particularly for studies that involve longer research sessions. Flexibility in scheduling and location can be particularly important for some users: enrolling professionals in your study may require that you travel to their workplace or allow for sessions outside of traditional working hours. If your study is fun and convenient, participants may be more likely to help your recruiting efforts by urging friends and colleagues to join in.

When working with human participants in any form of HCI research, you must pay careful attention to your role as a researcher. Participants may be impressed or intimidated by your presence, your use of language, your technical skills, the context of the experiment, or any of a variety of related factors. This is particularly true for observations and contextual inquiry, where you will spend a great deal of time in close contact with one or more participants. Although you should make every reasonable effort to help participants feel as at ease as possible, you should also be aware that your presence may have an impact on observed performance. In some cases, participants may exhibit the "demand characteristics" described above, trying to behave in the manner that they think you are looking for.

Others have claimed that the mere act of participating in an experiment will influence user behavior, in the so-called "Hawthorne effect" (Macefield, 2007). Although this effect has been the subject of significant debate among scientists (McCambridge et al., 2014; Levitt and List, 2011), some suggested responses are appropriate. Researchers should never give feedback regarding user performance during the course of a study and experiments involving the comparison of multiple interfaces should be controlled and "blind"—participants should not know if one of the alternatives is favored by the researchers (Macefield, 2007).

More generally, these concerns about the influence of researchers on experimental results point towards a need to be modest about the results of our research. All experiments have flaws and no single study establishes incontrovertible facts on its own. When reporting results and drawing conclusions, we should avoid overstatement, admit the flaws in our research, and point the way for future work that will bring greater understanding.

15.3.6 ADDITIONAL CONCERNS

15.3.6.1 Potentially deceptive research

Does respect for persons always require complete disclosure regarding research goals and design? Although it might seem as if withholding key details from research participants might be somewhat less than fully honest, complete transparency might not be appropriate in some cases, particularly if knowledge of the goals of the study might influence participant behavior. When this happens, researchers might resort to a bit of misdirection. Deceptive studies ask participants to perform tasks that are described as relating to a particular goal, when the researcher is actually interested in addressing a different question unrelated to the goal presented to the user. Although concealing the true nature of the study does present some concerns regarding the validity of informed consent, this practice is often necessary, particularly in situations where full disclosure might compromise the realism of the study.

A study involving security and usability provides an example of the use of deception in HCI research (Schechter et al., 2007). This study had two goals: to determine the influence of security feedback and to see if participants using their own data would behave more or less securely than those who were role-playing using someone else's data. As the researchers were concerned that study participants would not behave naturally if they were told that usability was being studied, they were told that the purpose of the study was to "help make online banking better" (Schechter et al., 2007). Participants were asked to perform online banking tasks. Some participants were "role-playing"—they were asked to pretend that they were a specific individual with specific goals in mind; others used their own bank accounts. In addition to finding that security indicators were not particularly helpful, this study found that people using their own bank accounts behaved more securely than those who were role-playing (Schechter et al., 2007).

Schechter et al. (2007) used deceit as a means of setting up conditions that maximized the realism of the experiment. By presenting users with real online banking tasks, they focused the experiment on how actual users might behave when using online banking on their own. If participants had been told that the experiment was examining their behavior regarding security and privacy, they might have paid extra attention to their behavior in these areas. This use of deception may be useful and valid, but it does have its limits. These limits arise from the established psychological concept of demand characteristics (Orne, 1962), which states that participants in a research study may act in a manner that attempts to validate the hypotheses being tested. In this study, participants may have taken the goal of improving online banking to heart, perhaps acting more insecurely than they otherwise might have (Patrick, 2007a).

A notable phishing study provides another example of the complexities of conducting research without full prior disclosure of goals and participant consent. Researchers at Indiana University harvested email addresses from publicly available sources and then conducted a phishing attack that encouraged students to log in to a university server that would verify (but not store) their authentication credentials. Arguing that no real harm would come to participants, and that disclosure and consent would sensitize participants to the goals of the project, and therefore invalidate results, the developers of this study worked closely with the appropriate IRB to carefully design a study protocol that would not require explicit consent. This process required extensive review of relevant regulations and legislation, leading to a novel study design that allowed the research to proceed without compromising on ethical concerns or participant privacy or security (Finn and Jakobsson, 2007a,b; Jagatic et al., 2007; Jakobsson et al., 2008).

Deception in HCI research should be used carefully and sparingly. As deception pushes the limits of the concept of informed consent, researchers should be careful to frame deceptions clearly, justify their use, and minimize any risks—particularly regarding discomfort and distress—that may be involved (see the Milgram's Experiment sidebar for a famous example of deceptive research). Participants in studies involving deception are usually thoroughly debriefed at the end of their participation. Debriefing has been shown to help deceived participants eliminate negative effects and even to have experiences that were more positive than those of participants who have not been deceived (Smith and Richardson, 1983).

15.3.6.2 Longitudinal studies

Many HCI studies necessarily involve designs that ask more of participants than a single visit to a usability lab for a relatively short (generally less than 2 hours) session. Ethnography, observations, case studies, and other in-depth qualitative studies often require repeated interactions with individual participants over weeks or months. Learnability studies might require multiple lab sessions in order to measure retention, while studies of technology in use might involve data collection over an extended time period, potentially including regular interactions with researchers (Azar, 2000; Harrison et al., 2014; Srinivasan et al., 2014). Long-term "field studies" of technologies such as mobile devices are particularly useful for developing understanding of emerging usage patterns that might be overlooked in a brief lab session (Kjeldskov and Skov, 2014).

As important as these studies may be, these longitudinal or "multiwave" studies are also challenging and time consuming. Recruiting, scheduling, and enrolling participants is often hard enough for relatively simple usability studies. When this challenge is extended to include the need for multiple visits or reports and potentially consistent use of a device, over a long period of time, the challenge is even more difficult. Researchers undertaking this challenge should expect a range of difficulties not seen in simpler studies: participants will either actively drop out or passively decline to respond to contacts, mobile devices will break or be lost (Harrison et al., 2014), research team members (particularly students) will move on, etc.

Longitudinal studies should be designed to account for the likelihood of these and other complications. Protocols and requirements for scheduled interactions with participants should be structured to decrease dropouts and nonresponses. Automatic or low-effort data collection through instrumented software (see Chapter 12) or online surveys can take the place of in-person or real-time telephone conversations whenever possible. Any measures that reduce demands placed on participants have the potential to increase your retention rates.

Appropriate incentives might encourage users to stick with a study—for example, users might be allowed to keep the mobile device under study if they complete all phases, or compensation might be "back-loaded", providing the bulk of the financial benefit at the end of the study. Conservative designs will also plan for attrition in both participants and equipment. Enrolling extra participants and purchasing spare devices will increase the likelihood of successfully completing the study, even in the face of attrition and device failure.

Although longitudinal studies may provide insight that is otherwise unavailable (Kjeldskov and Skov, 2014), the costs can be significant. Researchers considering such complex endeavors might ask themselves whether a subset of their goals might be met by simpler lab studies (Kjeldskov et al., 2004), leaving more complex designs for those challenges that simply cannot be addressed in any other way.

15.3.6.3 Working with children

Over the past 20 years, HCI research focusing on children has grown substantially, with regular conferences such as Interaction Design and Children showcasing the work of many research groups, and an exploding number of apps and products engaging children in both recreational and educational activities. As all parents know, working with children can be deeply rewarding and intensely frustrating (often at the same time!). Careful consideration of the differences between child and adult participants will help increase the reward while minimizing the difficulties.

Perhaps most important is the need to ensure that children understand what it means to participate in a research study in general, and in your studies in particular. Although this understanding is, of course, vital for all research participants, it is of particular concern for children who may not be able to understand many of the abstract concepts surrounding research, risk, and consent. When children participate in research studies, parents or legal guardians are generally asked to consent to the participation. When possible, children may also be asked to "assent"—to agree to participate—even if they are not capable of giving informed consent (Society for Research in Child Development, 1991; United States Department of Health and Human Services, 1993). This assent is generally in addition to—not instead of—parental consent.

Similar questions relate to the conduct of the study itself. For studies involving younger children, inviting parents to be in the room while the study is ongoing might be the best way to inspire confidence in the safety and security of the proceedings. When extending such an invitation, you might find that appropriate instruction to the parents is necessary to avoid interference that might bias results. For example, you might suggest that parents not interfere unless the child is clearly upset or distressed. The tables may turn completely in studies involving older children, who might prefer that parents not be present. In these cases, you should be prepared to respectfully discuss potential biases that might be associated with parental observations.

Other seemingly small details might become important when dealing with children in research studies. As children are often very (some parents might say excessively) concerned that their viewpoints are considered and their participation is valued, you might take extra effort to let them know that they are a vital part of a complex process, and that their participation is needed. These concerns are particularly challenging for studies involving children in design activities (Read et al., 2014). As many children are reward-driven, age-appropriate incentives (books are great) can be a great motivator for sitting still and completing tasks. Of course, given limited attention spans, experimental sessions should be designed with the age of the child in mind: 3-hour sessions for 4-year-olds might be doomed from the start.

Given the concern over the safety and security of children, these differences in consent and study design may lead to greater scrutiny of proposed studies by IRBs. Discussing your projects with your local IRB and modeling your materials on previous studies where possible might help ensure appropriate safeguards for underage participants and facilitate the approval process.

An understanding of childhood cognitive development can be invaluable for building a early understanding of what children of various ages can be expected to know and how they might view the world. Juan-Pablo Hourcade's book on Child-Computer Interaction (Hourcade, 2015) provides an invaluable overview. When possible, you might also consider including a child development expert on your research team.

15.3.6.4 Populations with specific concerns

Children are not the only research participants who may need special care and handling. Many HCI research projects involve needs assessments, tool development, and evaluation for projects that either specifically focus on certain groups of users, or aim for universal usability across broad ranges of ability, expertise, and technologies (Lazar, 2007). These populations might include older individuals, members of specific ethnic groups, patients with specific health concerns, families, and many other groups. Working with these "nontraditional" research participants can be both rewarding and challenging, requiring both flexibility and creativity.

Recruitment is often the first struggle, particularly for academic researchers who have traditionally relied on readily available pools of undergraduates as study participants. Finding participants for these more specific studies might require interacting with community organizations (as suggested for working with participants with disabilities, Chapter 16), reaching out via online and print resources, encouraging word of mouth and referrals from friends, and numerous other creative approaches. Experience indicates that there is no "silver bullet": many studies rely on a combination of approaches to meet enrollment goals. Perhaps the only consistent observation is that recruitment will often take longer and cost more than expected, making realistic plans necessary for success.

Finding appropriate subjects from these groups is only a part of the challenge. Scheduling and transportation can be difficult for families, elders, and others, just as they are for individuals with disabilities (Chapter 16). Flexibility is key—anything that you might be able to do to accommodate diverse schedules and living arrangements will be helpful. Consider your experimental design and data collection requirements—lab-based studies that work for some subjects might be inappropriate for studies with diverse user populations. Designs that simplify data collection—preferably simple enough to run on a laptop—will enable the enrollment of participants in participant homes, community centers, and libraries, potentially removing or reducing logistical barriers that might discourage some participants.

Studies involving these user populations should also give careful consideration to specific needs and limitations that might impact participants' ability to meaningfully participate in research studies. Some participants might struggle with informed consent forms and research project descriptions that might be straightforward for undergraduates. Patients considering participation of studies of medically-related systems might have privacy concerns. Families might be limited in their ability to participate in long sessions. Careful planning and review of proposed protocols, pilot participants, and planning of supplies and materials are particularly vital for studies involving these participants.

15.3.7 INTERNATIONAL CONCERNS

We apologize to readers from outside the United States who might have found themselves frustrated that the discussions of informed consent and IRBs earlier in this chapter are overly focused on the conduct of research in the USA, with little attention paid to matters in other countries. We plead guilty—this chapter is indeed heavily influenced by our experiences in conducting research in the US.

Although the above discussion may seem somewhat parochial, protecting participants in research studies is a global concern. A 2015 listing of human research standards lists dozens of countries with relevant standards (Office for Human Research Protection, 2017). Many international organizations, such as the World Health Organization (World Health Organization, 2015), have their own policies, protocols, and terminologies. For example, outside of the US researchers generally work with "Research Ethics Committees" instead of "Institutional Review Boards."

Despite these differences, overall perspectives are generally fairly well aligned. The European Commission's policies on protecting human participants cites precedents from the European Charter of Fundamental rights, including the "right to the integrity of the person," "respect for private and family life," "protection of personal data," and "Freedom of the Arts and Sciences" (European Commission, 2013). The differences between these rights and the three pillars of US policy as outlined in the Belmont Report—beneficence, respect for persons, and justice—lead to subtle differences in emphasis, but little that would be in substantive disagreement with American policy. For example, the European Commission's policy discussion explicitly covers data protection measures (European Commission, 2013) that would be familiar to many researchers in the US, even though those matters are not discussed in the Common Code.

Given these differences, researchers conducting human studies experiments should always be careful to ensure that they are appropriately versed in the local understanding of human subjects' protections and the related regulatory requirements. This preparation may be particularly important for those conducting research in a culture with which they are unfamiliar, as misunderstandings may lead to difficulties.

Cultural sensitivity is a particular concern for research projects conducted by foreigners working in developing countries. Work in the area known as Information and Communication Technology for Development (ICT4D) often involves the participation of researchers from relatively affluent locales in projects in developing countries, often with participants who do not share their levels of affluence or education. Some commentators have raised the question of whether or not informed consent is possible in the face of these disparities (Sharma, 2005), while others have developed materials that might use field training of local field workers to help promote research ethics in challenging situations (Merritt et al., 2010). HCI efforts in such circumstances should carefully consider how questions of imbalances in education and financial resources might bias research. Working with local partners is generally a necessity, as is compliance with local regulations. Although requirements will vary across contexts, project review by both the researchers' "home" institution and an appropriate board at the site of the study might be necessary.

15.4 HUMAN SUBJECTS RESEARCH AND THE PUBLIC TRUST

Human Subjects research can be alternatively rewarding and infuriating. The distances between the excitement of a novel insight or a statistically significant result and the frustration of dealing with participants who miss appointments or IRBs who misinterpret studies are all often very short indeed. Although all research endeavors face their share of difficulties, the bureaucratic issues in dealing with IRBs and related paperwork are particularly problematic, as the ever-present temptation to cut corners presents a tantalizing way out. We have all heard excuses like "I don't really need an IRB review for this study" or "we can reuse an existing IRB approval." We've also experienced the difficulties of securing IRB approval, with projects delayed weeks or even months in a seemingly inscrutable bureaucratic process. The temptation to end run these processes may be strong, but it should be avoided.

Although the practical costs of such approaches—including potential difficulties in publication and risk of losing grant funding—are significant, the real problem in short-cutting human-subject protection lies in the abuse of the public trust. Certainly, many years have passed since the Tuskegee experiments, Milgram's experiments, and Zimbardo's prison in a Stanford psychology building, and the overwhelming majority of scientific studies are conducted carefully, ethically, and appropriately. However, ethical questions in research conducted are far from fully settled. The Facebook (Kramer et al., 2014) and OKCupid controversies (Rudder, 2014) illustrate the difficulties that researchers might face if they fail to consider ethical questions before they tackle novel problems. Moving beyond individual researchers, professional norms can also be the source of great controversy. A 2015 study commissioned by the American Psychological Association found that changes to the APA's ethics policies enacted in the early 2000s may have been conducted with undue deference to the goals of the US Central Intelligence Agency and Department of Defense, and may have provided a veneer of approval to torture practices (Hoffman et al., 2015). The ensuing controversy led to substantial upheaval at the APA (Bohannon, 2015).

Researchers involved in these studies—or, for that matter, in prior studies we now think of as abusive or inappropriate—were not necessarily acting in bad faith or out of lack of concern. This is exactly why we need careful, independent review to ensure respect for persons, beneficence, and justice (The National Commission for the Protection of Human Subjects of Biomedical and Behavioral Research, 1979), and to justify the trust that society requires when we ask individuals to participate in our studies and governments and foundations to financially support our work.

15.5 SUMMARY

Working with human subjects is one of the most challenging and informative aspects of HCI research. Finding appropriate participants; informing them of their rights; protecting their privacy; and answering their questions can be time consuming and often tedious, but the results are more than worth the effort. Even when study participants criticize our designs or fail to confirm our cherished experimental hypotheses, they provide invaluable insight that provides a rigorous foundation for our work.

Whatever type of study you are running, it is never too early to plan for recruiting, informed consent documentation, and other aspects of human participation. Proper planning will keep your study from becoming one of the many that have been delayed by unforeseen circumstances including difficulty in finding participants, or delays in IRB approval.

Recruiting entails finding the right number of the right kinds of participants. For usability studies, ethnographic observations of users, interviews, focus groups, and other approaches aimed at gathering requirements or evaluating design proposals, this may mean understanding the audience of users and identifying a sample of participants that is broad enough to reflect the needs and behavior of potential users. Designers and professional developers conducting research of this sort might work with collaborators, marketing teams, professional organizations, or others with appropriate understanding and context to identify both the range of viewpoints that would be needed and possible sources of the appropriate individuals.

Empirical studies require consideration of both the diversity of potential participants and any confounding factors that might contribute to performance differences. Characteristics of desirable participants might both be informed by and influence experimental hypotheses. Students and researchers conducting these studies should be careful to plan their data analysis and recruiting together, to ensure that the participants will be selected to increase the power of the statistical analysis.

Appropriate respect for participants is a cornerstone of all research involving human subjects. These issues are particularly relevant for studies that involve deception. Even when not required by institutional policy to do so, designers and developers would be advised to use formal informed consent forms to help participants make informed decisions. Students and researchers should take the time—again, as early in the process as possible—to understand the regulations in force in their institution, and to make sure that their approvals are in order before starting any project.

Human subjects research in HCI can be an unpredictable and often unsettling process. Unforeseen problems, including misinterpreted tasks and goals, systems failures, and missed appointments, are routine: it's rare that a study (of any sort) goes off completely without a hitch. These matters can complicate data collection and interpretation: if a user chooses an interpretation of a written task that differs from your intent and then completes the task correctly, how do you interpret the result—is it correct or not? What should be done with results from a user who decides to withdraw from a study after completing only a portion of the tasks? As hard and fast rules for handling situations like these are few and far between, you may have to handle each issue on a case-by-case basis. The specific decisions that you make may be less important than how they are enforced: consistent application of policies and procedures will ensure your ability to make meaningful comparisons.

All participants in HCI research studies should be well treated and approached with an open mind. Participating in HCI studies should be fun and engaging whenever possible: by making our studies positive experiences, we encourage people both to participate and to provide useful feedback. As researchers, we should "expect the unexpected": software will crash, devices won't work, and (perhaps most distressingly) users will hate our beloved inventions. High-quality HCI research takes these setbacks in its stride, all the while striving to observe carefully while maintaining respect for the people who give a bit of their time to help our studies along. By watching and listening carefully, we can learn from what users do and how they do it. That, after all, is the point of conducting user studies.

DISCUSSION QUESTIONS

1. University researchers occasionally ask students in a class to participate in research studies. However, this practice may involve elements of coercion, as students may be concerned that refusal to participate may negatively impact their grade. Is voluntary informed consent possible in such a situation? What steps might be taken to reconcile the researcher's need for subjects with the students' right to decline to participate?

2. The virtual reprise of Milgram's experiment (see Section 15.2.1) asked participants to inflict harm upon a computer-generated avatar. This approach eliminates some of the potential ethical concerns associated with the original experiment, but may raise additional questions. As user behavior was similar to what was observed in the original experiments, it is possible that participants in the "virtual" versions would experience similar patterns of nervousness and distress. Do you consider this sort of research to be appropriate? What might be done to protect participants in this sort of experiment?

3. As part of a larger study of how various aspects of interaction in online worlds impact the offline lives of participants, you are interested in observing participants both online and offline. As you know, participants in online games

such as these may not represent a broad cross-section of society. The race and gender of online characters may not reflect those of the real individuals involved and some may choose to hide their "real" identity. Given these challenges, how might you go about finding a group of participants that would be interesting to work with? How might these challenges affect the conclusions that you might be able to draw from your observations and your ability to generalize from those conclusions?

RESEARCH DESIGN EXERCISES

1. You are designing a study to evaluate the effectiveness of a new text entry method for messaging on cell phones. Due to the popularity of messaging among college students, you decide that the undergraduate student body at your school would be an appropriate pool of potential participants. What would you want to know about the habits of these students regarding text messaging? You might be interested in comparing the performance of computer science students against students from other fields. Are there any other attributes of the students that might make for interesting comparisons? Given the male-female imbalance in computer science, what problems might this comparison involve?

2. Your research design for the study of text entry on cell phones involves asking users to perform a set of tasks in a laboratory. As they will not be using their own phones, there is little, if any, privacy risk. What other risks might this study pose, and how would you inform users about them?

3. Find the website or other information about your IRB. Examine the policies and procedures specific to your institution, and write a draft informed consent form for the study described in Exercise 1.

4. Studies of how users respond to events that interrupt their work (Gluck et al., 2007) present a challenge in design. If participants are told that the study is investigating reactions to interruptions, they may be more sensitive to those events than they would otherwise be. A deceptive study, in which the subjects were provided with an alternative description of the goals of the study, might be one way to get around this problem. How might you describe a deceptive study for examining reactions to interruptions? How would you describe this study in an informed consent form? What would you discuss in the debriefing sessions?

REFERENCES

Asan, O., Montague, E., 2013. Technology-mediated information sharing between patients and clinicians in primary care encounters. Behaviour & Information Technology 33 (3), 259–270.

Azar, B., 2000. Online experiments: ethically fair or foul? Monitor on Psychology 31 (4).

Beskow, L.M., Dombeck, C.B., Thompson, C.P., Watson-Ormond, J.K., Weinfurt, K.P., 2015. Informed consent for biobanking: consensus-based guidelines for adequate comprehension. Genetics in Medicine 17 (3), 226–233.

Beskow, L.M., Friedman, J.Y., Hardy, N.C., Lin, L., Weinfurt, K.P., 2010. Developing a simplified consent form for biobanking. PLoS One 5 (10), e13302.

Bohannon, J., 2015. APA Overhauling Policies and Leadership After Torture Report. Retrieved from http://news.sciencemag.org/brain-behavior/2015/07/apa-overhauling-policies-and-leadership-after-torture-report (30.08.15).

Centers for Disease Control and Prevention, 2007. U.S. Public Health Service Syphilis Study at Tuskegee. Retrieved from http://www.cdc.gov/nchstp/od/tuskegee/ (31.05.07).

Cohen, I.G., Lynch, H.F. (Eds.), 2014. Human Subjects Research Regulation: Perspectives on the Future. MIT Press, Cambridge, MA.

Cook, T.D., Campbell, D.T., 1979. Quasi-Experimentation: Design and Analysis Issues for Field Settings. Houghton Mifflin Company, Boston.

Davis, T.C., Holcombe, R.F., Berkel, H.J., Pramanik, S., Divers, S.G., 1998. Informed consent for clinical trials: a comparative study of standard versus simplified forms. Journal of the National Cancer Institute 90 (9), 668–674.

Department of Health and Services, 2009. Federal Policy for Protection of Human Research Subjects. Retrieved from http://www.hhs.gov/ohrp/humansubjects/guidance/45cfr46.html.

European Commission, 2013. Ethics for Researchers: Facilitating Research Excellence in FP7. Retrieved March 20, 2017 from https://ec.europa.eu/research/participants/data/ref/fp7/89888/ethics-for-researchers_en.pdf.

Federal Register, 2015. Federal Policy for the Protection of Human Subjects, United States Government. Retrieved March 20, 2017 from https://www.federalregister.gov/documents/2015/09/08/2015-21756/federal-policy-for-the-protection-of-human-subjects.

Finn, P., Jakobsson, M., 2007a. Designing and Conducting Phishing Experiments. IEEE Technology and Society Magazine (Special Issue on Usability and Security). pp. 1–21.

Finn, P., Jakobsson, M., 2007b. Designing ethical phishing experiments. IEEE Technology and Society Magazine 26 (1), 46–58.

Fiske, S.T., Hauser, R.M., 2014. Protecting human research participants in the age of big data. Proceedings of the National Academy of Sciences 111 (38), 13675–13676.

Gluck, J., Bunt, A., McGrenere, J., 2007. Matching attentional draw with utility in interruption. In: Proceedings of ACM CHI 2007 Conference on Human Factors in Computing Systems, ACM, San Jose, CA, pp. 41–50.

Goel, V., 2014. Facebook Tinkers With Users' Emotions in News Feed Experiment, Stirring Outcry. The New York Times. Retrieved March 20, 2017 from https://www.nytimes.com/2014/06/30/technology/facebook-tinkers-with-users-emotions-in-news-feed-experiment-stirring-outcry.html?_r=0.

Haney, C., Banks, C., Zimbardo, P., 1973. Interpersonal dynamics in a simulated prison. International Journal of Criminology and Penology 1, 69–97.

Harrison, D., Marshall, P., Berthouze, N., Bird, J., 2014. Tracking physical activity: problems related to running longitudinal studies with commercial devices. In: Proceedings of the 2014 ACM International Joint Conference on Pervasive and Ubiquitous Computing: Adjunct Publication. ACM, Seattle, Washington, pp. 699–702.

Hochheiser, H., Lazar, J., 2010. Revisiting breadth vs. depth in menu structures for blind users of screen readers. Interacting with Computers 22 (5), 389–398.

Hoffman, D.H., Carter, D., Viglucci Lopez, C.R., Guo, A.X., Latfif, S.Y., Craig, D., 2015. Report to the Special Committee of the Board of the American Psychological Association: Independent Review Relating to APA Ethics Guidelines, National Security Investigations, and Torture. Retrieved March 20, 2017 from http://www.apa.org/independent-review/revised-report.pdf.

Hourcade, J.P., 2015. Child-Computer Interaction. CreateSpace Independent Publishing Platform ISBN 978-1514397251. Available from http://homepage.divms.uiowa.edu/~hourcade/book/child-computer-interaction-first-edition.pdf (accessed March 19, 2017).

Hwang, W., Salvendy, G., 2010. Number of people required for usability evaluation: the 10+/−2 rule. Communications of the ACM 53 (5), 130–133.

Jagatic, T.N., Johnson, N.A., Jakobsson, M., Menczer, F., 2007. Social phishing. Communications of the ACM 50 (10), 94–100.

Jakobsson, M., Finn, P., Johnson, N., 2008. Why and how to perform fraud experiments. IEEE Security and Privacy 6 (2), 66–68.

Jones, J.H., 1993. Bad Blood: The Tuskegee Syphilis Experiment. Free Press, New York.

Kjeldskov, J., Skov, M., Als, B., Høegh, R., 2004. Is it worth the hassle? Exploring the added value of evaluating the usability of context-aware mobile systems in the field. In: Brewster, S., Dunlop, M. (Eds.), Mobile Human-Computer Interaction—MobileHCI 2004, vol. 3160. Springer, Berlin Heidelberg, pp. 61–73.

Kjeldskov, J., Skov, M.B., 2014. Was it worth the hassle? Ten years of mobile HCI research discussions on lab and field evaluations. In: Proceedings of the 16th International Conference on Human-Computer Interaction With Mobile Devices' Services. ACM, Toronto, ON, Canada, pp. 43–52.

Kramer, A.D.I., Guillory, J.E., Hancock, J.T., 2014. Experimental evidence of massive-scale emotional contagion through social networks. Proceedings of the National Academy of Sciences 111 (24), 8788–8790.

Larson, K., Czerwinski, M., 1998. Web page design: implications of memory, structure and scent for information retrieval. In: SIGCHI Conference on Human Factors in Computing Systems Los Angeles. ACM Press, CA, United States.

Lazar, J. (Ed.), 2007. Universal Usability: Designing Computer Interfaces for Diverse User Populations. John Wiley and Sons, Chichester, UK.

Levitt, S.D., List, J.A., 2011. Was there really a Hawthorne effect at the Hawthorne plant? An analysis of the original illumination experiments. American Economic Journal: Applied Economics 3 (1), 224–238.

Luger, E., Rodden, T., 2013a. An informed view on consent for UbiComp. In: Proceedings of the 2013 ACM International Joint Conference on Pervasive and Ubiquitous Computing. ACM, Zurich, Switzerland, pp. 529–538.

Luger, E., Rodden, T., 2013b. Terms of agreement: rethinking consent for pervasive computing. Interacting with Computers 25 (3), 229–241.

Macefield, R., 2007. Usability studies and the Hawthorne effect. Journal of Usability Studies 2 (3).

McCambridge, J., Witton, J., Elbourne, D.R., 2014. Systematic review of the Hawthorne effect: new concepts are needed to study research participation effects. Journal of Clinical Epidemiology 67 (3), 267–277.

Merritt, M.W., Labrique, A.B., Katz, J., Rashid, M., West Jr., K.P., Pettit, J., 2010. A field training guide for human subjects research ethics. PLoS Medicine 7 (10), e1000349.

Milgram, S., 1963. Behavioral study of obedience. Journal of Abnormal and Social Psychology 67, 371–378.

National Academies of Sciences and Medicine, 2016. Optimizing the Nation's Investment in Academic Research: A New Regulatory Framework for the 21st Century. Retrieved March 20, 2017 from https://www.nap.edu/catalog/21824/optimizing-the-nations-investment-in-academic-research-a-new-regulatory.

National Institutes of Health, 2014. Request for Comments on the Draft NIH Policy on the Use of a Single Institutional Review Board for Multi-Site Research. Retrieved from http://grants.nih.gov/grants/guide/notice-files/NOT-OD-15-026.html (29.08.15).

Nielsen, J., 1992. Finding usability problems through heuristic evaluation. In: Proceedings of the SIGCHI Conference on Human Factors in Computing Systems. ACM, Monterey, CA, USA, pp. 373–380.

Nielsen, J., Molich, R., 1990. Heuristic evaluation of user interfaces. In: Proceedings of the SIGCHI Conference on Human Factors in Computing Systems. ACM, Seattle, Washington, USA, pp. 249–256.

Office for Human Research Protection, 2017. International Compilation of Human Research Standards, 2017 Edition. Retrieved March 20, 2017 from https://www.hhs.gov/ohrp/sites/default/files/international-compilation-of-human-research-standards-2017.pdf.

Office for Human Research Protections, 1998. Informed Consent Checklist. Retrieved from https://www.hhs.gov/ohrp/regulations-and-policy/guidance/checklists/index.html (01.01.17).

Orne, M.T., 1962. On the social psychology of the psychological experiment: with particular reference to demand characteristics and their implications. The American Psychologist 17 (11), 776–783.

Patrick, A., 2007a. Commentary on Research on New Security Indicators. Retrieved from http://www.andrewpatrick.ca/essays/commentary-on-research-on-new-security-indicators/ (22.06.07).

Patrick, A., 2007b. Privacy Practices for HCI Research. Retrieved from http://www.andrewpatrick.ca/essays/privacy-practices-for-hci-research/ (04.06.07).

Pellegrino, E.D., 1997. The Nazi doctors and Nuremberg: some moral lessons revisited. Annals of Internal Medicine 127 (4), 307–308.

Puschmann, C., Bozdag, E., 2014. Staking out the unclear ethical terrain of online social experiments. Internet Policy Review 3 (4).

Read, J.C., Fitton, D., Horton, M., 2014. Giving ideas an equal chance: inclusion and representation in participatory design with children. In: Proceedings of the 2014 Conference on Interaction Design and Children. ACM, Aarhus, Denmark, pp. 105–114.

Ross, M., 2014. Do research ethics need updating for the digital age? Monitor on Psychology 45.

Rudder, C., 2014. We Experiment On Human Beings!. Retrieved from http://blog.okcupid.com/index.php/we-experiment-on-human-beings/ (27.09.15).

Schechter, S., Dhamija, R., Ozment, A., Fischer, A., 2007. The Emperor's New Security Indicators: an evaluation of website authentication and the effect of role playing on usability studies. In: IEEE Symposium on Security and Privacy. IEEE, Oakland, CA.

Schmettow, M., 2012. Sample size in usability studies. Communications of the ACM 55 (4), 64–70.

Schrag, Z.M., 2015. Institutional Review Blog. Retrieved from http://www.institutionalreviewblog.com/ (20.09.15).

Sharma, K., 2005. Can clinical trials ever be truly ethical? The Hindu. Retrieved April 10, 2017 from http://www.thehindu.com/2005/12/06/stories/2005120603081000.htm.

Shavers, V.L., Lynch, C.F.L., Burmeister, L.F., 2000. Knowledge of the Tuskegee study and its impact on the willingness to participate in medical research studies. Journal of the National Medical Association 92 (12), 563–572.

Shneiderman, B., Plaisant, C., Cohen, M., Jacobs, S., Elmqvist, N., Diakopoulos, N., 2016. Designing the user interface, sixth ed. Pearson Addison Wesley, Boston.

Slater, M., Antley, A., Davison, A., Swapp, D., Guger, C., Barker, C., Pistrang, N., Sanchez-Vives, M.V., 2006. A virtual reprise of the Stanley Milgram obedience experiments. PLoS One 1 (1).

Smith, S.S., Richardson, D., 1983. Amelioration of deception and harm in psychological research: the important role of debriefing. Journal of Personality and Social Psychology 44 (5), 1075–1082.

Society for Research in Child Development, 1991. Ethical Standards for Research with Children. Retrieved from http://www.srcd.org/about-us/ethical-standards-research (08.04.17).

Srinivasan, V., Moghaddam, S., Mukherji, A., Rachuri, K.K., Xu, C., Tapia, E.M., 2014. MobileMiner: mining your frequent patterns on your phone. In: Proceedings of the 2014 ACM International Joint Conference on Pervasive and Ubiquitous Computing. ACM, Seattle, Washington, pp. 389–400.

Steriadis, C.E., Constantinou, P., 2003. Designing human-computer interfaces for quadriplegic people. ACM Transactions on Computer-Human Interaction 10 (2), 87–118.

The National Commission for the Protection of Human Subjects of Biomedical and Behavioral Research, 1979. The Belmont Report: Ethical Principles and Guidelines for the Protection of Human Subjects of Research. Retrieved from https://www.hhs.gov/ohrp/regulations-and-policy/belmont-report/index.html (08.04.17).

United States Department of Health and Human Services, 1993. Institutional Review Board Guidebook: Chapter VI: Special Classes of Subjects. Retrieved from https://archive.hhs.gov/ohrp/irb/irb_chapter6.htm (20.03.17).

Verma, I.M., 2014. Editorial expression of concern: psychological and cognitive sciences. Proceedings of the National Academy of Sciences 111 (24), 10779.

Weibel, N., Rick, S., Emmenegger, C., Ashfaq, S., Calvitti, A., Agha, Z., 2015. LAB-IN-A-BOX: semi-automatic tracking of activity in the medical office. Personal and Ubiquitous Computing 19 (2), 317–334.

World Health Organization, 2015. Ethical standards and procedures for research with human beings. Retrieved from http://www.who.int/ethics/research/en/ (27.09.15).

Zimbardo, P., 2008a. The Lucifer Effect: Understanding How Good People Turn Evil. Random House.

Zimbardo, P., 2008b. Stanford Prison Experiment. Retrieved from http://www.prisonexp.org/ (08.04.17).

Working with research participants with disabilities

16

16.1 INTRODUCTION

Chapter 15 talks about the approaches for and issues that arise when working with human participants in research. As the number of research projects involving users with disabilities grows, it is important also to examine the specific concepts, issues, and challenges of doing human-computer interaction (HCI) research involving users with various disabilities. Computer technology is now being used everywhere, by everyone, on a daily basis, for work, for pleasure, for communication, and for overall living. This includes users with perceptual disabilities (e.g., hearing and visual), motor disabilities (e.g., limited or no use of hands, arms, legs, or mouth), and cognitive/intellectual disabilities (whether lifelong impairments, such as Down syndrome and autism, impairments that develop over time, such as dementia and Alzheimer's disease, or event-based impairments, such as aphasia). It is important that users with disabilities be directly involved with research. When researchers don't directly involve people with disabilities, they often make assumptions, which wind up being stereotypes. For instance, one common assumption is that all people with disabilities use a form of assistive technology (an alternate or modified input or output device or approach), which is not true. As another example, some researchers may not know that Blind people can use power tools to build furniture and can also drive cars! Those are two examples of how assumptions can be wrong!

The grouping of "users with disabilities/impairments" is itself somewhat artificial. It encompasses lots of different individuals with different impairments, abilities, and strengths; all they may have in common is that they have the label "impairment" or "disability" attached to them. For instance, individuals who are Blind, and individuals who have Alzheimer's disease may have practically nothing in common. And people that are often grouped together in research may be exact opposites. For instance, in evaluating technologies for people with cognitive impairment, some researchers have grouped together young adults with Autism and Down syndrome, when they are often polar opposites in social skills, motor skills, and in some cases, intellectual skills. This is important to remember: you can't just group together people with different disabilities under that one large umbrella. While research on users with perceptual and motor disabilities has existed since the 1970s, only recently have researchers tackled the challenges of designing computer interfaces for users with cognitive disabilities (Lazar, 2007b) and only rarely have researchers worked with people having multiple impairments. It is important to note that in some countries, a mental health challenge is also considered a disability under national laws, but that is outside the scope of this chapter (for more information on working with users with mental health issues, see Johansson et al., 2015).

It is also important to note that as people in general change their information consumption habits, they are often switching to interaction techniques primarily utilized by people with disabilities. For instance, captioning (which is known in much of Europe as subtitling) of video on television was used primarily for people who are Deaf or Hard of hearing, but as consumption patterns change, more of the general public (without disabilities) now get their news watching web-based video, and using the captioning, especially when they are in a location where they cannot play sound (Crabb et al., 2015). The same flexibility that allows digital information to work properly for someone with a disability will also allow for flexibility for someone without a disability who either has a situational impairment, or is just accessing information in a different way (e.g., from a smart phone) (Lazar et al., 2015). Many technologies that start out as assistive technology for a specific population of people with disabilities, such as audio books, speech recognition, and captioning, wind up later becoming popular among the general population (Lazar et al., 2015). So, for many reasons, researchers are interested in developing new accessibility techniques, and evaluating them with users both with and without disabilities. All products and interfaces should be designed for user diversity; disability should be a part of that!

It is important to note that different groups prefer different terminology. For instance, most communities of people with disabilities prefer people-first language (e.g., people WITH disabilities), however, two communities, Blind people and Deaf people, generally prefer language that is not people-first, and the Deaf community (capital D Deaf), meaning those who use sign language, and are a part of Deaf culture, do not consider themselves to have a disability, but consider themselves linguistically different. Also, the terminology for Autism has recently changed in the medical literature, so "Autism Spectrum Disorder" is preferred to a specific term like "Asperger's syndrome." Different countries have different usage of terms, as well, so, for instance, in much of Europe, Blind=no residual vision, and visually impaired=low vision, but in the United States, Blind=no vision or low vision. Even the choice of using the term impairment versus disability can sometimes be controversial and there is no general agreement. While writing this chapter (and throughout the book), we strive to use the most respectful language, but acknowledge that what is considered most respectful by one community may not be considered the best choice by another community.

The goals of HCI research involving users with disabilities are the same as research with other users, to understand the phenomena surrounding computer interfaces and usage patterns. It's not sufficient just to take guidelines from the research on interface design for people with disabilities (such as the Web Content Accessibility Guidelines), and you can't just take proxy users (nonrepresentative users who do not meet the inclusion criteria) to represent the users with disabilities. You must work directly with users with disabilities.

This chapter describes how research involving people with disabilities, may differ from research with the general population. There are three areas which researchers need to pay careful attention to: (1) participants, (2) research methodology, and (3) logistics. Due to the diversity of disability, researchers need to pay careful attention to ensuring that the participants are the "right" participants for a study, meaning that the participants meet all of the inclusion criteria. Participant recruitment will likely be a challenge, and this chapter describes both methods for recruitment, as well as communication strategies. The overall research methods (experimental design, surveys, time diaries, case studies, etc.) are often the same as for research involving other users. However, the logistics of performing this type of research are generally what makes it different (e.g., where you perform your research, how you get participants to sign IRB forms, and how you pay users with disabilities for their participation). For people with cognitive disabilities, individual modifications to the research methods may sometimes need to be made (discussed in detail later in this chapter). There also may be factors in the research that you should be aware of, as they may bias your data in one direction or another. Due to these complex logistics, it is realistic to say that it may take more time to do research involving participants with disabilities. It is intensive, but you should do it anyway! And as mentioned earlier in this chapter, research that leads to improved interface and design experiences for people with disabilities may eventually lead to interfaces that are better for the general population!

16.2 PARTICIPANTS
16.2.1 INCLUSION CRITERIA

When recruiting users with disabilities for research, you must be very clear on the criteria for inclusion in the research study. Just saying that someone has a disability isn't sufficient, as the population of people with disabilities is not monolithic, and in fact, even within the population of people with the same specific disability, there is great diversity. Table 16.1 displays the types of inclusion criteria that must be considered when doing HCI research involving people with disabilities. The goal of the research study, and the research methods involved, will help determine which of these inclusion criteria are relevant for the study. Some of the criteria simply relate to the representativeness of participants. So, for instance, people with a specific disability who are also employed in a certain field (e.g., people who are Deaf or Blind and also are lawyers). Some inclusion criteria relate to history of, or severity of a disability (e.g., people who have been Blind since birth versus people who lost vision later in life). Other inclusion criteria relate to experience and frequency of using a technology. Often, new users of assistive technology, without years of experience, or who do not utilize the technology on a frequent basis, will not be familiar enough with the technology to effectively use it in any type of research project. Other inclusion criteria may relate to communication methods: do your participants need to be fluent in sign language? Or in Braille? Keep in mind that it is estimated that only 10%–20%

Table 16.1 Typical Types of Inclusion Criteria When Doing HCI Research Involving People With Disabilities

Inclusion Criteria

Technology
- Which assistive technologies do the participants use or not use?
- How many years of experience do participants have using a specific technology (assistive or otherwise)?
- How many hours a week do participants utilize a specific technology?
- Do participants have experience with certain brands of assistive technology, or do they use it in certain combinations?

Education
- What level of education is required? Secondary school (high school)? An undergraduate (bachelor's) degree? A graduate degree?
- Is formal training in computer usage (e.g. software applications, OS, keyboarding) required for participation?

Employment
- Must the participants be employed in certain job roles?
- Must the participants be involved in paid employment?

Disability
- Is there a certain medical diagnosis that is required? (e.g., Trisomy 21 or Mosaic Down Syndrome?)
- Is there a certain severity of a disability required for participation (e.g., no residual vision or some vision?)
- Can participants be allowed to use aids (e.g., are people who use cochlear implants acceptable for the research study?)
- How long must participants have had the disability (e.g., born Blind or lost vision as an adult?)
- Have participants previously participated in rehabilitation training activities (e.g., such as orientation and mobility for Blind people?)
- Do participants use any electronic prostheses?

Communication
- Must participants be able to independently communicate?
- Must participants be fluent in sign language or Braille?

of Blind adults are fluent in Braille (which tends to surprise most people who don't work regularly in the blindness community).

It is important to note that, it may be hard to get detailed information about the medical status of someone with a disability (e.g., their cognitive level, their visual acuity, or range of motion), because of sensitivity involved in sharing personal health data, or national laws that limit the sharing of health data. However, there can be substitutes, described in assistive technology terms, for ensuring the same qualities in participants. For instance, rather than stipulating the visual acuity data, participants can be recruited by asking for those who are "screen reader users, unable to use screen magnification" meaning that there is close to no residual vision. Or asking about the use of tools such as magnifiers and closed-circuit television (CCTV), indicates that someone is low vision (Zhao et al., 2015). Sometimes, automated data collection of typing speed, or pointing performance, can help in measuring motor performance (Hurst et al., 2013). Furthermore, it is important to note that due to policies in some countries, people with certain disabilities may not be allowed to earn over a certain amount of money or they will lose their government benefits, so there are people who are employed in respectable positions, but are not being fully paid, or people who are underemployed, because they will lose their health benefits if they are fully employed. This may also mean that participants, in limited circumstances, may not be able to accept large payments for participation in a research study.

16.2.2 DIFFERING LEVELS OF ABILITY

Ability levels may vary widely among users with a specific disability (Jaeger, 2009). Assumptions should never be made, for instance, about "what users with aphasia are capable of." Since many disabilities are due to underlying medical or health causes, the severity of the impairment will vary among different users. Most impairments are not binary, that you either have them or don't. People can have partial impairments (such as partial hearing or visual impairment). People can have varying severity of impact (for instance, mild, moderate, or severe Aphasia, Alzheimer's disease, or dementia). So for instance, if Aphasia was caused by a stroke or head injury, the severity of the stroke or head injury, as well as the time elapsed from the Aphasia-causing event, can both impact on the severity (Miller et al., 2013). Even impairments that at first seem to be very clear and binary are actually not. For instance, there are different types of amnesia, based on what type of memory capability has been lost. While trisomy Down syndrome is the most common form (95%), there is another type of Down syndrome, called "mosaic Down syndrome," that is much rarer, but generally has a lesser impact on cognitive performance. Autism Spectrum Disorders even note the diversity ("spectrum") in their name. In all of these situations it is important to fully understand the nature and diversity of the population, by consulting experts in that specific impairment. In addition, standardized tests that measure the severity of the impairment can be very useful, as long as they are properly conducted and interpreted (Moffatt et al., 2004). Not only does the severity of the impairment influence interface design, but even for people at the same level of impairment, there are a number of other factors that influence performance on interface-related tasks, including: confidence, self-efficacy, and previous experience with using computers. The results are not always what they seem and it takes a lot of experience with a specific user population to understand this.

For instance, research tasks that might take user A only 1 hour might take user B 3.5 hours. In a typical population without disabilities, this would lead the researcher to believe that either users B's skills and task performance are lower, or maybe there is a problem with the equipment that user B is utilizing (e.g., it is older equipment or slower network connections). However, this would not necessarily hold true for populations with disabilities. For instance, newer users of a certain application or tool (such as head tracking) might be satisfied with completing a series of tasks in 3.5 hours. This same amount of time might be frustrating to someone who has utilized the equipment for years. Each user with a disability (or a combination of disabilities) is a unique individual, with a unique performance speed that they alone consider to be their average "default speed." The "default speed" should be taken into consideration to determine individual usability. However, the "default speed" can also be a complication when trying to compare the performance of a group of users with a specific disability. For instance, typical data input and output speeds vary more greatly for users with disabilities than for the general user population. As an example, Blind users listen to their screen readers (e.g., JAWS, VoiceOver, and Window-Eyes) at varying rates, and tend to think that any speed that is not their pre-set speed is either too fast or too slow. In experimental studies with Blind users, you may want to remove the potential confounding factor of having various screen reader speeds in the mix by using one screen reader speed for every participant, although this may frustrate the individuals who participate. Alternatively, you might check the speech rate that each user has set on their computer, but note that they will not be comparable across different screen reader brands.

In another example of the complexity of user differences within a specific impairment population, for a screen reader user who listens to the screen reader at a very rapid rate, they may be frustrated if a task takes more than 5 minutes to complete. Another user, who listens to the screen reader at a much slower speed, may be very satisfied if the same task takes 20 minutes to complete. Their personal expectations of performance may not always be obvious to the researcher and this may be hard to measure. Experience with the computer and confidence may also play a role. For instance, imagine three Blind users, all of whom are attempting the same task. User A may give up after 2 minutes of attempting the task, because they know that they typically can only find information using four different navigation methods, and once they have attempted all four navigation methods, it is pointless to continue, as they are confident that they would not be able to use any other method and succeed. User B may also give up after 2 minutes, but because they have low confidence. They are not confident in their abilities and think it is unlikely that they will be able to complete a task. User C does not give up, even after 45 minutes of attempting a task. While the computing skill set of user C might be high or low, they are confident in their abilities, and they repeatedly say, "I am not a quitter. I will keep going until I am able to complete the task." The authors of this book have personally witnessed all three behaviors. In this example, time is not directly correlated to technical experience or confidence, but rather, is influenced by both.

Experience can also play a factor in how people with disabilities perceive the user experience. For instance, Blind users often do not subjectively rate interface problems as being as bad as the objective performance ratings document (Trewin et al., 2015). One possible reason for this is that their previous experience with technology includes so many barriers to be overcome, that their expectations for their interaction experience are a low baseline, and interface problems may not be perceived as bad as they really are (Trewin et al., 2015). For instance, the research documents that Blind users may generally have a positive outlook (Trewin et al., 2015), and interface barriers may only impact on mood when it interferes with work (Lazar et al., 2006). Due to how participant baselines and expectations may differ, it is important that, if researchers use the terms "low accessibility" and "high accessibility" at any point interacting with participants, the researchers should be clear to define what the working definitions of those terms are. Does high accessibility mean true ease of use, or simply compliance with international technical standards such as the Web Content Accessibility Guidelines (WCAG) 2.0? Does low accessibility mean that a task can technically be accomplished but it is hard to use, or does low accessibility equate to inaccessible because there are so many barriers which make task completion impossible? Use of terminology must be clear.

Given that users with disabilities are really a mosaic of different communities with different needs, it is sometimes important to test an interface with either multiple groups, or a combination of users with and without disabilities. There are generally two approaches for developing interfaces for users with disabilities (Lazar, 2007a):

- Try to make an interface (for a website, digital library, application, or operating system) that works well for a majority of users (both with and without disabilities). Usually, this is the scenario where all users have the same end task goals (such as accessing an article or purchasing a song online), and they are simply utilizing alternative input or output devices (Slatin and Rush, 2003). This could be called the universal design approach.
- Design an interface that is optimized for a specific user group. This is the approach that tends to be used for people with severe cognitive disability, including children with autism and adults with Alzheimer's disease or aphasia (Cohene et al., 2005; Moffatt et al., 2004; Tartaro, 2007). The needs of the population are so specific, that the interface, and the corresponding task scenarios and applications, are so focused on the specific needs of the user population that they are unlikely to meet the needs of other populations. This is often used for Augmentative and Alternative communication devices, where the device is designed to meet the needs of one user or a group of users.

16.2.3 RECRUITMENT OF PARTICIPANTS WITH DISABILITIES

One of the greatest challenges of doing research involving users with disabilities is the recruitment of participants. There are a number of complex aspects of recruiting participants with disabilities into your research study. You can't just place signs in the computer science department or on campus saying, "we want users with spinal cord injuries to take part in our research study," as there are often not a sufficient number of individuals with specific disabilities on university campuses. The same holds true for research labs at corporations and government agencies. It's not likely that there are a sufficient number of people with the specific disabilities at your company or government agency (unless you work for a very large company or government agency). Certain offices at a university or a company (e.g., the Disability Student Services office, or the Compliance Office) may have a list of all people with disabilities in an organization, but you can expect that they will be reluctant to share that information with you, and according to the laws of some countries, it may be illegal to share that information. Also, depending on the national or regional laws of a country, an individual may not be required to identify that they have a disability. So the concept of being presented with a list of all people with disabilities within an organization, is simply not a realistic concept.

Some academic departments (often in Psychology and Education) have "pools" of potential participants for research studies, but again, they rarely will have a sufficient number of people with disabilities in those pools. The often-used (but often-not-appropriate) practice of recruiting students in computer science for research studies, will not help you reach this goal. When there are a few people with disabilities within an organization, they are often repeatedly asked to participate in every study, leading to those users becoming very experienced in research (Dee and Hanson, 2014). Some researchers choose to use "simulated impairments," where people without disabilities, say, are blindfolded or have their hands tied behind their back, but this should not be done, even for portions of a study. There are limited situations where using proxy users are appropriate, and they are discussed in later sections (specifically, Section 16.2.6).

PARTNERING WITH ADVOCACY GROUPS

The best way to recruit users with disabilities is usually to partner with a community-based group that focuses on the disability of interest to the research. Most people with disabilities have some sort of organization, support group, or coordination point. For instance, there are organizations of people with visual and hearing impairments, organizations of people with spinal cord injuries, and organizations of people with Alzheimer's disease. In cases where the disabilities impact the ability to live an independent life, these organizations often include caregivers and family members. It is usually good to approach these organizations for help in recruiting users. However, simply saying, "we want to do some research, and we need your help in recruiting users" is not sufficient, and it is hard to establish immediate trust (Feng et al., 2005). If you really care about these user populations, then you need to become involved with the community-based group for the long term. Most of these organizations get multiple requests for help, and they may be leery of "drive-by research," where you ask for their help, do the research, and then never show up or contact them again. When people feel a sense of reciprocity, they are more likely to participate in research (Dee and Hanson, 2014).

Some organizations are geographically based and you may want to contact their national offices. For instance, the Royal National Institute of Blind People in the United Kingdom and the National Federation of the Blind in the United States are leading organizations for Blind individuals. The

National Association of the Deaf, the Alexander Graham Bell Association for the Deaf and Hard of Hearing, the Alzheimer's Association, the National Down Syndrome Congress, National Spinal Cord Injury Association, and the Autistic Self Advocacy Network, rank among some of the better-known groups. While national organizations are common, other organizations may work at the grassroots, with local city-based groups that do not coordinate with each other. If possible, you should become a part of these organizations: go to their meetings, meet people, get involved in their community, and take part in fundraisers. If there is a regional or national convention, it is important to attend that gathering. At these gatherings, it is possible to better understand the logistics and challenges involved for that population, which can help with the planned research in the future. But it isn't sufficient to go to the meetings just to learn about issues such as Braille handouts or physical room limitations for individuals in wheelchairs. The end goal should not simply be to further your research, but to further the cause of these individuals and their quality of life. Your research is simply a piece of that long-term goal. As such, your partnership needs to be a two-way street. If you are asking for their help, then they should be able to expect your help. You should find a way to compensate the organization for their assistance to you. When your research is complete, you should make sure that the organization receives copies of any final reports. Rehabilitation centers that are often sponsored by local governments or industry, provide training and modifications to help adults with certain impairments move into the workforce. These organizations can often be sources of participants for research.

If you are working with a community-based organization that specializes in a certain impairment, the goal of your research is to further their cause and improve the quality of life for individuals with the specific impairment by improving understanding of HCI issues for the user population. If the only goal you have is to further your own professional career, with little concern for the needs of the population, look elsewhere. Working with users with disabilities is a long-term, emotional, involved process, with great societal benefit and long-term payoffs in the quality of life for individuals. Expect that the organizations involved will come to count on you and consider you a part of their cause. Invest in the long term or get out of the game. <End of sermon>.

16.2.4 COMMUNICATING WITH PEOPLE WHO ARE DEAF OR HARD OF HEARING

If a research study involves participants who are Deaf or Hard of hearing, then it is important to ascertain whether the participants will need sign language interpretation. It is possible that other forms of accommodation may be necessary (e.g., oral interpretation, induction/hearing loops), but sign language is a necessary accommodation for people who are Deaf (meaning that they are a part of Deaf culture and primarily use sign language). It is important to note that people who identify as Hard of hearing may not be sign language users.

If multiple researchers are fluent in the relevant sign language, that may be sufficient, but often, it may be necessary to bring in sign language interpreters, to ensure full communication with your participants. For instance, Shiver and Wolfe (2015) brought in sign language facilitators (who were themselves Deaf), to lead interviews with Deaf participants via videophone. Typically, sign language interpreters are brought in as pairs (e.g., so that they can substitute for each other and take breaks), but if there are multiple Deaf people taking part in multiple conversations at the same time, multiple interpreters may be necessary. Or if there is a presentation that will be made to a large number of people as a part of the research, perhaps real-time captioning (CART) might be a useful addition to sign language interpretation. If teleconferencing or telepresence will be involved in the research, and the group is mixed both in terms of hearing and in terms of physical location, we suggest that the reader consult (Vogler et al., 2013) for detailed advice. It is important to note that there are many different national sign languages (e.g., American Sign Language, Brazilian Sign Language, Mexican Sign Language, Norwegian Sign Language, etc.) which may be relevant depending on the participants and geographic location. However, it is NOT sufficient to say that researchers can just write messages on paper and text messages to their Deaf participants. That would be insulting and rude, to ask for the participation of Deaf participants, without ensuring that sign language interpreters will be present.

16.2.5 COMMUNICATING WITH PEOPLE WITH MODERATE TO SEVERE SPEECH IMPAIRMENTS

It is important to consider that some participants may have moderate to severe speech impairments and be unable to communicate orally (note that we are not including people who can communicate using sign language in this classification). Some of these people may simply be using an Augmentative and alternative communication (AAC) device. AAC devices are primarily used to allow people with communication challenges, to communicate more effectively using selection devices and computer-synthesized speech output. It is important to determine what the expressive language skills are, of potential participants, and then plan for multiple possible approaches for communication. Plan for participants to use AAC, and also think about whether more of the data collection should be in written format, where participants can fill out surveys or time diaries over a period of time, rather than be rushed to fill out text on the spot (Mahmud and Martens, 2015).

Be aware that because someone has challenges with speaking or expressive language skills, that does not necessarily mean that they have challenges with understanding spoken language (receptive language skills). In their study of an email application designed specifically for people with Aphasia, Mahmud and Martens (2015) note that there are two general kinds of Aphasia: nonfluent Aphasia and fluent Aphasia. People with fluent Aphasia have trouble with language comprehension, whereas people with nonfluent Aphasia (the focus of their study) are generally able to understand verbal communication.

16.2.6 **PROXY USERS**

In the past, some researchers would use "proxy users," where individuals without disabilities would represent individuals with disabilities during design or research. This could include people with no connection to the disability and people with some knowledge of the disability. Examples of people with no connection to the disability include blindfolding people who can see, or tying people's hands behind their back to simulate users with motor impairments (Sears and Hanson, 2012). These "simulations" or "temporarily impaired users" are generally not encouraged for any type of research as, over time, users with perceptual or motor impairments learn to compensate by becoming more reliant upon their other senses or body parts (Sears and Hanson, 2012). Someone who is Blind has learned to rely more on their hearing than someone who can see. Even if the users of interest and users without any disabilities are considered to have equal skill in some area (for instance, good quality speech), the impairment makes users perceive the technology differently. So, for example, it is inappropriate to test speech-recognition solutions for users with spinal cord injuries, by using users without any impairment, based on the claim that they have similar quality speech (Feng et al., 2005). Since users often compare a new technology to a previously used technology or option, the comparisons are very different. Domain experience also is an important factor. For instance, in testing technologies for Blind people to drive cars using nonvisual techniques, it would be inappropriate to have participants who can see but are wearing blindfolds, as they have, in many cases, years of experience driving cars (Sucu and Folmer, 2014).

There are some limited situations where it may be appropriate to use people who are familiar with the users and impairments to represent the users themselves. These are generally situations where users are unable to communicate, or are unable to process information due to their impairment. For instance, one study used speech language pathologists who worked closely with individuals with aphasia, instead of the actual users themselves, to get an understanding of user needs (Boyd-Graber et al., 2006). In another study, caregivers and family members were used as the primary information sources for designing technology for individuals with Alzheimer's disease (Cohene et al., 2005).

Another model of proxy users is to use pairs of users and their caregivers or therapists. For instance, in a study about designing walking technology for people with Dementia, pairs of people with dementia, and their primary family caregivers, were involved in the research (Holbø et al., 2013). In another study related to tools for therapy relating to childhood apraxia of speech, both children with apraxia of speech and their speech therapists, were paired up for the research (Parnandi et al., 2013). In some cases, children answered subjective questions, but in other cases, since the children were 3–7 years old and had childhood apraxia of speech, their parents answered for them. Another situation where proxy users might be appropriate is when a specific application or tool is being developed and it is undergoing multiple iterations before a proof-of-concept is complete. If users with the specific disability would not be available to take part in all stages and all iterations of design, then proxy users might be suitable in limited stages and limited circumstances, for preliminary evaluation, although this is not ideal. They should closely be followed up by evaluations with users who actually are representative and do have the relevant disability. Some authors have gone as far as to say that all studies being published in archival venues must have representative users (Sears and Hanson, 2012).

Note that, even with a cognitive or motor impairment, many participants can communicate by using some form of AAC device (as described in earlier sections). You should never use proxy users when participants can communicate but the researchers don't "speak their language" (such as people who are Deaf and use sign language or Deaf-blind users who use Braille or finger-spelling), or the participants utilize AAC.

16.3 METHODOLOGICAL CONSIDERATIONS

In general, the research methods described in other chapters of this book can be utilized in any research involving people with disabilities. However, when doing research involving people with disabilities, there are a number of methodological issues that a researcher should consider when planning for data collection.

In experimental research with the general population of users, it is often expected that a research study would have a minimum of 30–40 users, to be considered valid (see Chapters 2–4 for more information on sample sizes in experimental design and Chapter 5 for more information on sample sizes in survey research). These expectations may not be realistic for users with disabilities, as it might be impossible to get access to so many users in one geographic area with a specific disability. The generally accepted approaches for dealing with the issue of access to appropriate participants for research focusing on users with disabilities are: small sample sizes, distributed research, and in-depth case studies. Choosing the most appropriate approach will depend on the nature of the research questions. For instance, highly controlled studies will often use small sample sizes or in-depth case studies where researchers can be physically present with the participants. Research of a more exploratory nature (with fewer controls) can use distributed research.

16.3.1 SMALL SAMPLE SIZES

For research focusing on users with disabilities, it is generally acceptable to have 5–10 users with a specific disability take part in a study. This is due to a number of reasons. For instance, it may be hard to find participants with disabilities that meet all of the inclusion criteria discussed earlier in the chapter (employment, education, technical expertise). Or it may be hard to find people with a specific disability in a given geographical area (e.g., Mosaic Down Syndrome) or people with a certain disability where they are still able to take part in the research (e.g., ALS). For example, in the recent proceedings of the ASSETS conference (well accepted as a high-quality conference on this topic), many of the research studies in which users with disabilities had to be physically present to take part in the research had 15 or fewer individuals taking part in the research.

Because of the small number of participants with disabilities who often take part, this means that if a classic experimental design is used, there will often be no more than one control group and one treatment group, as the number of participants does not allow for statistical tests for multiple treatment groups, so repeated measures designs tend to be used if experimental design is used at all (see Chapters 2–4 for more information on experimental design). Because of the sample size issue, experimental design is used less often in research involving people with disabilities, though it can be used. One common approach is to have a group of participants with a specific disability, and a group of participants without a disability as the control group (Sears and Hanson, 2012). Care needs to be taken in justification and interpretation of results in these experimental designs; for instance, if demographic data does not identify significant differences between the groups (e.g., in age or education), that does not mean that the groups can be considered equivalent (Sears and Hanson, 2012). Experimental design methodologies involving people with disabilities can be done. However, due to the sample size issue, research involving people with disabilities, is often exploratory (rather than strict experimental design), a hybrid of quantitative and qualitative research, or primarily qualitative. There are not many users involved, but the data collection is certainly deep. For example, Mcintyre and Hanson (2014) describe how they used a combination of in-person interviews involving researchers and Blind individuals, before and after a navigation task within a building, while a digital recorder, not researchers, recorded data as 10 Blind and low vision participants were performing the navigation task within the building.

16.3.2 **DISTRIBUTED RESEARCH**

If not enough participants with disabilities, who meet the inclusion criteria, are available in a local area, another approach is to do distributed research, where the users do the research in their own home or office, without researchers present, and data is collected via time diaries, surveys, keystroke logging, or another method. Remote data collection generally allows for higher numbers of users (100 users or more) to take part in the research, because you can draw from potential participants over a much wider geographical area. In addition, a number of the challenges discussed later in the chapter (such as scheduling and transportation) may not be present for distributed research. However, there are drawbacks to remote data collection (see Chapters 10 and 14). It lowers the control that the researchers have over the study, and generally, the amount and richness of data collection will not be comparable to a research study done in-person (Petrie et al., 2006). Furthermore, it may not be possible to ascertain much detail about the specific technical environment utilized by the participant, when the data is collected remotely (Petrie et al., 2006). If software needs to be installed remotely, in a technology environment that researchers do not have direct access to, and may not be 100% aware of the configurations, this may pose a logistical problem. One hybrid approach is to have participants come to a centralized location to get trained on how to do the data collection, and then to remotely collect data and send the data results back to the researchers (Petrie et al., 2006).

There are multiple ways to do distributed research. For instance, one approach is to go for a high number of participants, using a standard data collection method, such as time diaries or surveys, which don't require researchers to be present. Lazar et al. (2007) describe how 100 Blind participants took part in a time diary study to examine what frustrating situations occur on the web, how they respond, and how it impacts on their work and time lost. Rich text format files were provided, with specified spaces for participants to enter their data. Surveys are often used for distributed research, because of the ease in getting a lot of responses. Feng et al. (2008) collected 561 surveys from parents, relating to the computer usage of their children with Down syndrome. Wentz and Lazar (2016) collected 150 surveys from Blind users, about the challenges they face when software updates or website redesigns are inaccessible. Porter and Kientz (2013) collected 55 surveys from people with various disabilities (primarily motor disabilities, but also visual, hearing, and cognitive), about the barriers that they faced in video gaming. Apart from surveys and time diaries, participants can be asked to perform tasks remotely on the web, with data being collected either via a remote usability testing application, video conferencing, or Javascript inserted into web pages. As an example, Bigham and Cavender (2009) had 89 Blind participants attempting to perform a series of tasks on audio CAPTCHAs, with data collected remotely. Another approach to distributed research is to analyze publicly available information (such as tweets), because although you may not be able to determine which individuals have disabilities, you can determine which tweets are about the topic of access for people with disabilities (Brady and Bigham, 2014).

Another approach to distributed research is to combine a remote data collection method, with interviews (either in-person or distributed). Shinohara and Wobbrock (2016) had 14 participants who were Blind, low vision, or Deaf and hard of hearing take part in a diary study related to social comfort of using assistive technologies, (which isn't a large sample), but which resulted in 97 diary entries and then 12 follow-up interviews done, mostly by phone.

16.3.3 IN-DEPTH CASE STUDIES

Yet another approach is to do in-depth case studies, in which fewer users (say, between three and 10) take part in a more intensive way. These studies might involve data collection over several days, or users being trained, or longitudinal studies. This is most appropriate when data cannot be appropriately collected in a short amount of time (say, 2–3 hours). For instance, for many complex software applications or devices, users really do need a period of training, as well as time to familiarize themselves with the tool. A 2-day period of research for each user can be seen as a minimum for a case study. Ideally, longitudinal studies would examine how users adapt to and utilize a new application over 3–6 months, although this is not always possible. There are multiple examples of how to do more in-depth and longitudinal case studies. For instance, Montague et al. (2014) describe their study, involving nine users with motor impairments (primarily due to Parkinson's disease), who utilized a mobile device for a period of 4 weeks while data was being collected. Buehler et al. (2015) describe a case study, over 11 weeks of training an individual with an intellectual disability and short-term memory loss, to independently design and print 3D models. Mahmud and Martens (2015) describe a study where people with Aphasia learn to use an email tool over a 3-month long period.

In some cases, a case study can provide an in-depth examination of only one person with a disability (see the sidebar in Chapter 7, relating to a case study of Sara). There can also be interesting twists in doing case studies. For instance, Torsten Felzer, who recently passed away, was a dedicated member of the community of researchers interested in accessibility. He himself had Friedreich's Ataxia, a neuromuscular disease, and as a researcher, he documented his own case study, of challenges that he faced, and new approaches that he tried, and which approaches worked, and how that changed over time as his disease progressed (Felzer and Rinderknecht, 2013).

16.3.4 CONSISTENT TECHNICAL ENVIRONMENT OR BEST CASE SCENARIO?

If your research study involves having people with disabilities interacting with a software application, operating system, or web site, one of the important methodological considerations is whether to use a standard technical configuration for all participants taking part, or to allow them to utilize their own technical setup. There are benefits and drawbacks to both situations. Many users with disabilities have spent time creating the optimal configuration for their usage. Because various assistive technologies (such as screen readers, Braille displays, and alternate input and output devices) are involved, sometimes it takes practice and tweaking to figure out the optimal configuration (which web browsers, operating systems, and which specific settings) that makes everything work together. Furthermore, there are also settings that are optimized for that specific user (e.g., speed of screen reader, level of magnification, color contrast, etc.). So the user likely has their own technical environment customized and optimized for performance. This may mean, for instance, that some component of the configuration (e.g., an operating system or application) is not the latest version.

In some cases, such as users testing a single software application or web site, or research focusing more on user behavior or performance, it may be possible to allow all users to utilize their own technical environment. There are benefits and drawbacks to doing this. The benefit of allowing users to utilize their own assistive technology and computer setup (with the associated settings), is that the data collected will be under the "best case scenario." This scenario will show users at what is most likely their peak performance level. Any usability problems identified will probably not be overestimated and will likely be conservative. Such an approach helps address doubters who will look at data and say, "the user experience isn't really this bad," as the problems reported will be as conservative as possible. Also, allowing users to use their own technical environment makes it more likely that, as only one or two new technical components are introduced to them, that you would have isolated the impact of the new items. In an extreme situation, if users were presented with new hardware, OS, application, and assistive technology at the same time, it would be hard to isolate the impact of any of the individual technologies.

However, this situation of allowing users to utilize their own technical environment may not be possible if part of what is being evaluated in research is a new set of technical configurations or applications. Another reason why allowing users to utilize their own technical environment may not be possible, is because the research involves a strict experimental design, and the technical environment needs to be controlled for. It would be a confounding factor in experimental design, if each user utilized a different technical environment. For instance, if a series of Deaf users had different screen sizes for reading the captioning, or Blind users were using different screen readers and listening at different rates of speech, these factors would clearly not be controlled for in an experimental design. It is important for researchers to plan ahead and consider if they want to allow users to utilize their own technical environment, or if they want to control the technical environment and make it consistent.

16.3.5 INTERVENTIONS

Researchers should consider when interventions, during data collection, may be appropriate and how they should be documented. Interventions, as described in the chapter on usability testing, are when there is an interface barrier that users are presented with, which does not allow the user to continue in the interface. These barriers are often accessibility barriers. So, for instance, if a login screen or an interface screen is inaccessible, it means that a participant with a disability may not be able to continue to use the rest of the web site or application. Generally, if researchers do not intervene, this means that the data collection is over, and that would be a missed opportunity to learn more about other aspects of an interface or other portions of data collection. An intervention is when a researcher helps the participant move forward by providing advice. Before beginning any data collection involving people with disabilities, a researcher should have a clear decision on if any interventions will be allowed, under what circumstances, how they will be documented, and how this will be accounted for in reporting the results.

16.4 LOGISTICS

16.4.1 COMMUNICATING WITH POTENTIAL PARTICIPANTS

When recruiting potential participants, it is important to understand their preferred method of communication and any related challenges. For instance, email may not be the preferred option for users with spinal cord injuries (SCI), as it may be harder for users with SCI to generate text. Instead, phone calls might be the preferred option (Feng et al., 2005). Obviously, phone calls would not work well for Deaf people, who may prefer email or text messaging, or sign language over video. You may need to engage with sign language interpreters to begin the conversation about potentially taking part in research. Other user populations may have different challenges in communication. For instance, email is often a preferred method of communication for Blind users. However, due to the large amount of time required for them to process spam email, Blind users tend to have very strong filtering on their email. Emails sent to multiple Blind users using the BCC option will not make it through the spam filter to most users (Lazar et al., 2005). So for Blind users, it is important to place the recipients' email address in the "To" line, not in the "CC" line or "BCC" line. Another approach for Blind users might be, if you have access to their phone numbers, to call them on the phone. For users with some types of cognitive impairment, it may be necessary to contact caregivers.

16.4.2 PILOT STUDIES

Due to the complex logistics involved in research involving participants with disabilities, it is a good idea, when possible, to do pilot studies before beginning any real data collection. Your simulations in the lab, or your expectations of how a user will interact, are likely to be very different from the reality. While this is true in any type of HCI research, it is especially true in working with users with disabilities. Since you may have access to a limited number of users and you won't have any opportunity to do the data collection a second time, you need to confirm or address your perceptions early on in the process by doing a pilot study with one or two users.

Pilot studies can uncover a number of problems. For instance, is the documentation accessible for the specific user population? Users with spinal cord injuries can't physically handle documentation, and Blind users may not be able to use printed materials or even Braille materials (approximately 10%–20% of Blind individuals are fluent in Braille). Users in wheelchairs will need physical settings, including computer desks, and buildings, that can accommodate their wheelchairs. Other technical problems may also arise. For instance, any text documents sent to users before a study, must work, for Blind users under multiple screen readers (Window-Eyes, JAWS, VoiceOver and NVDA), multiple operating systems (OS X, Win XP, Win 7/8/10), and multiple text editors (MS-Word, OpenOffice, etc.), as well as various combinations of screen reader, operating systems, and text editor (Lazar et al., 2005). Sometimes the file format that works best is Rich Text Format, which tends to work with most text editors. In doing a pilot study, you may find out that the participants expect to use aids (such as a portable notetaker, voice recorder, or electronic device) or expect you to have aids available to them (Sauer et al., 2010). Consider that different assistive technologies are not equal, for instance, some screen readers have OCR (optical character recognition) built into them to analyze graphic documents, whereas other screen readers do not. Generally, you need to be aware if all participants are using certain aids; if only some of them do, you need to find a way to compensate for that in your data collection. Also there may be conceptual misunderstandings, for instance, the coauthors of this book had the experience of running a pilot study, where the two Blind users in the pilot study, did not have the awareness of the structure of menu design that was expected. The coauthors adjusted the methodology accordingly.

One or two participants in the pilot study are generally enough, just to confirm that you are on the right track and that there are no major problems with logistics. If you have worked with a specific user population for a long time, you may have a few users that you collaborate with regularly, who are comfortable with you, and are willing to help you test out materials, be brutally honest, and serve as your "reality check." Whatever flaws or problems are discovered during the pilot study should be modified and accounted for, before the main study begins.

16.4.3 SCHEDULING DATA COLLECTION INVOLVING USERS WITH DISABILITIES

Transportation may be an issue for some users with disabilities. It is important to remember that users with some perceptual, cognitive, or motor disabilities may not drive a car, or may live in a location where having a car is not feasible. They may rely on rides from others, public transportation, taxis, Uber/Lyft, paratransit, and other scheduled services to get from point A to point B. Therefore, these users must typically be scheduled for data collection enough in advance to secure transportation. It is often not possible for these participants to make transportation plans, or change them, at the last minute.

Rather than asking participants to come to a university or remote location, it may be preferable for researchers to offer to go to a home or workplace location. To help ensure the safety and security of researchers entering participant homes, it is preferable to go in teams of at least two researchers. By visiting users in their home or workplace, it alleviates the need for the user with a disability to schedule transportation to a new location. In addition, getting a glimpse of the user in their own environment, using their own technical setup, is likely to lead to a more ecologically valid data collection effort. Note the previous section in this chapter, about using consistent technology, versus a user's own technical configuration. Visiting the user in his or her natural environment allows the user to be most relaxed and productive and yields the most ecologically valid data. However, it is possible to either have users bring their own technology to a research lab, or to bring a standardized technology configuration to a user's workplace or home. The physical environment and the technical environment are not necessarily linked.

The major drawback of visiting users in their work or home environment is that you tend to have less control over the environment (Feng et al., 2005). If users are able to come to a research lab, this offers the researchers more control over the layout and noise in the environment. However, apart from the transportation challenge, there is another major challenge: the accessibility of the researchers' building. Researchers must be completely certain that the building that they expect users to come to, is fully accessible. This means that the doors must be wide enough, restrooms must have accessible stalls, elevators must be present, and Braille must be available on all signs. In addition, some users may have service animals working with them (Feng et al., 2005).

It is also important to note that some users with disabilities are not involved in paid employment. Because employment is an important point of pride, those who are employed may be very sensitive about missing work for an outside research project. They are unlikely to let a research study interfere with their job performance (Lazar et al., 2006). It may be necessary to schedule research sessions during evenings or weekends. If, as researchers, you visit users in their workplace, be sensitive about not requiring more time for the research study than you had indicated to users, so that it will disrupt their work. In such circumstances, perhaps, it might be preferable to visit users at their homes, rather than their workplaces.

It is important for researchers to understand that the variety of users and the various levels of severity of the disability (see previous sections in this chapter) mean that the time involved for a user to take part in a research study might be relatively unpredictable. The researcher's schedule should be left flexible enough that it is not a problem if a participant takes much longer for data collection than is expected. In addition, many people with disabilities are determined to prove that they can accomplish tasks. This means that if the time period is limited for the specific participant's data collection, they may still want to continue and may feel the need to complete the task. For a researcher to tell the user that "time is up" may be met with resistance. This is generally not a problem, except that it needs to be accounted for in the scheduling of users.

16.4.4 INVOLVING PARTICIPANTS WITH COGNITIVE DISABILITIES/ INTELLECTUAL IMPAIRMENTS

When involving people with various disabilities in research, the research methods are generally the same, but often the logistics are what change. There's a concreteness that people with cognitive disabilities often need for participating in research. For instance, Erazo and Zimmermann (2015), in evaluating a simplified banking interface for people with cognitive disabilities, noted that nearly all of their 11 participants wanted to have a printed confirmation of a banking transaction for their records. In their evaluation of multitouch screens by people with Down syndrome, Kumin et al. (2012) noted that it is important to use real accounts, and real data (rather than fake or test accounts), because for people with cognitive disabilities, they may not feel comfortable using "someone else's account."

There are other adjustments that may need to be made. For instance, in their research study which used eye-tracking devices to measure document reading in people with Autism, Yaneva et al. (2015) noted that participants with Autism sometimes asked for the lights to be diminished due to some sensory issues. Other researchers experienced how participants with Autism, when evaluating mobile phone apps for independent living, may be sensitive to noise and smells, such as those that commonly occur in the kitchen (Tang et al., 2016). Typical workplace distractions, such as open workspaces with cubicles, colleagues talking, and software notifications (such as the sound when a new email message arrives) can also be distracting for people with Autism (Morris et al., 2015). For people with cognitive disabilities who are taking part in research, researchers should be aware of issues such as a dramatically different length of attention span between participants with the same disability, and some participants may need multiple breaks or frequent reminders to stay focused on the task, or more time to understand and answer the questions (surveys or interviews). Asking those familiar with the specific cognitive disability may help, for instance, in their study of email applications for people with Aphasia, Mahmud and Martens (2015) were told by speech pathologists, to design questionnaires such that there were no items on the far right of the page, where people with Aphasia might miss them.

It is important to ask people with cognitive disabilities, if they will be utilizing their own accounts, to bring the passwords written out on paper. Often, people with cognitive disabilities may have challenges related to memory or processing, and you must ask them to bring the passwords written out, because otherwise (1) they may forget the passwords, or (2) they may be saved on their computer at home (so that they typically will not need to login and remember the passwords) (Kumin et al., 2012; Ma et al., 2013).

For people with some cognitive disabilities (if they have visual strengths), it may be helpful to utilize a visual Likert scale (see Figure 16.1), which participants can simply point to. In their study of touchscreen usage by adults with Down syndrome, to help build on the visual strengths of people with Down syndrome, the following visual Likert scale was used (Kumin et al., 2012).

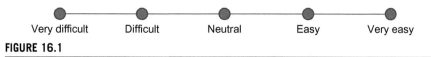

| Very difficult | Difficult | Neutral | Easy | Very easy |

FIGURE 16.1

Visual Likert scale.

From Kumin, L., Lazar, J., Feng, J.H., Wentz, B., Ekedebe, N., 2012. A usability evaluation of workplace-related tasks on a multi-touch tablet computer by adults with Down syndrome. Journal of Usability Studies 7 (4), 118–142.

Sometimes, when doing research involving people with cognitive disabilities, you need to be flexible about the research methodology. Due to either the concreteness mentioned earlier, or challenges in social interaction or understanding, participants may sometimes ask researchers to do something different from the task that they were asked to do. Being flexible allows for the participant engagement to be high. For instance, participants may argue about data entry, because they were asked to write about winter clothing but it's currently summer, or they were asked to enter a party into a calendar application with a one hour length, but the participant says that a party must last at least 4 hours (Kumin et al., 2012). Researchers can be flexible, since the task is only slightly modified, to allow for participants to be more comfortable with the tasks.

It is sometimes hard to determine the level of cognitive impairment. So, cognitive or behavioral testing can be done, however, for many reasons, it's impractical for

HCI researchers to get results (for participants who have undergone cognitive testing, they may not want to share the results, and Institutional Review Boards (IRBs) may not approve the collection of cognitive testing data as a part of HCI research). Furthermore, for some cognitive disabilities, such as Autism, there may be people with Autistic traits who are not aware of their traits or who are not "out" as being people with Autism, primarily because of the discrimination that they worry they may face (Morris et al., 2015). The reader of this book should consult (Morris et al., 2015) for details on how to appropriately recruit people with Autism from within a specific company, where the individuals may not be publicly identified as having Autism.

One consideration that researchers often must make when doing research involving people with cognitive disabilities, is whether to focus on just one cognitive disability in their research, or to focus on the general category of "cognitive disability." It is tempting to focus more broadly on cognitive disability, rather than on a specific cognitive disability, because recruiting participants with a specific cognitive disability can be a challenging experience. It's much easier to find 20 people to participate in research with "a cognitive disability" than to find 20 people with, say, "Traumatic Brain Injury" to participate. That's the reality. However, because someone has a cognitive disability doesn't mean that they are necessarily similar to other people with cognitive disabilities. So, for some participants, they may have varying levels of difficulty with memory, understanding, communication, visual, hearing, or social interaction (Ma et al., 2013). People with different types of cognitive disabilities generally are not similar. So, when possible, it's preferable to do research studies focusing on a population with a specific cognitive disability, recognizing, of course, that there are varying levels of severity within that population of users. It also needs recognizing that many of these individuals with a cognitive disability may not use any type of assistive technology, despite the public perception that all people with disabilities use assistive technology!

16.4.5 DOCUMENTATION FOR USERS WITH DISABILITIES

Often, there are a number of documents that are required for participation in a research study. These include IRB forms (also known as human subjects forms—see Chapter 15 for more information), instructions, task lists, and questionnaires. In traditional paper format, these forms may pose a problem for users who have what are known as "print disabilities," people that have trouble seeing print (e.g., blind or low vision), handling print (e.g., users with spinal cord injuries), or cognitively processing print (e.g., users with dyslexia). It's also important to note that in some cases, if children with disabilities are involved in the research, then the researchers themselves may be required to submit their own approval paperwork related to criminal record background checks.

Depending on the regulations of the country in which the research is taking place, research projects involving human participants may require that participants sign a form, in which they understand that they are taking part in a research experiment or project (see Chapter 15 for detailed information on what rights human participants have). Most human subjects forms require handwritten signatures, as per university or institutional requirement. This may be a problem for a number of user populations. Users with motor impairments, especially those that are unable to use their arms, may not be able to use a pencil or pen to sign a form or handle a form. An audio recording, or a video of the user, agreeing to take part in the study, hopefully will be acceptable to the institutional review board. For users with certain types of cognitive disabilities, it's questionable whether they would be able to sign a legal document. A caregiver, who has legal standing, might need to provide the signature. For children with a disability, often the parents need to give their approval for participation in the research project. Blind participants can sign paper forms, but it's questionable whether we should ask participants to sign a form that they cannot read. For participants that either cannot read or handle the form, it is standard practice to send an electronic version of the form beforehand, so that the participant can read and be comfortable with it. Note that the informed consent is especially important for participants with disabilities, as they are used to being tested so often, that it is especially important to make them aware, for instance, that in much of HCI research, they are helping to inform design or improve usability, but they themselves are not being tested. If Blind participants are being asked to sign a paper form, the text on the form should be reread to them, and they will need guidance on where to sign the form. Be sure to understand the specific policies relating to IRB forms from the organization that approved the research study (usually a university). For instance, many universities accept nothing but a signed, paper-based form. Some universities are beginning to accept electronic versions of informed consent (again, see Chapter 15). It is helpful to check if your institutional review board can accept some modified form of informed consent, which may be more appropriate for your participant population. If the institutional review board or similar research authority will not accept audio or video recording of a user giving consent, there are workarounds that can be utilized.

If a sponsoring organization requires signed forms from Blind users, there are two popular ways of guiding Blind users to the appropriate place to sign on the form. One method is to provide a signature guide (a small piece of plastic with a window in the middle, to indicate where the signature should be—see Figure 16.2). The other method is to attach a Braille label right below the signature line. The Braille label could say something along the lines of "sign above" (Lazar et al., 2005). While this might not be meaningful for the majority of Blind individuals who are not able to read Braille, the tactile information provided by the top line of the label can provide useful information on where the signature should be placed. Careful attention to details such as these can help build trust and confidence with participants, as they may appreciate that you've made the effort to make things work smoothly for them.

While human subjects forms are often the trickiest to deal with, this is primarily because there is often a legal requirement for a signed paper form. There is typically additional documentation in the research study, but there generally is

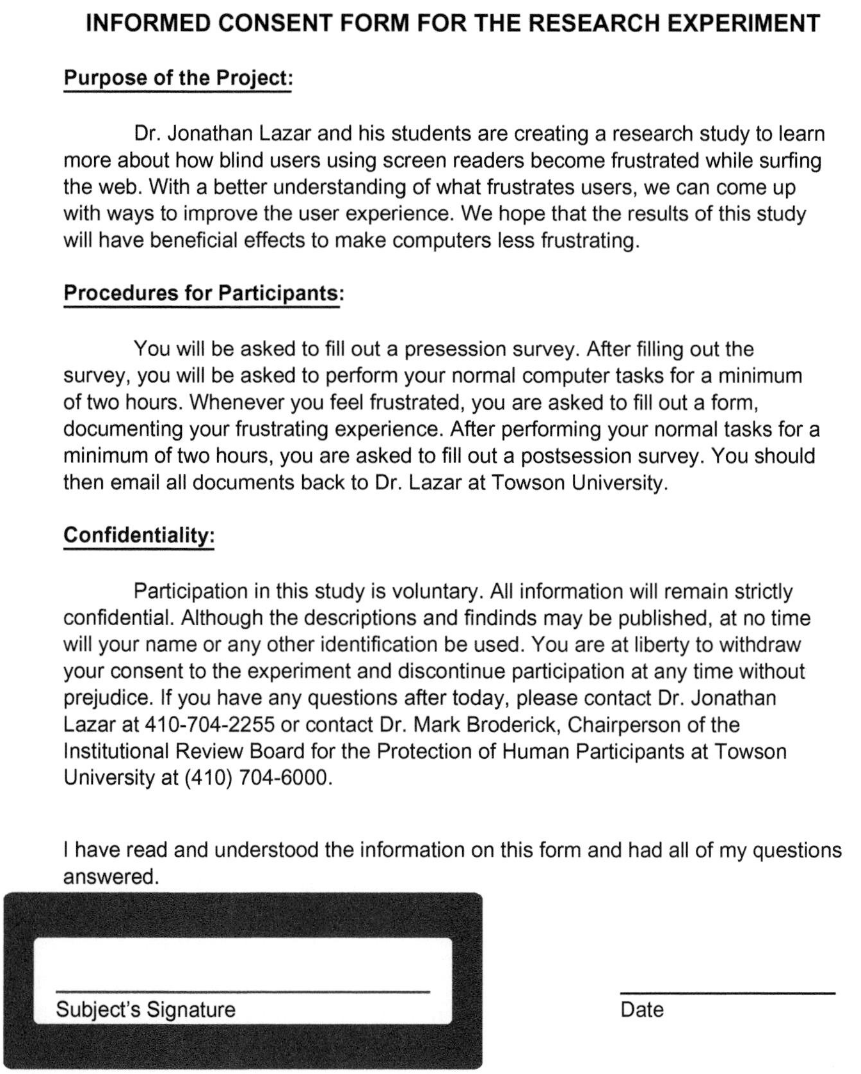

INFORMED CONSENT FORM FOR THE RESEARCH EXPERIMENT

Purpose of the Project:

Dr. Jonathan Lazar and his students are creating a research study to learn more about how blind users using screen readers become frustrated while surfing the web. With a better understanding of what frustrates users, we can come up with ways to improve the user experience. We hope that the results of this study will have beneficial effects to make computers less frustrating.

Procedures for Participants:

You will be asked to fill out a presession survey. After filling out the survey, you will be asked to perform your normal computer tasks for a minimum of two hours. Whenever you feel frustrated, you are asked to fill out a form, documenting your frustrating experience. After performing your normal tasks for a minimum of two hours, you are asked to fill out a postsession survey. You should then email all documents back to Dr. Lazar at Towson University.

Confidentiality:

Participation in this study is voluntary. All information will remain strictly confidential. Although the descriptions and findinds may be published, at no time will your name or any other identification be used. You are at liberty to withdraw your consent to the experiment and discontinue participation at any time without prejudice. If you have any questions after today, please contact Dr. Jonathan Lazar at 410-704-2255 or contact Dr. Mark Broderick, Chairperson of the Institutional Review Board for the Protection of Human Participants at Towson University at (410) 704-6000.

I have read and understood the information on this form and had all of my questions answered.

Subject's Signature   Date

FIGURE 16.2

An IRB form with a tactile signature guide for Blind users.

much more flexibility with the format of the other documentation. For instance, participants in research studies must often either read material, or record their responses, on paper. If users are unable to read printed documents or have trouble handling physical documents, then there are other options for use during the actual data collection. One option is to provide all of the materials in electronic format, which can be used both for reading and for recording responses. Plain text versions of all documentation can be made available to the participants at the time of the research study. Only the IRB form should be made available beforehand, as providing actual study documents beforehand could lead to learning effects. Electronic formats may introduce another potentially complicating factor into the research study. For instance, what happens if some participants are more experienced with text readers or word processors than other users? Will that difference, even though it is not being measured or controlled for, make a difference in the outcome of the research?

The other option is to verbally instruct the participant on what to do and ask them to respond verbally. While this is very appropriate, the major caveat here is to make sure that rules are created to guide the researchers on what they do and do not say. For instance, is there a limit on the number of times that the researcher can repeat instructions? Do the researchers refuse to answer questions outside the scope of the instructions? Can they spell out words? For instance, if the research study was investigating web searching habits, it would not be appropriate for the researchers to give hints or provide guidance to the participants. Therefore, there should be clear rules for the researchers on what they can and cannot say, so that there is consistency across all participants taking part in the research study. Obviously, you must tailor the instructions and documentation to the needs of the participants. For instance, if participants have a motor disability, such as a spinal cord injury, in which case handling documents and recording responses on paper might be problematic, then audio recording might be a good option. If participants are Deaf-blind, Braille may be the preferred option. As always, you must know your participant population very well.

16.4.6 BRINGING EXTRA COMPUTER PARTS

When visiting users with disabilities in their home or workplace, it's important to understand that their setup may not be what most researchers are used to, and if utilizing the user's own technology, the technical setup will be out of the researcher's control. For instance, Blind users may not have a working monitor, Deaf or Hard of hearing users may not have working speakers, and users with motor disabilities may not have a working mouse. Since many of these participants have purchased a "standard package" of CPU, monitor, and peripherals from a computer company, if pieces of hardware that are useless to them break, there is no real incentive for the participants to replace them. However, researchers often rely on these tools to understand the participant interaction. For instance, often researchers who are visual will need to see the screen to understand what the screen reader is reading. If this is the case, you need to carry extra computer parts with you when you visit the users. For instance, bring a monitor with you if you are visiting Blind users in their workplace or home. Also bring standard cables (such as video and USB cables). If doing multiple on-site visits, it is good practice to take extra parts (monitors, cables, speakers, mice, external keyboards) with you at all times, as you never know when you may need them.

WHEN USERS GET FRUSTRATED

What happens if a user with a disability is taking part in a study, is not successful at completing any of the tasks, and is getting frustrated? This person is getting agitated, is still trying to complete the tasks, but clearly is not making any progress. What happens next? This is a realistic question. For the researcher who is observing this participant, it is an upsetting time. Although our research studies in HCI typically do not endanger health or leave lasting emotional effects, it is certainly possible that a situation of this nature could occur which could leave the user angry and upset. Apart from a few rare studies designed to frustrate people on purpose, such as (Riseberg et al., 1998), HCI research is generally not designed to aggravate the users who take part.

There are a few options. The researcher can remind the participant that they have the right to end their participation in the experiment, at any time, with no adverse consequences (which is typically a standard requirement in IRB forms). As part of this reminder, the researcher should note that whatever payment is due for participation will be given to the individual, regardless of when they end their participation. But if the participant does not want to end the session, what happens next? Perhaps the participant can be offered a short break or a period of rest, which would allow him or her a few minutes to calm down. The researcher technically has the right to end the experiment if they feel that someone is beginning to be harmed. However, for the researcher to unilaterally end the participation of the participant also sets some bad precedents. If researchers frequently end user participation, there could be some bias injected into the research study. This is a tricky situation. Especially when working with users with disabilities, who are often hard to recruit and replace.

16.4.7 PAYMENT

When paying participants for taking part in research, it is important to make sure that the form of payment will be useful to the participants. For instance, gift cards for a specific store (such as a local bookstore) may not be useful for some participants if they cannot use standard print materials. Also, gift cards that only work at a certain store may not be useful, if transportation is required to visit the store and use the gift cards. Gifts that are typically used to recruit university students for research, such as iPods, may also not be appropriate, as many users with disabilities have very specific technical needs and may not want to use new devices. The best forms of payment are either cash or cash equivalents, such as cash cards. If those are not viable options, then at least a gift card should be given at a store that has online ordering options and an accessible website (such as Amazon) or that has many local branches and many types of merchandise. It is also important to note that users with disabilities are typically paid more than users without disabilities for their participation in HCI research. One mistake of novice researchers is that they often assume that people with disabilities do not need to be paid for their participation, but instead are "waiting around" to participate in research. This is not the case, and assuming such a scenario will not lead to either good long-term relationships, or people actually signing up to participate in your research.

16.5 SUMMARY

Research involving participants with disabilities can be challenging but it offers many rewards. The computer usage of many of these populations has not been explored in as much depth as with the general population of users, so there are many important research questions that remain unexamined, and people with disabilities should be involved in all types of HCI research. Before even recruiting people for a research study, it is important to learn more about the specific population of people with disabilities that you are interested in, and determine what their preferred terminology is, in terms of how their disability is referred to. Then, there are three areas which researchers need to pay careful attention to: (1) participants, (2) research methodology, and (3) logistics.

It's important to determine the specific inclusion criteria, what specific qualities (such as technology usage, education, occupation, employment, and severity of disability) would qualify someone to participate in the study. When recruiting participants with disabilities, it's a good idea to form long-term partnerships with disability advocacy organizations, and to think carefully about the best way to reach out to potential participants (in terms of technological communication and speech communication). Most research involving people with disabilities has a smaller number of participants, unless distributed approaches are used. It's also important to determine, for the participants in your study, if you want to use a consistent technical environment or instead use a "best case scenario," both of which can be appropriate, depending on the specific research design. Pilot studies are especially important for research involving people with disabilities because there are so many logistical factors that must be considered and planned for in advance. It is especially important to consider transportation, and the accessibility of a research location, to ensure that participants can actually participate! There may also be modifications to a data collection method that need to be made when involving participants with cognitive or intellectual impairments. Documentation will often need to be presented in different formats, and it is important to ensure that participant payment is also in a format that is usable. With appropriate planning and attention to the participants themselves, the research methodologies, and the logistics, HCI research involving users with disabilities can be very successful.

RESEARCH DESIGN EXERCISE

Imagine that you are going to start doing research focused on people with a disability that has not yet received attention in the HCI research literature, for example, people with Fragile X Syndrome. What are the first steps that you would take? Are there important considerations related to gender and communication? What groups could you reach out and connect with? What might the considerations be for recruiting participants? As a population of users without any preexisting research on computer usage, what research methods might be most appropriate? What modifications might you need to make to your methodology and logistics?

DISCUSSION QUESTIONS

1. What are five commonly used categories of inclusion criteria for determining whether someone with a disability can be included in a research study?

2. How do experience, confidence, technical environment, and previous barriers, influence perceptions of usability by participants with disabilities in research studies?

3. For what types of participants will you need to bring in sign language interpreters? How many sign language interpreters are typically needed?

4. Why are proxy users generally not considered valid for research? What are the limited circumstances where proxy users may be considered acceptable?

5. Why are small sample sizes considered acceptable in research involving people with disabilities?

6. What are the strengths and weaknesses of doing distributed research involving people with disabilities?

7. What are the strengths and weaknesses of doing case study research involving people with disabilities?

8. The chapter discusses the choice of using a consistent technical environment or using each user's individual technology environment. In what research scenario, and using what types of methods, would you want to utilize a consistent technical environment? In what research scenario, and using what types of methods, would you want to utilize each user's own technical environment?

9. What is a research intervention, and why might one be necessary when doing research involving people with disabilities?

10. What are three benefits of doing pilot studies involving participants with disabilities?

11. What are four methodological or logistical adjustments that you might need to make, when doing research involving people with cognitive disabilities?

12. What might three modifications be, to allow for people with disabilities to officially provide informed consent for participation in the research study?

REFERENCES

Bigham, J.P., Cavender, A.C., 2009. Evaluating existing audio CAPTCHAs and an interface optimized for non-visual use. In: Proceedings of the SIGCHI Conference on Human Factors in Computing Systems, pp. 1829–1838.

Boyd-Graber, J.L., Nikolova, S.S., Moffatt, K.A., et al., 2006. Participatory design with proxies: developing a desktop-PDA system to support people with aphasia. In: Proceedings of the ACM Conference on Human Factors in Computing Systems, pp. 151–160.

Brady, E., Bigham, J.P., 2014. How companies engage customers around accessibility on social media. In: Proceedings of the 16th International ACM SIGACCESS Conference on Computers & Accessibility, pp. 51–58.

Buehler, E., Easley, W., McDonald, S., Comrie, N., Hurst, A., 2015. Inclusion and education: 3D printing for integrated classrooms. In: Proceedings of the 17th International ACM SIGACCESS Conference on Computers & Accessibility, pp. 281–290.

Cohene, T., Baecker, R., Marziali, E., 2005. Designing interactive life story multimedia for a family affected by Alzheimer's disease: a case study. In: Proceedings of the ACM Conference on Human Factors in Computing Systems, pp. 1300–1303.

Crabb, M., Jones, R., Armstrong, M., Hughes, C.J., 2015. Online news videos: the UX of subtitle position. In: Proceedings of the 17th International ACM SIGACCESS Conference on Computers & Accessibility, pp. 215–222.

Dee, M., Hanson, V., 2014. A large user pool for accessibility research with representative users. In: Proceedings of the 16th International ACM SIGACCESS Conference on Computers & Accessibility, pp. 35–42.

Erazo, M., Zimmermann, G., 2015. Design and evaluation of a simplified online banking interface for people with cognitive disabilities. In: Proceedings of the 17th International ACM SIGACCESS Conference on Computers & Accessibility, pp. 309–310.

Felzer, T., Rinderknecht, S., 2013. How someone with a neuromuscular disease experiences operating a PC (and how to successfully counteract that). In: Proceedings of the 15th International ACM SIGACCESS Conference on Computers and Accessibility, pp. 29.

Feng, J., Sears, A., Law, C., 2005. Conducting empirical experiments involving participants with spinal cord injuries. In: Proceedings of the Universal Access in Human-Computer Interaction Conference [On CD-Rom].

Feng, J., Lazar, J., Kumin, L., Ozok, A., 2008. Computer usage and computer-related behavior of young individuals with Down syndrome. In: Proceedings of the ACM Conference on Assistive Technology (ASSETS), pp. 35–42.

Holbø, K., Bøthun, S., Dahl, Y., 2013. Safe walking technology for people with dementia: what do they want? In: Proceedings of the 15th International ACM SIGACCESS Conference on Computers and Accessibility, pp. 21–28.

Hurst, A., Hudson, S.E., Mankoff, J., Trewin, S., 2013. Distinguishing users by pointing performance in laboratory and real-world tasks. ACM Transactions on Accessible Computing 5 (2), 5.

Jaeger, P., 2009. Persons with disabilities and intergenerational universal usability. Interactions 16 (3), 66–67.

Johansson, S., Gulliksen, J., Lantz, A., 2015. User participation when users have mental and cognitive disabilities. In: Proceedings of the 17th International ACM SIGACCESS Conference on Computers & Accessibility, pp. 69–76.

Kumin, L., Lazar, J., Feng, J.H., Wentz, B., Ekedebe, N., 2012. A usability evaluation of workplace-related tasks on a multi-touch tablet computer by adults with Down syndrome. Journal of Usability Studies 7 (4), 118–142.

Lazar, J., 2007a. Introduction to universal usability. In: Lazar, J. (Ed.), Universal Usability: Designing Computer Interfaces for Diverse User Populations. John Wiley & Sons, Chichester, pp. 1–12.

Lazar, J. (Ed.), 2007b. Universal Usability: Designing Computer Interfaces for Diverse User Populations. John Wiley & Sons, Chichester, UK.

Lazar, J., Allen, A., Kleinman, J., Lawrence, J., 2005. Methodological issues in using time diaries to collect frustration data from blind computer users. In: Proceedings of the 11th International Conference on Human-Computer Interaction (HCI) (on CD-ROM).

Lazar, J., Feng, J., Allen, A., 2006. Determining the impact of computer frustration on the mood of blind users browsing the web. In: Proceedings of the 8th International ACM SIGACCESS Conference on Computers and Accessibility, pp. 149–156.

Lazar, J., Allen, A., Kleinman, J., Malarkey, C., 2007. What frustrates screen reader users on the web: a study of 100 blind users. International Journal of Human–Computer Interaction 22 (3), 247–269.

Lazar, J., Goldstein, D., Taylor, A., 2015. Ensuring Digital Accessibility Through Process and Policy. Morgan Kaufmann, Amsterdam.

Ma, Y., Feng, J., Kumin, L., Lazar, J., 2013. Investigating user behavior for authentication methods: a comparison between individuals with Down syndrome and neurotypical users. ACM Transactions on Accessible Computing 4 (4), 15.

Mahmud, A.A., Martens, J.B., 2015. Iterative design and field trial of an aphasia-friendly email tool. ACM Transactions on Accessible Computing 7 (4), 13.

McIntyre, L.J., Hanson, V.L., 2014. Buildings and users with visual impairment: uncovering factors for accessibility using BIT-Kit. In: Proceedings of the 16th International ACM SIGACCESS Conference on Computers & Accessibility, pp. 59–66.

Miller, H., Buhr, H., Johnson, C., Hoepner, J., 2013. AphasiaWeb: a social network for individuals with aphasia. In: Proceedings of the 15th International ACM SIGACCESS Conference on Computers and Accessibility, pp. 1–8.

Moffatt, K., McGrenere, J., Purves, B., Klawe, M., 2004. The participatory design of a sound and image enhanced daily planner for people with aphasia. In: Proceedings of the ACM Conference on Human Factors in Computing Systems, pp. 407–414.

Montague, K., Nicolau, H., Hanson, V.L., 2014. Motor-impaired touchscreen interactions in the wild. In: Proceedings of the 16th International ACM SIGACCESS Conference on Computers & Accessibility, ACM. pp. 123–130.

Morris, M.R., Begel, A., Wiedermann, B., 2015. Understanding the challenges faced by neurodiverse software engineering employees: towards a more inclusive and productive technical workforce. In: Proceedings of the 17th International ACM SIGACCESS Conference on Computers & Accessibility, pp. 173–184.

Parnandi, A., Karappa, V., Son, Y., Shahin, M., McKechnie, J., Ballard, K., Gutierrez-Osuna, R., 2013. Architecture of an automated therapy tool for childhood apraxia of speech. In: Proceedings of the 15th International ACM SIGACCESS Conference on Computers and Accessibility, pp. 5–12.

Petrie, H., Hamilton, F., King, N., Pavan, P., 2006. Remote usability evaluations with disabled people. In: Proceedings of the SIGCHI Conference on Human Factors in Computing Systems, pp. 1133–1141.

Porter, J.R., Kientz, J.A., 2013. An empirical study of issues and barriers to mainstream video game accessibility. In: Proceedings of the 15th International ACM SIGACCESS Conference on Computers and Accessibility, ACM. pp. 1–8.

Riseberg, J., Klein, J., Fernandez, R., Picard, R., 1998. Frustrating the user on purpose: using biosignals in a pilot study to detect the user's emotional state. In: Proceedings of the ACM Conference on Human Factors in Computing Systems, pp. 227–228.

Sauer, G., Holman, J., Lazar, J., Hochheiser, H., Feng, J., 2010. Accessible privacy and security: a universally usable human-interaction proof tool. Universal Access in the Information Society 9 (3), 239–248.

Sears, A., Hanson, V.L., 2012. Representing users in accessibility research. ACM Transactions on Accessible Computing 4 (2), 7.

Shinohara, K., Wobbrock, J.O., 2016. Self-conscious or self-confident? A diary study conceptualizing the social accessibility of assistive technology. ACM Transactions on Accessible Computing 8 (2), 5.

Shiver, B., Wolfe, R., 2015. Evaluating Alternatives for Better Deaf Accessibility to Selected Web-Based Multimedia. In: Proceedings of the 17th International ACM SIGACCESS Conference on Computers & Accessibility, pp. 231–238.

Slatin, J., Rush, S., 2003. Maximum Accessibility. Addison-Wesley, New York.

Sucu, B., Folmer, E., 2014. The blind driver challenge: steering using haptic cues. In: Proceedings of the 16th International ACM SIGACCESS Conference on Computers & Accessibility, pp. 3–10.

Tang, Z., Guo, J., Miao, S., Acharya, S., Feng, J., 2016. Ambient intelligence based context-aware assistive system to improve independence for people with autism spectrum disorder. In: 49th Hawaii International Conference on System Sciences (HICSS). pp. 3339–3348.

Tartaro, A., 2007. Authorable virtual peers for children with autism. In: Proceedings of the ACM Conference on Human Factors in Computing Systems, pp. 1677–1680.

Trewin, S., Marques, D., Guerreiro, T., 2015. Usage of subjective scales in accessibility research. In: Proceedings of the 17th International ACM SIGACCESS Conference on Computers & Accessibility, pp. 59–67.

Vogler, C., Tucker, P., Williams, N., 2013. Mixed local and remote participation in teleconferences from a deaf and hard of hearing perspective. In: Proceedings of the 15th International ACM SIGACCESS Conference on Computers and Accessibility, pp. 30–34.

Wentz, B., Lazar, J., 2016. Exploring the impact of inaccessible redesign and updates. In: Langdon, P., Lazar, J., Heylighen, A., Dong, H. (Eds.), Designing Around People, Springer, London, UK, pp. 3–12.

Yaneva, V., Temnikova, I., Mitkov, R., 2015. Accessible texts for autism: an eye-tracking study. In: Proceedings of the 17th International ACM SIGACCESS Conference on Computers & Accessibility, pp. 49–57.

Zhao, Y., Szpiro, S., Azenkot, S., 2015. ForeSee: a customizable head-mounted vision enhancement system for people with low vision. In: Proceedings of the 17th International ACM SIGACCESS Conference on Computers & Accessibility, pp. 239–249.

Index

Note: Page numbers followed by *f* indicate figures *t* indicate tables and *b* indicate box.

CPI Antony Rowe
Chippenham, UK
2017-04-28 21:49